FUNK & WAGNALLS
STANDARD REFERENCE
ENCYCLOPEDIA

FUNK & WAGNALLS
Standard REFERENCE
ENCYCLOPEDIA

VOLUME 6

CELLULOID—COLORADO

JOSEPH LAFFAN MORSE, Sc.B., LL.B., LL.D.
Editor in Chief

Standard Reference Works Publishing Company, Inc., New York

Frontispiece photo credits: Top left, East-
photo; Top right and center left, Charbon-
nier from Photo Researchers; Center right,
Francis G. Mayer, courtesy of the Minne-
apolis Museum of Arts; Bottom, Ergy Lan-
dau from Rapho-Guillumette.

Funk & Wagnalls
Standard Reference
Encyclopedia

LIST OF ABBREVIATIONS USED IN THE TEXT

abbr.	abbreviated	Gael.	Gaelic	OHG.	Old High German
a-c	alternating current	gal.	gallon	ON.	Old Norse
A.D.	Anno Domini	Gen.	General	ONF.	Old Norman French
alt.	altitude	Ger.	German	O.T.	Old Testament
A.M.	ante meridiem	Gr.	Greek	oz.	ounce
anc.	ancient	Heb.	Hebrew	Phil.	Philippine
Ar.	Arabic	Hind.	Hindustani	P.M.	post meridiem
AS.	Anglo-Saxon	Hon.	Honorable	Pol.	Polish
A.S.S.R.	Autonomous Soviet	h.p.	horsepower	pop.	population
	Socialist Republic	hr.	hour	Port.	Portuguese
at.no.	atomic number	Hung.	Hungarian	prelim.	preliminary
at.wt.	atomic weight	I.	Island	pron.	pronounced
b.	born	i.e.	that is	q.v.	which see
B.C.	before Christ	in.	inch	r.	reigned
bev	billion electron volts	Ind.	Indian	R.	River
b.p.	boiling point	Ir.	Irish	rev.	revised, revision
B.T.U.	British Thermal	It.	Italian	Rev.	Reverend
	Unit	Jr.	junior	Rum.	Rumanian
bu.	bushel	K.	Kelvin	Russ.	Russian
Bulg.	Bulgarian	kg	kilogram	S.	south; southerly;
C.	centigrade	km	kilometer		southern
cent.	century	lat.	latitude	sec.	second
Chin.	Chinese	Lat.	Latin	Skr.	Sanskrit
cm	centimeter	lb.	pound	Sp.	Spanish
Co.	County	lit.	literally	sp.gr.	specific gravity
colloq.	colloquial	long.	longitude	sq.	square
cu.	cubic	m	meter	S.S.R.	Soviet Socialist
Czech.	Czechoslovakian	m.	mile		Republic
d.	died	M.	Middle	Sum.	Sumerian
Dan.	Danish	mev	million electron volts	Sw.	Swedish
d-c	direct current	mg	milligram	temp.	temperature
Du.	Dutch	min.	minute	trans.	translation,
E.	east; easterly; eastern	M.L.	Medieval Latin		translated
ed.	edition	mm	millimeter	Turk.	Turkish
e.g.	for example	mod.	modern	U.K.	United Kingdom
Egypt.	Egyptian	m.p.	melting point	U.N.	United Nations
Eng.	English	M.P.	Member of	U.S.	United States
est.	estimated		Parliament	U.S.A.	United States of
et seq.	and following	m.p.h.	miles per hour		America
ev	electron volt	Mt.	Mount, Mountain	U.S.S.R.	Union of Soviet
F.	Fahrenheit	N.	north; northerly;		Socialist Republics
fl.	flourished		northern	var.	variety
fr.	from	N.T.	New Testament	W.	west; westerly;
Fr.	French	OE.	Old English		western
ft.	foot	OF.	Old French	yd.	yard
g	gram				

Note.—The official abbreviations for the States of the Union are used throughout. For academic degrees, see article DEGREE, ACADEMIC. For additional abbreviations of units of measure, see article WEIGHTS AND MEASURES. Some abbreviations which are self-explanatory have been omitted.

CELLULOID, originally the trade name of the first synthetic plastic, invented as a substitute for ivory, bone, hard rubber, or coral, by the brothers J. W. and I. S. Hyatt of Newark, N.J., in 1869. The material is made by mixing pyroxylin (cellulose nitrate) with pigments and fillers in a solution of camphor in alcohol. While the substance is warm, and until the alcohol evaporates, it is plastic, and is molded into a variety of shapes, but after cooling and drying it is hard. The term "celluloid" is now used for pyroxylin plastics made in this way by any manufacturer. Celluloid varnishes for lacquering on metal are also extensively manufactured. These are solutions of pyroxylin in mixtures of wood alcohol, acetone, and amyl acetate. Any color can be given to celluloid by the use of coloring matter during the process of manufacture. Some of the advantages of celluloid, besides its cheapness and durability, are that it takes a high polish, does not warp or discolor, and is impervious to moisture. As ordinarily manufactured, it is highly inflammable; but various modifications of the original processes of manufacture have been made, largely by the use of mineral fillers or other esters of cellulose in place of the very inflammable nitrate. Celluloid has now been generally replaced by cellulose acetate (see CELANESE) and other less inflammable plastics. See PLASTICS.

CELLULOSE (Lat. *cellula*, "little cell"), the chief constituent of the cell wall of all vegetable cells. These walls constitute the plant skeleton and also form a protective covering for the sensitive, living protoplasm. The term "cellulose" covers a number of bodies of similar chemical nature, the relative composition of which may be represented by the formula $C_6H_{10}O_5$; their molecular structures are, however, exceedingly complex. In plants cellulose is normally combined with woody, fatty, or gummy substances. A typical form, from which pure cellulose can be easily isolated by chemical methods, exists in cotton and flax fibers. Certain plants, such as peas, beans, the coconut palm, and Arabian coffee, store reserve food in the walls of their seeds as a pseudo-cellulose, which in this form undergoes hydrolysis more readily than other celluloses.

With some exceptions in the insect world, true cellulose is not found in animal tissues. Much of it is digested and absorbed by the herbivora, but the amount which man assimilates is usually relatively small. No digestive enzyme has been observed in the animal body having a specific action upon cellulose; it is considered probable that for its disintegration a co-operation of the living cell wall of the intestine and bacteria of the alimentary tract are necessary. The chief value of the digestion of cellulose by the animal organism has been assumed to be that the true foodstuff of the plant cells is thus liberated and rendered available.

Cellulose makes up more than one third of the entire vegetable matter in the world. Its stability is so great that considerable quantities are preserved unaltered through the process of formation of coal, in which its presence may be demonstrated by means of suitable reagents. It is manufactured on a large scale from wood, cotton, linen rags, hemp, flax, and similar materials of vegetable origin. Being insoluble in all ordinary solvents, it may be readily separated from the other constituents, which are soluble in water, alcohol, ether, dilute alkalies, or acids. It is soluble in an ammoniacal solution of cupric oxide (Schweitzer's reagent), from which it separates out in a pure state on addition of acid; the precipitate is washed with alcohol, and the cellulose is thus obtained in the form of a white, amorphous powder.

Sulfuric acid acts upon cellulose to produce, depending upon its concentration, glucose, soluble starch, or amyloid; the latter is a form of starch used for the coating of parchment paper.

When cellulose has been treated with an alkali, as in the mercerizing process, and then exposed to the fumes of carbon disulfide, it goes into solution as cellulose xanthate. By further treatment this solution yields viscose films and threads. Rayon is cellulose regenerated from such solutions. Viscoid, a hard mass obtained by mixing viscose with various substances, is used for moldings. Cellulose acetates are obtained by the action of acetic anhydrides on cellulose in the presence of sulfuric acid. They can be spun into fine filaments for the manufacture of such fabrics as Celanese (q.v.); they can also be used for photographic safety film, as a substitute for glass, for the manufacture of safety glass, and as a molding material in the manufacture of many plastic objects. Cellulose ethers, such as ethyl cellulose and benzyl cellulose, are used in paper sizings, adhesives, soaps, and synthetic resins. They are stable, inexpensive, and soluble in a wide variety of inexpensive solvents.

With mixtures of nitric and sulfuric acids, cellulose forms a series of inflammable and explosive compounds known as nitrocelluloses, the composition of which depends on the strength of the acids and the duration of the treatment. Pyroxylin (q.v.), or pyro cotton, is a cellulose nitrate used in various lacquers and plastics. It is an important constituent of most military propellants. When pyroxylin is dissolved in a mixture of alcohol and ether, it yields collodion, a cellulose nitrate used in medicine and photography, and in the manufacture of artificial silk, leather, and some lacquers. Guncotton is cellulose nitrate of more than 12.6 percent nitration. It is a high explosive, used in blasting gelatin, demolition blocks, and various other military explosives. (See EXPLOSIVES.)

The most important use of cellulose is in the manufacture of paper. For the cheaper grades of paper, the impure cellulose of wood pulp is employed; better grades are manufactured from cotton and linen rags. In the U.S. alone, more than 17 million tons of paper are produced annually. See PAPER; PLASTICS; WOOD: *Chemical Products of Wood.*

H.A.N.

CELSIUS, ANDERS (1701–44), Swedish astronomer, born at Uppsala. From 1730 to 1744 he was professor of astronomy in Uppsala University, built the observatory there in 1740, and was appointed its director. In 1733 was published his collection of 316 observations of the Aurora Borealis. In 1737 he took part in the French expedition sent to measure one degree of meridian in the polar regions. In his monograph *On the Measurement of Heat* (1742) he presented the first idea of the centigrade thermometer. He wrote, among other scientific treatises, *De Observationibus pro Figura Telluris Determinanda in Gallia Habitis Disquisitio* (Uppsala, 1738).

CELSUS, AULUS CORNELIUS (1st cent. A.D.), Latin physician and writer. He was called the Roman Hippocrates, because he introduced the Hippocratic system of medicine among the Romans. Celsus wrote an encyclopedic work on the subjects of medicine, rhetoric, history, philosophy, warfare, and agriculture. Only part of this work, the eight books on medi-

The Metropolitan Museum of
Gold chalice from Ardagh, Ireland

cine, *De Medicina,* survives, and is valued because in it Celsus has indicated the opinions and observations of the Alexandrian school of medicine.

CELT or **KELT.** See CELTIC PEOPLES AND LANGUAGES.

CELTIC ART, works of art produced in pre-Christian and early Christian times by Celts (see CELTIC PEOPLES AND LANGUAGES) inhabiting the British Isles and the European continent. The earliest Celtic art was created late in the Iron Age (q.v.) by Celtic tribesmen living on or near the Lake of Neuchâtel, in present-day Switzerland. The products of this era, known as the La Tène period, in-

The Metropolitan Museum of
A Celtic brooch of bronze, found in Tara, Ireland, is gold-plated and ornamented with enamel and pieces of coral.

clude pottery, metal, and woodwork ornamented with spiral and S-shaped figures, as well as other geometric designs. The early, or Pagan, period of Celtic art in Britain dates from about three centuries before the beginning of the Roman occupation (55 B.C.). Notable remains from the period include rude but impressive stone monuments which seemingly played an important role in fertility rites and other folk practices. Such monuments are found in many parts of Scotland, Ireland, Brittany, Wales, and Cornwall. Other pre-Christian artifacts include shields, swords, sheaths, helmets, armlets, and similar articles of personal use and adornment. The basic material was generally bronze, but occasionally silver and gold were utilized. The principal motifs employed were elliptical curves, divergent spirals, and chevrons; they were formed in high or low relief by the use of chased or engraved lines and dots on plates and of champlevé enamels of red, yellow, blue, and green. The patterns were of a highly intricate nature. Many articles of great beauty, found in various places throughout England, Scotland, and Ireland, are in the National Museums of London, Edinburgh, and Dublin. Pottery took the form of cinerary urns, food vessels, drinking cups, and incense cups, turned by hand and imperfectly baked but of fine workmanship.

With the introduction of Christianity into the British isles, Celtic art became religious in character. The priest took the place of the warrior, and the vessels used in the service of the church replaced those of the battlefield. This period produced illuminated pages of manuscript copies of the Gospels, the most famous of which are the Book of Kells in Trinity College, Dublin, and the Lindisfarne Gospels in the British Museum. Specimens of metal work of this period include chalices, crosiers, bells, and shrines. Examples of sculpture in stone are the incised cross slabs and monumental stones of Scotland and Ireland, which are similar in decorative characteristics to the metal work and manuscripts. See RUNES.　　　　　　　　　　A.S.

CELTIC PEOPLES AND LANGUAGES.

The Celtic peoples, so designated because their languages belong to the Celtic branch of the Indo-European family of languages, comprised an ensemble of different racial groups predominant in central and western Europe in antiquity. The characteristic of Celtic languages that most conspicuously distinguishes them from other Indo-European linguistic groups is their loss of the original Indo-European sound *p*. In most other Indo-European linguistic groups the sound was preserved. Thus, a Latin, Greek, or Sanskrit word containing an initial or medial *p* will appear in the Celtic family without that consonant (e.g., Latin *porcus*, Goidelic *orc*; Latin *plenus*, Breton *leûn*). In relation to the other members of the Indo-European family of languages, the Celtic group is closest, linguistically as well as geographically, to the Italic and Germanic.

The geographical and ethnological origins of the Celts are obscure. Their name is derived from *Keltoi*, the Greek form of a Celtic word meaning, possibly, "heroes" or "lofty ones". When they made their first appearance in northern Europe, probably in the 2nd millennium B.C., the Celts doubtless comprised one or more tribes of the Indo-European linguistic family. At an early stage of their subsequent development the Celts probably merged with non-Indo-European tribes. Eventually they became the dominant military and cultural force in north-central Europe, giving their language, customs, religion, and traditions to the peoples they subjugated. More than 150 distinct Celtic-speaking tribes, of whom the Britons and the tribes of Gaul (qq.v.) were the most prominent, ultimately emerged in Europe. Late in the 2nd millennium B.C. the Goidels, or Gaels, moved westward from the Continent and occupied the islands known later as Britain, Ireland, and the Isle of Man. Scholars are not certain whether the Goidels' occupation of Britain antedated or followed their settlement of the latter two islands. The Goidels were the ancestors of the modern Irish, Manx, and Scottish Gaels, many of whom still speak a Celtic language (see GAELIC LANGUAGE; MANX LANGUAGE AND LITERATURE).

The Goidels were succeeded in Britain, probably in the 5th or 4th century B.C., by a Celtic tribe known as the Brythons. During the Roman occupation of Britain the Brythons retained their language and their culture, although both were modified extensively by Roman influences. Though the Brythons were later overwhelmed by invading Teutonic tribes, the Brythonic variation of the Celtic language survives in Welsh, the most thriving Celtic language (see WELSH LANGUAGE; WELSH LITERATURE). Cornish, a variation of Brythonic spoken in Cornwall, became practically extinct about the end of the 18th century (see CORNISH LANGUAGE AND LITERATURE). A form of Brythonic, known as Breton, is also spoken in Brittany, the Amorican peninsula of w. France settled in the 5th and 6th centuries A.D. by refugees escaping from the Germanic invaders of Britain. See BRETON LANGUAGE AND LITERATURE.

The Goidelic and Brythonic groups of Celtic languages differ in that Goidelic preserves the velar element of the Indo-European labiovelar *qu* sound (later hard *c*), whereas Brythonic renders this sound as *p*. Thus Irish *mac* (son) corresponds to the Middle Welsh *map* (*mab* in modern Welsh); Irish *coic* (five) corresponds to Welsh *pump*. The Brythonic *p* is not, however, identical with the original Indo-European sound *p*, which dropped out of Celtic long before the differentiation of that tongue into separate languages. For convenience, the Goidelic family is known as Q-Celtic and the Brythonic as P-Celtic. Most Gaulish dialects were probably closely related to Brythonic. Toward the close of the 2nd millennium B.C., or at some time early in the 1st millennium B.C., the Gauls, the largest grouping of the Celtic tribes on the Continent, became dominant in the territory to which they gave their name. Between the 5th and 2nd centuries B.C., they swept over most of Europe, invading the Iberian peninsula, northern Italy, Macedonia, and Thessaly. They plundered Rome in 390 B.C., sacked Delphi in 279 B.C., and penetrated Asia Minor, where they founded Galatia (q.v.). As a result of these far-flung deployments, their positions in central Europe became increasingly vulnerable to the Germanic tribes E. of the Rhine. About the end of the 2nd century B.C., the Romans, under Gaius Marius, inflicted two disastrous defeats on the Gauls in northern Italy. Gaius Julius Cæsar subjugated the remainder of the Gallic tribes, notably the Belgæ (q.v.), beween 58 and 50 B.C., concluding the era of Celtic supremacy in western Europe. Celtic continued to be the universal language of Gaul until the end of the 2nd century A.D., but thereafter Latin became the predominant tongue. By the 4th century A.D., Celtic languages had virtually ceased to exist on the European continent.

The Celtic tribes of the Continent were bound together by common speech, customs, and religion, and by a characteristic physical type rather than by any well-defined central government. The absence of political unity contributed substantially to the extinction of their civilization, which, in many respects, was considerably further advanced than that of the Teutonic tribes in the east. Their social system was dominated by fiducial and religious factors, as illustrated by the hierarchic power of the Druids (see DRUIDISM), an order of priests who performed sylvan and magical ceremonies, and by the deep-rooted tribal or clan system, still clearly traceable in the Scottish clans. Their mythology, which included earth gods, various sylvan genii, and sun deities, was peculiarly rich in elfin demons and tutelaries, beings that still pervade the lore of peoples of Celtic ancestry. The art of the Continental Celts attained a remarkable degree of perfection, notably in the early phase (about 550 to 420 B.C.) of the period known in archeology as the La Tène period. Excavated specimens of their pottery and horse harness, and bronze swords, helmets, and jewelry, reveal that their craftsmen excelled in technique and ornamentation.

The most ancient Celtic-speaking peoples left no literature, their tradition having been purely oral. The few examples of Gaulish in existence consist mostly of inscriptions on monuments and coins, which yield proper names as well as scattered clues to the nature of Gaulish grammar and phonology. References to Gaulish proper names are also found in the works of Greek and Roman historians. The germ of Celtic literature appeared in the oghamic inscriptions of Ireland, simple records of men and events carved in stone and wood. Before the development of a formal alphabet the Goidelic tribes employed a symbolic system of writing which utilized the cross, the fylfot or swastika, the trefoil or trivet, and other figures. To some extent the symbolism included the use of colors and weaves, later exemplified by the Scottish tartans. The music and poetry of the insular Celtic-speaking peoples of ancient times were preserved by bards and other entertainers, who chanted tribal traditions, sang patriotic songs, and recited folk tales. The literary talent and heritage developed in this fashion eventually found expression in the literatures of the various insular Celtic peoples, particularly during the Middle Ages. See NEO-CELTIC MOVEMENT.   R.A.F.

CEMENT, any material which, after application in a plastic form, later becomes tenaciously adhesive. Some types, such as Portland cement, are used to bind together separate particles of other substances, such as sand or gravel, into a coherent mass, such as concrete; others are used for uniting the surfaces of various materials; still others, for coating surfaces to render them smooth or impervious to foreign substances. Cements are made in a wide variety of compositions, and for a wide variety of uses. Some are named for their composition, as calcareous cements and siliceous cements; others, for the materials they join, as glass cement and rubber cement; others for the object to which they are applied, as aquarium cement and boiler cement; others, for their characteristic property, as acid-resisting cement, quick-setting cement, and rapid-hardening cement; others, for their reputed place of origin, as Roman cement; and others, for their resemblance to other materials, as Portland cement, which resembles Portland stone. The "setting" of some types of cement is accomplished by the evaporation of the water, oil, alcohol or other liquid with which they were plasticized; of others, by cooling and solidification from a hot, molten condition; of others, by internal chemical change, hydration, or the formation of a network of interlacing crystals; and of others, by combining with the oxygen or carbon dioxide of the atmosphere. Cements which resist high temperature are called refractory cements. See CONCRETE; GLUE; MORTAR; CEMENT, PORTLAND.

CEMENT, PORTLAND, a powder composed of silicates and aluminates, which hardens chemically after being mixed with water. It is a hydraulic cement, that is, it will harden under water, and is the type of cement almost universally used for structural concrete. Typical Portland cements are mixtures of tricalcium silicate ($3CaO \cdot SiO_2$), tricalcium aluminate ($3CaO \cdot Al_2O_3$), and dicalcium silicate ($2CaO \cdot SiO_2$), in varying proportions, together with small amounts of magnesium and iron compounds. Gypsum is also commonly added to cement to slow the hardening process.

These active compounds in cement are unstable, and when water is added rearrange their structure. The initial set or hardening of the cement is due to the hydration of tricalcium silicate, which forms jellylike hydrated silica and calcium hydroxide. These substances ultimately crystallize and bind together the particles of sand or stone, which are always included in a mortar or concrete mixture, into a hard mass. Tricalcium aluminate acts in the same way to produce the initial set, but does not contribute to the ultimate hardening of the mixture. The hydration of dicalcium silicate proceeds similarly, but far more slowly, gradually increasing in hardness over a period of years. The process of hydration and setting of a cement mixture is known as curing; during this period heat is evolved.

Portland cement is manufactured from lime-bearing materials, usually limestone, together with clays, shales, or blast furnace slag containing alumina and silica, in the proportions 61.5% lime, 22.5% silica, and 7.5% alumina. Some rocks, called cement rocks, are naturally composed of these elements in approximately suitable proportions, and can be made into cement without the use of large quantities of other raw materials. In general however, cement plants rely on mixed materials.

In the manufacture of cement the raw materials are ground together, the mixture is heated until it fuses into a clinker, and the clinker is ground into a fine powder. The heating is usually accomplished in rotary kilns as much as 400 ft. long and 12 or more ft. in diameter. The kilns are slightly tilted from the horizontal, and the raw material is introduced at the upper end, either in the form of a dry rock powder or as a wet paste composed of ground-up rock and water. As the charge progresses down through the kiln it is first dried and heated by the hot gases from a flame at the lower end. As it comes nearer the flame, carbon dioxide is driven off, and in the area of the flame itself the charge is fused at temperatures between 2800° F. (1538° C.) and 2900° F. (1593° C.). The material takes 6 hours to pass from one end of the kiln to the other. After it leaves the kiln, the clinker is cooled quickly and ground, and then conveyed by a blower to packing machinery or storage silos.

In a modern kiln 100 lbs. of raw material will make 60 to 65 lbs. of cement. The weight lost is largely carbon dioxide and water. Kilns usually burn coal in the form of powder, but oil and gas are also used as fuels. With coal as a fuel about 1 lb. is consumed for every 2 lbs. of cement produced.

Cement is a grayish-green powder so fine in texture that 90% or more of its particles will pass through a sieve with 200 openings per inch. It is packed in bags containing 94 lbs., or in barrels of 376 lbs.

A number of tests are used to check on the quality of the cement. A common one is to make up a mortar specimen of one part of cement and three parts of sand and measure its tensile strength after a period of a week in air and under water. A good cement will show a tensile strength of 275 lbs. per sq. in. under these conditions.

Special Cements. By varying the percentage of its normal components or adding others, Portland cement can be given various desirable characteristics, such as rapid hardening, low heat during hydration, and resistance to alkalis. Rapid-hardening cements, sometimes called high-early-strength cements, are made by increasing the proportion of tricalcium silicate or by finer grinding, up to 99½% through a 325-mesh screen. Some of these cements will harden as much in a day as ordinary cement does in a month. They have the disadvantage, however, of producing much heat during hydration, which makes them unsuitable for large structures where the heat of hydration may cause cracks. For massive pourings of concrete, special low-heat cements, which usually have a large proportion of dicalcium silicate, are generally used. Where concrete work must be exposed to alkaline soils or water, which attack concretes made with ordinary Portland cement, resistant cements with a low aluminum content are generally employed. Cements for use under salt water may contain as much as 5% iron oxide. Cements with as much as 40% aluminum oxide are used to resist the action of sulfate-bearing waters.

Production. It was not until the 20th century that the U.S. produced Portland cement in any great quantity. In 1910, 76,550,000 barrels were manufactured. After 1910, production rose steadily until 1928, when 176,300,000 barrels were made. There was a sharp drop in the early 1930's, then production began to rise again. In 1961 the cement industry produced a total of 324,100,000 barrels. California ranks first among the States of the United States in the production of cement; other leading producers are Pennsylvania, Texas, and Michigan. See CONCRETE.

History. Hydraulic cements made from lime and clay have been used since the middle of the 18th century. The name Portland cement was first used in 1824 by Joseph Aspdin, an English cement maker, because of the resemblance between concrete made from his cement and the so-called Portland stone, which was much used in building in England. The first modern Portland cement, made from lime and clay or shale materials calcined to a clinker and then ground, was produced in England in 1845. At that time cements were usually made in upright kilns where the raw materials were spread between layers of coke, which was then burned. The first rotary kilns were introduced about 1830.

A.G.H.D.

CENCI, BEATRICE (1577–99), Italian noblewoman, called "the beautiful parricide". She was the daughter of Francesco Cenci, a Roman nobleman of wealth. According to legend, now stated to be without historic basis, he persecuted her, after his second marriage, with incestuous advances until circumstances enabled him to gratify his lust. She besought the help of her relatives, and in company with her stepmother and her brother, Giacomo, planned the murder of her father (1598). She and Giacomo were put to the torture. Gia-

como confessed but Beatrice persisted in declaring her innocence. All, however, were condemned and beheaded (1599). The story has been the theme of numerous literary works, notably a tragedy by Percy Bysshe Shelley, *The Cenci* (1819).

CENIS, MONT, or MONTE CENISIO, mountain of the Alps, on the French-Italian border. The culminating point of the pass over Mont Cenis reaches an elevation of about 6850 feet above sea level. The mountain is composed of schist, limestone, and gypsum, and is covered with a rich vegetation. The road over the pass, constructed in 1803–10 under Napoleon's orders, has a total length of 40 miles. The tunnel, constructed in 1857–70, is nearly 8 miles long and varies in altitude from 3775 to 4245 feet. See TUNNELS.

CENOZOIC ERA, the last great division of geologic time, lying between the Mesozoic Era and the present. In this era were deposited the strata including the Tertiary and Quaternary systems (qq.v.). See also GEOLOGY, SYSTEMATIC.

CENSORSHIP, supervision and control of newspapers, books, theatrical productions, motion pictures, and other mediums of communication for the purpose of preventing the dissemination of information and ideas held to be pernicious. The word "censorship" derives from "censor", the title of ancient Roman magistrates whose original function when the office was instituted in 443 B.C. was to supervise the enumeration of the population for the purpose of levying taxes. The duties of the censors were in time extended to include the supervision of citizens in their performance of public obligations, and eventually the censors became also the guardians of public morals.

In modern times agencies of censorship have been maintained by the state, the church, and certain private groups.

The State as an Agency of Censorship. State censorship is established in the interests of political stability or of national security. It is at present the most far-reaching and effective of all types of censorship, although it varies in degree of control among the different types of states.

In general, totalitarian states determine more or less directly the kind of information or cultural material that may be communicated by the press, book publishers, motion pictures, the theater, schools, and the like. Among such states are the U.S.S.R., the neighboring countries under Communist domination, the People's Republic of China, and Spain. In those states in which the ruling authority is elected for a limited term and is limited in power (United States, Great Britain, France) censorship is generally designed to prevent the publication or dissemination of material considered obviously obscene or seditious. In the United States, for example, the Post Office Department is empowered to prevent the passage of such types of material through the mails. In the different States of the United States varying degrees of censorship have been authorized by legislative enactments. Similarly, U.S. cities exercise censorship powers by licensing regulations.

During certain periods of emergency, as in time of war, the extent and intensity of censorship increases nationally and locally. The purpose of wartime censorship is to keep data about military preparations and movements from the enemy, to safeguard public order and morale from agitation that may foster defeatism or subversion, and to prevent news of adverse military developments from affecting the national morale. For these reasons, both the mails proceeding to and from fields of military training and operations and news dispatches about military or political subjects are carefully scrutinized; and the dissemination of ideas considered obstructive to the prosecution of the war or dangerous to the stability of the government is forbidden or restricted.

The Church as an Agency of Censorship. Church censorship can be traced back to ancient societies in which priests or priest-kings guarded the secrets of ritual and doctrine. In modern times church censorship is widely effective only in those states in which an established or sole church is recognized and is permitted to participate in or even control public education, public welfare, and other social and cultural services. In the United States and certain other countries various religious denominations, acting as private groups, bring their views on material considered by them to be objectionable to the attention of the communications industries. By such means they frequently succeed in precluding the presentation of the offending material. When material held to be objectionable is presented, religious groups often advise their members not to read, watch, or listen. A number of private groups associated with neither church nor state are also influential in certain nations, notably the United States, in preventing the presentation or restricting the circulation of material.

Attitudes Toward Censorship. In general, the proponents of state censorship maintain that the national or public welfare should be protected against sedition and immorality even at the expense of individual liberty. Those who are in favor of church and private censorship argue that in some cases the individual is unable to distinguish as well as church authorities or highly informed citizens harmful material in what is offered to him as information, doctrine, or entertainment.

Opponents of censorship generally do not advocate outright abolition of all censorship. They are concerned rather with the difficult questions of when, where, and how to apply censorship. Few would deny, for example, that some degree of military censorship is unavoidable in time of war, or that some degree of moral censorship is necessary to keep obscene material out of general circulation. Nevertheless, the opponents of censorship maintain that, carried beyond certain minimal limits, its infringement on freedom of expression is an actual harm, far graver in its consequences than the potential harm that might ensue from the comparatively unlimited circulation of ideas and information.

CENSORSHIP IN THE UNITED STATES

During the pre-Revolutionary period the press in the American colonies was subject to licensing laws similar to those of Great Britain. After the Revolution and the adoption (1788) of the Constitution freedom of speech and of the press was guaranteed in the Bill of Rights (1791) by the First Amendment, which states, "Congress shall make no law . . . abridging the freedom of speech or of the press . . .".

Within seven years of the ratification of the Bill of Rights, Congress violated the First Amendment by passing the four Alien and Sedition Acts (q.v.) of 1798. The acts were designed to keep out of the United States the seemingly dangerous ideas of the French Revolution and, in particular, the advocates of such ideas, but were also invoked to jail editors for printing articles critical of President John Adams and his administration. Three of the laws expired in 1800–01, and the last was repealed in 1802.

The constitutions adopted by each of the thirteen original States, and by the thirty-five new states created between 1790 and 1912, generally guarantee freedom of the press. At various times, however, many States have violated their own constitutions in regard to this freedom. Some of the most flagrant of these violations occurred in pre-Civil War days, when certain southern States outlawed abolitionist literature.

Moral Censorship. Moral censorship of

books became increasingly frequent in the latter half of the 19th century. In 1873 Congress passed the Comstock Law, named for the American reformer Anthony Comstock (q.v.), which forbade the sending or receiving of so-called indecent matter through the mails. It was soon followed by similar laws in most of the States. The Comstock Law still obtains, but it has been less rigidly enforced in recent years.

Court Rulings Affecting Censorship. The tendency to avoid applying the Comstock Law was due largely to a series of court decisions, in the first of which, rendered in 1933, a federal judge ruled that *Ulysses*, a work by the Irish novelist James Joyce, was not pornographic and therefore could be admitted into the United States. Subsequent decisions, including a number by the Supreme Court, have established that a book must be shown to be the direct cause of an illegal act before it can be constitutionally banned (1949) ; that it cannot be banned for sale to adults merely because it is considered harmful for children (1957) ; that it must be judged in its entirety rather than on the basis of isolated passages; and that the test of obscenity is whether the work as a whole, judged by contemporary standards, appeals to the "average man's prurient interest" (1957). In the spirit of the latter decision, a U.S. district court ruled in 1959 that an unexpurgated edition of the novel *Lady Chatterley's Lover,* by D. H. Lawrence, was mailable and not obscene.

Moral censorship of motion pictures in the United States derives from a Supreme Court decision of 1915, which declares that films are "merely entertainment" and are thus not entitled to the protection guaranteed by the First Amendment to certain other means of communication. The effect of this ruling was to strengthen existing State and local movie-censorship laws and to encourage the enactment of new ones. However, only four States (Kansas, Maryland, New York, and Virginia) and about twenty municipalities presently maintain local censorship boards to screen motion pictures, and their judgments are frequently overruled when appealed to the courts.

In 1952 the Supreme Court reversed its stand of thirty-seven years earlier in a case involving the Italian film *The Miracle*, which the N.Y. State Board of Censors had found sacrilegious. The Supreme Court ruled that government has no right to "suppress real or imagined attacks upon a particular religious doctrine". The court also recognized officially that motion pictures had developed into a medium for communicating worthwhile ideas and, as such, were entitled to the protection of the Bill of Rights. Although in succeeding years the court dealt with a number of other films (*Pinky, La Ronde, M, The Moon Is Blue,* and *The Game of Love*) and found each to be not obscene, in none of these rulings did the court attempt to define obscenity. It held merely that the film in question had been improperly censored.

Private Censorship. Private censorship of motion pictures is carried on by various groups which contend that the representation of certain ideas will be harmful to their own sincere interests and to that extent may distort the truth. A number of religious bodies are active in this way, notably the Legion of Decency, an agency of the Roman Catholic Church. The Legion has been influential in preventing the exhibition of certain motion pictures by theater owners.

Private groups such as the National Office for Decent Literature, organized in the 1930's by the Roman Catholic Church in the United States, attempt to make certain books considered objectionable unavailable to the general public. In addition, the office often encourages Church members to boycott objectionable books.

Radio and television in the United States are not censored. However, radio and television stations may operate only by license from the Federal Communications Commission, an independent agency of the U.S. government. The commission assigns radio wave lengths and television channels to private stations "in the public interest", and requires that the programs presented be above a certain minimum cultural standard. It requires also that stations present both sides of current issues in news and discussion programs and provide broadcasting opportunities to all candidates during political campaigns. An industry code and the advertisers' fear of offending customers have generally eliminated the need for censorship. On occasion the broadcasting companies practice self-censorship. For example, in 1956 a Chicago television station cancelled the film *Martin Luther* because of expected protests from members of the Catholic Church.

Political Censorship. Very little political censorship has been exercised in the United States since the 19th century. Neither Republican nor Democratic administrations have attempted to stifle public expressions of opinion by the party not in power. In some States, however, there have been occasional acts of censorship which reflect social attitudes of political importance. For example, in 1956 the South Carolina legislature, having discovered that a book which was held to favor racial integration had been purchased by State funds, asked the State library board to remove from circulation all volumes "antagonistic and inimical to the traditions and customs of the state".

The Federal government imposed censorship for reasons of national security during World War I and World War II. During World War II the restrictions upon the release of government information to the press were especially severe. During the postwar period, as relations between the United States and the Soviet Union worsened, censorship was continued.

A more controversial form of censorship in the interest of national security was exercised from 1952 through 1954, when the Senate Permanent Investigation Subcommittee, headed by Senator Joseph R. McCarthy (1908–57) of Wisconsin, conducted investigations into communism in the United States. The committee's findings led directly and indirectly to the removal from the United States Information Service libraries abroad of thousands of books written by alleged communists and to similar acts of censorship at home. The atmosphere of suspicion prevailing during that period subsided substantially after the Senate formally censured McCarthy in December, 1954.

In the early 1960's political censorship continued to exist in the United States chiefly in the form of restrictions on military information available to the public. (See also PRESS, FREEDOM OF THE; RIGHTS, CIVIL; LIBERTY.)

HISTORY

Censorship has existed from earliest times wherever the rule of a church or a state has been powerful enough to impose its authority upon society. Perhaps the first distinct form of censorship can be seen in the taboo (q.v.), commonly found among primitive peoples. The taboo is an interdiction originating in custom and imposed by tribal priests or rulers upon such things as specified foods, forms of intermarriage, clothes, and names which are believed to be forbidden by the gods or spirits, or the use of which would put someone in mortal danger. Among some Australian aborigines, for example, even a warrior's personal name is kept from general knowledge in the belief that an enemy can magically do harm to the warrior merely by uttering it.

Antiquity. In all ancient civilizations, such as the Egyptian, Babylonian, Persian, Hindu, and Chinese, different forms of religious and moral censorship often may be traced to their origin in taboos. At the same time, however, the autocratic rulers of those civilized states imposed their own types of political censorship in order to restrain the expression of opposition to their power. The principle of free and uncontrolled expression of ideas or communication of information was generally alien to the ancient world.

By contrast, the citizens of Athens enjoyed the political rights of free men during the Golden Age (4th and 5th centuries B.C.) of Athenian democracy. The citizens of Rome under the republic (6th–1st centuries B.C.) were also granted considerable political freedom. However, with the establishment of the empire (about 43 B.C.) censorship was extended and intensified.

The Middle Ages. In the Middle Ages the most powerful control of censorship was that of the Roman Catholic Church. In the Papal States directly under the political rule of the Church, and in localities where the bishop was the feudal lord, Church censorship was official and absolute. Elsewhere it was more limited in application. Censorship in the Middle Ages was concerned primarily with suppressing heresy, all manifestations of which were severely punished. In 1233 Pope Gregory IX instituted for that purpose the Inquisition (q.v.). The Church established a network of tribunals which examined accused heretics, sometimes resorting to torture, burnt heretical literature, and imposed upon convicted offenders death sentences that were carried out by the secular authorities. For almost five hundred years the Inquisition remained an influential agency of religious censorship. In 1600 the Italian philosopher Giordano Bruno was burned at the stake by the Inquisition for questioning certain dogmas of the Church and expressing a belief in pantheism. In 1633 the Italian scientist and father of modern astronomy Galileo Galilei was forced by the Inquisition to recant the Copernican theory, confirmed by his telescopic observations, that the earth revolves around the sun.

Perhaps the best-known example of church censorship has been the *Index of Prohibited Books* (q.v.) of the Roman Catholic Church. To this index, or list, first issued in the 16th century, has been added periodically the titles of new publications deemed heretical, obscene, or immoral. The Church continues to prohibit its members, on pain of excommunication, from reading such material.

During the 16th and 17th centuries the authorities of the various Protestant churches of Europe, England, and America suppressed everything they held to be heretical with a fervor equal to that prevailing during the Inquisition. Men and women were burned at the stake in many countries in which Calvinist and Puritan leadership was in authority. Under the rule of the Lord Protector Oliver Cromwell, severe moral censorship was instituted in England, and it was extended to the American colony of Massachusetts. In particular, the theaters were closed and all other forms of popular entertainment were outlawed.

The innovation of printing from movable type in the 15th century brought about a more scrupulous censorship of books and pamphlets than had ever before been exercised. Laws were enacted throughout most of Europe prohibiting all printing except by governmental license. For almost two centuries these laws encountered little opposition. One of the first and most famous denunciations of such laws was made by the English poet John Milton. In 1644, without a license from the crown, he issued *Areopagitica*, an influential pamphlet in favor of freedom of the press. In it he protested that "he who destroys a good Booke, kills reason itself . . .". Although the statutes to which he objected expired in 1695 and were never renewed in England, similar forms of censorship of the press remained in force throughout the rest of Europe.

The Age of Enlightenment and Later. The right of the state to censor was not generally questioned in Europe until the latter half of the 18th century, when the political philosophy of the Enlightenment gained currency among European thinkers. However, except for a brief period in France after the Revolution of 1789, political censorship continued to flourish until the latter half of the 19th century. Its decline during that period generally corresponded to the decline in the powers of European monarchs.

Coincident with the ebb of political censorship was a widespread increase in moral censorship, particularly stringent in Great Britain under Queen Victoria, whose reign lasted from 1837 to 1901. By the end of the century, however, this form of censorship generally had subsided also, both in Great Britain and the rest of Europe.

In the years preceding World War I censorship of all kinds declined in most of the civilized world.

During World Wars I and II, military censorship inevitably was imposed in all belligerent countries. However, political censor-

ship has been rare since World War I except in such totalitarian states as the Soviet Union, Italy under the Fascist dictator Benito Mussolini, and Germany under the National Socialist dictator Adolf Hitler. Since World War II censorship has become minimal in Germany and Italy, but remains severe in the Soviet Union, where direct operation of the economy and all social and cultural services enables the government to censor all communicable information at its source.

J.E.F.

CENSUS (Lat. *censere*, "to assess"), a term meaning primarily the official and periodical counting of the people of a country, or section of a country; also the printed record of the counting. In actual usage the term is applied to the collection of information on the size and characteristics of population, as well as information on the numbers and characteristics of dwelling units, various business enterprises, and governmental agencies.

References to counting the population are found in accounts of ancient peoples, such as the Hebrews and the Romans. The early form of census differed from the modern, however, in that it involved a count of the people solely for purposes of taxation or military conscription. Thus, widespread resentment toward census taking was engendered. In western Europe, however, as autocratic government changed to constitutional, the census became a statistical review for information on populations. This development, which took place in Sweden in 1749, in the United States in 1790, and in Great Britain, the Netherlands, Norway, and France in 1801, marked the beginning of the modern census.

During the 19th century and the first half of the 20th, the practice of census taking spread throughout the world. International organizations, such as the United Nations and the International Statistical Institute, have encouraged all countries to adopt uniform standards in taking their censuses. Decennial censuses are taken presently by a considerable number of countries throughout the world, usually in or near years ending in "0".

The first census of the United States was taken in order to provide, in accordance with Article I, section 2, of the Constitution, an enumeration of the "respective numbers" of people in the several States to serve as a basis for the apportionment of representation in Congress and of direct taxes. The Constitution provides that the first actual enumeration should be made within three years of the last meeting of the Constitutional Con-

Bettmann Archive

A census taker questions an American farm family in the late 19th century.

vention and within every subsequent term of ten years.

Procedure. The first national U.S. census recorded by name only the heads of families and grouped the members of the family into the following classes: free Whites, males sixteen years and over, males under sixteen years, females, other free persons, and slaves. Until 1850 no essential change was made in the manner of enumeration, though the classes were enlarged to embrace age, occupation, physical infirmity, and other data.

In this early period no combinations of statistics other than those given in the original schedule were made, and facts given under one head (e.g., age) were not correlated with those given under another (e.g., illiteracy). By 1850, however, for the first time, every inhabitant was recorded by name, the questions being answered for each person specifically, and not for the family group of which he was a part. This change in the manner of asking the questions, and the establishment of a central office in Washington brought about greater uniformity of reports and made numerous cross-tabulations possible. The 1850 census is regarded as the first scientific census in the United States.

The census of 1880 marked the next major improvement in the census procedure. Previously, United States marshals, and a temporary force of assistants appointed by the marshals, had conducted the census. In 1880, however, the work was taken from the marshals and placed in charge of the Census Office at Washington. In 1902, after it had been recognized that the nature and importance of the modern census was such as to require constant investigation, not merely decennial work, the Census Office, now known as Bureau of the Census, was made a permanent bureau of what is now the Department of Commerce. Until 1950, however, the field organization for carrying out the decennial censuses was recruited especially for each census and completely disbanded at the end of the undertaking. In 1950, for the first time, the field organization was based upon a small permanent field staff created to carry out the continuing work needed for the various monthly, quarterly, and annual surveys of the Bureau of the Census.

In most cases, answers to census questions are legally compulsory, but the bureau has traditionally stressed voluntary co-operation, making it clear that the answers to questions are held in strictest confidence and cannot be used to the detriment of any individual or organization. All Bureau of the Census employees are sworn to secrecy with respect to such information when they enter upon their duties, and no material is published except in such combinations of statistics as can be useful without revealing confidential material.

Scope. The decennial census has from the beginning been utilized to secure information beyond the mere number of inhabitants. As early as 1810, additional inquiries were introduced in an attempt to gather statistics on industry. Information was first collected on dependent and delinquent persons in 1830. Agriculture, mines, commerce, manufactures, and schools appeared as subjects of inquiry in 1840. A separate schedule for manufacturing and mechanical industries was adopted in 1850, and in that year the census first included such vital statistics as those relating to birth, marriage, and mortality. Because of the unwieldy complexity of the censuses of 1880 and 1890, the 1900 census was limited in subject matter to population, mortality, agriculture, and manufactures; provision was made, however, for extensive investigations in other fields after the completion of the decennial work. Since 1902 there have been supplemental decennial censuses of the wealth, public debt, and taxation of State and local governments; financial reports of States, and of cities with a population of 100,000 or more, have been issued annually by the Bureau of the Census.

The Fifteenth Census of the United States (1930), as published, contained statistics of population, occupations, unemployment, agriculture, irrigation and drainage, manufactures, mines and quarries, and, for the first time on a national scale, statistics of wholesale and retail distribution, of construction, and of hotels and other service establishments. The population schedule reported the sex, color, age, marital status (whether single, married, widowed, or divorced), place of birth, and occupation of each person. It also carried questions as to school attendance, and ability to read, write, and speak English; and in the case of the foreign-born it asked whether naturalized or alien, and the year of immigration to the United States. Under population were also included questions in regard to unemployment.

In addition to new information on the types of material gathered in previous censuses, the 1940 compilation included a special census of housing which covered the conti-

nental United States and all outlying possessions. Many of the phases of census taking were based upon the principles of modern sampling. For example, one person in twenty was asked several additional questions, covering matters of interest only to the Federal government, States, and large cities.

Data for the Eighteenth Census of the United States (1960) was gathered by methods that differed from those used in previous censuses. For the first time, reporting forms were mailed to households in advance of the census date so they could be completed before the census taker arrived to collect them. Compilation and cross-tabulation of the millions of items were carried out with the aid of electronic equipment. In the fields of population, housing, and agriculture, it was the most comprehensive survey yet taken, and publication of the statistical information about the 179,323,175 persons residing in the United States required many volumes. The census revealed a population increase of 27,-997,377 during the decade, the largest ever recorded by a decennial census, and a number more than seven times greater than the entire population counted in the first census in 1790. The highest rate of growth of any State was that of Florida, a 78.7 percent increase over 1950 which advanced the State from twentieth to tenth place in population rank. The greatest numerical growth took place in California; its gain of 5,130,981 accounted for nearly one fifth of the total population increase of the United States. The increase in urban growth was a continuing trend; about 85 percent of the increase in the total population between 1950 and 1960 occurred in standard metropolitan statistical areas.

Especially during recent years, the scope of the supplemental inquiries of the Bureau of the Census has been enlarged to cover industry and commerce. At the beginning of the 20th century the only industrial statistics collected were those on manufactures and mines and quarries, gathered every ten years. In order to meet modern statistical requirements, the Bureau of the Census subsequently began to conduct a dozen censuses each decade on a variety of subjects. These included the census of population and of housing, conducted in the year ending in "0"; the census of governments, covering the years ending in "2" and "7"; the census of business, manufactures, and mineral industries for the years ending in "3" and "8"; and the census of agriculture, for the years ending in "4" and "9".

Among the improvements in the handling of mass data is the application of electronic equipment to large-scale processing of figures. The 1954 censuses of manufactures and business were the first to be carried out almost entirely with the aid of electronic equipment.

The results of the various censuses in the United States are widely used by government, business, and the general public. At all levels of government, many decisions, regarding legislation, the building of schools, roads, and other facilities, and the allocation of funds, are based quite directly upon the results of one or more of the nation's censuses. In rapidly growing areas, many special censuses are taken in order to provide more up-to-date population totals for the distribution of State revenues. There has been an increasing use of census statistics for many kinds of business decisions. Such statistics provide a measure of potential markets for consumer goods and industrial goods, give a sound basis for advertising and marketing programs, and help in making decisions regarding the location of new plants and facilities of various kinds.

Among the publications of the Bureau of the Census are *Current Population Survey,* issued monthly, the *Monthly Survey of Current Business,* and the annual *Statistical Abstract of the United States* with its supplements, the *County and City Data Book* and the *Historical Statistics of the United States.* The *Statistical Abstract,* in one volume, presents the more important statistical studies prepared by the bureau and by other public and private agencies.

CENTAURS, in Greek mythology, a race of monsters, half man and half horse, which was believed to have inhabited the mountain regions of Thessaly and Arcadia. They were supposedly the descendants of Ixion (q.v.) and Nephele ("Cloud"). They were savage beings, symbolizing for the Greeks the destructive forces of nature. However, two of them were beneficent creatures: Chiron, the instructor of the hero Achilles and of the physician Æsculapius; and Pholus, the friend of Hercules. The best-known legend concerning the centaurs is the story of their battle with the Lapithæ. In art they were at first represented as men to whose bodies were attached the body and hind legs of a horse; later, and more usually, they were represented as human down to the waist only, and with the body and four legs of a horse. They are shown on vases and bronzes and in reliefs as drawing the chariot of Dionysius, the god of wine, and accompanied by cupids, satyrs, and nymphs; as being ridden by the god of love Eros; or as fighting with a human being.

CENTAURUS, a constellation of stars, the centaur, in the southern hemisphere of the sky, and visible chiefly from places south of the equator. The brightest star in this constellation, Alpha Centauri, is also the third brightest and the closest, of all visible stars in the heavens, to our solar system. Its large parallax (q.v.) of 0.75″ early attracted the notice of astronomers, and the measurement of its distance on the basis of this parallax was undertaken at the Cape of Good Hope Observatory in 1881–83. Its distance from the earth is 4.35 light-years. The star is actually a double, with a third star, its distant companion Proxima Centauri, revolving around the other two. The constellation also contains ω Centauri, the closest globular star cluster, about 20,000 light-years away. The line which joins Alpha and Beta Centauri points nearly to the south pole of the heavens.

CENTER COLLEGE. See CENTRE COLLEGE OF KENTUCKY.

CENTIGRADE. See THERMOMETER.

CENTIMETER. See C.G.S. SYSTEM.

CENTIPEDE, general name for the members of the class Chilopoda of the phylum Arthropoda. The centipedes are segmented animals bearing jointed appendages, having a head furnished with feelers and jaws, and breathing by means of air tubes or tracheae.

Structure. The centipede is like a primitive insect in its general structure. The body is divided into well-marked rings, but the region behind the distinct head is not divisible into thorax and abdomen. The number of rings varies from twelve to more than a hundred. The head, which is covered by a flat shield above, bears a pair of antennae, usually of considerable length, and consisting of from twelve to over one hundred joints; a pair of small, strong, toothed, and bristly mandibles; and a pair of under jaws, usually with palps. The next appendages are limblike, and are followed by a modified pair of legs, the basal pieces of which generally meet in the middle line, while the strong joints terminate in a sharp claw, at which a poison-gland opens. These appendages are used for seizing and killing prey. The legs of the other segments are usually seven-jointed, sometimes bearing spurs and glands, and are generally clawed.

The large brain is connected with a ventral chain of ganglia. Compound eyes occur in one family, and simple eyes in many; the feelers, certain bristles, and portions of the skin are also sensory. The alimentary canal is straight, and has associated with it salivary and digestive glands, and excretory (Malpighian) tubules. The heart is represented by a chambered dorsal vessel. Tracheae or air tubes open on the sides of the body, and are connected to one another on each side by a longitudinal stem.

Life and Habits. Centipedes are nocturnal in their food hunting, and remain under stones or wood during the day. Only in one family (Scutigeridae) are there compound eyes; most forms have only simple eyes, and many none at all. They are all carnivorous and not vegetarian like the millipedes.

Development. In some cases the males are said to deposit their reproductive elements in packets (spermatophores) fixed by a web to the ground. In most cases copulation probably occurs. *Scolopendra* is viviparous, the others lay eggs.

Classification and Forms of Interest. The class Chilipoda is distinguished from the Diplopoda, or millipedes, by having no more than one pair of legs on any one segment. The principal families of centipedes are Scutigeridae, Lithobiidae, Scolopendridae, and Geophilidae. The first of these includes forms with compound eyes, long feelers, eight shields along the back, and fifteen pairs of very long legs. The feelers and the last pair of legs are longer than the body; there are external generative appendages. In Lithobiidae, simple eyes alone are present; there are fifteen pairs of legs, antennae measuring a third or more of the body length, and fifteen dorsal shields. The genus *Lithobius* includes over one hundred species; *L. forficatus* (of a reddish-brown color, and about 1 in. long) is common throughout America and Europe. *L. mutabilis,*

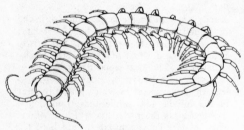

Centipede, Scolopendra cingulata

also common, has the habit of feigning death. The Scolopendridae have over a score of legs; short, many-jointed antennae, not more than one fifth of the total length of the body; and simple eyes, not over four pairs in number, or altogether absent. The poisonous bite of some of the larger forms is dangerous to man. *Scolopendra* is the most important genus. The

Geophilidae are long, wormlike centipedes, of somewhat sluggish habit, with 31 to 173 pairs of legs, short feelers, and no eyes. Well-developed spinning glands are seen in this family, and their secretion cements together ova and spermatozoa.

Distribution. Centipedes are world-wide, but abound especially in warm regions. Somewhat unsatisfactory fossil remains have been obtained from the American carboniferous strata; better-preserved centipedes have been obtained from the Solenhofen strata, but there is no certainty that centipedes existed before Tertiary times.

CENTRAL AFRICAN REPUBLIC, republic of the French Community (see COMMUNITY, THE), situated in central Africa. It is bounded on the N. by the Republic of Chad, on the E. by the Republic of Sudan, on the S. by the former Belgian Congo and the Republic of the Congo (former Middle Congo), and on the W. by Cameroun. The capital and most important town is Bangui (pop., 1960 est., 78,412). The republic is on the N. edge of the Congo Basin on a plateau 2000 to 3000 ft. above sea level. Savanna, or grassland, predominates over most of the country, especially in the N., and dense virgin forest covers the major part of the S. area. Parallel rivers traverse the country in a N.-S. direction. The climate is tropical and healthful. The country's largely undeveloped natural resources include many species of industrially valuable trees. The chief agricultural crop is cotton. In addition to cotton, the leading exports are palm oil, rubber, peanuts, coffee, and forest products. Cattle and other livestock are raised, and, in the S.W., gold and diamond mines are worked. A network of roads, covering about 300 m., supplements the waterways as the most important means of transportation. There are no railroads, but there is an airport in Bangui.

The region was visited by French explorers in the 19th century, and in 1910 it became part of the French colony of Ubangi-Shari-Chad (after 1920, Ubangi-Shari). In 1946 the colony attained Territorial status. On Dec. 1, 1958, the Territory was proclaimed a semi-autonomous republic within the French Community. In May, 1960, the nation joined the republics of Chad and the Congo (former Middle Congo) in a loose federation, the Union of Central African Republics. On Aug. 13, 1960, the republic became a fully autonomous state in the Community. Area, about 238,200 sq.m.; pop. (1960 est.) 1,193,000.

CENTRAL AMERICA, term applied to the southern portion of the North American con

INDEX TO MAP OF CENTRAL AMERICA

Continued on page 1914

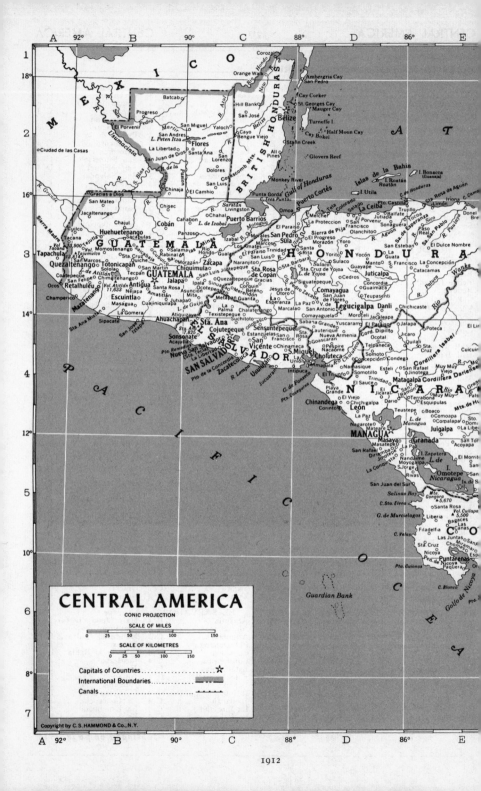

CENTRAL AMERICA

CONIC PROJECTION

SCALE OF MILES

0 25 50 100 150

SCALE OF KILOMETRES

0 25 50 100 150

Capitals of Countries...................☆
International Boundaries..............
Canals.....................................

1912

Index to Map of Central America—cont.

tinent lying N. of Colombia, South America, and S. of Mexico, and consisting of Costa Rica, Guatemala, Honduras, Nicaragua, Panama, El Salvador, and the British crown colony of British Honduras. See articles on these respective countries, and NORTH AMERICA.

CENTRAL CITY, county seat of Gilpin Co., Col., 8515 ft. above sea level, and 40 m. by rail W.N.W. of Denver. It was founded in 1859 after the first important gold discovery in Colorado was made in the Central City area. Gold and silver are still mined in the surrounding region. The city is the site of the Central City Historical Museum and Opera House Museum, and the Teller House, built in 1872, at a cost of $107,000, to house miners during the gold rush. Pop. (1960) 250.

CENTRAL FALLS, city of Providence Co., R.I., adjoining Pawtucket, on the Blackstone R., about 4 miles N. of the city of Providence. It was settled about 1763, and was called Chocolateville from 1780 to 1827. In 1847 it became the Central Falls Fire District of the town of Smithfield; in 1871 it was incorporated with the town of Lincoln; and in 1895 it became a separate city. Textile mills and glassworks are the principal industrial establishments. Pop. (1960) 19,858.

CENTRAL INTELLIGENCE AGENCY. See NATIONAL SECURITY COUNCIL; ESPIONAGE.

CENTRAL POWERS, designation applied during World War I to the German Empire and Austria-Hungary, and, by extension, to their allies, Bulgaria and Turkey. In its original meaning the term referred to the geographical position of Germany and Austria-Hungary in Europe.

CENTRAL PROVINCES AND BERAR. See MADHYA PRADESH.

CENTRE COLLEGE OF KENTUCKY, coeducational institution of higher learning, located in Danville, Ky., and founded in 1819. Courses of study are offered in the arts and sciences leading to the degree of A.B. In 1962 the enrollment at Centre College totaled 538, almost all of whom were full-time students. In the same year the faculty numbered 44.

CENTRIFUGE, a mechanical device consisting of a container which, spinning very rapidly, exerts large centrifugal forces on its contents. The mechanical problem of spinning a large container rapidly is comparatively simple, so that the only limit to the force which can be achieved with a centrifuge is the strength of the metal of which the device is made. It is thus not difficult to achieve centrifugal forces thousands of times as great as the force of gravity.

Centrifuges may be used for rapid separation of substances which would normally separate slowly under the influence of gravity. The draining of water from a wet solid, for example, may be accelerated by spinning the solid; this principle is used on a small scale in the dryer of an ordinary automatic washing machine and on a large scale in industrial filtering and drying. Similarly the separation of cream from milk, which takes many hours under the influence of gravity, may be accomplished in a few seconds in a centrifuge; the operation may be continuous, cream being constantly withdrawn from the center and skim milk from the periphery. Cream separators operating on this principle, introduced about 1880, were the first industrial centrifuges. Since then, numerous other industrial applications of centrifugation have been made; for example, the separation of sugar from syrup, and of wax from lubricating oil.

Ultracentrifuge. The smaller the diameter of a centrifuge, the more rapidly it may be spun without breaking and the greater the forces and accelerations exerted on its contents. For this reason, the most powerful centrifuges are long, narrow tubes rotated at enormous speeds. Such devices are known as ultracentrifuges. The ultracentrifuge was developed about 1920 by the Swedish chemist The Svedberg (q.v.), and further developed by the American chemist J. W. Beams (q.v.).

In the Beams ultracentrifuge, the rotor (the spinning part of the centrifuge) is suspended in a vacuum by magnetic means, with nothing touching it, and driven electrically. Friction is thus reduced to a negligible amount; for example, if a 1/16-in. rotor is spinning in a vacuum of 1/400,000,000th atmospheric pressure at 100,000 revolutions per second, and the driving force is turned off, it will lose only 100 revolutions per second in an hour. The greatest forces thus far achieved, 428,-000,000 times as great as those of gravity, were obtained with a 1/50-in. rotor spinning at 38,000,000 revolutions per minute.

See COLLOIDAL DISPERSION.

CENTURY PLANT. See AGAVE.

CEPHAËLIS. See IPECAC.

CEPHALIC INDEX. See INDEX, CEPHALIC.

CEPHALONIA (Gr. *Kephallēnia,* anc. *Cephallenia*), largest of the Ionian Islands of Greece, in the Ionian Sea, opposite the Gulf of Patras. Together with the nearby island of Ithaca and a number of other islands, it constitutes the department of Cephalonia. The department capital, Argostolion, is situated on the island of Cephalonia, which is about 30 miles long and from 3 to 20 miles wide. Cephalonia Island is mountainous; its highest point, Monte Negro, or Elato (anc. Mount Ænos), is 5315 ft. above sea level. The principal crops are currants, olives, cotton, and grapes. Industry, which is largely undeveloped, includes boatbuilding, the making of lace and baskets, and the weaving of carpets. The ancient Greek poet Homer mentioned the Cephallonians in his poems. The island was successively a possession of the Athenians, Romans, Byzantines, Normans, Venetians, Turks, and French. In 1809 it came into the possession of the British, who ceded it to Greece in 1864. During World War I it was occupied by the French and British in 1915. During World War II it was occupied by the Italians in 1941. Area of department, 306 sq.m.; of Cephalonia Island, 289 sq.m. Pop. of island (1961) 39,790.

CEPHALOPODA (Gr., "head-footed"), the highest class of mollusks, and in some respects the highest invertebrates. They are usually large animals, exclusively marine, with well-developed head-region but with the "foot" or ventral surface grown round the mouth, and split up into "arms," which (with one exception) bear suckers. Another part of the foot is modified to form a funnel through which water is squirted. Two or four gills are present in the usual mantle cavity. The eyes are peculiarly large, and their ferocious aspect has earned for many common forms the title of "devilfish." The mouth, in the midst of the arms, has a parrotlike beak, with a rasping ribbon on the tongue. The central nervous system, with its closely associated ganglia, is surrounded by a protective cartilaginous sheath, analogous, though in no way homologous, with a vertebrate brain box. The sexes are separate.

The cephalopoda are divided into two orders, Tetrabranchiata and Dibranchiata. The former is represented at present only by the genus *Nautilus*, although numerous fossil animals of this order are known. The Dibranchiata differ from other mollusks by having the shell rudimentary or absent. They are further subdivided into the Octopoda or eight-footed animals, such as the octopus (q.v.), and the Decapoda or ten-footed animals, such as the squid and cuttlefish (qq.v.).

CEPHEUS, a northern constellation, situated between Cassiopeia and Draco near the north celestial pole. Its brightest star, Alderamin, is of the third magnitude. More important, however, is the fainter δ Cephei, which is the type star of the class known as Cepheid Variables.

CEPHISODOTUS, name of two Greek sculptors. **1.** CEPHISODOTUS THE ELDER (early 4th cent. B.C.), the elder brother, or possibly the father, of Praxiteles (q.v.). His works mark the transition from the art of the 5th century to that of the 4th and are known only through an extant ancient copy of his group "Irene and Plutus". **2.** CEPHISODOTUS THE YOUNGER (late 4th cent. B.C.), the son of Praxiteles. Of his works only scanty mention has been preserved. He and his brother Timarchos made a statue of Menander which was set up in the theater at Athens; its base has been found bearing the signature of the artists.

CERAM, island of the Moluccas, in the Malay Archipelago, lying between New Guinea on the E. and Buru on the W., and forming part of the Republic of Indonesia. It adjoins the Ceram Sea on the N. and the Banda Sea on the S. Ceram is about 216 m. long from W. to E., is mountainous, and has jungles containing ironwood trees and sago palms. Most of the island's many rivers drain to the Ceram Sea and are dry part of the year. The climate is tropical, being hot and humid, with heavy rains in the wet season. Earthquakes sometimes occur. The greater part of the interior is unexplored. A majority of the population live along the coasts. The principal towns, Amahai and Tehoru on the S. coast, Bula Bay on the E. coast, Wahai on the N. coast, and Piru on the W. coast, are ports of call.

The people along the coast are principally Malay immigrants from the islands of Macassar, Java, and Ternate, and are engaged chiefly in fishing and as workers on plantations devoted to the cultivation of coconuts, spices, rice, corn, sugar cane, and tobacco. They are also employed in the production of sago flour and cajuput oil. Trade is dominated by Chinese, Arab, and Macassarese merchants; copra is the principal export. The prevailing religions are Malayan, Christian, and Mohammedan. The people of the interior are descendants of intermarriages between Malayans and Papuans; they live chiefly by hunting and fishing, and observe pagan religious rites. Under Dutch rule, which began in the middle of the 17th century, Ceram was included, for administrative purposes, in the Residency of Amboina. In 1946, following the uprising of the Indonesians against Dutch rule, Ceram became a part of the self-governing state of East Indonesia. (See REPUBLIC OF INDONESIA.) Area, 6621 sq.m.; pop. (1949 est.) 100,000.

CERAMICS (Gr. *keramos*, "potter's clay"), originally the art of making pottery, now a general term for the science of manufacturing articles prepared from plastic earthy materials and then made rigid by high-temperature treatment. Ceramics now thus includes the manufacture of clay, earthenware, china, porcelain, bricks, and some kinds of tile and stoneware. Ceramic products are used not only for artistic objects and tableware, but also for such utilitarian purposes as sewer pipe and the walls of buildings. See CLAY; BRICK; POTTERY.

CERASTIUM. See CHICKWEED.

CERBERUS, in Greek mythology, the many-headed dog who guarded the portal of the infernal regions. Orpheus charmed him by the magic of his lyre, and Hercules overcame him by strength and dragged him to the upper world.

CERCIS. See JUDAS TREE.

CEREALS or **CEREAL PLANTS,** the various species of the Grass family cultivated for their seed as an article of food. The name is derived from Ceres, the Roman goddess of grains and of the harvest. The cereals proper do not belong to any particular tribe of the grasses, but the employment of particular species as bread-plants seems to have been determined chiefly by the superior size of the seed, or by the facility of procuring it in sufficient quantity and of freeing it from its inedible envelopes. The most extensively cultivated grains are wheat (*Triticum*), barley (*Hordeum*), rye (*Secale*), oats (*Avena*), rice (*Oryza*), maize or Indian corn (*Zea*), different kinds of millet (*Setaria, Panicum, Paspalum, Pennisetum,* and *Penicillaria*), and durra or Guinea corn (*Sorghum* or *Andropogon*). These have all been cultivated from time immemorial. Barley, oats, and rye are the grains of the coldest regions, the cultivation of the former two extending even within the Arctic circle. Wheat is next to these, and in the warmer regions of the temperate zone its cultivation is associated with that of corn and rice, which are extensively cultivated within the tropics. The millets belong to warm climates, and durra is tropical or subtropical. See separate articles on plants mentioned.

The seeds of plants of other families, notably buckwheat, are sometimes incorrectly called cereals.

CEREBELLUM. See BRAIN.

CEREBRAL HEMORRHAGE. See APOPLEXY.

CEREBRAL PALSY, term applied to any of five pathological neuro-muscular conditions of the human body, caused by damage to the brain before, during, or immediately following birth, and frequently accompanied by impaired sensation, especially in the sense of hearing and sight. The five conditions are all characterized by various degrees of loss of muscular control resulting in facial grimaces, drooling, and awkward gait and speech in its victims. This awkwardness of manner has led many people to classify victims of cerebral palsy as feebleminded; actually, only about one third of them have suffered damage to the thinking centers of the brain.

Two of the cerebral-palsy conditions, the *athetoid* and the *spastic,* account for about eighty-five percent of all victims. The athe-

Cereals. From left to right: Wheat; oats; rye; barley; rice.

toid palsied manifest involuntary uncontrolled movements of the affected muscles; such movements are accentuated in states of excitement. Children with this condition tense their muscles in an effort to stop the movements, sometimes resulting in permanent muscular tenseness. The spastic palsied do not manifest involuntary movements; however, when they attempt to move, their movements are exaggerated. All forms of cerebral palsy are popularly, but erroneously, called "spastic paralysis". The other three cerebral-palsy conditions are *ataxia,* in which balance is disturbed, *tremor,* in which involuntary rhythmic contractions of the muscles occur, and *rigidity,* in which the muscles are stiff and inelastic.

About 550,000 individuals in the United States suffer from cerebral palsy; each year, about 10,000 children develop one or more of the five cerebral-palsy conditions as a result of trauma at birth, congenital malformation of the brain, blood disturbances such as those caused by incompatible Rh factors (q.v.) in the mother and child, or infectious diseases such as encephalitis or meningitis. Approximately one out of seven of these children die before the age of six. Educational and rehabilitational programs instituted after 1945 have resulted in increased acceptance of the intelligence of most of the cerebral palsied, and in training of victims of these conditions in speech and the pursuance of normal activities. M.J.E.S.

CEREBRUM. See BRAIN.

CERES, in Roman mythology, goddess of the grain and of agriculture, identified with the Greek goddess Demeter (q.v.). Her father was Saturn; her mother, Ops. A famine in 496 B.C. led the Romans to adopt her cult, and a temple to her was built on the Aventine in 493 B.C. The plebeians especially worshiped Ceres. Her great festival was the Cerealia, which was celebrated from April 12 to 19.

CEREUS, genus of plants of the family Cactaceae, containing 100 or more species. Various species of *Cereus* abound in the s.w. United States, extending through Mexico and Central America into South America. *C. speciosus,* one of the most spectacular greenhouse plants in the United States, has large flowers of a scarlet color, with violet-tinged inner petals. The fruit, when well ripened, is of a delicious flavor. The plant is a native of Mexico.

A number of species are grown under the name of night-blooming cereus. Of these, *C. nycticalus, C. triangularis,* and *C. grandiflorus*

are the best known. Some of the species are arborescent, the suwarro, *C. giganteus,* of Arizona, California, and N. Mexico, attaining a height of 50 feet or more and 18 inches to 2 feet in diameter. *C. pasacana,* of Argentina, is a similar treelike form. They branch sparingly

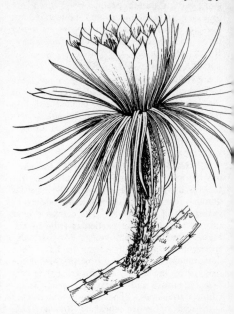

Night-blooming cereus, Hylocereus undulatus

and resemble huge candelabra in outline. The night-blooming forms have cylindrical or angled stems and are trailers and climbers. Some modern botanists classify the species of this genus in several related genera, such as *Heliocereus, Hylocereus, Silenicereus,* and *Carnegeia.*

CERINTHUS (fl. about 100 A.D.), a Christian heretic considered a Gnostic by modern scholars; see GNOSTICISM. He had a number of followers in Asia Minor, where he taught that the world was created by angels, one of whom gave the Ten Commandments to Moses, and that Jesus was the natural son of Joseph and Mary. He also preached the belief that the spirit of God, called Christ, descended on Jesus and enabled him to work miracles and proclaim the unknown Father, but that Christ left Jesus before the Passion and Resurrection.

CERIUM, a metallic element, symbol Ce, at. no. 58, at. wt. 140.13, m.p. 640° C. (1184° F.), b.p. 1400° C. (2552° F.), sp. gr. 6.90, valences 3 (cerous) and 4 (ceric). It was discovered independently in 1804 by the Swedish chemist Berzelius (q.v.) and by the German chemist

Martin Heinrich Klaproth (1743–1817); the pure metallic element was not isolated until 1875.

Cerium is the most abundant of the "rare-earth elements" (see RARE EARTHS); it is more abundant in the earth's crust than the more familiar metals zinc, lead, or tin. It occurs with the other rare-earth metals in monazite sand and samarskite in the U.S.S.R. (Ural Mountains), Norway, Brazil, and the U.S. (North Carolina). It also occurs in the minerals cerite, found in Sweden, and allanite, found in Greenland and New York State. Cerium is the only one of the rare-earth metals which can be easily separated from the others.

Metallic cerium is most familiar in the form of an alloy with iron which composes the "flints" used in cigarette lighters. Large quantities of ceric oxide were formerly employed in the manufacture of gas mantles. Compounds of cerium are employed in small quantities in the manufacture of glass, ceramics, arc-lamp electrodes, and photoelectric cells. Cerous nitrate has been used medicinally in the treatment of seasickness and chronic vomiting. Ceric sulfate is employed in chemistry laboratories as an oxidizing agent.

CERNĂUȚI. See CHERNOVTSY.

CERRO DE PASCO, town and former capital of Junín Department, Peru, situated about 14,000 ft. above sea level, 138 miles N.E. of Lima, with which it is connected by rail. The town was noted as one of the world's richest silver-mining centers, but is more important now for the mining of copper, which began there in 1898, and is chiefly managed by a U.S.-controlled mining corporation. Gold, lead, and bismuth are also mined at Cerro de Pasco. The mining corporation has built a railroad to Oroyo, 81 miles S., where smelting is carried on in its metallurgical plant, one of the largest in the world. The town consists chiefly of adobe houses. The inhabitants are largely Indian laborers and their families. A model village, some 200 ft. above the mining plant, houses the staff of the mining corporation. Pop. of town (1958 est.) 28,484.

CERTHIIDAE, a family of birds in the order Passeriformes, with stiff, pointed tail feathers which act as props and assist the birds in climbing. The family includes the various species of creeper (q.v.).

CERTIORARI, a common-law writ issued by a superior court to an inferior one, or by any court having jurisdiction to a body acting in a quasi-judicial capacity, such as commissioners, magistrates, and assessors of taxes, to obtain a review of the proceedings of the tribunal or body to which the writ is directed. The writ issues only when there is no other adequate remedy, and it is used in both criminal and civil cases. It requires the record of a proceeding in the inferior court to be certified by that court and returned to the court issuing the writ, for the purpose either of reviewing the same or of removing the action or proceeding to the higher court for trial. When certiorari is used as a means of review, it raises only a question of law for the consideration of the reviewing tribunal—the question whether or not the inferior tribunal had jurisdiction or proceeded in accordance with law.

CERUSSITE, or WHITE LEAD ORE, a mineral consisting of lead carbonate. In its pure form it is colorless and transparent, but it is usually yellow or greyish, because of various impurities. It has hardness 3, sp. gr. 6.5, and crystallizes in the orthorhombic system. It is formed by the alteration of galena or lead sulfide, which, as it oxidizes to sulfate, may be changed to a carbonate by means of solutions of calcium bicarbonate. The most famous sources of cerussite are the lead mines of Siberia and the Altai region, and various places in Sweden and Germany; fine crystals are found in Cornwall, England. In the United States it occurs at Phoenixville, Pa., and in lead deposits in Virginia, North Carolina, Missouri, Wisconsin, Colorado, Utah, and Arizona.

CERVANTES SAAVEDRA, MIGUEL DE (1547–1616), Spanish novelist, born in Alcalá de Henares, and educated at the College of the City of Madrid. His father was an indigent doctor with a large family. Although Cervantes grew up in poverty, he managed to obtain a fair education. In 1568 a number of his poems appeared in a volume published in Madrid to commemorate the death of the Spanish queen Elizabeth of Valois (1545–68). He went to Rome in 1569, and there in the following year he entered the service of Giulio Cardinal Acquaviva. Soon afterward Cervantes joined a Spanish regiment in Naples. He fought in 1571 against the Turks in the naval battle of Lepanto, in which he lost the use of his left hand. While returning to Spain in 1575 Cervantes was captured by Barbary pirates. He was taken to Algeria as a slave and held there for ransom. During the next five years he made several heroic but unsuccessful attempts to escape, and was finally ransomed in 1580 by his family and friends.

Back in Spain at the age of thirty-three, Cervantes, despite his wartime service and

Bettmann Archive

Miguel de Cervantes Saavedra

Algerian adventure, was unable to obtain employment with a noble family, the usual reward for veteran soldiers who had distinguished themselves. Deciding to become a writer, he turned out poems and plays at a prodigious rate between 1582 and 1585. Only two of the plays of this period, *El Trato de Argel* and *La Numancia*, are extant. His pastoral novel *Galatea* (1585) gained him a reputation, but the proceeds from its sale were insufficient to support him. Cervantes then took government jobs, first as a Seville commissary furnishing goods to the fleet of the Armada, and later (1594) as a tax collector in Granada. In the latter capacity he entrusted a large sum of government money to a merchant who absconded with it. Cervantes managed to make good the loss, but the government imprisoned him for three months because he failed to render a satisfactory account of his activities as tax collector.

While in prison he conceived the idea for a story about an amusing madman who imagines himself a knight-errant performing the splendid feats described in medieval tales of chivalry. In 1605 the first part was issued under the title *Don Quijote de la Mancha* (Eng. trans., *Don Quixote de la Mancha*, 1612). It became such an immediate success that within two weeks after publication three pirated editions appeared in Madrid. Partly because of the pirating and partly because of his lack of financial acumen, the enormous success of the work never brought Cervantes any substantial wealth.

His *Novelas Ejemplares* ("Exemplary Novels", 1613), a collection of twelve short stories, includes romances in the Italian style, de-

scriptions of criminal life in Seville, and sketches of unusual events and characters. Two of these stories, "Rinconete y Cortadillo" and "El Coloquio de los Perros" ("The Talking Dogs"), are renowned for their prose style. The second part of *Don Quixote* was published in 1615. Four days before he died Cervantes completed the fantastic novel *Persiles y Sigismunda* (1617).

Cervantes' masterpiece *Don Quixote* is generally regarded as the first modern novel and as one of the greatest novels ever written. Influenced somewhat by the epic poem *Orlando Furioso* by the Italian poet Lodovico Ariosto, *Don Quixote* is a brilliant satire, not only of the chivalric romances of the Middle Ages and early Renaissance, but also of the sentimental and pastoral novels popular in Cervantes' own time. Its protagonists, Don Quixote, the country squire, and his servant Sancho Panza, represent two profoundly contrasting aspects of human nature. Don Quixote is the incurable romantic, cherishing the chivalric ideals of a bygone age; Sancho Panza, by contrast, emerges as the quintessence of folk simplicity and worldly astuteness. The tale of their adventures together ranges across a broad panorama of 16th-century Spanish life, brilliantly depicting the

Bettmann Archive

Illustration by the French artist Honoré Daumier for Don Quixote *by Cervantes*

countryside with its bare landscape and dusty roads, the wretched inns and crafty innkeepers, the seedy aristocrats and stubborn peasantry. The folk irony, the puns, and the witty repartee which enliven the writing form an integral part of Cervantes' style in *Don Quixote*.

Despite the sadness and disillusionment expressed by Don Quixote's misadventures, the novel is fundamentally an optimistic work. The concept of a man who seeks to live by the chivalric ideals of manhood, virtue, and honor is only partially satirical. In the person of Don Quixote it is also a basic affirmation of those humanistic values which were under attack in Cervantes' Spain by the Inquisition (q.v.). *Don Quixote* has influenced, either directly or indirectly, nearly all subsequent novels; such famous British novelists, for example, as Tobias Smollett, Henry Fielding, and Charles Dickens owe much to Cervantes' clear-sighted, comic approach to reality.

E.F.

CERVERA Y TOPETE, PASCUAL, CONDE DE JEREZ, MARQUES DE SANTA ANA (1839–1909), Spanish naval officer, born in Medina-Sidonia, Cadiz Province, and educated at San Fernando Naval Academy. He won distinction in Morocco in 1859, and subsequently served in many foreign campaigns, notably in Cochin China, the Philippines, and Cuba. For a brief period, beginning in 1892, he was secretary of the navy. Following the outbreak (1898) of the Spanish-American War, he was made commander of a cruiser squadron and assigned to duty in American waters. The squadron arrived (about May 19) in the harbor of Santiago de Cuba, where it was later blockaded by an American fleet under Admiral William Thomas Sampson. On July 3, 1898, while attempting to break through the blockade, Cervera's squadron was destroyed and he was taken prisoner. He was court-martialed after his return to Spain, but was acquitted. In 1901 he attained the rank of vice-admiral. He became chief of staff of the Spanish navy in 1902.

CESALPINO, ANDREA, or (Lat.) **ANDREAS CÆSALPINUS** (1519–1603), Italian botanist and physician, born in Arezzo, Tuscany. He was educated at the University of Pisa and, in 1555, was appointed director of the botanic garden and professor of materia medica at the University. In 1592 he became the physician of Pope Clement VIII in Rome. Cesalpino is said to have anticipated later discoveries of the circulation of the blood in the human body. He was the author of *De Plantis* (16 vols., 1583), which was, in part, the basis of the system of botanical classification of Linnaeus (q.v.). His other works include *Quaestionum Medicarum* (2 vols., 1593) and *De Metallicis* (1596).

CESARION. See PTOLEMY XIV.

CESIUM, a chemical element, symbol Cs, at. no. 55, at. wt. 132.91, valence 1, m.p. 28.5° C. (83° F.), b.p. 670° C. (1238° F.), and sp. gr. 1.873 at 20° C. This white, soft, alkali metal was discovered in 1860 by Bunsen and Kirchhoff in mineral waters by means of the spectroscope, in which it shows two bright blue lines as well as fainter red, yellow, and green ones. The natural source yielding the greatest quantity of cesium is the rare mineral pollux (or pollucite). Ores of this mineral found on the Isle of Elba contain 34% of cesium oxide; American ores of pollux, found in Maine and South Dakota, contain 13% of the oxide. Cesium also occurs in lepidolite, carnallite, and certain feldspars. Its extraction is accomplished by separation of the cesium compound from the mineral, transformation of the compound thus obtained into the cyanide, and electrolysis of the fused cyanide. Cesium may also be obtained by heating its hydroxides or carbonates with magnesium or aluminum, and by heating its chlorides with calcium. Commercial cesium usually contains rubidium, with which it usually occurs, and which resembles it so closely that no effort is made to separate them. Like potassium, cesium oxidizes readily when exposed to air, and it is on this account used as a "getter" to remove residual oxygen from radio vacuum tubes. Because of its property of emitting electrons when exposed to light, it is used in the photosensitive surface of the cathode of the photoelectric cell. The radioactive isotope cesium-137, which is produced by nuclear fission, is a useful by-product of atomic-energy plants. Cs-137 emits considerably more energy than radium and is employed in present-day medical and industrial research; see TRACERS.

ČESKÉ BUDĚJOVICE (Ger. *Budweis*), city, port, and rail junction of the region of Jihočeský, Czechoslovakia, situated on the Moldau River, about 77 miles s. of Prague. It is the trade center of s. Bohemia. Among its principal articles of commerce are lignite, iron ore, and other raw materials produced in the surrounding region, and a variety of products manufactured in the city, including beer, porcelain, earthenware, and lead pencils. The city was founded in the 13th century. In the 18th century it became an episcopal see. Among the city's notable buildings are the Gothic Church of St. Mary, the bishop's palace, and the town hall. Pop. (1961 prelim.) 65,249.

CESTODA, a class of the phylum Platyhelminthes, consisting of tapeworms and similar endoparasites. They are characterized by the absence of cilia and intestines, and the presence of numerous testes and ovaries, with occasional yolk glands. Cestodes are widely distributed, but are especially abundant in warm climates. They occur as intestinal parasites in species of all the classes of vertebrates, especially mammals, but the complete life history is known for comparatively few species. The group contains two orders, the Cestodaria or Monozoa, unsegmented individuals (rare), and the Merozoa or Polyzoa, segmented tapeworms. See TAPEWORM.

CESTROTUM. See PAINTING, ENCAUSTIC.

CESTRUM. See PAINTING, ENCAUSTIC.

CETACEA, an order of aquatic mammals, comprising the whales, dolphins, and porpoises. The members of this order, in becoming more perfectly adapted to an aquatic life, have evolved the external structure of fish. Their bodies are fishlike, with smooth skins. Their pectoral or forelimbs are reduced to paddles that perform the functions of the pectoral fins of fish; their pelvic or hind limbs have disappeared entirely, and the pelvis itself has become reduced to a pair of horizontal bones that are remnants of the ischia. The tail is provided with a horizontal caudal fin, and a posterior dorsal fin is usually present on the back. There are also important modifications in the vertebral column and skull. The order comprises three suborders: Archaeoceti, all extinct animals, with long snouts, forward nostrils, and heterodont teeth; Odontoceti, including several families and about 60 species, comprising the toothed whales, including the small-sized porpoises, dolphins, belugas, and killers, and the huge sperm whales; and Mystacoceti, with nostrils far back, and their jaws bearing whalebone instead of teeth, as in the whalebone whale.

Fossil forms of the Cetacea are not common, and the evolution of the order cannot be satisfactorily traced. The earliest representative is the genus *Zeuglodon,* the only member of the suborder Archaeoceti. This genus appears in the Eocene rocks of Europe, North Africa, and North America, and its skull presents closer resemblances to the normal mammalian skull than are to be found in that of any other cetacean. Its teeth are of two kinds: conical, simple incisors and compressed, serrated two-rooted molars. See WHALE; DOLPHIN; PORPOISE.

CETRARIA. See ICELAND MOSS.

CETTE. See SÈTE.

CETUS, THE WHALE, an equatorial constellation lying to the south of Aries, the Ram. Its two brightest stars are normally β-Ceti, a second-magnitude star also called Deneb Kaitos (Arabic, "the tail of the whale"), and α-Ceti, a third-magnitude star also called Menkar (Ar., "nose"). Its most remarkable star is ο-Ceti, called Mira (the wonderful), a variable star first discovered in 1596. It has a six-hundredfold change in brightness, regularly increasing and diminishing over a period of about 11 months. On some occasions it reaches a brightness of second magnitude. Interferometer measurements have indicated that Mira is one of the largest stars known, with a diameter of about 220,000,000 miles, slightly larger than the diameter of the earth's orbit.

CEUTA, Spanish seaport and military and penal station on the N. coast of Morocco, 14 miles S. of the Rock of Gibraltar, from which it is separated by the Strait of Gibraltar. For administrative purposes Ceuta is included in the province of Cadiz in Spain. The city is situated on a headland consisting of seven peaks, at the end of a narrow isthmus. The highest of these peaks, Monte del Hacko, thought to be the ancient Abyla, is one of the two Pillars of Hercules (q.v.).

The port of Ceuta is built on the site of a Carthaginian settlement on which a Roman colony was later built. The Vandals took it from the Romans and lost it to Byzantium. It later became successively a possession of the Visigoths and of the Arabs. The latter called it Sebta or Cibta, whence the modern name is derived. Under later Berber and Spanish-Moorish rulers Ceuta became an important center for the manufacture of brassware and for trade in slaves, gold, and ivory. The Portuguese captured the city in 1415 and the Spaniards in 1580. Moors laid siege to it unsuccessfully several times, one siege lasting from 1694 to 1720.

Pop. (1960 est.) 73,182.

CÉVENNES, a mountain range in southern France, consisting of two divisions, the Northern Cévennes and the Southern Cévennes. The Cévennes form the watershed between the river systems of the Rhone and Saône on the E. and those of the Garonne and Loire on the W. The general direction of the range is from N.E. to S.W., commencing at the southern extremity of the mountains of Lyonnais and extending under different local names to the Canal du Midi where it approaches the northern spurs of the Pyrenees Mountains. The central mass of the Cévennes lies in the departments of Lozère and Ardéche and contains Mont de Mézenc (elevation 5754 feet), the highest peak of the range. The average height of the Cévennes is from 3000 to 4000 feet. The mountains were the scene of the persecutions of the Albigenses and the Waldenses in medieval times and of the Camisards (qq.v.) in the 17th century.

CEYLON (anc. *Taprobane*), island and independent state within the Commonwealth of Nations, situated in the Indian Ocean about 50 m. of off the S.E. coast of India, from which it is separated by the Palk Strait and the Gulf of Mannar. Lying between Ceylon and India is a discontinuous chain of tiny islands known as Adams Bridge. Ceylon has the shape of an irregular triangle with its apex in the N. and its base extending from s.w. to N.E. The greatest length from N. to s. is about 272 m.; the greatest width is about 137 m. The total area is approximately 25,322 sq.m. and the population (1961 est.) is 10,-167,000.

Nearly all of the Ceylonese coast, especially on the w., s., and S.E., is palm fringed and indented by lagoons and inlets. The more rugged N.E. coast contains Trincomali harbor, one of the best natural harbors in the world. Other harbors include the largely artificial one at Colombo (q.v.), the national capital, and at Galle (q.v.), both on the s.w. coast. Colombo has a population (1957 est.) of 480,800 and is the only city in Ceylon with more than 90,000 persons. Other important towns are Jaffna and Kandy (qq.v.).

Physical Characteristics. The outstanding feature of the topography of Ceylon is a mountainous mass in the south-central part. The peak of Pidurutalagala (8281 ft.) is the highest point. In the upland area there are two plateaus, Nuwara Eliya and Horton Plains, both of which are noted for their cool and healthful climate and are major centers of commercial tea plantations. North of the mountains is an arid and mostly level or gently rolling plain known as the dry zone, which also extends southward to the E. of the mountains. The dry zone was relatively densely populated in ancient times when it was ingeniously irrigated by a system of large and small storage tanks or reservoirs and by canals. It is now more thinly settled, although the government of Ceylon has made considerable progress in resettling the area and in restoring its ancient irrigation works (see *Land Resettlement*, below).

Rivers and streams are numerous, especially in the south-central region, but with few exceptions they are mountain torrents, broken by rapids. The largest river in Ceylon is the Mahaweli-Ganga, which flows eastward about 200 m. from the w. slopes of the central mountain mass to empty into the sea near Trincomali. Other rivers include the Kelani-Ganga, with its mouth near Colombo; the Kala-Ganga, which reaches the sea near Kalutara on the s.w. coast; and the Malwatu Oya, which flows N.w. across the dry zone to near Mannar.

Climate. Ceylon, being close to the equator, has a generally hot and humid climate throughout the year; however, a number of hill or mountain areas are cool at all seasons, and humidity is relatively lower in the dry zone. The annual temperature averages about 90° F. in the lowlands. In the higher mountainous regions the annual average is about 70° F. Precipitation is characterized by wide seasonal and regional variations. During the southwest monsoon, extending from May to November, rainfall is exceptionally heavy in the s.w. section, where the moisture-laden winds are interrupted by mountain barriers. Little moisture is deposited in the dry zone during the southwest monsoon. Precipitation in that region (about 40 in. annually) occurs mainly during the northeast monsoon, which begins about the first of November. Most crops in the dry zone require irrigation to survive. The hills and the lowlands of the s.w. section, known as the wet zone, normally have some rainfall at all seasons, but with peaks in May and June and in October and November.

Plants and Animals. The flora of Ceylon is noted for its beauty and variety. Dense tropical jungles occupy extensive areas in the s.w., and the upper mountain slopes are thickly forested. Many varieties of palm, including the areca, coconut, and palmyra, flourish in the lowlands along the coast. Mangroves and screw pines abound in various coastal areas. Numerous varieties of timber trees, notably mahogany and many species of the family Dipterocarpaceae, are indigenous to the wet zone. Among timber trees common to the drier sections of the island are ebony and satinwood. Ferns, water hyacinths, orchids, acacias, eucalypti, and cypresses flourish in various regions. Domesticated nonnative vegetation includes coffee, tea, rubber, and rice.

The animal life of Ceylon is also varied and is similar in many respects to that of India. Largest among the quadrupeds is the elephant, which is often tuskless. Work elephants are captured wild, often with much

Ewing Galloway

Plantation worker in Ceylon makes incision in rubber tree to permit flow of latex.

damage to the herds; further destruction is caused by illicit shooting of elephants by villagers protecting their crops and by others. The elephants in Ceylon are decreasing in number and may be in danger of extinction. Bears, leopards, and several species of monkey are somewhat more abundant. The island contains over 3000 species of birds and many species of reptiles, including the cobra and daboia (Russell's viper). Crocodiles and pythons are other indigenous reptiles.

Nationalities, Languages, and Religions. About three quarters of the population consists of Singhalese (q.v.) and the remainder consists of native-born and immigrant Tamils (q.v.) from s. India; the Tamils are employed chiefly as workers on the tea and rubber plantations. Other peoples include the descendants of the aboriginal Veddas (q.v.), and Malayans, Eurasians, and Europeans. Singhalese, a derivate of Sanskrit, is the predominant language; Tamil, a Dravidian language of s. India, is spoken by about 750,000 people. Buddhism, which was introduced into Ceylon in the 3rd century B.C., is the prevailing religion, but as observed in Ceylon it includes pre-Buddhist rites, the worship of some Hindu gods, and a number of Mohammedan customs. According to the census of 1953, there were 5,217,143 Buddhists, 1,164,-004 Hindus, 714,874 Christians, and 541,814 Moslems.

Education. The public-school system provides free education at all levels. Government and government-aided primary, secondary, and religious-training schools in the early 1960's numbered more than 8275, with about

2,224,800 enrolled pupils. In addition there were about 415 collegiate schools with approximately 291,225 pupils, 22 teacher-training colleges, and 99 unaided schools. The outstanding schools of higher learning are Ceylon Technical College, which provides courses in science, engineering, commerce, arts, and arts and crafts, and the University of Ceylon, with faculties of arts, science, medicine, veterinary medicine, law, agriculture, engineering, and Oriental studies.

Mineral Resources. The principal mineral resources of Ceylon are graphite and gem stones, including sapphires, rubies, topazes, and garnets. Thorium and uranium compounds are found on the island, which contains also small deposits of iron ore, mica, sand suitable for the manufacture of glass, and fine clay used in the production of chinaware. The total of all mineral resources is, however, of little economic importance.

Agriculture. Agriculture is the principal economic activity of the island, although due to rapid population increases Ceylon must import more than half of its food. By far the largest acreage is occupied by commercial plantations growing crops for export, primarily tea, rubber, and coconuts. In the aggregate these crops account for nearly 90 percent of Ceylonese exports by value. Tea is grown mainly at higher elevations because it thrives in a cooler and moister climate and in better-drained soils. Rubber is concentrated at lower levels, on the fringes of the hills, and often on the gentler slopes. Coconuts are principally a lowland- and coastal-area crop. Coconuts are grown on plantations for the commercial market and on small household plots for local domestic consumption.

Rice, the dominant food crop, occupies the more fertile soil in the wet-zone lowlands or the irrigated areas of the dry zone. Plantains, bananas, and vegetables, as well as coconuts, commonly are grown in small amounts by most farmers for their own use. Pineapples and mangoes are less widespread but are increasing in commercial importance. Horned cattle, buffaloes, and goats are raised in large numbers.

Manufacturing Industries and Fisheries. Modern manufacturing establishments are comparatively few and are largely confined to Colombo. Most of the factories in Colombo produce consumer goods, such as cotton textiles, rubber goods, food products, and glass, paper, and wood products. Fishing is generally restricted to a small coastal fringe and contributes relatively little to the economy as a whole, although efforts were made in the

1950's to develop large-scale commercial fishing.

Trade and Communications. The exports of Ceylon in descending order of value are tea, rubber, coconut products, and graphite. The principal imports are rice and other foodstuffs; manufactured goods, including textiles, machinery, transport equipment, and cement; and raw materials, chiefly petroleum, coal, and other minerals.

There is an excellent system of paved roads communicating with most parts of the island; the system is especially well developed in the plantation areas. However, parts of the dry zone and of the s.e. region are deficient in roads. Main railroads connect Colombo with Kandy, Trincomali, Jaffna, and Galle, and there are several smaller lines, again most highly developed in the plantation areas. Much of the s.e. is without railroads, but there is rail connection with India by means of a ferry across the Gulf of Mannar.

Government. Ceylon is governed according to the constitution of 1948. By the terms of this document, promulgated (1946) by an order in council, executive power is vested in a governor-general, who is a Ceylonese national appointed by the British government, and a prime minister, who heads a council of ministers. The governor-general's office is mainly formal and ceremonial. Legislative authority is exercised by a bicameral Parliament consisting of a House of Representatives and a Senate. Members of the House are elected by universal adult suffrage, except six who are appointed by the governor-general. Half of the Senate is elected by the House of Representatives; the other half is appointed by the governor-general.

Defense formerly was provided mainly by British bases at Trincomali and elsewhere. In 1957 these bases were reclaimed by Ceylon, and defense was left largely in the hands of the small, British-trained Ceylonese army and navy. There are no Ceylonese territories outside Ceylon, except for some tiny islands near the coast. The Maldive Islands, 400 m. s.w. of Ceylon, were formerly a Ceylonese dependency, but presently form a British-protected sultanate.

Land Resettlement. One of the major accomplishments of the government of Ceylon was the virtual elimination by 1950 of malaria, formerly an endemic scourge, thus permitting considerable progress in resettling the dry zone and bringing its long-abandoned land into food production. The aim of the Ceylonese government was to lessen the country's dependence on food imports, to diversify an economy dominated by commercial plantations, and to provide additional agricultural land. However, the rapid rise of the population, especially after the elimination of malaria, makes self-sufficiency in food production appear unattainable.

History. According to Hindu legend the greater part of Ceylon was conquered in prehistoric times by Ramachandra, seventh incarnation of the supreme deity Vishnu. The written history of Ceylon begins with the chronicle called *Mahavamsa*. This work was started in the 6th century A.D. and provides a virtually unbroken narrative up to 1815. The *Mahavamsa* was compiled by a succession of Buddhist monks; because it often aims to glorify or to degrade certain periods or reigns, it is not a wholly reliable source despite the wealth of historical material which it contains.

The *Mahavamsa* relates that the island was conquered (504 B.C.) by Vijaya, a Hindu prince from N.E. India. After subjugating the aboriginal inhabitants, a people now known as Veddas, Vijaya married a native princess, encouraged emigration from the mainland, and made himself ruler of the entire island. The realm (called Sinhala after Vijaya's patrimonial name) inherited by his successors consisted, however, of the arid region lying to the N. of the south-central mountain system.

Members of the dynasty founded by Vijaya reigned over Sinhala for several centuries. During this period, and particularly after the adoption (about 307 B.C.) of Buddhism as the national religion, the Singhalese developed a magnificent civilization. Extant evidence of their engineering skill and architectural achievements include remnants of vast irrigation projects, a number of ruined cities, notably the ancient capital Anuradhapura (q.v.), and numerous ruined shrines (dagobas). Beginning late in the 3rd century B.C. the Singhalese were involved for hundreds of years in successive struggles with invaders from s. India and with chieftains of the s. part of the island. Indian potentates and Tamil kings controlled all or part of Sinhala almost without interruption until 1155, when a Singhalese prince was restored to the throne. A cultural renaissance occurred during his reign, and many notable irrigation works and religious edifices were constructed. Sinhala was again subjugated by Indian invaders early in the next century, but part of the kingdom was regained by a native prince in 1235. During the next two and a half centuries the island was partitioned into seven kingdoms. Chinese forces occupied all of

Ceylon from 1408 to 1438.

The Portuguese soldier and viceroy in India Francisco de Almeida visited Ceylon in 1505. Twelve years later the Portuguese, having established friendly relations with one of the native monarchs, founded a fort and trading post at Colombo. Their sphere of influence expanded steadily thereafter, mainly as a result of successful wars of conquest, and by the end of the 16th century they controlled large sections of the island. Armed resistance to their encroachments centered chiefly in the mountain kingdom of Kandy, but Portuguese greed, cruelty, and religious bigotry alienated the population of the subjugated areas. Consequently, when the Dutch launched (1638–39) the first of a series of attacks on Portuguese strongholds in Ceylon they found numerous allies among the natives. The struggle ended (1658) with the Dutch in control of most of the island; the kingdom of Kandy remained independent.

Though concerned primarily with the development and protection of their trading monopolies, the Dutch introduced many beneficial administrative and economic reforms.

They established a stable and efficient government, instituted a uniform code of laws, and initiated a comprehensive program of public works, including the construction of highways and inland waterways. Their taxation system was oppressive, however, and they engendered considerable ill will by systematically persecuting native Roman Catholics.

In 1795, following the occupation of the Netherlands by revolutionary France, the British government dispatched an expeditionary force against Ceylon. The Dutch capitulated early in the next year, and in 1798 the British made all of Ceylon, except the kingdom of Kandy, a crown colony. By the provisions of the Treaty of Amiens (1802), which terminated the second phase of the Napoleonic Wars, the island was formally ceded to Great Britain. Kandy was occupied in 1803 and annexed to the crown colony in 1815. The British period of rule was marked by abortive native rebellions in 1817, 1843, and 1848; the development of coffee plantations, which prospered for a time but were finally ruined by plant diseases; the importation of Tamils for coolie labor; the introduction of

Rice, the leading food crop of Ceylon, is grown in the wet lowlands and in the dry region, where fields are flooded artificially. The elephant is the common draft animal.

British Information Services (Lubinski)

tea and rubber estates; and despoliation of forest resources. In this period also occurred violent social-religious struggles between the Singhalese peasants, mostly Buddhists, and the moneylenders and traders, chiefly Mohammedans; and a continual struggle by all the native peoples for representative government and national freedom. The first substantial victory in the struggle for self-government came in 1931, when Great Britain promulgated a new constitution for the colony. Among the outstanding features of this document were provisions granting the natives semiautonomous control over national affairs.

During World War II Ceylon was an important base of operations against the Japanese and a major source of rubber, foodstuffs, and other materials vital to the Allied war effort. On Feb. 4, 1948, the colony became a self-governing dominion of the British Commonwealth of Nations; Sir Henry Moore and D. S. Senanayake of the United National Party were installed respectively as governor-general and prime minister, at ceremonies held in Colombo; and an ancient Singhalese flag was adopted as the flag of the new state.

The foreign ministers of the Commonwealth of Nations assembled at Colombo in January, 1950, for the purpose of drafting a tentative plan for the economic development of southeastern Asia. As finally formulated, the plan (known officially as the "Colombo Plan") allocated nearly $340,000,000 of Commonwealth funds for a variety of Ceylonese projects, notably irrigation works and hydroelectric plants. In June, 1951, the Ceylonese government rejected a request from the United Nations that every country in the world refuse to sell arms and strategic materials to Communist China. D. S. Senanayake died in March, 1952, and his son Dudley Senanayake, who belonged to the same party, was named prime minister. During the year it was necessary to import rice from the United States to relieve a severe food shortage. In August, 1953, twenty-one persons were killed in riots in Colombo over the government's action in discontinuing its subsidy on rice and thereby causing the price to increase threefold. On Oct. 12 Sir John Kotelawala, also of the United National Party, became prime minister.

Ceylon declined in 1954 to join the Southeast Asia Treaty Organization, which was formed as a defensive alliance by the United States, Great Britain, and six other anti-Communist nations. However, in April, 1955, Prime Minister Kotelawala, speaking at a

Ewing Krainin

Masked Ceylonese dancers in costume

conference of Asian and African nations held in Bandoeng (Bandung), Indonesia, stated that he regarded Communist expansion as a menace. On Dec. 14, 1955, Ceylon was admitted to membership in the United Nations.

The United National Party lost the elections held in April, 1956, and S. W. R. D. Bandaranaike of the socialistically oriented People's United Front became prime minister. Under his administration agreement was reached to establish closer trade and other relations with the Soviet Union and with Communist China.

The 2500th anniversary of the death of Buddha was observed in Ceylon with great ceremony for one year beginning in May, 1956, and ending in May, 1957. In the United Nations during 1957 Ceylon adopted a policy of neutrality in the disputes between the Communist and non-Communist countries. Ceylon abstained from voting in the U.N. General Assembly on the resolution (passed Sept. 13) condemning the Soviet Union for its action in suppressing the Hungarian revolt of 1956. The United States agreed on Feb. 7, 1958, to provide Ceylon with technical assistance and a grant of about $780,000 for economic projects. The Soviet Union and Ceylon signed a trade agreement on Feb. 8 and an agreement for economic and other assistance to Ceylon on Feb. 25. On March 4 Ceylon accepted a loan of about $10,500,000 from Communist China.

On Sept. 25, 1959, Bandaranaike was shot by a Buddhist monk; he died the following day. His immediate successor as prime minister was Wijayananda Dahanayake, the former minister of education. In the general elections of March 19, 1960, the United National Party won the greatest number of votes, and two days later Dudley Senanayake became prime minister in a minority cabinet, which quickly lost parliamentary confidence. New general elections held on July 20 resulted in a near majority of parliamentary seats being won by the Sri Lanka (or Freedom) Party, headed by Bandaranaike's widow, Mrs. Sirimavo Bandaranaike, who was sworn in as prime minister the next day. On Dec. 31 a bill was passed making Singhalese the only official language of Ceylon. Spokesmen for the Tamil-speaking minority led mass demonstrations against the measure in early 1961. To cope with the situation, a state of emergency was declared on April 17 and remained in force until October. Among other steps, the Tamil Federal Party was forbidden to operate and strikes were declared illegal.

CÉZANNE, PAUL (1839–1906), French painter, born at Aix-en-Provence. In the college of his native town he formed a friendship with Emile Zola, whom he followed to Paris and on whose advice he took up painting. He failed in the entrance examinations to the École des Beaux-Arts and entered the École Suisse. There he became acquainted with the Impressionist painter Camille Pissaro, who introduced him to the work of Gustave Courbet. Cézanne also worked with Claude Monet and Pierre Renoir of the Impressionist school. Cézanne joined the Impressionists, exhibiting with them in 1874 and again in 1877, when he sent in 17 oil paintings. Discouraged by the ridicule of critics and by his differences with the Impressionists, Cézanne retired in 1879 to Aix, where he spent the remainder of his life. He broke with all his old friends, even with Zola, and seemed to be forgotten by the world.

In this seclusion he developed a style of painting destined to exert a great influence on modern art. Cézanne differed from both Impressionists and Academicians. Both of these schools were primarily concerned with selective representation of nature in the guise of reality, the Impressionists emphasizing particularly the scientific study of light and color vibration. In his later period Cézanne tended more and more to employ natural forms as a part of graphic architectonic structure. In all his work, which included still life, portraiture, and landscapes, Cézanne sought to abstract the elements of nature from their temporary and accidental semblances, and to build them deliberately into three-dimensional compositions, which had esthetic rather than realistic validity. His emphasis on formal values, which had been dissipated by the representational and emotional aims of the realists and the stress on color and atmosphere of the Impressionists, led to a new school in painting, Postimpressionism (q.v.); from this school in turn developed many of the types of painting of the 20th century.

Cézanne is sometimes known as "the father of Modernism". During his lifetime, however, he remained unknown except to a few connoisseurs. It was not until a retrospective exhibition of his work in Paris in 1904 that his reputation as one of the most original geniuses in painting began to be established. His works are in many private collections and museums. Among those in museums are "La Maison du Pendu" and "L'Estaque" (Louvre, Paris), "La Vallée de l'Arc" (Metropolitan Museum of Art, New York City), "La Montagne Saint Victoire" (Museum of Occidental Art, Moscow), "Le Jas-de-Bouffan" (Prague Museum), and "Pines and Rocks" and "Oranges" (Museum of Modern Art, New York City).

C.G.S., or CENTIMETER-GRAM-SECOND SYSTEM, the universal system of units of measurement used by all scientists, and in daily commercial use by most nations, except the United States and Great Britain. The unit of length is the *centimeter*, that of mass, the *gram*, and that of time, the *second*. Such diverse quantities as density, acceleration, and viscosity can be expressed in C.G.S. units.

The meter, which is 100 centimeters, was established as the basis of the metric system (q.v.) in the 1790's. It was originally supposed to be one ten-millionth of the distance from the equator to the pole, but for greater convenience was later defined as the distance, measured at 20° C. (68° F.), between two fine lines on the "International Prototype Meter", a platinum-iridium bar in Paris. The gram, originally supposed to be the weight at 4° C. (39.2° F.) of one cubic centimeter of water, was later defined as one thousandth of the weight of the "International Prototype Kilogram", a platinum-iridium cylinder in Paris. Exact duplicates of these international

Culver Service
"Self-portrait" by Paul Cézanne

Museum of Modern Art (Sunami)
"Boy in a Red Waistcoat" by Paul Cézanne

standards are kept in other places, notably the U.S. Bureau of Standards in Washington. Moreover, scientists have compared them with certain invariant physical quantities so that the standards could be accurately reproduced if they were ever all destroyed; the meter has been measured against the wave length of light produced in a lamp containing mercury transmuted from gold, and the gram against the exact weight of one cubic centimeter of water, which is actually slightly less than one gram. See WEIGHTS AND MEASURES.

The second is defined as one sixtieth of a minute, which is one sixtieth of an hour, which in turn is one twenty-fourth of a mean solar day. See DAY.

CHABRIER, ALEXIS EMMANUEL (1841–94), French composer, born at Ambert, Puy-de-Dôme. He was largely self-educated musically. His music is characterized by rich color, vivacity, humor, and strongly marked rhythm. Among his works are the operas *Gwendoline* (1886) and *Le Roi malgré Lui* (1887), and the orchestral pieces *España* (1883) and *Joyeuse Marche* (1888). He also composed choral works, music for piano, and music for voice and piano.

CHACMA. See BABOON.

CHACO CANYON NATIONAL MONUMENT. See NATIONAL PARK SERVICE.

CHACO, EL or **GRAN CHACO,** a region of central South America, also known as CHACO BOREAL, lying N. of the Pilcomaya R. and W. of the Paraguay R. It is 100,000 sq.m.

in extent, and embraces parts of southeastern Bolivia and northern Paraguay, and is contiguous to the Chaco Central region of Formosa Territory in northern Argentina. The Chaco is a low alluvial plain inhabited chiefly by Samucan and Guaycuruan Indian tribes. That part of the Chaco which is in Paraguay is noted for the production of quebracho logs from which tannin is extracted. No census of the population was ever taken, but the number of people living in the Chaco region of Argentina was estimated in 1958 to be 672,900.

From 1870 the exact position of the boundary between Bolivia and Paraguay across the Chaco was a disputed issue between those countries. Both Bolivia and Paraguay claimed the entire territory. Bolivia, eager to secure an outlet on the navigable waters of the Paraguay R., had gradually pushed its frontier in a southeasterly direction. Finally, after occupying more than half of the disputed territory, Bolivia was prevented from advancing further by a chain of Paraguayan blockhouses established in a N.-S. line along the 60th meridian. Bolivia built similar fortifications, and along this frontier full-scale war broke out in July, 1932. No declaration of war was ever made by either side.

The League of Nations Council repeatedly reminded the disputants of their obligations under the Covenant and supported the Commission of Conciliation formed by the neutral Pan-American members in 1931 to negotiate a settlement, but without success. In December, 1932, the Commission proposed a settlement by arbitration. This proposal was accepted provisionally by Bolivia but was rejected by Paraguay.

Indeterminate fighting continued in the Chaco, with heavy loss of life, until June, 1935, when an armistice was finally arranged. A peace treaty was drawn up and signed in July, 1938, and in Oct., 1938, an arbitration commission delimited the frontier, giving Paraguay a major part of the Chaco region.

CHAD, LAKE, body of fresh water in central Africa, situated at the junction of the Republic of Chad, Cameroun, Nigeria, and the Republic of the Niger, about 800 ft. above sea level. The principal affluents of Lake Chad are the Shari and Yobe rivers. Although the lake has no visible outlet, it is steadily decreasing in size as a result of evaporation and underground seepage. In the rainy season its area is as much as 10,000 sq.m., but in the dry season it shrinks to as little as 5000 sq.m. In open water the depth of the lake varies from 3 ft. in the N.W. to more than 20 ft. in the S. Numerous islands, which are inhabited by native tribesmen, lie along the E. shore of the lake.

CHAD, REPUBLIC OF, republic and member of the French Community (see COMMUNITY, THE), in north-central Africa, bounded on the N. by Libya, on the E. by the Sudanese Republic, on the S. by the Central African Republic, and on the W. by Cameroon and the Republic of the Niger. The W. boundary passes through Lake Chad (q.v.). Fort-Lamy (pop. in 1961, 58,179) is the capital. Much of Chad consists of desert land typical of the Sahara, of which it forms a part. The highest point is Emi Koussi (11,204 ft.), a peak of the Tibesti Mountains in the N.W. Another highland area is the Ennedi Plateau in the N.E., which attains a maximum altitude of about 4800 ft. There is a large lowland area known as the Bodélé depression between Lake Chad and the Tibesti Mountains. The Shari and the Logone, which are navigable by steamship for part of the year only, are the principal rivers of Chad. The climate of the country is subject to cyclical changes, and rainfall is scanty. In the desert zone of the N. region, temperatures fluctuate as much as 100° F. in a single day. A leading occupation of the people is the raising of cattle, asses, horses, sheep, camels, and ostriches. The most important agricultural crop is cotton. In addition to cotton, the principal exports of the republic include dates, ivory, butter, hides, and ostrich feathers.

The African kingdoms of Kanem, Wadai, and Baguirmi were situated in the region oc-

cupied by the present-day Republic of Chad when the first European explorers visited it in the 19th century. In 1910 the area became part of the French colony of Ubangi-Shari-Chad; after 1920 it was governed as a separate colony. The colony attained Territorial status in 1946. On Nov. 28, 1958, as the result of a plebiscite, the Territory was proclaimed a semiautonomous republic within the French Community. In May, 1960, the Republic of Chad joined the Central African Republic and the Republic of the Congo (former Middle Congo) to form the Union of Central African Republics, a loose federation of states. On Aug. 11, 1960, the Republic of Chad became a fully independent state within the French Community. Area, 495,624 sq.m.; pop. (1961) 2,674,990.

CHADWICK, FLORENCE (1918–   ), American swimmer, the first woman to swim the English Channel in both directions, born in San Diego, Calif. On Aug. 8, 1950, she swam from France to England in 13 hr. 20 min., breaking the women's record set by the American swimmer Gertrude Ederle in 1926. Florence Chadwick made the crossing from England to France on Sept. 11, 1951. In an attempted round-trip, nonstop Channel passage on Sept. 4, 1953, she set a new world record of 14 hr. 42 min. for the southward crossing, but was unable to complete the return trip. On Oct. 12, 1955, she swam from England to France in 13 hr. 55 min., again establishing a world record for the southward crossing. On Aug. 5, 1957, she swam the Bristol Channel from Wales to England, a distance of 14 miles, in the world record time of 6 hr. 7 min.

CHADWICK, SIR JAMES (1891–   ), British physicist, born in Manchester. In 1908 he entered the Victoria University of Manchester, where the following year he met and commenced working under the great physicist Lord Ernest Rutherford. After graduating, he remained at Manchester until 1913, when he went to Germany to study at Berlin. He was in Germany at the outbreak of World War I, and was interned there throughout the war. He then returned to Manchester, but the following year went to Cambridge University with Rutherford, with whom he continued fruitful collaboration until 1935. In that year he became professor at the University of Liverpool. From 1948 to 1958 he was master of Gonville and Caius College, Cambridge University. In addition to the work which he performed with Rutherford, Chadwick is best known for his discovery in 1932 of one of the fundamental particles of matter, the neu-

American Museum of Natural History
Chaffinch, Fringilla coelebs

ron, a discovery which led directly to nuclear fission and the atomic bomb. Chadwick himself was one of the first in England to stress the possibility of the development of such a bomb, and was the chief scientist associated with the British atomic-bomb effort, spending much of his time from 1943 to 1945 in the U.S., principally at the Los Alamos laboratory. Chadwick was a fellow of the Royal Society, by which he was awarded the Hughes Medal in 1932. He received the Nobel Prize in physics in 1935, and was knighted in 1945.

CHÆRONEA, a town of ancient Bœotia, Greece, memorable for the disastrous defeat there of the Athenians by Philip of Macedon in 338 B.C. This defeat struck a deathblow to the liberties of ancient Greece. There, also, in 86 B.C., Sulla, the Roman general, defeated Archelaus, the general of Mithridates VI of Pontus. Plutarch was a native of Chæronea.

CHAFFEE, the name of two American military officers, father and son: **1.** ADNA ROMANZA (1842–1914), born in Orwell, Ohio, and educated in the public schools of Ohio. He served in the Civil War and in the Spanish-American War; as major general of volunteers during the Boxer Rebellion in China (1900), he was in command of the American contingent of the allied forces that captured Peking. Thereafter he commanded the American forces in the Philippines (1901–02), was commander of the Department of the East (1902–03), and, until his retirement, was lieutenant general and chief of staff of the U.S. Army (1904–06). **2.** ADNA ROMANZA (1884–1941), born at Junction City, Kan., and educated at the U.S. Military Academy, West Point, and at other American military institutions. During World War I he was a staff officer in France. He became a brigadier general in 1938. He was known as "the father of the mechanized forces" principally for his work in mechanizing the 7th Cavalry Brigade.

CHAFFINCH, a common European bird, *Fringilla coelebs,* of the family Fringillidae.

It is a small bird, 5 to 6 inches long. The head and neck are blue gray; the back is chestnut; and the wings are almost black, with conspicuous white bars. The chaffinch is valued for its song, and is one of the commonest cage birds, especially in Germany. In the colder northern countries it is migratory, but spends the winter in flocks in England and in countries around the Mediterranean.

CHAGALL, MARC (1889–   ), French painter, born in Vitebsk, Russia, and educated in art in Saint Petersburg (later Petrograd, now Leningrad) and Paris, France. He remained in Paris until 1914 and traveled subsequently in Germany. Between 1915 and 1917 he lived in Petrograd; after the Russian Revolution he was director (1918–19) of the Art Academy in Vitebsk and art director (1919–22) of the Moscow Jewish State Theatre. Chagall painted several murals in the theater lobby and executed the state settings for numerous productions. Except for a period (1941–49) of residence in the United States, he lived in France after 1922.

Chagall's distinctive use of color and form derives partly from Russian expressionism and was influenced decisively by French cubism (see CUBISM; EXPRESSIONISM). He crystallized his style early, as in "Candles in the Dark" (1908; owned by the artist), but later developed subtle variations. His numerous works represent characteristically vivid recollections of Russian-Jewish village scenes ("I and the Village", 1911; Museum of Modern Art, New York City) and incidents in his private life, as in the series of prints "Mein

Culver Service
Marc Chagall

Culver Service

"The Violinist" by Marc Chagall, an impression of his own Russian-village childhood rendered in bright colors and semi-cubist style

Leben" (1922), as well as treatments of Jewish genre subjects ("The Praying Jew", 1914; Art Institute of Chicago, Ill.) and Biblical material, as in the ambitious series of etchings which he executed between 1925 and 1939 to illustrate the Old Testament.

Among Chagall's other works are "The Cattle Dealer" (1912; private collection, Switzerland); "Paris Through the Window" (1913) and "The Birthday" (1915–23), both in the Solomon R. Guggenheim Museum, New York City; "The Circus" (1926; private collection, Brussels, Belgium); "Cock and Harlequin" (1928; private collection, Paris), "Time Is a River Without Banks" (1930–39; Museum of Modern Art); and "The Window" (1959); owned by the artist). He has executed many prints illustrating literary classics.

Chagall is recognized as one of the most significant contemporary painters and graphic artists. He treats his subjects in a vein of humor and fantasy that draws deeply upon the dreamlike resources of the subconscious and distinguishes him as a master of surrealistic inventiveness; see SURREALISM. The personal and circumscribed imagery dominating his work is suffused often with exquisite poetic fancy.　　G.A.

CHAGRES RIVER, a river of Panama, rising about 30 miles N.E. of Panama City, and entering the Caribbean Sea at Chagres. The river supplies the water required to operate the locks of the Panama Canal, which follows the bed of the stream from Mindi to Gamboa. The tremendous rise of this river during freshets, as much as 32 feet in 24 hours, presented one of the most formidable engineering problems in connection with the construction of the canal. The building of the Gatun Dam, which formed Gatun Lake, solved the problem.

CHAILLU, PAUL DU. See DU CHAILLU.

CHAIN, ERNEST BORIS (1906–　　), German-British biochemist and pathologist, born in Berlin and educated at the University of Berlin. Being Jewish, he left Germany after Hitler's accession to power, in 1933, and went to England, where he engaged in research at Cambridge University on enzymes. He became a British citizen in 1939. In 1935 he went to Oxford University, where he collaborated with Sir Howard Florey on the investigation of antibiotic substances produced by molds. By 1941 this investigation had resulted in the production on a small scale of penicillin, and the demonstration in hundreds of laboratory animals and five human patients of the three important characteristics of penicillin as a germicide: that it was potent, nontoxic, and widely effective. After 1950 Chain was professor of biochemistry and scientific director of the International Research Center for Chemical Microbiology at the Higher Institute of Health, Rome, Italy. In 1961 he became professor of biochemistry at the University of London. Chain shared the 1945 Nobel Prize for medicine and physiology with Florey and Sir Alexander Fleming. In 1949 Chain became a fellow of the Royal Society.

CHAIN MAIL. See ARMOR; COAT OF MAIL.

CHAIN SNAKE, a harmless king snake, *Lampropeltis getulus,* of North America, so called because of the chainlike markings on its skin. Its color and markings vary in different districts. In the east and south of the U.S. the color is black, crossed by yellow lines. The chain snake is 4 to 5 feet in length.

ts habits are nocturnal, and its principal food consists of other snakes and rodents.

CHAIN STORES, groups of retail establishments, handling in general the same kind of merchandise, and operated under a central management and common ownership. The Bureau of the Census of the United States defines as chain-store groups only those consisting of a minimum of 11 units; prior to 1951 the minimum was 4 units. A number of States, on the other hand, in imposing taxes on chain stores, define chain-store groups as consisting of a minimum of 2 units.

The first important chain-store system in the United States was probably the Great American Tea Co., founded as a single store in 1858, which later became the Great Atlantic and Pacific Tea Co. chain of food stores. By 1962 it had about 4400 stores. The F. W. Woolworth Co., now an international chain of variety stores specializing in low-priced items, was founded in 1879; the James Butler chain of grocery stores, in 1882; the United Cigar Stores Co., in 1901; and the J. C. Penney Co. chain of variety stores, in 1902. After 1919, chain-store systems developed rapidly in the United States. During 1962 chain-store groups comprising 11 or more stores accounted for about one fourth of all retail sales. Chains of gasoline stations, department stores, variety stores, drug stores, and grocery stores account for approximately 60 percent of all business done by chain-store systems in the United States.

CHAIR, a movable seat, ordinarily with legs and a back, and sometimes with arms, designed for the use of one person. Chairs date back to very ancient times. For many hundreds of years they were used only by royalty, nobility, the priesthood, and the wealthy nonofficial classes. During these centuries other persons used stools, chests, and benches for sitting purposes. Chairs did not become a common article of furniture until the 16th century.

Chairs in Ancient Times. The ruling classes of Babylonia used chairs made of palm wood, which was easily worked, and strong light and soft. The chairs of Assyrian monarchs were elaborate. The massive chair or throne of King Sargon II (722–705 B.C.) had sides on which three representations of the king himself were carved, and below them a figure of his war horse in harness. The sides of the royal chair of King Sennacherib (705–681 B.C.) consisted of three rows of carved figures, each set bearing supporting crossbars. On the walls of ancient Egyptian tombs are painted and carved representations of chairs of many kinds.

Greek chairs were made of bentwood (wood that is bent and not cut into shape) and frequently had sloping backs. The *cathedra,* a portable Greek and Roman chair originally used only by women, gave its name to a type of chair from which philosophers lectured. In early Christian times the term *cathedra* was applied to the chair in which the bishop sat, and the churches in which this chair stood came to be known as cathedrals.

The chairs used by officials and dignitaries in Rome were known as *sellæ,* and the most important type of these was the *sella curalis.* At first the *sella curalis* was a prerogative of royalty. When Rome became a republic, only consuls, censors, and magistrates might use a *sella curalis.* During the days of the Empire, it was a seat for the emperors, and during their absence from Rome it was occupied by their statues. The *sella curalis* generally had two pairs of bronze legs, sometimes made to imitate elephants' tusks. The chairs used in Roman homes or in amphitheaters were named *sedilia.* The term *sedilia* is now usually restricted to certain seats in a church, most often 3 in number, used by the officiating clergy. In medieval times *sedilia* designed for the use of important clerical dignitaries were generally enriched with painting and gilding. The most famous extant chair of Roman times is the portable chair supposedly used by St. Peter, now in the Vatican, Rome. It is of wood, with ivory carvings that portray the labors of Hercules. The chair is placed on exhibition once a century. Another famous chair of ancient days is the "Chair of Dagobert", a Frankish king of early Merovingian times (7th century). It is constructed of cast bronze and has legs in the form of animal heads and feet.

One of the oldest chairs extant in England is the elaborate oak chair used for the coronation of Edward I (13th century) and of most of the kings who followed him. Under this chair, which stands in Westminster Abbey, London, is the stone, known variously as the "Stone of Destiny" and "Stone of Scone", on which early Irish and later Scottish kings sat while being crowned.

Modern Chairs. The change from the conception of the chair as a sign of power to that of an article for common use came about during the Renaissance.

Until the middle of the 17th century, ordinary European chairs were of oak and were not upholstered. Later, leather was used for upholstery and then velvet and silk. The oak

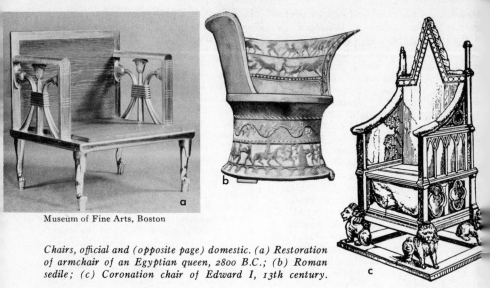

Museum of Fine Arts, Boston

Chairs, official and (opposite page) domestic. (a) Restoration of armchair of an Egyptian queen, 2800 B.C.; (b) Roman sedile; (c) Coronation chair of Edward I, 13th century.

Bettmann Archive

chairs were at first massive and heavy; later, cane backs and seats were introduced, as in the Louis XIII chair in France in the first half of the 17th century.

The earliest chairs for ordinary use in England were low, with heavy, carved backs. Many examples of chairs of this type of the Tudor period are in the Victoria and Albert Museum, London. With the beginning of the 17th century, English chairs, imitating French models, were made taller and lighter, and the carving on them was limited to the framework. The English chair of the periods of Charles I and Charles II was characterized by spiral turnings, and by seats and backs with cane panels of needlework upholstery. The most elegant English chairs of the 17th century were those made during the Restoration (q.v.). Heavy and inelegant chairs again came into vogue in the reigns of William and Mary (1689–1702) and Queen Anne (1702–14).

In the 18th century several notable English cabinetmakers greatly modified the typical heavy English chair. The first and most famous of these cabinetmakers was Thomas Chippendale (q.v.). He replaced the solid splat, or back-piece, of the chair with a splat that was pierced and artistically carved, and substituted well-proportioned cabrioles or sometimes square legs for the massive legs of the chairs of the preceding period. Chippendale chairs are characterized by elegance as well as solidity. George Hepplewhite, Robert Adam, and Thomas Sheraton (qq.v.) made

chairs less massive than those of Chippendale.

Many new varieties of chairs were made in the 19th and 20th centuries, but in the main these new types were derived from those designed in the second half of the 18th century.

The first chairs made in the American colonies were of oak or pine and were modeled on the chairs of the various countries from which the colonists came, chiefly England, Holland, Sweden, and Germany. In time, variations of these models appeared. One of the best-known typically American chairs of early Colonial days was the "Carver" chair, an armchair with turned spindles. The original "Carver" chair is preserved at Plymouth, Mass. In general, Colonial chairs followed the changing styles of chairs in England. The Windsor chair, a strong rail-back chair, made of oak, ash, or hickory, on English models, was popular in Colonial days. Important American chairmakers of the 18th century were William Savery, Jonathan Gostelowe, Benjamin Randolph, and James Gillingham, all of Philadelphia; and, in the first half of the 19th century, Duncan Phyfe (q.v.) of New York City.

At the beginning of the 20th century a new type of chair was developed in various European cities. One of the most important of the centers for this development was the Bauhaus, a school for architectural and industrial design located in Weimar and later in Dessau, both in Germany. In the Bauhaus a number of furniture designers, including Le Corbusier and Miës van der Rohe, designed chairs with

(d) German Renaissance chair: (e) Sheraton chair, 18th century; (f) Early American spindle chair; (g) Modern chair by Eero Saarinen.

Knoll Associates, Inc.

simple, functional lines, built for use and comfort and to blend with modern interiors. A great impetus was given to the development of this "modern" type of chair by its exhibition at the Paris Exposition of Decorative Arts in 1925. In 1927 a number of department stores in New York City imported the new chairs and placed them on sale. Soon many American furniture factories were making such chairs.

Wood is the principal material out of which modern chairs are made. Aluminum, chromeplated tubular steel, and other metals are also used. Rust-proofed wrought iron and cast iron, and other materials are utilized in making modern chairs for outdoor use. See also FURNITURE.

CHALCEDON or **CALCHEDON,** an ancient seaport of Bithynia, Asia Minor, on the Sea of Marmora, at the southern end of the Bosporus strait, opposite Byzantium (now Istanbul). It was founded in 677 B.C. by Megarians from Greece; in the 2nd century B.C. it became a Roman possession. In 451 A.D. Pope Leo I convened the Fourth Ecumenical Council in Chalcedon, to combat the heretical doctrine of the Monophysites (q.v.). After the capture of the city in 616 by the Persians under Khosrau, the city declined, and finally was demolished by the Turks, who used its building stones for Constantinople (Istanbul).

CHALCEDONY, a fibrous crypto-crystalline variety of quartz of various shades of white, yellow, brown, green, and blue. It is transparent or translucent, but some of the milk-white varieties are opaque. It occurs in mammillary, botryoidal, and stalactitic shapes, and as a lining or filling of cavities in rocks. Its principal varieties are *agate,* which is banded and striped, having alternating layers of chalcedony and opal, jasper, or other forms of quartz; *carnelian,* which is clear and of various shades of red; *chrysoprase,* an apple-green variety, in which the color is due to nickel oxide; *heliotrope* or *bloodstone,* of a dark-green color, with small spots of jasper; *onyx,* consisting of bands of opal and chalcedony of different colors, usually black and white; *plasma,* of a deep-green color; and *sardonyx,* a red-and-white-banded variety of chalcedony. (See separate articles on most of the above varieties.) Its many colors and the high luster that it takes by polishing render chalcedony valuable for brooches, necklaces, and other ornaments, and some varieties of it are cut as seal stones. Chalcedony is found in Great Britain, in Brazil, and in the United States in Colorado and California. The formation of the famous agatized (also called silicified or petrified) wood of Chalcedony Park, Ariz., is caused by a natural replacement of the woody fiber by chalcedony from siliceous waters.

CHALCID FLIES, a large group of hymenopterous insects constituting the superfamily Chalcidoidea. They are small, rarely more than 0.1 inch in length, and are characterized by elbowed antennae. Thousands of species make up the group, and their larvae are parasitic on the eggs, larvae, or pupae of other insects. Since so many of these hosts are destructive to plants, the chalcid flies are beneficial economically. Asparagus beetles, gall wasps, scale insects, cicadas, Hessian flies, and cabbage butterflies are among the types preyed upon by the chalcid flies. Many millions of chalcid flies are raised in laboratories and released for the control of such injurious insects.

CHALCIS or **CHALKIS** (Gr. *Khalkis*), capital of the Ægean island department of Eubœa, Greece, on the Strait of Euripus, which is there very narrow. Chalcis is connected with the mainland of Greece by a bridge over the strait, and is situated about 40 miles N.N.W. of Athens, with which it is connected by rail. The ancient city, inhabited by Ionians, was an important commercial and industrial center. In the 7th–8th centuries A.D. it was a base for the establishment of colonies in Macedonia (there giving name to the peninsula of Chalcidice) and in Sicily. It was successively, thereafter, an Athenian, Macedonian, and Roman possession. In the Middle Ages it was a prosperous community under the Venetians, who held it from 1209 until its conquest by the Turks in 1470. Pop. (1961) 24,745.

CHALCOCITE, or COPPER GLANCE, a mineral consisting of copper sulfide. It crystallizes in the orthorhombic system, and has hardness 3 and sp. gr. 5.6. It is an important ore of copper and is frequently met with in granular or compact masses. The luster is metallic, and the color lead gray, which tarnishes to dull black on exposure. Chalcocite occurs commonly associated with other copper min-

erals, as in the Cornwall mines, where beautiful specimens are found. It also occurs in Czechoslovakia, Germany, Mexico, South America, and the U.S. at Bristol, Conn. See COPPER.

CHALCOPYRITE, or COPPER PYRITES, the most widely distributed mineral of copper and one of the principal sources of copper. It consists of a copper-iron sulfide which crystallizes in the tetragonal system, with hardness 4 and sp. gr. 4.2. It has a metallic luster, is of a brass-yellow color, and is often tarnished or iridescent. It occurs widely disseminated in metallic veins and in the older rocks, frequently with pyrite or iron sulfide, and sometimes with nickel and cobalt sulfide. This mineral occurs in large deposits in Sweden, Germany (in the Harz Mountains), Czechoslovakia, Hungary, New South Wales, South Africa, and the United States. When tarnished, it is sometimes called *peacock ore,* owing to the iridescent film of brilliant colors with which it becomes coated.

CHALDEANS. See BABYLONIA.

CHALDIANS. See KHALDIANS.

CHALIAPIN, FEODOR IVANOVITCH (1873–1938), Russian dramatic bass singer, born at Kazan. He received his training in Tifls (1892–93), and made his debut in grand opera at the Marinsky Theater (St. Petersburg, 1894). He became world-famous for his roles in Russian operas, including *A Life for the Czar,* by Glinka; *Prince Igor,* by Borodin; and *Sadko* by Rimski-Korsakov. He was also notable for his roles in operas by Mozart, Rossini, Boito, and Massenet. He first appeared at the Metropolitan Opera House, New York City, in 1909, and scored his most notable success there when he appeared as Boris Godunov in 1921. He also had many successful seasons with the Chicago Civic Opera Company. He left Russia after the Bolshevik revolution, and settled in France, where he was naturalized. His writings include *Pages From My Life* (1927) and *Man and Mask: Forty Years in the Life of a Singer* (1932).

CHALK, a soft white or whitish form of limestone composed of the remains of small marine organisms such as foraminifera and cocoliths. Chemically it is almost pure calcium carbonate with traces of other minerals. It ranges in hardness and texture from very soft, porous varieties to harder close-grained types. It is particularly common in strata of the Cretaceous Period (Lat. *creta,* "chalk"). Chalk is plentiful in the British Isles and is exposed in the white cliffs on either side of the English Channel. Large deposits of chalk occur in Iowa, Texas, and Arkansas. See CAL-CITE; LIMESTONE.

CHALLONER, RICHARD (1691–1781), English Roman Catholic churchman, born at Lewes, in Sussex. He was educated at Douai, France, and taught philosophy and divinity there from 1713 until 1730, when he settled in London. There he served as a missionary priest and, after 1741, as bishop; 17 years later he became vicar apostolic of the London district. His works include a popular prayer book, *Garden of the Soul* (1740); *Memoirs of Missionary Priests and Other Catholicks of both Sexes who Suffered Death or Imprisonment in England on Account of their Religion* (1741); biographies of British saints, *Britannia Sancta* (published anonymously, 1745); and an edition of the Douai Bible (1749–50).

CHALMERS, THOMAS (1780–1847), Scottish theologian and preacher, born at Anstruther and educated at St. Andrews University. In 1803 he was minister of the parish of Kilmany, Fifeshire, and in 1815 he was called to Tron Church, Glasgow, as pastor. During the following years he became one of the most popular preachers in England and Scotland, and was noted also for his social work. He became minister of St. John's parish in 1819, and there established schools, revived church attendance, and reduced relief expenditures. In 1823 he accepted a professorship of moral philosophy at St. Andrews, and after 5 years at that university joined the faculty of Edinburgh University as professor of theology. There he taught until 1843, when he led a group of 470 Scottish clerics in a movement of secession from the Scottish Church. The new organization, the Free Church of Scotland, which took a position of independence from civil authority in spiritual matters, founded a college at Edinburgh of which Chalmers became the first principal. His chief writings are *Christian and Civic Economy of Large Towns* (1826), *Political Economy* (1832), *The Adaptation of External Nature to the Moral and Intellectual Constitution of Man* (1833), *and Institutes of Theology* (1843–47).

CHÂLONS-SUR-MARNE, city in N.E. France, capital of the department of Marne and the seat of a bishopric. The city is located on the Marne River, 107 miles E. of Paris by rail. The plain between Troyes and what is now Châlons-sur-Marne was the scene (451 A.D.) of the defeat of Attila (q.v.) and the Huns by the allied forces of Romans and Visigoths. Notable public buildings in the city are the cathedral of Notre Dame (12th

and 13th centuries), the cathedral of St. Étienne (chiefly 13th century), and the Hôtel de Ville (18th century). The chief industry of the city is brewing. Other industries are the manufacture of shoes, wall paper, brushes, and woolen and cotton goods, and the making of champagne. The city has a considerable trade in grain, hemp, and rapeseed oil. Pop. (1962) 39,794.

CHALON-SUR-SAÔNE (anc. *Cabillonum*), city in E. central France, in the department of Saône-et-Loire, on the Saône River where it joins the Canal du Centre. The church of St. Vincent, originally a cathedral (12th to 15th centuries) and the church of St. Pierre (17th century) are among the notable buildings of the city. It is an important railroad junction and is the second most important industrial city of the Burgundy region. The chief industries of the city are the manufacture of glass, straw hats, hosiery, vinegar, pottery, jewelry, tiles, and chemicals. It contains copper and iron foundries and dyeing plants. The city has an extensive trade in corn, timber, and wine. Pop. (1954) 37,399.

CHALYBITE. See SIDERITE.

CHAMBAL RIVER, a river of central India. It flows in a general northeasterly direction for a distance of 650 miles from the Vindhyan Mountains to the Jumna River, of which it is the principal tributary.

CHAMBERLAIN, (ARTHUR) NEVILLE (1869–1940), British statesman, son of Joseph Chamberlain and half brother of Sir Joseph Austen Chamberlain (qq.v.). Neville Chamberlain was educated at Rugby, and at Mason College, Birmingham. He was a member of the Birmingham city council and chairman of the town planning committee (1911), an alderman (1914) and lord mayor (1915–1916). In national politics, he was a member of the Central Control Board (1915), director general of national service (1916–1917), and postmaster general (1922–23). He was successively paymaster general, minister of health, chancellor of the exchequer (1923–24), and again minister of health (1924–29), in which latter capacity he carried out extensive social legislation. He again became chancellor of the exchequer in 1931, and was successful in balancing the British budget. Succeeding Stanley Baldwin (q.v.) as prime minister, in 1937, with the avowed object of avoiding a European war, he followed a policy of appeasement toward the European dictators Adolf Hitler of Germany and Benito Mussolini of Italy. This policy culminated (September, 1938) in the Munich Pact (q.v.), which resulted in the cession of part of Czechoslovakia to Germany. Chamberlain was also instrumental in the establishment of a committee for nonintervention on the part of the various powers in the Spanish Civil War (1936–39). In November, 1938, he brought about British recognition of Italian sovereignty over Ethiopia, which Italy had conquered and annexed in 1936, and in 1939 recognition of the Franco government which had seized power in Spain. The appeasement policy failed, however, to prevent additional acts of aggression, and after Germany invaded Poland, Chamberlain announced his country's declaration of war on Germany (Sept. 3, 1939). Following the defeat of the British forces by the Germans in Norway (1940), Chamberlain was forced to resign as prime minister, and Winston Churchill (q.v.) assumed the office. Chamberlain served as lord president of the council under Churchill and was also leader of the Conservative Party until October 3, 1940, when ill-health forced his resignation from both offices.

CHAMBERLAIN, HOUSTON STEWART (1855–1927), German author, born at Southsea, England. He was a resident of Germany from 1885 to 1889, when he settled in Vienna, Austria. In 1908 he married Eva Wagner, the youngest daughter of the German composer Richard Wagner. He lived in Bayreuth, Germany, from 1908 until his death, and in 1916 he became a naturalized German citizen. Chamberlain's best-known work is *Die Grundlagen des Neunzehnten Jahrunderts* (1899–1901). In this work he proclaimed the superiority of peoples, particularly the German people, who were descended from so-called "Aryan" stock. Among his other works are *Das Drama Richard Wagners* (1892), and other books on Wagner and his work; *Heinrich von Stein* (1903); *Immanuel Kant* (1905); and *Goethe* (1912).

CHAMBERLAIN, JOSEPH (1836–1914), British statesman, born in London and educated at University College School, London. Until he was 38 years old he devoted himself to a business career, from which he retired with great wealth. During the later years of this period he also became active in the local politics of the city of Birmingham, and in 1869 he was elected to the town council, on which he served until his election in 1873 to the office of mayor. His administration, during which gas and water supplies were taken over by the city and slums were cleared, was regarded as a turning point in the history of Birmingham and a model for other contemporary cities.

Chamberlain's long parliamentary career began in 1876. Four years later, as a representative of the radical wing of the Liberal Party, he was given a seat in Gladstone's cabinet as president of the Board of Trade. His principal interest at this time was in British policy in Ireland; he advocated a partial Home Rule which was not entirely acceptable either to Gladstone or to the Irish Nationalists, and which resulted in his leaving the cabinet in 1885. He re-entered it in 1886 as president of the Local Government Board, but resigned the same year because of Gladstone's advocacy of Home Rule. In 1887–88 he visited the United States as member of a commission to settle a fisheries dispute between the U.S. and Canada. He returned to the cabinet under Lord Salisbury in 1895 as secretary of state for the colonies, a post he held for seven crucial years. Until this period Chamberlain had been considered a radical in municipal politics and a social reformer in Parliament. He maintained his interest in domestic reforms, as evidenced by the Workmen's Compensation Act sponsored by him and passed in Parliament in 1897; but he soon became noted as a champion of imperialism. His conduct in the period immediately preceding the Boer War (see SOUTH AFRICAN WAR) of 1899–1902 was bitterly assailed by some and ardently admired by others in England. Most controversial was the question of his complicity in the Jameson Raid of 1896 and his relationship with President Kruger of Transvaal. After the war he set a precedent by visiting the colonies in South Africa in person as secretary of state. His chief interest between 1902 and his retirement from public life was the colonial policy, now known as "imperial preference", which was designed to tighten the economic bonds of the British Commonwealth. His program, which involved an end to the traditional free-trade policy of England, was unpopular and resulted in his entering the opposition to the government, but he was returned to Parliament and remained a member until his death. His interest in Birmingham, where he founded and became chancellor of Birmingham University, continued throughout his life, and there his sons, Joseph Austen and Arthur Neville Chamberlain (qq.v.), began their political careers.

CHAMBERLAIN, SIR (JOSEPH) AUSTEN (1863–1937), British statesman, born at Birmingham, and educated at Rugby and a Cambridge University and in Berlin and Paris. He was the eldest son of Joseph Chamberlain (q.v.) and was his father's secretary for time. Austen Chamberlain became a member of Parliament (Unionist) in 1892. He was chancellor of the exchequer from 1903 to 1906 and again from 1919 to 1921, and secretary of state for India from 1915 to 1917. From 1921 to 1923 he was Conservative leader of the House of Commons and lord privy seal; from 1924 to 1929 he was foreign secretary, and in 1931 became first lord of the admiralty. During his second term as chancellor, he strengthened British credit by imposing heavy income taxes, supertaxes, and excess-profit taxes. His 1919 budget reduced by one sixth the duties on articles from British colonies; he thus made the principle of imperial preference, which his father had advocated 15 years previously, a regular part of the British financial system. As lord privy seal he advocated and assisted in the establishment (1921) of the Irish Free State. While foreign secretary he was instrumental in bringing about the signing (1925) of the Locarno Treaties (see LOCARNO), and for this effort toward maintaining peace he was awarded the 1925 Nobel Peace Prize (jointly with the American Charles G. Dawes). Austen Chamberlain was vitally interested in the League of Nations and attended all the meetings of its Assembly and its Council. He was a strong advocate of the Kellogg-Briand Pact (q.v.) and played an important part in Germany's entrance into the League of Nations in 1926. His speeches on European and Empire questions were published (1928) as *Peace in Our Time.*

CHAMBERLAIN, NEVILLE. See CHAMBERLAIN, (ARTHUR) NEVILLE.

CHAMBERLIN, THOMAS CHROWDER (1843–1928), American geologist and educator, born at Mattoon, Ill., and educated at Beloit College and the University of Michigan. In 1869 he became the professor of natural science at the State Normal School at Whitewater, Wis.; from 1873 until 1882 he held the professorship of geology at Beloit College; from 1882 until 1887 he was in charge of the glacial division of the U.S. Geological Survey; from 1887 until 1892 he was president of the University of Wisconsin; and from 1892 until his retirement in 1919 he was professor of geology and director of the Walker Museum at the University of Chicago. He accompanied the Peary Relief Expedition of 1894 to Greenland as geologist. Chamberlin was one of the originators of the so-called planetesimal hypothesis of the origin of the earth. In 1893 he founded the *Journal of Geology,* which he edited for 30 years. His major works include *General Treatise on Geology* (with Rollin D. Salisbury, 1906), *The Origin of the Earth*

(1916), and *The Two Solar Families* (1928).

CHAMBER MUSIC, a term designating music that is suitable for performance in a moderate-sized auditorium or room. The term originally meant the music composed for a nobleman's household and performed for him and his guests. In modern usage it generally signifies works written for groups of from 2 to 10 instruments, and played with only one performer to each part. In the earliest period of chamber music (end of the 16th and be ginning of the 17th centuries), the voice was used in conjunction with the instruments, but from the time of Joseph Haydn (1732–1809) voice parts were discontinued in chamber music. Some modern composers, however, have restored the voice as one of the components of a chamber-music ensemble. The favorite instrumental combination for chamber music has always been the string quartet, consisting of first and second violins, viola, and cello. Other popular chamber-music combinations are the trio, consisting of piano, violin, and cello; and the quintet, consisting of the string quartet with the addition of the piano. Compositions written for such ensembles are called "trios", "quartets", and "quintets".

Practically every composer of note since the end of the 16th century has written some form of chamber music.

CHAMBER OF COMMERCE, local, national, or international association of entrepreneurs, established to promote the interests of its members. Originally, the membership of chambers of commerce comprised principally merchants, but now it consists chiefly of bankers, manufacturers, and merchants. The first chamber of commerce was probably that founded in Marseille, France, in 1599, as a branch of the town's government, with wide powers, including the appointment and supervision of French consulates in the Near East. In 1700 King Louis XIV of France decreed the establishment of other chambers of commerce, with more limited powers, in other towns. They were all suppressed in 1791, during the French Revolution, but were restored by Napoleon in 1804, and ever since have been an integral part of the French economic and governmental structures. Chambers of commerce in a number of other European countries resemble those of France.

Chambers of commerce in the British Isles and the United States have, from the first, had no governmental functions. The first of these chambers were founded in the British isle of Jersey, and in New York City, in 1768. The first chamber in England was the Commercial Society of Manchester, established in 1794.

The London chamber came into being in 1881.

The early chambers of commerce were concerned principally with problems of domestic and foreign trade, and with governmental policies and political events affecting trade. With the development, in the 19th and 20th centuries, of large-scale industry and large and powerful banks, chambers of commerce also became concerned with a wider range of economic and political matters, including labor problems.

An international chamber of commerce, composed of representatives of manufacturing, banking, and commercial interests in a number of leading countries, was organized in 1920, and provision was made for a congress to be held every second year, in the country of one of its members.

CHAMBER OF COMMERCE OF THE UNITED STATES, a federation of local chambers of commerce, national trade associations, and individuals prominent in the business and banking worlds, established in 1912, with the aid of President William Howard Taft. It supplies information on matters of interest to its members, and gives expression to the views of its members on governmental policies affecting their interests. Membership in 1960 was about 25,000 business firms, corporations, and individuals, and 3600 organizations. The policy of the Chamber is determined at its annual meetings, and, between these meetings, by a referendum vote of the membership. The Chamber publishes a monthly, *The Nation's Business,* and other publications.

CHAMBERSBURG, county seat of Franklin Co., Pa., on Conococheague and Falling creeks, in the Cumberland Valley. The surrounding region is noted for its apple and peach orchards, and also contains deposits of freestone, marble, and blue limestone. The borough has a large trade in farm produce, and contains railroad shops and factories producing tomato and apple products, flour and flour-milling machinery, steam presses, power-transmission machinery, clothing, hosiery, and paper towels. Chambersburg was first settled in 1730 by Benjamin Chambers, an immigrant from Ireland, and for many years was called Falling Spring. In Chambersburg, John Brown and his associates planned their raid on Harpers Ferry. During the Civil War, Chambersburg was taken by Confederate forces three times, the last seizure ending in the burning of the city (1864) upon its refusal to pay $100,000 in gold to Confederate Gen. John McCausland. The borough is the site of Wilson College (Presbyterian) and of Penn Hall School, both for girls. Government is by a chief burgess and a council of ten. Pop. (1960) 17,670.

CHAMBEZI RIVER, a river of Africa, 250 m. long, forming a remote headstream of the Congo River. It rises in a plateau, 6000 ft. above sea level, in Northern Rhodesia, between lakes Tanganyika and Nyassa and, flowing southwest, enters Lake Bangweulu in the wet season, but during the dry season skirts the southern border of the shrunken lake and flows directly into the Luapula River.

CHAMBORD, CHÂTEAU DE, a celebrated château, one of the best examples extant of French Renaissance architecture, located in the department of Loir-et-Cher, France, about 9 m. from Blois. The château contains 440 rooms and stands in the midst of a park of 13,000 acres, which also contains the village of Chambord. The structure, originally a hunting lodge of the counts of Blois, was begun by order of Francis I and completed in the reign of Louis XIV. Napoleon presented the château and its domain to Louis Alexandre Berthier. In 1821 his widow sold the property to the Legitimists, who had raised the money by public subscription. They presented it to the Duchesse de Berry, and she in turn bestowed it on her infant son, Henri de Berry, whose claim to the French throne the Legitimists supported. He bequeathed it to a Spanish branch of his family, the dukes of Parma.

CHAMELEON, any lizard of the family Chamaelontidae, found chiefly in Africa and Madagascar, especially the type species *Chamaeleon vulgaris,* which is also found in Europe and Asia. The body is very compressed and the dorsal line sharp, the skin being rough with granules. The head, elevated into the form of a cone, rests on a very short neck, which does not permit the head being turned. To compensate for this handicap, the eyes are large and prominent and can move independently of each other. The legs raise the body from the ground; the toes, of both the fore and hind feet, are divided into two sets, one directed forward, the other backward, so that each foot has the power of grasping like a hand. The tongue is remarkably extensile, and viscous at the end, enabling the chameleon to easily capture insects, which are

Chameleon, Chamaeleon vulgaris

its main food. The ability of the animal to change color is due to layers of contractile pigment-bearing cells which can be pressed toward the surface of the skin, and to the inflation of air vessels in connection with the lungs. Other characteristics are the absence of an external eardrum or tympanic membrane, and of a columella or epiterygoid skull bone in which the chameleon differs from all other lizards except the Amphisbaenae.

The name chameleon is popularly given in the U.S. to several lizards capable of changing color, especially to the genus *Anolis* of the Iguana family.

CHAMISSO, ADELBERT VON or LOUIS CHARLES ADELAIDE DE (1781–1838), German poet and naturalist, born at Boncourt, in Champagne, France. His parents took him with them to Germany in flight from the French Revolution, settling in Berlin. After a career with the Prussian army (1798–1808), he turned to literature, writing his best-known novel, *Peter Schlemihls Wundersame Geschichte* (1814), on the theme of a man who sold his shadow. From 1815 to 1818 he sailed as botanist on the Russian vessel *Rurik* on a scientific circumnavigation of the world; on his return he was appointed curator of the botanical gardens in Berlin. Aside from his scientific works and the above-mentioned novel, Chamisso is known for his lyrical poetry, especially the cycle *Frauenliebe und -leben* (1830), for which Robert Schumann composed music.

CHAMOIS, common name of a goat-antelope of the genus *Rupicapra* in the family Bovidae (q.v.). The genus contains only one species, *R. tragus,* which inhabits the Alps and other high mountains of Central and South Europe. The chamois is about the size of a large goat, but the neck is longer in proportion, and the body shorter. The horns of both sexes are seldom more than 6 or 7 in. long, black, rising nearly straight up from the forehead, and so bent back at the tip as to form a hook. The summer color is reddish brown, with a darker dorsal band, and a yellowish ventral surface. The winter color is a darker brown, but white below. A dark brown band runs from the eye along each cheek. The rest of the head is pale yellow. The short tail is black.

The usual summer resort of the chamois is in the higher regions of the mountains, not far from the snow line, and it is often to be seen lying on the snow. In winter it descends to the higher forests. The aromatic and bitter plants of the mountain pastures, and young twigs of rhododendron, willow, and juniper

Chamois, Rupicapra tragus

are its favorite food. The chamois is gregarious. It is an animal of extraordinary agility, and flocks may often be observed sporting in a remarkable manner among the rocky heights. It passes readily up or down precipices which almost no other quadruped could attempt. The scent, sight, and hearing of the chamois are extremely keen. When a flock is feeding, one animal is always on the watch, and by a sort of whistle announces apprehended danger. The flesh is highly esteemed as venison, and chamois hunting has been so popular as sport that the animal is becoming rare.

CHAMOMILE. See CAMOMILE.

CHAMONIX or **CHAMOUNI,** valley and town in the Alps Mountains, in the department of Haute-Savoie, S.E. France. The valley, about 3400 feet above sea level, is 14 m. long and from 1 to 2½ m. wide. It runs from N.E. to S.W., and its entire length is traversed by the Arve River. In the northwestern part of the valley rise Mont le Brévent and the Aiguilles Rouges mountain chain; in the s.w. is Mont Blanc and its glaciers. The principal agricultural products of the valley are potatoes, oats, flax, barley, and honey. The chief industries are the manufacture of hats and textiles, and the carving of articles of wood. The town of Chamonix, lying 39 miles S.E. of Geneva, Switzerland, at an altitude of 3415 feet, is a tourist resort, serving as a starting point for expeditions to explore the glaciers of Mont Blanc or to ascend the mountain. Pop. of the town (1962) 7206.

CHAMPAGNE. See WINE: *Champagne.*

CHAMPAGNE, an ancient province of N.E. France, now forming the departments of Marne, Haute-Marne, Aube, and Ardennes, and also comprising part of the departments of Yonne, Aisne, Seine-et-Marne, and Meuse. The province was about 180 miles long by 150 wide. It was noted for its vineyards and, in the 12th and 13th centuries, for its fairs. Its chief towns were Troyes, Bar-sur-Aube, Laon, and Reims.

CHAMPAIGN, city in Champaign Co., Ill about 127 miles s.w. of Chicago, in a rich agricultural region. It is a retail trading center and contains a soybean-processing plant, a hybrid-corn plant, a railroad shop, a planing mill, and factories producing **trailers,** industrial machinery, forgings, concrete culverts and sporting goods. The University of Illinois is located in the adjoining city of Urbana. Pop. (1960) 49,583.

CHAMPAIGNE or **CHAMPAGNE,** PHILIPPE DE (1602–74), Flemish painter, born in Brussels. He went to Paris in 1621, and there collaborated with Nicolas Poussin in decorating the Luxembourg Palace. He became official painter to Marie de' Medicis, Queen of France, and rector of the Academy of Paris, and at various times served King Louis XIII and Cardinal Richelieu; the latter commissioned Champaigne to decorate his palace and the dome of the Sorbonne. He was principally noted as a portrait and religious painter. Among his works are "Richelieu" and "The Last Supper" (both in the Louvre), a series of pictures depicting the life of St. Benedict (Brussels Museum), and "Arnaud d'Andilly" (Boston Museum of Fine Arts).

CHAMPLAIN, SAMUEL DE (1570–1635), French explorer, called "The Father of New France", born at Brouage. In 1599 he undertook his first voyage to the New World, visiting the West Indies and Spanish America. In a report of his observations, which he made to King Henry IV of France, he suggested that a canal across the Isthmus of Panama might "shorten the voyage to the South Sea (Pacific) by more than 1500 leagues". The king sent him in 1603 to accompany an expedition fitted out for the purpose of colonizing the New World. On this trip Champlain explored the St. Lawrence to the Lachine Rapids, and on a successive voyage in the following year explored the Bay of Fundy and the New England coast as far south as the shores of Massachusetts. His accounts and maps of the territory explored by him have been of great value to historians, and some of them are especially interesting for their descriptions of the habits and characteristics of the Indians. In

1608 he sailed from France for the fourth time, on this occasion as lieutenant governor of New France, and on July 3rd of the same year founded the first European settlement on the site of the present city of Quebec. He formed alliances with the Indians of Canada and helped them in their wars with the Iroquois of northern New York, thus establishing friendly relations between the French and the Canadian Indians which continued as long as the former held Canada. While on an expedition with the Indians (1609) he discovered the lake which bears his name, and two years later he built a trading station at Montreal. In subsequent years he explored the inland waterways of what are now southern Ontario and northern New York State. In 1629, when a British raiding party captured the settlement of Quebec, Champlain was taken prisoner and held in England until 1632. He was governor of New France from 1633 until his death. Among the most interesting of the many accounts by Champlain of his travels are the *Bref Discours des Choses plus Remarquables que Samuel Champlain de Brouage a Recognues aux Indes Occidentales* (1601), first published more than 250 years after it was written, and preserved in manuscript at Dieppe; and *Des Sauvages, ou Voyage de Samuel Champlain de Brouage Fait en la France Nouvelle* (1604).

CHAMPLAIN, LAKE, lake in North America, situated along the N. part of the boundary between the States of New York and Vermont, and extending about 6 m. into Quebec Province, Canada. It is about 125 m. long, varies in width from about ¼ m. to 14 m., and has a maximum depth of about 600 ft. and an area of about 600 sq.m. An important link in an extensive waterway, it is connected with the New York State Barge Canal System and the Hudson R. by the Champlain Canal and with the St. Lawrence R. by the Richelieu R. and the Chambly Canal. Approximately fifty islands are located in the lake; among the larger islands are Grand Isle, North Hero Isle, and Isle La Motte. Lying in an extremely picturesque region between the Adirondacks and the Green Mountains, Lake Champlain is the site of numerous summer and winter resorts. Salmon, pike, and shad abound in its waters. Burlington, Vt., is the principal port. Other towns on the lake include Plattsburg, Port Henry, Whitehall, and Crown Point, all in New York, and Chimney Point, in Vermont. Lake Champlain was discovered in 1609 by the French explorer Samuel de Champlain, whose name it bears. On Sept. 11, 1814, during the War of 1812, an American fleet won a decisive victory over the British off Plattsburg.

CHAMPOLLION, Jean François (1790–1832), French Egyptologist, born in Figeac, brother of Jean Jacques Champollion-Figeac. He became professor of history at the Lyceum of Grenoble when he was only nineteen years old. In 1824, King Charles X of France sent him to Italy to study Egyptian antiquities in the museums of that country, and on his return to France, made him director of the museum of Egyptian antiquities in the Louvre, Paris. In 1828 Champollion was co-director, with Ipollito Rosellini, of a scientific expedition to Egypt.

Champollion's greatest achievement was the deciphering of the Egyptian hieroglyphic "sacred writing" of the Rosetta Stone (q.v.), which enabled him to work out the grammar and compile a dictionary of the ancient Egyptian language. Because of his achievements, Egyptian hieroglyphics, theretofore a baffling mystery to archeologists, were readily deciphered, and an immense amount of knowledge of ancient Egyptian civilization was acquired.

Champollion's many writings include *L'Égypte, sous les Pharaons* (2 vols., 1814), *Précis du Système Hiéroglyphique des Anciens Égyptiens* (1824), and the posthumously published *Grammaire Égyptienne* (1836) and *Dictionnaire Égyptienne* (edited by his brother, 1841).

CHANCE, Frank Leroy (1877–1924), American professional baseball player, born in Fresno, Cal. From 1901 to 1912 he was first baseman for the Chicago National League team; from 1905 to 1912 its manager. He played 1220 games for Chicago, in which he had a batting average of 298. Evers achieved fame as a member of the "Tinker-to-Evers-to-Chance" double-play combination (see Tinker, Joseph Bert; Evers, John Joseph). In 1946 he was elected to the Baseball Hall of Fame.

CHANCELLORSVILLE, BATTLE OF, important engagement of the American Civil War, fought on May 2–3, 1863, at the village of Chancellorsville (now Chancellor), Spotsylvania Co., Va., about 10 miles w. by s. of Fredericksburg. The Union forces, the Federal Army of the Potomac, under General Joseph Hooker, numbered about 130,000; the Confederate forces, comprising the Army of Northern Virginia under General Robert E. Lee, numbered about 60,000.

Following the Union catastrophe late in 1862 at Fredericksburg Hooker, who superseded General Ambrose Everett Burnside as commander of the Army of the Potomac, had succeeded in thoroughly reorganizing the army, restoring its morale, and preparing it for action. During this period the Federal and Confederate armies lay facing one another across the Rappahannock R. at Fredericksburg. Planning to turn the Confederate left flank and to destroy Lee's communications with Richmond, Hooker began operations by sending (April 27) his Ist and VIth Corps, under General John Sedgwick across the Rappahannock below Fredericksburg, with orders to contain the enemy; he then moved the remainder of his army westward about 25 miles to Kelly's Ford, crossed the Rappahannock and Rapidan rivers, and during the night of April 30 concentrated at Chancellorsville, on Lee's left flank. The Confederate leader, regarding Sedgwick's arrival below Fredericksburg as a diversionary maneuver, had meanwhile begun to marshal the bulk of his forces, notably a corps under General Thomas "Stonewall" Jackson, against the main Union force. On the morning of May 1 Hooker started to march on Fredericksburg, but on meeting advance elements of the Confederate army returned to his strongly fortified positions around Chancellorsville.

Early on May 2 Lee ordered Jackson's corps (about 26,000 men) to make a wide detour around the extreme right of Hooker's position and assault his flank. The purpose of this movement was not apparent to the Federals. About 6 P.M., after a march of some 15 miles, Jackson suddenly attacked the flank and rear of General Oliver Otis Howard's XIth Corps, which constituted the right flank of the Federal army, and stampeded it. Jackson, while in advance of his troops, was fired upon and mortally wounded by his own men, who mistook his escort for a detachment of Federals.

During the progress of this movement Lee made a series of successfully diversionary attacks on Hooker's frontal positions, thus immobilizing the bulk of the Federal army. On the morning of May 3 Lee vigorously attacked the Federal front and flank, with Jackson's force, now commanded by General J. E. B. Stuart, figuring prominently in the action. The brunt of the assault fell upon units under General Daniel Edgar Sickles, on the Federal right, and General Henry Warner Slocum, at the center. Hooker showed indecision, and the Federal army withdrew to strong defensive positions. Lee was deterred from immediately following up his advantage by the news that his position was threatened on the right by an advance of the Federal force un-

From left to right: Irish chandelier (late 18th century); crystal and bronze chandelier of the English regency period (early 19th century); French chandelier (early 19th century).

der Sedgwick. Confederate reinforcements checked Sedgwick's advance, and on the night of May 4–5, he was driven across the Rappahannock. Lee then prepared to advance against Hooker on the 5th, but the latter hastily withdrew his army across the river during a heavy storm. The Confederate victory frustrated Federal plans for an assault on Richmond and made possible Lee's subsequent invasion of the North. Union casualties in the battle totaled about 17,300, including about 1600 killed and 9800 wounded; Confederate losses were about 12,800, including about 1650 killed and 9100 wounded.

CHANCRE. See SYPHILIS.

CHANDELIER (Lat. *candelabrum*, "candlestick"), a frame designed to hold lights, and generally suspended from a ceiling. Originally the light of a chandelier was supplied by candles. Candles were in time superseded by gas lights, and these by electric lights.

The earliest chandeliers were made of wood, but this type was so easily damaged by candle grease that horn, and metal, including copper, wrought iron, brass, and sometimes silver, were used instead. Some early chandeliers were in the form of a cross; in the 12th century, chandeliers in the form of a crown became popular. A notable example of the crown chandelier was that presented to the cathedral of Aix-la-Chapelle in 1168 by the Holy Roman Emperor Frederick I. In the 17th century the bronze or brass chandelier was popular in northern Europe. The most magnificent chandeliers of the 18th century were made in France.

In the second half of the 17th century, a vogue for rock-crystal (transparent quartz) and cut-glass pendants and other decorations on chandeliers came into being. These decorations achieved their greatest popularity in the 18th and the first half of the 19th century. Cut glass from Bohemia (present-day Czechoslovakia) was at first the principal glass used. After the middle of the 18th century, cut glass manufactured in Great Britain took the place of Bohemian cut glass to a large extent. The decorations of such chandeliers became in time extremely ornate. Modern ideas of decoration have resulted in chandeliers of simple design, usually of metal.

CHANDRAGUPTA or **CHANDRAGUPTA MAURYA** (d. 286 B.C.), the first king (322?–298 B.C.) of the Maurya dynasty of the ancient kingdom of Magadha, (present-day province of Bihar, India). He was known to the Greeks as Sandrocottus. He was the son of a king of Magadha, but was driven out of the kingdom by the kinsman who had succeeded his father. While in exile, Chandragupta reputedly met the Macedonian king Alexander the Great (about 325 B.C.) and urged him to invade India. After Alexander's death, Chandragupta wrested the Punjab region from the Macedonian forces; then he conquered Magadha, killed the king, and assumed the royal power. By conquest he extended Magadha until it comprised Afghanistan and all of northern India between the Bay of Bengal and the Arabian Sea. In 305 Seleucus Nicator invaded Northern India, but was defeated by Chandragupta, who thereupon added to his lands some territory north of the Indus. Chandragupta reputedly abdicated and, a voluntary exile in the south of India, committed suicide. The Maurya dynasty was carried on by his son Bindusara (reigned 298–273).

CHANGAN. See SIAN.

CHANGCHIAKOW or **CHANGKIAKOW**. See KALGAN.

CHANGCHOW. See LUNGKI.

CHANGCHOW or **CH'ANG-CHOU**, municipality of Kiangsu Province, China, situated on the Grand Canal, about 100 miles W.N.W. of Shanghai. It is a manufacturing center, with plants engaged in the production of combs, textiles, flour, and machinery. From 1912 to 1948 Changchow was known as Wunsin. Pop. (1953 est.) 296,500.

CHANGCHUN, city of Kirin Province, Manchuria, China. In 1934, during the Japanese undeclared war on China and the conquest of Manchuria, Changchun became the capital of the puppet state of Manchukuo and was renamed Hsinking. After the defeat of the Japanese in World War II the Chinese recovered possession of the city and restored its former name. Pop. (1957 est.) 975,000.

CHANGE OF LIFE. See MENOPAUSE.

CHANG HSUEH-LIANG (1898–   ), Chinese soldier, known as "the Young Marshal", son of the military leader Chang Tsolin, educated at Mukden Military Academy. In 1928, on his father's death, he succeeded him as commander in chief in Manchuria. He was forced to leave Manchuria in 1933, following the Japanese occupation of the region. After a visit (1933–34) to Europe he received command of a Nationalist army in Shensi Province. Chinese Communist forces, then in the vanguard of the anti-Japanese movement in China, became increasingly active in the northwestern provinces during the next two years, and in the fall of 1936 General Chiang Kai-shek, head of the Chinese Nationalist (Kuomintang) government, ordered General Chang to drive the Red armies from Shensi. Several of Chang's units deserted to the Communists during the ensuing campaign, which ended in a stalemate; vigorously anti-Japanese himself, General Chang then began to fraternize with the Reds. General Chiang Kai-shek went to Sian, capital of Shensi, early in December, 1936, for the purpose of dismissing Chang and initiating a new offensive against the Communists. On December 12, shortly after his arrival, General Chiang was kidnaped by troops under Chang's command, and several generals in his entourage were executed. General Chang notified the Nationalist government that its leader would be released subject to fulfillment of certain conditions, notably an immediate declaration of war against Japan and readmission of the Communists to the Kuomintang. The Nationalist government refused to deal with the rebels, but private negotiations for Chiang's release continued until Dec. 25, when Chang capitulated, probably on the basis of an unofficial agreement by Chiang to terminate the war against the Communists. General Chang was sentenced (Dec. 31, 1936) by a courtmartial to ten years' imprisonment and five years' loss of civil rights. Pardoned in January, 1937, he later retired to private life.

CHANGSHA, river port and capital of Hunan Province, China, on the Siang R., about 320 miles N. of Canton. The city is a center for the export of rice, eggs, and coal produced in the surrounding region. In 1911 Changsha was one of the centers of the revolution which resulted in establishment of the Chinese republic. Pop. (1957 est.) 703,000.

CHANGTEH, city of Hunan Province, China, on the Yuen R., about 300 miles E. of Chungking. It has an extensive river trade in the produce of Hunan and Kweichow provinces. Pop. (1953 est.) 94,800.

CHANNEL CAT. See CATFISH.

CHANNEL ISLANDS, a group of small islands belonging to the British Crown, in the English Channel, about 10 to 30 miles off the N.W. coast of France and 50 to 120 miles S. of England. The principal islands of the group include Jersey (area, 45 sq.m.; pop., 1961 est., 57,200), Guernsey (area, 24.5 sq.m.), Alderney (area, about 3 sq.m.), and Sark (area, about 2 sq.m.); Guernsey, Alderney, and Sark have a combined pop. (1961 prelim.) of 47,159. The temperate climate of the Channel Islands (the mean annual temperature is 51.7°) and picturesque scenery attract tourists; the tourist trade plays an important role in the economy of the islands.

The people, especially in Guernsey and Jersey, adhere to their old speech, a dialect of the old Norman French. French and English are the official languages. English is spoken chiefly in the towns, of which the largest is Saint Helier (q.v.), on the island of Jersey.

The produce is principally agriculture, and the islands are famous for cattle. Horticulture and floriculture are successfully followed, especially in Guernsey, and granite is quarried. During World War II the islands were occupied by German troops on June 30, 1940, but restored to the British on May 9, 1945. Area of Channel Islands, about 75 sq.m.; pop. (1961 est.) 104,398.

CHANNING, EDWARD (1856–1931), American historian, born in Dorchester, Mass., and educated at Harvard University, where he later became professor of history. Among his works are *Town and County Government in the English Colonies of North America* (1884); *A Student's History of the United*

States (1897); and *History of the United States* (in 6 vols., 1905–25), of which the 6th volume, *The War for Southern Independence* (1925), won the Pulitzer Prize for U.S. history in 1925.

CHANNING, WILLIAM ELLERY (1780–1842), American Unitarian clergyman, known as the "Apostle of Unitarianism", born in Newport, R.I., and educated at Harvard College. He was pastor of the Federal Street Congregational Church, in Boston, Mass., from 1803 until his death. Channing was the spokesman of those New England Protestants who were unable to accept the Calvinistic doctrine of man's inherent evil. Although at first reluctant to break with orthodox Congregationalism, he found his views and those of his followers in such conflict with it that the formation of a new sect became unavoidable. Channing formulated the basic tenets of Unitarianism in a sermon delivered in Baltimore, Md., in 1819 at the ordination of the American historian Jared Sparks, later president of Harvard College. In 1820 Channing convoked the Berry Street Conference of liberal ministers; the conference led to the formation (1825) of the American Unitarian Association.

Channing's interest and influence extended beyond the domain of religion. Throughout his career he denounced slavery and war, devoting much of his writing to these subjects. He was an eloquent speaker and a prolific writer whose works are characterized by sincerity and moral fervor. Among his more important writings are the antislavery tract *Slavery* (1835) and the essays "Remarks on the Character and Writings of John Milton" (1826), "Remarks on the Life and Character of Napoleon Bonaparte" (1827), and "Essay on the Character and Writings of Fenelon" (1829). *The Perfect Life,* a collection of his sermons, was published in 1872.

CHANTILLY, a town in the department of Oise, France, 26 miles by rail N.E. of Paris. It possesses two noted châteaux, one of which contains a library and art collection belonging to the Institut de France. Chantilly was noted formerly as a lace-manufacturing center, but is now a pleasure resort, with a notable park and a well-known race course. Pop. (1962) 8190.

CHANUKAH. See HANUKKAH.

CHANUTE, OCTAVE (1832–1910), American engineer, born in Paris, France, and educated in the United States. He was a successful construction engineer and was noted for his work in the construction of iron bridges. In 1889 he became interested in aviation and made a number of contributions to the art, among them studies of the strength of air currents. He built a five-plane glider which was an improvement over the designs of Otto Lilienthal, and suggested to the Wright brothers the use of movable surfaces to control the direction of flight. He wrote *Progress in Flying Machines* (1894).

CHAOS, in ancient Greek cosmogony, the original infinite space, filled with clouds and darkness, from which sprang all things that exist. It gave birth to Erebus and Nyx (Night). Later, in Roman cosmogony, the word was applied to the confused mass out of which the universe was formed into a *cosmos,* or harmonious order. Philosophically, chaos is a condition in which chance rules, and in which all evidence of cause and effect, law, or ideal ends, is lacking.

CHAPALA, LAKE, the largest lake of Mexico, about 70 m. long and 20 m. wide, on a high plateau in the state of Jalisco. Its western end is about 30 miles s. of Guadalajara. Lake Chapala is encircled by precipitous mountains and contains a number of islands. The Rio Lerma is the lake's principal tributary stream, and the Rio Grande de Santiago is its outlet. Area, about 1400 sq.m.

CHAPARRAL, a thorny, dry-ground type of thicket, characteristic of s.w. United States and N. Mexico. It consists of trees and shrubs stunted by short, wet winters followed by long, dry summers. These plants include more than 150 species, but the greater part of the growth is made up of buckthorn, chamiso, scrub oak, sumac, and sage.

CHAPARRAL COCK. See ROAD RUNNER.

CHAPBOOKS, tracts written for popular reading, usually in the form of pamphlets of 16 or 32 pages stitched together and bound in paper, widely circulated in England and Scotland from the early part of the 16th century, and later in the American colonies. They were sold in small bookshops and by chapmen or traveling peddlers. Chapbooks contained popular tales such as *Reynard the Fox, Jack the Giant Killer,* and *Tom Thumb;* abstracts of popular books such as *Robinson Crusoe* and *Don Quixote;* the lives of heroes and martyrs; ghost stories and tales of witchcraft; stories of murders and executions; historical narratives, travel tales, and religious treatises; information on fortune telling and the interpretation of dreams; and information on other subjects. The earliest English chapbooks were translations of 15th-century popular French writings circulated in cheap pamphlet form in France. Chapbooks flourished in Great Britain and America until the beginning of the 19th century, when they were largely supplanted by inexpensive magazines and other publications.

CHAPEL, a structure, other than a church or cathedral, designed for worship. It may be within a church or annexed to it, or form part of a group of structures, as in a monastery, college, or palace, or it may be isolated. Worship in a chapel is usually carried on with less elaborate ceremony than worship in a church. The term "chapel" was derived from the *capella,* the designation for the shrine in which the *cappa* ("cloak") of St. Martin was transported by the kings of the Franks in early medieval days. Later the term was applied to any sanctuary containing sacred relics, and the priest in charge of the sanctuary was termed the *capellanus* ("chaplain"). By further extension the expression "chapel" came to have its present meaning.

The earliest sanctuaries to which the term "chapel" may be applied were probably the crypts erected in the catacombs to contain memorials to martyrs. Before the 8th century it was rare for chapels to form an integral part of any church. But after this time, with the multiplication of relics and the increased worship of saints, the practice of building chapels in churches became widespread. In Greek churches the chapels were placed in aspses to the right and left of the main apse. The Blanskenoy church in Moscow has 8 chapels thus located, each equipped for separate Mass. In French churches chapels dedicated to various saints were placed between the buttresses off the apse, with the chapel devoted to Mary, the "Lady Chapel", the most eastern, and thus behind the altar. Notable examples of French cathedrals with many chapels are the cathedral at Le Mans, which has 13 chapels, and that of Notre Dame, Paris, which has a continuous line of chapels opening out of the side aisles. In English churches the apse usually has a straight wall and the chapels are located in extensions of the transepts.

In medieval times, hospitals, courthouses, and all religious houses usually had chapels annexed to them. Episcopal palaces had their chapels. One of the earliest of these was the chapel (5th century) of the episcopal palace at Ravenna, Italy. "Palatine" chapel was the name given to the chapel in the palace of a

Rosary Chapal, Vence, France, decorated by Henri Matisse in a new interpretation of chapel tradition. On the far wall the story of the Crucifixion is recounted. The fish on the altar cloth are a modern use of the ancient symbol for Christ's name.

French Government Tourist Office

The Cloisters, N.Y.C.
Sections of the 12th-century chapel of the Romanesque church of Notre-Dame-du-Bourg, Langon, France, in a modern restoration at The Cloisters, New York City

Brandeis University News Bureau
Berlin Chapel, Brandeis University, Waltham, Mass. Traditional symbols of Jewish faith, Menorah (left), Eternal Light (above), and Ark (center), are interpreted in modern design.

civil ruler, or to a chapel for his private use in a religious structure. The Popes had a private chapel (6th century) in the Lateran palace, Rome. During the period when the city of Avignon, France, was the papal seat (1309–77), the Popes had a palatine chapel in the papal palace in that city. The Sistine Chapel, in the Vatican, Rome, was constructed by Pope Sixtus IV (1471–84) and was decorated by the Italian painters Raphael, Michelangelo, and others. Among England's royal chapels are the chapel of St. George, at Windsor, and the chapel at Hampton Court.

Most universities and colleges have chapels, either detached from or a part of other buildings on the grounds. A notable example of the college chapel is that of King's College, Cambridge, England. With its length of over 300 feet, width of 45, and height of 80, this chapel approaches cathedral size. Other important collegiate chapels are the Appleton Chapel at Harvard University, the Battell Chapel at Yale University, the Marquand Chapel at Princeton University, and St. Paul's Chapel at Columbia University.

CHAPELAIN, JEAN (1595–1674), French man of letters and poet, born in Paris. He was one of the organizers (1635) and leading members of the Académie Française (see INSTITUTE OF FRANCE); he established a code of laws to govern the Académie and organized its project of compiling a dictionary and gram-

mar of the French language. Chapelain assisted Cardinal Richelieu in the writing of his dramas; and in 1662, at the request of Jean Colbert (q.v.), he drew up a memorial for the guidance of the French king (then Louis XIV) in pensioning literary men. Chapelain was the author of an epic poem *La Pucelle,* 12 cantos of which were published in 1656, and the rest (posthumously) in 1882.

CHAPEL HILL, town in Orange County N.C., 28 miles N.W. of Raleigh. It is the site of the University of North Carolina, founded in 1793. Pop. (1960) 12,573.

CHAPLAIN, a clergyman attached to a household, society, or public institution. The term was probably first applied to the ecclesiastic in charge of the cape (*capella*) of St Martin, which was preserved by the kings of France as a sacred relic and carried onto the battlefield in wartime by an official called the *capellanus.* Later any cleric charged with custody over relics, or over a chapel (q.v.) where relics might be kept, was called a chaplain. In modern times the name is given to clergymen in the service of the armed forces attached to a hospital, prison, college, legislature, or similar public or semipublic institution, or employed to minister to a royal, noble or other private household.

CHAPLIN, CHARLES SPENCER (1889–)
British motion-picture actor, director, and producer, born in London, England, and edu-

ated there. He went to the United States in 1910 as a leading comedian with a pantomime company and appeared (1913) first in motion pictures as a comedian with the Keystone Film Company. In *Kid Auto Races at Venice* (1914) he originated the role of "Charlie", a little tramp wearing baggy pants, enormous shoes, and a bowler hat, and carrying a bamboo cane, which he played in more than seventy films during his subsequent career. He was associated later with the Essanay Film Company (1915) and the Mutual Film Company (1916) as actor, writer, and director and with the First National Film Company (1918) also as producer. During these years Chaplin gradually developed the tramp character from a jaunty, slapstick stereotype into the compassionate human figure which endeared him, in this role, to audiences throughout the world. In 1919 he helped found the United Artists Corporation, with which he was associated until 1952. His first independent venture for United Artists was *Woman of Paris* (1923), his only production in which he had no acting part. Among the most important pictures which Chaplin produced, directed, and starred in are *The Kid* (1921), *The Pilgrim* (1923), *The Gold Rush* (1925), *The Circus* (1928), *City Lights* (1931), *Modern Times* (1936), *The Great Dictator* (1940), *Monsieur Verdoux* (1947), *Limelight* (1952), and *A King in New York* (1957). In the late 1940's and early 1950's Chaplin was attacked by various organizations in the United States for alleged procommunist activities. He went to Europe in 1952 and the following year he established permanent residence in Switzerland.

Chaplin perfected a personal style of acting which derives from the theatrical tradition of the clown and the mime (see PANTOMIME) and combines acrobatic elegance, expressive gestures, facial eloquence, and impeccable timing. His portrayals of the little tramp, who soon became a universally recognized symbol of indestructible individuality, won him critical renown as a tragicomedian. However, the advent of motion-picture sound recording in 1927 soon imperiled the effectiveness of the pantomime on which much of Chaplin's creative imagination depended; at the same time he became concerned with themes of contemporary significance. He gradually abandoned the role of the tramp and relied more upon specific character portrayal in a particular time and setting. *The Great Dictator,* his first film to use all the resources of sound recording, marks this transition. Chaplin's treatment of his subjects is compounded of satire and pathos. At first his thematic material and characterization emphasized the victory of courage and resourcefulness over social adversity and injustice. His films produced after 1936 deal with the triumph of man over evil in society. Thus in *Modern Times* he attacked mechanization, in *Monsieur Verdoux* he indicted social hypocrisy and dishonesty, and in *A King in New York* he satirized life in the United States. His satire gained in depth and force as his criticism of the modern world became more incisive. See also MOTION PICTURES: *History.*   G.A.

CHAPMAN, FRANK MICHLER (1864–1945), American ornithologist, born in Englewood, N.J. He became curator of the American Museum of Natural History, in New York City, to which he donated specimens of his own collecting. He was president of the Burroughs

Culver Service
Charlie Chaplin in characteristic role of a tramp in the movie The Gold Rush

Memorial Association (1921–25). Among his writings are *Handbook of Birds of Eastern North America* (1896), *The Economic Value of Birds to the State* (1903), and *The Travels of Birds* (1916). He founded and edited the magazine *Bird Lore.*

CHAPMAN, GEORGE (1559–1634), English dramatist and classical translator, born near Hitchin, Herfordshire. His earliest play was *The Blind Beggar of Alexandria,* produced in 1596 and printed in 1598. His comedy *All Fools,* printed in 1605, was probably produced in 1599. In 1610 appeared the first of his translations of Homer, and in 1616 appeared *The Whole Works of Homer, Prince of Poets, in his Iliads and Odysseys,* which was followed (about 1624) by *The Crowne of all Homer's Workes, Batrachomyomachia, or the Battaile of Frogs and Mice: His Hymns and Epigrams.* While he was busy with his translations, Chapman was also writing for the stage. He joined Jonson and Marston in the composition of *Eastward Ho* (1605), and wrote a graceful comedy, *The Gentleman Usher* (1606). Chapman's other plays include *Bussy d'Ambois* (1607), *The May Day* (1611), *The Widow's Tears* (1612), and *Cæsar and Pompey* (1631). Among his translations are those of Petrarch's *Seven Penitential Psalms* (1612), the *Divine Poem* of Musæus (1616), and Hesiod's *Georgics* (1618). Chapman, though considered one of the major Elizabethan dramatists, is best remembered today for his translations of Homer, the first in English and still regarded among the best. This reputation was undoubtedly promoted by the celebrated poem by John Keats, *On First Looking Into Chapman's Homer.*

CHAPMAN, JOHN. See APPLESEED, JOHNNY.

CHAPU, HENRI MICHEL ANTOINE (1833–91), French sculptor, born at Le Mée. He studied at the École des Beaux-Arts, Paris, under Francisque Joseph Duret and James Pradier, and won the Prix de Rome in 1855. Important among his works are the statues "Jeanne d'Arc Écoutant Ses Voix" (Luxembourg Museum, Paris) and "La Jeunesse" (in memory of Henri Regnault, courtyard of the École des Beaux-Arts).

CHAPULTEPEC, rocky height surmounted by a historic castle, situated about 3 miles s.w. of Mexico City, with which it is linked by the boulevard Paseo de la Reforma. The terrace of the castle affords a magnificent view of Mexico City. In the surrounding area, called Chapultepec Park, are lakes and fountains, a zoo, an astronomical observatory, stately boulevards, and cypress trees many centuries old.

Chapultepec was known to the ancient Aztecs as Grasshopper Hill. Perhaps as early as 1248 it was a seat of the Aztec emperors. In 1783 the hilltop was chosen as the site of the Spanish viceroy's residence, and construction of the castle was begun in 1783. Though still unfinished, the castle was used as a fortress throughout the colonial period. After years of neglect the castle became the home of the National Military Academy in 1842. Its fortifications were modernized shortly before the outbreak (1847) of the Mexican War. Chapultepec Castle was captured by American troops on Sept. 13, 1847, in the final battle of the war. The victory led to the immediate surrender of Mexico City and the opening of negotiations for a peace settlement.

Emperor Maximilian made the castle his residence in 1864. The building was remodeled, the interior was furnished with imperial splendor, and the grounds were beautified. After the downfall (1867) of Maximilian the castle became the summer residence of the presidents of the republic. In 1937 the property was converted into a national museum and public park. The National Military Academy subsequently was rehoused in part of the castle.

From Feb. 21 to March 8, 1945, during World War II, delegates to the Inter-American Conference on Problems of War and Peace met at Chapultepec Castle and there affixed their signatures to the Act of Chapultepec (see CHAPULTEPEC, ACT OF).

CHAPULTEPEC, ACT OF, an agreement adopted at Chapultepec, Mexico, March 3, 1945, by the Inter-American Conference on Problems of War and Peace, by the provisions of which the signatories bound themselves to give each other aid against aggressors who might hinder their efforts in World War II by attacks upon their political independence or territorial integrity. At the Conference all the nations of North and South America, excepting Argentina, were represented and signed the Act. Argentina signed it on April 4, 1945. Declarations of a similar nature, directed against aggression by non-American countries, had been adopted at various times by the American republics. The novel feature of the Act of Chapultepec was that it was aimed also at aggressive acts on the part of an American state toward other American states. The Act of Chapultepec also provided for a treaty to be drafted after the end of World War II continuing into the postwar period the guarantes of the Act concerning aggressors. The treaty pledge of the Act was

Char, or brook trout, Salvelinus fontinalis

fulfilled by the Treaty of Rio de Janeiro (q.v.), signed on September 2, 1947.

CHAR, or CHARR, common name of the many varieties of *Salvelinus,* a genus of the Salmon family similar to the trout. The char has smaller scales than the true trout (*Salmo*), differs in the structure of the vomer, and has red instead of black spots, especially during the breeding season. The color is grayish or green above, the lower parts red, especially in the male; the lower fins are anteriorly margined with white. Its sides are marked with round red spots, and its back is not marbled. This species has a wide distribution, occurring in cold lakes and mountain streams of central and northern Europe, of northeastern America, and probably also in Siberia. It is extremely variable, and has consequently received a host of specific names, such as "saibling", "sälbling", "ombre chevalier", and "Greenland trout". The chars are by far the most active and handsome of the trout, and live in the coldest, clearest, and most secluded waters. They weigh up to 100 pounds. The best-known of the distinctively American chars is the brook trout, or speckled trout; but trout of the Rangeley Lakes, in Maine, is somewhat nearer the European type. See TROUT.

CHARACINIDAE. See SALMONIDAE.

CHARACTERISTIC. See LOGARITHMS.

CHARADE, a riddle consisting of a word of two or more syllables, which is to be guessed from the representation, by word of mouth or by pantomime, of a meaning suggested by its separate syllables and then by the entire word. Spoken charades may be verse or prose. The following is an example of the spoken charade:

"My first is to ramble;
"My next to retreat;
"My whole oft enrages
"In Summer's fierce heat."

Answer: *Gadfly.*

A simple example of the pantomimic charade is as follows. For the first syllable the participant opens a closet and indicates an insect flying about. He then appears to remove a garment and shows a hole made in it. For the second syllable one participant acts the part of an employer, the other, his secretary. The secretary brings him a number of letters and the employer angrily points out

places in them that cause his displeasure. In the third, a participant dons an imaginary hood. For the entire word, a participant uses the gestures of rocking a baby to sleep.

Answer: *Moth--err--hood*: Motherhood.

Pantomimic charades are a popular game at parties in the United States and Great Britain. The participants are generally divided into two competing groups, and each acts out a number of charades which the other must guess. Charades reputedly originated in France in the 18th century.

CHARCOT, JEAN MARTIN (1825–93), French neurologist, born in Paris. In 1856 he was appointed physician to the Central Bureau of Hospitals. In 1860 he became professor of pathological anatomy in the faculty of medicine in Paris. Two years later he established his connection as a physician at the Salpêtrière Hospital, where he opened the most highly regarded neurological clinic of his day. He specialized in the study of hysteria, locomotor ataxia, hypnosis, and aphasia; cerebrospinal sclerosis was named *Charcot's disease* after him. His writings include *Leçons sur les Maladies du Système Nerveux* (5 vols., 1872–93) and *Leçons du Mardi à la Salpêtrière* (2 vols., 1889–90).

CHARD, SWISS CHARD, or SEA KALE, a form of the common garden beet in which the edible portion is the enlarged fleshy stalk and midrib of the leaves. Unlike garden beets, the roots are small and woody. Chard is used for cooked greens and for salad. It is grown in the same manner as garden beets. See BEET.

CHARDIN, JEAN BAPTISTE SIMÉON (1699–1779), French painter, born in Paris, and trained principally under the French painter Noël Coypel. Chardin's still-life paintings established his reputation and gained him admission to the Académie des Beaux-Arts. After 1733 he did genre paintings also, excelling in the portrayal of children, as in "Boy Blowing Soap-Bubbles" and "Girl with Cherries". He was equally famous for his scenes of family life, of which the celebrated "Le Bénédicité" is an outstanding example. Among the best of his portraits are pastels of himself and his wife. Between 1765 and 1767 he painted a series of decorative panels for the chateaux of Choisy and Bellevue. Chardin's works are characterized by naïve and charming realism. His domestic interiors are unsurpassed, as is his treatment of light and atmosphere. The Louvre, Paris, has most of his paintings, and some are owned by various American museums, including the Metropolitan Museum of Art, New York City, and the National Gallery, Washington, D.C.

CHARENTE, a river in the w. central part of France. It rises in the department of Haute-Vienne, about 14 miles N.W. of Châlus, and then flows N.W. to Civray, at which point it turns S. into the department of Charente to Angoulême. Thence it flows w. past Châteauneuf, Jarnac, and Cognac and enters the department of Charente-Maritime. It flows N.W. past Saintes and empties into the Bay of Biscay below Rochefort, opposite the Ile d'Oléron. The river is 224 m. long and is navigable from its mouth to Angoulême, a distance of 104 m.

CHARING CROSS, a district of the city of Westminster, in the county of London, England, on the N.W. bank of the Thames River, between the Strand and Saint Martin's Lane It stands upon the old site of the 13th-century village of Cherringe, where in 1291 a Gothic cross was erected by Edward I as a token that the bier of his wife, Eleanor, had been set down there during its journey from Grantham, Lincolnshire, to Westminster Abbey. In 1647 the cross was demolished by the Roundheads (q.v.). The present copy was erected near the original site in 1865. The actual site, as near as it can be determined, is now occupied by Le Sueur's equestrian statue of Charles I, which was cast in 1633 and erected in 1674. The great cross, which is 1¼ m. from St. Paul's, stands within the square that faces Charing Cross Railway station. See CROSS.

CHARIOT, in ancient times, a kind of carriage upon two wheels used both in peace and in war. The Roman form, the *currus,* was entered from behind and was closed in front and uncovered. It was drawn by two, three, or four horses, and carried either one or two persons, both standing. The word *biga* is often applied to a two-horse chariot for battle or for racing; *triga* was a name for a chariot drawn by three horses yoked abreast, of which two drew from the pole; while the *quadriga* was drawn by four horses abreast, the two center horses (*jugales*) only yoked, the two outside horses (*funales*) being attached by ropes. The *currus triumphalis,* in which Roman generals rode during their triumphal entrance into the city, was round in form, without any side open, and had panels richly decorated with carvings in ivory. Roman writers recorded the use among the Britons and some other foreign nations of war chariots carrying iron blades or scythes fixed to the end of the pole and axletree. The oldest war chariots known from writings are those of Pharaoh, mentioned in the Bible (Exod. 14:7). Many Assyrian tablets represent heroes, such as Sennacherib or Esarhaddon, riding in triumph at the head of their armies in chariots much heavier than, but otherwise not unlike, the Roman forms of chariots.

CHARLEMAGNE, or CHARLES THE GREAT, or CHARLES I (Lat. *Carolus Magnus*) (742–814), King of the Franks and Emperor of the West. His birthplace is unknown, but from the fondness which he displayed for Aix-la-Chapelle and Ingelheim, it has been conjectured that he was born in one of those cities. He was the eldest son of Pepin the Short, King of the Franks, and the grandson of Charles Martel (qq.v.). On Pepin's death (768) Charlemagne and his brother Carloman jointly succeeded to the throne. Carloman died in 771, whereupon Charlemagne became sole king of the Franks.

In 772 Charlemagne was called to the aid of Pope Hadrian I, whose territories had been invaded by Desiderius, King of the Lombards. Charlemagne crossed the Alps from Geneva with two armies in 773 and overthrew the kingdom of the Lombards in 774. He deposed Desiderius, made himself king of the Lombards, and thus extended his domain southward into Italy.

From 772 through 799 Charlemagne conducted a series of campaigns to subjugate and Christianize the Saxons. Despite their fierce resistance and frequent rebellions, he finally succeeded in vanquishing them. In 788 he forced the duke of Bavaria, whose territory had been an autonomous duchy, to become his vassal. Between 791 and 796 Charlemagne conquered the Avars, whose land lay between the Carpathian plain and the Danube.

Charlemagne invaded Spain in 778 for the purpose of driving the Moslems out of Europe. The expedition ended in failure, and the entire rear guard of his army was destroyed by the Basques during its retreat over the Pyrenees. The tale of the disastrous expedition gave rise to the medieval French epic *Chanson de Roland,* which with similar stories, forms one of the three great groups or cycles into which literary historians have divided the epic French verse of the Middle Ages.

After 785 Charlemagne waged systematic warfare against the Moslems of northeastern Spain. He captured Barcelona in 801 and spent the last years of his reign consolidating Spanish gains.

In 799 Charlemagne granted refuge at his court to Pope Leo III, who had been accused of adultery and perjury and driven out of Rome. The following year Charlemagne went to Rome to investigate the charges. He presided over a tribunal before which the pope formally cleared himself. On Christmas Day,

Culver Service

Above: The coronation of Charlemagne as emperor of the Romans in 800. Left: A portrait of Charlemagne.

800, the pope crowned Charlemagne emperor of the Romans. The coronation marked the beginning of the Holy Roman Empire (q.v.).

Charlemagne's empire extended from the Ebro R. to the Elbe R. Besides enlarging the bounds of Christendom, he had fulfilled his self-appointed role as guardian of the Christian faith.

Charlemagne improved, but did not radically alter, the administrative institutions he had inherited. The empire was divided into districts ruled by counts, called *Markgrafen,* or counts of the marches, who defended the frontiers against attacks. Imperial unity was maintained by officers, the *missi dominici,* who were sent out in all directions as the organs of the imperial will. Charlemagne zealously endeavored to promote education, agriculture, the arts, manufactures, and commerce. He projected great national works, including a canal to connect the Rhine and the Danube rivers.

Learned men from all parts of the empire were encouraged to come to his court, and he established a famous palace school for his own children and the sons of noblemen. He collected and preserved in his libraries original Greek and Roman manuscripts, which otherwise might not have survived. He himself possessed an amount of learning unusual in his age; he could speak Latin and read Greek, and he attempted to draw up a grammar of his own language. He was succeeded by his son Louis, known as the Pious or the Debonair. See also CAROLINGIANS; FRANCE: *History.*

CHARLEROI, town in Hainaut Province, Belgium on the Sambre R. about 30 miles s. of Brussels, with which it is connected by canal. It is the center of the most important coal-mining region of the country. Mining, metalworking, and glass manufacturing are the principal industries. The Spanish founded the town on the site of the village of Charnoy in 1666, during their occupation of what is now Belgium, and named it after Charles II of Spain. It was subsequently a French possession in the 17th and again in the 18th cen-

1953

turies. In 1914, during World War I, Charleroi was the scene of a furious battle between German and French troops in the course of which the town was almost entirely destroyed. Pop. (1960 est.) 25,768.

CHARLES, the name of several European rulers. Brief accounts of less important monarchs are included in this article under the name of the countries which they ruled. The more important rulers are described in separate biographical sketches, to which the reader is referred below.

From *Karl* in German and the Scandinavian languages, and Latinized as *Carlus* (*Karlus*) or *Carolus* (*Karolus*), come the spellings *Carlo* in Italian, *Carlos* in Portuguese and Spanish, *Carol* in Rumanian, and *Charles* in English and French. See also CARLOS; CAROL.

AUSTRIA

Charles I (1887–1922). See CHARLES I, Emperor of Austria.

ENGLAND

Some historians list Charles I (reigned 1625–49) and Charles II (reigned 1660–85) as kings of Great Britain and Ireland rather than as kings of England, Scotland, and Ireland. Although the thrones of Scotland and England were united in 1603, when Charles I's father, James VI of Scotland (reigned 1567–1625), became James I of England (reigned 1603–25), the legislative union of England and Scotland was postponed until 1707, when the two kingdoms officially were designated Great Britain.

Charles I (1600–49). See CHARLES I, King of England, Scotland, and Ireland.

Charles II (1630–85). See CHARLES II, King of England, Scotland, and Ireland.

FRANCE

Charles the Great (742?–814). Charlemagne usually is not included in the numeration of French kings. See CHARLEMAGNE.

Charles I (823–77). See CHARLES II, Holy Roman Emperor.

Charles II (839–77). See Charles III, under *Holy Roman Empire*, below.

Charles III, called CHARLES THE SIMPLE (879–929); King (898–923). He was the posthumous son of King Louis II. Charles claimed the French throne during the reign (888–98) of Eudes, or Odo, Count of Paris, but was not acknowledged king until 898. His reign was marked by raids of Norsemen to whom he finally ceded in 911 much of what later was called Normandy. Charles was deposed in 922 by his chief vassals and imprisoned in Peronne from 923 until his death.

Charles IV, called CHARLES THE FAIR (1294–1328); King of France as Charles IV and King of Navarre as Charles I (1322–28). He was the third son of King Philip IV. In 1327 Charles helped his sister Isabelle to dethrone her husband King Edward II of England. During his reign Charles increased taxation, exacted burdensome duties, debased the coinage, and confiscated estates. He died without male issue, and as a result the direct line of Capetian dynasty ended.

Charles V (1337–80). See CHARLES V, King of France.

Charles VI, called CHARLES THE WELL-BELOVED and later CHARLES THE SILLY (1368–1422); King (1380–1422). He was the son of King Charles V. After his father's death in 1380, he was under the guardianship of a ducal council until 1388, when he rejected its regency and began to reign in his own right. Charles ruled well until 1392, when he became insane. In the ensuing contest for control of the kingdom, France suffered grievously from civil wars between the Armagnacs (house of Orléans) and the Burgundians. The English, taking advantage of the internal strife, invaded France, won the Battle of Agincourt (1415), conquered Normandy in 1417, captured Rouen in 1419 and Paris in 1420, and imposed on Charles the Peace of Troyes (1420). Under this treaty Charles was compelled to marry his daughter to King Henry V of England.

Charles VII (1403–61). See CHARLES VII, King of France.

Charles VIII, called CHARLES THE AFFABLE (1470–98); King (1483–98). He was the son of King Louis XI. His sister, Anne de Beaujeu, served as regent from 1483 to 1491, when he began to reign in his own right. The chief event of his reign was his invasion of Italy in 1494 and his temporary occupation (1495) of Naples. As a result of that invasion and several subsequent French invasions of Italy, Italian cultural influences were introduced into France.

Charles IX (1550–74). See CHARLES IX, King of France.

Charles X (1757–1836), King (1824–30). He was the grandson of King Louis XV and younger brother of kings Louis XVI and XVIII. Charles was known as Charles Philippe, Comte d'Artois, until he became king. During the French Revolution he led the *émigrés* and subsequently (1795–1814) he lived in Great Britain. After the Restoration (1815) Charles headed the ultraroyalist party of reaction. During his reign he attempted to rule as an absolute monarch and aroused so much unpopularity that he was deposed by a revolutionary outbreak in July, 1830; see JULY REVOLUTION. Charles abdicated and went into exile in Great Britain. Later he lived on the Continent.

GERMANY

The title "King of Germany" or "King of the Germans" was borne by several Holy Roman emperors named Charles. See below; see also HOLY ROMAN EMPIRE.

HOLY ROMAN EMPIRE

Charles I (742?–814). See CHARLEMAGNE.

Charles II (823–77). See CHARLES II, Holy Roman Emperor.

Charles III, called CHARLES THE FAT (839–88); Emperor (881–87); King of part of Germany (876–87); and as Charles II, King of France (884–87). He was the grandson of Emperor Louis I and son of Louis II, King of Germany. Charles was deposed from his three thrones in 887 by Arnulf, Duke of Carinthia. His deposition marked the dissolution of the Frankish Empire.

Charles V (1500–58). See CHARLES V, Holy Roman Emperor.

Charles VI (1685–1740). See CHARLES VI, Holy Roman Emperor.

Charles VII (1697–1745). See CHARLES VII, Holy Roman Emperor.

HUNGARY

Charles I (1288–1342). See CHARLES I, King of Hungary.

Charles II (1345–86). See Charles III, under *Naples*, below.

Charles III (1685–1740). See CHARLES VI, Holy Roman Emperor.

Charles IV (1887–1922). See CHARLES I, Emperor of Austria.

NAPLES

Name of four kings of Naples or of the Two Sicilies.

Charles I (1226–85). See CHARLES I, King of the Two Sicilies.

Charles II (1246–1309); King of Naples (1285–1309). He was the son of King Charles I. A prisoner of the Spaniards from 1284 to 1288, Charles succeeded to the throne while still in captivity. During his reign he waged an unsuccessful war (1296–1302), which was fought furiously on land and on sea, with Frederick II, King of Sicily, for possession of that island.

Charles III, known also as CHARLES OF DURAZZO (1345–86); King of Naples (1381–86) and King of Hungary as Charles II (1385–86). He was the great-grandson of King Charles II. His reign was marked by his murder in 1382 of his foster mother Queen Joanna I of Naples, and by his war (1382–84) with Louis I, the titular king of Naples.

Charles IV (1716–1788). See Charles III, under *Spain*, below.

NAVARRE

Charles I (1294–1328). See Charles IV, under *France*, above.

Charles II, called CHARLES THE BAD (1332–87); King (1349–87). He was the son of Queen Joanna. His reign was characterized by disputes with relatives, disregard for treaties, rupture of alliances, and intermittent interference in French and Spanish politics.

Charles III, called CHARLES THE NOBLE (1361–1425); King (1387–1425). He was the son of King Charles II. During his reign, which was peaceful, he increased the prosperity of his kingdom by construction of many public works.

Charles IV, usually called DON CARLOS and known also as PRINCE OF VIANA (1421–61). He was the son of King John II of Aragon and Princess Blanche of Navarre. Charles was expelled from Navarre in 1441 by his father although his title to the kingdom, which he inherited from his mother, had been recognized by the Cortes. After nine years of civil war Charles was captured in 1452 and was imprisoned. Released later, he lived in France and Italy, then returned to Navarre, and again was incarcerated in 1459. A renewal of revolt compelled John II to recognize his son's succession in 1461, but within three months Charles died, perhaps of poison. He won fame as a poet and as the author of *Cronica de Navarra* ("Chronicle of Navarre").

NORWAY

The Norwegian kings named Charles were also kings of Sweden. See under *Sweden*, below.

SPAIN

Charles I (1500–58). See CHARLES V, Holy Roman Emperor.

Charles II (1661–1700); King (1665–1700). He was the son of King Philip IV. Spain was controlled by a regency during the decade of his minority and then alternately by French or Austrian factions in his court. During his reign Spain rapidly declined as an international power. Charles, who died without issue, willed the throne to Philip, Duke of Anjou and grandson of King Louis XIV of France, thereby precipitating the War of the Spanish Succession (see SPANISH SUCCESSION, WAR OF THE).

Charles III (1716–88); King of Spain (1759–88) and King of the Two Sicilies as Charles IV (1734–59). He was the son of King Philip V. Charles became duke of Parma as Charles I in 1731. In that capacity he conquered the Kingdom of the Two Sicilies, which he ruled as Charles IV. During his Spanish reign Charles assisted agriculture and commerce, established military academies, strengthened the navy, reformed the fiscal administration, curbed the Inquisition, and expelled the Jesuits. His friendship with France and his dislike of Great Britain led to the Spanish-French alliance (1779) in support of the American Revolution.

Charles IV (1748–1819); King (1788–1808). He was the son of King Charles III. His wife, Princess Maria Louisa of Parma, and ministers, especially Manuel de Godoy, his wife's paramour, profoundly influenced Spanish foreign policy during his reign. As a consequence Spain became involved disastrously in the French Revolutionary Wars (1792–95) and was forced to retrocede Louisiana to the French (1800); in addition, the Spanish navy was destroyed at Trafalgar and France invaded Spain (1807). He abdicated in 1808, after which he lived in France for a while and then resided in Italy.

SWEDEN

Charles I-VI. These six kings are of dubious authenticity based mainly on early medieval legends.

Charles VII (d. 1167); King (1161–67). He was the son of Sverker. Charles assumed the title "King of Swedes and Goths" in 1161; he was assassinated.

Charles VIII, known as KARL KNUTSSON (1408?–70), King of Sweden (1448–57, 1464–65, 1467–70) and King of Norway as Charles I (1449–50). He served as regent of Sweden from 1436 to 1440. Charles' intermittent reign was marked by his flight into Germany in 1457, his temporary recovery of the sovereignty after King Christian I's reign (1457–64), and his later recall to power in 1467.

Charles IX (1550–1611). See CHARLES IX, King of Sweden.

Charles X Gustavus (1622–60). See CHARLES X GUSTAVUS, King of Sweden.

Charles XI (1655–97). See CHARLES XI, King of Sweden.

Charles XII (1682–1718). See CHARLES XII, King of Sweden.

Charles XIII (1748–1818); King of Sweden (1809–18) and King of Norway as Charles II (1814–18). He was the son of King Adolphus Frederick and younger brother of King Gustavus III. As high admiral, he defeated a Russian fleet in the Gulf of Finland in 1788. He was regent from 1792 to 1796 during the minority of King Gustavus Adolphus IV and again in 1809 after that king had lost his throne through revolution. During Charles' reign Sweden lost Finland to Russia in 1809, but was united with Norway in 1814.

Charles XIV John (1763?–1844). See CHARLES XIV JOHN, King of Sweden.

Charles XV (1826–72). See CHARLES XV, King of Sweden.

WÜRTTEMBERG

Charles, full German name KARL FRIEDRICH ALEXANDER (1823–91); King (1864–91). He was the son of King William I. Charles aided Austria in the Austro-Prussian War (1866), but sided with Prussia and the other German states in the Franco-German War (1870–71). His reign was noted for liberal reforms.

P.R.C-N

CHARLES I (1887–1922), Emperor of Austria and, as Charles IV, King of Hungary from 1916 to 1918. He succeeded the Emperor Francis Joseph, and was the last of the Hapsburg rulers. Although he was the eldest son of the Archduke Otto, he was little known until after his marriage with Princess Zita of Parma, in 1911. During World War I, he nominally commanded the army that invaded Romania. On the death of the Emperor Francis Joseph in 1916, Charles proclaimed himself Emperor of Austria, and he and his consort were crowned King and Queen of Hungary in Budapest, Dec. 30, 1916. During the war he addressed a letter to his brother-in-law, Prince Sixte of Bourbon-Parma, in which he supported the claims of France in Alsace-Lorraine and proposed the restoration of Belgium and Serbia. Charles disavowed the letter when it was published in April, 1918, but it had a disheartening effect on the Central Powers. After the political and military collapse of Austria-Hungary, on Nov. 11, 1918, Charles abdicated the throne of Austria, and two days later that of Hungary. In March, 1919, he left Austria and in April of that year the Austrian Parliament formally deposed him, annulled the sovereign rights of the House of Hapsburg, and exiled its members from Austria. Twice in 1921 Charles

ent to Hungary, where his efforts to regain
ower caused him to be taken on a British
arship, with his wife, to Madeira, where he
ied.

CHARLES I (1600–49), King of England,
cotland, and Ireland from 1625 to 1649. He
vas the second son of James I of Great Brit-
in and became heir-apparent when his elder
rother Henry died in 1612. In 1623, at the
uggestion of the Duke of Buckingham, who
ccompanied him, he made a visit to Spain
o press in person his suit for the hand of the
nfanta of Spain. In this he was unsuccessful,
nd he subsequently excited popular enthusi-
sm by advocating war with Spain. On the
eath of James (1625), Charles succeeded to
he throne.

Until this time popular with his subjects,
harles aroused their ill-will by marrying
rincess Henrietta Maria of France, a Roman
atholic. His reign was doomed to failure.
Ie was a puppet in the hands of his favorite,
uckingham, whom he had appointed prime
inister in defiance of public wishes and
vhose warlike schemes ended ignominiously.
'hree Parliaments, convoked in four years,
vere dissolved in royal exasperation at their
efusal to comply with his arbitrary measures,
nd public feeling became embittered. The
hird Parliament met in 1628 and presented a
tatement of its position known as the Peti-
on of Right. At first the king temporized,
hen made concessions, and finally dissolved
'arliament, although the assassination of
'uckingham removed one of their grievances.
n addition to the dissolution, Charles had
leven of the parliamentary leaders impris-
ned. Influenced by the queen, and with Arch-
ishop Laud and Sir Thomas Wentworth
later Earl of Strafford) as chief adviser,
harles governed without a Parliament for
1 years, the despotic Star Chamber and High
'ommission courts giving semblance of legal
inction to forced loans, poundage, tonnage,
hip money, and other extraordinary measures
o meet governmental expenses. His attempt
o impose episcopacy provoked the Scotch to
estore Presbyterianism and to adopt the
olemn League and Covenant, Feb. 28, 1638.
n 1639 Charles assembled an army to en-
orce his will and summoned the "Short
'arliament", which refused his demands and
rew up a statement of public grievances,
emanded an inquiry into Eliot's death, and
nsisted on peace with Scotland. Obtaining
noney by irregular means, Charles advanced
gainst the Scots, who crossed the border,
efeated his army at Newburn-upon-Tyne,
nd soon afterward occupied Newcastle and

Culver Service
Charles I, King of England

Durham. His money exhausted, the king was
compelled to call the "Long Parliament"
which met Nov. 3, 1640. Led by John Pym,
it proceeded to redress grievances and showed
its resolution by impeaching and imprisoning
the instigators of royal despotism, Laud and
Strafford. The peers, before whom Strafford
was tried, refused to condemn him, but a
luckless plot to overcome Parliament by military force sealed the fate of the ministers.
A bill of attainder was passed, and Charles,
in trepidation for the life of his queen, which
he considered in danger from mob violence,
signed Strafford's death warrant, and confirmed a bill by which Parliament was not to
be dissolved without its own consent. The
king visited Scotland, hoping by concessions
to win favor and armed support.

On his return from Scotland Charles, learning of the impending impeachment of his
queen, who had sought assistance from Rome,
appeared in the Commons with an armed
force and, accusing Pym and several other
members of treason, demanded their arrest
and delivery to him. The country was aroused
and the king fled with his family to Hampton
Court. Seven months later civil war commenced and proceeded, although arbitration
was vainly attempted from time to time. The
Royalists under Prince Rupert were the vic-
tors at Worcester, Sept. 23, 1642; but after

Culver Service

Charles II, King of England

CHARLES II (1630–85), King of Englan
Scotland, and Ireland from 1660 to 1685. F
was the second, but eldest surviving, son c
Charles I, and was Prince of Wales fro
birth. He took his seat in the House of Lor
in 1641, held a nominal command in the ear
campaigns of the Civil War, and was prese
at Edgehill in 1642, where he narrowly e
caped capture. Appointed general of the wes
ern forces, he parted from his father a
Oxford, March 4, 1645, and remained i
safety in Somerset, Devon, and Cornwa
after the defeat of the Royalists at Naseb
he escaped by way of Scilly and Jersey an
joined his mother in Paris, where he re
mained for two years. In July, 1648, he saile
from Helvoetsluis with a small fleet for th
Thames, where he captured several prize
He issued a proclamation of conciliation t
the Londoners and Scots, and returned t
The Hague, where during his father's tri
he did his utmost to save him, forwardin
a blank charter with his signature attache
for Parliament to inscribe its own terms c
clemency.

At his father's death in 1649 he assume
the title of king and was proclaimed in Scot
land, Ireland, the Channel Islands, and eve
one or two places in England, then ruled b
Oliver Cromwell. After spending some time i
Holland, France, and Jersey, with the inte
tion of invading Ireland, he returned to Ho
land, and, embarking at Terheyden for Scot
land, landed in Cromarty Firth, June 2
1650. He was crowned at Scone, Jan. 1, 165
after an acknowledgment of his father's faul
and various declarations and concessions c
a feeble character. He suddenly invaded Eng
land the following August with 10,000 me
and was proclaimed king at Carlisle and othe
places on his advance. Cromwell hastene
to meet and surround him and after two er
counters routed his army at Worcester, Sep
3, 1651. Charles was hunted and a price wa
put upon his head, but he safely embarke
at Shoreham on October 15 and landed a
Fécamp, Normandy, the next day.

He spent eight years of impecunious an
profligate exile in France and at Cologne an
Bruges. After Oliver Cromwell's death (1658
when Richard Cromwell had indicated h
readiness to resign the office of Protector, th
restoration of royalty was consummated b
General Monck. In the Declaration of Breda
Charles announced his intention to accep
a parliamentary government and grant an
nesty to his political opponents. He was pro
claimed king at Westminster, May 8, 166
He landed at Dover on the 26th, and wa

several reverses the Parliamentary forces acquired experience and discipline, and Oliver Cromwell and Baron Fairfax, the Parliamentary leaders, defeated Prince Rupert at Marston Moor, July 2, 1644, and annihilated the Royal army at Naseby, June 14, 1645. Guerrilla warfare continued until Charles gave himself up to the Scottish army at Newark, on May 5, 1646. He was delivered to the English Parliament, who assigned him a residence at Holmby House, near Northampton. After three months he escaped to the Isle of Wight, where he hoped to receive aid from the governor of Carisbrooke Castle, but was imprisoned. The Independents, doubting the sincerity of Cromwell's support of the national cause, compelled Parliament to pass an act of treason against further negotiation with the king, who was removed to Hurst Castle.

Parliament appointed a court to try the king. He was moved from Hurst Castle to Windsor on Dec. 23, 1648, and on Jan. 20, 1649, was taken to Westminster Hall, where the court was opened with great solemnity. Charles denied its legality and refused to plead. On the 27th he was sentenced to death as a tyrant, murderer, and enemy of the nation, by 67 out of the original 70 judges. Scotland protested, the royal family entreated, France and the Netherlands interceded, in vain. He was beheaded at **Whitehall on Jan. 30, 1649.**

elcomed, at Whitehall, by the two houses ' Parliament on May 29, 1660.

Charles was crowned on April 23, 1661. His rst Parliament, noted for subservience and sistence on "royal prerogative", gave him a untrammeled course. Edward Hyde, Earl ' Clarendon, his dignified companion in ex-, was appointed chief minister. Episcopacy as restored, and English and Scotch Non-nformists and Presbyterians subjected to rsecution. Charles extended an indemnify-g Act, dating from Jan. 1, 1637, to June , 1660, to all political offenders, excluding e regicides, of whom 13 were executed, while e bodies of Cromwell and Ireton were hung chains, and the remains of Blake, Brad-aw, and others were cast out of Westminster bbey into potter's fields. Extravagant, and ways in want of money, Charles assented the abolition of the feudal rights of knight rvice, wardship, and purveyance in consid-ation of an annuity of $6,000,000, which, owever, was never fully paid. On May 20, 62, he married Catherine of Braganza r her large dowry. The failure of the bsidies to produce the amount agreed on d the chronic mismanagement of the Eng-sh finances brought the king to a desperate ed of money. The choice faced him of se-ring this from Parliament or else of selling e control of England's foreign policy to e highest bidder. To accept the first al-rnative meant to become the slave of Par-ament. On the other hand, a ready purchaser f the foreign policy was found in Louis XIV, ho desired to extend French power on the ontinent and needed England's aid, or at ast England's neutrality, for the success of s plans. In return for French subsidies harles plunged England into a war with olland in 1672, from which the country as whole had little to gain.

The war, however, was not unpopular; ommercial rivalry had already brought about vo wars between the two countries, the last ne having occurred in the early years of the ign (1665–67). The Dutch War of 1672 did ot prove a success, and some knowledge of e negotiations with France, joined with harles' efforts towards absolutism, brought im into conflicts with his Parliament, which sted nine years, until Charles, aided by rench subsidies was able to dissolve his last arliament (1681). The last years of the strug-le were especially embittered on account of ar of Roman Catholicism, toward which urch the king was suspected to have lean-gs and to which his brother and heir, the uke of York, confessedly belonged. This feeling culminated in the so-called Popish Plot (see OATES), which resulted in the execution of many innocent victims. From 1681 to his death Charles ruled as an absolute king. In his dying hours he received absolution from a Roman Catholic priest, although he had not previously avowed his attachment to that religion.

CHARLES V (1337–80), known as CHARLES THE WISE, King of France from 1364 to 1380. He was the son of King John II, the Good, and on his father's being made prisoner by the English at the Battle of Poitiers (Sept 19, 1356) he assumed the regency. The most significant event of his rule was the vigorous effort of the peasants, aided by a part of the bourgeoisie, to deliver themselves from the tyranny of nobles and the court, which resulted in the popular uprising called the Jacquerie (q.v.). Upon the death of his father, in 1364, Charles ascended the throne. War with England raged for a number of years, but with results highly favorable to Charles, who stripped his enemies of all their conquests in France except a few fortified places. Charles was a generous patron of literature and the arts, founded the Bibliothèque Royale, and increased the privileges of the university. During his reign the building later known as the Bastille (q.v.) was added to the fortifications of Paris.

CHARLES VII (1403–61), King of France from 1422 to 1461. He was the fifth son and the successor of Charles VI. When his father died, Paris and almost all the north were in the hands of the English, who proclaimed,

Charles VII, King of France

as king, Henry VI of England, who was then 18 months old; and made the Duke of Bedford regent. During the first six years Charles was compelled by the English to evacuate Champagne and Maine. In 1427 the English failed in their siege of Montargis; but in October, 1428, they besieged Orléans, and on Feb. 12, 1429, the French met with a disastrous defeat at Harengs. At this critical moment Joan of Arc (q.v.) came to the king's aid, and the siege of Orléans was raised on May 8, 1429. Charles was consecrated king at Reims, July 17, 1429. The English gradually lost their possessions in France, and the Duke of Burgundy, their ally, went over to Charles. The latter entered Paris in 1436, and in the following years the English lost all their French possessions except Calais. The last battle, a disastrous defeat for the English, was at Castillon, July 17, 1453.

CHARLES IX (1550-74), King of France from 1560 to 1574. He succeeded his elder brother, Francis II, at the age of 10, under the regency of his mother, Catherine de Médicis (q.v.). Even after Charles assumed active rule, he remained under his mother's domination. Intrigues and civil wars between Catholics and Huguenots marked the whole course of his reign, of which the barbaric St. Bartholomew Massacre was the most memorable event (see SAINT BARTHOLOMEW, MASSACRE OF).

CHARLES (1433-77), known as CHARLES THE BOLD, the last Duke of Burgundy, the son of Philip the Good, of the house of Valois, and of Isabella of Portugal, born in Dijon. During his father's life he bore the title of Count of Charolais. He was of an ambitious and violent disposition. From early life he was an enemy of Louis XI of France, the nominal feudal superior of Burgundy, and when Louis caused Philip to deliver up some towns on the Somme, Charles left his father's court and formed an alliance with the Duke of Brittany for the maintenance of feudal rights against the crown. Their forces ravaged Picardy and Île de France, threatened Paris, and defeated the king at Montlhéry (1465). The result was a treaty by which the Count of Charolais obtained the towns on the Somme and the counties of Boulogne, Guines, and Ponthieu. In 1467 he succeeded his father as Duke of Burgundy, thus becoming the ruler of Flanders, Brabant and nearly all the rest of the Netherlands, in addition to Burgundy and Franche-Comté. Richer and more powerful than any other prince, Charles conceived the plan of restoring the old Kingdom of Burgundy, which had once included

Lorraine, Provence, Dauphiné, and part o Switzerland. A series of intermittent war with France resulted from this ambition. I 1475 he made himself master of Lorraine. I the following year he invaded Switzerland but was defeated. Three months later he ap peared again in Switzerland with a new arm of 25,000 men and laid siege to Morat, wher he suffered a still more severe defeat. Never theless he refused to listen to terms and lai siege to Nancy in the fall of 1476. His arm was small, and he was defeated and killed His daughter and heiress, Mary, married th Emperor Maximilian I.

CHARLES I, Holy Roman Emperor. Se CHARLEMAGNE.

CHARLES II (823-77), known as CHARLE THE BALD, Holy Roman Emperor (875-77) and King of France (840-77) as Charles He was the son of Louis the Piou by his second wife, Judith. The determi nation of Judith to secure a kingdom fo her son led to repeated wars between th sons of Louis, until, by the Treaty of Verdu in 843, Charles received the western portio of the empire, which from this time may b called the Kingdom of France, or, mor strictly, the West Frankish Kingdom. Th government of Charles was weak; the grea nobles were rapidly becoming independent the Northmen pillaged the country, almos without resistance on the part of Charle who bribed them to depart. Yet on the deat of Emperor Louis II, in 875, Charles receive the imperial crown through the favor of th pope. See CAROLINGIANS.

CHARLES V (1500-58), Holy Roman Em peror and, under the title of Charles I, Kin of Spain. He was born at Ghent, the elde son of Philip, Archduke of Austria, and J anna, the daughter of Ferdinand and Isabel of Spain. Philip's parents were Emperor Ma imilian and Mary, daughter and heiress Charles the Bold, Duke of Burgundy. On t death of his father in 1506, Charles, at t age of six, inherited the Burgundian real which included the Netherlands. On the dea of his grandfather, Ferdinand, in 1516, became King of Spain, as his mother, Joann was of unsound mind. Spain at this time w suzerain over the states of Naples, Sicily, a Sardinia.

On the death of his grandfather, Ma milian, in 1519, Charles conjointly with younger brother, Ferdinand, succeeded to t possession of the hereditary dominions of t house of Hapsburg, which included the arc duchy of Austria. On June 28, 1519, Charl was designated Holy Roman emperor the choice of the electors, the rival candidates being Francis I of France and Henry VIII of England. Charles was crowned at Aix-la-Chapelle, Oct. 23, 1520. Owing to the jealousy of his Spanish connections, he was required to sign an election agreement (*wahlkapitulation*) guaranteeing certain rights to the German nation—a practice followed by his successors in the imperial office.

Charles was now by far the most powerful sovereign in Christendom. He ascended the imperial throne at a time when Germany was agitated by the religious revolt under the leadership of Martin Luther (q.v.). To restore tranquillity, a great diet was held at Worms in 1521, before which Luther made a memorable defense of his doctrines. Just at this moment the great struggle between France and Spain broke out afresh, Francis I taking up arms against Charles, whose attention was drawn away from the internal affairs of Germany.

The war between Charles and Francis, in which the former had Henry VIII of England as an ally, and was strengthened by the support of the powerful Charles of Bourbon, proved disastrous to France. The French were swept out of Lombardy, and Francis was taken prisoner. He was forced to sign a humiliating treaty at Madrid, January, 1526; but hardly had he been set at liberty when he prepared to renew the struggle, with Henry VIII now on his side and with the support of Pope Clement VII, of the house of Medici, who, alarmed at the victories of the Emperor Charles, was anxious to rid Italy of the imperial armies and induced some of the Italian states to join him.

The emperor's forces, under Georg von Frundsberg and Charles of Bourbon, took Rome itself by storm (1527), plundered it, and made the Pope a prisoner. Charles pretended great regret, went into mourning with all his court and caused prayers to be said for the Pope's liberation, while by his own direction the Pope was kept for seven months a captive. The Peace of Cambrai, between Charles and Francis, in 1529, deprived France of Lombardy. In 1530 Pope Clement VII, into whose scheme for the restoration of the Medici in Florence Charles had entered, crowned the victorious monarch at Bologna as King of Lombardy and Emperor of the Romans (the last coronation of a German emperor by the pope). Previous to this, in 1521–22, Charles had relinquished to Ferdinand of Hungary the sole sovereignty over the principal portion of the old hereditary Austrian dominions.

After his coronation at Bologna, Charles attempted to put an end to the religious differences in Germany and to repel the Turks, who had overrun Hungary and laid siege to Vienna. But the diet at Augsburg, in 1530, proved how vain was the hope of settling the religious revolt in Germany; and when the emperor refused to recognize the confession of the Protestants (see AUGSBURG CONFESSION), they refused to help him against the Turks. In 1531 the Protestant princes formed the League of Schmalkald and allied themselves with France and England for their own protection. This, and the continued assaults of the Turks, compelled the emperor to yield in some measure to the demands of the Protestants and to conclude the Peace of Nuremberg (1532).

In 1535 Charles undertook an expedition against the pirate Barbarossa in Tunis, and set free about 22,000 Christians who had been held as slaves. War again broke out with France. An armistice for 10 years was concluded at Nice in 1538, which left most of the Duchy of Savoy in the hands of Francis. In 1541 Charles undertook an unsuccessful expedition against Algiers.

From 1542 to 1544 he was engaged in a fresh war with France, Henry VIII being once more his ally. It was terminated by the Treaty of Crespy, advantageous to the emperor. The victory of Mühlberg, April 24, 1547, placed the Protestants at the mercy of Charles, who deprived John Frederick, Elector of Saxony and Protestant leader, of his territories. In 1548 the Augsburg Interim was published,

Culver Service

Holy Roman Emperor Charles V

fixing the degree of religious toleration to be accorded in Germany pending the decision of the Council of Trent, which had been opened in 1545. In 1551 Magdeburg, a great stronghold of Protestantism, succumbed to the arms of Duke Maurice of Saxony. But Maurice, who had previously supported the Emperor, suddenly deserted Charles, allying himself with Henry II of France. Charles was compelled to flee before the Protestants, and in 1552, through his brother Ferdinand, he concluded with them the Peace of Passau, by which the Lutheran states were allowed the exercise of their religion. A more definite settlement was made, in the Peace of Augsburg, in 1555. In the meanwhile King Henry II seized the three bishoprics of Toul, Metz, and Verdun (1552), and an attempt of the emperor to reconquer Metz failed miserably.

Weary of the constant struggles and heavy responsibilities of his scattered realms, Charles in 1555–56 resigned the Netherlands and Spain to his son Philip, and in 1557 abdicated the imperial crown in favor of his brother Ferdinand and retired to the monastery of Yuste, in Estremadura. By his wife, Isabella, daughter of King Emmanuel of Portugal, he had one son, his successor, Philip II of Spain, and two daughters. Charles V was a prince of remarkable executive powers. While he spared his Protestant subjects in Germany for political reasons, he persecuted heresy unsparingly in Spain, where policy imposed upon him no restraint.

CHARLES VI (1685–1740), Holy Roman Emperor (1711–40), titular King of Spain as Charles III (1703–14), and King of Hungary as Charles III (1712–40). He was the son of Emperor Leopold I. Charles was proclaimed king of Spain by his father in opposition to Duke Philip of Anjou, who had been willed the Spanish throne by King Charles II. Philip's accession (1700) as King Philip V precipitated the War of the Spanish Succession (see SPANISH SUCCESSION, WAR OF THE), which continued from 1701 to 1714. Charles had numerous allies and Philip was aided only by France, but after alternate successes and reverses Charles renounced his claim to Spain by the Treaty of Rastatt (1714). Meanwhile, Charles had succeeded his brother Joseph I as Holy Roman emperor in 1711 and in 1713 had issued the Pragmatic Sanction to secure the succession of his daughter Maria Theresa to his dominions in the event that he should die without a male heir. This proclamation later led to the War of the Austrian Succession (see SUCCESSION WARS: *War of the Austrian Succession*). After a successful war against the Turks (1714–18), from whom he wrested some territory by the terms of the Treaty of Passarowitz (1718), Charles engaged in the War of the Polish Succession (see SUCCESSION WARS: *War of the Polish Succession*) from 1733 to 1735. Under the provision of the Treaty of Vienna (1738), which terminated that conflict, he ceded Spain the kingdoms of Naples and Sicily in exchange for the duchies of Parma and Piacenza. Following a second war (1737–39) with the Turks Charles lost most of the territory he had won in 1718.

CHARLES VII, or CHARLES ALBERT (1697–1745), Holy Roman Emperor (1742–45). He was the son of Elector Maximilian Emanuel of Bavaria; he succeeded to the electorate in 1726. During the War of the Spanish Succession (see SPANISH SUCCESSION, WAR OF THE) his father supported the claim of Louis XIV of France, which resulted in the invasion of Bavaria by Joseph I of Hapsburg. Joseph I took both Charles and his brother Clement, later Archbishop of Cologne, as his prisoners to Vienna where they were educated by the Jesuits. Charles was released after the Peace of Baden (1714), and in 1717 he led his father's auxiliaries in the war against the Turks. He was married in 1722 to the younger daughter of Joseph I, and although he had committed himself, at the time of his marriage, to respect the Pragmatic Sanction, by which the European powers agreed that the possessions of the Austrian crown should pass to Maria Theresa, he immediately contested it after the death of Charles VI in 1740. This brought on the War of the Austrian Succession (see SUCCESSION WARS) and a brief interval of glory for Charles Albert. He became King of Bohemia in 1741 and the following year was unanimously elected Holy Roman Emperor and crowned Charles VII by his brother Clement. Even while the coronation was taking place, the Austrian army was invading the Emperor's home territory in Bavaria; Charles VII was obliged to spend the greater part of his "rule" in refuge in Frankfort. He was reinstated by Frederick the Great in October, 1744, but died a few months later.

CHARLES I (1288–1342), also known as CHARLES ROBERT OF ANJOU, or CAROBERT, King of Hungary (1308–42). He claimed the throne of Hungary as the grandson of Stephen V (q.v.) and was supported by Pope Boniface VIII. Charles was crowned king in 1301 but was forced to abdicate the same year. He was elected king by the diet in 1308 and was enthroned the following year, but his reign did not officially begin until his formal investiture in 1310, when he founded the Anjou line of Hungary. He levied direct taxes to support his army, encouraged trade and the mercantile expansion of cities, and raised Hungary to a power of the first rank.

CHARLES I (1226–85), King of the Two Sicilies (1286–85). He was the seventh child of King Louis VIII of France, and married Beatrice, heiress of Provence. After 1246 he was Count of Anjou and of Provence. In 1248 he went on a Crusade with his brother, King Louis IX of France, suffered captivity in Egypt, and returned to Provence in 1250. Exceedingly ambitious, he sought opportunities to increase his possessions. For aid rendered Margaret of Flanders he was promised the Province of Hainaut, but Louis interfered, and Charles was compelled to relinquish Hainaut for a sum of money. In 1262 Pope Urban IV invited Charles to assume the crown of the Two Sicilies and to assist in the overthrow of its king, Manfred. In 1263 Charles was made Senator of Rome and in 1266 was crowned King of the Two Sicilies. A crusade was preached against Manfred, who was overwhelmed and slain in the battle of Benevento. In 1268 Conradin, the legitimate heir, was defeated at Tagliacozzo, captured and executed; a like fate was dealt out to many Italian nobles; estates were confiscated to reward the French mercenaries, and Charles established himself firmly in power. In 1270 Charles participated in the disastrous Crusade of his brother, Louis IX, and later (1282), when he was preparing for another expedition, news was brought of the rebellion afterward known as the Sicilian Vespers (q.v.). Charles sent his fleet against Messina, refusing all offers of capitulation; but the city held out until assistance came from Don Pedro of Aragon, and Charles's fleet was burned. He died at Poggio.

CHARLES I, King of Spain. See CHARLES V, Holy Roman Emperor.

CHARLES IX (1550–1611), King of Sweden from 1604 to 1611. He was the son of Gustavus Vasa. In 1560 he became Duke of Södermanland, and in 1592 regent of the kingdom, after the death of his brother, John. He favored introduction of the Reformed religion into Sweden, and in 1593 he secured the adoption of the Augsburg creed as the basis of the national religion. He confirmed the position of Protestantism by his victory at Staongebro in 1598 over his nephew Sigismund of Poland, who was rightful King of Sweden, but who, as a partisan of Catholicism, was objectionable to the mass of the people. After many attempts at compromise, Sigismund was formally deposed in 1599 and Charles was offered the royal title. At first he merely accepted the regency, but in 1604 he yielded to the popular demand and was crowned King of Sweden. He engaged in wars with Poland, Russia, and Denmark, but his people did not share his ambitions and denied him the support he desired. He founded the University of Gothenburg and made a new code of laws.

CHARLES X GUSTAVUS (1622–60), King of Sweden from 1654 to 1660. He was born at Nyköping, the son of Catherine, eldest sister of Gustavus Adolphus, and of John Casimir, Count Palatine of Zweibrücken (Deux Ponts). On the abdication of Christina in 1654 he succeeded to the throne of a kingdom in an almost bankrupt condition. In 1655 he invaded Poland, whose king, John Casimir, indulged in pretensions to the Swedish crown. Charles compelled the Elector of Brandenburg to enter into an alliance with him, defeated the Polish army at Warsaw, and overran the country; but retired when Russia and Austria prepared to assist the Poles, while the King of Denmark invaded the Swedish territories in Germany. He attacked Denmark in 1658 and obtained the provinces of Scania, Halland, and Blekinge by the Treaty of Roeskilde. During this war he accomplished the famous exploit of leading an army across the ice of a channel between the Danish islands and the mainland. Renewing the war in the same year, Charles laid siege to Copenhagen. However, the Dutch came to the assistance of the Danes and defeated the Swedish fleet. Charles was defeated also in Pomerania by the Elector of Brandenburg, who had turned against him.

CHARLES XI (1655–97), King of Sweden from 1660 to 1697. He was the son of Charles X and Hedwig Eleonora of Holstein. During his minority the government was entrusted to his mother, Hedwig, as regent. From 1661 to 1672 the kingdom was free from foreign wars, but it was misgoverned by the regency, and the education of the young king was neglected so that he might longer be prevented from asserting himself. Until he reached manhood he could neither read nor write. In 1672 he assumed the reins of government. In 1674 he was called upon by Louis XIV of France, under a treaty made by the regency, to engage in the war of France on the German princes and Holland. The Swedes invaded Brandenburg and met defeat at Fehrbellin. Charles overthrew the Danes at Halmstadt, Lund, and Landskrona; but his fleet was defeated by the Dutch near Oeland, and again by the Danes at Blekinge and Kiöge. Much territory was

Charles XII, King of Sweden

wrested from Sweden, but was, however, restored by the Peace of Saint-Germain-en-Laye (1679). In 1680 a struggle between the crown, supported by the burghers and peasants, and the nobles, resulted in a considerable diminution of the power of the nobles. In 1682 the king was invested with absolute authority. By a judicious administration of revenues, he wiped out the public debt, reorganized the fleet and army, and by 1693 dispensed with extraordinary subsidies. Though he had absolute power, he never imposed a tax without the consent of the estates; and he published every year a detailed account of revenue and expenditure.

CHARLES XII (1682–1718), King of Sweden, known as "The Madman of the North". He was the son of Charles XI, and succeeded to the throne at the age of 15. Soon after his succession, Sweden, with extensive possessions on the shores of the Baltic, was threatened by a coalition of Frederick IV of Denmark; Augustus the Strong, Elector of Saxony and King of Poland; and Peter I of Russia. The war that was brought on by the coalition was at first, on Sweden's part, a war of defense; then, through the successes of Charles, a war

of conquest; and, finally, through his failure, a struggle for existence. In a six weeks' campaign, Denmark was brought to terms, and Frederick signed the Peace of Travendal (1700). Hastening to Riga, Charles compelled the Poles to raise the siege of that place, and then by forced marches brought his army of a little over 8000 men to the relief of Narva in Esthonia, which was beleaguered by 40,000 Russians, while Peter himself had gone to hasten the advance of 20,000 more. The disciplined Swedish troops, although they were wearied by forced marches, administered a severe defeat to the Russians. Charles did not follow up his success against Peter. He turned to conquer Poland, which was overrun by the Swedish troops. Augustus was driven into Saxony, and Charles obtained the election of Stanislas Leszczynski as King of Poland in 1705.

Charles then marched into Saxony, through Silesia, hailed as the protector of the Protestants. Seeing his hereditary dominions in danger, Augustus sued for peace. Charles exacted from him renunciation of the Polish crown and all alliances, and recognition of Stanislas. Charles was at the height of his power, with a disciplined army of 40,000 men, encamped near Leipzig, holding Germany in awe. But he was determined to humble Russia, and turned eastward with 46,000 men with that object in view. He penetrated into the interior of Russia, his army harassed on the way, and, finally, on July 8, 1709, while besieging Poltava, was attacked by the Russian army in force, and the entire fabric of his military success was shattered in one disastrous engagement. He barely escaped into Turkish territory, with 300 of his guard. He prevailed upon the Sultan to take up arms against Russia, and in 1711 Peter found himself in a precarious position on the banks of the Pruth. The Swedish monarch spent the next three years in intrigues to induce the government to attack Russia again. When he found that his plots were of no avail, he defied the Turkish power, and was made a prisoner. He escaped in 1714, and reached Stralsund, a Swedish possession in Pomerania. The city was besieged by a combined force of Danes, Prussians, and Saxons for a year before it surrendered. Charles escaped, reached Sweden, and raised another army, with which he invaded Norway in 1717 and 1718. During this struggle he was killed by a cannon ball at the siege of Fredrikshald.

CHARLES XIV JOHN (1763–1844), King of Sweden and Norway from 1818 to 1844, and before his elevation to the throne, Gen.

Jean Baptiste Jules Bernadotte, a celebrated marshal of Napoleon. He was born in Pau, France, the son of a French lawyer. He fought in the revolutionary wars (from 1794 as general of division) in Belgium, Germany, and Italy, and in 1799, in the last year of the Directory, was minister of war. In 1800 he suppressed a rising of the Chouans, and in 1804 Napoleon created him marshal. He bore a distinguished part in the victory of Austerlitz in 1805, for which he was made Prince of Pontecorvo, and won fresh laurels in the campaign against the Prussians in 1806-07 and at Wagram in 1809. He was chosen by the Swedish Diet in 1810 Crown Prince and successor of Charles XIII. The only condition of moment was that he should become a Protestant. Bernadotte agreed, changed his name to Charles John, and soon began to exercise many of the royal functions. The Crown Prince resisted the efforts of Napoleon to involve Sweden in his designs against England. The country was soon engaged in war with France, and at the head of the northern troops Prince Charles joined the allies in the final struggle with Napoleon and contributed to the victory of Leipzig (1813). He forced Denmark in the Treaty of Kiel to give up Norway, and conducted the campaign for its subjugation (1814). Charles XIII died in 1818 and was succeeded by Prince Charles John as Charles XIV John. The period of his administration was prosperous and peaceful.

CHARLES XV (1826-72), King of Sweden and Norway from 1859 to 1872. He succeeded his father, Oscar I, who was a son of Charles XIV John. The rule of Charles was liberal and popular. He instituted numerous legal reforms. The most important event was the change (in 1866) in the constitution of the parliament, which has since consisted of two chambers, one elected by the provincial representatives and the other by the people. He had a taste for literature and art, and wrote a volume of poems. In 1850 he married Louisa, daughter of Prince Frederick of the Netherlands.

CHARLES, Jacques Alexandre César (1746-1823), French chemist, physicist, and aeronaut, born at Beaugency, Loiret. In 1783 he made the first balloon using hydrogen gas (called *Charlière*, as distinguished from the *Montgolfière*, or fire balloon), and on Dec. 1, 1783, made a successful ascent to a height of nearly two miles. He invented a thermometric hydrometer and a number of optical instruments. In 1787 he published a statement, concerning the expansion of gases under the influence of heat, very similar to that later published by Gay-Lussac. The modern statement of the law is known sometimes as Gay-Lussac's Law (q.v.) and sometimes as Charles' Law. He was elected to the French Academy in 1785, and later became a professor at the Conservatoire des Arts et Métiers.

CHARLES, CAPE, a cape at the N.E. side of the entrance of Chesapeake Bay, Va., comprising the southernmost part of Northampton Co. On Smith's Island, N.E. of the cape, is a lighthouse with revolving light 180 ft. above high water.

CHARLES EDWARD. See Stuart, Charles Edward Louis Philip Casimir.

CHARLES LOUIS JOHN (1771-1847), Archduke of Austria, the third son of Emperor Leopold II, born in Florence. He was entrusted, in 1796, with command of the Austrian Army of the Rhine. After inflicting defeats on the French generals Jean Victor Moreau, Comte Jean Jourdan, and Jean Bernadotte, he drove the French across the Rhine and captured Kehl. In 1799 he was again at the head of the Army of the Rhine; he was several times victorious over Jourdan, protected Suabia, and successfully opposed Masséna, but suffered defeat at Zürich. Appointed governor general of Bohemia, he formed a new army there. After the battle of Hohenlinden (1800) he was again called to the chief command and succeeded in staying the progress of Moreau, but signed an armistice, which was followed by the Peace of Lunéville. In 1805 he commanded the army opposed to Marshal André Masséna in Italy and fought the battle of Caldiero, but, upon bad tidings from Germany, retreated from the left bank of the Adige to Croatia. This retreat was one of his greatest military achievements. Made generalissimo of the Austrian forces, he won in 1809 the battle of Aspern, which first showed Europe that Napoleon was not invincible; but he did not promptly follow up his victory, and Napoleon, who hastened to re-enforce his army, retrieved his fortunes at Wagram. The Archduke was compelled to give way, till he reached Znaim, where an armistice was concluded. He lived in retirement till his death. He wrote *Grundsätze der Strategie* (1814).

CHARLES MARTEL (688?-741), a Carolingian ruler of the Franks. His father, Pepin of Herstal, was ruler of the Frankish kingdom of Austrasia and mayor of the palace under the last Merovingian kings. When Pepin died in 714, Charles, an illegitimate son, was imprisoned by his father's widow, but escaped in 715 and was proclaimed mayor of the palace by the Austrasians. A war between Austrasia and Neustria followed, which ended in Charles becoming undisputed ruler of all the Franks. He was engaged in wars against the Alemanni, Bavarians, and Saxons, but his importance is chiefly due to his war against the Saracens, who, having conquered Septimania from the Visigoths in 720, advanced into Aquitaine, and in the succeeding years conquered Bordeaux, defeated the Duke of Aquitaine, crossed the Garonne, advanced to the Loire, and threatened Tours. Charles overthrew them near Poitiers, in 732, in a great battle, in which their leader, Abd-er-Rahman, fell, and their progress, which had filled all Christendom with alarm, was checked for a time. He drove them out of the Rhone valley in 739, when they had again advanced into the Burgundian territories as far as Lyons, deprived them of Languedoc, which he added to the Kingdom of the Franks, and left them nothing of their possessions north of the Pyrenees beyond the river Aude. Charles died at Quiercy on the Oise, leaving the kingdom divided between his two sons, Carloman and Pepin the Short (q.v.). See also CAROLINGIANS.

CHARLES OF ORLEANS. See ORLÉANS, CHARLES OF.

CHARLES PHILIP ARTHUR GEORGE, PRINCE OF WALES (1948–   ), heir apparent to the throne of Great Britain and Northern Ireland, the son of Queen Elizabeth II and Philip Mountbatten, Duke of Edinburgh.

CHARLES RIVER, a river of Massachusetts, separating Boston and Cambridge. It rises in the southern part of Middlesex and the western part of Norfolk counties, and, after a winding, 47-mile-long course, flows into Boston Bay between Boston and Charlestown. The waters of the Charles are used to generate electricity for the factories in the cities situated on its banks.

CHARLESTON, seaport, third-largest city of South Carolina, and county seat of Charleston Co., about 112 m. by rail S.E. of Columbia. It is about 7 m. from the Atlantic Ocean, on a low peninsula between the Ashley and Cooper rivers, which unite to form a broad bay. The bay is almost entirely landlocked and makes an excellent harbor, along the shores of which are noted bathing beaches and facilities for water sports. On two islands at the entrance to the bay are forts Moultrie and Sumter (see FORT SUMTER), and about 6 miles north of the city is the Charleston Navy Yard. In the city and its vicinity are a number of notable gardens, parks, and recreation centers. Charleston is a noted tourist center.

The city's notable buildings, some of historic interest, include a museum, founded in 1703 as the Powder Magazine; Dock Street Theater, opened in 1736; St. Michael's Episcopal Church, built in 1752–61; the Unitarian Church, dating from 1772; the Charleston Orphan House, erected in 1792–94; a number of fine 18th-century colonial homes; the city hall, built in 1801; Market Hall, now a Confederate Museum, erected in 1841; Beth Elohim Synagogue, built in 1840; and the United States Custom House, built in 1849–79. Educational and cultural institutions include the College of Charleston, which was founded in 1770 and, in 1837, became the first municipal college in the U.S.; the Medical College of the State of South Carolina, founded in 1824; The Citadel, a State military college, founded in 1842; the Porter Military Academy, an Episcopalian institution, dating from 1867; and Gibbes Art Gallery, constructed in 1905.

A network of rail, air, bus, and truck lines, and inland waterway, coastal, and transoceanic steamship lines connect Charleston with other cities on the Atlantic seaboard and in the interior, and with foreign ports. Charleston is an important center of domestic and foreign trade, and has the headquarters of a United States customs district. Among the principal exports of the city are coal, petroleum products, tobacco, and cotton and cotton goods; imports include petroleum, sugar, and chemicals used in the production of fertilizers. The storage and transshipment of petroleum is an important industry in Charleston. Other industries include shipbuilding, canning, and the manufacture of fertilizers, turpentine, rosin, coke and coke by-products, soap, foods, beverages, cigars, and textiles.

In 1670, English colonists under Gov. William Sayle came to Albemarle Point, on the west bank of the Ashley R., three miles from the present city, and named their settlement Charles Town in honor of King Charles II of England. Two years later a town was laid out on the site of the present city; and in 1680 it became the seat of government of what was then the proprietary Province of Carolina. A majority of the inhabitants of the earlier settlement moved to the new town, which subsequently was named Charles Town, and still later, Charleston. Huguenot refugees from France joined the colony in 1680 and other Huguenots after the revocation of the Edict of Nantes (q.v.) in France in 1685. Acadian exiles increased the town's population by about 1200 in 1755.

In 1775 Charleston was one of the chief cities and the third seaport in America, and it was the first Southern city to join the revolutionary movement against the English crown. In February, 1776, the Provincial Congress of South Carolina met in Charles Town and on March 26 adopted the first independent State constitution. On June 28, 1776, the garrison on Sullivan's Island, under Colonel Moultrie, repulsed an attack by the British fleet; and in 1779 the city was again successfully defended, against General Prévost; but on May 12, 1780, with its garrison of 7000 under General Benjamin Lincoln, it was captured after a siege of six weeks by a British force of 16,000 under Sir Henry Clinton, its loss being regarded as one of the greatest disasters of the Revolutionary War. On Dec. 14, 1782, the British evacuated the city and the Americans again took possession of it.

Charleston was incorporated in 1783 and until 1790 was the capital of the State. In 1784 the first bale of cotton exported from America to Europe was shipped from there. Between the conclusion of the War of 1812 and the outbreak of the Civil War the importance of Charleston as a shipping center declined, following the growth of other ports, notably Philadelphia and New York City. The city, however, progressed as a result of the development of the cotton industry and the construction of railroads.

Charleston was the center of the nullification (q.v.) movement of 1832; and the Democratic State convention which, on December 20, 1860, passed the first ordinance of secession, met there. On April 12–13, 1861, the Civil War was opened by the Confederate bombardment and capture of Fort Sumter. In 1863 a Federal fleet under Admiral Samuel Francis Dupont de Nemours unsuccessfully attacked the fortifications of the harbor, and, though closely besieged and frequently bombarded, the city remained in possession of the Confederates until Feb. 17, 1865, when it was evacuated. On the following day the Union forces under General Sherman took possession. On Aug. 31, 1886, Charleston suffered from an earthquake. Most of the houses were rendered unfit for habitation, many persons were killed, and property valued at over $8,000,000 was destroyed. In 1924 Charleston became the official port of the State. Pop. (1960) 65,925.

CHARLESTON, capital and second-largest city of West Virginia, and county seat of Kanawha Co., situated at the confluence of the Elk and Kanawha rivers, about 50 m. by rail E. of Huntington. It is the leading commercial and industrial center of the State. Bituminous coal, hardwood timber, petroleum and natural gas are produced in the sur-

rounding region. Industrial establishments in the city include plants engaged in the manufacture of plastic goods, nylon, acetate rayon, chlorine and numerous other chemicals, glass, furniture, mining equipment, and foundry products. Among the principal points of interest are the State capitol, an edifice in the Italian Renaissance architectural style; and Morris Harvey College, founded at Barboursville in 1888 and removed to its present site in 1935.

In 1788 an outpost known as Fort Lee was built on the site of the present-day city to protect the settlers of the Kanawha Valley. Scotch-Irish and German immigrants later settled in the vicinity of the fort. Charles Town (later shortened to Charleston) was incorporated as a town in 1794; in 1870 it was incorporated as a city and made the State capital. Charleston lost this status in 1875, but regained it ten years later. Pop. (1960) 85,796.

CHARLESTOWN, formerly a separate city, and, since 1874, a part of Boston, Mass. Charlestown was settled in 1629 by a small company from Salem and was organized as a town in 1634. Territory originally within its limits has been divided up to form the towns of Woburn, Malden, Stoneham, Burlington, and Somerville, and parts of Medford, Cambridge, Arlington, and Reading. The Battle of Bunker Hill was fought in Charlestown in 1775, when the British set fire to the town, destroying 320 buildings, valued at $525,000. The battle is commemorated by the Bunker Hill Monument. Charlestown was the home of John Harvard, the earliest benefactor of Harvard University (then Harvard College); and the birthplace of Samuel F. B. Morse, inventor of the telegraph.

CHARLES TOWN, town and county seat of Jefferson Co., W.Va., 55 miles N.W. of Washington, D.C. It is a residential and industrial community, in a rich agricultural region. Harness, brass products, and fertilizer are among the principal manufactures. Points of interest in or near Charles Town include "Mordington", originally the home of Charles Washington, founder of the town and brother of George Washington, first President of the United States; and the Courthouse (dating from 1801), scene of the trial and conviction for treason of the American abolitionist leader John Brown. Brown was hanged at Charles Town on Dec. 2, 1859. Pop. (1960) 3329.

CHARLOCK, a popular name for wild mustard, *Brassica arvensis,* in the family Cruciferae. It has rough, dentate leaves and small yellow, four-petalled flowers. The seedpods are long, knotty, and tapering; the seeds are sometimes used as a substitute for table mustard. Charlock is an annual weed common in the U.S. and Europe.

CHARLOTTE, largest city of North Carolina and county seat of Mecklenburg Co., about 174 miles s.w. of Raleigh, and about 20 miles N. of the South Carolina boundary. It is an important commercial, industrial, banking, and educational center, the whole-sale-distribution point for a large part of the South, and a leading center of the Southern textile industry. Cotton, peanuts, and tobacco, the chief crops of the surrounding region, are shipped from the city in large quantities. In addition to textiles, especially cotton yarn and cotton goods, the principal manufactures include food products, machinery, furniture, wearing apparel, and chemicals. The city is also a center of the construction industry in the South, many national companies maintain branch offices and warehouses there, and it is the site of a branch of the Federal Reserve Bank and of various regional offices of the State and Federal governments.

Educational and cultural institutions include the North Carolina Medical College, for white students; the Johnson C. Smith University, for Negroes, founded in 1867; Queen's College, for women, a Presbyterian institution established in 1857; Charlotte College a coeducational junior college; and the Mint Museum of Art.

Charlotte was settled about 1750, incorporated in 1768, and in 1774 was made the county seat. In September, 1780, during the Revolutionary War, the British General Charles Cornwallis entered the city and occupied it for several days. He referred to it as a "hornet's nest", a representation of which was later adopted as the city's emblem. The city was the last meeting place of the full Confederate cabinet, on April 10, 1865. In 1866 Charlotte was chartered as a city. Pop. (1960) 201,564.

CHARLOTTESVILLE, city and county seat of Albemarle Co., Va., situated on the Rivanna R., about 69 miles w.N.w. of Richmond, in a rich farming, catttle-raising, and fruit-growing region. Industrial establishments in the city include woolen, silk, flour and planing mills, and plants engaged in the production of clothing, machinery, pens and pencils, and fruit wines and brandies. Monticello, the home of Thomas Jefferson, third President of the United States, is 3 miles to the E., and Ash Lawn, which was the home of James Monroe, fifth President of the United States,

is nearby. The city is noted for its educational facilities. It is the site of the University of Virginia, St. Anne's School for Girls, Jefferson School of Commerce, Miller Manual Labor School, and the Institute of Textile Technology.

Charlottesville was settled about 1737 and named in honor of Queen Charlotte of Great Britain. It was incorporated as a town in 1762. In 1781, during the American Revolution, British troops under Colonel Banastre Tarleton raided the town in an unsuccessful attempt to capture Thomas Jefferson, then governor of Virginia. The town was chartered as a city in 1888. Pop. (1960) 29,427.

CHARLOTTETOWN, city, capital, and seaport of the province of Prince Edward Island, Canada, and county seat of Queen's County, situated on Hillsborough Bay, on the s. central coast of the island. Industrial establishments in Charlottetown include textile mills, lumber mills, foundries, canneries, and the shops of the Prince Edward Island railway. Fishing is an important industry. Prince of Wales College and Normal School, founded in 1860, and St. Dunstan's College (1831), a Roman Catholic educational institution, are located in the city. Charlottetown was founded by the French in 1750 as Port la Joie, and later, under British rule, was renamed in honor of Queen Charlotte of Great Britain. It became the provincial capital in 1765. Pop. (1961) 18,318.

CHARM, any formula, act, or object supposed to have a magical power to ward off danger or to bring good luck. Originally, the term meant the chanting of a verse, supposed to exert occult influence; by extension, it came to mean an object worn or carried for protection or good fortune.

CHARON, in Greek mythology, the ferryman who conveys souls of the dead across the River Styx in Hades. To pay the soul's fare, a small coin (*obolus*) was placed in the mouth of the dead before burial. If this rite was neglected, Charon refused to convey the shade across, and it was doomed to wander restlessly on the shore of Acheron. From the 5th century B.C. Charon appears frequently in literature. He is depicted on Athenian white lecythi, vases buried with the dead, as a bearded old man wearing the short tunic and pointed cap of a seaman, in a skiff with a single oar. On Etruscan monuments Charon is represented as a demon of death, with bestial face, huge tusks, and pointed ears, carrying snakes or, more commonly, a large hammer. In Roman times, the bodies of fallen gladiators were dragged from the arena by a man disguised as this demon. In modern Greek superstition Charon survives as *Charos* or *Charontas*, who, as a black bird of prey or winged horseman, bears victims to the world of the dead.

CHARPENTIER, GUSTAVE (1860–1956), French composer, born in Dieuze, Meurthe-et-Moselle, and educated at the Paris Conservatory under Jules Émile Frédéric Massenet. His fame rests mainly on the opera *Louise* (1900), for which he also wrote the libretto. An overwhelming critical and popular success when first produced at the Opéra Comique in Paris, *Louise* subsequently was presented in all the leading opera houses of the world. The composer also set to music verses of the French impressionist poets Charles Baudelaire and Paul Verlaine. He was elected a member of the Académie des Beaux-Arts in 1912. Two of his best-known compositions are an orchestral suite, *Impressions d'Italie* (1890), and a symphonic drama, *La Vie du Poète* (1892). His later works, which include the opera *Julien* (1913), never achieved the critical acclaim accorded *Louise*.

CHARR. See CHAR.

CHARTER, a formal document by which rights or privileges are conferred. The term formerly applied to a written conveyance of land, and property held under such an instrument was, in Anglo-Saxon law, called "charterland", "bookland", or "bocland". In this sense the word has given way to deed. The term charter is used to describe a grant of land or special privileges by the state, or a solemn guaranty by the sovereign of popular rights. Magna Charta (q.v.), or the Great Charter, issued by King John in 1215, is one of the chief constitutional documents of Great Britain.

It was the custom of the British government for centuries to grant political charters to some of its colonies. In American Colonial history, grants of franchise, governmental privileges, and estates to companies for the purpose of establishing colonies, to the inhabitants of colonies in general, or to individual proprietors, were embodied in charters. Of the first sort were the charters of Massachusetts Bay, granted by Charles I (1629), and the charter of Georgia, granted by George II (1732). Of the second sort was the charter of Connecticut, granted to the people of the colony by Charles II (1662). Of the third sort were the original charter of New York, granted to the Duke of York by Charles II (1664), and the charter of Maryland, granted to Lord Baltimore by Charles I (1632).

In the United States, corporations are chartered, as a rule, by legislative acts of a State, either by a special statute which confers upon a particular corporation the special powers and privileges named therein, or under a general law which provides the method to be pursued by persons who would organize a corporation. In the latter case the articles of association, taken in connection with the provisions of the general statute, constitute the charter. If the corporation is a public one, such as a city, county, or town, its charter may be changed at will by the legislature. Such a corporation is a mere agency of the State for the exercise of governmental powers within a particular area. It has no vested right to any of its powers or franchises. Its charter "is not a contract, but a law for the public good". On the other hand, the charter of a private corporation is a contract between the State and the corporators. As such, it is protected from repeal or modification by the provision of the Federal Constitution which declares that "no state shall . . . pass any . . . law impairing the obligation of contracts" (Art. I, Sec. 10). The State granting the charter may, however, reserve the right to alter, amend, or repeal it. See CORPORATION.

In England, towns, universities, schools, banks, and joint-stock companies often derived their privileges from royal charters. Now, however, Parliamentary sanction is generally obtained for grants of important privileges. In the case of companies, Parliament has passed a general act, by complying with the provisions of which any body can obtain the privileges of incorporation.

CHARTER OAK, a large tree that stood in Hartford, Conn., until blown down, August, 1856, when its age was computed to be nearly 1000 years. The tradition relating to it is as follows: When Sir Edmund Andros (q.v.) was appointed governor general of New England, he went to Hartford in 1687 to receive the Colonial charter. The colonists were loath to surrender the document, but, appearing to submit, carried it to the council chamber. During the debate the lights were extinguished and in the ensuing confusion the charter was carried from the room to its hiding place in the hollow of the tree. There it remained until 1689, when the deposition of Andros made further concealment unnecessary.

CHARTIER, ALAIN (1385?–1433?), French poet and diplomat, born in Bayeux, and educated at the University of Paris. He served the French dauphin, later King Charles VII, in various official capacities, including those of secretary and negotiator. After the crushing defeat (1415) of France by England in the Battle of Agincourt, Chartier wrote *Le Quadrilogue Invectif* (1422), a passionate appeal to all French classes patriotically to unite in support of their king. One of his most famous poems, "La Belle Dame sans Merci", set a literary fashion and suggested the poem of the same title by the British poet John Keats. Chartier's works include *Livre des Quatre Dames,* a collection of lyrics; *Livre d'Espérance* (1429), an outspoken attack on corruption among the nobility and clergy; and *Bréviaire des Nobles,* which was so greatly admired by his contemporaries that court pages were required to memorize parts of it. His works, which strongly influenced the literature of his century, show a boldness and freedom of thought that foreshadow the Renaissance.

CHARTISM, political reform movement in Great Britain from 1838 to 1848. The word is derived from "People's Charter", designation applied to a legislative program submitted to Parliament in 1837 by the London Workingmen's Association. The Chartist movement, which the Association sponsored, resulted from widespread dissatisfaction with the Reform Bill of 1832 and the Poor Law of 1834, legislation which workingmen considered discriminatory.

The People's Charter contained six specific demands, including suffrage for all male citizens 21 years of age and over, elections by secret ballot, and annual Parliamentary elections. These demands were rejected by the House of Commons. The Association launched a nation-wide campaign for its program, and more than 1,250,000 persons signed a petition to Parliament, requesting that the Charter be enacted into law.

In February, 1839, the Chartists assembled in London in a representative convention for the purpose of developing a program of action. When, in the next July, Parliament again rejected the Charter, the Convention issued orders for a general strike. However, the orders were withdrawn a few days later. A Chartist insurrection broke out at Newport, Monmouth County, on November 4, 1839, but the rebels, numbering about 3000 men armed chiefly with picks, were betrayed by police informers and were ambushed, suffering numerous casualties. Many Chartist leaders were arrested and sentenced to prison terms of one or two years.

In 1840 a new organization, the National Charter Association, was organized for the furtherance of Chartist aims. Another petition to Parliament, signed by about 3,315,000 citizens, was rejected in May, 1842. A protracted period of decline ensued, until a new wave of enthusiasm and militancy, stimulated by the revolutions in Europe, developed in 1848. A fourth petition to Parliament was initiated and plans were made for a public demonstration in London, to be climaxed by a march on the House of Commons. Alarmed by the public support accorded the petition, which, according to Chartist leaders, received 6,000,000 signatures, the authorities prohibited the march and prepared for possible insurrection. The demonstration, held without violence on April 10th, was attended by more than 50,000 persons, but the petition was again rejected by the House of Commons. Although the Chartist movement gradually disintegrated thereafter, all of its program, except the demand for annual Parliamentary elections, eventually became law.

CHARTRES (anc. *Carnutes; Autricum; civitas Carnutum*), city in N.W. France, capital of the department of Eure-et-Loir, and the seat of a bishopric. The city is situated on the Eure River, 55 miles S.W. of Paris by rail. Chartres consists of an upper and lower town connected by steep streets. The highest point of the city is crowned by the cathedral of Notre Dame (10th to 13th centuries) noted for the beauty of its two spires, its statuary, its 13th-century stained glass, and its Renaissance choir screen. Henry IV was crowned king of France at Chartres in 1594. The principal industries of the city are brewing, distilling, dyeing, the milling of flour, and the manufacturing of machinery, leather goods, hosiery, and stained glass. Chartres is a market center for the surrounding agricultural region. Pop. of the city (1962) 31,169.

CHARTREUSE, a liqueur, named after the Carthusian monastery La Grande Chartreuse, where it was made. When the Carthusian monks were driven out of France in 1903, the secret of its preparation was taken with them to Tarragon, Spain. The monks were readmitted to France in 1938. The formula is said to be known only to the Father Superior of the order. Three kinds are made: green, yellow, and white.

CHARYBDIS. See SCYLLA AND CHARYBDIS.

CHASE, MARY ELLEN (1887–), American educator and author, born at Blue Hill, Me., and educated at the universities of Maine and Minnesota. After teaching English at the University of Minnesota from 1918 to 1926, she was associate professor (1926–29) and professor (1929–55) of English at Smith College. She wrote textbooks; works of literary criticism, including *The Bible and the Com-*

Cathedral of Notre Dame, Chartres, of classic Gothic style, was constructed over a period of several centuries, the spire at right in 1145 and the spire at left in 1506.

1971

mon Reader (1944); the autobiographical works *A Goodly Heritage* (1932), *A Goodly Fellowship* (1939) and *The White Gate* (1954); the novels *Mary Peters* (1934), *Silas Crockett* (1935), *Dawn in Lyonesse* (1938), *Windswept* (1941), *Plum Tree* (1949), *The Edge of Darkness* (1957), and *Lovely Ambition* (1960); the biography *Abby Aldrich Rockefeller* (1950); and *Life and Language in the Old Testament* (1955) and *The Psalms for the Common Reader* (1962).

CHASE, SALMON PORTLAND (1808–73), American statesman, born at Cornish, N.H. In 1830 he settled as a lawyer in Cincinnati, where he defended numerous fugitive slaves. An uncompromising opponent of slavery, he was largely instrumental in founding the Liberty Party, which in 1844 brought about Henry Clay's defeat. Chase was elected to the U.S. Senate in 1849 by the Ohio Democrats, but separated from the party in 1852 when it committed itself to slavery. He was twice elected governor of Ohio (1855–59) by the newly formed Republican Party, of which he was one of the founders.

From 1861 to 1864 he was secretary of the treasury in Lincoln's wartime cabinet. In that office Chase rendered many important services, including the maintenance of national credit and the supply of funds with which to prosecute the war, the provision and regulation of a currency system, and the development of a national banking system. In 1864 he was appointed chief justice of the United States Supreme Court.

CHASE, SAMUEL (1741–1811), American jurist, born in Somerset Co., Md. He was admitted to the bar in 1761 and became prominent during the Revolutionary War. As a member of the Assembly he opposed the Stamp Act, and subsequently was a delegate to the Continental Congress (1774–78; 1784–85). In 1776 he was a member of the deputation which endeavored unsuccessfully to induce the Canadians to declare war against Britain, and it was very largely owing to his efforts that Maryland was prevented from espousing the cause of the mother country. In 1776 he was one of the signatories to the Declaration of Independence. In 1791 he became chief judge of the Maryland General Court and in 1796 associate justice of the Supreme Court of the United States. He was impeached for his conduct in criticizing Jefferson's administration during a charge to a grand jury, but was strongly defended and ultimately acquitted by the Senate. He continued to serve as a member of the Supreme Court until his death.

CHASE, STUART (1888–), American social scientist and writer, born at Somersworth, N.H., and educated at the Massachusetts Institute of Technology and Harvard University. He was an investigator of the meat industry for the Federal Trade Commission from 1917 to 1922 and was consultant to various Federal commissions on economic matters from 1934 to 1941.

His works include *The Tragedy of Waste* (1925), *Your Money's Worth* (with F. J. Schlink, 1927), *Men and Machines* (1929), *A New Deal* (1932), *The Tyranny of Words* (1938), *A Primer of Economics* (1941), *Men at Work* (with Marian Tyler, his wife, 1945), *For This We Fought* (1946), *Proper Study of Mankind* (1949; rev. ed., 1956), *Roads to Agreement* (with Marian Tyler, 1951), *The Power of Words* (with Marian Tyler, 1954), *Guides to Straight Thinking* (1956), *Some Things Worth Knowing* (1958), *Live and Let Live* (1960), and *American Credos* (1962).

CHASIDIM or **HASIDIM** (Heb., "the saintly ones"), in history, a name given to especially pious persons among the Jews. From passages in the Psalter, the books of Maccabees, and the Talmud it seems evident that the term was used for those who distinguished themselves by loyalty to the law and by charitable deeds. They opposed all Hellenizing tendencies and clung closely to the teachings and practices of Judaism. The Chasidim suffered death in preference to transgressing the tenets of their religion.

In modern times the name Chasidim is applied to a mystical sect established in Poland about 1750 by the religious leader Israel ben Eliezer (d. 1760) and after his death led by Beer of Mizricz (d. 1772). Rabbi Israel was called "Baal Shem-Tob" (q.v.) or "master of the Holy Name". His followers were characterized by, among other things, a belief in miracles, by participation in extremely enthusiastic prayer services, by devotion to the ideal of brotherly love, and by emphasis on emotional piety as opposed to strictly disciplined ritual. The sect grew rapidly, numbering about 50,000 in 1770. It provoked great opposition on the part of the Talmudists, those who studied and practiced the body of Jewish law as written down in the Talmud (q.v.) and the various other codes. In Vilna, Poland, in 1781 the Talmudists denounced the Chasidim as heretics. The sect continued to flourish, however, and has many adherents. N.N.G.

CHASTELARD, PIERRE DE BOSCOSEL DE (1540–64), French poet at the court of King Francis II. After the king's death he accompanied Francis' widow, Mary, Queen of Scots, back to Scotland as a page of Marshal Damville. He fell in love with the queen, to whom he conveyed a poem, *Regrets,* by Pierre Ronsard, and with whom he exchanged amatory verses. His conduct became so rash that he was seized in her bedchamber and sentenced to hang; he was executed at Edinburgh.

CHASUBLE, an ecclesiastical vestment. See COSTUME, ECCLESIASTICAL.

CHAT, common name applied to the North American bird *Icteria virens,* the largest species of the wood warbler family; see WOOD WARBLER. Known also as the yellow-breasted chat, it breeds in the eastern United States and winters in Mexico and Central America. It is 7½ inches in length and has a bright-yellow breast and throat, a white abdomen, and olive-green upper parts. A variety of yellow-breasted chat, found in the western States, has a longer tail and is called the long-tailed chat.

The chat feeds on insects and builds its nest in thickets near the ground. The eggs, usually five in number, are white and spotted with brown. Like the mockingbird, the chat has a wide variety of imitative calls. The male has a clownish reputation because of his behavior during the mating season; he mounts into the air and performs droll gymnastics accompanied by a mixture of whistles, toots, and clucks.

The name "chat" is applied in Europe to several genera of birds belonging to the thrush family, Turdidae.

CHÂTEAU, CHÂTEL, or CASTEL, names applied in France and other parts of the Continent to the residences of the feudal lords of the soil. The name *château-fort* is applied to the fortified castles erected before the 15th century. The term *château* is also applied to the modern French country house, when the proprietor is also the owner of extensive adjoining landed property.

CHATEAUBRIAND, VICOMTE FRANÇOIS RENÉ DE (1768–1848), French writer and statesman, born at St. Malo, Brittany. He entered the French army in 1786, and from 1791 to 1792, as a member of a French expedition to search for the Northwest Passage (q.v.), he traveled widely in North America. Though he believed in political reform, the excesses of the French Revolution led him to join the Royalists. In 1792 he fought with the Royalist army and was wounded at Thionville; then he became an émigré and from 1792 to 1800 lived in England. Returning to France, he found favor with Napoleon, who gave him a diplomatic post which he resigned, however, in 1804 in protest against Napoleon's execution of the Duc d'Enghien (q.v.). After the Bourbon restoration Chateaubriand was made a peer of France (1815), was ambassador to Great Britain in 1822, and from 1823 to 1824 was minister of foreign affairs. He was one of the most important French writers of the first half of the 19th century. In his works he dispensed with the imitation of 18th-century literary models prevailing at the time. He introduced into French literature new and exotic types of character and background, principally the Indians and scenery of North America; and an emphasis on introspection, generally of a pessimistic nature, exemplified in his novels *Atala* (1801) and *René* (1802). These new literary elements mark him as a forerunner of the Romantic period in French literature. In addition, his assertion of the superiority of Christianity over other religions not only in its moral but its esthetic aspects (*Le Génie du Christianisme,* 1802), had a profound influence on the religious and literary life of his time. Among others of his important works are *Les Martyrs* (1809), *Les Natchez* (1826), *Le Dernier des Abencérages*

TWA Photo

The Château de Chambord, France, was built as a Renaissance hunting lodge. The fenestrated towers contrast gracefully with the long horizontal lines of the main building.

(1826), and his autobiography, *Mémoires d'Outre-tombe* (1849–50).

CHÂTEAU-THIERRY, BATTLE OF, a part of the Second Battle of the Marne, in World War I. It is notable in American history as the first victorious action of American troops in that war. See MARNE, BATTLES OF; WORLD WAR I: *The Campaigns and Other Events of 1918.*

CHATHAM, city, river port, and county seat of Kent Co., Ont., Canada, on the Thames R., about 11 miles N. of Lake Erie, and about 40 miles E. of Detroit, Mich. It is situated in a fertile farming region; has a large export trade via lakes St. Clair, Erie, and Huron; and contains lumber mills, flour mills, and factories for the manufacture of binder twine, woven-wire products, and engines. Pop. (1961) 29,826.

CHATHAM, city and river port of Kent, England, on the Medway R., contiguous to the city of Rochester and 34 m. by rail E.S.E. of London. Chatham has important naval establishments, including nine dry docks, a naval hospital, and a barracks. A large retail trade is carried on, owing chiefly to the presence of naval personnel. Manufactured products include flour and bricks. Chatham was incorporated in 1890, and includes the suburb of Luton. Pop. (1961 prelim.) 48,989.

CHATHAM, EARL OF. See PITT, WILLIAM.

CHATHAM ISLANDS, group of two small islands and a number of islets in the Pacific Ocean, situated about 536 miles E. of Christchurch, New Zealand, and forming a county of South Island, New Zealand. Chatham (or Whairkauri) Island, the largest of the group, is about 38 miles long and has a maximum width of 25 miles. Of volcanic origin, it has elevations up to 1000 ft. above sea level and contains numerous small lakes. Pitt (or Rangihaute) Island, the next-largest, has an area of 25 sq.m. Waitangi (pop. in 1961, 147), on Chatham I., is the chief settlement. Sheep and cattle are raised on the islands, and fishing is an important industry. Wool and frozen fish are exported. The islands were discovered in 1791 by an English naval commander. Most of the aboriginal inhabitants, a Polynesian people known as Moriorios, were killed by Maoris who took possession of the islands in 1831. The present population comprises Maoris, Europeans, and a few aborigines. Area, 372 sq.m.; pop. (1961) 487.

CHATI. See WILDCAT.

CHATSWORTH, the name of the mansion of the dukes of Devonshire and one of the most splendid private seats in England. It is in Derbyshire, on the Derwent R. Sir William

Cavendish in 1570 began the old mansion, which was finished by his widow, afterward Countess of Shrewsbury. In this building Mary, Queen of Scots, was imprisoned for 13 years. The present edifice includes the Ionic pile, built by the 1st Duke of Devonshire. The façade is 720 feet long; with the terraces, 1200 feet. The grounds of Chatsworth are 9 miles in circuit and are surpassed only by those at Versailles.

CHATTAHOOCHEE, river of the United States, rising in the Appalachian Mountains, in N.E. Georgia. About 410 m. long, and navigable, it crosses the State in a southwesterly direction to West Point, Ga., where it turns south; in this section of its course it forms part of the boundary between Georgia and Alabama and part of the boundary between Georgia and Florida. At the southwestern corner of Georgia it unites with the Flint R. to form the Appalachicola R. of Florida.

CHATTANOOGA, city, port of entry, and county seat of Hamilton Co., Tenn., on the Tennessee R., about 110 miles S.W. of Knoxville, and adjoining the Georgia State boundary on the S. It is located in the area served by the Tennessee Valley Authority (q.v.), which furnishes cheap, abundant hydroelectric power, and in close proximity to rich coal and iron-ore fields. The city is one of the leading industrial centers of the South. Manufacturing is highly diversified; the chief manufactures include iron and steel products, nonferrous-metal products, machinery, cement, textiles, hosiery, farm equipment, furniture, stoves, chemicals, bottles, ceramics, and foodstuffs and beverages.

Among the city's principal structures are the post office, which also houses the main headquarters of the Tennessee Valley Authority; the Federal courthouse, constructed in 1934; Union Station; and Soldiers and Sailors Memorial Auditorium. Noteworthy educational institutions include the University of Chattanooga, founded in 1886, the Chattanooga College of Law, and the Cadek Conservatory of Music.

Both in the vicinity of and within Chattanooga are many historic landmarks and scenic attractions, and the city is a popular tourist center. Several of the most sanguinary battles of the American Civil War were fought in the environs (see CHATTANOOGA, BATTLE OF; CHICKAMAUGA, BATTLE OF). The sites of these battles are largely preserved in the Chickamauga-Chattanooga National Military Park, a beautiful wooded tract covering 8149 acres. Situated mostly in Georgia, the park contains nearly 2000 battle-line tablets, regimental markers, and other guides inscribed with detailed descriptions of the military actions. Other features of the park include Signal Mountain, site of a Confederate observation post; Orchard Knob, scene of the first Union success in the Battle of Chattanooga and headquarters of General Ulysses S. Grant, the Union commander; Lookout Mountain, on which was fought the battle's second phase, popularly known as the "Battle above the Clouds"; and parts of Missionary Ridge, where the fiercest and most decisive phase of the battle took place; Chattanooga National Cemetery, with the graves of more than 13,000 Union soldiers; and a large Confederate cemetery. An inclined railway, which attains a grade of 72 percent, affords access to the summit of Lookout Mountain.

Among additional points of interest in and near the city are "the General", a locomotive (on diplay in Union Station) which figured in one of the most dramatic episodes of the Civil War; Lake Chickamauga, a 59-mile-long lake created (1940) by the construction of Chickamauga Dam across the Tennessee R.; Lookout Mountain Caverns, containing remarkable stalactite and stalagmite formations and Ruby Falls, a 145-foot underground waterfall; and Fort Oglethorpe, a U.S. military reservation in nearby Catoosa Co., Ga.

The name of the city is an Indian designation for Lookout Mountain, i.e., "rock rising to a point". Protestant missionaries were active among Indians living in the area as early as 1817, but the site of the present-day city was not permanently settled until 1835. Chattanooga was chartered as a town in 1839, and it subsequently became an important river port. In 1849 the extension of a railroad line to Chattanooga spurred its development; in 1851 it became a city. During the Civil War the city was extensively damaged in the battles cited above. Pop. (1960) 130,009.

CHATTANOOGA, BATTLE OF, battle of the American Civil War, fought on Nov. 23, 24, and 25, 1863, between a Union army of about 60,000 men under General Ulysses Simpson Grant and a Confederate force of approximately 40,000, under General Braxton Bragg. Following its earlier defeat in the Battle of Chickamauga (see CHICKAMAUGA, BATTLE OF) on Sept. 19–20, 1863, the Union Army was bottled up in Chattanooga and cut off from its sources of supply. Bragg's army was entrenched on Lookout Mountain (q.v.), 3 miles s.w. of Chattanooga, and on parts of Missionary Ridge (q.v.), running parallel to Lookout Mountain, about 3 miles E. and s.E. of Chattanooga. The Confederates also held the plain between Lookout Mountain and Missionary Ridge.

On Oct. 27–28, Union engineer units commanded by General William Farrar Smith seized Brown's Ferry on the Tennessee R., w. of Chattanooga, opening a supply route into the city, and forces of the XIth and XIIth Corps, under General Joseph Hooker, seized the valley of Lookout Creek, an affluent of the Tennessee situated w. of Lookout Mt., and effected a junction with Smith's troops. General Grant then halted further operations until the arrival of reinforcements (four divisions) under General William Tecumseh Sherman.

On Nov. 23 the Army of the Cumberland, led by General George Thomas, captured Orchard Knob, an elevation in the plain between Chattanooga and Missionary Ridge, and during the night of Nov. 23–24 Sherman forces began the occupation of positions fronting the N. extremity of Missionary Ridge. The Union assault on Lookout Mountain was launched at 8:00 A.M. on November 24, and by the morning of the 25th the Union force, about 9000 men under General Hooker, had driven the Confederates from their positions. During the night of the 24th–25th General Bragg shifted the bulk of his forces to Missionary Ridge.

The decisive phase of the battle began (7:00 A.M., Nov. 25) when Sherman's force, consisting of six divisions, attacked Confederate intrenchments on the N. slopes of Missionary Ridge. Various Federal units succeeded in reaching the crest in the course of the next six hours, but on each occasion the enemy rallied and drove them back. Finally, at about 3:30 P.M., Grant ordered a diversionary assault on the Confederate earthworks along the w. base of the ridge. The assaulting force, four divisions under General Thomas, took these positions at bayonet point; simultaneously, Hooker's forces, having descended Lookout Mountain, stormed the southern and eastern flanks of Missionary Ridge. Thomas's men, disregarding orders to advance no farther than the first line of earthworks; continued on up the steep slopes and, in one of the most remarkable charges known in military history, carried the enemy fortifications along the crest. The panic-stricken Confederates fled in disorder; during the night the remnants of Bragg's army withdrew northward.

Grant's victory forced the Confederates to evacuate Tennessee and made possible Sherman's subsequent march through Georgia. Union casualties in the battle were estimated at about 5800, including approximately 750 killed, 4700 wounded, and 350 missing; Confederate casualties were estimated at about 8700, including approximately 360 killed, 2200 wounded, 2000 prisoners, and 4150 missing.

CHATTEL, in law, a term nearly coextensive with "personal property". A chattel is property, the title to which, upon death of the owner, passes to the executor or administrator of the estate, as distinguished from real property, the title to which passes directly to the heir. By chattel is meant that species of personal property capable of physical delivery and possession. Thus, choses (things) in possession are chattels, but choses in action (legal claims for moneys due), although personal property, are not chattels in the technical sense.

Chattels are classified as chattels real and chattels personal. A chattel real is any interest or property in land less than a fee interest. As opposed to ownership in fee, chattels real are regarded as personal property; but, as being interests in real property, they are called chattels real to distinguish them from other chattels, which are called, simply, chattels.

Certain objects which are a part of real estate may become chattels upon being severed from it, as timber which has been cut, or ore mined and removed from the land; and certain other objects which are still attached to and form a part of real property such as growing crops or emblements, are for some purposes regarded as chattels. On the other hand, in general, chattels which become attached to the land or are used as a part of the real estate lose their character as chattels and become real estate. Thus materials used in constructing a house or other structure forming a part of real estate are real estate. Certain chattels, however, affixed to the real estate but capable of removal, as machinery and articles of furniture, retain their character as chattels for some purposes, while for other purposes they are deemed real estate. See GIFT; SALE.

CHATTERTON, THOMAS (1752–70), English poet, born at Bristol and educated at the Colston Free School, Bristol. As a boy he learned to read from the Gothic characters of an old, black-letter Bible, and studied the inscriptions and escutcheons on the tombs of the ancient Church of St. Mary Redcliffe and the medieval English manuscripts in the muniment room of the church. At 14 he was apprenticed to an attorney in Bristol, but devoted all his spare time to writing manuscripts in imitation of those he had studied. From 1765 to 1770 he wrote a series of poems in imitative Middle English, purporting to have been written by Thomas Rowley, a priest of Bristol in the 15th century, a character of his own invention. In 1768 when the new Bristol bridge was opened, he attracted attention by his contribution to a newspaper of an account of the opening of the old bridge in 1248. This account, his own composition, he claimed to have found in a 13th-century manuscript in Redcliffe Church. In 1769 he sent to Horace Walpole a manuscript entitled *The Ryse of Peyncteyne yn Englande wroten by T. Rowleie, 1469, for Mastre Canynge.* Walpole upon investigation found this account of medieval English painters spurious and rejected it with severe censure.

Chatterton did not find the study of law congenial and went to London in 1770 to engage in literary work. He wrote at a furious rate, producing squibs, political essays, satiric poems, tales, letters, and the burletta *Revenge* (1770). His work earned him little and finally, rather than starve, he killed himself by taking poison. He is known chiefly for his *Poems, Supposed to have been Written at Bristol, by Thomas Rowley, and Others, in the Fifteenth Century* (first collected edition, 1777). Important in this collection are the poems *The Battle of Hastings, Balade of Charitie, Bristowe Tragedy, Aella,* and *On Happienesse.* Though all the poems are impostures, they are characterized by rich invention, intensely romantic imagination, and sensitive feeling. They had considerable influence on the work of John Keats, Samuel Taylor Coleridge, and other poets of the English Romantic movement, and on the English Pre-Raphaelite poets.

CHAUCER, GEOFFREY (1343?–1400), first major English poet, born in London, and educated probably at Saint Paul's Cathedral School in London. In 1357 he was a page in the household of Lionel, the youngest son of King Edward III. Chaucer served (1359–60) during the Hundred Years' War with the English army in France and was taken prisoner and later ransomed. Between 1361 and 1366 he may have studied law at one of the Inns of Court in London. He married, probably in 1366, Philippa de Roet, whose sister, Catherine Swynford, became the third wife of John of Gaunt (q.v.), another of the king's sons and a patron of Chaucer. Between 1360 and his death Chaucer held a number of official appointments and traveled on diplomatic missions, so presumably he had become a substantial man of affairs. He journeyed often to France on government business and at least twice (1372–73, 1378) to Italy, where, it is supposed, he first came under the influence of the works of the Italian writers Dante Alighieri, Francesco Petrarch, and Giovanni Boccaccio. Chaucer held the important and lucrative post of controller of the customs of wools, skins, and hides for London from 1374 to 1386, and during that time he had the use of a house above Aldgate, one of the gates of the city. He seems to have maintained residence thereafter mainly in Kent, for which he served as justice of the peace (1385) and member of Parliament (1386). In 1389 he was appointed clerk of the king's works, in charge of the building and repair of extensive royal establishments. This office proved to be hazardous, for he was assaulted once and robbed at least twice during a period of four days in 1390; he resigned in 1391. He then was appointed deputy forester of the royal forest of North Petherton. Toward the end of his life he apparently enjoyed the favor of King Richard II and King Henry IV, although records suggest that he was then in financial difficulties. Chaucer is buried in Westminster Abbey (q.v.), in what is known at present as the Poets' Corner.

The works Chaucer wrote before about 1382 are dominated by a prevailing literary mode of the later Middle Ages, which is characterized by a symbolic interaction among allegorical or fanciful personages who often are in a garden closed off from the world or in a dream landscape. Most of these early poems are composed in the octosyllabic couplet characteristic of early medieval narrative verse.

Chaucer's translation of the popular 13th-century work *Le Roman de la Rose* by the French poets Guillaume de Lorris (q.v.) and Jean Clopinel, known as Jean de Meung, belongs probably to this period. Another early work is *The Book of the Duchess* (1370?), a sensitive and evocative elegy in the form of a dream vision, written in honor of Blanche, the first wife of John of Gaunt. The unfinished poem *The House of Fame* (1372?–80?) is a partly humorous, very fanciful dream vision in which Chaucer himself, in imitation of a more solemn scene in Dante's *The Divine Comedy,* is carried by a talkative eagle from earth to a strange realm. In *The Parlement of Foules* (1380?–86?), or *The Parliament of Birds,* he is led in a dream into a garden, where he first enters a temple dedicated to the goddess Venus and devoted apparently to romantic and sensual love, and then sees the judgment of Dame Nature in distributing mates to various birds representing various kinds of people. Part of his intention here is

Culver Service

Geoffrey Chaucer

to portray love in marriage.

Chaucer's later works, written between about 1382 and his death, generally depict concrete individuals in the everyday world and contain notable technical innovations. During this period he made extensive use of the rime-royal stanza in his conservative, formal, or religious narratives, and he introduced the iambic pentameter couplet into English verse, using it in his more secular or satirical compositions. See VERSIFICATION: *English Versification.*

At the beginning of *The Legend of Good Women* (1380?–86?) Chaucer relies again upon the dream vision but passes to the successive stories of famous women whose love was villainously betrayed by men. *Troilus and Criseyde* (1385?), a romance of ancient Troy, reflects another romance on the same subject by Boccaccio. However, Chaucer's work differs in representing sensitively the psychological stages of the noble but inconstant Criseyde's love for and desertion of the warrior and prince Troilus. The poem succeeds in relating these occurrences to a larger view of man's fate, partly through the reactions of the wordly-wise and middle-aged character Pandarus. Chaucer's masterpiece, *The Canterbury Tales,* written approximately between 1386 and 1400, comprises a series of extraordinarily diverse tales and viewpoints tied together by revelations of the characters of the tellers, a band of pilgrims. Chaucer exhibits in this work his mastery of story form and his understanding of the human condition. See

CANTERBURY TALES, THE. He also wrote shorter poems, prose treatises, and other translations, some of which have been lost.

From his time onward, Chaucer has been considered among the greatest of English poets. The qualities which have endeared his work to generations of readers are his breadth of human understanding and his loving and often jovial creation of individual human character. He brought together in literary works of a new subtlety and urbanity the courtly and idealized view of life common to medieval romance (see ROMANCE), the spiritual insight common to medieval religious works, and the robust and lusty perception of human frailty common to medieval satire.

From the Norman Conquest in 1066 to Chaucer's time French and Latin were the languages used by the upper classes of England. Subsequently such popular and pre-eminent works as *The Parlement of Foules, Troilus and Criseyde,* and *The Canterbury Tales* proved more influential than those of any other writer in establishing English as a literary language; see ENGLISH LANGUAGE: *History.* Chaucer's poetry also set the style, vocabulary, and metrics of English and Scottish verse for more than a century after his death. The widespread esteem in which his poetry has been held in all succeeding ages is attested by the adaptation of some of his works into Modern English by the poets John Dryden in the 17th century, Alexander Pope in the 18th century, and William Wordsworth in the 19th century.　　　　　　　　　A.K.H.

CHAUDIERE RIVER, a river in Quebec, Canada. The head streams of the Chaudière rise in Maine, and flow into Lake Megantic, Quebec, from which the river proper issues. It flows generally N.N.W. and joins the St. Lawrence River about 7 m. above the city of Quebec. The Chaudière is about 120 m. long. The falls of the same name are 2½ m. above the mouth of the river.

CHAULMOOGRA, any tree of the genera *Taraktogenos* and *Hydnocarpus,* growing in Burma and the East Indies. The large, soft fruits have a hairy surface and contain a few large seeds. From these seeds is expressed a clear, yellow oil, chaulmoogra oil, which has been much used in medicine, particularly in the treatment of skin diseases. Intramuscular injection of the purified oil was formerly the only known treatment for leprosy (q.v.). The principal active constituents of the oil are esters of chaulmoogric acid, $C_{18}H_{32}O_2$, and hydnocarpic acid, $C_{16}H_{28}O_2$.

CHAUSSON, ERNEST (1855–99), French composer, born in Limay. In 1880 he studied under Jules Massenet at the Paris Conservatoire, and from 1880 to 1883 was a pupil of César Franck, whose style and technique strongly influenced his work. Chausson wrote operas, choral works, songs, chamber music. church music, and compositions for orchestra and voice, and for piano. His best-known works are *Symphony in B Flat* (1890) and *Poème* (for violin and orchestra 1896).

CHAUTAUQUA INSTITUTION, a center for popular education, located in the village of Chautauqua, N.Y. The institution carries on its work by means of summer assemblies and schools and through home studies. The institution was established in 1874 at Fair Point, later Chautauqua, by the Methodist Episcopal minister Dr. John Heyl Vincent (q.v.) and the philanthropist Lewis Miller as a center for the study of the Bible and the training of Sunday-school teachers; the first assembly, which was in the form of a camp meeting, met for a period of two weeks. With successive years the educational scope of the annual assembly greatly widened. At the present time it takes place during the entire months of July and August and its educational work comprises four main divisions: about 100 courses for which New York University gives university credit, including English, history, speech and the dramatic arts. foreign languages, science, mathematics, and business education; a school of music; a summer high school; and a department for adult education. Other features of the institution include lecture courses on the university extension model; public lectures and addresses by prominent men and women; and various forms of artistic entertainment, including about 30 symphony concerts given each summer by a symphony orchestra composed of 60 musicians from leading American orchestras; concerts by a chorus; and performances of plays and operas by resident companies. Many of the artistic events of Chautauqua are broadcast over nation-wide radio hookups.

Chautauqua exerts an educational influence throughout the United States by means of a system of home reading in literature, science, and other subjects carried on by the Chautauqua Literary and Scientific Circle (C.L.S.C.), organized in 1878. The four-year course is divided into the *Modern European Year,* the *Classical Year,* the *English Year,* and the *American Year.* In general, each year's course covers reading in the history, literature, social institutions, and other aspects of the learning and life of the particular period or nationality designated. The study of exact science or of languages is not taken up by the home reading course. Those enrolling in the C.L.S.C. read at home and meet in neighborhood groups once a week for discussion conducted by local leaders. The number of Chautauqua readers enrolled at one time has been as high as 750,000. Most of the readers do not finish the entire four-year course; about one half read for two years. Over 75,000 have gained the certificate that is granted with the completion of the entire course.

The physical plant of the institution covers about 350 acres and comprises about 85 public buildings, including the Hall of Philosophy; an amphitheater seating 6000; the Norton Memorial Hall, seating 1400 and used for plays, chamber music, and opera; the Smith Memorial Library; a building for religious teaching and conferences; a motion-picture theater; and a number of music studios. In addition, Chautauqua has for the use of students and visitors a large hotel, 40 smaller hotels and boarding houses, and several hundred cottages. The population of the village, a little over 300, is augmented to about 9000 each summer; in addition, about 40,000 people visit the institution each season.

The term *chautauqua* is applied in general to any assembly for educational purposes which is modeled after the summer assembly and schools of Chautauqua, N.Y.

CHAUVINISM, the name given to a policy of excessive national self-glorification, accompanied by an attitude of aggressive hostility to everything foreign. The word is of French origin, from the name of a French soldier, Nicolas Chauvin, who adored the memory of Napoleon and continually talked of Napoleon's achievements at Austerlitz and Jena, and of his own determination to take a brilliant revenge for the battle of Waterloo. The vaudevillists of the day seized upon him as a subject for the comic stage, and since then the term *Chauvinist* has come to have its present meaning.

CHAVANNES, Puvis de. See Puvis de Chavannes.

CHAVEZ, Carlos (1899–), Mexican composer and conductor, born in Mexico City. He studied music with Manuel Chavez, his brother, and with Asunción Parra and Padro Ogazon. In 1928 he was appointed director of the National Conservatory of Music in Mexico and the same year he organized and became the conductor of the Mexican Symphony Orchestra. Chavez was guest conductor of leading orchestras of the United States. Among his compositions are the ballet *H. P.* (1926–27), and the orchestral works *Sinfonia de Antigona*

(1933) and *Sinfonia India* (1936). He is the author of *Toward a New Music* (1942) and *Musical Thought* (1961).

CHAZARS. See Khazars.

CHEAPSIDE, a street in London extending from St. Paul's Churchyard east to Poultry and thence to the Mansion House. It is famous for fine stores, especially of jewelers and mercers, and for its historic past. It was originally an open square, where fairs and markets were held during the Middle Ages; its name is derived from this use. In the 14th century it was a tournament ground. Following the Great Fire of 1666 the square was narrowed down into a street. The well-known Church of St. Mary-le-Bow is one of the landmarks of Cheapside.

CHEAT. See Brome Grass.

CHEAT RIVER, a river of West Virginia, formed of four confluents, rising in the eastern part of the State, in the Allegheny Mountains, and uniting in Tucker Co. It flows through a region rich in iron and coal and joins the Monongahela R. in Pennsylvania, 4 m. from the State line. It is about 125 miles long, but drains a rather narrow area. It furnishes abundant water power and in parts of its course flows through narrow gorges and magnificent scenery.

CHECHEN or **TCHETCHEN,** a mountaineer people of the eastern Caucasus (see Caucasia), numbering about 435,000 and comprising the Chechens proper, who form the bulk of the population, and the Ingushes and other small groups. Their language, Tchetchentsish, is one of the independent non-Indo-European languages of Caucasia. Under their native Mohammedan chiefs, the Chechens fought against Russian aggression in the 18th and 19th centuries. In 1859, after the surrender of the chieftain Shamyl, many of them fled to Armenia. A considerable number of those who remained adopted the Greek Orthodox religion. In 1936 the Chechen area was organized as the Chechen-Inguish A.S.S.R. of Soviet Russia. This republic was dissolved in 1944 and then reconstituted in 1957.

CHECKERBERRY. See Partridgeberry.

CHECKERS, or Draughts, a game played on a checkered board, made square, divided into 64 equal square spaces colored alternately black and red or any two strongly contrasted colors. The draughts, or checkers, are circular and flat. There are many varieties of checkers, including Chinese, English, Polish, Spanish, Italian, and Turkish. A similar game was played by the Egyptians as early as 1600 B.C., and a form of it was popular in ancient Greece. The game is found among natives of New Zealand.

Two persons play the game, each having a set of 12 men, one set black, the other white, or red. The men may be placed either on the black or light squares, but they must all be placed on one color only. The men may be moved diagonally only, and one square at a time. If an enemy's man stands in the way, no move may take place unless there is a vacant square beyond into which the piece can be lifted. The one leaped over is "taken" and removed from the board. If there is an enemy's man in front of the new position, with an empty space beyond, the second man may also be taken; this maneuver is called a double jump. Triple and longer jumps are possible.

When a man on either side has made its way to the last row on the opposite side, it is entitled to be "crowned", that is, made into a "king". To indicate a king, a second man is placed on top of the first. Kings, like other men, can move only diagonally, and only one square at a time except when jumping opponent's men; however, they may move either backward or forward, and this additional power gives a great advantage to the player with the greatest number of kings.

The object of the game is to clear the board of all the opponent's men, or to hem them in so that they cannot be moved. If, when it is one player's turn to move, he has no piece which can be moved, he loses the game.

CHEDDAR, town of Somersetshire, England, on the s. side of the Mendip Hills and 22 m. by rail s.w. of Bristol. It lies at the entrance of the rocky Cheddar gorge, nearly 1 m. long and noted for the stalactite caverns in its limestone cliffs. Prehistoric remains have been discovered in the caverns, and Roman remains are found in the vicinity. Cheddar is noted for the cheese made there and named for it. See CHEESE. Pop. (1951) 2600.

CHEDUBA or **MAN-AUNG,** an island in the Bay of Bengal, about 10 m. off the coast of Arakan, Burma, of which it forms a part. It is of volcanic origin, about 20 m. long from N. to S., and about 17 m. wide. Along the coast are earthy cones, which emit mud and gas. The soil is fertile and there are deposits of silver, copper, and iron; the principal product, however, is petroleum. The port and chief village is Cheduba (pop. in 1953, 2635). Area, 220 sq.m.

CHEESE, a solid or semisolid food product prepared from milk. In the U.S. today it is almost invariably prepared from cow's milk, but the milk of ewes, mares, female goats, or other mammals is equally suitable for cheese making, and has been so used since prehistoric days.

The principal solid constituent of milk is casein (q.v.), a protein. The casein can be made to precipitate by the addition to milk of acid, or of rennet (q.v.) prepared from the gastric juice of calves. When milk is allowed to stand in a warm place, it "sours" because of the presence of bacteria which convert milk sugar into acid. This acid causes the casein to separate as a curd, leaving a thin, watery portion called whey. This was undoubtedly the earliest method of making cheese and is still used for making pot cheese and cottage cheese, although curd prepared with rennet is today preferred. The curd, however prepared, contains, in addition to protein, most of the other food value of the milk, including fat, minerals, sugar, and vitamins. It is compact, can easily be made solid, and can be preserved over long periods of time, advantages over milk which make cheese an important item in the diet of almost all primitive and many civilized peoples.

Cheddar or American cheese, which makes up about two thirds of U.S. cheese production, is manufactured from whole milk, and contains a small amount of fat. Cottage cheese and pot cheese, constituting about 20% of U.S. production, are made from skim milk, and contain very little fat. Cream cheese, constituting about 5% of U.S. production, is made from cream or cream-enriched milk, and contains from 10% to 50% of fat.

Cheese may be hard or soft, according to the amount of water left in it and the character of the curing. The ripening of cheese, on which the characteristic flavors of the different kinds depend, is due to the action of various kinds of bacteria. The principal hard cheeses are the common Cheddar cheese, the English Cheshire and Stilton, the Dutch Edam and Gouda, the Schweitzer (Swiss) or Emmenthaler (French product, known also as Gruyère), and the Italian Parmesan and Gorgonzola. Among the soft cheeses are Brie (*Fromage de Brie*), Camembert, Neufchâtel, and Limburger. Roquefort is a semisoft cheese made in France from sheep's milk.

In the U.S., cheese making was formerly a domestic operation conducted on farms. The first cheese factory was opened at Rome, N.Y., in 1851, and cheese factories have now practically superseded the making of cheeses on farms. About two thirds of the total national production is now in Wisconsin, and about half of the remainder is in New York. The average annual production amounts to more than 1 billion pounds. In addition, about 50 million pounds are imported yearly.

CHEETAH, or HUNTING LEOPARD, any feline carnivore of the genus *Acinonyx*. The cheetah is about the same weight as the leopard, but has a longer body and longer, slender limbs. It is also distinguished by its claws, which are short and almost nonretractile. The color is yellowish brown with black spots. The cheetah takes its prey by running, rather than by leaping from ambush. Deer and antelope are

Rapho-Guillumette (Ylla)
Asian cheetah, Acinonyx venatica

its chief prey, and the cheetah is often tamed and used for such hunting in India. The cheetah is widely distributed in the Old World tropics: *A. venatica* in Asia, and *A. jubatus* in Africa. Another African species, *A. rex*, is striped, rather than spotted.

CHEFOO, seaport of Shantung Province, China, on the N. shore of the Shantung peninsula, about 110 miles N.E. of Tsingtao, and about 100 miles S.S.E. of Port Arthur on the opposite shore of the Gulf of Pohai. Across the harbor on which Chefoo is situated is the village of Yentai, which is the actual port. In 1863 Chefoo was opened to foreign trade and later became a center for the export of raw silk. In Chefoo, in 1876, representatives of Great Britain and China signed the Chefoo Convention, opening a number of Chinese ports to foreign trade. Chefoo remained a treaty port until 1943, when treaties with the U.S. and Great Britain ended foreign trading rights in China. Pop. (1953 est.) 116,000.

CHEKA (from Russian *Chrezvychaĭnaya Komissiya,* "Extraordinary Commission"), former name for the secret police of the Union of Soviet Socialist Republics. The Cheka was founded December 20, 1917, to cope with sabotage and other counterrevolutionary activities against the Bolshevik government, which had come into being through the revolution of November 7. The Cheka's function was

at first limited to making preliminary investigations of people suspected of counterrevolutionary activities. But after the revival of terrorist activities against the government, including the wounding of Nikolai Lenin (q.v.) in Moscow on August 30, 1918, the Cheka was granted more extensive powers. These included the power of making summary arrests, and of judging and executing those found guilty. In 1922 the Cheka was reorganized as the G.P.U. (from the initial letters of the Russian words for Special Government Political Administration).

CHEKHOV, CHEKOV, or TCHEKHOV, ANTON PAVLOVICH (1860–1904), Russian dramatist and short-story writer, born in Taganrog, and educated at the University of Moscow. He wrote humorous stories and sketches for magazines while at the university. In 1884 he graduated with a degree in medicine. Afterward he lived in Moscow and continued to write for periodicals, practicing medicine very little. The first collection of his humorous writings, *Motley Stories,* appeared in 1886, and in the next year his first play, *Ivanov,* was produced in Moscow. In 1890 Chekhov visited eastern Siberia and wrote *Sakhalin* (1891), an exposure of the cruel penal system in force in the convict settlement on Sakhalin Island in the Pacific Ocean. Shortly after his return he went to live in Melikhovo, a country place near Moscow, where he remained with his family from 1892 to 1897. During a cholera epidemic (1892–93) he served as district supervisor of medical aid. In 1897 he discovered that he had tuberculosis, whereupon he moved to the Crimea, which has a salubrious climate; later he made frequent trips to health resorts in France and Germany. Toward the end of the century he met the brilliant Russian actor and producer Stanislavski (1863–1938), director of the Moscow Art Theater, which produced (1898) his play *The Sea Gull* (1896). This association of playwright and director, which continued until Chekhov's death, led to the production of his other famous plays, *Uncle Vanya* (1899), *The Three Sisters* (1901), and *The Cherry Orchard* (1904), as well as of a number of one-act dramas.

Chekhov began writing as a humorist, but after his first stories were collected in 1886 he experimented in a more serious vein, developing an allusive prose style and a distinctive use of scene and character strongly evocative of mood and atmosphere. After 1889 his grasp of form in both drama and fiction became assured. His greatest plays, cited above, and such short-story masterpieces as *Ward No. 6* (1892), *Peasants* (1897), and *The Teacher of Literature* (1904) belong to this last period. Among his collections of short stories are *The Kiss and Other Stories* (1910), *Darling and Other Stories* (1910), and *Duel and Other Stories* (1916).

Chekhov is one of the finest masters of the short story in modern literature. The themes he writes about originate in the ordinary course of life, principally among the landed gentry and the professional middle class. His characters express the insecurity of their status during the period before the 1905 revolution. Demoralized by self-doubt and a sense of futility, they can only react to situations, not create them. In this respect they are early examples of character types encountered later in 20th-century fiction, whose lives are disoriented by the complexity of the modern world. Although Chekhov seems most sympathetic to those of his characters who are sensitive enough to suffer, he lets them fulfill their own destinies. In the irony of this artistic detachment, he inherits the tradition of the French novelist Gustave Flaubert, i.e., he refuses to "play God" to them.

The innovation of the modern type of short story depending for its esthetic effect on mood and symbolism rather than on plot was largely due to Chekhov. He departed radically from treatment of the short story as a miniature novel with climax and resolution; his narratives are rather a thematic arrangement of impressions and ideas ending in a state of muted feeling. The effect of this new literary conception was very strong outside Russia and of decisive importance in the work of such later short-story writers as Katherine Mansfield, James Joyce, and Sherwood Anderson.

In the Russian theater Chekhov is pre-eminently the greatest representative of naturalism (q.v.), and *The Cherry Orchard* is one of the masterpieces of European prose drama. His plays, like his stories, are studies of spiritual failure, but they develop more fully the interaction of characters against the background of a society in disintegration. Chekhov carried the realism of the Norwegian poet and dramatist Henrik Ibsen a step further by making patterns of inconsequential action achieve dramatic force on the stage. The acting method Stanislavski perfected for the Moscow Art Theater is characterized by the sensitive emotional identification of the actor with his role, in contrast to the calculated portrayal of the role that typified the dominant French tradition. Chekhov found the new method a fitting ve-

Culver Service
Anton Pavlovitch Chekhov

hicle for his untheatrical plays. This marked departure from tradition was momentous in the history of the theater.

Chekov's work is not ambitious in design or extraordinarily profound; his achievement lies within the rational bounds of psychological subtlety. The height of his influence was reached in the 1920's, but his short stories are still widely read and his plays continue to appear frequently in theatrical repertories.

CHELAN LAKE, a lake in Chelan Co., Wash., in the Cascade Mountains. It is about 55 m. long and averages about 1 m. in width, and is the longest lake in the northwestern United States and one of the deepest in the country. It is of glacial origin, is fed by the Stehekin R., and empties into the Columbia R. at Chelan Falls. Chelan State Park is on the lake.

CHELSEA, a city of Suffolk Co., Mass., and a northern suburb of Boston, from which it is 3 m. distant. It is situated on a peninsula between the estuaries of Chelsea Creek and the Mystic R. On the north it adjoins the city of Everett. It is connected with Charlestown by a bridge across the Mystic R., and with Boston by ferry and rail. The city's principal buildings include the city hall, the courthouse, the United States naval and marine hospitals, the Massachusetts Soldiers' Home, and Ye Old

Pratt House. The U.S. Coast Guard Station in Chelsea is a supply depot for lighthouses.

Chelsea is principally a manufacturing city; its industries are lithography, fish canning, and the manufacture of shoes, elastic webbing, wallpaper, furniture, paints, chemicals, rubber goods, marine clocks, machine-shop and foundry products, and bakery products. It is an important center for trade in waste materials and junk.

Chelsea was founded in 1624 as Winnisimmet, and was a part of Boston until 1739 when it was incorporated as a township. In 1857 it was incorporated as a city. In 1908 a fire destroyed most of the city, which was rebuilt within two years. Pop. (1960) 33,749.

CHELSEA, a southwestern metropolitan borough of London, England, on the N. bank of the Thames River. Among its landmarks are the Royal Hospital, Chelsea (for disabled soldiers), begun in the reign of Charles II (1660–1685) and completed under the supervision of the architect Christopher Wren in 1692; the Sloane Botanic Gardens; and the Chelsea Embankment, on the Thames (laid out in 1871–74), a tree-lined promenade flanked by fine houses. Chelsea is noted principally for the manufacture, in the 18th century, of Chelsea china, and for its literary, artistic, and political associations. At various times in the 18th and 19th centuries, Chelsea was the home of Jonathan Swift, Richard Steele, Tobias Smollett, Robert Walpole, Joseph Turner, Dante Gabriel Rossetti, James MacNeill Whistler, Leigh Hunt, and Thomas Carlyle. Pop. (1961 prelim.) 47,085.

CHELTENHAM, a municipal and parliamentary borough, and resort town, of Gloucestershire, England, about 8 miles N.E. of the city of Gloucester. It lies in a picturesque valley, on the Chelt, a small stream which rises in the adjacent hills and flows into the Severn. Among the numerous churches of the town is the parish church of St. Mary, dating from the 14th century. Among the schools are the free grammar school (1576); Cheltenham College (1843), a private school for boys; and Ladies' College, Cheltenham (1854), a private school for girls.

Roman remains have been discovered at Cheltenham. In the 13th century the town was noted for its fairs and markets. After 1716, when mineral springs were discovered there, Cheltenham began to rise to importance as a health resort. The visit of George III in 1788 set upon it the seal of fashion. Pop. (1961 prelim.) 71,968.

CHELYABINSK, name of a Region and of its administrative center, in the Uralsk area of the Russian Soviet Federal Socialist Republic. The Region is situated in southwestern Siberia and borders on the European part of the Soviet Union. The Region is partly forested and contains many lakes and marshes. More than half of the land is under cultivation. Wheat, rye, oats, millet, and peas are grown; cattle, horses, sheep, and pigs are raised; and coal is mined. Industrial establishments include flour mills, breweries, distilleries, and the largest iron and steel works in Europe. The city of Chelyabinsk is the site of one of the largest tractor-building works of the Soviet Union and is an important railroad center. Other industries in the city include the manufacture of agricultural tools and leather products. Area of Region, 33,900 sq.m.; pop. (1959 est.) 2,979,000. Pop. of city (1960 est.) 709,000.

CHELYUSKIN, CAPE, a cape in northern Siberia, forming the northernmost point of the Asiatic continent. It is a portion of the tundra extending northward from the Taimir Peninsula to lat. 77° 35′ N.

CHEMICAL ANALYSIS, the separation of a compound substance into simple and elementary constituents. The term is opposite in meaning to *chemical synthesis*, which treats of the union of simple or elementary bodies to produce more complex compounds. Chemical analysis is of two kinds: *qualitative analysis*, which determines the quality or nature of the ingredients of a compound; and *quantitative analysis*, which estimates the exact proportion, by weight or volume, in which the several constituents are united.

The divisions of inorganic chemistry and organic chemistry (see CHEMISTRY: *Divisions*) have led to a corresponding classification of chemical analysis into *inorganic analysis*, comprehending the processes followed and the results obtained in the investigation of the atmosphere, water, soils, and rocks; and *organic analysis*, treating of the modes of isolation and the nature of substances composed principally of carbon compounds. Both these departments afford examples of what are called *proximate* and *ultimate analysis*. Proximate analysis is the resolution of a compound substance into components which are themselves compound; whereas ultimate analysis comprehends the disunion of a compound into its elements. Organic analysis affords good examples of each class: thus, ordinary wheat flour, when subjected to proximate analysis, yields, as its proximate components, gluten, albumen, starch, sugar, gum, oil, and mineral matter; each of these proximate ingredients is in itself compound, and when they undergo ultimate analysis, the gluten and albumen yield, as their ultimate elements, carbon, hydrogen, oxygen, nitrogen, sulfur, and phosphorus; the starch, sugar, gum, and oil contain carbon, hydrogen, and oxygen.

There are three fundamental methods used in analysis: the volumetric, in which the volumes in solution of the elements present are determined; the gravimetric, in which the substance is precipitated and weighed; and the spectroscopic, in which the influence of the substance on the spectrum is recorded. Electrolytic methods are those involving the decomposition of substances by means of an electric current; see ELECTROCHEMISTRY. Modern developments in the field of analysis include microanalysis, which is used when the size of the sample is extremely minute. Techniques of this kind are employed extensively in the field of atomic energy (q.v.); see MICROCHEMISTRY; RADIOCHEMISTRY.

Organic Analysis. The chemical analysis of organic compounds differs from inorganic analysis because of the enormous number of organic compounds which have the same ultimate analysis but differ in structural formula. In inorganic chemistry it makes little difference whether the formula of the mineral realgar is written As_2S_2 or AsS; it is frequently given in either form. In organic chemistry, on the other hand, there is little similarity between acetylene, C_2H_2, and benzene, C_6H_6. Moreover, there are other compounds besides benzene which have the formula C_6H_6: divinylacetylene, for example.

Analysis of an organic compound which has not previously been analyzed, must, therefore, proceed through the stages of ultimate analysis and molecular weight determination to establish the empirical formula, and must then proceed to an elaborate proximate analysis to establish the structural formula. Synthesis is always the final test of correctness of the formula. The synthetic product is then proven identical with the substance analyzed by a "mixed melting point" (see FREEZING POINT).

In analysis for identification, physical properties are useful, melting point is a particularly valuable aid, and a "mixed melting point" is positive proof of identification.

Proximate analysis of organic compounds establishes the presence or absence of such groups as alcohol, amine, double-bond, rings, or inorganic constituents such as chlorine. It may be either qualitative or quantitative. Quantitative analysis of acid, for example, might be used to determine the number of acid groups in a molecule of undetermined

structure, or to determine the strength of a sample of acetic acid (vinegar).

Ultimate analysis of organic compounds is concerned chiefly with carbon, hydrogen, and nitrogen. Other elements, if present, are determined in the same fashion as in inorganic analysis. When the amounts of other elements in a compound have been measured, oxygen is usually determined by difference, i.e., by subtracting the known percentages of other elements from 100.

Techniques of Quantitative Ultimate Organic Analysis. Carbon and hydrogen are measured at the same time. A small sample of the substance is placed in a long glass tube and heated; oxygen, obtained from carefully purified air or copper oxide, converts the carbon into carbon dioxide and the hydrogen into water. The carbon dioxide is absorbed in a strong alkali and the water in calcium chloride or similar dehydrating substance. The absorbents are weighed before and after absorption, and the amounts of carbon and hydrogen calculated.

The amount of nitrogen may be determined in two ways. In the Dumas method, the substance is heated in a glass tube, as above, in a stream of carbon dioxide gas. The substance is decomposed into nitrogen, water, and carbon dioxide. The carbon dioxide is absorbed, and the nitrogen collected over a solution of potassium hydroxide and its volume measured. In the Kieldahl method, the nitrogen is converted into ammonia, the amount of ammonia being determined by application of standard acid-alkali volumetric methods.

The modern tendency in organic analysis is to use "micro methods", in which the sample to be analyzed may be as small as a few micrograms (less than a millionth of an ounce). Microanalysis is essential in chemical investigations of such substances as trace elements and vitamins (qq.v.) and in the examination of foods and drugs.

Industrial Applications. Industrial analysis involves the examination of substances in industrial laboratories to determine their nature and purity. It includes commercial analysis, pharmaceutical analysis, and other practical types of analysis. Although it may use any of the techniques of an academic laboratory, and is both qualitative and quantitative, it is generally restricted to proximate analysis. Industrial analysis differs from inorganic or organic analysis in dealing usually with complex mixtures, to which it is impossible to apply tests having sufficient specificity to respond to the presence of a given ingredient without being influenced by the other substances present in the mixture. To such a mixture it is necessary to apply many physical processes in the hope that these will so separate the constituents as to render it possible to recognize them either by appearance, odor, or specific test. Thus a knowledge of experimental physics, no less than of chemistry, is essential to the successful analyst. The following paragraphs indicate the physical processes which yield the most information about an unknown commercial mixture.

Distillation. The mixture being placed in a glass flask furnished with a thermometer, heat is applied, and the boiling point noted. If the boiling point gradually rises, then the mixture contains more than one volatile liquid; and by separating the various portions of distillate, according to the temperature at which they pass over, it is often possible to obtain samples sufficiently pure to be recognized. The term *fractionation* or *fractional distillation* is applied to this method. If a nonvolatile residue remains in the flask, it must be examined from other points of view.

Density. If the unknown substance is a liquid, its density may be determined merely by noting the level at which a hydrometer floats in it. Commercial acids, sugar solutions, and solutions of many other chemicals are regularly measured in this way to determine their concentration. Measurement of the density of solids is more difficult, but often useful.

Solution. Substances may frequently be identified by the nature of the chemicals which attack them or the solvents which dissolve them. For instance, a drop of nitric acid will attack brass but not gold. A solvent, such as water, alcohol, ether, or benzene, may be shaken with the substance under examination, and in many cases will dissolve one ingredient, to the exclusion of others.

Rotation of the Polarized Ray. Many substances have the power of rotating the plane of polarization of a ray of light and this rotation is often sufficient to detect the presence and the proportion of the substance to which it is due. Such substances as albumen, alkaloids, camphor, sugar, and turpentine exhibit this property.

Fluorescence. This phenomenon is often helpful in commercial analysis. For example, when fluorescence is not present it is possible to pronounce the intense bitterness of a sirup to be due not to quinine, which fluoresces, but to some other bitter ingredient. See FLUORESCENCE AND PHOSPHORESCENCE.

Melting and Solidifying Point. The knowledge of such data is important, as in the case in which common or other resins have been mixed with small pieces of amber. In such cases the more fusible resin melts and runs away, leaving the bodies of higher melting point. In cases in which no separation takes place, as with various kinds of wax, determination of the melting point enables the presence of paraffin or other foreign bodies to be detected.

Ignition on a piece of platinum or a porcelain dish is the simplest method of removing organic matter from inorganic, the latter usually remaining behind as a residue.

Sublimation. When carefully heated under a watch glass, many substances yield sublimates having a characteristic crystalline form, which is easily recognized when examined under the microscope.

Medical Applications. A type of chemical analysis called medical, or physiological, analysis is applied in the investigation of vital fluids, such as blood, sputum, and urine. Medical analysis actually antedated ordinary chemical analysis; the present scientific names of the two types of diabetes, *insipidus* and *mellitus* (Lat. *mel*, "honey"), derive from an ancient method of diagnosis by a crude analysis of the urine for sugar. Modern diagnosis leans heavily on accurate analysis, and many laboratories specialize in physiological analyses and such special analyses as biopsy (q.v.) and blood counts(see BLOOD). Chemical analysis is applied also to identification of drugs and measurement of their strength and purity. In many cases such analysis follows the routine methods of industrial analysis. For such drugs as vitamins which act in minute amounts, the only available methods of procedure are biological assay, the actual testing of the drug on laboratory animals, or microbiological assay, in which the test is made on microorganisms. S.Z.L.

CHEMICAL ENGINEERING, that branch of engineering which encompasses the design, construction, and management of factories in which the essential manufacturing operations consist of chemical reactions. The province of the chemical engineer includes such diverse operations as the manufacture of nitric acid, the brewing of beer, and the processing of textiles. He must be conversant with other branches of engineering, particularly mechanical, but his field is set apart by the study of the so-called "unit operations". The operation of drying, for example, is based on essentially the same principles whether it is applied to saltpeter, malt, or wool. The chemical engineer divides an entire manufacturing process into separate unit operations, each of which he studies quantitatively and also in its relation to the rest of the process.

Among the important classical unit operations of chemical engineering are: flow of fluids; flow of heat; chemical reactions (divided into classes, depending, for example, on whether the reactants are liquid and solid, or solid and gas); combustion (a specific type of chemical reaction); crystallization; sedimentation; filtration; crushing and grinding; screening; and the various processes involving vaporization and condensation, notably evaporation, absorption, extraction, distillation, drying, and air conditioning. Among the more recently developed unit operations are gaseous diffusion (employed in the production of uranium fuel for atomic-energy plants; see DIFFUSION) and molecular distillation (used, for example, in the purification of vitamins). Further information on most of these unit operations will be found under individual headings; see, for example, DISTILLATION; FILTRATION.

CHEMICAL GARDENING. See HYDROPONICS.

CHEMICAL REACTION. See REACTION, CHEMICAL.

CHEMICAL SENSE IN ANIMALS, the capacity of an animal for receiving and reacting to a stimulus of a purely chemical nature. The criterion of the chemical sense is to be found in the specialized mode of behavior with which the animal responds to the particular class of objects concerned. Many of the lowest forms of animals (e.g., ameba) respond to the presence of chemicals in their environment in the same way that they respond to mechanical contact with a solid object; they cannot, however, be said to give evidence of a chemical sense, since the identity of response to mechanical and chemical stimuli shows no indication of a special experience concomitant with the one kind of stimulation and not with the other. A little higher in the biological scale the specialized response is found; while still higher there seems to be a difference in the reaction of the animal to substances in solution and to those diffused in air, a difference which has led to the discrimination of two senses, taste and smell.

Among the coelenterates is first found evidence of a separate chemical sense. The hydra responds to food by seizing it with its tentacles, a performance never elicited by mechanical stimulation. Sea anemones exhibit at least two responses to chemical substances. In the one, the positive reaction, a particle of food is seized by the outer tentacles and passed on by means of the inner tentacles to the mouth; in the other, the negative reaction, the tentacles withdraw in the presence of certain chemicals, such as quinine. In both of these animals the difference in the character of response to chemical and mechanical stimulation indicates an independent chemical sense. In other members of the group, however, the response to both sorts of excitation is the same, although the chemical stimulus seems to be more readily effective, or, as is the case in jellyfish, effective only in certain parts of the creature.

Higher in the evolutionary scale, the evidences of the chemical sense become more abundant and more striking. The flatworms show a complex feeding reaction. One form of earthworm will burrow only in the presence of the juices from manure, which constitutes its usual environment. There is some evidence of both taste and smell in snails; starfish perceive food at a distance. Most of the Crustacea show a general restlessness when in the presence of food, and it is thought that in some forms chemical stimulation is effective in guiding the male to the female. Spiders give evidence of smell, in that they will move away from glass rods, dipped in certain oils, which are held behind them.

In insects there is a development in the sense of smell, both in respect to sensitivity and in respect to the number of discriminable smell qualities. Evidence of extreme olfactory sensitivity is seen in the mating of moths. A male moth, when liberated over a mile away from the only female in the region, has been known to find her within a very short time. In another instance, a female hatched in a region where her species was practically nonexistent was visited, within a few hours after she became mature, by 60 males. When the female was placed in a tightly sealed box, however, no males were attracted. Ants appear to be sensitive to a considerable number of different smell qualities, which play a part apparently distinguish the smell of food and in determining their complex behavior. Ants of their larvae, and discriminate between nest mates and foreigners also in terms of smell. They are guided in the paths to and from the nest largely by smell, and it has been suggested that the ability of certain forms to recognize, upon coming at random across a path, the direction to the nest as distinct from the direction from it, is in some way due to an olfactory perception. The fact that the antennae, which bear the organs of smell, are movable, makes it possible that ants may have an olfactory space perception not unlike

U. S. Army Photo

Testing a flame thrower, a military device used in chemical warfare. This light, compact type of one-shot flame thrower is designed for inclusion in a paratrooper's equipment.

tactual space perception in man. Bees are, perhaps, no less well endowed for olfactory discrimination, although vision plays a more important role in their habits than it does with ants. One investigator finds evidence of a large number of specifically different smell qualities, such as those of the individual workers, the queen, the drones, the larvae, food, wax, and honey.

There is no conclusive evidence for a chemical sense in fishes, amphibia, or reptiles, although it is suspected in fishes. Most birds are probably without the power of smell.

Mammals may be said to possess capacity for taste and smell. Such aquatic animals as whales, porpoises, and seals form a probable exception as regards smell. In other members olfactory sensitivity is great. Animals, such as the dog, which are dependent upon smell in daily life, sense faint odors and appear to isolate a single smell component within a complex mixture.

For details of behavior of particular forms, see articles under names of those animals. See TROPISM.

CHEMICAL WARFARE, a term popularly synonymous with gas warfare, but technically including also the use of smoke, incendiaries, and similar chemical agents which, in the U.S. Army, are under the jurisdiction of the Chemical Warfare Service. See PYROTECHNY.

The Greek historian Thucydides records a battle in the year 431 B.C. in which a town was attacked with burning pitch and sulfur; the fumes presumably acted as a poison gas while the burning materials acted as incendiaries designed to set fire to the town. Incendiaries were occasionally used in warfare after that time, but poison gas was not effectively used before April, 1915.

The standard incendiary bomb at the be-

ginning of World War II consisted of a case of magnesium metal filled with thermite, a mixture of aluminum and iron oxide. The burning of such a bomb cannot be extinguished with water; it will burn its way through a steel plate almost as quickly as a rock sinks in water. In the autumn of 1940 a large part of London was gutted by fires started by such bombs dropped from German aircraft.

The incendiary bomb developed by the U.S. during World War II consisted of gasoline gelatinized by several substances, the most important of which is called *Napalm* and consists of soaplike chemicals. These bombs have the advantage not only of being violently incendiary and inextinguishable by water, but of being extremely sticky; the bomb explodes on impact and scatters burning blobs of jelly which cling to any surface they strike. With such bombs, the U.S. Army Air Force devastated most of the large Japanese cities during 1945. Flame throwers, containing jellied gasoline or other combustible oils, were particularly valuable in World War II and in the Korean War for routing enemy troops from pillboxes and other strong positions. A small flame thrower was carried on a man's back, while large ones were mounted on tanks. Another incendiary substance, white phosphorus, was used as an antipersonnel agent; artillery shells filled with phosphorus, exploding near personnel, spattered them with small pieces of material which continued to burn even when imbedded in the flesh.

Screening smokes are used to screen movements and activity on land or at sea, to blanket the enemy, to inactivate observers, to spot artillery fire and bombing, and to disguise clouds of poison gas. The most important chemical smokes are white phosphorus and a hexachlorethane-zinc mixture, both of which are solids producing smoke on burning; and titanium tetrachloride and a sulfur trioxide-chlorsulfonic acid mixture, both of which are liquids producing smoke when exposed to a humid atmosphere.

The term "poison gas" is used to include gases, liquids, and solids which produce a toxic or irritating physiological effect (see GAS WARFARE). The use in warfare of chemicals produced by bacteria or other living organisms is included under the term "biological warfare" (q.v.).

CHEMISTRY, the science of the composition of substances, and of changes in their composition. The outer limits of this science cannot clearly be demarcated, for it underlies all other natural sciences to the extent that the properties of the material bodies considered by other sciences are influenced by their chemical composition. Thus, chemistry merges with physics in such subjects as the behavior of solids, liquids, and gases; the nature, production, and effects of heat; the chemical production and chemical effects of electricity; and the constitution of the atom. Chemistry provides the fundamental principles of the biological sciences insofar as the life processes of plant and animal organisms are dependent upon the substances which compose their bodies or furnish their food, and upon the changes which occur within their bodies in the maintenance of life. To the geologist, chemistry supplies data concerning the materials which form the earth, and to the astronomer it furnishes information about the composition of the sun, stars, and other celestial bodies.

History. *Ancient Period.* Among the earliest chemical operations consciously performed by primitive man were the production of fire, the tanning of skins, the firing of clay, the fermentation of fruit juices, and the making of glass, soaps, poisons, perfumes, cosmetics, and pigments. The handicrafts of primitive man led him to the discovery of rocks from which metals, chiefly copper, tin, and iron, could be extracted with the aid of fire. Steel was made as early as 3000 B.C. The first man known to history to propose a theory of the composition of substances was Thales, of Miletus in Asia Minor, who in the 6th century B.C. upheld the idea that all things are composed of water. This theory was probably suggested to him by such observations as that water is necessary for plant growth, that plants are moist within, that plants form the ultimate source of the food of animals, that soil is deposited from water, that water dries

and forms an atmospheric gas, and that water freezes into a hard solid. Philosophers who succeeded Thales identified the primary element of all things with air or breath; fire; a combination of earth, air, fire, and water; undifferentiated matter; and abstract concepts such as the infinite, number, and being. In the 5th century B.C., two Greeks, Leucippus and Democritus, anticipated the modern atomic theory by declaring that material bodies are composed of tiny, indivisible particles of different kinds, which by combining in many ways, form all the substances of the universe, much as all the words of a language may be formed by different combinations of the same letters of its alphabet (see ATOM AND ATOMIC THEORY). Subsequent philosophers directed attention to problems of the social, rather than the natural sciences, and further speculation on the composition of matter was abandoned until the Middle Ages.

Medieval Period. The medieval "alchemists" struggled chiefly with two problems: the transformation of other metals into gold; and the preparation of an "elixir" which would restore youth and prolong life. Most of their wizardry was futile, cryptic, and fraudulent. However, their labors led to the discovery of previously unknown substances. For example, among the acids, they prepared oil of vitriol (the modern sulfuric acid), aqua fortis (nitric acid), and muriatic acid (hydrochloric acid), in addition to the oldest known acid, acetic acid (vinegar or sour wine). Soda and potash (now sodium carbonate and potassium carbonate) were their "mild alkalis"; caustic soda and caustic potash (now sodium hydroxide and potassium hydroxide), their "caustic alkalis", produced by dissolving the mild alkalis in water and adding lime, a material obtained by roasting limestone or chalk. They learned that mixtures of acids and alkalis yielded salts upon evaporation. The alchemists also invented chemical apparatus of various types and devised techniques of laboratory manipulation. The Swiss physician Philippus Paracelsus in the 16th century sought to turn chemical investigations to the service of medicine, and thus founded the school of iatrochemistry. He and his followers adopted the theory, held by some alchemists, that the basic elements of all things are mercury, sulfur, and salt, rather than earth, air, fire, and water, as the ancients had taught.

Rise of Modern Chemistry. Modern chemistry began with the work and writings of the British scientist Robert Boyle, who drew attention to the chief errors of al-

"The Alchemist," a painting by David Teniers the Younger

chemical theory impeding the development of a scientific chemistry. He held that the language in which both alchemists and iatrochemists expressed their principles was so mystical as to be devoid of sense; that specific terms were employed in such a variety of meanings as to produce hopeless confusion; and that it was futile to try to analyze the composition of myriad substances while limiting such composition to a few elements chosen arbitrarily. He proposed definitions of compound and element: a compound is a substance which can be decomposed into simpler ingredient substances, elements; an element is a substance which cannot be separated into simpler components by chemical methods.

The erroneous phlogiston (q.v.) theory introduced by the German chemists Johann Joachim Becher and Georg Ernst Stahl in the 17th century was an attempt to combine a multitude of observed facts under a single explanation. According to this theory, when a substance burns, an ingredient called phlogiston departs in the flame, leaving a "calx" or ash. As early as the 8th century the Arabian scientist Geber reputedly observed the fact that lead or tin, when heated in air, is converted into a calx (now called oxide) which is heavier than the original metal; by the 17th century it was known that the extra weight came from the air, and also that the weight did not increase indefinitely.

Among the first to study chemical changes by careful experiment, to produce evidence opposed to the phlogiston theory, and scientifically to establish chemical facts, was the British chemist Joseph Black. Others, such as the British chemists John Mayow (1640–79) and Joseph Priestley, established a number of important facts regarding the chemistry of combustion.

It was the French chemist Antoine Laurent Lavoisier who forced the abandonment of the erroneous phlogiston theory and built the foundation of modern chemistry. In 1770 Lavoisier, using accurate balances and weighing techniques, found that metals increased in weight when burned and that the increase in weight was equal to the air (oxygen) that disappeared. Phlogiston consequently would have to possess a negative weight. In the course of these experiments, Lavoisier enunciated the law of conservation of matter, which had been tacitly assumed by Black: that matter is uncreatable and indestructible by human agency, and that there is thus an equal quantity of matter both before and after any chemical change.

A gas which bubbles up from metals immersed in dilute acids was named "inflammable air" by Priestley in 1781, after its most curious property. He noticed that the explosion of this gas in air formed dew, and the British chemist Henry Cavendish, by burning large quantities of "inflammable air", proved that this combustion produced a

English chemists. Left to right: Robert Boyle, who established some of the first principles of modern chemistry; Joseph Priestley, who conducted experiments in combustion; John Dalton, first man to teach the atomic theory of the constitution of matter.

The French chemist Antoine Lavoisier instructs the young Éleuthère Irénée du Pont.

Alessandro Volta demonstrates his electro-chemical cell to Napoleon I.

A 19th-century chemical laboratory in the town of Giessen, Germany

liquid in no way different from water. Lavoisier, who also performed the experiment, renamed inflammable air "hydrogen" (Gr., "water-former"), and recognized water as its oxide.

Chemical Principles. Early in the 19th century the French chemist Joseph Louis Proust distinguished and defined a compound, a mixture, and a solution: a chemical *compound* is a homogeneous substance in which the properties of its ingredient elements have quite disappeared, and in which new properties are found, unpredictable from those of its elements; a *mixture* is a substance in which the ingredients retain their properties, and the properties of the whole are the average properties of the ingredients; and a *solution* is a mixture in which the ingredients are distributed homogeneously. Proust also proposed the "law of fixed proportions": that the proportions of the elements in any pure compound are invariable. A "law of multiple proportions" proposed by the British chemist John Dalton and a "law of reciprocal proportions" advanced by the German chemist Jeremias B. Richter (1762–1807), maintained that to every element can be assigned a "combining weight", in which, or in simple multiples of which, it combines with others.

These facts led Dalton to his atomic theory of the constitution of matter: that all elements are composed of tiny, invisible particles which Dalton called "simple atoms". The simple atoms of an element join with those of other elements in definite ways, and thus form "compound atoms" of the resulting compound.

The combining weights of elements, that is, the ratios among the weights of elements which consistently enter into combination. could be determined experimentally. However, from these combining weights the chemist could not deduce (nor did Dalton's atomic theory disclose) the atomic weights, that is the relative weights of individual atoms, since it was uncertain how many of each kind of simple atom were joined in the compound atom. This knowledge was desirable for mathematical calculation of the quantities of reagents and products involved in a chemical change. A clue to the problem was furnished by the French chemist Joseph Louis Gay-Lussac, who observed that gases at the same pressure and temperature react in simple ratio by volume, and that if the product of the reaction is a gas, its volume bears a simple numerical ratio to those of its elements, but is not the sum of the volumes of its elements. Thus, two volumes of ammonia gas can be decomposed into one volume of nitrogen and three of hydrogen. If the atoms of all gaseous elements, at equal pressure and temperature, were equally spaced, as Gay-Lussac thought, so that equal volumes of gases contained equal numbers of simple atoms, this could not be true also for compound atoms. This difficulty was resolved by the Italian chemist Amedeo Avogadro by the simple expedient of supposing the ultimate particles of an elementary gas each to consist of two atoms joined together. He called such a combination a "molecule", and applied this name also to the "compound atoms" of Dalton; see AVOGADRO'S LAW. On this assumption, the number of atoms which join in composing a molecule becomes obvious, and the relative atomic weights of elements can be determined. However, the hypothesis of Avogadro was neglected for 50 years, during which time hopeless confusion characterized the subject of atomic weights, and during which time a chemist regarded it as a mark of independence of thought to have his own table of atomic weights. Finally, the theory of Avogadro was revived by his countryman Stanislao Cannizzaro, who composed the first modern table of atomic weights.

Chemical Symbolism and Equations. Since medieval times, chemists have used symbols to denote the substances they considered elements. The present symbols consist of the initial letter, or initial two letters, of the Latin name of the element or, in the case of a recently discovered element, of its name in some modern language. The same symbols are adopted by all chemists throughout the world. A chemical reaction is expressed by an "equation" in which atoms of the reacting elements are expressed by symbols, with numerical subscripts following them to denote the numbers of each atom in the molecule. Numbers are prefixed to denote the least number of atoms or molecules which can be involved in the transformation. An arrow separates the reacting substances from their products. Thus, the combination of one volume of nitrogen, represented by the symbol N, with 3 of hydrogen, represented by H, to form ammonia, NH_3, is represented thus:

$$N_2 + 3H_2 \rightarrow 2NH_3.$$

In other words, molecules of hydrogen and nitrogen are, according to Avogadro's hypothesis, diatomic; this fact is acknowledged by the subscripts 2. Ammonia is a compound the molecule of which consists of one atom of nitrogen linked to 3 of hydrogen; this combination is expressed as NH_3. The least number of atoms which may be involved are one diatomic molecule of nitrogen, N_2, and 3 diatomic molecules of hydrogen; their combination will produce 2 molecules of ammonia; see NITROGEN FIXATION. An equation is "balanced" when the number of atoms of each kind in the reacting substances equals the number of atoms of that kind in the products. Thus, the 6 atoms in the 3 diatomic molecules of hydrogen, in the above example, equal the 6 atoms of hydrogen in the 2 molecules of ammonia, each of which contains 3.

The proportionate weights both of reagents and of products in a reaction depend upon the number of atoms of each kind involved and the relative weights (atomic weights) of each kind of atom. Calculation of such proportionate weights may therefore be accomplished by multiplying the number of each kind of atom by its atomic weight (see ELEMENTS, CHEMICAL), and adding the products to obtain the molecular weights of the compounds. In the illustrative reaction, nitrogen has an atomic weight of 14, and hydrogen of 1. (Whatever the actual weight of a nitrogen atom is, it is approximately 14 times as heavy as a hydrogen atom.) Hence, 2 atoms of nitrogen have a proportionate weight of 28; 3 molecules of diatomic hydrogen, a weight of 6; and each molecule of ammonia, a weight of 14 plus 3, or 17. Thus, 28 parts by weight of nitrogen and 6 of hydrogen form 34 parts by weight of ammonia. See REACTION, CHEMICAL.

Radicals. Among the earliest facts learned from the analysis of organic compounds was that a certain group of elements may be found together in different compounds and enter as a group into chemical changes. For example, sulfuric acid (H_2SO_4), copper sulfate ($CuSO_4$), sodium sulfate (Na_2SO_4), and other sulfates all contain the group SO_4, known as the "sulfate radical". Such groups, called "radicals", could be replaced as a whole by elements or other radicals. A study of such replacement in organic compounds led the French chemist Jean B. Dumas (q.v.) to enunciate his theory of "types", series of compounds which are structurally analogous. The theory was extended by other chemists, chiefly the German August W. Hoffmann and the Frenchman Charles Frederic Gerhardt (1816–56).

Isomerism. Another remarkable result of the early analyses of organic compounds was the discovery that two compounds, might nonetheless be composed of the same elements in precisely the same proportions. The identity of composition of substances with dissimilar properties was noticed, in the case of tartaric and racemic acids, by the Swedish chemist Jöns Jacob Berzelius, who in 1827 speculated that either the molecules of two substances contain the same number of the same kinds of atoms linked together in different arrangements (isomerism), or that the kinds and relative numbers of atoms in the molecules of isomers are the same, but the absolute numbers of atoms are different (polymerism). Many cases of both types occur.

Valency. Restatement by Cannizzaro of Avogadro's theory made apparent a property of elements known as valency, the number of atoms of hydrogen with which one atom of the element can combine, or which it can replace. See VALENCE. The English chemist Edward Frankland, who is commonly regarded as the author of the theory of valency, pointed out that the inorganic compounds of nitrogen, phosphorus, and arsenic are consistently formed by the union of their atoms with 3 or 5 atoms of monovalent elements. That oxygen has a valency of two is seen in its compounds such as water, H_2O, in which the oxygen atom holds two atoms of a univalent element. In the oxide of phosphorus, P_2O_5 (phosphorus pentoxide), phosphorus has evidently a valency of 5, while the valency of oxygen is 2.

The concept of valency furnished the clue to the structure of organic compounds. This problem was finally completely solved by the German chemist Friedrich August Kekule, who supposed carbon to have a valency of 4. His idea was based on a study of marsh gas, now called methane (q.v.), a gas which forms from the decomposition of organic matter. When Kekule adopted, with Cannizzaro, the atomic weight of 12 for carbon, he stated the formula of marsh gas as CH_4. In this compound, carbon has evidently a valency of 4, and Kekule pointed out that in all the simplest compounds of carbon, one atom of carbon holds 4 atoms of a univalent, or 2 atoms of a divalent element, and that the sum of the valencies of all the atoms united with one atom of carbon is always 4. In a molecule which contains 2 carbon atoms, the combining power of the two atoms is not 8, according to Kekule, but 6, since two of the affinities of the carbon atoms are used in holding each other. Kekule's realization of the quadrivalency of carbon permitted a visualization of the spatial arrangements of the atoms within the molecule. He devised graphic formulas, known as "Kekule's sausages", which represented atoms as ovals with appropriate numbers of bulges to represent the valencies. These diagrams were simplified by the Scottish chemist Alexander Crum Brown (1838–1922), who, in 1863, represented valencies by lines radiating from the symbol of the element. The phenomena of isomerism could now be explained by determining experimentally, in various reactions, the structural arrangements of the atoms in the molecules of isomeric substances.

Divisions. Chemistry is divided into two parts, inorganic and organic, treating, respectively, substances that are not now, and never were, ingredients of living things; or substances in, or derived from, living things. Practically all organic compounds are composed of carbon and hydrogen; in most cases together with oxygen, often with nitrogen, and sometimes with other elements. Inorganic compounds comprise all the compounds of other elements. It was once thought that organic compounds could be synthesized only by the life processes of plants and animals, and that it was no more possible to make them in the laboratory than to make living substances. When in 1828 the German chemist Friedrich Wöhler synthesized urea, a typical animal product, he demonstrated that the separation between the organic and inorganic divisions was not as fixed as was supposed. Since then, thousands of organic substances have been found capable of chemical synthesis. The division of chemistry into two groups, one comprising the compounds of a single element, carbon, the other the compounds of the remaining elements has persisted for convenience.

Physical chemistry deals with the application to chemistry of physical laws capable of mathematical treatment; electrochemistry, with the chemical production and chemical effects of electricity. Like other sciences, chemistry may be divided into pure and applied branches. In applied chemistry are found such specialized fields as agricultural, industrial, and pharmaceutical chemistry; and the chemical techniques developed for specific materials, such as plastics, rubber, dyes, explosives, and others. Analytical chemistry is concerned with methods of determining the chemical ingredients of compounds, mixtures, and alloys.

Analysis. Analysis of a material the composition of which is unknown is accomplished by decomposing it, or by causing it to react with a known substance in order to form a product with a distinctive color, odor, or physical appearance. Thus, the British scientist William Nicholson (1753–1815) decomposed water, by means of an electric current, into hydrogen and oxygen. Thus, Antoine Lavoisier proved that organic compounds contain carbon and hydrogen by combining them with oxygen (burning them) and showing that the combustion produced "fixed air", which he recognized as an oxide of carbon, and water, which he identified as the oxide of hydrogen. The quantity of an element present may be determined by weighing, if it is a solid or liquid; by calculating its weight from its pressure, temperature, and volume, if it is a gas; or by calculating its weight in the compound it forms. See CHEMICAL ANALYSIS.

Electrochemistry. The science of the chemical production and effects of electricity began with the invention of the electric cell and battery by the Italian physicist Alessandro Volta in 1800. With the voltaic cell, many experimenters tested the electrical conductivity of various substances, and the British scientist William Nicholson (1753–1815) observed that the passage of electric current through water decomposes it into hydrogen and oxygen. He observed further that certain substances (acids, bases, and salts) increased the electrical conductivity of water remarkably and, in so doing, were in most cases decomposed by the electric current. Any substance which thus conducts electricity is called an electrolyte. The British scientist William Cruikshank (1745–1800) found that electric current precipitates silver and copper from solutions of their compounds; from his observation has developed the process of electroplating (q.v.). The quantitative laws of electrolytic decomposition (see ELECTROCHEMISTRY) were investigated about 1830 by the British chemist Michael Faraday, who concluded that the weight of an element liberated depends only upon the amount of current and the length of time that it flows, although other factors, such as the voltage and resistance of the circuit, affect the strength of the current. He discovered also that the weights of different elements liberated are proportional to their combining weights. In 1806, Theodor Grotthus (1785–1822) proposed the theory that molecules of electrolytes exchange atoms with one another all along the line from the anode (positive terminal) to the cathode (negative terminal). Faraday later assigned the name "ion" (Gr., "traveler") to such moving atoms. In 1887, the Swedish chemist Svante Arrhenius (q.v.) proposed the theory that the freedom of ions (either ionized atoms or ionized radicals) to move exists not only while current passes, but also permanently. He declared that when an electrolyte is dissolved, its molecules separate into two types of ions, of equal and opposite electric charges.

When current passes, the electrodes attract the ions of opposite charge, causing the decomposition of the electrolyte, and the deposition of material. The charge on an ion is proportional to its valency. The current is carried by these ions, and may actually consist of the migration of these charged particles. See IONIZATION.

This theory of ionization explained also the fact that an electrolyte in solution causes an abnormally large rise in the boiling point of its solvent, an abnormally large depression of its freezing point, and abnormally large effects on its vapor pressure and osmotic pressure (see OSMOSIS), behaving as if more molecules are present than actually are dissolved.

Physical Chemistry. This branch of the science deals with the borderline between physics and chemistry, and in particular with those aspects of chemical phenomena which are subject to mathematical analysis. The two most fertile fields for this type of analysis are *chemical kinetics,* the study of the mechanism and speed of chemical reactions, and *thermodynamics,* the study of the energy produced or absorbed by chemical reactions, and the effects of heat and other forms of energy on these reactions. These two fields, which absorb most of the attention of physical chemists, are mutually exclusive: thermodynamics is concerned solely with the materials and products of a reaction, and the energy relationships involved, without concern for the mechanism or intermediate products; kinetics is concerned solely with the mechanisms and the intermediate products of the reaction.

In addition to those phenomena which can be studied mathematically, physical chemists have undertaken the study of such miscellaneous chemical subjects as colloid chemistry (see COLLOIDAL DISPERSION), atomic theory (see ATOM AND ATOMIC THEORY), crystals and crystal structure (see CRYSTAL), and those spectroscopic and X-ray phenomena which are caused by molecules or other aggregates of atoms (see SPECTRUM; X RAY).

See also BIOCHEMISTRY; CHEMICAL ENGINEERING; CHEMISTRY, INDUSTRIAL; CHEMISTRY, INORGANIC; CHEMISTRY, ORGANIC; MICROCHEMISTRY; RADIOCHEMISTRY; THERMOCHEMISTRY.

G.D.P

CHEMISTRY, AGRICULTURAL. See AGRICULTURAL CHEMISTRY.

CHEMISTRY, BIOLOGICAL. See BIOCHEMISTRY.

CHEMISTRY, INDUSTRIAL, the practical application of the science of chemistry to industry. Industrial chemistry is applicable not only to strictly chemical industries, which generally produce bulk materials, but also to most other manufacturing industries, which generally produce fabricated articles. In some industries the processes of synthesis and fabrication are combined under a single roof; thus, a typical plastics factory uses as raw materials chemicals such as formaldehyde and carbolic acid, or agricultural products such as cotton and corncobs, and turns out as finished products toothbrushes, electrical insulators, or rayon fabrics.

Industrial chemistry is contrasted with laboratory chemistry, from which it differs principally in three points: cost, purity, and amount of the final product. A typical laboratory reaction yields at most a few ounces of product; in some cases where large amounts of material are unavailable, as in the original atomic-bomb experiments on plutonium, experiments must be done on less than a millionth of an ounce of material. In a typical industrial installation, on the other hand, production may reach many tons, or even thousands of tons, each day. The laboratory chemist, because of the negligible cost of the small quantities involved, uses materials of the utmost purity, and carries on his reactions in vessels of glass, platinum, or other substances which will not contaminate his products. He is interested in determining whether a particular product can be made or whether a particular reaction will take place. He assumes that if he can find a way to solve his problem, he can leave to the industrial chemist the method of its practical application. The industrial chemist, however, must bear costs constantly in mind; if the process cannot be operated economically it cannot be operated industrially. He must therefore find a way of using inexpensive raw materials, which will frequently be somewhat impure; he must employ reaction vessels of iron, wood, or similar inexpensive substances, and yet keep contamination down to permissible limits; he must arrange the reactions so that control will be simple and automatic, lest labor costs become prohibitive; and he must examine the effects of various irregularities in raw materials, climatic conditions, and numerous other factors, so that the product will be of uniform quality.

Even when all of these problems have been solved in an industrial laboratory, the transition from ounces to tons is difficult and requires extensive experimentation, for numerous unpredictable variations occur between small-scale and large-scale production. For example, a process for the manufacture of glue may have been evolved in the laboratory, in which the glue is boiled in a one-gallon vessel. If the same reaction is now tried in a vessel of the same shape but ten times as large in each dimension, it can be seen that although the volume of the vessel is one thousand times as great, the area of the surface is only one hundred times as great. Under such circumstances, the formation of foam may exceed the rate at which the foam breaks down, and it may be impossible to boil the glue without having it overflow the vessel.

For such reasons, after an industrial chemist has demonstrated a process to be practical in the industrial laboratory, he does not directly build a full-scale production plant, but first builds an experimental factory of intermediate size, called a *pilot plant*. With the experience gained in building and operating the pilot plant, it is possible to design a full-scale factory with reasonable assurance that it will work satisfactorily. Generally, therefore, after the first test-tube experiment has been successfully performed, a period of from five to ten years elapses before full-scale industrial operation can take place. In some recent developments, however, this period has been remarkably shortened. In many cases, processes which seem to operate satisfactorily at the test-tube level have never become satisfactory for industrial manufacture. For example, chemists of the 19th century knew how to make synthetically what is now called 100-octane gasoline; nonetheless this substance is still prepared from natural products (petroleum), no practical industrial synthesis having as yet been developed.

Among the most important industrial chemicals are the so-called *heavy chemicals,* chemical raw materials which are shipped in large quantities (carload lots), such as sulfuric acid, salt, caustic soda, ammonia, and chlorine. To list all of the applications of industrial chemistry would be to list virtually all the products of modern civilization, but among the more important products, both natural and synthetic, which industrial chemists have brought into existence, or for the processing of which they have invented improved methods, are: coke, alloys, rubber, glass, plastics, adhesives, paints, varnishes, lacquers, insecticides, fungicides, disinfectants, pigments, dyes, inks, photographic materials, food products, fertilizers, ceramics, refrigerants, cements, explosives, textiles, soap and detergents, hormones, sulfa drugs, antibiotics, and vitamins. See

articles on most of the above substances; see also CHEMICAL ENGINEERING.   H.A.N.

CHEMISTRY, INORGANIC, a branch of chemistry which, technically, deals with the compounds of all of the 100-odd elements other than carbon. The carbon compounds are set apart chiefly because of the almost unique chain-forming and ring-forming properties of the carbon atom; see CHEMISTRY, ORGANIC. Actually a few simple carbon compounds, such as carbon dioxide, are usually considered under inorganic chemistry, and in a few rare compounds the elements silicon, boron, and germanium (qq.v.) form chains of atoms, and these compounds are usually considered with the organic chemicals.

Inorganic chemistry is too heterogeneous an assemblage of knowledge to form a convenient unit of study; the term would be of little importance except for the tendency in schools to entitle courses Inorganic Chemistry when a better title would be Elementary Chemistry. The subject matter of such courses includes the elementary laws of chemistry, its symbolism and nomenclature, and an introduction to the experimental method as applied to physical science, including practice in many of the laboratory manipulations which are important in experimental chemistry. The student is made acquainted with such fundamental chemical concepts as valency, ionization, and activity, and given an introduction to atomic theory and the kinetic theory of gases. Particular attention is paid to the properties and reactions of substances in aqueous solution.

On the basis of their behavior in aqueous solution, most inorganic compounds can be conveniently classified as acids, salts (qq.v.), or bases. The properties of such compounds can usually be approximately predicted on the basis of their constituents; for example, ordinary table salt (sodium chloride, $NaCl$) has many properties in common with all sodium compounds on the one hand, and with all chlorides on the other. Oxygen is the most important inorganic element, geologically, biologically, and industrially; its compounds with the elements, called oxides, can be classified as acidic and basic, inasmuch as the oxides of the metals form bases when combined with water, and the oxides of the nonmetals form acids.

The number of industries depending primarily on inorganic compounds is small in comparison with those depending on organic compounds, or on both. Whereas the number of professional chemists who call themselves organic chemists is large, relatively few call themselves inorganic chemists. A chemist who does confine himself to inorganic substances must further specialize. He may specialize in one of the available techniques, becoming, for example, an analytical chemist, an electrochemist, or a physical chemist. Or he may specialize in a particular industry such as the manufacture of concrete, glass, ferrous or nonferrous metals, adhesives, or ceramics. Even in these industries some knowledge of organic chemistry is required. See CHEMISTRY.

S.Z.L.

CHEMISTRY, ORGANIC, branch of chemistry which deals with the compounds of the element carbon. The study of these compounds was originally set apart because they were derived from living *organisms*; until 1828, chemists thought that such compounds required an essential "vital force" for synthesis and therefore could not be made in the laboratory. Although urea, a typical animal product, was made in a test tube in that year, and chemists in the succeeding years have synthesized numerous organic compounds, the division of chemistry into organic and inorganic is still a convenient one, and is generally accepted.

There are a great many different types of organic compounds because of the peculiar ability of carbon atoms to attach themselves to one another. Such compounds as the hydride of carbon, CH_4 (see METHANE), and the oxide of carbon, CO_2 (see CARBON DIOXIDE), are not essentially different from the hydrides and oxides of other elements. But carbon also forms hundreds of other hydrides; for example, two atoms of carbon may be combined to form a molecule of ethane, C_2H_6, ethylene, C_2H_4, or acetylene, C_2H_2. When more than two atoms of carbon are combined in a molecule, more variations are possible. Thus, there are two different compounds with the formula C_4H_{10} and the name butane, depending on whether the carbon atoms are combined in a straight or branched chain; these two compounds are called respectively *n-* (for normal) and *i-* (for iso) butane. In larger molecules, an almost infinite number of different chains or rings, with branches, of carbon atoms are possible, and an extremely large number of such different structures are found in nature and have been prepared in the laboratory. See HYDROCARBONS.

Chemists have prepared and studied about a million different organic compounds, approximately ten times more than the total known number of different compounds which contain any of the other elements but which do not contain carbon. Whereas most of the elements may be present in organic compounds, the vast majority of these compounds contain only carbon, hydrogen, oxygen, nitrogen, sulfur, bromine, chlorine, and iodine. Any organic chemist can easily prepare hundreds of new compounds, but only if time can be spent in studying their properties is such research profitable. Sulfanilamide, for example, had been known to organic chemists for many years before its germicidal properties were discovered. Saccharin, hundreds of times as sweet as cane sugar, was prepared in the course of routine research, and its properties of sweetness were discovered only accidentally. Tyrian purple, the royal dye of the ancients, was prepared by a chemist some years ago in accordance with the classical formula, but he then discovered that it was identical with a compound which had been previously synthesized and discarded as inferior to certain other synthetic dyes. Hundreds of organic compounds of great potential value to mankind are doubtless resting unused on laboratory shelves because their possibilities are unsuspected.

Because of the possible variations of structure, organic chemical reactions rarely follow a single course. For example, ethylene, C_2H_4, may react with chlorine in numerous ways: being "unsaturated" (because two of the valence bonds of each carbon atom are attached to one another) it may add HCL or Cl_2 to form respectively C_2H_5Cl or $C_2H_4Cl_2$; chlorine may substitute for hydrogen to form C_2H_3Cl, $C_2H_2Cl_2$, or other variations; there may be a combination of these two reactions; or two or more molecules may combine to form complex derivatives. The extent to which one or another of the foregoing reactions will predominate will depend on the relative concentrations, the temperature and pressure, the presence or absence of light, whether or not the reaction takes place in solution and the nature and concentration of the solvent, the presence of acids or alkalies, and numerous other factors. By controlling such factors the organic chemist may direct the reaction along desired lines, but his product will always require purification. The organic chemist must not only control his reactions, but must also develop methods for purifying his products and for testing their purity. Moreover, he needs special methods for determining the structure of his compounds, and for proving the validity of his conclusions regarding structure. See CHEMICAL ANALYSIS.

Divisions. Organic compounds are conveniently separated into two groups, the *aliphatic,* in which the carbon atoms in a molecule are connected to one another in chains, straight or branched, and the *cyclic,* in which the carbon atoms are connected in rings. The latter include: the *aromatic,* in which the rings are highly unsaturated, such as that of benzene (C_6H_6); the *alicyclic,* in which the rings are saturated, and the properties of the compounds are intermediate between the aliphatic and the aromatic; and the *heterocyclic,* in which other atoms than carbon, such as nitrogen, enter into the ring structure. For further details on all of these groups, see AROMATIC COMPOUNDS.

Classes. Just as inorganic compounds can be classified, the most important classes being acids, bases, and salts, so organic compounds fall naturally into groups which contain similar radicals and have properties in common. Organic acids contain the carboxyl radical, -COOH. The most familiar, and one of the simplest, of organic acids is acetic acid, CH_3COOH, the active principle of vinegar. The next member of this group is propionic acid, C_2H_5COOH, followed by butyric acid, C_3H_7COOH. The formula of successive members in a given group differs by the same amount of C_1H_2. Most organic acids are, like acetic acid, far weaker than such inorganic acids as hydrochloric or sulfuric. Some organic substances which do not have the carboxyl group may nevertheless have acidic properties; for example, phenol, C_6H_5OH, is sometimes called "carbolic acid".

The organic analogs of bases are the aliphatic alcohols, such as ethyl (or "ordinary") alcohol, C_2H_5OH, and the aromatic phenols, such as carbolic acid. The reaction of an organic acid with an alcohol yields an ester, the organic analog of a salt. In organic chemistry, however, such reactions are slow and incomplete, while in inorganic chemistry they are almost instantaneous. Other important classes of organic compounds are ethers, aldehydes, ketones, amines, nitro compounds, and sulfonic acids (see separate articles on each of these classes). Many compounds have two or more such active groups, and their properties partake of those of all the constituents. For example, the amino acids (q.v.) have both a carboxyl and an amine group.

Complex Compounds. Although no clear dividing line exists, organic compounds with as many as fifty carbon atoms are usually considered "simple". Many important organic compounds, however, have enormous molecules, of indefinite size containing thousands of carbon atoms. The amine group of one molecule of an amino acid, for example, can combine with the carboxyl group of another, to form a molecule twice as large. Then the amine group of the second can combine with the carboxyl group of a third, and so on. In this way, protein (q.v.) molecules are built up within the bodies of both plants and animals. An identical chemical process under controlled conditions is responsible for such synthetic complex compounds as nylon (q.v.). Other textile fibers, both synthetic and natural, consist of complex, polymeric compounds formed by different reactions. Carbohydrates such as cellulose are similarly built up by the combination of many molecules of simple sugars. Rubber (q.v.), both natural and synthetic, consists of polymeric organic molecules, as do most plastics, resins, and gums.

Most organic chemical reactions have some tendency toward the building up of such giant molecules, and the organic chemist is accustomed to find in the bottoms of his flasks small amounts of "gunk", consisting of tars of indeterminate, complex nature. The exact structure of any such complex molecule is almost impossible to ascertain, and consequently an exact duplicate of a natural complex molecule is almost impossible to synthesize. Thus, although the first systematic work on proteins started in the 1830's, the exact duplication of a natural protein, such as albumin or hemoglobin, is still unlikely. Proteins are considered to be made up of many amino acid molecules. From amino acids man has synthesized products called peptides, itermediate between amino acids and natural proteins. Recently compounds that approach the formulas and complexity of natural proteins have been produced in the laboratory, but these products are not the same as those found in nature. This failure to synthesize a natural protein is in marked contrast to the success of the organic chemist in synthesizing such compounds as vitamins and hormones (qq.v.), which, although "simple" in the sense here considered, are often of bewildering complexity. See CHEMISTRY.

G.D.P.

CHEMNITZ. See KARL-MARX-STADT.

CHEMNITZ or **KEMNITZ,** MARTIN (1522–86), German Lutheran theologian, born in Brandenburg and educated at Frankfort on the Oder and Wittenberg. He was placed in charge of the library of the Duke of Prussia at Königsberg (now Kaliningrad) in 1550, but three years later returned to Wittenberg to lecture on Melancthon's exposition of Lutheran doctrine, *Loci Communes,* on which his own posthumously published *Loci Theo-*

logici (1591) was based. In 1554 he became a preacher at Brunswick, and in 1567 was given the post of superintendent there. He was influential in inducing the Lutherans of Saxony and Swabia to unite in accepting the statement known as the Formula Concordiæ, which ended a split in that sect. Chemnitz' chief works besides that already mentioned include his *Examen Concilii Tridentini* (4 vols., 1565–73) and, in collaboration with his predecessor as superintendent, Joachim Mörlin, *Corpus Doctrinæ Prutenicum* (1567).

CHEMOTHERAPY, the use of chemical agents in the treatment of disease. In its widest sense, chemotherapy includes the use of any therapeutic drug, but in general usage it is confined to those chemicals, especially synthetic chemicals, which have a specific toxic effect against a specific parasitic microorganism (the causative agent of an infectious disease) without serious toxic effect upon the host (the diseased individual).

Cinchona (q.v.) bark has been used for the treatment of malaria at least since 1638, and the specific chemicals, principally quinine, which are the active principles of cinchona have been known since 1820. The first synthetic chemotherapeutic agent was salvarsan (q.v.), discovered by the German bacteriologist Ehrlich in 1909. Ehrlich had discovered that certain dyes, when injected into an animal, were highly selective, dyeing only a particular organ of the body. Later he discovered a dye, trypan red, which, when injected into a syphilitic animal, would dye the causative organisms without affecting the host. He reasoned that a suitable chemical composed of a combination of a dye such as trypan red (which would attach itself to the germ), and a poison such as arsenic (which would kill the germ), would comprise a "magic bullet" for the cure of syphilis. He prepared hundreds of such chemicals, and the 606th chemical was salvarsan, also known as arsphenamine or 606. This drug effected almost miraculous cures of syphilis and related diseases.

The next important advance in chemotherapy came with the discovery of the antibacterial action of sulfanilamide (see SULFA DRUGS), information on which was first published in 1935. Penicillin (q.v.) was first used to treat diseases in human beings in 1940, and since that time numerous other chemotherapeutic agents produced by microorganisms have been discovered; these substances are known as antibiotics (q.v.).

Extensive research on chemotherapy was carried out in the U.S. during World War II, particularly on sulfa drugs, antibiotics, and antimalarials. Quinine, the traditional antimalarial drug, became unavailable early in 1942 when the Japanese conquered the cinchona-producing areas. The Germans, having experienced a similar situation during World War I, had done research on synthetic antimalarials, and had developed plasmochin in 1924 and atabrine (q.v.) about 1930. Neither of these chemicals was entirely satisfactory, but both were useful, especially when combined with quinine. By the end of the Korean War various synthetic drugs had been developed for the cure and prevention of all types of the disease; see MALARIA.

In the mid-1950's various drugs called tranquilizers (q.v.) were applied in the field of psychiatry as aids in the treatment of mental illness. Another group of drugs known as psychic energizers was introduced during the same period. Biochemical research is in progress to discover specific drugs for the cure of mental diseases; see MENTAL DISORDERS: *Current Research.*

Ehrlich envisaged the medical treatment of the future as a simple matter of diagnosis, followed by injection, ingestion, inunction, or inhalation of the particular chemical which would cure the particular disease. Chemotherapy has a long way to progress before this end can be achieved; although many serious infectious diseases have been brought under control, no drug has yet been found to cure such viral diseases as poliomyelitis (q.v.). Among the unsolved medical problems confronting present-day chemotherapy are cancer, certain types of heart disease, and mental illness. See MEDICINE.

CHEMOTROPISM, sensitiveness of certain plant organs by virtue of which they change the direction of their growth when acted upon by chemical substances. If an organ bends so as to grow toward the source of a substance, it is said to be positively chemotropic to that substance; if it turns away from it, it is negatively chemotropic. The organ tends to place itself so that it shall be equally stimulated on all sides by the diffusing chemical substance. In elongating organs, such as roots and fungus filaments, the reaction is one of growth; the curvature is brought about either by the retardation of growth on one side or by its acceleration on the other, or by both together. The reaction is seen in case of many gases, liquids, and solids when dissolved in water. The term "aerotropism" has been applied to the power of responding to gases in this way. An example of chemotropism is the following: if fungi are grown in a plate of moist gelatin, and an excess of sugar is added to a certain part of the gelatin plate, the filaments will bend and grow from all parts of the medium toward the part which is richer in sugar. The diffusion of the sugar into the surrounding material is the occasion of the response.

CHEMULPO. See INCHON.

CHEMURGY, a branch of applied chemistry dealing with the use of agricultural products as raw materials for industrial manufacturing. The word *chemurgy* was only recently coined; it came to the attention of the American public during the 1930's, a period when consumption of farm products was particularly low and the chemurgical use of such products offered a new demand. Spokesmen for farm interests suggested, for example, that the government subsidize the conversion of cornstarch into alcohol for use as a diluent in gasoline for motor fuel. Although this particular suggestion was never followed, a similar program was adopted during World War II to supply alcohol for synthetic rubber manufacture.

During the same period an enormous improvement in the farm economy of the southeastern U.S. was effected by crop rotation, alternating the planting of peanuts or sweet potatoes with the staple crop, cotton. This rotation was made economically possible by the development of hundreds of chemurgical uses for peanuts and sweet potatoes by George Washington Carver (q.v.) a pioneer in the development of chemurgy.

Vegetable oils are an important chemurgic raw material, used in the manufacture of lubricants, paints, and soaps. Cottonseed oil, the most important, is now an economically indispensable by-product, used for both food and chemurgic purposes. Other oils, such as castor and tung, are used almost entirely for industrial purposes. The enormous development of the synthetic textile industry has created a demand for farm products, first for the manufacture of rayon, and more recently for the manufacture of nylonlike fibers. The progress of synthetic chemistry has opened up new uses for such former waste products as oat hulls, from which are now derived a group of chemicals called furfural derivatives, with many industrial uses. Other products of chemurgy are newsprint from slash pine, synthetic wool from milk, and plastics from a wide variety of farm products and by-products.

CHENAB, river of the Indian subcontinent, about 590 miles in length. It rises in the Himalaya mountains in the E. Punjab, traverses the S. part of Kashmir, and flows in a generally S.W. direction to join the Sutlej R.

CHENGTEH, or JEHOL, city of Hopeh Province, China, on the Lwan R., about 130 miles N.E. of Peking, in a fertile farming region. In former times Chengteh was the summer residence of the Manchu emperors of China. From 1931 to 1945 it was occupied by the Japanese invaders of China. Following World War II, Chengteh was one of the centers of conflict in the Chinese civil war. Prior to 1956 the city was the capital of the former Jehol Province. Pop. (1953 est.) 92,000.

CHENGTU, capital of Szechwan Province, China, about 175 miles N.W. of Chungking. It is situated on a plain, 2000 ft. above sea level, which forms the Min R. delta. The plain is made fertile by an irrigation system dating from the 3rd century B.C. Chengtu is the commercial and cultural center of the agricultural region extending eastward, known as the Red Basin, and of the pastoral country to the west. The city is the site of West China Union University. Pop. (1961 est.) 1,135,000.

CHÉNIER, ANDRÉ MARIE DE (1762–94), French poet, born at Constantinople of a Greek mother and a French father, and educated at the Collège de Navarre, Paris. From 1787 to 1790 he was in England as secretary to the French ambassador. For the next four years he wrote articles and poems on political subjects. Although he was in sympathy with the French Revolution, he was alarmed by its excesses. His writings against the Reign of Terror aroused the anger of Maximilien Robespierre, leader of the popular radical party. Chénier was arrested and executed.

Only two of his poems were published in his lifetime, *Le Jeu du Paume à David Peintre* and *Hymne aux Soldats de Châteauvieux,* both written sometime between 1790 and 1794. A number of his poems were published after his death, including *La Jeune Captive* (1795), written during the four months he was in prison awaiting execution, and *La Jeune Tarentine* (1801). The first complete edition of his collected works was published in 1819. Chénier is regarded as one of the most important of French classical poets and also as a forerunner of the French romantic poets. An opera, *Andrea Chénier,* based on his life during the French Revolution, was written by the Italian composer Umberto Giordano and first produced in 1896.

CHENNAULT, CLAIRE LEE (1890–1958), American army officer, born in Commerce, Texas. In 1917, during World War I, he joined the U.S. Army Air Corps and in 1925 became commandant of the 19th Pursuit Group, stationed in Hawaii. He was one of the originators of the idea of using parachute troops ("paratroops"), and in 1926 conducted demonstrations of their utility. In 1937 he resigned from the army and became aviation adviser to the Chinese government, then at war with Japan. For the Chinese Air Force he organized volunteer American aviators into a corps known as the "Flying Tigers", which did notable work in defending the Burma Road, China's avenue of supply from India, from Japanese air forces. During World War II he was placed in command of the U.S. Army Air Forces in China in 1942, with the rank of brigadier general; he was made a major general in 1943. The following year he became commander of the 14th U.S. Air Force in China and also chief of the air staff of the Chinese Air Force. He resigned the latter command in 1945. The following year he returned to China and organized a commercial air line, of which he was chairman of the board after 1950. He wrote *Way of a Fighter* (autobiography, 1949).

CHENONCEAUX, a celebrated castle in the department of Indre-et-Loire, France, built on piles in the river Cher, 4 miles E. of Bléré. Its foundations were laid in 1515. It became crown property in 1535 and was a favorite occasional residence of Francis I. Henry II presented it to the celebrated Diana of Poitiers, who lavished much money on its embellishment, as did also Catherine de Médicis, after she had dispossessed Diana. Mary Stuart, Queen of Scots, spent her honeymoon at Chenonceaux with Francis II in 1559. The castle became private property in the 18th century and was an attractive resort for the distinguished literary and scientific men of that time, including the French philosophers Montesquieu, Voltaire, and Jean Jacques Rousseau, the naturalist Georges Louis Leclerc, De Buffon, and the English statesman Henry St. John, Viscount Bolingbroke.

CHENOPODIUM, a genus of herbs in the family Chenopodiaceae, many of which are familiar and annoying weeds. The species are mostly annuals, the under sides of the leaves often covered with a mealy hoariness. They are widely distributed throughout most of the world, many of the species common in the U.S. and Canada being naturalized from Europe or tropical America. The names goosefoot or pigweed are applied to all of the species, while many of them have specific common names. Among the latter are *C. botrys,* Jerusalem oak; *C. bonus-henricus,* good King Henry or wild spinach; *C. ambrosioides,* Mexican tea; *C. anthelminticum* (perhaps a variety of the last mentioned); wormseed;

C. album, lamb's-quarters; *C. vulvaria,* stinking goosefoot. Wormseed seeds were formerly used in medicine as an anthelmintic. The leaves of wild spinach have been used as food, as have the seeds of *C. quinoa,* a species which has not been naturalized in the United States.

CHEOPS. See KHUFU.

CHERBOURG, seaport and naval station of the department of Manche, France, situated on the English Channel, at the mouth of the Divette R., and about 232 m. by rail W.N.W. of Paris. It is an important fishing and industrial center, with shipbuilding yards, iron and copper foundries, lumber mills, and rope factories, and one of the principal ports of call for transatlantic steamers on the European mainland. Protected by a breakwater over 2 m. long, Cherbourg harbor is accessible to the largest ocean-going vessels and includes a large roadstead, outer and inner basins for commercial shipping, and an extensive basin for naval craft. Among the naval installations, largely grouped in a section known as Port Militaire, are dry docks, barracks, magazines, a hospital, and heavy fortifications. The chief exports include eggs, butter, and paving stones; the chief imports are Algerian wine, phosphate fertilizers, and coal.

Cherbourg is built on the site of what was probably the ancient Roman camp of Coriallum. In the 11th century the town was known as Carusbar. It was sacked by the English in 1295, and during the next two centuries withstood several English sieges. Projects for the fortification and improvement of the harbor were initiated in the 17th century. In 1758 Cherbourg was captured by the British, and its military installations were destroyed. A vast construction program, launched during the reign of Emperor Napoleon I, was finally completed late in the 19th century. The city became a part of German-occupied France during World War II, according to the terms of the Franco-German armistice of June 1940; its harbor installations, used by the German navy, became a frequent target of the Allied air forces. Following the invasion (June 6, 1944) of western Europe by the Allies, the city was the scene of severe fighting. The German occupation troops wrecked many of the harbor works before capitulating (June 27). Pop. (1962) 37,096.

CHEREMKHOVO, city of the Russian Soviet Federated Socialist Republic, in s. central Siberia, near the Angara R. It is situated on the Trans-Siberian Railway, about 75 miles N.W. of Irkutsk, in an area, the Cheremkhovo Basin, noted for the production of coal and lime. The production of grain and livestock is also an important industry of the region surrounding Cheremkhovo. The building of the city (1928–38) was a part of the Soviet Union's industrialization program of the first and second Five Year Plans. Following World War II, during the fourth Five Year Plan, the surrounding region was developed as the center of atomic energy production in the Soviet Union. Industry in the city is based on an abundance of coal, lime, and hydroelectric power. Pop. (1959 est.) 123,000.

CHERIBON, city and seaport of the Republic of Indonesia, situated on the N.E. coast of Java, about 130 miles E. of Batavia. It is the center of a large export trade in tea, rice, sugar, coffee, essential oils, teak, and other products of the surrounding region. Tjareme (10,098 ft.), an active volcano, is located a short distance s.s.w. of the city. Prior to the termination (1949) of Dutch paramountcy in Indonesia, Cheribon was the capital of a residency of the same name. Pop. (1951 est.) 54,079.

CHERIMOYA, CHIRIMOYA, or CHERIMOYER, common names of the tree *Annona cherimolia,* native of equatorial America, or of its fruit. The word cherimoya is derived from a Quichua (native Peruvian) word meaning round, cold fruit. It is closely related to the custard apple (q.v.), and its fruit is highly esteemed in Brazil, Ecuador, and Peru, where it is widely cultivated. It has also been cultivated in the East Indies and extreme southern U.S. Both flowers and fruit emit a pleasant fragrance, but when the tree is covered with bloom the odor is so strong as to be almost overpowering. The fruit varies from the size of an orange to 16 ounces or upward in weight. It is roundish or heart-shaped. Externally it is nearly smooth, greenish or brownish yellow when ripe, and often with a reddish cheek. The skin, thick and tough, is marked off into pentagonal or hexagonal areas. The flesh is snow-white and juicy and contains a number of brown seeds.

CHERKASSY, city of Kiev Region of the Ukrainian Soviet Socialist Republic, near the Dnieper R., about 100 miles s.E. of Kiev. Its industrial establishments include lumber mills, and factories for the manufacture of sugar and tobacco produced in the surrounding district, and for the production of bricks and nails. Pop. (1959 est.) 85,000.

CHERNIGOV, capital of a Region of the same name, Ukrainian Soviet Socialist Republic, situated on the Desna R., about 78 miles N.N.E. of Kiev. The city is an industrial center with flour mills and plants engaged in the manufacture of shoes and other leather products. Chernigov Region lies in the N. part of the Ukraine; its terrain is generally level, with forested and marshy tracts in the N.W., and is watered mainly by the Dnieper and Desna rivers. Hemp, tobacco, oats, rye, honey, and wheat are the chief agricultural products, and lumbering is an important industry. Other industries include the production of tar and pitch, and wooden and leather goods.

Chernigov was an important city early in the 10th century, and in the 11th century it became the capital of the principality of Syeversk. In 1240 it was destroyed by Mongol invaders, but it was subsequently rebuilt. Lithuania annexed the city in the 14th century. Thereafter it was a Polish possession until captured by the Russians in 1686. During World War II the city and the Region were occupied by the Germans from 1941 to 1943. Area of Region, about 4120 sq.m.; pop. (1959) 1,553,000. Pop. of city (1959) 89,000.

CHERNOVTSY (Rumanian *Cernăuţi*), CHERNOVITZ, or CZERNOWITZ, administrative center of a Region of the same name, Ukrainian Soviet Socialist Republic, situated on the Prut R., near the Rumanian border, and about 245 miles s.w. of Kiev. Before 1918 the city was the capital of the Austrian crownland of Bucovina; following the defeat of the Central Powers in World War I, it was the capital of the Rumanian province of Bucovina from 1918 to 1940. After the cession of Bessarabia and northern Bucovina to the Soviet Union in 1940, during World War II, the city and the surrounding district were included in the Chernovtsy Region of the Ukrainian S.S.R., except for an interval during the war when they were again held by the Rumanians. The chief industries of the Region are the cultivation of cereal grains and general farm crops and the raising of cattle and sheep. Lumber is also produced. Pop. of city (1959 est.) 145,000.

CHERNYSHEVSKY, NICOLAI GAVRILOVICH (1828?–89), Russian author and political leader, born at Saratov, and educated at the University of St. Peterburg. During his early career he became widely known as a literary critic. His philosophy of criticism, notably expressed in *Aesthetic Relations of Art to Reality* (1855), stressed the importance of social values in literature. In the period of social unrest that followed the Crimean War (1854–56), he championed political and economic reform in Russia, expounding his views in *The Contemporary,* an influential periodical. He soon became prominent in the radical wing of the Russian reform movement. As a result of his attacks on the government, he was arrested, in 1862, and imprisoned in the St. Petersburg fortress. There he wrote his best-known work, *What Is To Be Done?* (1863), a novel dealing with the Russian Revolutionary movement. In 1864 the government exiled him to northern Siberia, where he was detained until 1883. He spent the final years of his exile, which ended shortly before his death, in Astrakhan. There he translated 12 volumes of *Universal History* (15 vols., 1857–80) by the German historian Georg Weber.

CHEROKEE INDIANS, North American Indians, of the Iroquoian family (q.v.), originally one of the most powerful native tribes of the southeastern region of the continent. Remnants of the tribe consist of a group of about 2000 living on a reservation in western North Carolina, and about 20,000 individuals living chiefly in Oklahoma. When European colonization of North America began, the Cherokees occupied the Allegheny and Appalachian mountain regions of what is now North Carolina, South Carolina, Tennessee, Georgia, and Alabama. The tribe consisted of seven clans, distributed among numerous permanent villages of substantially built log houses, whose members subsisted by hunting and farming. During the struggles between the French and English for colonial supremacy in North America, the Cherokees sided generally with the English, and in 1730 the leaders of the tribe declared their allegiance to the English throne. However, their relations with the colonists were marked by occasional periods of warfare, notably from 1758 to 1761, when fierce fighting took place in South Carolina. In most instances hostilities resulted from seizure of Cherokee territory by the American colonial authorities. Animated by hatred of the latter, the tribe aided Great Britain during the American Revolution. Representatives of the tribe negotiated a formal peace treaty with the United States Government in 1785, but Cherokee resistance to American sovereignty continued for 10 years after the war. Between 1790 and 1817 about 3000 of the tribe emigrated w. of the Mississippi, settling in what later became Indian Territory (q.v.), now part of Oklahoma. In 1791 the tribal chieftains, confirming the previous treaty, ceded to the U.S. government part of their territory. This was the first of a series of similar cessions. The government of the U.S., in return, recognized the tribe's ownership rights in the territory remaining,

establishing prohibitions against trespassing thereon.

Early in the 19th century, Christian missionaries began to work among the Cherokees, converting and educating many of them. The tribes established, in 1820, a representative form of government, similar to that of the United States, consisting of an elective principal chief, a Senate, and a House of Representatives, and they also established a public-school system. This achievement was followed, in 1825, by the adoption of a syllabic alphabet of 85 characters, a system invented by Sequoya (q.v.), a member of the tribe. In 1827 the Cherokees drafted a constitution, officially incorporating the tribe as The Cherokee Nation. About the same time they began publication of a newspaper, the first Indian periodical to appear in the continental United States.

Meanwhile, valuable gold deposits had been discovered in tribal territory, an area reduced by cessions and other losses to about 7,000,-000 acres located in n.w. Georgia, s.w. North Carolina, and e. Tennessee. In 1819 Georgia appealed unsuccessfully to the U.S. government to remove the Cherokees from their lands. Attempts then were made to acquire the territory by purchase. The Indian Nation retaliated with a law which made any such sale by one of its citizens punishable by death. Finally, in contravention of U.S. laws which guaranteed the Indians possession of their lands, the Georgia State Legislature, in 1828–30, enacted legislation which outlawed the Cherokee government, deprived its citizens of their fundamental rights, and confiscated their territory. Indian appeals to the U.S. government for protection were rejected by President Andrew Jackson. In 1832 a majority of the U.S. Supreme Court, including Chief Justice John Marshall, ruled that the legislation enacted by the Georgia State Legislature was unconstitutional. The Federal authorities ignored the decision. Although a small group of leading Cherokees agreed, in 1835, to cede the territory in exchange for $5,700,000 and land grants in the Indian Territory, their action was repudiated by more than nine tenths of the tribe and a number of the group members were put to death as traitors.

Troops of the United States government began military operations against the Cherokees in 1838, forcibly evicting them from their lands. In the confusion and fighting a substantial number of the Indians escaped. Later they settled in western North Carolina, where they purchased 56,000 acres of land, entailed the acreage to the tribe, and incorporated under the laws of the State. These settlements laid the foundations of contemporary Cherokee communities in North Carolina. Meanwhile most of the tribe, estimated to number 16,000, were driven west in a forced march, in the course of which several thousands died as a result of hunger and hardship. On their arrival in Indian Territory the survivors, under the leadership of John Ross their chief, re-established their government, with Tahlequah (now county seat of Cherokee Co., Okla.) as their capital. The nation flourished until the outbreak of the American Civil War (1861), when fratricida divisions and economic dislocations developed. The Cherokees provided large contingents of soldiers to both the Union and Confederate armies. After the war the Nation concluded a new treaty with the United States, granting freedom and Cherokee citizenship to Negro slaves belonging to members of the tribe. Except for a few minor land disputes, the Nation thereafter maintained friendly relations with the United States. In 1892 the Cherokees sold to the U.S. government their western territorial extension known as the "Cherokee Outlet", and in 1906 they disbanded their Nation, becoming citizens of the United States. Their residual tribal lands were forcibly broken up and parceled out by the government largely to whites.   J.C.

CHERRA PUNJI, small village in the Khasi Hills, Assam, India. It stands on a plateau, exposed to the full force of the monsoon driving N. from the Bay of Bengal, and is noted as having one of the heaviest rainfalls in the world. Over 900 in. of rainfall were registered in 1861; the mean annual average is 429 in.

CHERRY, common name for several trees of the genus *Prunus,* or for the edible fruit of these trees. The genus *Prunus,* in the Rose family, also contains the plums, and since many of these plants have been cultivated for thousands of years and widely hybridized, their classification is complex. Some botanists classify several species of plums and cherries in other, closely related genera, notably *Cerasus* and *Padus.*

The ancestors of most of the modern cultivated varieties of cherry are probably *Prunus avium* (sweet or dessert cherry) and *P. cerasus* (sour or pie cherry), the former attaining a height of 40 or 50 ft., and having its leaves and peduncles drooping, with small austere fruit; the latter having erect, smooth, shining leaves and a more juicy fruit, but being a much smaller tree. Both have white flowers in clusters or nearly sessile umbels, and both are generally regarded as natives of middle and s. Europe, if not also of Britain, where both are naturalized. According to the Roman writer Pliny, *P. cerasus* was introduced by the general Lucullus from Cerasus in Pontus to grace his triumph after his victory (71 B.C.) over Mithridates, King of Parthia. *P. avium* is frequently planted, not only because of its fruit and because it is exceedingly ornamental when in flower, but also on account of its value as a timber tree, being of rapid growth, with firm, strong, close-grained wood, suitable for the purposes of cabinetmakers, turners, and musical-instrument makers. Double varieties of both species are also grown.

The cultivated varieties of the cherry are very numerous, and differ considerably in size, color, and flavor. Among important varieties in cultivation are Mazzards, quick-growing trees used as stock for grafting other varieties; Hearts and Bigarreaus, sweet cherries, the latter being firmer and less juicy; Amarelles and Morellos, sugar cherries, the latter being darker colored and sourer; and Dukes, hybrids between the sweet and sour forms. Among the native species with very sour fruit which are occasionally cultivated is the chokecherry (q.v.), *P. virginiana*. The fruits of all these varieties are eaten fresh, or used for making preserves and liqueurs. A variety of cherry brandy made from fermented cherries with crushed pits (which give the brandy

Monkmeyer (Borsig)

Japanese flowering cherry, Prunus serrulata

a bitter flavor) and known as *Kirschwasser* is made in several European countries.

Cherries are grown in many parts of the U.S.; sweet cherries, more difficult to grow, are cultivated mainly in California, and sour cherries are common in the east. There are about 13,000,000 trees in cherry orchards in the U.S., with an annual production of about 200,000 tons of cherries. The amount canned varies greatly from year to year, but averages from 2 to 4 million standard cases of 24 No. 2½ cans.

Although all cherry trees are very attractive when in bloom, some species with inferior fruit are cultivated especially for their flowers. Most notable of these are the Oriental cherry, *P. serrulata*, and the Nanking cherry, *P. tomentosa*. Thousands of trees of these species, presented by Japan to the U.S. have been planted in Washington, D.C., around the Potomac Basin, where the cherry blossoms attract considerable attention each year in April.

CHERSO. See CRES.

CHERT, or HORNSTONE, a variety of quartz (q.v.), not unlike flint, but more brittle, and sometimes more fibrous. It is common in limestones of Paleozoic age. Its colors are gray, white, red, yellow, green, or brown. The name chert is very commonly given to the siliceous concretions in limestone rocks. Some varieties of chert are organic in origin.

CHERUB (Heb. *k'rūbh*, pl. *kerubim*), in the Bible, a winged creature represented as in attendance upon Yahwe, and as belonging to the court of heavenly beings around his throne. According to Ex. 25: 18–22; 36: 7–9, there were two cherubs made of gold on top of the covering of the ark of the Covenant, and pictures of cherubs were woven into the veil and elsewhere (Ex. 26: 31; 36: 35). In Ezek. 1, four cherubs, represented as animals with the legs and feet of oxen, two pairs of wings, and different faces—one that of a man, another that of a lion, another that of an ox, and another that of an eagle—carry the vault of heaven on which rests the throne of Yahwe. This gave rise at an early period of the Church to the symbolic figures of the four evangelists —the human countenance being associated with Matthew, that of the lion with Mark, that of the ox with Luke, and that of the eagle with John.

In the developed system of Hebrew angelology the cherubs form one of the 10 highest classes of angels. Cherubim, seraphim (q.v.), and ophannim (wheels) are mentioned in the Parables of Enoch. Their function becomes more and more that of offering praise to the Most High. Dwelling so near to the source of all knowledge, they also become examples of most perfect knowledge. This is emphasized by Philo and by many Christian teachers. In the hierarchical gradations established by these theologians the cherubim rank next to the seraphim as the second order of angels.

CHERUBINI, MARIA LUIGI CARLO ZENOBIO SALVATORE (1760–1842), Italian composer, born at Florence. Before the production in 1780 of his first opera, *Quinto Fabio*, at Alessandria, he had written several church works which were performed in Florentine churches. In 1784 he was invited to London, and held the post of composer to King George III of England for one year. He settled in Paris in 1788 and wrote several operas which were produced with success. He visited Vienna in 1805, and made the acquaintance of Haydn, Beethoven, and Hummel. In 1808 he composed the first of his great church works, the *Mass in F*. From 1821 to 1841 he was director of the Paris Conservatory, in which position he exerted great influence on the musical life of his time. His works include light Italian operas, such as *Armida* (1782) and *Ifigenia in Aulide* (1787); dramatic French operas, such as *Médée* (1797), *Les Deux Journées* (1800), *Faniska* (1806), *and Ali Baba* (1833); masses, requiems, motets, cantatas, and choral works; and several string quartets. His treatise, *Cours de Contrepoint et de la Fugue,* which appeared in 1835, is believed to have been largely the work of the composer Halévy.

CHERVIL, an annual herb, *Anthriscus cerefolium,* of the Parsley family. It is a native of Europe, where it is cultivated as a pot-herb, and used in soups and for a garnish, in the same manner as parsley. Sweet chervil, *Myrrhis odorata,* a native of s. Europe, is quite common throughout the British Isles. In Scotland it is sometimes called myrrh; its smell is attractive to bees, and beehives are rubbed with the plants to induce swarming.

CHESAPEAKE, in United States naval history, a forty-gun frigate which figured in one of the episodes leading to the War of 1812 and in one of the memorable battles of that war. On June 22, 1807, the *Chesapeake,* en route to the Mediterranean Sea from Norfolk, Va., on a training cruise, was overtaken on the high seas by the British man-of-war *Leopard.* The commander of the British vessel, a fifty-two-gun frigate, halted the *Chesapeake* and demanded the restitution of several alleged deserters from the royal navy. Commodore James Barron, the American commanding officer, denying there were deserters on the *Chesapeake,* refused to allow a British search party to board her. The British frigate then fired, killing and wounding a number of her crew. Totally unprepared for battle, Commodore Barron was obliged to submit to a search, with the result that four men, including three Americans, were arrested as deserters from the British navy. The United States government promptly demanded explanation, apology, and reparation, and public indignation, popularly expressed in the slogan "Reparations or War", contributed substantially to the gradually worsening relations between the two countries, but Great Britain failed to take action on the American demands until 1811.

On June 1, 1813, during the War of 1812, the *Chesapeake,* then under Captain James Lawrence, sailed from Boston to engage the British ship *Shannon,* which was stationed in Massachusetts Bay. The first broadside from the *Shannon* killed several officers of the *Chesapeake* and carried away part of her rigging. Out of control, she drifted alongside the *Shannon,* whereupon a British boarding party gained possession of her deck. The Americans fought fiercely and sustained heavy losses, among them Captain Lawrence. His final command was "Don't give up the ship"—a cry which became an American watchword during the remainder of the war. Shortly after Lawrence fell the *Chesapeake* surrendered. American casualties in the engagement included 61 killed and 85 wounded; British casualties were 33 killed and 50 wounded.

CHESAPEAKE AND OHIO CANAL, an inland waterway 184 miles long, extending through the Potomac valley from Georgetown, D.C., to Cumberland, Md. The project was initiated by George Washington in 1774, but was not completed until 1850. Parallel railroads, opened in the 1890's, absorbed most of the traffic, and by 1924 the canal was abandoned.

CHESAPEAKE BAY, largest embayment on the Atlantic coast of the United States, entering deeply into Virginia and Maryland. It extends inland in a generally N. and s. direction for a distance of 200 m., ranging between 4 and 40 m. in breadth. Its mouth, a passage between Cape Charles, Va., on the N., and Cape Henry, Va., on the s., is about 12 m. wide. The bay is indented by the estuaries of numerous streams, including the James, York, Rappahanock, Potomac, and Patuxent rivers on the w. and the Susquehanna River on the N. On the N.E., the estuary of the Elk River is linked to the Delaware River by means of the Chesapeake and Delaware Canal, a waterway which provides

shipping with a short route to and from the Camden-Philadelphia port area. The most important ports on the bay, which is navigable by deep-water vessels throughout its length, are Newport News, Va., Norfolk, Va., Portsmouth, Va., and Baltimore, Md. Chesapeake is noted for its oyster fisheries, and yields large quantities of crabs and other sea food.

CHESAPEAKE BAY RETRIEVER. See RETRIEVER.

CHESHIRE, a N.W. county of England, bordering on the w. on Flint and Denbighshire in Wales, from which it is separated in part by the river Dee; and on the N.W. on the Irish Sea. The northwestern part of the county consists of the Wirral peninsula, formed by the estuaries of the Dee and the Mersey. The Weaver, a tributary of the Mersey, is the principal river within the county. Cheshire forms an extensive, nearly level plain between the Derbyshire and Welsh mountains and contains many grazing tracts and dairy farms. Cheese making is an important agricultural industry.

In addition to its river navigation, the county has an excellent system of canals, and contains part of the Manchester Ship Canal. The chief mineral products are rock salt and coal. The latter is mined near Chester and on the eastern borders of the county. In almost every part of Cheshire, freestone, limestone, millstone, and marl are quarried. The principal towns include Birkenhead, Stockport, Wallasey, Crewe, and Chester (qq.v.). Area, 1015 sq.m.; pop. (1961 prelim.) 1,367,860.

CHESS, game played by two players, or by two opposing groups of players, on a square board divided into sixty-four squares, called a *chessboard,* with thirty-two variously shaped pieces, called *chessmen.* It is an intellectual contest with the element of chance reduced to a minimum. The essentials of chess are easily learned; because of its value as a recreation and as a mental discipline, the game is included in the curriculum of educational institutions and military schools in a number of countries. Chess as played by masters of the game, however, requires complex and subtle analysis, as well as a minute knowledge of chess theory and its applications in hundreds of critically analyzed games. Such play is possible, therefore, only to players who devote a large part of their time and energy to study and practice of the game and to competitive play.

Chess is a truly international game; among the nations which have produced masters of world-wide repute are Turkey, Italy, Spain,

Chessmen in the classic Staunton pattern. From left to right: King, queen, bishop, knight, rook, and pawn.

France, Ireland, Great Britain, Poland, India, Cuba, the United States, and the Soviet Union. Transoceanic matches between players in different countries are conducted occasionally by means of such media as cablegrams and radio messages and quite regularly by airmail letters.

The game probably originated in Persia (present-day Iran) in the 6th century A.D. From Persia chess spread eastward to India and, later, into the Near Eastern countries. Traders and other travelers are believed meanwhile to have introduced the game into southern Siberia and China. The Arabs brought chess into Europe from the Near East late in the 10th century, and European colonists subsequently carried it to the New World.

The form and rules of chess became stabilized shortly after its introduction into India; there were virtually no changes thereafter until the 16th century. At that time the modern form of the game began to develop, with several significant European modifications gaining acceptance. Notable among these were the optional two-square first move of the pawns (see *Rules,* below) and, consequently, the *en passant,* or "in passing", capture; the introduction of castling as a means of removing the king to relative safety; and the extension of the bishops' and, particularly, of the queens' moves. These changes not only quickened the play but the last-named modification also altered the strategical objectives of the game. The queen, which had hitherto been the weakest piece, now became by far the most powerful, and the advance of pawns to become queens became correspondingly more important.

By the 18th century the new rules had gained general acceptance and masters of international fame had begun to emerge, first as the result of matches contested between individuals, and then from tournaments held among teams. For many decades chess competition and ratings varied in form from country to country. In Russia and Germany, for example, organized chess societies sponsored formal tournaments between players who were graded on the basis of their skill; tournament winners were awarded a certain number of points, and consistent winners gradually accumulated enough points to merit the title "master". By contrast, tournament and match play were sponsored in the United States and Great Britain by various private groups on a sporadic, unorganized basis, and the title of master was applied only informally to players who won such matches or tournaments against outstanding competition.

The first major international tournament, held in London in 1851, was won by the German Adolph Anderssen (1818–79). The first official U.S. champion was the American chess genius Paul Morphy (1837–84), who gained his title in 1857 by winning the Grand Tournament of the First American Chess Congress, held in New York City. Morphy then toured Europe for almost two years, defeating all comers, and retired shortly thereafter. In 1866 the Czech-Austrian Wilhelm Steinitz (1836–1900) defeated Anderssen, proclaimed himself world chess champion, and was generally recognized as such after winning matches with the leading players of his time. When Steinitz finally lost in 1894 to the German Emanuel Lasker (1868–1941), the latter's claim to the world chess title was universally recognized; during the next half century, the world championship was won by a succession of chess masters.

In 1914, after a great international championship held in St. Petersburg (now Leningrad), Russia, the Russian czar Nicholas II created and bestowed on the five leading players in the tournament the title "grandmaster". Among the five grandmasters named was the American player Frank James Mar-

hall (1877–1944). The new title was later
applied informally to winners of tournaments open only to players recognized as mas-
ers; by the 1930's the title had been earned
by three other Americans, Isaac Kashdan
(1905–   ), Samuel Reshevsky (1911–   ), and
Reuben Fine (1914–   ). The four American
grandmasters were mainstays of the American
teams which won the International Team
Championship in 1931, 1933, 1935, and 1937.
Other members of the winning U.S. teams included, at various times, the American chess
masters Arthur W. Dake (1911–   ), I. A.
Horowitz (1907–   ), and Herman Steiner
(1905–55). Meanwhile the American title,
succession to which had at various times been
a matter of dispute, was formalized in 1935
by the establishment of a biennial championship tournament sponsored by the U.S. Chess
Federation. The first biennial tournament,
held in the following year, was won by Samuel Reshevsky.

World chess competition was severely curtailed during World War II, but the postwar
era proved an eventful period in the history
of the game. In 1946 the world titleholder, the
Russian-born, naturalized French grandmaster Alexander Alekhine (q.v.), died undefeated, leaving the world championship vacant
for the first time in fifty-two years. Subsequently, the International Chess Federation,
the world governing body, organized a mul-
tiple-round world-championship tournament
designed to find a successor to Alekhine. In
addition, the federation set up a program of
lesser tournaments designed to produce a
challenger for the world title at least once
every three years. The winner of the first
world tournament, held in 1948, was the
Soviet master Mikhail Botvinnik (q.v.). In
the same year the American championship
matches, which had been biennial, were placed
on a triennial basis.

During the decade following the war the
International Chess Federation assumed the
responsibility of electing grandmasters and
by 1957 had awarded the title to fifty of the
world's outstanding players. Nineteen of
these players were from the Soviet Union
and five were from the United States. The
American grandmasters were Kashdan, Reshevsky, Fine, Larry Evans (1932–   ), and
Arthur B. Bisguier (1930–   ).

From 1945 on, the Soviet Union dominated
world chess play. Soviet teams entered and
won the international team contests for the
first time in 1952, and subsequently won almost all other major tournaments which they
entered. Soviet players dominated also the in-

ternational women's, junior, and students'
team championships. The Soviet successes
were attributed largely to a sustained, multi-
faceted campaign by the Soviet government
to produce champions. First, the U.S.S.R.
combed its satellite states for chess talent, re-
cruiting chess masters from such countries
and constituent states as Hungary, Czechoslovakia, Latvia, Estonia, and Poland. Second, Soviet chess masters were subsidized,

Chess Review

*A typical opening sequence in chess. Each
player made his first move. White, who always
moves first, advanced the pawn before the
king (known as the king pawn) to the fourth
square. Black did the same.*

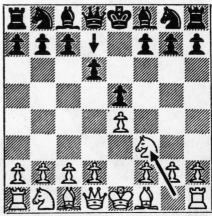

Chess Review

*Here, each player has made his second move.
First, White moved his knight as indicated,
attacking Black's advanced pawn. Then Black
protected that pawn by moving his queen
pawn as shown on the board.*

honored as "masters of sport", and permitted such a high standard of living that at mid-century they were among the few Soviet citizens who owned automobiles. Third, chess instruction and competition were important activities in all Soviet schools and factories. Chess instruction was mandatory in the schools, and the ability to mate with king and two bishops against a king was reputedly a passing requirement in the Soviet equivalent of the third grade. In addition, every Soviet factory was required to maintain a chess team. Finally, the government made every possible effort, through the press and other communication media, to stimulate popular interest in the game. As a result many hundreds of thousands of persons annually attended or participated in various local and national Soviet chess tournaments. An important chess tournament attracted almost as much popular interest in the Soviet Union as a major-league baseball game did in the United States.

United States Chess Champions, as winner of the Grand Tournament of the First American Chess Congress in 1857, Paul Morphy of New Orleans became the first official U.S. champion. When Morphy retired several years later, the title remained vacant until

Bobby Fischer, American boy who became an International Grand Master of chess, contemplates his next move in a tournament.

The New York Times

1871, when George H. Mackenzie (1837–91) won the championship. From about 1875 to 1909 the title was frequently in dispute. Outstanding championship players of the period included Max Judd (1852–1906), Jackson W. Showalter (1860–1935), Simon Lipschuetz (1863–1905), Albert B. Hodges (1861–1944), and Harry Nelson Pillsbury (1872–1906). Frank J. Marshall defeated Jackson Showalter in 1909 and reigned as the acknowledged American champion until 1935, when he retired undefeated. The next American titleholder was Samuel Reshevsky, who won in 1936, 1938, 1940, 1942, and 1946. Reshevsky did not compete in 1944, when the tournament was won by Arnold S. Denker (1914–). After the 1948 tournament, won by Herman Steiner (1905–55), the next three competitions were held triennially, and were won by Larry Evans (1951), Arthur Bisguier (1954), and Robert J. Fischer (1944–), in 1957–58. Fischer won the next four yearly tournaments.

WORLD CHESS CHAMPIONS

Player	Year
François André Philidor (France)	1747–1795
Alexandre Deschapelles (France)	1815–1820
Louis de la Bourdonnais (France)	1820–1840
Pierre de Saint-Amant (France)	1840–1843
Howard Staunton (Great Britain)	1843–1851
Adolph Anderssen (Germany)	1851–1858
Paul Morphy (United States)	1858–1859
Adolph Anderssen (Germany)	1859–1866
Wilhelm Steinitz * (Austria)	1866–1894
Emanuel Lasker (Germany)	1894–1921
José Raul Capablanca (Cuba)	1921–1927
Alexander Alekhine (France)	1927–1935
Max Euwe (Netherlands)	1935–1937
Alexander Alekhine (France)	1937–1946
Mikhail Botvinnik (U.S.S.R.)	1948–1957
Vassily Smyslov (U.S.S.R.)	1957–1958
Mikhail Botvinnik (U.S.S.R.)	1958–1960
Mikhail Tal (Latvia)	1960–1961
Mikhail Botvinnik (U.S.S.R.)	1961–

* First officially recognized world champion

Chess game in progress in medieval Italy (from 15th-century woodcut)

Rules. The sixty-four squares of the *chessboard* are colored alternately light (usually white) and dark (usually black). In playing, the chessboard must be so placed that a white square is at the right-hand end of the row of squares nearest each player. The rows of squares extending from left to right, when the board is in the correct position, are called *ranks*. The rows of squares extending from a player to his opponent, are called *files*. The rows of squares extending diagonally are called *diagonals*.

The chessmen consist of two sets of sixteen *men*, one set being light-colored and called *White*, the other being dark-colored and called *Black*. Each set of men consists of eight *pawns* and eight *pieces*.

P	P	P	P	P	P	P	P
R	Kt	B	K and Q		B	Kt	R

P, pawn; R, rook; Kt, knight; B, bishop; K, king; Q, queen.

The white queen is placed on a white square, and the black queen at the opposite end of the file; the kings are placed in the remaining vacant spaces.

The object of each player is to capture his opponent's king. Regardless of the number of other pieces on the board, when the capture of one player's king becomes inevitable, he has lost the game. The king is not actually captured; when it is directly threatened with what would be capture in the case of the other chessmen, it is *in check*. If it is in danger of capture, the king must be removed from check, either by removal to a square where it is no longer in check, by interposition, or by immediate capture of the attacking man. When none of these alternate defenses is possible the king is *checkmated,* and the game is over. If a player can continue indefinitely to check his opponent's king on successive moves, the game is *drawn* (tied) by *perpetual check*. If the king is the only legally movable man that a player has on the board, and is not in check, but cannot be moved without moving into check, the game is stalemated. Stalemated games are drawn.

On the other hand, a player who has captured one or two of his opponent's pieces without sacrificing pieces of equal value has a great advantage, and can usually win the game. For this reason much of the strategy of chess involves attempts to capture pieces other than the king. To make a capture a player moves one of his men to the square occupied by an opposing man and removes the opposing man permanently from the board. Except when capturing, a man may be moved only to a square unoccupied by any other chessman.

White makes the first, or opening, move of each game. The players move alternately, and may move only one man at a time except in *castling,* as explained below.

The king is moved one square per move along any rank, file, or diagonal. Once in each game the king may make an alternate move: castling. In castling, the king is moved two squares to either side of its original position; simultaneously the rook on that side of the board is placed just to the other side of the king. A player may not castle if he has previously moved the castling rook or the king, or if, at the time, any of the squares between king and rook are occupied; nor may he castle if in so doing the king must move out of, into, or across a square under attack by an opposing man.

The *queen* can be moved one or more squares along an open file, rank, or diagonal. The *rook* is similarly moved along either a rank or a file.

The *bishop* is similarly moved, but only diagonally.

The *knight* is moved one square along either a rank or file, and then one square diagonally to a square of a different color which is not adjacent to the square from which the move began.

All the foregoing pieces may be moved forward and backward across the board. *Pawns* may never be moved backward. A pawn may be moved only along its original file, and only one square per move, with two exceptions: when moved for the first time from its original position, it may be moved either one or two squares; a pawn may capture an opposing chessman only if the latter occupies a square diagonally adjoining that of the capturing pawn. When a pawn reaches the eighth rank it must be exchanged for a queen, bishop, knight, or rook of the same color, at the player's option. Thus a player may have two or more queens on the board at the same time. If, in being moved for the first time, a pawn is moved two squares and is thereby moved abreast of an opponent pawn on an adjoining file, it may be moved back one square by the opposing player and captured by the opposing pawn *en passant* ("in passing"), on the opponent's next move.

The queen, because of its mobility, is the most valuable piece on the board. It is worth more than a rook and a bishop, but less than

two rooks. Though the values of the men, especially the pawns, vary somewhat as the game progresses, a practical scale of values is the following: queen, nine pawns; rook, five pawns; bishop, three $\frac{1}{3}$ pawns; and knight, three $\frac{1}{4}$ pawns. The king is inexpendable, but has a "playing value" of three pawns.

Chessmen, with the exception of the knight, may not move over occupied squares. It is thus possible, in some cases, to defend a man under attack by interposition of another man between the attacking man and the man to be defended. Interposition as a means of defense against attack by a knight is impossible.

Chess play is divided into three general phases: the opening; the middle game; and the end game. In the *opening,* White, having the initiative, strives to bring his pieces into play rapidly, gain control of the squares in the center of the board to assure mobility for his forces, and construct a solid position as a base from which to launch an attack. *Black's opening* efforts are generally devoted to the development of an impregnable defense through the rapid deployment of men to hold the center, and to a concurrent search for opportunities to wrest the initiative from White and to pass from defense to attack.

Systems of opening play, the variations of which number several hundred, are called *gambits* (e.g. "Queen's Gambit," "Queen's Gambit Declined"), *counter-gambits* ("Center Counter-Gambit"), *defenses* ("Alekhine's Defense"), *openings* ("English Opening", and *games* ("Queen's Pawn Game"). A number of these systems bear the names of the men who developed them ("Ruy Lopez"). Opening play has been subjected to persistent and exhaustive analysis, which has been embodied in a voluminous literature that is revised constantly as new theories and occasional passing fads periodically upset conventional styles of play. Success in opening play depends greatly on knowledge of this literature.

The *middle game* generally finds the opposing players locked in battle and striving to convert initial advantages into decisive ones in position or in numbers of men. The middle game offers a practically, if not mathematically, unlimited field for the application of strategical plans, variations in tactical lines of play, subtle traps, and deliberate sacrifices of valuable pieces resulting in unexpected checkmates of the opposing king. While the literature in this department of the game is considerable, it is not as precise nor as extensive as that of the opening phase.

In the *end game* a player generally utilizes advantages won in the middle game, to im-

se checkmate on his opponent; while the
tter attempts to neutralize and overcome
ose advantages. There are usually fewer
eces on the board in the end game; the king
comes an active and sometimes decisive
ctor, in both attack and defense; and the
awns greatly increase in value as they
reaten to decide the issue by becoming
ueens. The utmost precision in calculating
oves is required for successful play in this
here. End-game play has been carefully
udied and reduced to a series of rules in a
terature which is more precise than but not
o voluminous as that on opening play.

J.S.B.

CHEST or THORAX, in anatomy, the upper
art of the body, lying between the neck
nd the abdomen. It is somewhat conical in
rm, flattened in back and in front. The
pex is formed by the structures of the neck;
e base is formed by the diaphragm (q.v.).
ackbone, sternum, and ribs form the frame-
ork of the chest; its walls are completed by
e intercostal muscles. The principal organs
closed in the chest are the heart and the
eat blood vessels, the lungs with the trachea
nd bronchi, the esophagus, and the thoracic
uct which is the terminus of the lymphatic
ystem, collecting the chyle and lymph and
scharging them into the blood.

CHESTER, city and port of entry of Dela-
are County, Pa., situated on the Delaware
., 13 miles s.w. of Philadelphia. It is served
y three railroads and by steamship lines,
nd is the trading and shipping center of a
ighly industrialized region. In Chester are
xtensive shipbuilding plants, steel mills and
oundries, munition works, locomotive works,
il refineries, automobile assembly plants, and
actories producing textiles, paper products,
oor coverings, and chemicals. Pennsylvania
lilitary College, founded in 1821, and the
rozer Theological Seminary (Baptist),
ounded in 1867, are located in the city. Of
istoric interest are Pusey House, built in
683; the Courthouse, built in 1724; and
Vashington House (1747), in which General
eorge Washington wrote his account of the
attle of Brandywine for the Continental
ongress. Founded as Upland in 1644 by
wedish settlers, Chester is the second-oldest
ommunity in Pennsylvania. The Dutch con-
rolled the settlement from 1655 to 1664,
vhen it was placed under English sovereignty.
Villiam Penn, founder of Pennsylvania, gave
he settlement its present name in 1682. In
701 Chester was incorporated as a borough,
nd from 1789 to 1851 it was the county seat
f Delaware County. It received its char-

ter as a city in 1866. Pop. (1960) 63,658.

CHESTER, county seat and episcopal see of
Cheshire, England, on the river Dee, about
16 miles s.e. of Liverpool. It is one of the
most picturesque towns in England. It stands
on a rocky sandstone height, and its still surrounded by the entire circuit of its ancient
walls, nearly 2 miles around, 7 or 8 feet thick,
and forming a promenade with parapets,
where two persons can walk abreast. The ancient gateways have been all rebuilt. The castle, with the exception of "Cæsar's Tower",
has been moved, its site being occupied by
barracks and county buildings. The two main
streets cross each other at right angles, and
were cut out of the rock by the Romans 4 to
10 feet below the level of the houses. These
streets exhibit the curious arrangement called
the "rows"; the front parts of their second
stories, as far back as 16 feet, form a continuous paved promenade or covered gallery.
There are a considerable number of the picturesque old timber houses of the 16th century, and many of the more modern buildings
are in the same style of architecture. Cheshire
cathedral is an irregular massive structure of
red sandstone, 375 by 200 feet, with a massive
tower of 127 feet. It was formerly the church
of the abbey of St. Werburgh, which for 650
years was one of the richest in England. The
present bishopric of Chester dates from the
reign of Henry VIII. About 3½ miles from
the city is Eaton Hall, seat of the Duke of
Westminster.

The tourist trade is an important factor in
the economic life of the city. Industry in Chester, and just outside its walls, includes metalworking and the manufacture of foods and
tobacco. Pop. (1961 prelim.) 59,283.

CHESTERFIELD, town in Derbyshire, England, at the confluence of the Hipper and
Rother rivers, 24 m. by rail N.N.E. of the town
of Derby. Chesterfield is of great antiquity; it
was mentioned in the *Domesday Book* (q.v.).
Among its notable buildings are the church
of St. Mary and All Saints, dating from about
1350; the grammar school, founded in 1574;
and the Stephenson Memorial Hall, constructed in 1879. Lead and iron ores are mined, and
slate and stone are quarried in the vicinity of
Chesterfield. Industrial establishments in the
town include iron and brass foundries, and
plants manufacturing machinery, textiles, and
earthenware. Pop. (1961 prelim.) 67,833.

CHESTERFIELD, 4th EARL OF, PHILIP
DORMER STANHOPE (1694–1773), English man
of letters and statesman, born in London and
educated at Cambridge. He was elected to the
House of Commons in 1715 as Lord Stanhope

of Shelford, and entered the House of Lords in 1726 when he succeeded his father as Earl of Chesterfield. From 1728 to 1732 he was ambassador to the Dutch Republic, during which period (1730) he was also appointed lord high steward. At first Chesterfield supported the Whig ministry of his friend Horace Walpole; but his opposition to that ministry's excise measures resulted in his dismissal from the stewardship (1733). During the next period he carried on vigorous opposition both in Parliament and, under the name of Geffery Broadbottom, in the public press against both Walpole and King George II; in 1743 a coalition including Chesterfield, sometimes known as the "Broadbottom Party", came into office, with Henry Pelham as prime minister, and Chesterfield was again sent to The Hague as British ambassador (1744). His most important post was that of lord lieutenant of Ireland (1745–46); his administration was characterized by its tolerance and by firmness in insisting on peace between the opposing factions. After his appointment as secretary of state in 1746 his relations with King George improved. He is credited with a major role in the calendar reform of 1751, when Great Britain adopted the Gregorian calendar; see CALENDAR REFORM.

His later career was identified with literature rather than politics. Chesterfield knew many of the leading literary figures of the period, including Voltaire, Pope, and Swift. His relations with the lexicographer Dr. Samuel Johnson were less cordial, Johnson having rejected in a famous letter Chesterfield's offer of patronage which came eight years too late. Chesterfield is best known as the author of *Letters to His Son*, addressed to his illegitimate son, Philip Stanhope (not to be confused with his godson of the same name, adopted after the death of the first Philip Stanhope). These *Letters* (published posthumously in 1774), noted for their graceful and witty literary style, faithfully depict the aristocratic society of the 18th century of which the Earl of Chesterfield was a conspicuous member.

CHESTERTON, GILBERT KEITH (1874–1936), English author, born in London and educated at St. Paul's School. He studied art and began his literary career as a reviewer of books on art. He later became a regular contributor to a number of English and American magazines and achieved distinction as a poet and literary critic. Chesterton was a defender, on the whole, of conservative ideas in religion, philosophy, economics, and politics. His literary style was brilliant and vigorous and his

powers of reasoning so ingenious that he was often termed a "master of paradox". In 1922 he became a Roman Catholic and subsequently wrote extensively in defense of that faith. Among his numerous writings are the volumes of poetry *The Wild Knight* (1900) and *The Ballad of the White Horse* (1911); books of essays on politics, religion, and other subjects, including *Heretics* (1905), *Orthodoxy* (1908), *What's Wrong with the World* (1910), and *All I Survey* (1933); the critical works *Robert Browning* (1903), *George Bernard Shaw* (1909), *St. Francis of Assisi* (1923), *Robert Louis Stevenson* (1927), and *Chaucer* (1932); the novels *The Napoleon of Notting Hill* (1904), *The Man Who Was Thursday* (1908), and *The Ball and the Cross* (1909); and the detective stories *The Club of Queer Trades* (1905), *The Innocence of Father Brown* (1911), *The Wisdom of Father Brown* (1914), *Incredulity of Father Brown* (1926), *The Man Who Knew Too Much and other Stories* (1922), and *The Scandal of Father Brown* (1935). See DETECTIVE STORY.

CHESTNUT, common name for trees of the genus *Castanea* in the Beech family, or for the fruit of these trees. The American chestnut, *C. dentata*, is a magnificent tree, reaching a height of 100 feet and a trunk diameter of 3 to 4 feet. It was formerly one of the commonest trees in forests from Maine to Michigan and southward to Louisiana, and was much valued both for its delicious nuts and for its timber, which was coarse-grained, light, and durable. These trees have been attacked by a disease called chestnut blight caused by a fungus, *Endothia parasitica*. The disease, probably imported from the Orient, started near New York City about 1904 and rapidly spread throughout the country. No cure has been found, and virtually every American chestnut tree in the U.S. has been killed. Although young shoots spring up around the dead trunks, they are killed before they become old enough to bear fruit.

Several foreign chestnut trees, notably the European chestnut, *C. sativa*, the Japanese chestnut, *C. crenata*, and the Chinese chestnut, *C. mollissima*, have been cultivated in the U.S. These three species are comparatively resistant to blight. They are smaller than the American chestnut, and have larger nuts, which, however, are less tasty. Some Japanese species with inferior nuts appear to be almost completely blight-resistant. Several varieties of hybrid, blight-resistant chestnuts are now on the market.

The chinquapin, *C. pumila*, is a native American species, much smaller than any of he above, which is attractive but has a very inferior nut. It has suffered extensively from blight. See also HORSE CHESTNUT; WATER CHESTNUT.

CHEVALIER, MAURICE (1889–), French actor and singer, born in Ménilmontant. He began his stage career at the age of 7, appearing as a singer in the Palais du Travail, at Belleville. Between 1909 and 1913, he appeared as a dancing partner of the comedienne Mistinguett at the Folies-Bergère, Paris. After World War I, he won wide popularity in various dramatic productions and revues. In 1929 he made his first American appearance, presenting a repertoire of songs at Ziegfeld's New Amsterdam Roof Garden, in New York City. Thereafter he played leading roles in numerous motion pictures, including *The Innocents of Paris, Paramount on Parade, The Beloved Vagabond,* and *Gigi,* and made additional music-hall and concert appearances in such cities as Paris, London, and New York. He wrote *Ma Route et Mes Chansons* (1946; Eng. trans., *Man in the Straw Hat,* 1949) and *With Love* (as told to Eileen and Robert Mason, 1960).

CHEVIOT HILLS, a mountain range in the counties of Northumberland and Roxburgh, in the English and Scottish borders, and extending 35 miles from near the junction of the Till and Tweed rivers in the N.E., to the sources of the Liddel River in the S.W. The highest point is Cheviot Hill (2658 ft.). The hills are noted for a valuable breed of sheep and for their connection with historic border warfare.

CHEVROTAIN, a small traguloid ruminant found in Africa and the East Indies, and intermediate between deer and swine. On account of their heavy hind parts they have the aspect of certain rodents, as the agoutis, but are often confounded with musk deer. Several species inhabit s. India and Ceylon and one inhabits the Philippine Islands; the best-known are the kanchil, *Tragulus kanchil,* of

Chevrotain, Tragulus kanchil

Bettmann Archive
Painting of a Cheyenne warrior by the American artist Frederic Remington

the Malayan Islands, and the Indian chevrotain or mouse deer, *Tragulus meminna.* A related species, the water chevrotain, *Dorcatherium aquaticum,* is found in w. Africa. All are shy, walking with an odd, tiptoe gait and standing about 12 inches high. They belong to a survival of a group widely distributed in Middle Tertiary times and are traceable to the same ancestry as the deer. See DEER.

CHEYENNE, a tribe of North American Algonquian Indians, formerly inhabiting Wyoming, but now living on reservations in Oklahoma and Montana. They lived at one time on the upper Cheyenne River, and according to tradition were friends of the Ojibway and the Dakotas while these two tribes were at war with each other. At last the Ojibway, becoming suspicious, set upon the Cheyenne and drove them down into the Dakota country. After this they finally divided into two bands, one of which became affiliated with the Kiowas of the south, and the other with the Dakotas of the north, forming respectively, the Southern and Northern Cheyenne.

CHEYENNE, the capital of Wyoming, and county seat of Laramie Co., situated about 105 miles N. of Denver, Colo., on a plateau, 6060 ft. above sea level, at the foothills of the Rocky Mountains. The city was first settled in 1867 when the Union Pacific Railroad reached that point. In 1869 it was selected as the capital of Wyoming Territory, and in the same year was almost entirely destroyed by fire. In 1890, on the admittance of Wyoming to the Union as a State, Cheyenne became the State capital. The city has a commission form of government.

Numerous parks and broad streets and boulevards give Cheyenne an attractive appearance. Notable buildings include the State Capitol, the governor's mansion, the city hall and county courthouse, the State Supreme Court Building, the Federal Building and Post Office, the Union Pacific Station, a veterans' hospital, the Convent of the Holy Child Jesus, and Saint Mary's Catholic Cathedral. One mile northwest of the city is Fort Francis E. Warren (formerly Fort D. A. Russell), a large permanent United States military post. Near the fort are the Pole Mountain Maneuver Grounds of the U.S. Army. West of the city is the Medicine Bow National Forest.

Coal, iron, and oil are mined in the vicinity of Cheyenne, and there are numerous large ranches, both cattle and sheep. Dry farming is also an important industry of the region. The city is noted for the shipping of beef cattle and sheep to the East, and is a supply center for hunting and sports equipment. In the city are railroad shops and, in the Municipal Airport, airplane repair shops. Pop. (1960) 43,505.

CHIABRERA, GABRIELLO (1552–1637), Italian poet, born in Savona, and educated in Rome. He enjoyed the patronage of the leading princes of Italy. He rigidly imitated Greek and Latin verse, thus inhibiting originality of thought, but the sculptural effect of his metrical studies widened the outlook of his contemporaries in matters of form. His methods influenced various modern Italian poets, notably Giuseppe Parini (1729–99) and Giosuè Carducci. Much of Chiabrera's verse actually was inspired by the 16th-century French poet Pierre de Ronsard and his associates, known as the Pléiade (see PLEIAD), whose spirit Chiabrera caught and transmitted to later Italian poets. Chiabrera has been called the "Italian Pindar". Several of his shorter lyrics are among the best in Italian literature.

CHIANG KAI-SHEK or, in Peking dialect, CHIANG CHIEH-SHIH, real name CHIANG CHUNG-CHENG (1886–   ), Chinese soldier and statesman, born near Ningpo (now Ninghsien), Chekiang Province, and educated at Paoting (now Tsingyuan) Military Academy and the Military Staff College, in Tokyo. He was married at the age of fourteen. During a visit to Japan in 1905 he became acquainted with the exiled Chinese revolutionary leader Sun Yat-sen (q.v.). Two years later, while still a student, he joined the Ko Min Tang ("revolutionist party"), founded by Sun and known later as the Kuomintang ("people's party"). Following the outbreak (September, 1911) of the revolution against the Chinese imperial government he entered the revolutionary army as a regimental commander and participated in the capture of Shanghai. He remained in the military service after the establishment (1912) of the Chinese Republic, aided Sun's abortive attempt (1913) to overthrow the reactionary Yüan Shih-k'ai regime, and fought in several of the ensuing civil wars and uprisings. Returning (1917) to civilian life, he engaged in various business activities until 1921, when he resumed his association with Sun, then president of the insurgent Southern Chinese Republic. He was selected (1923) by Sun, a close friend of the newly organized Russian Bolshevik government, to visit Russia and study its military and social systems.

In 1924, on his return to South China, he organized and became head of the Whampoa Military Academy, training center for the leading cadres of the Kuomintang army. Appointed commander in chief in September, 1925, several months after President Sun's death, he retained the services of the Soviet military specialists serving with the Kuomintang army and otherwise adhered to Sun's policies, notably the policy of vigorous prosecution of the war against the northern Chinese regime. His forces overran two of the northern provinces during the final months of 1925, and in 1926 he led an expeditionary force through Hunan Province to the banks of the Yangtze River and established Kuomintang headquarters at Wuchang, one of the chief centers of the revolutionary movement in the north. He was elected to the Central Executive Committee of the Kuomintang in 1926 and appointed chairman of the Military Affairs Commission.

During the spring of 1927, a period of bitter dissension between the conservative and radical wings of the Kuomintang, Chiang assumed leadership of the conservative faction. His initial acts in this capacity included removal of the Kuomintang capital to Nanking, proscription of the Chinese Communist Party (then a part of the Kuomintang), and expulsion of the Soviet mission. In a crucial action (April), Chiang's forces entered Shanghai, thwarted an attempted Communist coup, and killed thousands of Reds. He retired to private life in August, 1927. Having previously divorced his first wife, he married (December) Soong Mei-ling, a sister of Sun's widow and a member of one of the wealthiest and most influential families in China. Through this marriage, Chiang formed valuable connections with important business interests. Originally a Confucianist, he was converted to Methodism, the religion of his wife's family, shortly after his marriage. Yielding to urgent appeals from the Kuomintang, he returned to his military command early in 1928. In October, after capturing Peking (subsequently called Peiping) and defeating the armies of the northern war lords, he was made president (chairman of the State Council) of the newly established Kuomintang government and generalissimo of the armed forces. His administration, lasting nearly three years, was characterized by the eradication of various social evils inherited from the empire, but prosecution of the war against the Communists imposed severe strains on national unity. In an effort to promote harmony among dissident groupings within the Kuomintang, he again withdrew to private life in 1931, being succeeded in the presidency by Lin Sên (1867?–1943). Chiang continued, however, to dominate the Chinese government.

Chiang was reappointed commander in chief of the armed forces in 1932, during the period of grave crisis engendered by the Japanese annexation of Manchuria. Except for a stubborn defense of Shanghai, the Kuomintang offered little more than token resistance to Japanese encroachments, however, and during the next few years Chiang was engaged chiefly in successive campaigns against the Communists. By the end of 1935 he had succeeded in driving them from their main stronghold (Kiangsi and Fukien provinces) into northwest China. Meanwhile Japan had begun to occupy sections of China proper.

Anti-Japanese sentiment was widespread in China during 1936, but Chiang, who had assumed the premiership in the previous year, continued his efforts to forestall further aggression by concessions to Japan, while attempting to organize the nation for an eventual decisive struggle. Willingly acceding to Japanese demands for more effective action against the Chinese Reds, the government ordered a general anti-Communist campaign early in December. To insure action in Shensi, where the Nationalist commander General Chang Hsueh-liang (q.v.) had been fraternizing with the Communists, Chiang flew to Sian (Chang's headquarters) for the purpose of removing him. On Dec. 12, soon after his arrival, Chiang was kidnaped on Chang's orders and five of the generals in his entourage were executed. The Nationalist government refused to negotiate with the insurgent leader regarding Chiang's release, which was promised subject to certain conditions, principally an immediate declaration of war against Japan and readmission of the Chinese Communist Party to the Kuomintang. Private negotiations for his release continued until Dec. 25, when Chang apparently capitulated and voluntarily left Sian as Chiang's prisoner. Chang received a ten-year prison sentence on Dec. 31, but at Chiang's request the government pardoned him a few days later.

In the half-year period following the Sian *coup* Chiang was instrumental in securing a complete reversal of Kuomintang policy toward the Chinese Communists and Japan. Armed resistance to further Japanese aggression was approved by the Central Executive Committee of the Kuomintang in February, 1937; Kuomintang-Communist agreements for united opposition to Japan were concluded at about the same time. Chiang took command of the national military establishment at the beginning (July 7, 1937) of the Sino-Japanese War and, employing positional and guerrilla military tactics, led a brilliant defensive struggle during the next four years. For most of this period he also served as premier. In January, 1942, after Japan entered World War II on the side of the Axis powers, he was made supreme commander of all Allied ground and air forces in the Chinese theater of operations (China, Indo-China, and Burma). He was elected president of China in September, 1943, following the death of Lin Sên. In November, 1943, he participated in the Cairo Conference (q.v.), which defined Allied war aims with respect to Japan.

Comprehensive programs for the institution of representative government and for the social and economic rehabilitation of China were enunciated by Chiang during the final year of World War II. His initial objective was accomplished with the promulgation (Jan. 1, 1947) of a republican constitution. In April, 1948, he was elected the first constitutional president of China. Meanwhile Kuomintang-Communist rivalries had erupted into large-scale hostilities, and the war-weary Chinese people rapidly lost confidence in Chiang's government. As a consequence of repeated Communist victories and in order to facilitate peace negotiations, he resigned as president and commander in chief in January, 1949. In the following December, after collapse of Nationalist resistance on the mainland and the removal of the republican capital to Formosa, he resumed the presidency. Given economic and military aid by the United States, which refused to recognize the Communist-led People's Republic of China, Chiang's regime grad-

Monkmeyer (Tiers)
Chiang Kai-shek

ually transformed Formosa into a strong defense bastion against the mounting power of Asiatic communism. Late in 1954 and early in 1955 Chiang's forces repulsed repeated Communist air raids against Quemoy, Matsu, the Tachens, and other Nationalist-held islands off the coast of China. Nevertheless, the Nationalists evacuated the Tachens in February, 1955. Despite this setback, Chiang periodically reiterated his determination to reconquer the Chinese mainland. His works include *China's Destiny* (1947) and *Soviet Russia in China* (1957).   E.O.R.

CHIANG KAI-SHEK, MADAME (1898–), Chinese sociologist, statesman, and writer, born in Shanghai, and educated at Wellesley College, Mass., U.S.A. She was Mei-ling Soong of the noted Soong family before her marriage to Chiang in 1927. She was a member of many commissions and councils for the improvement of social and economic conditions in China. During World War II she assisted Chiang Kai-Shek in military campaigns, defense work, and foreign affairs. She frequently visited the United States on missions to secure aid for the Nationalist cause. Among her writings are *China Shall Rise Again* (1941) and *Sure Victory* (1955).

CHIAROSCURO (It. *chiaro,* "light"; *oscuro,* "shade"), the distribution of lights and shades in a painting or drawing. The term was applied initially to a method of wood engraving (q.v.). The first great master of chiaroscuro in Italian painting was Leonardo

da Vinci, and it was the chief characteristic of the art of his pupils. It was also practiced extensively by the Italian painters Correggio and Caravaggio and by the German painter Matthias Grünewald (qq.v.) and was an outstanding characteristic of Dutch painting. Its greatest master was Rembrandt (q.v.). The term *chiaroscuro,* as used today, refers generally to the light and dark effects obtained by the old masters; the term *values* has replaced it in modern art usage.

CHIBA, city in the prefecture of the same name, Honshu Island, Japan. The city is at the northeastern extremity of Tokyo Bay and forms a suburb of the city of Tokyo 17 m. to the w. Extensive fisheries are in the vicinity. Area of prefecture, 1960 sq.m.; pop. (1960) 2,306,010. Pop. of city (1960) 241,615.

CHIBCHA, or MUYSCA, an important South American Indian nation or confederacy centering, at the time of the Spanish Conquest, on the upper Magdalena River, about Bogotá, Colombia. Detached tribes of the same stock were found along the isthmus and in Costa Rica. In culture the Chibchas ranked close to the Quechuas, practicing agriculture by the aid of an extensive system of irrigation, weaving cotton cloth, and working gold with a high degree of skill, although they were ignorant of the use of copper and bronze. They offered heroic resistance to the Spaniards, but were finally subdued and nearly exterminated. See AMERICAN INDIAN LANGUAGES; AMERICAN INDIANS: *Indians of South America: Andean Area.*

CHICAGO, county seat and port of entry of Cook Co., Ill., and second-largest city in the United States, on the s.w. shore of Lake Michigan, 908 miles by rail w. of New York City and about 2275 miles by rail E. of San Francisco. Chicago is one of the principal industrial cities of the nation. The site of the city, 225 sq.m. in area, is low, flat and crescent-shaped, and approximately 600 feet above sea level. It extends along Lake Michigan for 26 m. in a N. and s. direction and is situated on both sides of the Chicago R. (q.v.), which divides less than a mile inland from its mouth into two branches, one extending N.W. and the other s.w. The river and its branches separate the city into three sections, known as the North, West, and South sides. These sections of the city are connected by a large number of bridges, a majority of which are movable, and by a system of rapid-transit subway tunnels. Local transportation facilities consist of an elevated and subway rapid-transit system.

nd motorbus lines.

Twenty-seven trunk-line railroad routes, onverge on Chicago, linking it with all major merican and Canadian cities. Its unsurpassed tatus as a distribution center, which resulted rom its position on the natural overland oute between the industrial areas of the East nd the agricultural regions of the West, and rom its proximity to the Mississippi valley, s further indicated by the fact that approximately 10% of the total freight tonnage of he United States is handled at Chicago terminals. The city has about 150 railroad yards, vith a capacity of more than 200,000 cars. A elt-line railway system, with approximately ?000 miles of track, connects the various trunk-line systems, facilitating intracity freight transfer. Notable among the railway passenger terminals in the city are the Central, Grand Central, Dearborn, Union, La Salle Street, and North Western stations. Chicago is also serviced by numerous cross-coun-

try motorbus and truck lines, and by most of the major U.S. air-transport systems.

The business section of the city largely centers on the South Side, near the lake front, in an area known as the Loop, which is so named because it is encircled by the elevated-railway system. Here are situated many of the leading railway passenger terminals, hotels, commercial firms, banks, theaters, newspaper-publishing plants, public buildings, and sky-scrapers. Among the best-known thorough-fares of the Loop area are State, Clark, Dearborn, La Salle, Market, and Madison streets. Notable Chicago buildings include the City Hall-County Building, twin structures of limestone in the French Renaissance style; the Board of Trade building, a massive granite edifice 612 feet high; the 24-story Merchandise Mart, a wholesale merchandising center covering two city blocks; the Tribune Tower, the Marshall Field and Co. department store; the U.S. Court House; the

Fred G. Korth

The Union Stockyards in Chicago, since 1865 a world center for livestock trading and meat packing. The famous stockyards occupy a square mile on the city's South Side.

The sky line of Chicago, viewed across Grant Park and a section of Lake Michigan. Behin the skyscrapers that line the lake front lies the famous business area known as the Loop.

Pittsfield, Kemper Insurance, Prudential, and Palmolive buildings, all more than 550 feet in height; and the Conrad Hilton, largest hotel in the world.

A large percentage of the well-to-do families of Chicago have their homes in the contiguous suburban areas. The exclusive residential neighborhoods in the city proper are principally in a narrow belt along the lake front. Chicago contains many slum areas. The largest of these lies to the s. of the Loop on the South Side, where more than 600,000 Negroes are concentrated. A number of other depressed neighborhoods are occupied chiefly by foreign-born residents, who total about 650,000. Among the principal foreign-born groups in a recent year were Poles (119,000), Germans (83,000), Russians (67,000), Italians (66,400), Swedes (46,000), Irish (40,000), and Czechoslovaks (33,000).

In addition to being the leading center in the world for livestock trading and slaughtering and for meat packing, Chicago is the chief grain market of the United States, with enormous storage and distribution facilities. World grain prices are largely determined at the Chicago Board of Trade, a speculative trading organization established in 1848. The city also ranks second in the nation in wholesale and retail trade, being exceeded only by New York City. Chicago is one of the principal American inland ports, easily accessible to the waterborne traffic of the Great Lakes. Most of the incoming shipments are bulk cargoes, notably iron ore, coal, coke, copper, and lumber. Outgoing cargoes include large quantities of grain, meat, and manufactured goods. Since 1959, Chicago has been connected with

the world's salt-water ports via the Sai Lawrence Seaway, for which it is the s.\ terminus. Chicago is linked to the Mississip R. and Gulf ports by the Illinois Waterway, barge route completed in 1933. Most of th dock-terminal facilities of the port are co centrated at Calumet Harbor, in the s.e. se tion of the city. Waterborne cargoes handle at Chicago in a recent year exceeded 75,00(000 tons.

Chicago has a large number of manufa turing industries. It ranks ahead of Pitt burgh, Pa., in the production of iron and stee and leads the nation in the manufacture c farming machinery and railway cars. Durin World War II three airplane-engine factorie including the largest factory of this type i existence, were in operation in the city Among other plants established in the cit during World War II were two large airplan factories, a factory producing tank parts, an an aluminum-fabrication plant. Addition important industries of the city include petrc leum refining, printing, publishing, brewin and soapmaking, and the manufacture telephone equipment, radio equipment, refri erators, motor vehicles and parts, men clothing, musical instruments, foundry an machine-shop products, furniture, paints an varnishes, confections, and bakery product The city has approximately 12,000 manufa turing establishments, and the annual val of all manufactured products exceeds $6,00(000,000.

The educational and cultural facilities Chicago are among the best in the natio In addition to a modern public-school sy tem, Chicago City Junior College, numero parochial schools, and many privately operated art and technical-training institutes, the city has a number of outstanding schools of higher learning. These include the University of Chicago (see CHICAGO, UNIVERSITY OF), the Illinois Institute of Technology, Loyola University (qq.v.), Mundelein College, De Paul University, Chicago Theological Seminary, John Marshall Law School, St. Francis Xavier College for Women, Pestalozzi Froebel Teachers College, and the Hebrew Theological College. The medical school of the University of Illinois (q.v.) and the medical and other professional schools of Northwestern University (q.v.) also are in the city.

Notable among the other educational facilities of Chicago are its libraries. The Chicago Public Library, established in 1872, has about 2,200,000 volumes, and maintains approximately 100 branches and sub-branches. Others include the Newberry Library, founded in 1887, which has a collection of more than 450,000 volumes dealing with literature, music, philology, and archeology; the John Crerar Library, founded in 1889, with about 820,000 volumes, mainly on scientific subjects; the Library of International Relations, founded in 1932; and the libraries of the various schools of higher learning, notably that of the University of Chicago.

Other cultural and educational institutions are the Art Institute of Chicago (founded as the Chicago Institute of Fine Arts, in 1879), which has outstanding collections of paintings, prints, ceramics, medieval sculptures, Oriental art, and other art objects, and maintains one of the leading art schools in America; the Chicago Natural History Museum (founded in 1893), noted for its Hall of Babylonian Archeology and for its ethnological, botanical, zoological, and geological exhibits; the Chicago Academy of Sciences, Museum of Natural History (founded in 1857), which contains habitat groups illustrating the natural history of the Chicago and other North American areas; the Chicago Historical Society (founded in 1856), with numerous exhibits and books relating to American history and an internationally famous collection of Lincolniana; the Adler Planetarium and Astronomical Museum; and the Museum of Science and Industry. Chicago is also the home of the Chicago Symphony Orchestra and Hull House, celebrated social settlement founded by Jane Addams (q.v.). Daily newspapers published in the city include the *Tribune,* the *American,* the *Daily News,* and the *Sun-Times.*

Chicago is the seat of an archdiocese of the Roman Catholic Church, and has more than 1500 Christian and Jewish places of worship. Notable among these are the church of St. Patrick, erected in 1856, the Second Presbyterian Church, built in 1874, and Temple Sholom, built in 1930.

The Chicago park system comprises about 135 public parks and a number of bathing beaches, recreation areas, and boulevards. Many of these occupy remarkably beautiful sites along the shores of Lake Michigan. The largest park in the city is Lincoln Park, about 1000 acres in extent, which has numerous recreational facilities, a Zoological Garden, and a bird sanctuary. Grant Park, consisting of 300 acres, has a number of notable features, including the John G. Shedd Aquarium, Buckingham Memorial Fountain (280 feet in diameter), and a seated figure of Abraham Lincoln, by Augustus Saint-Gaudens. Adjoining Grant Park is Soldier Field, a stadium with a seating capacity of 100,000, which commemorates the Chicago war dead of World War I. Among other well-known Chicago parks are Burnham Park, Jackson Park, Union Park, and Garfield Park. Chicago Zoological Park, popularly known as Brookfield Zoo, is located in Brookfield, a village 14 miles s.w. of the city. The Cook County Forest Preserve, a woodland belt of 33,000 acres on the outskirts of the city, provides further recreational facilities.

The name "Chicago" is probably derived from *She-kag-ong* (Ojibway Indian, "wild onion place"), a term applied originally to what is now the Chicago R. The first Europeans to visit the *She-kag-ong* were Louis Joliet and Jacques Marquette, French explorers, who arrived there in 1673. Later the locality was visited by other French explorers, notably Robert Cavelier, Sieur de La Salle. Following 1684 the river and the surrounding territory were called *Chekagou* by the French, who controlled the region until 1763, when it was ceded to the British at the end of French and Indian War. After the American Revolutionary War the British ceded it, along with the other western territories, to the United States.

Jean Baptiste Point de Saible, a fur trader and native of Santo Domingo (now the Dominican Republic) built the first house on the site of the present city in 1779. In 1803, Federal troops of the U.S. established a stockade, called Fort Dearborn, near the mouth of the Chicago R., and the next year John Kinzie, of Quebec, acquired the property built by de Saible, becoming the first permanent settler of North American origin.

While attempting to evacuate Fort Dearborn, in August, 1812, the garrison was ambushed, with many casualties, by hostile Indians, who burned the fort. It was rebuilt 4 years later. By 1830 a village consisting of 12 families had developed near Fort Dearborn. Chicago was incorporated as a town in 1833, when its population was 550. In March, 1837, when the number of inhabitants totaled 4170, it was incorporated as a city.

Chicago rapidly became one of the busiest ports on the Great Lakes, and this process was accelerated by the completion, in 1848, of its first railroad, the Chicago and Galena Union R.R., and of the Illinois and Michigan Canal (q.v.). The population was 29,963 in 1850, and within the next 10 years it increased about 360%. In 1860, Chicago was the scene of the historic National Convention of the Republican Party, which nominated Abraham Lincoln for the Presidency of the United States. Ten years later the population was 298,977.

On October 8–9, 1871, one of the most disastrous fires in the history of the nation swept the city, destroying 17,450 buildings and causing property damage of about $200,000,000. This represented nearly one third of the city, covering an area of 3½ sq.m. Approximately 300 persons perished and more than 100,000 were made homeless before the blaze was extinguished. Within a year the city was largely rebuilt, with the aid of contributions from the rest of the U.S. and from other countries.

The workmen of Chicago were among the first in America to attempt collective bargaining with employers, and the first to demand an 8-hour working day. Since 1877, when a walk-out of railroad workers occurred, the city has been the scene of a number of major strikes. One of the more notable of these took place at the McCormick Harvester Company on May 3, 1886. Several strikers were killed by the police on this occasion, and the violence led to a protest demonstration, afterward known as the Haymarket Square Riot (q.v.), in which 7 police were killed. Despite failure of the authorities to produce incriminating evidence, seven leaders of the demonstration were convicted of murder and four were hanged.

In 1893 the World's Columbian Exposition, commemorating the 400th anniversary of the discovery of America, took place in Chicago. By 1900 the population of the city was 1,698,575. Alternate periods of corruption and reform characterized the political history of Chicago for many years. After the election as mayor, in 1915, of William Hale Thompson a protracted period of municipal graft and corruption ensued, for which both the Republican and Democratic organizations of the city shared responsibility. Serious race riots, which caused the death and injury of many Negro and white citizens, occurred in the city in 1919. Crime increased following the adoption of the 18th (Prohibition) Amendment to the Constitution of the United States, and Chicago won a reputation for its bootleggers and gangsters. Anton Joseph Cermak (q.v.), who was mayor from 1931 to 1933, initiated a reform movement that helped to reduce crime in the city. Another world's fair, the Century of Progress International Exposition, was held at Chicago in 1933. In June, 1945, the voters of the city authorized the Chicago Transit Authority, a municipal body, to purchase the privately-operated rapid-transit and street-car systems. Pop. (1960) 3,550,404.

HAROLD M. MAYER, UNIVERSITY OF CHICAGO

CHICAGO NATURAL HISTORY MUSEUM, or FIELD MUSEUM OF NATURAL HISTORY, one of the most important natural science museums in the world, located in Chicago and founded in 1893 with money donated by many Chicago citizens, including Marshall Field (q.v.), who subscribed $1,000,000 to the project. The museum, originally called the Columbian Museum of Chicago, opened in 1894 in the Fine Arts Building of the 1893 Chicago World's Fair Columbian Exposition. The present museum building in Grant Park, Chicago, was financed by a bequest of $4,000,-000 provided by the will of Marshall Field. His will also granted the museum an endowment of $4,000,000.

CHICAGO RIVER, river in northeastern Illinois, situated chiefly within the city of Chicago. Its main branch divides, about 1 m. inland from its mouth on Lake Michigan, into 2 forks, one extending s.w. and the other N.W. The normal direction of flow, into Lake Michigan, was reversed during construction of the Chicago sewage disposal system, the principal feature of which was the Chicago Drainage Canal. The canal extends from a point on the South Branch of the river to a point on the Desplaines River at Lockport, Ill., providing an outlet for effluent from the purification plants of the Chicago Sanitary District. Together with the canal the river forms a link of the Illinois Waterway, a system which joins the Great Lakes to the Gulf of Mexico via the Illinois and Mississippi rivers. The Chicago River also is connected to the Illinois River by the Illinois and Michigan Canal (q.v.), which extends from the South Branch, at a point in the Bridgeport section of Chicago, to La Salle, Ill., nearly 100 m.

CHICAGO, UNIVERSITY OF, a co-educational, privately endowed institution of higher learning situated on the Midway Plaisance, between Washington and Jackson parks, on the South Side of Chicago. Though the university is nonsectarian, its charter requires that one of the members of the Board of Trustees must be a representative of the Baptist Theological Union. John D. Rockefeller founded the university in 1890. His own gifts amounted to $35,000,000 over a period of 20 years. The university was also liberally endowed by the Rockefeller Foundation and by many citizens of Chicago. Its organizer and first president (1890–1906), Dr. William Rainey Harper, divided the university year into four quarters rather than the usual two semesters, founded the university's summer school, sponsored the university press, and emphasized graduate study and research. In 1931, under Robert Maynard Hutchins (q.v.), who became president in 1929, Chicago University was reorganized according to a plan thenceforth known as the "Chicago Plan". Under this system, in place of the undergraduate college and the graduate school, the university established a college division, for general education; four upper divisions for research and advanced study—one each for the social, physical, and biological sciences, and one for the humanities; and professional schools, including schools of divinity, library work, law, medicine, and social service administration. To obtain a bachelor's degree students were required to pass fourteen comprehensive examinations in various fields. The examinations in a given field were taken after preparation which might consist either of undergraduate courses or of independent study. The guiding principle behind the Chicago Plan was that the bachelor's degree represented the accumulation of a certain body of knowledge. The means and the time required to obtain that body of knowledge were of secondary importance. Thus, one of the most important features of the system was the so-called placement tests, administered on entrance to the college. If the placement tests indicated that a student's knowledge was already sufficient to pass the comprehensive examination in a particular field, he was automatically exempted from taking it. It was possible, therefore, for a student to earn the bachelor's degree in less than four years. However, even if a student were exempted from all fourteen comprehensive examinations, he was required to complete at least one year of study, often on a graduate level. Under the provisions of a change adopted

in 1953 most undergraduates presently complete four years of undergraduate study that combines, in about equal parts, work in general education with work in a department of specialization. Ten year-long courses in general education are required of all students in the college. Students are still eligible for advanced standing on the basis of placement tests, however.

The graduate divisions of the university grant all advanced academic degrees. More than half of the student body consists of graduate students.

In connection with research on atomic energy, the university maintains the Enrico Fermi Institute, the Institute for the Study of Metals, and the Institute of Radiobiology and Biophysics. Members of the department of astronomy staff Yerkes Observatory (q.v.) and the McDonald Observatory of the University of Texas.

The total enrollment of the university in 1962 was about 6000 full-time students, including approximately 4000 graduate students; the faculty numbered about 860. The endowment was approximately $139,000,000, and the library contained 2,142,000 bound volumes. The University of Chicago Press, established in 1892 to provide facilities for the publication of scholarly works, issues about 100 books a year and a number of journals.

CHICHEN ITZA, the most important of the ancient ruined cities of Yucatan, situated 18 miles S.W. of Valladolid in the northern part of the peninsula. The name, meaning "Mouth of the Wells of Itza", is derived from the Itza tribe of Mayan stock which formerly occupied it, and from the two natural wells which formed the water supply and around which centered the religious and cultural life of the city. Chichén Itzá was founded early in the 6th century A.D. and abandoned about the year 670. Rebuilt some 300 years later, when the Itza returned to the region, it became the most important city of N. Yucatan and a center of Mayan culture. About 1200 A.D. the city was conquered by Toltec and Aztec invaders from Mexico, and under their influence it achieved an even greater development. It was abandoned a century or more before the coming of the Spaniards.

The principal ruins cover an area of one square mile. The general structural type is that of the platform pyramid, ascended by means of broad stairways leading to vaulted chambers the walls of which are covered with sculptured figures and hieroglyphic inscriptions, or vividly colored paintings resembling the Aztec codices. The material is white limestone with the walls made of mortar and broken stone, faced with cut stone.

Each prominent structure is known by the natives under distinct names, as the "Tennis Court" or "Ball Court", which is formed of two parallel walls, each 274 ft. long and 30 ft. thick, standing 120 ft. apart. Projecting from each wall 25 ft. above the ground is a sculptured ring of stone in the form of two entwined serpents. From Spanish descriptions it is certain that this was a courtyard devoted to the playing of a favorite game, in which the players strove to send the ball through the ring.

Another important ruin is the "Castle" (*Castillio*), a pyramidal mound one acre in area and rising to a height of 100 ft. The "Palace" or "Nunnery" (*Casa de las Monjas*), the "House of the Dark Writing" (*Akabtzib*), the "Red House" (*Chin-chan-chob*), the "Caracol" or Round Tower, and the temples of the Tables, the Tigers, and the Cones are among other notable ruins.

CHICKADEE. See TITMOUSE.

CHICKAHOMINY RIVER (Algonquin Indian, "river of the coarse-pounded corn"), a river of Virginia, about 90 m. long. It rises northwest of Richmond and flows in a general southeasterly direction, parallel for a number of miles to the James River, with which it merges about 8 miles west of Williamsburg. In the Civil War, during the Peninsular Campaign (q.v.) of 1862 to capture Richmond, the battles of Williamsburg, Hanover Court House, Fair Oaks, Mechanicsville, Gaines's Mill, Savage's Station, Frazier's Farm, and Malvern Hill, were fought on or near the banks of the Chickahominy, as was the Battle of Cold Harbor in 1864.

CHICKAMAUGA, BATTLE OF, the most sanguinary battle of the American Civil War, fought on September 19–20, 1863, near Chickamauga Creek, about 12 miles E. of Chattanooga, Tenn., in northern Georgia. The battle involved General William Starke Rosecrans' Army of the Cumberland, which numbered about 55,000 men, and a Confederate army, about 70,000 strong, commanded by General Braxton Bragg. The prize at stake was Chattanooga, which Rosecrans had occupied on September 9, following Bragg's withdrawal from the city. In the mistaken belief that Bragg had begun a general retreat southward, Rosecrans ordered pursuit. Reconnaissance soon established the fact that the Confederate command was preparing to launch an enveloping movement, which, if successful, would cut off the Union army from Chattanooga. To meet this threat, Rosecrans rapidly concentrated his three corps

along the upper Chickamauga. Five brigades of the Confederate army, which had deployed along the opposite bank of the creek, forced a crossing on the afternoon of September 18. These units were followed by others during the night. The battle began about 9:00 A.M. on the next day, with a heavy Confederate assault on the Union left, held by troops under General Henry Thomas. Severe losses were suffered by both sides in the subsequent action, most of which took place at point-blank range in heavy underbrush. By sunset, Rosecrans had committed his entire army to the action, while Bragg held in reserve three divisions, later reinforced by several brigades commanded by General James Longstreet.

The battle was resumed, with a Confederate attack, early on September 20. Because of a tactical error by Rosecrans, which resulted in the weakening of his right flank, and a misinterpreted order, which caused the withdrawal of a division from his center, Confederate forces under Longstreet broke through the Union line, rolling back its right flank. This section of the Union line, about 7000 men, escaped annihilation chiefly because of a heroic counter attack by two relief brigades under General Gordon Granger. About 4:30 P.M., General Thomas, later known as "the Rock of Chickamauga", who had withstood repeated attacks on the Union left, began a general withdrawal, occupying positions from which the Confederate pursuit was halted before nightfall. The Union army fell back to Chattanooga on the following day. Union casualties during the battle numbered 16,179, in killed, wounded, and missing, and Confederate losses were about 18,000. The percentage of total casualties exceeded that of any other battle of the war.

CHICKASAW, a Muskhogean tribe of North American Indians, formerly occupying northern Mississippi and the adjacent part of Tennessee, and later the western part of Oklahoma, under the name of the "Chickasaw Nation". They are now citizens of the United States. Originally they were a warlike people, and throughout the Colonial period adhered to the English side as against the French, who tried unsuccessfully to subdue them. From the close of the Revolution they maintained friendly relations with the United States. In 1832 they sold their lands E. of the Mississippi and moved to their present location. They joined the Confederacy during the Civil War, and at its close were obliged to free their slaves and admit them to equal Chickasaw citizenship. See AMERICAN INDIANS: *Southeastern Area*.

CHICKASHA, county seat of Grady Co., Okla., on the Washita R., about 40 miles s.w. of Oklahoma City. In the surrounding region, the fertile Washita Valley, cotton, corn, wheat, alfalfa, and sorghum are grown, and cattle are raised. The region is noted also for its large deposits of natural gas and oil, the Chickasha gas field being one of the largest in the world. In the city are cotton gins, cottonseed-oil mills, flour mills, machine shops, and factories for the processing of dairy and poultry products. Chickasha is the site of the Oklahoma College for Women, a State institution. Pop. (1960) 14,866.

CHICKEN. See FOWL; POULTRY.

CHICKEN POX or **VARICELLA,** in medicine, an acutely contagious disease, chiefly of children, being characterized by early fever, an eruption of papules and vesicles, and mild constitutional disturbances. In most cases fever is present 24 hours before the eruption appears. The eruption comes out in crops, on the face, scalp, or shoulders, as red, widely scattered papules, spreading slowly over the body, one crop maturing while another is appearing. Pitting is rare and generally occurs on the face, where the lesions are apt to become infected with pus germs. Chicken pox is extremely contagious, but very rarely dangerous and complications or serious sequelae are rare. Isolation of cases is necessary till all crusts separate and fall off. Chicken pox bears no relation to smallpox.

CHICKLING VETCH. See LATHYRUS.

CHICK-PEA, a plant of the genus *Cicer,* of the family Leguminosae. It has pinnate leaves, solitary axillary stalked flowers, and two-seeded pods, inflated like bladders. The common chick-pea, *C. arietinum,* is a native of southern Europe. It is an annual, 1½ to 2 feet high. The seeds are rich in starch and have a slightly bitterish taste; they are about the size of common peas. The ripe seeds are eaten, either boiled entire or made into pea soup. They are sometimes roasted as a substitute for coffee. A red-seeded variety is grown both for table and for stock food.

CHICKWEED, any of several plants used as food for cage birds, especially those of the genus *Stellaria* in the Pink family. One of the common weeds of gardens and cultivated fields is the species called also "stitchwort", or "starwort", *S. media.* It is a native of most parts of Europe and of Asia, and introduced into America. It is an annual, with a weak procumbent stem and ovate leaves, always characterized by having the stem curiously marked with one or two lines of hairs. The leaves of chickweed afford an instance of the "sleep of plants", in that they close up on the young shoots at night. Although generally regarded as a troublesome weed, chickweed is a good substitute for spinach or greens. A number of species of a nearly allied genus, *Cerastium,* also bear the name of "chickweed", or "mouse-ear chickweed", and the name is occasionally given to other allied plants, as *Holosteum umbellatum,* introduced into the United States from Europe, and called "jagged chickweed".

CHICOPEE, a city in Hampden Co., Mass.. 3 miles N. of Springfield, on the E. bank of the Connecticut R. and at the mouth of the Chicopee R. It is an industrial city, deriving hydroelectric power from the Chicopee R. Manufactured products include cotton and knit goods, textile machinery, firearms, automobile tires, and sporting goods. Chicopee was settled about 1652 and was a part of Springfield until 1848; it became a city in 1890, for a time known as Cabotville. The present city includes the separate divisions of Chicopee, Chicopee Falls, and Willimansett, and is the site of the College of Our Lady of the Elms (Catholic), and the location of Westover Air Base. Pop. (1960) 61,553.

CHICORY, or SUCCORY, a perennial herb, *Cichorium intybus,* of Europe, naturalized in the United States. It has heads of large, bright blue flowers and dandelionlike roots. The roasted and pulverized root is used in adulterating coffee, or as a substitute for it. The endive (q.v.) belongs to the same genus. *Cichorium* is the type genus of the family Cichoriaceae, which is regarded by some authorities as a tribe of the Compositae.

CHIEF JUSTICE, in the U.S. judicial system, the title of the presiding justice of the U.S. Supreme Court and of the presiding justices of the highest tribunals in most of the States. The Chief Justice of the United States is the highest judicial officer of the republic and is appointed for life by the President with the approval of the Senate. He orders the business of the Supreme Court and administers the oath of office to the President and Vice-President on the occasion of their inauguration. He is also invested with the function of presiding over the Senate in the event that it sits as a court to try an impeachment of the President of the United States.

The chief justices of State tribunals order the business of the courts over which they preside; they are chosen in a number of ways: in Massachusetts and a number of other States, the chief justice is appointed by the governor with the consent either of the upper house of the legislature or of a gubernatorial advisory body; in Pennsylvania, Missouri, Colorado, and a number of other States, the oldest judge in point of service on the supreme tribunal of the State is generally made chief justice; in Illinois, the judges of the Supreme Court choose one of their number to serve as chief justice; and in Florida, the judges of the highest State tribunal select one of their number by lot as chief justice. In New York State and in Maryland the title of the presiding justice of the supreme tribunal, the Court of Appeals, is Chief Judge.

In the English judicial system, the titles Lord Chief Justice of England and Chief Justice of the Court of Common Pleas (see COMMON PLEAS, COURT OF) are the equivalent of the U.S. title Chief Justice.

CH'IEN LUNG or KIEN LUNG (1711–99), Chinese emperor, fourth of the Ch'ing dynasty. His dynastic name was Kao Tsung. His reign, begun in 1736, following the death of his father, Yung Chêng, was marked by numerous achievements. He secured control of Tibet in 1751, and between 1755 and 1760 he conquered the Ili Valley region and Kashgaria, substantially increasing the imperial domain. An advocate of friendly policies toward the western nations, he approved, in 1784, a trade agreement with the United States. His domestic policies included encouragement of the arts, notably literature and pottery making. He abdicated in favor of his son, Chia Ch'ing, in 1796.

CHIETI, archiepiscopal city and capital of the province of the same name in Abruzzi e Molise, Italy. The city, 140 m. by rail E.N.E. of Rome, is situated more than 1000 ft. above sea level, and the Apennine Mountains rise above it on three sides; on the E., it faces the Adriatic Sea. There are a few remains in Chieti of ancient *Teate Marrucinorum,* the most important seat of the Sabelli, which fell into the hands of the Romans in 305 b.c. After Roman occupation, the city was held successively by the Lombards, Franks, and Normans. The religious order of the Theatines (Order of Clerks Regular), founded in 1524, takes its name from the city. The cathedral of Chieti is noted for its Gothic campanile. The modern city contains factories producing silk and woolen textiles, and is an important center of trade in wine, olive oil, grain, silk, and other products of the surrounding agricultural region. Pop. (1957) 43,841. Area of province, 997 sq.m.; pop. (1961) 379,319.

CHIGGER, the larva of any of several mites, particularly *Trombicula irritans,* which clings to the skin of men and animals, some-times burrowing under the skin. Chiggers, which are also called red bugs, jiggers, harvest mites, harvest lice, or harvest bugs, are common in southern U.S. They cling to grass stems and foliage and attach themselves to any animal that brushes against them. Their

Monsanto magazine
American chigger, Trombicula irritans
(greatly magnified)

bite is irritating but not dangerous. The term chigger is also applied to the chigoe (q.v.). See MITE.

CHIGOE, a tropical American flea, *Tunga* or *Sarcopsylla penetrans,* sometimes also called jigger, jigger flea, or chigger. Chigoes are smaller than common fleas, but otherwise resemble them. The female flea burrows under the skin of men and animals to lay her eggs. As the eggs develop, a painful and sometimes dangerous ulcer is formed. Chigoes are particularly likely to attack the skin of the feet.

CHIHUAHUA, a small, voiceless dog descended from the ancient breed known to the Toltec Indians of the 9th century. The modern breed was first discovered about 1850 in the state of Chihuahua, Mexico, from which it took its name. Two types of the breed exist, one with a smooth coat and one with a long-haired coat. The chief characteristics of both types are a well-rounded head, a slightly arched neck, a level back, and a moderately long tail. The Chihuahua weighs from one to eight pounds, may be of any color from white to black, and is alert and swift-moving.

CHIHUAHUA, capital of the state of Chihuahua, Mexico, 225 miles s. of El Paso, Texas. It is situated at an elevation of 4635 ft. above sea level, on the Chihuahua R., in a plain surrounded by mountains on all sides except the north. It has a fine public square, in which stands a monument erected to Miguel Hidalgo (q.v.) and his generals, the leaders of the revolution of 1810. The city is the center of a mining district and contains important textile mills. Chihuahua was founded about 1704 and became a prosperous mining community. In 1864 it was, for a time, the provisional capital of Mexico, under President Benito Juárez. Pop. (1960) 144,653.

CHILD, LYDIA MARIA (1802–80), American author and abolitionist, born in Medford, Mass. She wrote her first novel, *Hobomok,* in 1821; started *The Juvenile Miscellany,* the first monthly magazine for children in the United States; and taught in her private school in Watertown (1824–28). In 1833 appeared her *Appeal for That Class of Americans Called African,* the first antislavery book published in the U.S. She afterward became editor of the *National Anti-Slavery Standard* (1840–43). Her other works include *The Rebels* (1822), *The American Frugal Housewife* (1829), *Autumnal Leaves* (1856), *The Freedman's Book* (1865), and *Aspirations of the World* (1878).

CHILDBIRTH. See OBSTETRICS.

CHILD LABOR, designation applied originally to the practice, highly prevalent during the 19th century, of employing preadolescent children in industry and agriculture; now used to denote the employment of minors generally.

The employment of young children in gainful occupations was practiced throughout the world as a matter of course until relatively modern times. The use of child labor was not regarded as a social problem until the introduction of the factory system into England during the latter part of the 18th century. Owners of the new English cotton mills of that period collected pauper children throughout the kingdom, obtaining their services for the cost of maintenance. In some cases children 5 years of age were compelled to work from 13 to 16 hours a day. Although English social reformers attempted as early as 1802 to obtain legislative restrictions against the worst features of the child-labor system, nothing positive was accomplished for many years. Conditions as bad as those imposed on pauper children rapidly developed in enterprises employing nonpauper children. Often with the approval of political, cultural, and religious leaders, children were permitted to labor in hazardous occupations, notably mining. The resultant social evils included illiteracy, further impoverishment of poor families, and a multitude of diseased and crippled children. Popular agitation for reform steadily increased, but no effective action to ameliorate

conditions was taken until 1833, when the Factory Act was passed by Parliament. This act, providing merely for inspection of factories, and several subsequent acts gave little protection to child workers, however. The first significant English legislation dealing with the problem was enacted in 1878, when the minimum age of employees was raised to 10 years and employers were required to restrict employment of children between the ages of 10 and 14 to alternate days or consecutive half-days. In addition to making every Saturday a half-holiday, this legislation also limited the workday of children between 14 and 18 years of age to 12 hours, with an intermission of 2 hours for meals and rest.

Meanwhile the industrial system developed in other countries, bringing abuses of child labor similar to those in England. In the United States the employment of young boys and girls was common practice in the early years of the 19th century. Community leaders, imbued with puritanical ideas regarding the evils of idleness among children, co-operated with employers, helping them to recruit young factory hands from indigent families.

Inasmuch as the average working day in the mills of that period extended from dawn to dusk, education of child laborers manifestly was impossible. Measures to correct this evil were taken for the first time in Connecticut, the legislature of which, in 1813, passed a law requiring mill owners to provide instruction in reading, writing, and arithmetic for their child workers. The next important legislation affecting child labor, adopted in Massachusetts in 1842, limited the working day for children under 12 years of age to 10 hours. In 1848 the Pennsylvania State Legislature placed restrictions, for the first time in the United States, on the age levels of youth employed in silk, cotton, or woolen mills, establishing a minimum age of 12 years. Connecticut adopted a 9-year minimum in 1855, and two years later Rhode Island established a 12-year minimum, with the further stipulation that children from 12 to 15 years old must attend school for 3 months each year. Several other States adopted similar legislation. However, the number of children in industry increased tremendously in the U.S. after the Civil War, when industrial expansion resulted in unprecedented demand for labor power. By the end of the 19th century nearly one fifth of all American children between the ages of 10 and 16 were gainfully employed. This state of affairs continued for the next decade. Then, chiefly as the result of the public-enlightenment activities of various organizations, notably the National Child Labor Committee, the legislative bodies of a number of States enacted restrictive legislation, leading to sharp reductions in the number of children employed.

Because of the lack of uniformity in child-labor standards established in the various States, a condition which placed industries in States with relatively high standards in a disadvantageous competitive position, the Congress of the United States, in 1916, passed a law which set a national minimum age of 14 in industries producing nonagricultural goods for interstate commerce. In 1918 the Supreme Court of the United States ruled, in a 5 to 4 decision, that the legislation was unconstitutional. Another child-labor law, enacted in 1918, was also declared unconstitutional by the Supreme Court, in 1922. In 1924 both Houses of Congress passed an amendment to the Constitution, empowering Congress to "limit, regulate, and prohibit the labor of persons under eighteen years of age." The number of State legislatures which ratified the proposed amendment was 28, 8 less than the 36 required.

Despite the reluctance of State legislators to ratify the child-labor amendment, legislative attempts to deal with the problem nationally continued, notably during the New Deal administration of President Franklin D. Roosevelt. The National Industrial Recovery Act, passed by Congress in 1933, established a minimum age of 16 for workers in most industries. In hazardous industries a minimum age level of 18 was established. This law contributed to a substantial decrease in the number of young workers, but the U.S. Supreme Court ruled the act unconstitutional, in 1935. In the next year Congress passed the Walsh-Healey Act, which prohibits firms producing goods under Federal government contract from employing males under 16 years of age and females under 18. The next important legislation on the problem was the Fair Labor Standards Act, better known as the Wage and Hour Law, passed by Congress in 1938. This law bans from interstate commerce all goods manufactured in industries which employ children under 16 and all goods manufactured in industries which employ children of 16 and 17 and are judged hazardous by the Children's Bureau. The act exempts children working in agriculture if they are not legally required to attend school; children employed by parents in enterprises other than mining and manufacturing; and children of 14 and 15 employed in enterprises other than mining and manufacturing, provided such employment does not interfere with well-being, health, or schooling. However, with young workers employed predominantly in establishments producing goods solely for intrastate commerce, the Wage and Hour Law displaced relatively few young workers from industry.

In the early 1960's about 1,050,000 children aged 14 and 15 and 1,620,000 children aged 16 and 17 were employed in the United States. An undetermined number of children under the age of 14, mostly belonging to families of itinerant farm workers, were employed in agricultural labor.

CHILD PSYCHOLOGY, study of the mental development of and the processes of behavior in children. Between the 17th and the 19th centuries occasional studies of children had been made by the Czech religious leader John Amos Comenius, the French philosopher and writer Jean Jacques Rousseau, the Swiss educational reformer Johann Heinrich Pestalozzi, and the German educator Friedrich Froebel. Their interest, however, was in improving the education of the child rather than in studying the child himself. See EDUCATION. The first systematic psychological studies of children began during the latter part of the 19th century. The pioneer work was done by the German physiologist and psychologist Wilhelm Thierry (1841–97) in *Die Seele des Kindes* (1882), a study of the child's mind, and by the American educator and psychologist Granville Stanley Hall, known as the "father of child psychology", in *Contents of Children's Minds on Entering School* (1891).

Through the influence of Hall in America and of the French educator Gabriel Compayré (1843–1913) in Europe, and of their associates, studies quickly followed of children's thinking, imagination, memory, and reasoning, without reference to their formal education. Hall's work, in particular, helped to establish the modern point of view that the child is not a miniature adult mentally, any more than he is physically. The interest in comparing children's intellectual capacities with those of adults gradually gave way to studies of the pattern of physical and mental development in children.

Finding a method suitable for studying children was one of the major problems that confronted the early researchers in child psychology. The work of the American psychologist John Broadus Watson and his associates at Johns Hopkins University in Baltimore, Md., beginning in 1917, is of historic importance. On the basis of studies of animals, which, like babies and young children, are incapable of expressing their thoughts, feelings, and emotions in words, Watson contended that observations of a child's behavior under carefully controlled conditions would enable the experimenter to draw conclusions about basic psychological processes. This method, known as the behavioristic method (see BEHAVIORISM), was influential in prompting a great number of research studies of newborn infants, babies, and young children. Many refinements later were made upon Watson's original approach. In 1926 the American psychologist Arnold Lucius Gesell of Yale University first used the moving-picture camera as an aid to observation, and a year later introduced the one-way-vision screen by means of which an observer could watch the behavior of a baby or young child without distracting him. In 1929 the experimental psychologist Albert Paul Weiss (1879–1931) and his associates and students at Ohio State University developed a sound-shielded, so-called experimental cabinet, lighted from within, regulated in temperature and humidity, and equipped with a device to record bodily movements. The use of some of these techniques was influenced by the spread of Gestalt psychology (q.v.) in the United States. The Gestalt point of view was brought to bear upon the study of children through the work of the German-born psychologist Kurt Koffka (1886–1941), whose *Growth of the Mind* (1921) was translated into English in 1924.

For the study of older children behaviorism did not prove as useful as standardized tests of intelligence, personality, and special aptitudes. Shortly after World War I group tests that had been used to measure the abilities of soldiers were revised for use with school children of all ages, from kindergarten through high school. The purpose of the tests was to determine changes in different mental capacities and in personality as the children grew older. In Switzerland the psychologist Jean Piaget (1896–) tested children by means of realistic problems rather than standardized questions, in order to follow their thought processes, especially in relation to their use of language. See PSYCHOLOGICAL TESTING.

Attempts to explain the individual differences which widespread testing revealed in children of the same age brought back into consideration the heredity-environment controversy. To supplement information supplied by the tests, the child psychologists turned to psychiatry, sociology, and anthropology for data about training methods, the position of the child in the family, marital adjustment of parents, and similar influences.

These studies have added weight to the psychological evidence that some basic differences are fundamentally due to heredity but are greatly influenced by environment. Even sexual differences in the ability to master school subjects and in patterns of interest may be due to heredity, although such differences develop to a great extent from training the child to behave according to standards considered appropriate for his sex.

An offshoot of the heredity-environment controversy was a long series of studies of twins by the British scientist Sir Francis Galton and later by Gesell at Yale, the child psychologist Myrtle B. McGraw (1899–) at Babies Hospital in New York City, the geneticist Horatio Hackett Newman (1875–1957) at the University of Chicago, and others. These studies revealed that identical twins, who come from the same germ cell that split into two shortly after fertilization, have physical and mental characteristics much more alike than those of nonidentical, or fraternal, twins, who come from two separate cells. Identical twins may show differences especially in personality, in which the role of environment seems more important than in physical and mental development. Furthermore, studies of groups of senescent twins by the psychiatrist Franz Josef Kallmann (1897–) reveal even more clearly the influence of environment. These studies show that the similarities of identical twins persist as they grow older whereas those of nonidentical twins decrease. See HEREDITY.

Early studies of development in children made use of the so-called cross-sectional approach, in which young children were compared with older children by distinct age groups. It soon became apparent, however, that there were individual variations among children of the same age. A new method was therefore adopted; called the longitudinal approach, it traces the development over a period of years of the same children chosen from the same age group. A pioneer longitudinal study of very bright children was begun by the American psychologist Louis Madison Terman (1877–1956) and his associates at Stanford University and provisionally reported (1926) in *Genetic Studies of Genius*. This investigation is still being carried on with the original group of subjects, who are now middle-aged men and women. Similar studies have been made of children of normal intelligence by Gesell at Yale, Walter F. Dearborn (1878–1956) at Harvard University, Nancy Bayley (1899–) and her associates at the University of California, and by many others.

These studies have made it apparent that all children undergo a course of development at different rates of advancement, depending mainly upon physiological and sociological factors. Another result is that child psychologists have been able to divide the entire period of development into the following characteristic stages.

Prenatal Stage: from conception to birth, the period when the most important factor is physical growth, more pronounced in the head region than in the rest of the body.

Neonatal Stage: from birth to about the end of the second week of life, when the infant does not gain weight or mature in behavior until he becomes adjusted to life outside the mother's body.

Infancy or Babyhood: from two weeks to two years, when the major developments consist of control over the muscles of the body and of the beginnings of speech. As the helplessness of the baby decreases, he desires to be more independent.

Early Childhood: from two to six years, when the child is learning skills to increase his independence, to enable him to gain control over his environment, to communicate with others through speech, and, in general, to fit into family and neighborhood life.

Late Childhood: from six to ten or twelve years, when the child becomes more integrated into society and associates closely with children of his own age.

Puberty: from ten or twelve years to thirteen or fifteen years, when the sex organs mature, the body grows to adult size and shape, and the so-called secondary sex characteristics, or features, that distinguish the adult male from the adult female body develop. Girls, on the average, become sexually mature at thirteen years, and boys a year or two later.

Adolescence: from the time of sexual maturity, at thirteen or fifteen years, to legal maturity, at twenty-one years, when the child prepares himself for later life by learning to think, feel and act like an adult.

There have been two important outgrowths of the longitudinal studies of children. The first is the establishment of norms, or standards, for physical, motor, speech, mental, emotional, and social development at different ages. By means of these standards it is possible to judge the development of individual children in order to determine how it compares with what is considered normal for their ages. The most widely used standards are known as the "Gesell Norms". The second outgrowth of longitudinal studies has been the construction of several age series of developmental tasks, or standards of what a child of a given age can be expected to learn. The best-known series is that of psychologist Robert J. Havighurst (1900–) of the University of Chicago. The physical and mental characteristics of adolescents had been studied as early as 1904 by Hall. A new scientific departure, developed during the 1930's, was motivated in part by the rise in juvenile delinquency (q.v.). Profiting by techniques devised for the study of older children, the important studies of adolescence presently use the longitudinal approach. The influence of physical changes upon the mental, emotional, and social behavior of children during the period of sexual maturing in early adolescence has been highlighted by studies of the age of maturing, especially that of Nancy Bayley and the psychologist Mary Cover Jones (1896–) of the University of California. Not only are children who begin to mature early more precocious in their physical development than those who begin late, but they show better personality adjustments and continue to mature even during the early years of adulthood. See ADOLESCENCE.

At present all areas of adolescent behavior are being investigated. Drawing heavily on research studies and theories of psychiatrists and sociologists, child psychology has been able to fill in gaps in its knowledge of social behavior, "dating", and courtship patterns. Marked contributions from the field of applied psychology have added information about the adolescent's vocational interests and his work adjustments. Studies in the field of social psychology have yielded valuable data about adolescent leadership, popularity, religious attitudes, and moral behavior. With the aid of this information from other fields the child psychologist has been able, in a relatively brief period, to acquire a fairly comprehensive understanding of typical adolescent behavior. See SOCIAL PSYCHOLOGY.

Recent studies of the aging process by gerontologists have thrown light on the importance of childhood as the foundation age of life. Studies of the normal aged have shown that attitudes and interests, patterns of behavior, and personality and character traits can be traced to the early years of their lives. No longer is it assumed that the early experiences of children are unimportant merely because they are not easily remembered. At present, it is recognized that child-training methods, discipline, early social relationships in and outside the home, and the methods used to learn skills and speech determine whether the child will develop into a happy, well-adjusted adult or into a social misfit.

As research in child psychology advanced and brought to light information that could be used profitably in the rearing of children, attempts were made to disseminate it through newspapers, magazines, books, and pamphlets, written especially for parents. Of the many books and pamphlets about babies which are available today, Benjamin M. Spock's *Common Sense Book of Baby and Child Care* (1946) and the child-care pamphlets issued by the U.S. government's Department of Health, Education, and Welfare are widely used. In recent years the scope of these books and articles has extended beyond the preschool years into adolescence. Such writings give advice to parents on common problems arising at every stage of growing up, problems that range from thumb-sucking, dawdling, and temper tantrums to lying, cheating, and sexual irregularities. Child psychologists also have written books directed to the adolescent himself in an attempt to explain what growing up means in terms of sexual changes and behavior patterns and to give advice on the problem of becoming an adult.

The research in child psychology which is presently conducted in university laboratories and in mental-health institutes is becoming increasingly important in the daily lives of American families. It provides useful information about the rearing of children and about maintaining them in mental and physical health.

See also JUVENILE DELINQUENCY.

E.B.H.

CHILDREN, EDUCATION OF. See EDUCATION, ELEMENTARY; EDUCATION, SECONDARY; KINDERGARTEN; NURSERY SCHOOL.

CHILDREN, EMPLOYMENT OF. See CHILD LABOR.

CHILDREN'S COURT. See JUVENILE COURT.

CHILDREN'S CRUSADE. See CRUSADE, CHILDREN'S.

CHILDREN'S LITERATURE, writings designed for children, or which children can read with interest, including fiction, poetry, biography, and history. Children's literature includes also riddles, precepts, fables, legends, myths, and folk poems and tales based upon spoken tradition. Primitive or very ancient literature, such as the Babylonian animal tales or the Homeric stories, is often adapta-

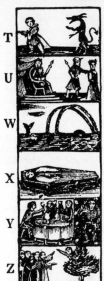

T Young TIMOTHY Learnt fin to fly.

U VASTHI for Pride, Was fet afide.

W Whales in the Sea, GOD's Voice obey.

X XERXES did die, And fo muft I.

Y While youth do chear Death may be near.

Z ZACCHEUS he Did climb the Tree Our Lord to fee.

Page from The New England Primer, *showing didactic verses alphabetically arranged*

ble to children's reading because of its simple narrative form.

Until the Renaissance the main sources of children's literature in the West were the Bible and the Greek and Latin classics. The expansion of literacy following the invention of printing in the 15th century increased the range of children's literature, and subsequently national history became a fresh source. After the 18th century archeologists, philologists, and anthropologists added material from Oriental and primitive cultures and European folklore. Typical of the developments generally were those in English and American literature for children, and these developments will be the subject of the present article, with occasional references to works and influences originating in other countries.

The Middle Ages. In England the earliest forms of oral literature, shared from generation to generation by young and old alike, were simple folk tales, usually of Celtic and Anglo-Saxon origin. These tales included the hearty folk ballads, among them the Robin Hood (q.v.) group, and the narratives sung by wandering bards about King Arthur and his knights (see ARTHURIAN CYCLE) and other heroes of chivalry.

The first books intended for the young were Latin collections of the 7th and 8th centuries. The best-known works, written by such outstanding ecclesiastical scholars as Aldhelm, Alcuin, and Bede, were used as lesson books in the monastery schools.

The Renaissance. With the development of vernacular literature, particularly after the invention of printing, more children's books appeared. Among the publications of the first English printer, William Caxton, was the *Book of Curtasye* (1477), a collection of rhymes which set forth rules of conduct for a "goodly chylde". Eight years later Caxton printed the English translator and compiler Sir Thomas Malory's *Morte d'Arthur*, which became the basis for later treatments of the Arthurian legends. Caxton also issued the *Fables* of Aesop, translated from the French, and the beast fable *Reynard the Fox*, translated from a Flemish version.

A new type of children's book, called the hornbook, appeared during the 16th century. It consisted of a printed page covered by a transparent sheet of horn and mounted on a square of wood with a handle at one end for the child to hold. Used for elementary instruction, the hornbook contained alphabets, the Lord's Prayer, Roman numerals, and the like. The chapbook, an unstitched pamphlet consisting usually of about seventy folded pages, appeared in the 17th century. Chapbooks, which were peddled from door to door throughout England, contained versions of popular literature ranging from nursery rhymes to medieval romances.

The 17th and 18th Centuries. Works of moral and religious instruction directed to children long had been in circulation, but under the influence of Puritanism in the 17th and 18th centuries such works became more important than any other type of writing for the young. *The New England Primer*, printed (1690) in Boston, Massachusetts Bay Colony, by the English-born publisher and journalist Benjamin Harris (fl. 1673–1716), is typical. It contained a rhymed alphabet, tables of syllables, the Lord's Prayer, the Apostles' Creed, the Ten Commandments, and an account of the burning of a Protestant martyr at the stake. Preparation for possible sudden death and departure to the next world was a feature of the rhymes and stories in earlier editions of the *Primer*. Among verses that became well known through their inclusion in the *Primer* was the prayer "Now I Lay Me Down to Sleep" and the English churchman Isaac Watts' "Cradle Hymn". Editions of *The New England Primer* were issued as late as the 19th century. The title of another contemporary children's book, *Spiritual Milk for Boston Babes,* further indicates the religious tone of most of the children's literature of the period.

One of the most significant developments in children's literature was the use of illustrations. *Orbis Pictus* ("The World in Pictures"), the first known children's picture book, was issued in 1657 by the exiled Czech Protestant educational reformer John Amos Comenius. An English translation appeared a year later. Its subject was natural history and the illustrations were woodcuts.

Among the classics of children's literature are adult books that appeal to children as well, or have been adapted for children. One is the English author and preacher John Bunyan's simple but forceful allegory of man's conflict between good and evil, *Pilgrim's Progress* (published in two parts, 1678 and 1684). Another is Daniel Defoe's *Robinson Crusoe* (1791), the story of an ingenious and self-reliant castaway. This masterpiece served as a basis for another children's favorite, *The Swiss Family Robinson* (1812; Eng. trans., 1814) by the Swiss writer, philosopher, and librarian Johann Rudolf Wyss. Jonathan Swift's *Gulliver's Travels* (1726), which adults enjoyed for its satire, is enjoyed by children for its fantasy. The first significant French children's book was *Historie ou Contes du Temps Passés avec des Moralités* (1698), a collection of traditional fairy tales, known also as *Contes de Ma Mère l'Oie*, by Charles Perrault. The tales included "Sleeping Beauty", "Cinderella", "Red Riding Hood", and "Blue Beard". These stories were soon afterward translated into English. "Mother Goose" became a lasting nursery name in England and America, as applied to nursery rhymes as well as fairy tales.

In the 18th century the British publisher John Newbery (1713–67) became the first to print attractive, cheap books for children. Containing stories, verses, puzzles, riddles, maxims, and lessons, the books sold for sixpence each in little paper-covered editions. Newbery's moral precepts were gentler and less forbidding than those of the previous century. His best-known publications are the *History of Little Goody Two Shoes* (erroneously credited to Oliver Goldsmith) ; *A Little Pretty Pocket Book*; and *Mother Goose's Melodies*, reprinted (1785) in Boston (1750–1831).

Until late in the 18th century no clear distinction had been made between instruction and entertainment in children's literature. Most stories and poems written for children were designed to convey useful information or moral advice. Largely because of growth of religious freedom, especially in Great Britain and in the newly established American nation, and because of the egalitarian principles spread by the French Revolution, children's literature eventually became less didactic in purpose. A major influence in this development was Jean Jacques Rousseau. In his *Émile* (1762) Rousseau became the first to point out that the child's mind is not merely the adult's in miniature and that it has to be considered in its own terms.

One effect of the ideas expressed in *Émile* was a tendency in the children's books influenced by it to overemphasize the guiding role of the wise and benevolent adult. In England *Sanford and Merton* (3 vols., 1783–89) by Thomas Day (1748–89) spread this portion of Rousseau's influence in the story of pampered little Tommy Merton who was reclaimed by good, rugged Harry Sanford under the wise supervision of a clergyman, Mr. Barlow. The story is constantly interrupted by lengthy sermons that stress its educational purpose. A similar product of the Rousseau movement was the work of the Irish novelist Maria Edgeworth, who wrote two collections of short stories for children, *Parent's Assistant* (1796) and *Moral Tales* (1801). A preachy and highly moral tone is maintained throughout these volumes, but it does not greatly interfere with the author's keen understanding of children and her skill in describing scenes and characters.

The *Songs of Innocence* (1789) and *Songs of Experience* (1794) by the British artist, poet, and mystic William Blake provide the first example of literature concerned with the essential goodness of children in the spirit of Rousseau's educational philosophy. Blake's ideas on children's innocence and on corruption of children by adult standards of belief and behavior derive less from Rousseau directly than from a blend of German mysticism, English Protestantism, and the political ideas of the French Revolution. Blake believed that passion, or feeling, according to the individual conscience, was superior to all intellectual rules. However, his writings and engravings were much too difficult for a youthful audience; instead of children, they influenced long after Blake's death other authors and artists in the field of children's literature. Blake, like William Wordsworth in the same years, made childhood seem a happy and virtuous time, and growing up a saddening and complicated process. Blake's work, ignored during his own time, became generally known only during the latter part of the 19th century.

Houghton Mifflin Company

Illustration by the 20th-century American illustrator N. C. Wyeth for Jack the Giant Killer. *Such imaginative interpretations add rich visual imagery to children's stories.*

The 19th and Early-20th Century. *Romantic Tales, Folk Tales, and Fantasy.* The romantic movement that swept European culture early in the 19th century also affected children's literature. In England the writings of the novelist Sir Walter Scott, noted for his tales of chivalry, were read with delight by older children. A revival of interest in William Shakespeare gave children one of their most fascinating books, *Lambs Tales from Shakespeare* (1806), consisting of versions of the Shakespeare stories by the essayist Charles Lamb and his sister Mary Ann Lamb. Two American authors of the same period, Washington Irving and James Fenimore Cooper, wrote with similar historical vividness about the more recent American past. Irving developed the legends of the Dutch country in New York State in *The Sketch Book* (1819), which contained "Rip Van Winkle" and "The Legend of Sleepy Hollow", and Cooper wrote about early American frontier life in his series known as the Leatherstocking Tales, the most famous of which is *The Last of the Mohicans* (1826).

Renewed interest in folklore, a tendency of the romantic movement, led to the enrichment of children's literature with myths, legends, and wonder stories. The German philologists, the brothers Jacob Ludwig Carl Grimm and Wilhelm Carl Grimm, made notable contributions in their volumes of stories known collectively as *Grimm's Fairy Tales.* Published between 1812 aind 1815, and circulated in translations throughout the world, the volumes include such tales as "Hansel and Gretel", "Snow White and the Seven Dwarfs", "The Valiant Little Tailor", and "Rapunzel". More creative and stylized versions of the folk tale were written by the Danish author Hans Christian Andersen, whose collections appeared between 1835 and 1872. Some of the more famous Andersen stories are "The Snow Queen", "The Nightingale", "The Red Shoes", "The Ugly Duckling", and "The Constant Tin Soldier". The classic myths of Greece were retold in *A Wonder Book* (1852) and *Tanglewood Tales for Boys and Girls* (1853) by the American novelist Nathaniel Hawthorne. In Great Britain, toward the end of the century, the man of letters Andrew Lang wrote one of the best-known collections of European fairy tales in a series of volumes beginning with the *Blue Fairy Tale Book* (1889).

The avid response of children to myth and fairy story made it clear that their minds have an unlimited range of imagination and that they do not distinguish sharply between reality and unreality. The British painter and author of limericks and nonsense verse Edmund Lear was among the first to appreciate these truths. His *The Book of Nonsense* (1846) and *More Nonsense* (1870) are landmarks of children's literature. The supreme combination of fantasy and humor was achieved by the British author and mathematician Charles Lutwidge Dodgson (Lewis Carroll) in *Alice in Wonderland* (1865) and *Through the Looking Glass* (1871). According to some theories, the success of these works is to be accounted for by the mathematical logic underlying their fantasy; according to others, by the profound psychological perceptions in the fantasy. In any case there is general agreement that the two books constitute the ultimate masterpiece of children's literature. The original illustrator John Tenniel's drawings are so apt that his name has become almost as well known as that of the author.

Another British writer who continued the creative fairy-tale tradition was Oscar Wilde (*The Happy Prince and Other Fairy Stories,* 1885). Two other notable late-19th-century British writers for children were Robert Louis Stevenson and Rudyard Kipling. Stevenson's *Treasure Island* (1883), *The Child's Garden of Verses* (1885), and *Kidnapped* (1886) have become classics, as have Kipling's animal stories in *Jungle Books* (1894–95) and *Just So*

Stories (1912), based upon the folk traditions of India. Separate lyrics by Kipling are to be found also in poetry anthologies for older children. In the United States during this period the most notable stories about animals were the dialect tales of Joel Chandler Harris in his *Uncle Remus* books (published between 1880 and 1906), which relied upon Negro folk traditions.

Fantasy continued to be a major mode of imaginative literature for children in the early-20th century. From his successful stage play *Peter Pan* (1904), a fantasy about a boy who would not grow up, the British novelist and dramatist James Matthew Barrie adapted *Peter Pan in Kensington Gardens* (1906) and *Peter and Wendy* (1911). Another fantasy that has become a classic is the British writer Kenneth Grahame's *Wind in the Willows* (1908), recounting the adventures of Rat, Mole, and their pompous friend Toad. A distinguished contribution to children's poetry was made by Walter de la Mare in his *Songs for Childhood* (1902) and other collections. His anthology of children's poems *Come Hither* (1923) remains the most comprehensive of its kind.

Among foreign children's classics which have enriched English and American children's literature also are *Heidi* (1881; Eng. trans., 1884) by the Swiss writer Johanna Spyri (1827–1901), whose heroine is a spirited little girl living in the Swiss Alps; *The Adventures of Pinocchio* (1882; Eng. trans., 1892) by the Italian writer Carlo Lorenzini (1826–90), better known as Carlo Collodi, whose hero is an irrepressible wooden marionette; and *The Wonderful Adventures of Nils* (2 vols., Eng. trans., 1906–07) by the Swedish author Selma Ottiliana Lovisa Lagerlöf, whose hero is a boy who rode over Sweden on a goose's back. In another vein are the science popularizations by the French naturalist Jean Henri Fabre, whose books, especially those about wasps, beetles, mason bees, and spiders, are models of their kind.

Illustrated Children's Books. A tradition of clear, colorful, and simple drawing for children in various styles gradually developed, especially in Great Britain. Among the more famous artists were Walter Crane, whose series of picture books was initiated in 1873 with *The Frog Prince*; Catherine (Kate) Greenaway, whose lovable children on flower-bedecked pages appeared in *Kate Greenaway's Almanacs* (1883–97) and other books; and Randolph Caldecott (1846–86), whose works include *Farmer's Boy, Diverting History of*

John Gilpin, Three Jovial Huntsmen, and *Come Lassies and Lads.*

Among other outstanding British illustrators are Leslie Brooke (1862–1940), best known for *Johnny Crow's Garden* (1903), *Johnny Crow's Party* (1907), *Johnny Crow's New Garden* (1935), and the collections *The Golden Goose Book* (1905) and *Ring O' Roses* (1922). Beatrix Potter (1866–1943) wrote and illustrated books that have been called "classics in miniature", among them *Peter Rabbit* (1902) and *Squirrel Nutkin* (1903). *Little Black Sambo* (1899) by Helen Bannerman (1866?–1946) is perhaps the classic example of text integrated with pictures. Sequels to the adventures of Sambo continued into the 20th century.

Children's Magazines and Notable Contributors. Magazines such as the American publications *Youth's Companion,* founded in 1827, and *St. Nicholas,* founded in 1873, were significant in the development of children's literature, and they continued their influence into the early years of the 20th century. The contributors included British writers, such as Kipling; the Americans Louisa May Alcott, Howard Pyle, who was noted also as an illustrator, Oliver Wendell Holmes, Lucretia Peabody Hale (1820–1900), and Samuel Langhorne Clemens (better known as Mark Twain); and the Canadian-born illustrator and author Palmer Cox (1840–1924).

Three of the American contributors became famous for their children's books. In *Little Women* (1867) Louisa May Alcott began a series of children's books about New England family life that have remained popular favorites. Mark Twain's *The Adventures of Tom Sawyer* (1871) provides a lively picture of boyhood escapades in a Missouri town on the Mississippi River in the period when frontier life was still a recent memory. The companion volume *The Adventures of Huckleberry Finn* (1884) is considered by critics the greatest boy's book ever written by an American and an enduring contribution to the national literature. Howard Pyle, although a lesser writer, made a notable contribution to children's literature by retelling English legends, notably in *The Merry Adventures of Robin Hood* (1883) and *The Story of King Arthur and His Knights* (1903). Both are illustrated with his own distinguished drawings.

Fiction for Older Boys and Girls. Various works of fiction written specifically for older boys and girls appeared in the mid-19th century and became increasingly popular during the 20th century. Among the best known of such books are those by Horatio Alger, such as *From Farm Boy to Senator* and *Brave and Bold,* based upon the theme of success achieved through hard work and thrift. Other popular examples of books for boys include the series, about a schoolboy athlete named Frank Merriwell, written by Gilbert Patten under the pseudonym Burt L. Standish, and the series of adventure stories entitled *Onward and Upward* by William Taylor Adams, who wrote under the pseudonym Oliver Optic. Love stories designed for teen-age girls also first became popular in this period, notably including *Ramona* (1884) by Helen Hunt Jackson and the series entitled *What Katy Did* by Sarah Chauncey Woolsey (1835–1905), who wrote under the pseudonym Susan Coolidge.

The Period after World War I. Notable among English postwar children's books were those by the writer and illustrator Hugh Lofting (1886–1947), whose "Doctor Dolittle" series, begun in 1922, has for its hero a doctor who preferred to treat animals rather than humans; *When We Were Very Young* (1924), and tales of whimsy in *Winnie-the-Pooh* (1926) and *House at Pooh Corner* (1928) by the poet and playwright Alan Alexander Milne have become classics; and the Australian-born Pamela Travers (1906–), whose "Mary Poppins" books (1934–52) have a nursemaid as their heroine.

The distinction between works written expressly for children and those which children could share with adults became more precise in the period after World War I, particularly in the United States. Important reasons for this development were the spread of compulsory education and psychological testing; thus it became possible for authors to write for children within specific age and intelligence groups. Under these influences and that of the educational theories of the American philosopher, psychologist, and educator John Dewey, children's literature began to emphasize the real world in terms of the child's experience.

The volume and quality of reading material for children increased trmendously in the postwar period, and school and public libraries made books, magazines, and reference works available without cost. The American Library Association was increasingly helpful to educational organizations in the selection of reading material for children. The annual observance of Children's Book Week, begun in 1919, acquainted the general public with the importance of books for the young. Annual prizes such as the Newberry and the Caldecott awards, for the best American children's book and the best illustrated book, respectively, focused attention on quality in children's literature. Encyclopedias for children were issued, among them the *World Book Encyclopedia* (19 vols., first published in 1917–18 as the *World Book*) and *Britannica Junior* (12 vols., 1934). Newspapers inaugurated regular departments in which children's books were reviewed. The *Horn Book* magazine, established in Boston in 1924, is devoted entirely to the evaluation of children's books and related subjects.

The imaginative tales, based on the prowess of such legendary figures as Paul Bunyan, Pecos Bill, John Henry, Mike Fink, and Tony Beaver and on episodes in the life .of the American pioneer David Crockett, continue to captivate the American juvenile reader. An outstanding collection in which some of these characters appear is *America Sings* (1942) by the poet and novelist Carl Lamson Carmer (1893–).

With the publication of *Millions of Cats* (1928), by the American artist and writer Wanda Gag (1893–1946), the picture narrative, in which text is reduced to a minimum, became a favorite with preschool children. Until 1930 most illustrated children's books were in black and white, but new printing developments made color illustration universal. Among leading color illustrators are Ludwig Bemelmans, Robert Lawson (1892–), and Dorothy Lathrop (1891–), and others continue to produce volumes of high craftsmanship, sometimes writing their own texts.

Notable among American children's writers of the 1940's and 1950's are James Grover Thurber, whose fantasies *Many Moons* (1943) and the *White Deer* (1945) are illustrated with his own drawings; and Elwyn Brooks White, whose *Stuart Little* (1945) and *Charlotte's Web* (1952) won praise and popularity. Other recent books of unusual interest are Ruth Krauss' *A Hole Is to Dig* (1952), a delightful attempt to recreate childhood experience through subtleties of language; *The Wheel on the School* (1954) by Meindert de Jong, a writer of keen perception; *Impunity Jane* (1954) by Rumer Godden (1909–), who writes for children with all the resources of a practiced novelist; and *The Cat in the Hat* (1957) by Theodore Seuss Geisel (1904–), who writes under the pseudonym Dr. Seuss. In the last-named book, conceived as a supplementary reader for school children and illustrated with boldly comic drawings, the story is told with a vocabulary of about three hundred words, but

it reveals the same extravagant fantasy which characterizes Geisel's other writings. A recent example of his original type of humor is *Yertile the Turtle and Other Stories* (1958).

By the mid-20th century the publication of children's books in the United States had increased both in quantity and in variety. Quantitatively, such books constituted a great proportion of the American book trade. Of the approximately 22,000 books issued in the United States in 1962, about 2600, forming the second-largest category among those published, were children's books. As a result of improved methods of manufacture and of mass distribution, new types of inexpensive children's publications appeared also, such as the Golden Book series for infants and children consisting of low-priced books profusely illustrated in color. For a discussion of other types of inexpensive books read also by children, see COMIC BOOK.

CHILD WELFARE. See MATERNAL AND CHILD WELFARE.

CHILE, republic of South America, bounded on the N. by Peru, on the E. by Bolivia and Argentina, and on the s. and w. by the Pacific Ocean. Chile lies from N. to s. between about 17°25′ S. lat. and 55°59′ S. lat. (Cape Horn). With an extreme length of approximately 2600 m., Chile is longer in a N.-s. direction than any other country in the world. Its width, ranging between 46 and 250 m., averages about 110 m. The total area of the country is 286,396 sq.m., making it the seventh-largest South American republic. This total includes the area of the chief islands and island groups, which extend along the coast from Chiloé Island to Cape Horn. Among these are Chonos Archipelago, Wellington Island, and part of Tierra del Fuego (q.v.), the E. portion of which is Argentine territory. Other islands belonging to Chile include the Juan Fernández Islands, about 400 miles w. of the coast, and Easter Island (q.v.), in the South Pacific. Chile also claims a section of Antarctica. The population of Chile (1960) is 7,339,546.

THE LAND

Physical Characteristics. The dominant physiographic feature of Chile is the Andes mountain system, which comprises about one third of the total area of the country. The western cordillera of this system, known as the Cordillera de los Andes, extends from the great Bolivian plateau in the N., southward along the E. boundary of Chile into Tierra del Fuego. The cordillera is volcanic in origin, has several active volcanoes, and contains

Entrance to the Chamber of Deputies in the capital city of Santiago, Chile

structural faults which result occasionally in severe earthquakes. In the N. portion of the cordillera average altitudes range from 12,000 to 15,000 ft., but many peaks exceed 20,000 ft. Among the notable mountains are Ojos del Salado (22,590 ft.), the highest peak in Chile, and Llullaillaco (22,057 ft.). Aconcagua, the highest peak outside of Central Asia, is partly in Chile and partly in Argentina. Uspallata Pass, the principal pass in the central cordillera, crosses the Andes at 12,000 ft. The cordillera is generally broad in the N., exceeding 100 m. in places. South of 33° S. lat., the cordillera is complicated by spurs and chains, and elevations decrease from the extreme at Aconcagua to about 6000 ft. at the s. extremity. This section of the range is considerably narrower than in the N., and many passes, which seldom exceed 5000 ft., provide access to Argentina. The peaks are perpetually snow capped and, below 1500 ft., heavily forested.

From the base of the N. portion of the cordillera an extensive plateau, broken by mountain spurs enclosing depressions known as pampas, slopes westward to precipitous escarpments along the Pacific. The escarpments vary from 600 to 1500 ft. in height. The plateau, particularly N. of 28° S. lat., is desert country and contains vast nitrate fields and rich mineral deposits. The plateau extends southward beyond Valparaíso, where a distinct mountain range, called the Cordillera Marítima, begins. Elevations of this chain, which slopes steeply on the w. and gradually on the E., seldom exceed 6000 ft. South of Chiloé Island the range sinks into the Pacific and its peaks constitute the long chain of islands and archipelagoes that project beyond the Strait of Magellan.

A longitudinal valley known as the Central Valley comprises the region between the coastal range and the Cordillera de los Andes. It extends southward from about the latitude of Santiago, dropping from an altitude of about 2300 ft. to sea level. The valley, approximately 600 m. long and from 25 to 50 m. wide, is the richest agricultural region of Chile.

Numerous rivers traverse Chile from the Andes to the sea; among the most important are (from N. to S.) the Loa, Elqui, Aconcagua, Maipo, Maule, Bío-Bío, and Imperial rivers. Although of limited value to navigation, the rivers are vital for irrigation and hydroelectric power.

Remarkably few natural harbors are situated on the Chilean coast N. of Chiloé Island. The chief exception is Concepción Bay, where several good harbors, notably that of Talcahuano, are located. North of Concepción Bay safe anchorages have been constructed, however, at several points, including San Antonio, Valparaíso, and several N. mining ports. The principal harbors s. of Concepción Bay are Coronel and Lota, near the mouth of the Bío-Bío R., Corral at the mouth of the Valdivia R., Puerto Montt on Reloncaví Bay; and Ancud on Chiloé Island. Other good harbors indent the coast s. of this point, but the region is stormy and commercially unimportant.

Climate. The climate of Chile is as diversified as its physiography. The region N. of 28° S. lat., situated in the rainless zone of the S.E. trade winds, is one of the driest areas in the world. However, some precipitation occurs along the w. slopes of the cordillera during the summer months, occasionally creating serious flood conditions in the rivers, which, with only one or two exceptions, are dry throughout the remainder of the year. In the N. coastal regions, monthly average temperatures range between 60° F. and 73° F. during the summer months and seldom fall below 52° F. in winter. Temperatures decrease about one degree for each 300 ft. of altitude in the Andes. South of 28° S. lat., precipitation, confined mainly to the winter months, increases from about 5½ in. annually at La Serena to more than 100 in. in the vicinity of Valdivia. The plateau region in the interior is characteristically dry to the latitude of Santiago, however. Precipitation attains a maximum of about 200 in. near the Strait of Magellan, where violent storms frequently occur. Heavy rainfalls also occur on the w. slopes of the s. extensions of the Andes. The climate in the Central Valley is temperate, with monthly average temperatures ranging from 68° F. in summer to 46° F. in winter in the N. portions, and from 61° F. in summer to 45° F. in winter in the s. portions. Temperatures in the regions S. of 45° S. lat. are considerably lower.

Places of Interest. The vacation resources of Chile attract visitors from neighboring countries and, with the advent of air travel, from more distant places as well. Among Chilean vacation offerings are the casino at Viña del Mar; ski resorts, notably Farellones (altitude 7400 ft.), which is a two-hour drive from Santiago, and Portillo; the s. lake region; many spas; fishing (swordfish, marlin, tunny in the N., trout and other fresh-water fish in the lakes and streams); and ocean swimming.

Natural Resources. *Plants.* The indigenous plant life of Chile differs in the various climatic zones. In the desert region of the N., cacti and drought-resistant shrubs are found. The Central Valley, with its considerable rainfall, supports the espino (a thorny shrub) and the Chilean pine, which bears edible nuts. In the s., where the rainfall is heaviest, there are dense forests containing laurel, magnolias, and various species of beech and conifers. Native food plants of Chile include the potato, bean, and peppers.

Animals. The Andes are a barrier to the penetration into Chile of many South American animal species. Monkeys, poisonous snakes, and jaguars, all of which are typical in other parts of the continent, are not found in the country. Among Chilean mammals are the vicuña, guanaco, numerous species of rodents (including the chinchilla), and the guemal, a small deer. The larger birds include the albatross, penguin, rhea, and condor. Fish and marine mammals abound in the coastal waters (see *Fisheries*, below).

Political Divisions. Chile is composed of 25 provinces; these are Aconcagua, Antofagasta, Arauco, Atacama, Aysén, Bío-Bío, Cautín, Chiloé, Colchagua, Concepción, Coquimbo, Curicó, Linares, Llanquihue, Magallanes, Malleco, Maule, Ñuble, O'Higgins, Osorno, Santiago, Talca, Tarapacá, Valdivia, and Valparaíso. Chile also lists an antarctic territory among its subdivisions (see ANTARTICA).

Largest Cities. The capital and largest city of Chile is Santiago (q.v.). Valparaíso (q.v.) is the second-largest city and chief port. Other important cities are Antofagasta, Osorno, Puerto Montt, Chillán, Concepción, Iquique, Talca, Talcahuano, Temuco, Valdivia, Viña del Mar, and Punta Arenas, the southernmost city in the world.

THE PEOPLE

Population. The population of Chile is predominantly urban, with 60 percent of the

INDEX TO MAP OF CHILE

Continued on page 2040

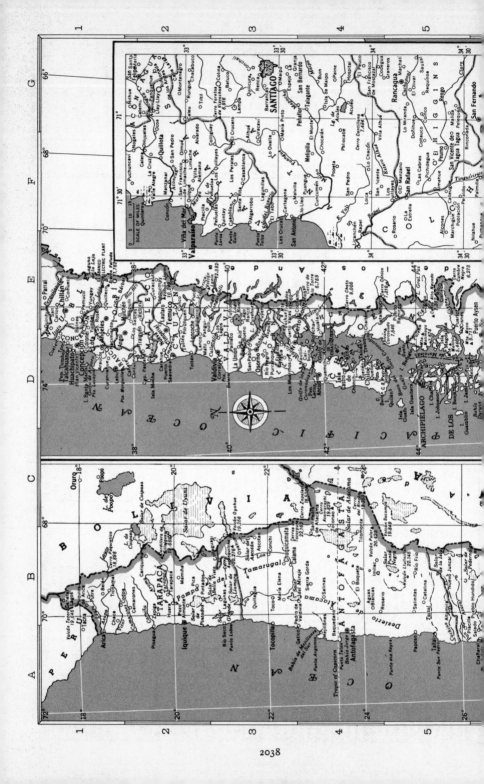

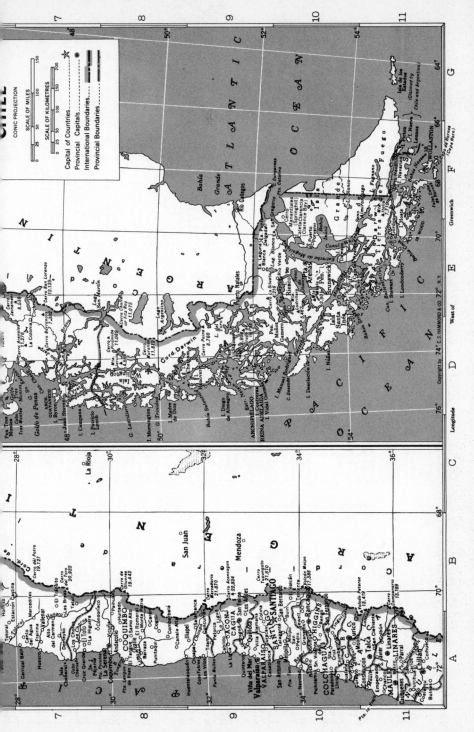

CHILE

CONIC PROJECTION

SCALE OF MILES

0 25 50 100 150

SCALE OF KILOMETRES

0 25 50 100 150 200

Capital of Countries................⭑
Provincial Capitals.................◉
International Boundaries............
Provincial Boundaries..............

Copyright by C. S. HAMMOND & CO. N.Y.

Index to Map of Chile.—cont.

people living in towns. Most of the Chilean people live in the Central Valley; there the distribution of population is fairly uniform. In the desert regions of N. Chile the population is clustered chiefly in mining towns, river valleys, and the mineral-exporting ports; vast unpopulated stretches lie between the settlements. In s. Chile, between Puerto Montt and Punta Arenas, the population is also dispersed in isolated settlements; in between there are unpopulated stretches of rain forest, glaciers, fjords, and rain-soaked islands. Expansion of the population into the N. and into most of the region s. of Valdivia started in the last half of the 19th century; settlers in the N. were mainly native Chileans, whereas most of the settlers in the s. were Germans and other immigrants.

Races, Religion, and Language. Most of the people of Chile belong to a homogeneous mixture of Spanish and Indian stock. The population includes a minority of descendants of immigrants from Germany, Austria, Italy, France, Switzerland, Great Britain, Yugoslavia, and the Middle East. The foreign-born, comprising less than 3 percent of the population, are chiefly Spaniards, Germans, Argentines, Italians, and Bolivians. The descendants of the original Indian inhabitants live in reservations in the s. provinces and total about 130,000; the Indians of the s. are referred to as Araucanians (see ARAUCANIAN) although they represent several tribes. The number of Indians has increased in recent decades. A few small Indian groups of other stock are found in the far N., including the Chango (q.v.). The Yahgan and the Onas, who once populated Tierra del Fuego, are virtually extinct.

Members of the Roman Catholic Church constitute 90 percent of the population of Chile. The Church maintains an archdiocese at Santiago. In 1925 the Church was disestablished. There is complete freedom of worship in Chile, and all faiths may maintain places of worship. A small portion of the population is Jewish.

Spanish is the official language of Chile.

Education. Chile has both a free public-school system and numerous private schools. All children between the ages of seven and fifteen must attend school. Enrollment in the early 1960's totaled about 1,160,300 primary-school and kindergarten pupils and about 125,500 secondary-school pupils. The literacy rate is about 80 percent, one of the highest rates in Latin America.

The University of Chile at Santiago had a total enrollment of approximately 12,350 students in the early 1960's. The university was founded in 1738 as the Royal University of San Felipe; the present name was adopted in 1843. Other institutions of higher learning include Concepción University, 2 Catholic universities, technical universities at Valparaíso and Santiago, and a number of colleges and lyceums maintained in the provincial capitals.

Libraries and Museums. The largest library in the country is the National Library in Santiago, with about 700,000 volumes. The University of Chile possesses about 450,000 volumes. Museums in Santiago include the National Historical Museum, the National Museum of Fine Arts, and the National Museum of Natural History.

Culture. Chile has one of the oldest newspapers in the Western Hemisphere, *El Mercurio,* which was founded in Valparaíso in 1827. The country pioneered in the establishment of teacher-training schools and the admission of women to professional schools. Among Chileans who have acquired fame abroad are José Toribio Medina (1852–1930), a historian and bibliographer; Claudio Arrau (1904–   ), a pianist; and Lucila Godoy de Alcayaga (1889–1957), a writer under the pen name of Gabriela Mistral, who was awarded the Nobel Prize for literature in 1945.

THE ECONOMY

Mining. Mineral deposits, located chiefly in the N. in Atacama and Tarapacá provinces, constitute the principal source of national wealth. Chile is the leading mineral producer of South America. It ranks second to the United States in the production of copper. Chilean copper deposits are the largest in the world. In the early 1960's annual production of this metal totaled more than 532,000 tons, approximately 95 percent of which was exported.

Prior to the development of synthetic processes of manufacturing nitrates, Chile led the world in nitrate production. Its deposits of this mineral are found mainly in the Atacama Desert. About 1,110,000 tons, almost all of which was exported, were mined annually in the early 1960's. A by-product of the industry is iodine; Chile produces about 60 percent of the world's supply of this mineral. Chile also has large deposits of sulfur, coal, and iron ore. The country has, in addition, productive deposits of silver, gold, cobalt, molybdenum, tungsten, mercury, zinc, manganese, and bauxite.

The Chilean government has made efforts to increase the production of copper and nitrates. A law in effect in 1955 abrogated practices that copper-mining companies felt had restricted their growth. The law established income-tax advantages for companies which kept production from falling below certain levels, improved dollar-exchange rates for copper companies, and allowed companies to sell their copper abroad directly instead of through the government. After this enactment the major United States companies initiated programs to expand production facilities and develop new copper deposits. The Chilean nitrate industry has declined. Formerly the world's primary source of nitrogenous fertilizers, it supplied less than 3 percent of the world demand in the 1950's. New production techniques included solar evaporation, a method particularly suited to the rainless nitrate areas. Plans are under consideration to establish heavy-chemical industries in the N., where the cities which grew with nitrate production have declined.

Limited petroleum deposits have been found in Chile. In the early 1960's the production of crude oil from wells s. of the Strait of Magellan totaled about 8,278,000 barrels annually. A refinery, in Concón, near Valparaíso, processes native and imported crude oils.

Manufacturing. Chile is one of the leading industrial nations of Latin America. Mineral, forest, and agricultural resources permit a wide range of manufacturing. Major industrial developments have been recent. Industrial production increased by 45 percent between 1940 and 1950 and by an almost equal amount during the next five years. Subsequently various economic problems, including inflation, slowed growth. Industrial output exceeds agricultural output in value. Almost 500,000 workers, comprising 21 percent of the labor force, are employed by industry.

Chile is one of five Latin-American nations which produce steel. A steel plant in Huachipato, near Concepción, produces about 325,-000 metric tons of pig iron, 381,000 metric tons of steel, and 268,000 metric tons of rolled products annually. On a per-capita basis Chile ranks first in Latin America in the production of electric power (86 percent is hydroelectric power), second in the production of shoes, and third in the production of cement. In total output, Chile is fourth in the production of plate glass and plywood. Other important manufactures include textiles (cotton, wool, rayon, nylon), clothing, chemicals, glassware, chinaware, explosives, processed foods, metal goods, beverages, pharmaceuticals, cosmetics, paints, paper and cardboard, cordage, cigarettes, and electrical equipment. There has

been an increase in the production of household appliances and of tires, tubes, and other rubber goods. In many consumer items Chile now supplies most of its own needs.

Industrial growth in Chile has been actively stimulated by the government through tariff protection and subsidies. In some instances the government has also assisted by becoming a stockholder in productive enterprises, e.g., in the Huachipato steel mill.

Agriculture. Agriculture and stock raising provide about 16 percent of the national income of Chile and employ about 27 percent of the labor force. Except for sheep raising, which is conducted in the far south, agricultural enterprises are concentrated in the Central Valley. The country has about 14,000,000 acres of potential farmland, but only 3,140,000 acres are used to plant major crops. The chief crops include wheat, potatoes, corn, oats, barley, beans, rice, lentils, and chick peas. Sugar beets, flax, hemp, onions, tobacco, alfalfa, clover, and nuts also are raised. The leading fruit crops are grapes (from which about 100,000,000 gallons of wine are produced in an average year), apples, melons, peaches, apricots, plums, and cherries.

Almost half of the farms in Chile are 12 acres or smaller, but such farms contain less than 5 percent of the cultivated area. About 25 percent of the cultivated area is in farms exceeding 2500 acres in size.

Sheep are raised in large numbers in Chile, particularly in Tierra del Fuego and the Magallanes pampas, where ranch acreage totals about 15,000,000. Flocks comprised about 7,520,000 head in the early 1960's. Annual wool output is about 25,800 tons. Other livestock in the country includes about 2,940,000 cattle, 980,000 pigs, and 528,000 horses.

Extensive forested areas are located in s. Chile, mainly in the region extending from Valdivia to Aysén. The total forest area in Chile is about 40,000,000 acres. Production of timber averages about 201,300,000 cu. ft. annually.

Chile does not produce enough food to meet its needs and must import sugar and wheat; however, it is engaged in improving its agriculture with the aid of foreign experts, some of whom were sent by the United States under the Point Four Program (q.v.). A major phase of the program in Chile is the Chillán Plan, which includes extensive experimental, demonstration, and educational work in farming, forestry, and rural health.

Fisheries. Over 200 varieties of fish are found within 30 m. of the Chilean coast. The country has one of the largest fishing indus-

The famous beach at Viña del Mar, a residential suburb of Valparaíso, Chile

tries in Latin America. Whaling in the s. brings in about 1000 whales a year. Seals and otters are hunted in Magallanes. Processing plants pack a good part of the fish catch and also produce fertilizers and other by-products. Recently Chile began shipping a frozen shellfish (*langostino*, a form of rock lobster) to the United States.

Currency, Finance, and Banking. The monetary unit of Chile is the escudo, which was introduced on Jan. 1, 1960, with an official value of about 90 cents in U.S. currency. The peso, which the escudo replaced, had become steadily inflated during the 1950's and at the time of its withdrawal stood at about 1000 to the U.S. dollar.

After World War II Chile began to suffer from a severe inflation, with the Santiago cost-of-living index, for example, increasing 1200 percent between 1950 and 1957. Factors responsible for the inflation include population growth which outstrips the agricultural capacity of the country, so that food must be imported; the expense of extensive social-welfare programs; and unbalanced government budgets. Another inflationary factor is the increase in prices caused by subsidies extended to native industries, by high exclusionary tariffs, by monopolies in some aspects of production and distribution, and by automatic adjustments of wages and salaries to cost-of-living rises. Early in 1956 laws were enacted to establish wage and price controls. On January 1, 1958, President Carlos Ibáñez del Campo stated that the cost of living had increased 84 percent in 1955, 38 percent in 1956, and 17 percent in 1957.

The Central Bank of Chile, established in 1926, controls the lending operations of the other Chilean banks and has exclusive power to issue bank notes. The capital of the Central Bank is owned by the Chilean Treasury, by domestic and foreign banks, and by the public.

Commerce. In the early 1960's the foreign trade of Chile was valued annually at about $1,110,000,000. Exports were valued at about $508,140,000, with minerals constituting over 85 percent of the value. Besides mining products, Chilean exports included (in order of value) agricultural products, animal products, and food products. The principal markets of the export trade of Chile were the United States, the United Kingdom, Germany, and Argentina. Major imports comprised machinery, chemicals and drugs, transportation equipment and vehicles, and metals and manufactures from the United States, Germany, and the United Kingdom; foodstuffs from Argentina; and cotton and raw sugar from Peru.

The Chilean merchant fleet, with about 100 vessels of 100 tons or more, aggregates approximately 230,000 gross tons.

Transportation. The railway lines of Chile total about 5400 m. and are entirely confined to the n. two thirds of the country. The main longitudinal system is connected by spur lines to important coastal towns and by trans-Andean lines to points in Bolivia and Argentina. Several international air-transport systems provide service between Santiago and major world points, and a government-owned airline furnishes domestic and foreign service, including flights to the United States. Passenger travel between Chile and all parts of the world is facilitated also by a number of steamship lines, which operate passenger vessels on regular schedules from Valparaíso.

The total length of the Chilean highway system is about 31,000 m. More than 80 percent of the system, which includes 1500 m. of first-class roads and 16,000 m. of dirt roads, may be used safely by motor vehicles. The country has about 46,000 automobiles, 38,500 trucks, and 5000 buses.

Communications. Chile has a federal postal service which operates about 1150 post offices. There are about 15,900 m. of telegraph lines and more than 145,000 telephones. The country also has 3 large radio-broadcasting stations.

Newspapers. The Chilean newspaper with the largest circulation is *El Mercurio.* Other newspapers, each with a circulation of more than 50,000 copies, are *Tercera de la Hora, La Nación,* and *El Diario Ilustrado.*

GOVERNMENT

Central Government. The central government of Chile is based on the constitution of 1925. The constitution vests executive power in a president, elected for a six-year term, and a cabinet, which is appointed by the president. The president cannot serve two consecutive terms. He has certain veto powers, which may, however, be overridden by a two-thirds vote of the Congress. Legislative power is vested in the latter, a bicameral body consisting of a Chamber of Deputies, whose members are elected for four-year terms on the basis of 1 for each 30,000 inhabitants or fraction of not less than 15,000; and a Senate of 45 members. Senators are elected for eight-year terms and represent either a single province or a group of provinces. Every four years the terms of some of the senators and of all the deputies come to an end. Judicial authority is vested in a High Court of Justice, appointed by the president; 9 Courts of Appeal; departmental courts; and various minor courts. All literate citizens twenty-one years of age or older are eligible to vote in national elections. Women received full voting privileges in 1949. Foreign residents may vote in local elections.

Local Government. The governmental structure of Chile is highly centralized, with the president appointing the administrative heads of the provinces and of the provincial subdivisions, the departments. These administrators are called intendants and governers, respectively. Municipalities, however, are governed by popularly elected officials, except that the mayors of large cities, including Santiago and Valparaíso, are presidential appointees.

Political Parties. Among the political parties of Chile are the Conservative and Liberal parties, which have been dominant in Chilean history; the Radical Party, which gained the majority in recent times; the Christian Democratic Party, which was re-

cently organized and has been growing in importance; and two Socialist parties. The political pattern is fluid, for elections have increasingly seen realignments of new and old groups, sometimes under new names. Labor's role in politics is important. The Communist Party was banned in 1948, but its former members participate through other groups.

Legislation. In modern times the central government has enacted legislation which gives it a dominant role in the economy. Social-welfare and labor legislation, first enacted in the 1920's, established numerous agencies to provide most of the country's workers with health, maternity, and unemployment benefits and with insurance, old-age pensions, family allowances, and housing assistance. The government controls all foreign trade, operates most of the transport and communication systems, including the airlines, and participates actively in many phases of the mining industry. The government is also the major promoter of new enterprises, such as hydroelectric plants, petroleum exploitation and refining, and steel manufacturing.

Defense. In Chile military service is compulsory and universal for men; there are eighteen months of active duty beginning at the age of twenty and followed by membership in the reserve until the age of forty-five. The Chilean army consists of 3 corps, 1 division, 1 cavalry division, and 1 railway regiment. The active army is about 20,000 strong. The Chilean navy includes 1 battleship, the *Almirante Latorre;* 2 cruisers, the *Capitán Prat* and the *O'Higgins,* both purchased from the United States in 1951; and destroyers, frigates, submarines, and other vessels. Naval strength, which includes coast-artillery units and marines, stands at about 13,000. The Chilean air force consists of 4 brigades.

HISTORY

The first European to visit what is now Chile was the Portuguese explorer Ferdinand Magellan, who landed at Chiloé Island following his voyage, in 1520, through the strait which bears his name. The region was then known to its native population as *Tchili,* an Indian word meaning "snow". At the time of Magellan's visit, most of Chile s. of the Rapel R. was dominated by the Araucanians, an Indian tribe remarkable for its fighting ability. The tribes occupying the northern portions of Chile had been subjugated during the 15th century by the Incas of Peru. In 1535, after the Spanish under Francisco Pizarro (q.v.) had completed their conquest of Peru,

Ewing Galloway

Aconcagua, on the Chile-Argentina border, is the highest peak in the Andes.

Diego de Almagro, one of Pizarro's aides, led a gold-hunting expedition from that country overland into Chile. The expedition spent nearly three fruitless years in the country, and then withdrew to Peru. Pedro de Valdivia, another of Pizarro's commanders, led a second expedition into southern Chile in 1540. Despite fierce resistance from the Araucanians, Valdivia succeeded in establishing several settlements, including Santiago (1541), Concepción (1550), and Valdivia (1552). However, in 1553 the Araucanians organized a successful uprising, killing Valdivia and many of his followers and devastating all of the towns except Concepción and La Serena. The rebellion was the initial phase of warfare which lasted nearly one hundred years. The Araucanians were the only important Indian people who did not succumb to Spanish attack. Strife continued intermittently during and after the Spanish colonial period and did not end until late in the 19th century.

In the Spanish colonial organization Chile originally was a dependency of the viceroyalty of Peru and later had its own government. Chile developed slowly because it did not have important silver deposits to attract the Spanish or natives who were willing to labor. Moreover it was far from the main centers of Spanish colonization in Peru and was difficult to reach because of its deserts and mountains. Farming in the Central Valley was the chief occupation, and Chile supplied Peru with foodstuffs, especially wheat. The agricultural pattern was of large landholdings, with much of the rural population living on and working the estates. Buildings in the towns were of adobe and rarely of architectural note. The townspeople lived by trade. At the end of the 18th century Chile had a population estimated at about 500,000, exclusive of the Indians in the s.

In 1810 Chile joined other Spanish colonies in breaking political ties with Spain. On Sept. 18, celebrated thereafter as the Chilean independence day, the Santiago town council deposed the colonial governor of Chile, delegating his powers to a council of seven. Although this act marked the formal establishment of Chilean independence from Spain, intermittent warfare against Spanish troops, dispatched from Peru, continued for more than 15 years. A royalist army was decisively defeated at Chacabuco on February

12, 1817, ending Spanish control of N. Chile, and one year later Bernardo O'Higgins (q.v.), one of the revolutionary leaders, proclaimed the absolute independence of Chile. However, royalist forces controlled nearly all of southern Chile until 1818, and were not completely expelled from the country until 1826.

O'Higgins, who had been named director general of Chile in 1818, ruled the country with dictatorial powers until 1823, when popular hostility to his regime forced his resignation. A liberal constitution, establishing a republican form of government, was then adopted, but political strife among numerous organizations contending for power kept the country in turmoil until 1830, when conservative elements, headed by General Joaquín Prieto (1786–1854), organized a successful rebellion and seized control of the government. In 1831 Prieto became president, but the leading person in the government was Diego José Victor Portales (1793–1837), who filled various cabinet posts during Prieto's administration. A new constitution, vesting immense powers in the executive department of the government, was adopted in 1833. Abortive armed attempts to remove the Conservatives from power were made by liberal groups in 1835, in 1851, and in 1859.

Despite its reactionary character, the Conservative Party government fostered domestic policies which contributed substantially to the commercial and agricultural development of Chile. In addition, steps were taken to exploit mineral resources, railroads were constructed, and immigration was encouraged. A school system and many other educational and cultural institutions were established. The chief developments in Chilean foreign relations during the period of Conservative dominance was a series of boundary disputes, beginning in 1843, with Argentina. Armed hostilities were narrowly averted on several occasions in connection with this problem, which was not settled until 1881. In that year a treaty was signed, granting half of Tierra del Fuego to Chile.

Divisions resulting from disagreements with the Roman Catholic Church had taken place, meanwhile, within the Conservative Party. Beginning in 1861 its liberal wing, in coalition with the Liberal Party, instituted a number of constitutional reforms, including prohibition of consecutive presidential terms. Endeavors to promote public welfare and the further development of national resources were intensified, notably by new railway and highway projects and the creation of a postal system. In 1865 Chile became involved in a war with Spain, the naval forces of which bombarded Valparaíso. Hostilities continued sporadically until 1869, when diplomatic representatives of the United States negotiated a settlement.

Chilean interests subsequently began the exploitation of the immensely valuable nitrate deposits in the Atacama Desert, an area located in indefinitely-bounded territory between Chile and Bolivia and Peru. Rejecting Bolivian claims to the region, the Chilean government, in Feb., 1879, ordered its military forces into the Bolivian port of Antofagasta. Two months later Peru, an ally of Bolivia, declared war on Chile, precipitating the War of the Pacific. As a result of its victory in this conflict, terminated in 1883, Chile acquired considerable territory, including the Province of Antofagasta from Bolivia and the Province of Tarapacá from Peru. Peru also yielded Tacna and Arica to Chile, on condition that after ten years a plebiscite be held. Although the two countries failed to agree on conditions for a plebiscite, disposition of the disputed areas was achieved in 1928 by peaceful negotiation, Tacna becoming a possession of Peru and Arica going to Chile. See TACNA-ARICA DISPUTE.

The next major development in Chilean history occurred in 1891, when political forces closely allied with the Roman Catholic clergy organized a revolt against the administration of President José Manuel Balmaceda, a Liberal Party leader. Under the leadership of Captain Jorge Montt, a naval officer, the rebels, who termed themselves "Congressionalists", seized the Chilean fleet and the rich nitrate provinces in the north. In August they defeated a government army near Valparaíso. This city then fell to the rebels, as did Santiago, virtually ending the war. More than 10,000 lives had been lost, and considerable property destroyed. Balmaceda committed suicide in September. Shortly thereafter Montt became president, and Chile entered an extended period of peaceful reconstruction, and ended by agreement another boundary dispute with Argentina. As a concession to liberal sentiment in the country, Montt instituted several reforms, notably democratization of the executive department. The following years were marked by increasing participation of the Chilean people in politics, and by mounting political turbulence.

In August, 1906, a disastrous earthquake virtually destroyed Valparaíso and extensively damaged Santiago, killing more than 3000 people and making about 100,000 homeless. The damaged areas were rapidly rebuilt, how-

The harbor of Valparaíso, the second largest city and the major seaport of Chile

ever. Another earthquake occurred on Jan. 24, 1939, killing about 50,000 people.

Chile was neutral in World War I. After the war great strife developed in the country between liberal and conservative elements. The liberals gained power with the election in 1920 of Arturo Alessandri Palma (q.v.), but he was unable to gain congressional adoption of his proposals for reform. In 1924 a group of military figures accomplished a *coup d'état*, ostensibly for the purpose of forcing liberal reforms, drove Alessandri from office, and established a military dictatorship. The dictatorship was overthrown early in 1925 in another military coup and Alessandri was restored to the presidency for less than a year. Under the next president, Emiliano Figueroa, governmental authority was actually wielded by an army officer, Carlos Ibáñez del Campo (1877–   ), who ruled as president from 1927 until 1931. Following additional coups and changes of administration, Alessandri was elected president again in 1932 and served until the end of his term in 1938.

In the elections of 1938 a liberal government, with Pedro Aguirre Cerda (1879–1941) as president, was elected by a coalition of democratic groups united in a popular front. This coalition was successful again in 1942, when Juan Antonio Ríos (1888–1946) was elected president. During World War II the government of Chile severed diplomatic relations with Japan, Italy, and Germany in January, 1943, and declared war on Japan on April 11, 1945. The country became a charter member of the United Nations in June, 1945. Significant developments during the war period included the emergence of the Communist Party as one of the strongest political organizations in Chile.

In the presidential election of 1946 a left-wing coalition consisting mainly of the Radical and Communist parties supported the candidacy of the Radical Party leader Gabriel González Videla (1898–   ). He won a plurality of the votes, but in accordance with Chilean electoral procedure providing that a successful candidate must poll as many votes as his opponents combined, the election of a president devolved on Congress. González Videla was confirmed as president in October.

Although González Videla appointed three communists to his cabinet, thereby establishing a precedent in the politics of the Western Hemisphere, the coalition endured for less than six months. The communist ministers, frequently at loggerheads with other members of the government, were removed from the cabinet in April, 1947.

In 1947 Chile was represented at the Inter-

Eucalyptus logs on their way from a forest to a shipping center in Chile

national Conference for the Maintenance of Peace and Security, held at Petropolis, Brazil. Chile approved the Inter-American Treaty of Reciprocal Assistance drafted by the conference. See Rio de Janeiro, Treaty of.

In 1947 diplomatic relations with the Soviet Union were severed. During the following year the government intensified its anticommunist campaign. Hundreds of Communists were incarcerated in concentration camps, and the government effectuated the "Law for the Defense of Democracy", which practically proscribed the Communist Party. Manifestations of social and labor unrest were frequent during 1949 and 1950. In 1951 strikes occurred in almost every sector of the national economy.

Industrial strife, the high cost of living, and nationalism with strong anti-United States overtones provided the backdrop for the 1952 presidential contest. A coalition of minor parties nominated former president Carlos Ibáñez del Campo, who appealed consistently to nationalist sentiments during the subsequent campaign. Among other things, Ibáñez promised eventual nationalization of the coal and copper industries. He emerged from the election, held in September, with a large plurality.

The Ibáñez administration was beset by the problem of inflation (see *Currency, Finance, and Banking,* above). The government made attempts to alleviate economic distress by encouraging production of copper and nitrates (see *Mining,* above). These efforts suffered a setback when there occurred a sharp drop in world prices of copper in 1956 and the worst drought in almost a century in 1957. Attempts to remedy the economic situation were hampered also by bitter rivalry among the political parties, by the president's precarious majority in Congress, and by the readiness of the Communists to exploit dissatisfaction.

On Feb. 7, 1958, the government granted a wage increase of 20 percent to all workers, whether employed privately or in civil service. Jorge Alessandri, the candidate of a conservative-liberal coalition, was elected to the presidency on Sept. 4 and took office on Nov. 4. Alessandri, who favored free enterprise and the encouragement of foreign investment, received a plurality of the votes but less than the combined total of his three left-wing opponents. On Dec. 24, 1959, the government announced that copper production during the year was the highest in Chilean history. On Jan. 1, 1960, a new monetary unit, the escudo, worth about 90 cents in U.S. currency, replaced the peso, then valued at about 1000 to the dollar. In congressional elections held in March, 1961, the parties supporting Alessandri retained control but by a reduced majority; both Communists and Socialists made substantial gains. At the inter-American economic and social conference held in Punta del Este, Uruguay, in August, Chile announced plans to raise living standards by 20 percent during a ten-year period through the expenditure of $2.5 billion. On March 8, 1962, it was announced that the U.S. Agency for International Development, under a program known popularly as the Alliance for Progress, would make $120 million available to Chile for the first phase of its plan for economic expansion.   E.K.J.

CHILEAN-PERUVIAN WAR. See Chile: *History;* Peru: *History.*

CHILI. See CAPSICUM.

CHILLÁN, city and capital of Ñuble Province, Chile, situated about 56 miles E.N.E. of Concepción. It is the commercial center of a rich agricultural region. Industries include brewing and flour milling. Chillán was founded by Spanish settlers in 1594. Pop. (1960) 82,947.

CHILLICOTHE, county seat of Ross Co., Ohio, in the foothills of the Allegheny Mountains, on the Scioto R., about 50 miles s. of Columbus. It is the trade center of a farming and grazing region, and is an industrial city, containing railroad shops and manufacturing paper products, shoes, dairy and other food products, furniture, chemicals, and concrete. Chillicothe was founded in 1796, and in 1800 became the seat of government of the Northwest Territory. It served as the first capital of the State of Ohio (1803–10; 1812–16). Near the city is the Mound City Group National Monument. Pop. (1960) 24,957.

CHILLON, ancient castle in Switzerland, at the east end of Lake Geneva. Dating from about the 8th century, it was partly rebuilt in 1238 by Amadeus IV of Savoy, and long served as a state prison. There for six years (1530–36) François de Bonnivard endured the captivity immortalized by Byron's poem *The Prisoner of Chillon* (1821).

CHIMBORAZO, an extinct volcano, the highest mountain peak of Ecuador, in the west Cordillera of the Andes, about 100 miles s. of Quito. It is covered with snow and its height is 20,702 ft.

CHIMES. See BELL.

CHIMKENT, city of the Kazakh Soviet Socialist Republic, in s.w. Siberia, about 75 miles N.E. of Tashkent. Wheat, cotton, petroleum, coal, lead, and zinc are produced in the surrounding region. The city contains lead-refining plants. Pop. (1959 est.) 153,000.

CHIMNEY SWALLOW, the common European house swallow, *Hirundo rustica.* It is about 7½ inches long, and has crescent-shaped wings and deeply forked tail. The upper parts are black; the throat is chestnut brown edged with black; and the under parts are pink. The chimney swallow ranges from Greenland to western China. In North America the name is applied to the chimney swift (see SWIFT).

CHIMNEY SWIFT. See SWIFT.

CHIMPANZEE, one of the highest of the anthropoid or manlike apes. It stands about four feet high, and has dark hair, a broad, leathery, reddish-brown face, small nose, large mouth, protruding lips, large brow ridges, and small ears. The face has an angle of 70 degrees and the head hangs down upon the chest.

There are no cheek pouches. The arms are unusually long, reaching the knee; their span is about half as much again as the height of the animal. The hand is narrow, but as long as the foot. The sole of the foot can rest flatly on the ground, and the animal readily stands or walks erect. The backbone exhibits the curves characteristic of man, and the chimpanzee is alone among anthropoids in having the spine of the second neck vertebra bifurcated as in man. It has one pair of ribs more than the twelve possessed by man. Chimpanzees have no tail, nor any ischial callosities. The brain is about half the minimum size of a normal human brain. All the *gyri* (ridges) of the human brain are represented in the chimpanzee, but are simpler and larger in proportion to the brain.

National Audubon Society (Thornton)
Chimpanzee, Pan styrus

The chimpanzee is found from the Atlantic coast of central Africa eastward through the forest region to the Nile, from about 10° s. to 12° N. of the equator. Throughout this great area it seems to be numerous and is known under many names. It occupies a wider area than the gorilla. It lives in forests, is an adept climber, but keeps on the ground most of the time. Its diet consists mainly of wild fruits with animal food occasionally added. Chimpanzees live in families or in small societies. They construct penthouses in the thick forests and make considerable noise, especially when provoked by other monkeys.

CHINA, or CHINAWARE. See POTTERY.

CHINA, country of central and E. Asia, bounded on the N. by the Mongolian People's Republic (Outer Mongolia) and the Soviet Union, on the E. by the Soviet Union, North Korea, the Yellow Sea, and the China Sea, on the S. by the China Sea, the Democratic Republic of Vietnam, the kingdom of Laos, the Union of Burma, the Republic of India, Bhutan, and Nepal, and on the W. by Afghanistan and the Soviet Union. The country extends from lat. 53° N. to lat. 18° N., a distance of about 2300 m., and from long. 73° E. to long 135° E., a distance of some 3500 m. This article deals with the Communist state known officially as the People's Republic of China (Chin. *Chung-Hua Jeṇ-Min Kung-Ho-Kuo*); for information about the Nationalist state known officially as the Republic of China (Chin. *Chung-Hua Min-Kuo*), see FORMOSA.

China ranks first in the world in population and second (after the Soviet Union) in area. The area of China is about 3,700,000 sq.m. and the population (1960 est.) is 660,-000,000. The capital is Peking (q.v.). The land borders of China have a total length of about 9000 m.; the coast line is about 7000 m. long.

POLITICAL DIVISIONS OF COMMUNIST CHINA

	Area (thousands of sq.m.)	Pop. (1957 est., in millions)	Capital (1957 est. pop., in thousands)	
Provinces				
Anhwei	56	33.6	Hofei	(304)
Chekiang	39	25.3	Hangchow	(784)
Fukien	46	14.6	Minhow	(616)
Heilung-kiang	180	14.9	Harbin	(1552)
Honan	65	48.7	Chenghsien	(766)
Hopeh	75	43.7	Tientsin	(3220)
Hunan	79	36.2	Changsha	(703)
Hupeh	72	30.8	Wuhan	(2146)
Kansu	135	12.8	Lanchow	(504)
Kiangsi	67	18.6	Nanchang	(508)
Kiangsu	40	45.2	Nanking	(1419)
Kirin	70	12.6	Changchun	(975)
Kwangtung	84	38.0	Canton	(1840)
Kweichow	66	16.9	Kweiyang	(504)
Liaoning	50	24.0	Mukden	(2411)
Shansi	60	16.0	Yangku	(1020)
Shantung	56	54.0	Tsinan	(862)
Shensi	74	18.1	Sian	(1310)
Szechwan	210	72.2	Chengtu	(1107)
Tsinghai	320	2.0	Sining	(300)
Yunnan	162	19.1	Kunming	(880)
Autonomous Regions				
Inner Mongolia	580	9.2	Kweisui	(314)
Kwangsi Chuang	84	19.4	Yungning	(264)
Ningsia Hui	30	1.8	Yinchwan	(84)*
Sinkiang Uigur	660	5.6	Urumchi	(275)
Tibet	580	1.3	Lhasa	(50)*
Independent Cities				
Peking	3.4	4.0		
Shanghai	0.4	6.9		

* 1953 estimate

The country includes about 3400 offshore islands. Hainan (q.v.), with an area of 13,000 sq.m., is the largest island. Besides the island of Formosa, other islands off the Chinese mainland which are not under the control of the Communist government are Hong Kong (q.v.), which, together with the mainland peninsula of Kowloon, constitutes a British crown colony, and the Portuguese island of Macao (q.v.).

THE LAND

Physical Characteristics. The surface of China is distinguished by a great variety of land forms, including snow-capped mountain ranges, vast plateaus, and low-lying plains. On the whole, a mountainous topography predominates, and lowlands occupy only 20 percent of the country.

The arrangement of the principal relief forms in China, excluding the N.E. region known as Manchuria, may be compared to a giant stairway of three steps rising from the depths of the Pacific Ocean. The base of the stairway is found in the waters of the Yellow Sea, the East China Sea, and the South China Sea. The first step is formed by the lowlands and plains along the coast. These lowlands project westward to a series of north-and-south-trending mountain ranges which rise to the second step. The second step is a zone of extensive uplands of medium elevation. The third step is represented by the highlands of Tibet, which are surrounded and traversed by great mountain chains.

Northeastern China, known in physical geography as Manchuria, is occupied by a plain which is bounded on the S. by the Yellow Sea and by mountains on the other sides. The mountains are the Great Khingan Mts. in the W., the Ilkuri Shan in the N., and the Little Khingan Mts. and the E. Manchurian uplands in the E. Low hill ranges divide the Manchurian plain into three sections, namely the Amur-Sungari lowland in the N., the central Manchurian lowland, and the S. Manchurian lowland, around Mukden.

The S. Manchurian lowland is connected on the S.W. by a narrow coastal pass, called the Shanhaikwan gateway, with the largest lowland of China, known both as the North China Plain and the Great Chinese Plain. This great lowland, which is watered by the lower course of the Hwang Ho (Yellow R.), is bounded on the S. by the Kwaiyang Mts., a range averaging about 1000 ft. in elevation. To the S. of these mountains lies the plain of the middle course of the Yangtze R. The plain, which contains 2 large lakes, Tungting

Part of the Great Wall of China, begun under the Ch'in dynasty (3rd century B.C.)

Hu and Poyang Hu, extends southward along the valleys of the Siang and the Kan rivers, 2 tributaries of the Middle Yangtze.

The part of China s. of the Yangtze R. consists largely of a complex system of low mountain ranges. The mountains are succeeded by hills along the valley of the Si R. and by coastal lowlands around the delta of the Si near Canton.

The portion of China bordering on Outer Mongolia consists of a vast upland of plateaus, mountain ranges, and intermontane basins. This region, called Inner Mongolia, has an average elevation of 3500 ft. The E. margin, a steppe land known as Barga, borders on the Great Khingan Mts. Along the s. margin are the Gobi and Ala Shan deserts.

To the s. of the desert belt lies a plateau ranging in elevation from 1500 to 6000 ft. and covering an area of 260,000 sq.m. The plateau bears a thick layer of loess, a fine-textured brown soil of high fertility. The Hwang Ho flows E. through the loess plateau and, encountering the solid bedrock of Inner Mongolia, turns s., forming a gigantic bend. The interior of the bend is occupied by the Ordos desert plateau.

Sinkiang (q.v.), the extreme w. section of China, is bounded on the s. by the ranges of the Kunlun and the Astin Tagh. Northern and southern Sinkiang is divided by the ranges of the Tien Shan, which rise to 15,000 ft. Among the E. outliers of the Tien Shan is the Turfan depression, which drops to 427 ft. below sea level. South of the Tien Shan lies the Tarim R. basin, with an area of 350,000 sq.m., much of which is occupied by the Takla Makan Desert. North of the Tien Shan is Dzungaria, a broad basin with rolling terrain. The border of Sinkiang and Tibet is formed by a series of mountain ranges which extend from w. to E. The ranges include the Kunlun (rising to 25,340 ft. in the Ulugh Muztagh), the Astin Tagh, the Nan Shan, and the Chin Ling Shan.

The s. part of Tibet (q.v.), which constitutes the s.w. section of China, is in the Himalaya mountain system. Much of Tibet consists of a rocky desert plateau with salt lakes and salt marshes.

The Kunlun system in its E. extension forms the Szechwanese Alps, which rise to heights of 15,000 to 20,000 ft. The E. outliers of these mountains enclose the Red, or Szechwan, Basin. The Szechwanese Alps drop toward the sea in the s.E., forming 2 gigantic terraces, the Yunnan plateau (7500 ft.) and the Kweichow plateau (5000 ft.).

River Systems. China has extensive river systems, including some of the longest rivers in the world. All the large rivers drain into the Pacific Ocean.

Rivers play an extraordinarily important role in the life of China. Chinese civilization began on the banks of some of the largest rivers, notably the Hwang Ho and the Yangtze R. (qq.v.). Because of irregular and usually inadequate precipitation, the rivers constitute an important source of water for irrigation. The rivers are also major transportation routes and, in addition, have a tremendous hydroelectric potential. However, the rivers of China have not had beneficial effects alone; over the centuries disastrous floods have caused millions of deaths, washed away fertile soils, deposited sand and gravel in agricultural areas, and produced large swamps. In recent times increasing attention has been given to flood-control measures, including the construction of dams, dikes, canals, and reservoirs.

The longest river of China is the Yangtze R. (3430 m. long), which is exceeded in length only by the Mississippi-Missouri system, the Nile R., and the Amazon R. The Yangtze R. rises in the Tibetan highlands, traverses mountainous country in its upper course, and enters the Red Basin. The river leaves the basin through the famous Yangtze gorges near Ichang, flows across the broad Yangtze plain, and empties into the East China Sea. The Yangtze R. receives its largest tributaries from the left; these tributaries are the Yalung, Min, Kialing, and Han rivers. From the right it receives the Siang and the Kan rivers. There are 2 large lakes in the middle Yangtze valley, namely Tungting Hu and Poyang Hu; these lakes serve as natural flood reservoirs during the summer, when the monsoon rains bring the river to its high-water stage. The Yangtze is the most important navigation route among the great rivers of China.

The Hwang Ho, the second-longest river of China, is about 2900 m. in length. The Hwang Ho, which also rises in the Tibetan highlands, flows through the loess country in a huge bend and then enters the North China Plain. The mouth is on a gulf of the Yellow Sea. The only important tributaries are the Wei and Fen rivers. Probably no other river has brought so much suffering to mankind as the Hwang Ho in its lower course. In the past 2500 years the river shifted its course nine times within a 450-m. zone extending from Tientsin to Shanghai. The last change in course occurred in 1938, when the river left its bed as a result of destruction of containing dikes. It turned s., joined the Hwai R., and finally merged with the mouth of the Yangtze R. The breach in the dikes was repaired in 1947, and the river returned to its previous course.

The third-largest Chinese river, the Si (West) R., is 1200 m. long. It rises in the plateau of Yunnan and flows through Kwangsi Chuang Autonomous Region and Kwangtung Province to the South China Sea. At Canton it forms a large joint delta with two other rivers, the Peh (North) R. and the Tung (East) R. Other major rivers within or bordering on China are the Sungari, Yalu, Amur (q.v.), and Tsangpo.

Climate. More than 90 percent of China lies in the Temperate Zone. Only the extreme s. of the country extends into the tropics. However, a number of factors give China a climate far different from that normally found in the Temperate Zone. The chief factor is the country's location between the continental land mass of N. Asia and the Pacific Ocean. The regular movement of a high-pressure center over the Asian continent in winter and over the ocean in summer produces seasonal atmospheric circulations known as the winter and summer monsoons.

In winter the climate of China is under the influence of cold, dry N.W. winds blowing from the interior of Asia. Almost all of China is colder during the winter than any other part of the world situated in the same latitudes. Light frosts occur even in Canton, which is in the Tropical zone and has an average January temperature of 55° F. Winter temperatures tend to be higher near the coast and lower in the interior. The coldest winters occur in the extreme N., where, at Lungkiang, a temperature of —41° F. has been recorded. The warmest winters occur in the s., especially in areas protected by mountain ranges against the cold winter monsoon. The winter winds bear almost no moisture, so that China has very little winter precipitation, either in the form of rain or of snow. Wind-borne sand from the Central Asian deserts covers the fertile soils of the Chinese plains. Windbreaks are being planted in an effort to halt the advance of sand.

In the tropical parts of China average July temperatures are as high as 85° F. Due to influences from the strongly heated interior of Asia, the Temperate Zone of China has higher summer temperatures than are commonly found at such latitudes. The July average rises as high as 93° F. in the Turfan depression of Sinkiang.

Far more precipitation is received by s. than by N. China. Annual rainfall exceeds 40 in. almost everywhere s. of the topographic barrier formed by the Chin Ling Shan. North of those mountains annual precipitation decreases rapidly. It is only 15 in. at Yangku in Shansi Province.

The amount of precipitation in any given area depends to some extent on the local relief; thus, rainfall often is heavy on the windward slopes of mountains in the way of the humid summer monsoon. For example, the s. slopes of Omei, in Szechwan Province, receive as much as 320 in. of precipitation a

INDEX TO MAP OF CHINA

Continued on page 2056

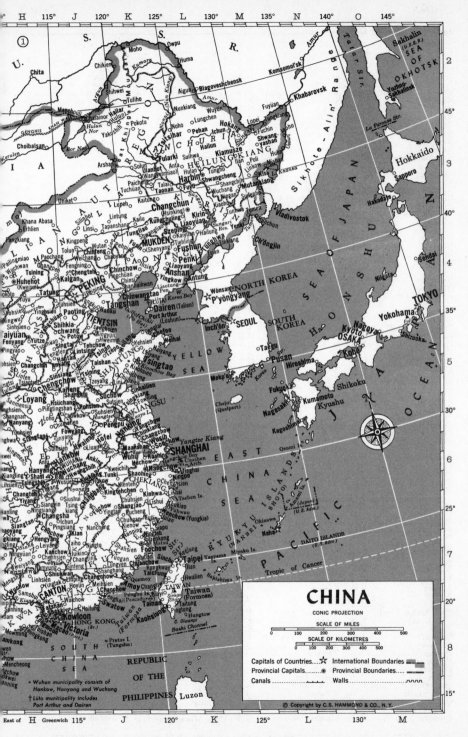

CHINA

CONIC PROJECTION

SCALE OF MILES

0 100 200 300 400 500

SCALE OF KILOMETRES

0 100 200 300 400 500

Capitals of Countries......☆ International Boundaries....
Provincial Capitals.........◉ Provincial Boundaries....
Canals.................. Walls..................

* Wuhan municipality consists of
Hankow, Hanyang and Wuchang

† Lüta municipality includes
Port Arthur and Dairen

© Copyright by C.S. HAMMOND & CO., N.Y.

East of H Greenwich 115°   J   120°   K   125°   L   130°   M

2055

Index to Map of China—cont.

year. On the other hand, the arid areas w. of the Great Khingan Mts. receive less than 15 in. annually. The lowest rainfall in China is recorded in the Takla Makan Desert of Sinkiang, which receives only 0.5 in. a year.

A distinctive feature of the climate of China is the typhoons which pass over the s.e. part of the country in August and September. These storms often produce great destruction along the coasts.

Geology. China consists geologically of the Chinese platform, a stable, rigid section of the earth's crust, and a series of enclosing unstable zones in which the crust has been folded to produce the great Himalayan, Kunlun, and Tien Shan uplifts. The Chinese platform comprises two distinct sections, the Sinian shield, in n. and n.e. China, and the South China massif. The rocks of the Sinian shield are largely of nonmarine origin. Occasional marine inundations have left only a thin sedimentary cover in some areas, with the more ancient rock of the foundation often appearing as outcroppings. The South China massif, in contrast, has a longer history of marine sedimentary deposits. The two sections of the Chinese platform are separated by a narrow zone of folding that gave rise to the Chin Ling Shan system in the Upper Paleozoic period. The greatest mountain-building period in the Chinese platform occurred during Cretaceous times. That period, known as the Yen Shan revolution, resulted in the breaking up of the platform into a series of separate blocks. The mountains formed during the Yen Shan revolution trend from n.e. to s.w., especially in the South China massif.

Soil. The most fertile soils in China are the alluvial, the loessial, and the so-called red soils. Alluvial soils predominate in the lowlands of n. and n.e. China and in the valley of the middle and lower Yangtze R. These soils were deposited by the rivers during floods in the form of silt enriched with organic residues.

Loessial soils cover the plateau along the middle course of the Hwang Ho. Loess is believed to have been formed of fine-textured sand and dust blown for thousands of years from the interior of Asia. The thickness of the loess layer ranges to more than 1000 ft. The layer covers not only depressions but also mountain slopes, smoothing their contours and making them suitable for the raising of crops. Loessial soils are very fertile but do not retain moisture well. Successful farming in loess-soil regions depends therefore on irrigation.

The so-called red soils, many of which are reddish or reddish yellow but which include also gray and black soils, are most common in s. China, particularly in Szechwan Province, part of which is called the Red Basin. The fertility of these soils, which were formed as a result of the weathering of rocks in a hot, humid climate, is due to the presence of decayed plant matter and soluble mineral salts. Red soils are especially suitable for the growing of subtropical crops, such as tea and citrus fruit.

Other types of soils in China are related to specific types of relief. In the s. parts of China, red soils give way to reddish-brown soils and then to brown soils at higher elevations. In n. China, chestnut-colored soils are common in lowlands and ash-colored soils are found in the mountains. In the arid w. areas sandy and salt-impregnated soils predominate. There are large areas of chernozem, or black soil, in n.e. China.

Plants. The variety of relief, climate, and soils in China has given rise to a wide range of vegetation, from the tropical to the n. forest types. Of a total of more than 5000 species of trees and shrubs that have been identified in China, about 50 tree species are native only to that country. In Szechwan, for example, there grows the ginkgo tree, which, except where transplanted, is found elsewhere in the world only in fossil form. China is the home of many of the world's cultivated plants, including millet, buckwheat, ramie, and the tung oil tree. In addition to the native vegetation, many plants brought from Japan, s.e. Asia, Europe, and the New World have been acclimatized in China. Cultivated crops have almost completely replaced the natural vegetation in areas of intensive agriculture. This process often has been associated with deforestation; only 5.2 percent of the total territory of China is in forest.

Four basic native vegetation zones can be distinguished in China if the extensive deforestation is disregarded. A zone of temperate deciduous forest lies in the e. part of the country n. of the Yangtze R. The largest forest stands have been preserved in the Khingan Mts. The most common tree types in this zone are oak, elm, birch, linden, ash, hornbeam, poplar, pine, and spruce. Wild apple and pear trees are also found there. The ginseng root, which traditional Chinese medicine credited as a panacea, also grows in this zone.

A zone of subtropical and tropical evergreen forest lies s. of the Yangtze. Typical plants are the tung oil tree, the camphor tree,

Eastfoto

Morning activity in a family of the Hui nationality of Kansu Province, northwest China

the lacquer tree, the wax tree, the rubber tree, citrus trees, the banana palm, and the pineapple, sugar cane, and tea plants. About 35 types of bamboo, which plays a major role in the life and economy of the Chinese people, grow in s. China. Bamboo is used to build homes and to make furniture, housewares, baskets, pipes, poles, farm implements, musical instruments, and many other items, including paper. Young bamboo shoots are used as food.

A steppe-vegetation zone covers part of the semiarid w. areas of China, including a portion of Tibet. Tall grass predominates in the more humid steppe and short grass in the drier section. A zone of sparse desert vegetation is found in the arid parts of Inner Mongolia, Sinkiang, and Tibet.

The almost complete absence of forest cover in the most highly developed farming areas has been responsible for the age-old natural catastrophes of China, such as floods and soil erosion. Deforestation has been especially serious in areas bordering on the deserts, where wind-blown sand encroaches on cultivated land. Forest shelter belts and windbreaks are being planted to prevent further inroads of sands.

Animals. Typical representatives of the fauna of the temperate deciduous-forest zone include the lynx, musk deer, Japanese deer, wild boar, hare, squirrel, sable, marten, ermine, and weasel. The fauna of this zone is closely related to that of the Siberian forests of the Soviet Union. South of the Chin Ling Shan divide, the evergreen forests harbor a tropical fauna, including tigers, leopards, giant pandas, monkeys, and porcupines. Birds

are represented by pheasants, peacocks, parrots, herons, and cranes. In the steppe and desert areas hoofed animals, rodents, and reptiles predominate. They include the antelope, wild ass, musk deer, camel, yak, and marmot, and lizards and snakes. There is relatively little trapping of the fur-bearing animals found in parts of China.

Water Power. According to preliminary estimates, the rivers of China have a hydroelectric power potential of 150,000,000 kilowatts. The greater part of the water-power potential (72 percent) is concentrated in the s.w. section of the country; the central and s. provinces, with 12.4 percent, rank next in potential water power. The Yangtze R. basin has 40 percent of the water-power potential, followed by the basins of the Hwang Ho and the Tsangpo. Only about 4 percent of the nation's water-power potential has been developed, mainly near the industrial centers in N. and N.E. China. The largest operating hydroelectric stations are on the upper Sungari and on the Yalu R. As part of the long-range development of the Hwang Ho, two 1,000,000-kilowatt stations were under construction on the river at the beginning of the 1960's. Of the total amount of electricity produced in China in the early 1960's, approximately 25 percent was derived from hydroelectric stations.

Political Divisions. The People's Republic of China is divided into twenty-one provinces, five autonomous regions, and two independent cities. In addition, Formosa is claimed by the republic. The provinces are Heilungkiang, Kirin, and Liaoning in Manchuria; Hopeh, Honan, and Shantung in the North China Plain; Kiangsu, Anhwei, Hupeh, Hunan, and Kiangsi in the middle and lower Yangtze R. basin; Chekiang, Fukien, and Kwangtung along the S.E. and s. coasts; Kweichow, Yunnan, and Szechwan in the s.w.; Shensi and Shansi in the loess region; and Kansu and Tsinghai in the N.W. The five autonomous regions, each inhabited largely by a major non-Chinese ethnic minority, are Inner Mongolia (Mongols), Ningsia Hui (Hui, or Chinese Moslems), Sinkiang Uigur (Uigurs), Tibet (Tibetans), and Kwangsi Chuang (Chuang). The two independent cities, which are directly under central government control, are Shanghai and Peking.

Largest Cities. According to the 1953 census, 103 cities in China have a population of more than 100,000. Of these cities 9 have a population of more than 1,000,000 and 16 a population between 500,000 and 1,000,000. The largest cities of China, with approximate population in 1961, unless otherwise indicated, are: Shanghai, 10,000,000; Peking, 6,000,000; Tientsin, 4,000,000; Mukden, 2,423,000; Wuhan, 2,226,000; Chungking, 2,165,000; Canton, 1,867,000; Harbin, 1,595,000; Lü-Ta (Dairen and Port Arthur), 1,590,000; Nanking, 1,455,000; Sian, 1,368,000; Tsingtao, 1,144,000; Chengtu, 1,135,000; Yangku, 1,053,000; Fushun, 1,019,000; Changchun, 975,000 (1957); Kunming, 880,000 (1957); Tsinan, 862,000 (1957); Anshan, 805,000 (1957); Tangshan, 800,000 (1957); Hangchow, 784,000 (1957); Chenghsien, 766,000 (1957); and Changsa, 703,000 (1957).

THE PEOPLE

Population Distribution. The census of June 30, 1953, was the first scientific census ever taken in China. Out of a total population of 582,603,417 persons, 98.5 percent were directly registered. The others, a total of 8,397,477, were reported indirectly by the local government authorities of outlying areas.

The average density of population in China is about 150 per square mile. The distribution of population is highly uneven. The E. part of China, with 25 percent of the total area, contains 70 percent of the population and has an average population density of 475 per square mile. The w. areas, on the other hand, are very sparsely populated, with less than 25 persons per square mile. There is a sharp difference not only between the densely settled E. provinces and the w. deserts, but even within the high-density areas. For example, in the E. province of Kiangsu the density varies generally from 1100 to 1200 per square mile, but in some rural districts attains 2000 or more.

The most densely populated parts of China are the lower reaches of the Hwang Ho, the lower and middle course of the Yangtze R., the Red Basin of Szechwan, the Canton delta, and the coastal zone of s.E. China. The densely populated sections of s. China were the source of Chinese emigration to s.E. Asia, notably to Indonesia, Malaya, and Thailand, and to other parts of the world, including the Western Hemisphere. According to the 1953 census, males outnumbered females by 107.5 to 100. This predominance of males, which may be attributable in part to a former practice among certain classes of female infanticide, has been typical of the Chinese population. A sample survey of population growth made in 1953 showed births at a rate of 37 per 1000 and deaths at a rate of 17 per 1000, or a natural increase of 20 per 1000. The national population thus is increasing at the rate of 2 percent, or about 12,000,000, annually. A breakdown by age groups shows that the population is relatively young, with persons less than four years old comprising 15.6 percent of the total, compared with 8.7 percent in the United States. The large percentage of persons of younger age results from a high birth rate and from improved sanitation, which has reduced infant and child mortality. The urban population, constituting more than 13 percent of the national total, has been increasing rapidly in recent years as a result of the Communist industrialization program, which attracts more people to the cities.

Nationalities. The 1953 census tabulates 35,300,000 persons, or 6 percent of the population, as belonging to national minorities. National minorities are groups distinguished from the Chinese chiefly by language or religion. The chief minorities are the Chuang (6,600,000) in Kwangsi Chuang Autonomous Region; the Turkish-speaking Uigur (3,700,000) in Sinkiang Uigur Autonomous Region; the Hui or Chinese Moslems (3,600,000) in Ningsia Hui Autonomous Region; the aboriginal Yi (3,300,000) in Szechwan and Yunnan provinces; the Tibetans (2,800,000) in Tsinghai, Szechwan, and Tibet; the aboriginal Miao (2,500,000) in Kweichow and Hunan provinces; the Mongols (1,500,000) in Inner Mongolia, Kansu, Tsinghai, and Sinkiang; the Puyi (1,250,000) in Kweichow; and the Koreans (1,100,000) in Kirin Province of Manchuria. Other national minorities are found in outlying areas of China. The 1953 census listed also 2,400,000 Manchus among the minorities. The Manchus, who are descendants of the people which conquered

Tibetan girls dress in festival costume for a celebration in Lhasa, capital of Tibet.

Eastfoto

China in the 17th century and established the Manchu dynasty, and the Chinese Moslems are almost indistinguishable from the Chinese proper, among whom they are settled.

The Chinese proper call themselves the Han people after the native dynasty which ruled China from 202 B.C. to 220 A.D.

Language. See CHINESE LANGUAGE.

Education. The educational system of China has undergone major changes under the Communists, whose policy is to make education widely accessible. Compulsory elementary education gradually is being enforced. The number of children in primary schools rose from a little over 20,000,000 in 1950 to about 90,000,000 in the early 1960's. In the same period the number of students in general secondary schools rose from about 1,500,000 to about 12,000,000. In institutions of higher education the number of students rose from about 117,000 to about 810,000 in the same period. Thousands of students are sent abroad for special training.

China has 227 higher educational institutions, including 15 general universities. The other institutions were specialized universities and colleges for instruction in engineering (48 institutions), languages (8), teaching (53), agriculture and forestry (31), medicine (37), economics and finance (5), political science and law (5), fine arts (16), physical culture (6), and other subjects (3).

The Chinese Academy of Sciences, established by the Communist government in 1949 as the successor to the Academia Sinica, is the center of scientific research activities in China. The academy maintains sixty-eight research institutes grouped in four departments: mathematics, physics, and chemistry; biology, geology, and geography; technical sciences; and philosophy and social sciences. Other research institutes set up by the Communist regime include the Chinese Academy of Medical Science and the Chinese Academy of Agricultural Science, both established in 1956.

The largest libraries of China are the Peking State Library (founded 1912), with 2,500,000 volumes; the Mukden Central Public Library (founded 1948), with 1,200,000 volumes; and the Shanghai Municipal Library (founded 1912), with 900,000 volumes. The principal museums are the former Imperial Palace and the National Revolutionary Museum in Peking, the Mukden Museum, and the Southwestern Museum in Chungking.

A Latin alphabet of thirty letters was adopted in 1956 to replace gradually the 30,000 characters of the old Chinese script.

Religion. The 3 principal religions of China traditionally are Buddhism, Taoism, and Confucianism (qq.v.). There are also Moslems and Christians, chiefly Roman Catholic. Lamaism (q.v.) is the religion of the Tibetans and the Mongols. The Thai peoples of s.w. China are predominantly Hinayana Buddhists. The government, as in other Communist countries, follows a policy of hostility to the practice of religion.

For other aspects of Chinese culture see CHINESE ART; CHINESE LITERATURE; CHINESE MUSIC; CHINESE PHILOSOPHY.

THE ECONOMY

The Communist government has gone farther toward achieving an integrated national economy than any previous regime. Some of the early dynasties, beginning with the Ch'in (255–202 B.C.), achieved a high degree of integration, because only an integrated economy could cope with the tasks of building defensive walls (see GREAT WALL) and other defenses against invaders and of controlling floods and improving irrigation and navigation on the great river systems. However, periods of relative economic integration always were followed by periods of disintegration, during which economic activity was organized on a local basis by feudal lords, by villages, and by families. No regime before that of the Communists was able to destroy the old family system or the system of at least partial village and provincial autonomy. Even under the Nationalist regime (1926–49) families were the basic units of economic activity, the villages were largely self-sufficient, and warlords in the provinces enjoyed virtual autonomy. The Communists succeeded, however, in destroying the old family system and in ending village and provincial autonomy.

The Communists have made striking advances in industrializing much of China. Modern industry, although introduced into China in the latter half of the 19th century, was largely confined to the coastal port cities and was under foreign auspices and control. The development of Manchuria, the most highly industrialized region of China, occurred during the 20th century under alternating Russian and Japanese control. The Nationalist government had impressive plans for industrializing China and for freeing its economy from foreign control; these plans were vitiated by Japanese invasion, by civil war, and by the chronic weakness of the Nationalist government in its relations with the provincial warlords and with foreign businessmen. The rapid progress of the Communists in industrializing China freed the economy from control by Japan and by the Western powers. Many experts hold that liberation was accomplished only at the expense of subjecting the Chinese economy to the overlordship of the Russian Communists. It is generally agreed, however, that Communist China enjoys more freedom in its economic activity, as well as in other aspects of its national life, than any of the other countries in the Soviet bloc of states.

The development of all branches of the national economy is controlled by five-year plans. The first plan went into effect early in 1953 and was completed toward the end of 1956, one year ahead of schedule. The second five-year plan was for the period from 1958 to 1962. All economic activities were directed and co-ordinated according to plan. By 1956 the Communists had nationalized a large percentage of the industrial enterprises of China and had eliminated nearly all private operation of industry. Virtually all industrial production is controlled by the state, either directly through state-owned plants or indirectly through joint state-private plants or co-operatively owned plants. More than 90 percent of the handicraftsmen are grouped into producer co-operatives. Despite the Communist emphasis on industrialization, about 80 percent of the population is engaged in agriculture.

The rate of growth of industry was rapid in recent years, even when account is taken of recovery from the chaos of civil war and of the generally low level of industrial output which had prevailed. The total value of industrial output more than doubled in a four-year period during the 1950's. At the same time priority was given to developing heavy industry as against producing consumer goods. Under the Communists industry has been shifted gradually from former areas of concentration along the coast to less developed areas in the interior in order to achieve a more even distribution throughout the country.

Manufacturing Industry. In 1949, when the Communists completed their conquest of the Chinese mainland, the steel industry had been reduced to less than 20 percent of its pre-World War II capacity as a result of dismantling by Soviet troops and of the civil war. Reconstruction of the steel industry received high priority under the Communist program. Prewar levels were attained by 1952 and then were surpassed. Under the Communists virtually all of the output of iron ore and pig iron is further processed within China; formerly much of these products had to be exported for processing because of insufficient steel-making capacity in China. In addition China began the production of steel products never before made in that country, such as special steels (tungsten steels and stainless steels), rails, heavy steel plate, and seamless pipe. The 3 main steel-producing areas in China are Manchuria, N. China, and the Yangtze R. valley. During the late 1950's Communist China annually produced about 5,000,000 tons each of pig iron and steel ingots and about 4,300,000 tons of rolled steel.

The Chinese Communists are expanding heavy industry as the key to the technological transformation of the country's backward economy. Among types of heavy industry are shipbuilding and the manufacture of locomotives, rolling stock, tractors, mining machinery, petroleum-drilling and -refining machinery, and heavy machine tools.

The cotton-textile industry of China in the early 1960's annually produced about 7,500,000 sq.yds. of cloth. Relatively small quantities of silk, woolen, and linen fabrics also are produced. Before the Communists came to power 80 percent of all the cotton mills in China were concentrated in a few large cities along the coast, with Shanghai alone containing almost half of the milling capacity. The main cotton-growing areas, located in the interior, had few mills. The Communists have constructed most of the new mills in the cotton-growing areas of Hupeh, Honan, Hopeh, and Shensi provinces.

Mining. The coal industry plays a major role in China's industrialization effort. The estimated reserves of well in excess of a trillion tons place China among the leading countries in coal resources; however, most of the Chinese coal is of low grade. Reserves of high-grade anthracite and lignite are relatively small. The greater part of the coal reserves is concentrated in Shansi and Shensi provinces. Most of the development, however, has been in Manchuria and N. China, where the country's heavy industry is concentrated. Annual coal production in the early 1960's was over 380,000,000 tons.

China must import the greater part of the petroleum products which it requires. The basic crude-oil resources are concentrated in the N.W. part of the country. The largest oil field is at Yumen in Kansu Province, where production began in 1939. The production of petroleum annually in the early 1960's was about 4,000,000 tons.

China is rich in a number of nonferrous metals, particularly tungsten, antimony, tin,

Children receive instruction on how to operate a disk harrow, one of the modern farm implements that have been introduced to increase agricultural production in China.

molybdenum, and mercury. All of these are produced beyond the country's own needs and the surplus is exported, chiefly to the Soviet Union. Copper, lead, zinc, and aluminum are produced also, but in insufficient quantities for the country's needs. About 32,000,000 tons of iron ore were mined annually in the early 1960's.

Agriculture. Agriculture, traditionally the economic mainstay of China, remains the most important sector of the national economy, despite the Communist emphasis on industrial production. Agriculture employs 75 percent of the population and produces half of the gross value of the national economic output. About 11 percent of the total territory of China is used for raising crops, 20 percent is pasture land, and 5 percent is woodland. In E. China N. of the Yangtze R. more than one third of the total area is under cultivation. South of the Yangtze R. in E. China the land is more mountainous and only 15 percent of the total area is cultivated. The percentage of land under cultivation is smallest in the arid W. parts of the country. About 30 percent of the cultivated land of China is irrigated. Irrigated lands are found mainly in S. China, but also on the margins of the arid regions. In an effort to expand the area under cultivation, the Chinese Communists are

planting virgin lands in N. Manchuria and in Sinkiang. A major flood-control program is designed to protect vast parts of the country against recurring floods.

The Chinese Communists inherited the traditional framework of rural China, with land privately owned and unequally distributed among the peasants. The average land holding per individual peasant in all China was ⅓ acre. The Communists classified rural families according to the extent of land ownership as follows: less than 1.6 acres, poor peasant family; 1.6 to 5 acres, middle peasant family; 5 to 8 acres, rich peasant family; more than 8 acres, landlord family. From 1950 to 1952 the Communists carried out a land reform in which they confiscated land from landlords and rich peasants and distributed it among middle and poor peasants. The land reform was followed by a drive to collectivize agriculture on the Soviet pattern. By the end of 1956 agricultural collectivization was virtually complete; more than 120,000,000 peasant households, or 96 percent of the national total, had joined collective farms. In addition to collective farms there are a number of state farms, worked by peasants who are paid regular salaries by the state; in contrast the peasants of the collectives share the proceeds. Mechanization of agriculture is still in an

Photos from Eastfoto

Agriculture and industry in modern China. Above: Sheepshearing in Sinkiang Province, an important livestock-raising area. Left, top: Coal miner descending a mine shaft in Kailan District, Hopeh Province, center of rich deposits of coal and iron ore. Bottom: Applegrower from Shantung Province.

early stage in China. In the late 1950's there were about 330 machine-and-tractor stations which supplied heavy farm machinery to collective farms. These stations had a total of less than 10,000 tractors (in terms of 15-horsepower units), sufficient only to work about 2 percent of the cultivated land. Most of the state farms are in the newly developed wheatlands of N. Manchuria.

Food crops occupy 90 percent of the sown area of China; annual output of food crops in the early 1960's was about 300,000,000 tons. The most important of these crops is rice, which occupies 20 percent of the total cultivated area. Rice is grown for the most part s. of the Hwai R., notably in the middle and lower valley of the Yangtze R., the Canton delta, and the Red Basin of Szechwan. Two harvests of rice are obtained annually in most places. The yearly production of rice in the late 1950's was about 80,000,000 tons.

The second most important food crop is wheat, which is grown mainly N. of the Hwai R. The chief wheat-growing areas are the North China Plain and the valleys of the Wei and Fen rivers in the loess region. Most of the wheat grown in these areas is winter wheat, which is sown in the fall and harvested in the spring. However, in Manchuria, Inner

Mongolia, and N.W. China, where winters are much colder, the spring wheat is sown in the spring and harvested in the fall. Although wheat, like rice, occupies 20 percent of the cultivated area of China, the yield is much lower than that of rice. The yearly output of wheat in the mid-1950's was approximately 25,000,000 tons.

The annual production in the mid-1950's of all other grains, including kaoliang, millet, barley, corn, and oats, exceeded 60,000,000 tons. Kaoliang and millet are important food crops in N. China and Manchuria. Each is sown to about 10 percent of the total cultivated area. Kaoliang, in addition to being a food crop, also is converted into alcohol and used as an animal feed; the stalks are utilized to make paper and as a roofing material. Barley and corn each occupy about 6 percent of the cultivated area. Oats are important chiefly in the w. parts of the country, notably Inner Mongolia and Tibet.

In addition to these grain crops, food crops also include sweet potatoes (about 21,-000,000 tons produced annually in the mid-1950's), Irish potatoes, and vegetables. Sweet potatoes predominate in the s. and Irish potatoes in the N. Fruit ranges from such tropical varieties as pineapples and bananas (grown on the island of Hainan) to apples and pears (grown in the N. provinces of Liaoning and Shantung). Citrus fruits, particularly oranges and tangerines, are major products of s. China.

Oil seeds play a major role in Chinese agriculture, supplying edible and industrial oils and an important share of exports. The most important oil crop is soybeans, which occupy about 10 percent of the total cultivated area, mainly in N. China and Manchuria. Half of the world's production comes from China, which annually raised about 10,000,000 tons the mid-1950's. China is also one of the world's leading producers of peanuts (annual production in the same period, about 3,200,-000 tons), second only to India. Peanuts are grown in Shantung and Hopeh. Other important oil crops are sesame seed and rapeseed. A valuable vegetable oil is supplied also by the tung tree. More than half of the tung oil of China originates in Szechwan.

Tea is a traditional export crop of China. Until the middle of the 19th century China had a virtual world tea monopoly. Subsequently, however, India, Ceylon, Java, and Japan gained control of the world market and Chinese production began to drop. Presently China is, after India and Ceylon, the world's third-largest tea producer, with an annual output in the early 1960's of about 155,000 tons. The principal tea plantations are on the hillsides of the middle Yangtze R. valley and in Fukien and Chekiang.

China obtains its sugar both from sugar cane and from sugar beets; the annual production of sugar from both these crops in the early 1960's was approximately 700,000 tons. Sugar cane has long been cultivated in China. It is grown mainly in the provinces of Kwangtung and Szechwan. Sugar beets, a relatively new crop for China, are raised in the Manchurian province of Heilungkiang and on irrigated land in Inner Mongolia.

The Chinese Communists have given increasing attention to the expansion of industrial crops for the textile industry. The most important of these crops is cotton; in the late 1950's about 2,650,000 tons were produced annually. Cotton, which can be grown in almost all parts of China, is raised principally in the North China Plain, the loess region, the Yangtze R. delta, and the middle Yangtze plain. The North China Plain yields about half the total Chinese cotton output.

Other fibers are ramie and flax, which are used for linen and other fine cloths, and jute and hemp, which are made into sacks and rope. Ramie, which is a native Chinese crop, is grown chiefly in the Yangtze R. valley.

Flax is a N. crop. The main jute-growing areas are Chekiang and Kwangtung.

Another traditional Chinese crop is raw silk. Silk growing is common in the central and s. areas, notably in the Yangtze delta, which yields half of the silk-cocoon crop. Other silk-growing areas are the Canton delta and the Red Basin.

China has more hogs than any other country in the world and is the leading exporter of hog bristles. In the drier w. parts of China, comprising about 40 percent of the country's total area, livestock raising by nomadic herders often constitutes the principal, if not the only, rural occupation. Most of the nomads' herds are made up of sheep, goats, and camels. In the Tibetan highlands the yak is the source of food and fuel (the dung is burned), and its hair and skin provide materials for shelter and clothing. Other livestock animals are donkeys, mules, and goats.

Forestry. Only about 5 percent of the total territory of China is in forest, compared, for example, with more than 30 percent in the Soviet Union. About 60 percent of the forest land is in Manchuria and the N.E. part of Inner Mongolia, but lumbering is not extensively carried on in these areas because of insufficient transportation facilities. In E. China reserves amount only to 5 percent of the national total; however, lumber production is high because of proximity to industrial centers.

Fisheries. The shallow seas which adjoin China abound in fish and other marine products and have favored the development of a large fishing industry along the entire coast. The most important food fish are cod, herring, sea perch, sardine, and mackerel. Other marine food include trepang (sea cucumbers), octopuses, oysters, shrimps, and seaweed. China obtains more than one third of its fish catch from rivers, lakes, and ponds. The main fresh-water fish are pike, bream, catfish, carp, whitefish, and loach. Carp ponds, a traditional Chinese food source for thousands of years, yield one third of the country's fresh-water fish. About 1,000,000 persons earn their living as full-time fishermen, but millions of peasants combine fishing with various agricultural pursuits. Under the Communists state and co-operative fisheries have taken over a substantial share of the industry.

Currency, Finance, and Banking. The Chinese Communist monetary unit is the yüan, which is equivalent to about 40 U.S. cents. In 1955 the government exchanged the former highly inflated currency at the rate of 10,000 units to 1 yüan.

Before World War II the yearly national budgets of China never exceeded the equivalent of $1,000,000,000 dollars in U.S. currency. The annual budgets under the Communist regime are substantially higher, having attained the equivalent of $29,000,000,000 in the early 1960's. The major sources of government revenue are direct taxes and earnings from state-owned business enterprises. Taxes, which make up about half the total revenue, are levied mainly on industry and commerce and also on agriculture. About 45 to 50 percent of the total budget is used for investment in economic development. Other important items of expenditure are for social services and education (15 to 20 percent), defense (15 to 20 percent), and governmental administration (10 percent).

The banking system is entirely under government control; all vestiges of private banking were abolished in 1952. The People's Bank of China is the chief bank. Its principal functions are to issue currency; to grant short-term loans to agriculture and industry; and to act as a depository of funds of governmental organizations, state enterprises, and co-operatives, and of private savings accounts. The other banks of Communist China are as follows: the People's Construction Bank, which specializes in financing major economic-construction projects; the Agricultural Bank, which makes loans to farmers and holds savings accounts; the Bank of Communications, which handles the state's investments in jointly owned state-private enterprises; the Bank of China, which specializes in foreign exchange and international settlements; and the Joint State-Private Bank, an amalgamation of former private banks into a jointly operated bank, which holds savings accounts.

Commerce and Trade. Domestic trade in Communist China is conducted almost entirely by state trading companies, and by trade co-operatives. Nearly all private retail stores were eliminated by 1956. The state trading companies have a virtual monopoly of the domestic wholesale trade and specialize in specific products or groups of products, such as grain, cotton textiles, salt, metals and machinery, and coal. The co-operative agencies are of two kinds: consumer co-operatives, which are mainly retail sales outlets in urban areas; and rural marketing and supply co-operatives, which operate as buying and selling agents of the state trading companies in rural areas.

Foreign Trade. Foreign trade underwent major changes after the Communist takeover

in 1949. Before World War II the principal trade partners of China were the United States, Japan, Germany, and Great Britain. Under the Communists Chinese trade has been chiefly with the Soviet Union and other countries in the Communist bloc of states. Of the total exports, valued at about $2,000,000,000 in the early 1960's, about 55 percent went to the Soviet Union.

The prewar imports of China were chiefly food (including rice, wheat, flour, sugar, and fish products), tobacco, cotton, wool, textiles, pharmaceuticals, and petroleum, paper, and wood products. Machinery and industrial equipment made up less than 15 percent of the total prewar imports. Exports in the prewar period consisted almost entirely of agricultural products and unprocessed minerals; relatively small quantities of light manufactures, chiefly textiles, also were exported. Under the Communists capital goods, including complete industrial plants, machinery, precision instruments, and rolling stock and other transportation equipment, comprise 85 to 90 percent of all imports. Petroleum products also are an important import. Agricultural products and minerals predominate among exports as in the prewar period; notable exports are tea, raw silk, tung oil, hog bristles, wool, soybeans, peanuts, egg products, walnuts, handicraft articles, tungsten, tin, antimony, molybdenum, and mercury. However, there has been a considerable increase in Chinese exports of manufactured goods, mainly to the less developed countries of S.E. Asia. Industrial exports include silk and cotton goods, canned goods, paper, sewing machines, bicycles, machine tools, irrigation equipment, diesel engines, construction materials, and chemicals.

Transportation. Railroads, by far the most important means of transportation in China, carry 80 percent of all freight. China has more than 18,000 m. of railroad lines. The railroad network, concentrated in Manchuria and in the E. half of the country, chiefly serves the areas of greatest industrial and agricultural production. As part of their industrialization program the Communists have undertaken an ambitious railroad-construction program. Among the important projects are a railroad linking Peking with the Trans-Siberian Railroad of the Soviet Union, as well as new lines connecting several important cities. The Chinese have also established through traffic to North Vietnam, both along the old Kunming-Hanoi railroad and along the new Hengyang-Hanoi line. In the mid-1950's the railroads of China carried about

409,450,000 tons of freight annually.

Although China appears to be abundantly supplied with waterways, only a few rivers are navigable for large vessels. The Yangtze R. is navigable by ocean-going vessels as far as Wuhan, and by large river boats as far as Chungking. The Siang R., the lower course of the Si R., and the Sungari R. also are navigable by large river boats. Other waterways can be negotiated only by small, flat-bottomed boats and junks. The total length of inland waterways is about 65,000 m., but most of this mileage is navigable only by small boats and junks. About one fourth of all the freight carried by water in China moves along the coasts. In the mid-1950's the total freight tonnage carried annually on inland waterways was about 39,130,000 tons; freight carried by coastal shipping totaled about 12,120,000 tons.

The total length of Chinese highways which can be used by trucks is more than 250,000 m. Highways play an especially important role in the w. areas which are far removed from the railroads. The Communist regime has built a number of major highways linking the w. provinces with the rest of the country. Trucks, used mainly for short hauls, carry more freight than that carried on the waterways. However, the total freight volume (weight of freight multiplied by average distance) transported by truck was considerably less than the freight volume transported by ship.

The airline network of China has an aggregate length of almost 19,500 m. Airlines radiate from Peking to most parts of China. Service is provided also to the Soviet Union, Burma, North Vietnam, and North Korea.

Communications. The first five-year plan (1953–57) called for the extension and improvement of communications between Peking and all the main cities of China as well as the newly founded industrial centers. In general the communications system of China is poorly developed except for postal routes.

The principal radio-broadcasting facilities of China are in Peking, from which programs are broadcast in the principal dialects of Chinese and also in Korean, Vietnamese, Burmese, Indonesian, Japanese, and other Asian languages, and in English. In the late 1950's the broadcasting system consisted of 107 radio stations and 3 television stations.

In the late 1950's there were published in China over 350 national and provincial newspapers and over 460 magazines. In addition, several periodicals were published in English and other foreign languages for distribution abroad. Some of the principal newspapers of China, with city of publication and circulation, are *Jen-min Jih-pao (People's Daily)*, the organ of the Central Committee of the Communist Party (Peking, 800,000); *Ta-kung Pao* (Peking, 280,000); *Nan-fang Jih-pao* (Canton, 200,000), *Tze-fang Jih-pao* (Shanghai, 200,000), and *Tientsin Jih-pao* (Tientsin, 70,000).

Labor. As a result of the policy of stressing industrialization, the number of industrial workers increased steadily in the years following the establishment of the Communist government. There are more than 32,000,-000 industrial and office workers, virtually all of them employed in state-owned enterprises or in co-operatives. All Chinese labor unions are combined into the Chinese Trade Union Federation, which has a total membership of about 16,500,000. The federation is completely controlled by the government.

The masses of the Chinese people were mobilized by the government in the service of the five-year plans of economic development adopted in 1953 and 1958. This mobilization involved mass transfers of population to areas of planned economic development, forced labor by many of those convicted of so-called counterrevolutionary activities, and the marshaling of large numbers of so-called volunteers to work special projects, such as road building, swamp drainage, and the extermination of flies, field mice, sparrows, and other destructive and disease-carrying animal life.

GOVERNMENT

Central Government. The structure of the central government of China is determined by the constitution of 1954, which is typical of those of Communist countries. According to this document, the supreme organ of state power is the national legislature, called the National People's Congress. Besides enacting legislation, its functions include electing the executive and judicial officers of the government. The National People's Congress is elected every four years and meets once a year. In practice, most of its functions are delegated to the Standing Committee, which operates during recesses. Among the officials elected by the Congress is the chairman of the republic, who is, in fact, the chief of state. The Congress and the standing committee routinely approve all actions of the chairman of the republic and of his appointees. The chairman appoints the State Council, which conducts the operations of the central government. The State Council is headed by the premier and includes a number of ministries.

Public Health. A ministry of the central government is in charge of all public health and medical institutions. China had, in the early 1960's, about 470,000 physicians schooled in traditional Chinese medicine and 80,000 trained in Western methods. Every county had a hospital, and the number of hospital beds in the country was about 440,000.

Local Government. The local governments of China are subordinate directly or indirectly to the central government. Each province elects its people's congress, which is responsible to the National People's Congress. Each provincial subdivision also elects a congress, which is responsible to the congress at the next highest level.

Some provinces contain autonomous *chou,* which are areas inhabited by a national minority. Provinces and autonomous *chou* are divided into counties (or autonomous counties) and cities under provincial jurisdiction, and counties are further divided into townships (or national townships) and small towns. There are about 2050 counties, 175 cities under provincial jurisdiction, 110,000 townships (including nationality townships), and 3600 small towns.

Political Parties. Communist China follows the practice of other so-called people's democracies in allowing parties other than the Communist to function. These parties, which participate in the government in a subordinate role, do not pursue an independent political policy. All the political parties are united in the Chinese People's Political Consultative Conference. The Communist Party of China, with a membership (1961) of about 17,000,000, is the predominant party and fully controls the affairs of the nation. The combined membership of the 8 other political parties is much less. The principal smaller parties are the Revolutionary Committee of the Kuomintang, formed in 1948 by members of the Kuomintang, the leading Nationalist party, who defected to the Communist side; the China Democratic League, formed in 1941 by middle-of-the-road sympathizers with the Communists; the China Democratic National Construction Association, founded in 1945 by pro-Communist industrialists and businessmen; and the Chinese Peasants and Workers Democratic Party, formed in 1928 by persons who opposed the Kuomintang's anti-Communist policies.

Defense. According to the 1954 constitution, the armed forces of China are under the command of the National Defense Council, which is headed by the chief of state and has about 90 members. The Chinese Communist military establishment is called the People's Liberation Army. It includes ground forces estimated at 3,000,000, a small navy, and an air force of about 5000 planes. Large contingents are engaged in economic-development projects, such as railroad construction and the development of virgin lands in Sinkiang and Manchuria.

HISTORY

The history of China until the modern period may be viewed as forming a cyclical pattern in which a highly civilized Chinese state is pitted against peoples of less developed culture whom the Chinese considered barbarians. The center of the older Chinese civilization, in this view, is found in the agriculturally favored valleys of the Hwang Ho and the Yangtze R. Typically, a native Chinese dynasty, after consolidating power in this area, proceeds to expand its territory at the expense of the peoples to the N. and S. and in Central Asia. Faced with resistance, however, the territory under Chinese control is steadily reduced; ultimately an alien people conquers the native dynasty and occupies and rules all the territory which is distinctively Chinese in culture. In a resurgence of national feeling the invaders are expelled from the river valleys, and after a period of disorder a new native Chinese dynasty assumes control. Thereupon the cycle is repeated.

In the traditional view which prevailed among Chinese scholars, the sequence of dynasties was explained in terms of obtaining and forfeiting the "mandate of Heaven" to rule. The mandate would be forfeited when the dynasty became corrupt and oppressive and failed to maintain public works. A new dynasty, by introducing reforms and re-establishing stable and fair government, in its turn would enjoy the "mandate of Heaven" to rule until the faults of the preceding dynasty were repeated.

China to the Manchu Dynasty. According to ancient Chinese tradition the history of the country began some 4500 years ago in the Hwang Ho valley. A legendary emperor, Fu Hsi, is believed to have been the first of a series of 10 rulers; although earlier rulers also are mentioned in ancient writings. The first royal house which, in the belief of modern historians, may have existed in China is that of Hsia; little is known of this house, however, except its possible dates (1994–1524 B.C.) and that it may have included 16 or 17 rulers. Several archeological sites in the Hwang

Chinese rulers. Left: The Mongol conqueror Genghis Khan. Center: The Manchu emperor K'ang Hsi. Right: The Dowager Empress Tz'u Hsi who suppressed reform movements.

Ho valley are tentatively identified as belonging to the Hsia. This royal house appears to have been succeeded by the Shang (sometimes called the Yin), which continued until approximately 1028 B.C. Shang remains have been found in more than 80 sites in the Hwang Ho valley from the vicinity of Sian, about 700 m. inland, to the coast. There is little knowledge about the first 2 centuries of the Shang period except that the rulers appear to have shifted their capital several times. After about 1300 B.C., when the capital city was established near modern Anyang in N. Honan Province, information concerning the Shang is abundant. The Shang practiced writing in a fairly well-developed form. A study of Shang inscriptions and remains indicates a relatively high degree of civilization. The people practiced agriculture and also went on hunting expeditions. Millet and rice were raised; domestic animals included cattle and pigs. Irrigation was practiced and pottery was well developed. Farming implements were of stone and wood, but the chariots, armor, and swords of the upper classes were made of bronze. The Shang "state" probably was the most powerful of a number of tribal areas then comprising China.

The royal house of Shang was followed by the Chou (about 1027–256 B.C.). Under the Chou the last traces of nomadic life disappeared, agriculture became universal, and great public works were built. At about the middle of the Chou period iron began to be used in place of bronze. The Chou period is known also as the classical period of China, because literature and the arts flourished and such great works were produced as the *Book of History* and the *Book of Songs*, which have shaped Chinese thought up to the 20th century. The great sages, Confucius, Lao-tse, Mencius (Meng-tse), and Mo Ti (Mo-tzu), flourished then. The Chou period is known also for the development of the feudal system in China.

Despite the humanitarian doctrines of the sages, a devastating series of wars between contending feudal states marked the close of the Chou period, and from N.W. China emerged the first imperial dynasty, the Ch'in dynasty, under Shih Huang Ti, who ruled from 255 to 206 B.C. The Ch'in restored order, abolished the feudal system, drove back the Hun Tatars into the desert, began to build the Great Wall (parts of which may have existed before) as a symbol both of defense and of a united China, and extended the empire s. of the Yangtze valley. Shih Huang Ti, the "First Emperor", built a capital near the present site of Sian, as a center of Ch'in power. To break utterly with the bonds of the past, the Ch'in ruler ordered a burning of all books except those on pharmacy, medicine, divination, agriculture, and arboriculture. For this deed his name has been held in reproach by later Chinese scholars.

After the death of Shih Huang Ti, rebellion broke out, and the Han line of rulers (202 B.C.–220 A.D.) came to power. The Han rulers were native Chinese.

Under the Han the Tatar hordes were driven as far back as Turkestan, and parts of Central Asia and Mongolia were added for a time to the empire. Overland trade was inaugurated, chiefly in Chinese silk, to Syria and the Roman market. The system of competitive examinations for entrance into civil service became an institution. Political centralization and territorial expansion of China under the Han was accompanied by cultural advances. These included the standardization of the forms of Chinese written characters, the recovery of the classics, the first dictionary, the first encyclopedic history of China, and tentative beginnings of porcelain manufacture. Buddhism was also introduced from India at about that time, marking the first strong influence of another culture upon that of the Chinese.

Rebellions and the weakening of the im-

Eastfoto   Wide World   Eastfoto

Modern Chinese leaders. Left: Sun Yat-sen, revolutionary leader. Center: Chiang Kai-shek, President of Formosa. Right: Mao Tse-tung, Chinese Communist Party Chairman.

perial line brought an end to the Han dynasty, but not to the concept of political and cultural unity imparted by the Hans; Chinese still call themselves the "Sons of Han". After the great Han period no dynasty occupied the throne for so long a period as three centuries, most of them lasting a much shorter time. The epoch of the Three Kingdoms (northern China; western China; and the region along the middle and lower Yangtze River), from 220–419 A.D., was one of war and misrule, but, owing to the adventures of its heroes, was also the romantic period of Chinese literature. During the Sui dynasty (589–618 A.D.) China again achieved unity, and during the great T'ang dynasty (618–907 A.D.) the country recovered much of the power it had had under the Han. The empire, for a time the strongest on earth, extended from the Caspian Sea to the Pacific Ocean; embassies from Persia, Japan, Korea, Tibet, and various other nations often met at the court of China, and commerce flourished.

On the fall of the T'ang dynasty through corruption and rebellions, five feeble dynasties ruled, between 907 and 960. Then the era of the Sung (960–1280) opened, with a fresh burst of literary splendor, and brought in the Augustan Age of China, with its activity in bookmaking and printing (both with wood blocks and with movable type) and the formation of libraries.

But another great change was impending. Under the leadership of Genghis Khan, the Mongols overran northern China. Under Kublai Khan (1260–94), grandson of Genghis, who established the Mongol (Yuan) dynasty in China, the empire reached its widest development. Kublai's realm extended from the Dnieper River in Russia to the Pacific Ocean and from the Arctic Ocean to the Straits of Malacca. The laws were codified, and literature and public works flourished. For a half-century there was considerable commerce with Italy. Marco Polo and his two uncles then lived in the empire, in the service of the Khan,

used paper money and passports, and traveled on the Grand Canal in China, at a time when paper money, passports, and canals were unknown in Europe. Intercourse with the Arabs and Persians was continuous, and the highway into Europe was maintained until the Mongols in Central Asia embraced Islam. The Mongol dynasty, one of various foreign dynasties of China, ended in 1368 with a series of peasant revolts in the Yangtze R. valley.

The last native Chinese imperial line was the Ming dynasty (1368–1644). Its founder, a former Buddhist priest, rose to power in a national reaction which followed the period of disorder due to the disintegration of the Mongol Empire under the successors of Kublai Khan. Under Ming rule Portuguese and Spanish traders entered China and settled in various ports. Tongking (Tonkin) and Cochin China were added to the empire in the south, while in the north the nation was continually harassed by the Tatars, and along the coast by Japanese freebooters.

Early Modern Period. In 1643 the warlike Manchus from the N.E. were besought to defend the country from its Tatar enemies. A Manchu prince established himself in Peking, and, in 1644, on the suicide of the last Ming emperor, took the imperial throne, founding the last imperial Chinese dynasty, known as the Ch'ing dynasty.

For a time Ming claimants opposed the Manchus, but were finally driven out. The enforced adoption by the Chinese of the plaited queue of the Manchus at first produced friction between the two peoples, but this gradually disappeared, and Manchus and Chinese assumed harmonious relations, although the former remained a distinct military and official class. In most cases the customs of the country and the methods of administration remained Chinese, as did the language, and, like most numerically weak conquerors, the Manchus gradually adopted the ways of the people whom they had subdued.

The Manchus conquered Mongolia and

The raising of sheep is an important part of the economy of Tibet.

ruled Manchuria. Under K'ang Hsi (1662–1722), perhaps the greatest of the Manchu rulers, Tibet was conquered, sciences and arts were encouraged, and a great dictionary of the Chinese language and other extensive literary compilations were begun. Under Ch'ien Lung (1736–95), Turkestan and Kashgaria were taken, Burma was penetrated, and Cochin China and Korea were compelled to pay tribute. Later Manchu emperors were not as vigorous, and there were numerous rebellions throughout the land. The most significant event of the Manchu dynasty, however, was the growing pressure of Europeans.

Portuguese traders had appeared in China as early as 1514, and Catholic missionaries had followed in their footsteps. The Chinese were never able to comprehend how adherents of the same religion could quarrel as did the missionary Jesuits, Franciscans, and Dominicans, and the churchmen lost credit accordingly. Nor did the Portuguese traders conduct themselves in a way to win the respect of the Chinese; the avarice, the violence, and the spirit of bitter rivalry exhibited by them, as well as by the Spanish, Dutch, and English, all of whom in the seventeenth century followed the Portuguese in the Chinese field and were quick to prevent Portugal from capitalizing on its initial advantage, tended to accentuate the suspicion with which foreigners were regarded. A narrow and exclusive policy, intended to protect China from the aggression of the "barbarians", was initiated before the close of the Ming period, and was developed by the Manchu emperors as time went on. Mutual misunderstandings due to the collision of diametrically opposed civilizations generated continual troubles. Since the liberal days of the Mongol rulers the Chinese had been retiring within themselves, and the admission of foreigners to privileges of trade and intercourse was regarded as a special grace

to inferiors. Diplomatic intercourse, in the Western sense, was not understandable to them, since the Emperor, the Son of Heaven, had no equals, and those who approached him could do so only as vassals. The Western nations failed to understand this point of view, with the consequence that friction increased. Only Russia, whose rapid march across Asia had brought it into contact with China in the 16th century, had any success in dealing with China officially before the first Anglo-Chinese war. The Russians, with their knowledge of Oriental peoples, conceded much to Chinese prejudices in nonessentials. The Treaty of Nertschinsk (1689), which halted Russia's advance in the Amur region, was the first treaty signed between China and a Christian power. The United States entered the China field in 1785; and in the days of the old Oriental trade the commerce of the United States was second in volume among the western nations; but the American government made no attempt to safeguard the interests of its citizens in China or to enter into relations with the Chinese government. England (until 1834 through the East India Company) began to trade with Canton in 1635, and by the end of the 18th century the English traders, and Protestant missionaries, were the most numerous of the foreigners in China, and also the most aggressive.

Despite restrictions imposed by the Chinese government (until the mid-19th century, Canton being the only port open to trade), commerce flourished. Early foreign trade in China was characterized by the purchase chiefly of Chinese silk, tea, and porcelain by foreign silver. To create a more favorable balance of trade, the western traders began to look for commodities which might be sold to the Chinese. American clipper ships would carry ginseng root (used by the Chinese as medicine), furs (received by the Americans from

Hsi-ling Gorge, the longest of the gorges on the Yangtze River

Pacific Coast Indians in return for the usual trade goods), and silver dollars (acquired in Mexico on the Cape Horn route to the Pacific coast). With the ginseng, furs, and silver dollars (hence the term "Mexican dollar" for the silver dollar in China), they would trade for Chinese goods. But the balance of trade continued to be unfavorable to western merchants until the British opened a market for opium from India.

With the dissolution of the East India Company in 1834 and, at about the same time, the bankruptcy of the *hong* merchants (a group of merchants in Canton to whom had been relegated control of China's trade), commerce became demoralized. The trade problem reached a climax over the question of opium. Late in the 18th century, opium traffic had been declared illegal by the Chinese government, but the decree was not enforced until 1837, when China became disturbed at the loss of silver the opium trade was causing. Attempts at enforcement, however, met, in 1839, with the opposition of the British merchants, backed in their stand by the British government, which was reluctant to interfere with a trade that was worth from $5,000,000 to $8,000,000 annually to the government of India. The situation resulted in the so-called Opium War (q.v.), which broke out early in 1840 and ended in a British victory. In 1842, by the Treaty of Nanking, which concluded the war, China was compelled to cede to Great Britain the island of Hong Kong, to open to British trade five of its chief ports, and to pay a war indemnity of $21,-000,000 to Great Britain, covering the expenses of that country in defeating the Chinese. The opium question which had engendered the conflict was not touched upon.

This first commercial treaty entered into officially by China was the opening wedge which was sought by other western powers.

Two years later the United States and France also concluded trade agreements with the Chinese.

In 1856, war with Great Britain was again precipitated when China refused to apologize to the British for the seizure, for alleged piracy, of a Chinese boat flying the British flag. The war closed temporarily in 1858 with the Treaty of Tientsin, which provided that England and France were to have ministers at the Chinese court, at least on special occasions, and China was to be represented at London and Paris; Christianity was to be tolerated in China; various inland trade privileges were to be granted to the British and French; China was to pay the expenses of the war; the term "barbarian" was no longer to be applied to foreigners in China; and a tariff was to be set on opium, legalizing importation. Two years later the war was renewed in an attempt to secure a ratification of the treaty by the Imperial government, which was obtained only when the allied armies took Peking. At the time of the conclusion of the Treaty of Tientsin with England and France, China signed a treaty also with Russia, ceding Amur to the latter power.

Meanwhile, in 1850, a rebellion, aimed at the overthrow of the Manchu dynasty, had broken out in southern China. This rebellion, known as the Taiping Rebellion (q.v.) was led by a religious fanatic, Hung Hsiu-chuän, who set himself up in Nanking as the head of a new Protestant dynasty. The rebellion was finally crushed in 1864 by a Chinese imperial army, known as the Ever-Victorious Army, partly under American and English army officers (see GORDON, CHARLES GEORGE).

The United States had watched with deep interest the progress of the second Anglo-Chinese war, and President Buchanan sent William B. Reed to China to conduct any negotiations which might become necessary. In its friendly attitude the United States was supported by Russia. The efforts of Reed resulted in a new treaty of friendship and commerce with China, signed on June 18, 1858. The United States minister to China from 1861 to 1867, Anson Burlingame, was so successful in winning the confidence of the Chinese administration, then in progressive hands, that upon his retirement, he was asked to head a Chinese embassy accredited to eleven leading nations. In 1868, Burlingame negotiated another treaty between the United States and China, by which China was recognized as a nation of full equality with western powers, and Chinese immigration was permitted into the United States. In 1873 the Chinese emperor granted a personal audience to representatives of Russia, the United States, Great Britain, France, and Holland. This marked the final breakdown of Chinese reserve, and the recognition of the powers of the western world as the equals of China.

France, meanwhile, was pursuing a vigorous course south of China. In 1884, attempting to make fast its protectorate over Annam, France became involved in a campaign against Chinese forces in Tongking (Tonkin). The war was ended in 1885 by a treaty giving France control over both regions, but leaving open the question of Chinese suzerainty.

In 1894 Japan took advantage of disorders in Korea, over which China claimed suzerainty, to revive ancient claims in that country, and sent an expeditionary force into the peninsula, resulting in the Sino-Japanese War. From the start of hostilities Japan had the upper hand, and by the Treaty of Shimonoseki in 1895 Japan was able to wrest from China its recognition of the independence of Korea (which remained, however, under direct Japanese control), the cession of Formosa and the Liaotung Peninsula (including Port Arthur), a large war indemnity, and a most-favored nation treaty. Russia, France, and Germany, however, protested against the cession of the peninsula of Liaotung, and brought such pressure to bear that Japan relinquished this part of its conquest.

In the closing years of the 19th century, Germany, Russia, and Great Britain took advantage of the weakness of China, as evidenced by its rapid collapse in the war with Japan, to secure territorial leases, additional concessions, and other special privileges in China. In return for loans to pay its war debts, China granted far-reaching railroad and trade concessions. The United States alone among the great powers did not engage in the scramble for spheres of influence, urging, in 1899,

that the powers observe an "open door and equal opportunity" policy.

The danger to China from foreign powers now became so evident that two Chinese factions appeared, divided upon the method of resistance. One was a nationalist reform group, the other a reactionary party inspired by the Dowager Empress and including among its adherents the so-called Boxers, an organization which had as a motto "Exterminate the Foreigners". For a time the reformers seemed to have gained control at the palace and influenced the young Emperor Kuang-Hsü, the nephew of the Dowager Empress. The Dowager Empress, however, kept the Emperor, whom she had placed upon the throne, in subjection, and in 1898 he issued a decree practically transferring the sovereign authority to her. From that time, the reformers were persecuted and violent antiforeign demonstrations sprang up in many quarters, culminating in the Boxer Rebellion (q.v.) of 1900, which was put down by the combined forces of Japan, Russia, Great Britain, the U.S., and France. In the peace protocol signed in Sept., 1901, the importation of arms and ammunition, or material for the manufacture thereof, was forbidden; Chinese membership in antiforeign societies was forbidden; a fortified legation district in Peking was provided for (but all foreign troops except legation guards were withdrawn); and heavy war indemnities were imposed (which China could meet only by giving the foreign powers still more control). The sole lessening of the burdens placed upon China after the Boxer Rebellion was the remission of a share of its indemnity by the United States, to be used for the education of Chinese students in the U.S.

The Boxer Rebellion had provided an opportunity for Russia to strengthen its hold on Manchuria. In 1898 China had leased Port Arthur to Russia, and during the Boxer Rebellion that country had sent troops into the region to widen its sphere of influence. In 1902 Russia agreed to evacuate Manchuria, but failed to do so, and as a result the Russo-Japanese War (q.v.) broke out in 1904. In 1905, by the Treaty of Portsmouth concluding this war, both powers agreed to evacuate Manchuria, though maintaining guards to protect their railroad interests.

The Republic. Despite some reforms and the promise of parliamentary government, the Manchu dynasty was doomed after the Boxer Rebellion. The person chiefly responsible for the movement which overthrew the Manchu government and founded the republic of China, was Dr. Sun Yat-sen (q.v.). He led the revolutionary movement from abroad (having left China because of persecution by the Dowager Empress for his liberal views), spending patient years organizing rebellions against the government, until finally, on Oct. 10, 1911 (now a national holiday), a revolution broke out which proved successful. A railway strike in Szechwan, called in protest against the introduction of foreign capital and material, had resulted in the sending of Imperial troops, and this furnished the ground for the general rising against the Manchus, which spread from province to province. The Imperial family was forced, on Dec. 28, 1911, to flee the capital, the boy emperor, Hsüan T'ung (Pu-yi), abdicating on Feb. 7, 1912, leaving the government in the hands of a national assembly set up by the revolutionaries, with Sun Yat-sen as first president of a provisional Chinese republic. On Feb. 12, 1912, China formally became a republic. The government was recognized by the United States in May, 1913. The policy of the new state was based on Sun's "Three Principles of the People": 1. Nationalism; 2. Democracy; 3. the People's Livelihood. To unify the country, however, in which there was still considerable dissatisfaction with the new government, Sun resigned the presidency, yielding in 1912 to Yüan Shih-k'ai (q.v.), former Imperial prime minister. Yüan Shih-k'ai, however, departed from the republican principles of Sun, suppressing him and his followers, dismissing parliament, and, in 1915, attempting, unsuccessfully, to restore the monarchy. (The western world, though not overly enthusiastic about the Chinese revolution, had done nothing to suppress it, being concerned at the time with the preliminary moves of World War I. Accordingly, their policy was chiefly one of aiding a "strong man", who, in return, would protect their investments. In this manner, Yüan Shih-k'ai had become the first of the modern "warlords" of China.) Yüan Shih-k'ai died in 1916, and was succeeded by Li Yüan-hung. It was during the period of Li Yüan-hung's rule that parliament was restored and work was renewed on framing a permanent constitution. Parliament, however, was largely ineffective, being composed of many conflicting elements.

For more than two decades after the revolution the warlords, political leaders with private armies, played the dominant role in Chinese politics, and China was in a constant state of upheaval and civil war. In this unsettled state, China was unable to meet the problems brought on by World War I. Japan moved quickly to take advantage of the situation. Occupying the German-leased territory in Shantung, Japan presented, in 1915, its "21 demands", requesting transfer to Japan of any German-leased territory in China, mining and railroad concessions, and control in southern Manchuria. Among other demands, Japan forbade cession of territory along China's coast to any other foreign power and required the appointment of Japanese advisors to the Chinese government. With Europe involved in war, China was forced to agree to many of the demands.

On Aug. 14, 1917, China entered World War I, so that it would have an opportunity to put an end to the unequal treaties signed with Germany and Austria-Hungary, and also to gain the right to be represented at the peace conference which would meet after the war. Because of internal disorders, China's actual role in the war was small.

On Nov. 7, 1917, notes of agreement were signed between the United States and Japan recognizing the fact that Japan had special interests in China. Both governments, however, agreed to maintain the principle of the "open door" (q.v.) in that country. This agreement was terminated in 1923.

China profited from World War I by seizing German and Austrian concessions in China and by the cancellation of the Boxer indemnity. Against these advantages, however, loomed a stronger Japan (the Peking government having in 1918 concluded military and naval agreements with Japan, whereby Japan, under the pretext of action against a Bolshevist danger, obtained a complete hold on northern China, including control of northern Manchuria and the Chinese Eastern Railway). The peace conference after World War I upheld Japan's actions in China during the war, when David Lloyd George and Georges Clemenceau, in accordance with secret pledges given to Japan in 1917, and Woodrow Wilson, in order to save the League of Nations, and relying on the Japanese promise eventually to evacuate Shantung, accorded to Japan all the former German "rights, title, and privileges in the province of Shantung". The Chinese delegates refused to sign the Versailles Treaty, which contained the article relating to Shantung, China becoming, however, a member of the League of Nations on the basis of a peace treaty signed with Austria.

At the Washington Conference (q.v.) of 1921–22, the Shantung problem was somewhat relieved with the return to China of the former German Leased Territory of Kiaochow, and all public properties therein, Japan being reimbursed by China for railroad properties and retaining partial control over mining interests in the region. The Nine Power Treaty signed at the Washington Conference (by Belgium, China's provisional government, France, Great Britain, Italy, Japan, the Netherlands, Portugal, and the United States) was designed to stabilize conditions in the Far East, safeguard certain of China's rights, and promote intercourse between China and other powers on the basis of equality and of equal commercial opportunity. Thus was finally adopted the long-advocated "open door" policy.

The prestige of the Chinese government was so far restored after the Washington Conference that China was able to conclude important agreements with Germany, in respect to financial and other matters; and with the Soviet Union, providing for recognition of the Soviet government, the right of China to purchase the Chinese Eastern Railway, renunciation by the Soviet Union of extraterritorial rights and of Boxer indemnity payments, and the return to the Soviet Union of legation and consular buildings. In June, 1924, the United States Congress passed a law remitting all further payments on the Boxer indemnity obligations.

Two other national developments were important. One was the growth of the spirit of nationalism, more or less closely allied at first with a deep interest in the political theories of the Soviet Union. The other was the steady and continued industrialization of China. Factories and mills multiplied, particularly along the coast and the inland transportation arteries, bringing in their train a revolution in the mode of life of millions of Chinese. Many of these mills were capitalized and operated by foreigners.

Sun Yat-sen, elected president again in 1921, engaged in organizing a modern government. Internal strife was too powerful, however, to permit unity. Sun had previously headed the government of the Kuomintang, with his capital at Canton. Opposed to his administration had been a separate one maintained at Peking in the north largely with the support of Manchurian warlords. Following World War I, despite the efforts of the Kuomintang to maintain stability, China became subject almost entirely to rule by warlords, while Sun was regarded by most of the western world as an ineffective idealist. He continued his work, however, although on many occasions the revolution was checked when its founder was abandoned by his political or military followers. Sun eventually turned to Soviet Russia

for aid. In 1924, with the aid of Russian advisers, the Kuomintang was reorganized, and the nationalist army was built up, coming under the leadership of Chiang Kai-shek (q.v.). In July, 1925, Gen. Michael Borodin, Russian Communist, was appointed adviser to the Nationalist government. While his connection with the Soviet government remained unknown to the public, it was later disclosed that the Soviet Embassy was supplying him with funds. Following the agreements of 1924, the Soviet Union made her Peking representative an ambassador; but relations with the Peking government were of uncertain friendliness. The open sympathy of the Soviet authorities with the Kuomintang brought very strained relations with such Northern leaders as Chang Tso-lin, who was bitterly opposed to Communism. The Soviet attitude led to a raid on Soviet Embassy buildings in April, 1927, and the seizure of secret documents, and to much friction over the control of the Chinese Eastern Railway.

In the meantime, a boycott against British trade in Hong Kong, which began in 1925, lasted for 15 months and for a time practically paralyzed foreign business. In other parts of China antiforeign demonstrations and rioting took place but gradually subsided into the more peaceful form of boycotts and strikes. The Shanghai shootings of 1925, however, were branded in the national consciousness and furthered the cause of the Nationalists. (On May 30, 1925, a Japanese overseer had killed a Chinese laborer in a Shanghai mill, and when a parade of strikers and students, which had been organized in protest, grew threatening, they were fired upon by Sikh police of the International Settlement on the order of a British police officer. Strikes and boycotts against British and Japanese goods were declared, and demonstrations in Peking and many of the treaty ports caused much further loss of life. On June 2, American, British, and Italian marines were landed at Shanghai to guard the International Settlement.)

The Nationalist Triumph. When Sun Yat-sen died in 1925, the Kuomintang made him a national hero and rallied the people around a program based on democracy, a higher standard of living, and the ousting of foreigners holding extraterritorial rights in China. Led by Chiang Kai-shek, and including in its number many Communists, the Nationalist, or Kuomintang army began its march to break the power of the warlords, in order to unite China under one flag. Rapid progress was made. By the close of 1926, Chiang held control of most of the territory south of the

Yangtze, including the greater part of the provinces of Fukien, Kiangsi, and Chekiang, and was threatening Shanghai. After the capture of Hankow, the seat of the Nationalist government was moved to that city from Canton.

The dramatic and spectacular success of the Nationalist armies brought swift repercussions in the foreign offices of the powers. So threatening was the situation that the American Minister, on Jan. 13, 1927, advised American citizens throughout the interior and the South to seek protection in the coast cities. The United States despatched naval vessels and marines to the Far East and other powers took similar action, Great Britain ordering 20,000 additional troops to Shanghai. Early in January, the British concessions in Hankow and Kiukiang were overrun by the Chinese.

Shanghai was finally occupied on March 21, 1927, when the General in command came over to the Nationalists. Two days later, Nanking was captured. At this time, Chiang split with the Communists over questions of policy and tactics; the Communists, a powerful factor in the building up of the Nationalist party, were denounced. The new Nationalist government estranged itself from the Soviet Union and drove the Communists from its ranks; such a policy was taken because, among other reasons, in facing the prospect of Japanese opposition to unification, the Nationalist government wanted the support of the other Treaty Powers, who were hostile to communism. The break with the Soviet Union and the Chinese Communists led to civil war with the Communists but to better relations with Great Britain and the United States.

In 1928 the Nationalists took Peking and changed its name to Peiping, meaning "northern peace", and the seat of the new government was established at Nanking. By 1928, recognition of the Nationalist government had come from the League of Nations, the United States, and most of the European nations. The complete tariff autonomy of the Nationalist regime was also recognized by twelve nations, some promising to abandon extraterritoriality by Jan. 1, 1930. (Late in 1942, the U.S., Great Britain, and soon afterward the Netherlands and Belgium, agreed to relinquish their extraterritorial rights. China signed treaties with the two first-named nations, Jan. 11, 1943, the question of Hong Kong remaining undiscussed. The U.S. in 1943 abolished Chinese exclusion laws, granting all Chinese in the U.S. the right of naturalization and permitting Chinese immigration under the usual quota restrictions. Canada relinquished its extraterritorial rights on April 14, 1944, and France, on Feb. 28, 1946. See EX-TRATERRITORIALITY.

The Nationalist government under Chiang Kai-shek faced two major problems: from within, that of the Communists, and from without, that of the Japanese, who had come more and more to consider China the legitimate aim of Japanese expansion. Though the government made steady progress toward a more stable and unified administration, the decade that followed Chiang's triumph in 1928 saw continued conflict in China. Chiang resigned his government posts in 1931 because of opposition from members of his own party, but he returned a year later when the Japanese menace assumed warlike proportions.

In Kiangsi, south-central China, the Communists, after 1927, had set up a number of Soviet communities and had built up a Red Army. Chiang led several military expeditions against them, but was unable to subjugate them. Finally, in 1935 and 1936, the Chinese Communists were dislodged south of the Yangtze, but, withdrawing in one of the greatest military feats in history, known as the "Long March", they moved far west to the border of Tibet, then swung north and east, and finally, after a journey of about 6000 miles, took up new positions in northern Shensi, just south of Inner Mongolia. Chiang attempted to dislodge them from this stronghold also, but failed. Nationalist troops in north China were under Gen. Chang Hsueh-liang (q.v.), who, having been driven out of Manchuria by the Japanese, had more cause to dislike the Japanese than to dislike the Communists. Chiang Kai-shek, rejecting a Japanese offer of co-operation against the Communists, agreed nevertheless to suppress the movement himself, and ordered a general campaign. But growing opposition to Chiang's policy of delaying action against the Japanese in Manchuria found its climax in a kidnap plot, engineered by Chang Hsueh-liang and other military leaders. Chiang was captured on Dec. 12, 1936, at Sian, capital of Shensi Province, and the price demanded for his return was amnesty to the Communists in the interest of a united front against the Japanese, and the settlement of other political and military issues. Although he did not yield officially to the demands, Chiang was shortly released; he eventually admitted Communists into the Kuomintang, and about a year later commenced active warfare against Japan. Chang, who accompanied the Generalissimo back to the National capital, was sentenced to imprisonment.

Conflict with Japan. The need to co-operate in resistance to Japan was an important factor in uniting China's strife-torn population. Already well established in Manchuria (q.v.) economically and militarily, the Japanese, taking as pretexts the shooting of one of their officers in August of 1931 and the destruction of a part of the Japanese-controlled South Manchuria Railroad, occupied Mukden during the night of Sept. 18–19. From then on, Japan continually threatened Chinese independence, forcing the government of the Kuomintang to acquiesce in every demand. Losing their best troops in useless but heroic efforts to defy the aggressor, and completely inadequately equipped to put up resistance, the Chinese surrendered more or less quickly to each fresh demand until in 1937 the Chinese forces under Chiang Kai-shek were able to offer resistance with some prospect of success; full-fledged warfare developed after the so-called Marco Polo Bridge incident near Peiping.

The seizure of Mukden was followed by the occupation of Tsitsihar, Chinchow, and Harbin and the establishment of an administrative council independent of the Chinese National government in Nanking. After Chengteh, the capital of Jehol Province, was captured, March 4, 1932, an armistice was signed at Tangku, May 31. The truce provided for demilitarization of a large section of China lying between the Great Wall, the Gulf of Chihli, and a line running roughly east and west a short distance north of Peiping and Tientsin.

Manchuria, then comprising the three provinces of Liaoning, Kirin, and Heilungkiang, was declared independent of China under the name of Manchukuo, March 1, 1932, and was later joined by Jehol Province.

In Jan., 1932, the conflict in Manchuria spread to Shanghai, primarily as a result of the anti-Japanese boycott which broke out in all of China after the occupation of Mukden. In Shanghai the boycott had been accompanied by attacks upon Japanese residents. Imperial troops immediately took steps to end the attacks and the boycott by force. The Chinese mayor of Shanghai capitulated, Jan. 28, to a note demanding satisfaction, while Nipponese warships and troops concentrated near the city. Nevertheless, shortly after midnight Japanese marines launched an attack upon the native borough of Chapei. The battle continued until, on March 2, the fall of Kiangwan forced the Chinese to withdraw from the environs of Shanghai.

It was not until May 5 that a truce was concluded under which the Japanese forces gradually withdrew while the Chinese troops retained their positions held at the time of the armistice. Japan again ordered contingents to Shanghai in the early fall of 1932, when renewed anti-Japanese outbreaks occurred.

Meanwhile, the League of Nations made various attempts to bring about a peaceful solution. All reports, including that of the Lytton Commission, were outspoken in condemning Japan for unprovoked aggression. The government in Tokyo, claiming self-defense, soon demanded the right to establish a "new order" in East Asia and undermined every attempt at reconciliation, finally resigning from the League, March 27, 1933. The United States expressed willingness to co-operate against Japan; however, none of the powers actively went to the aid of China.

On March 1, 1934, Manchukuo was declared an empire. To head the puppet state, the Japanese selected Henry Pu-yi, who, as the boy Emperor Hsüan T'ung (q.v.), had abdicated the throne in 1912; he was now called Kang Teh.

China refused to recognize the independence of Manchuria as had been urged by Tokyo, but economic advantages were granted to Japan. On July 3, 1934, China capitulated further by lowering tariff rates on Japanese goods while those on practically all other imports were raised.

In 1935, Japanese troops moved south of the Great Wall and partially detached Hopeh Province in China proper and Chahar in Inner Mongolia from the control of the Nanking government. Japanese military control was established at Ningsia Province in western Inner Mongolia, and Nipponese troops battered at the door of Outer Mongolia, under Soviet Russian protection and control.

On May 29, the Japanese Kwantung Army demanded the evacuation of the Peiping-Tientsin region by Chinese forces, elimination of officials hostile to Japan in North China, and the suppression of all anti-Japanese activities including the closing of Kuomintang offices in this region. The terms were accepted on June 12. Agreements made later in the same year provided for further removal of Chinese troops and the establishment of a new demilitarized area in eastern Chahar. Kalgan in Chahar fell victim to Japanese attack, Dec. 14.

In Jan., 1936, Nanking's refusal to accept a three-point program of collaboration with Japan brought additional Japanese troops into North China. The Japanese, on Nov. 5, renewed their drive into Suiyuan, anxious to prevent a junction of Chinese Communists with Outer Mongolian and Soviet forces. This Japanese force was thrown back at Taolin, 40 miles w. of the Chahar border. The Chinese then drove the Mongol-Manchukuo forces out of Pailing-miao, capital of the semi-autonomous Mongol state set up in 1935.

Chiang Kai-shek continued his efforts to prevent further military action by concessions to Japan, at the same time attempting to organize the country for an eventual struggle. In July, 1937, five years after the start of the war, the Japanese were in possession of nine tenths of the Chinese railways, all the chief ports, and most of the large interior cities, occupying those parts of China which they considered of importance in their economic exploitation of the vast Chinese realm. China's richest lands, industries, and mines were devastated; Japanese looting and the Chinese "scorched-earth" policy of leaving only ruins to the invader added to the destruction.

The Sino-Japanese death struggle came to a head in 1937. With the United States indicating by its neutrality legislation that it would not intervene, and with Europe occupied with internal affairs, Japan seized on a minor clash between Japanese and Chinese troops at the Marco Polo Bridge near Peiping, July 7, to try to put an end to Chinese defiance. After this move Chiang was forced by political pressure (the Sian kidnapping incident and its consequences) to abandon the tactics of evasion and delay. A Japanese ultimatum was rejected at the end of July. Thereupon, 35,000 Japanese troops in North China undertook to oust the Chinese from the entire Tientsin-Peiping area. On July 28, a Japanese detachment was annihilated at Peiping, but the city surrendered the next day. Japan's advance was rapid; the two chief cities of North China were in Japanese hands by Aug. 2. A puppet government was established at Peiping and the city was renamed Peking. The Chinese, defeated at Nankow Pass, retreated south into Shansi Province, leaving the Peiping-Kalgan railway to the Japanese. Driving west from Kalgan, the Japanese invaded Suiyuan Province, Inner Mongolia, following the railway to its terminus at Paotow, which fell Oct. 17. Tatung in North Shansi was captured Sept. 14, and the heavily fortified Yenman Pass was taken, Oct. 2. Progress was slowed thereafter by Chinese guerrilla tactics, particularly those of the Communist army. Reinforced Japanese troops conquered Taiyuan, Nov. 9.

Meanwhile, some 300,000 Japanese crossed the Yungting River south of Peiping, Sept. 14, easily shearing through the 400,000 opposing Chinese who, about 100 miles s. of Peiping, attempted a stand behind a strong line of fortifications extending east from Paoting, capital of Hopeh Province, which was taken together with Tsangchow, Sept. 24, rendering the entire line untenable. Then advancing on the strategic railway junction of Shihkiachwang, the Japanese crushingly defeated the Chinese, Oct. 10, and in about a week's time reached the Hopeh-Honan border. Japanese crossed the Hopeh-Shantung border early in Oct., and on Oct. 11 seized Hucheng, 30 miles n. of Tsinan, capital of Shantung; crossing the Yellow River, Dec. 25, they occupied Tsinan, Dec. 27. Tsingtao was abandoned by Chinese forces, Dec. 31.

A sensational conflict grew out of a minor incident in Shanghai suburbs, Aug. 9, 1937, when a Japanese naval officer and a seaman were shot. On Aug. 12, 16 Japanese warships arrived in Shanghai; China sent some 30,000 crack troops into the Shanghai-Woosung area bordering on the International Settlement. On Aug. 13, following a clash in the suburb of Chapei, Japanese warships on the Whangpoo River opened fire. On Aug. 14 the Chinese planes attempted to bomb the vessels anchored off the Bund of the Settlement, but the bombs fell in the most populous part of the Settlement, killing 1,142 persons and injuring 1,400 more. Desperate fighting continued for a month before Japan gained an indisputable grip on the salient between the Yangtze and the Whangpoo rivers, and the Chinese withdrew west to a line extending about 20 miles n. from the Settlement opposite Chapei to the Yangtze near Liuho.

About 200,000 Japanese troops, supported by hundreds of planes and heavy artillery, on Oct. 27, drove 500,000 Chinese from their new line. Japan then landed about 30,000 men at Hangchow Bay and struck north to the rear of the Chinese position near Shanghai, and the Chinese retired about 50 m. from Shanghai to a line running south from the Yangtze through Soochow and the Tai-Hu lake region to Hangchow Bay.

Nanking was surrounded by the Japanese from the south by Dec. 9, 1937, and some 50,000 troops of Gen. Tang Sheng-chi allowed themselves to be trapped in the city. After three days of intense street fighting, Tang and his staff made a secret getaway by boat, leaving the troops leaderless. A few thousand of them managed to escape to the north shore of the Yangtze but most of the Chinese were trapped and annihilated. After crushing the last resistance, Dec. 15, the Japanese exterminated thousands; foreign and Chinese properties were looted and destroyed, and thousands of civilians were shot. Similar atrocities were repeated on a lesser scale when Hangchow capitulated, Dec. 25.

The Japanese navy seized islands off South China flanking the British shipping routes to Hong Kong. Pratas Islands, off the south tip of Formosa and but 500 m. from Manila, P.I., were occupied early in Sept. Quemoy Island, dominating the entrance to Amoy, was taken late in Oct., and Taikam and Chikkai Islands in Nov. Beginning Aug. 26, a blockade of the entire Chinese coast south to Swatow (extended on Sept. 5 south to Indo-China) was declared by the Japanese. Nevertheless, considerable quantities of armaments reached China via Hong Kong, and a military highway across Chinese Turkestan to facilitate the imports from the Soviet Union was begun.

A nonaggression treaty between China and Russia was signed, Aug. 21, and on Sept. 10 an agreement was concluded with the Chinese Communists under which their armies were formally incorporated into Chiang's forces.

Foreign properties were heavily damaged throughout the campaigns and American and British warships and their crews fell victim to attacks. Among these, the *Panay* incident was the most serious. On Dec. 12, Japanese planes bombed, machine-gunned, and sank the U.S. gunboat *Panay* which had sailed 28 m. up the Yangtze from Nanking to avoid the fighting. Japan later apologized and paid an indemnity to the U.S.

Japan registered further gains in 1938 in the face of stubborn Chinese resistance. The Japanese offensive may be divided into three major campaigns located roughly (1) north of the Yangtze River in Kiangsu, Anhwei, and Shantung provinces, (2) in the Yangtze River valley, and (3) in South China.

The campaign north of the Yangtze had as its objective the closing of the gap between Japanese forces in North China and the Yangtze valley. Japan captured the port of Tsingtao, Jan. 10, 1938, and most of Shantung Province soon after. Hangchwang was seized in March, but the Chinese prevented the crossing of the Grand Canal at this point. Taierchwang, also on the Grand Canal 20 m. to the southeast, was occupied, Mar. 31; on Apr. 6 and 7, however, the Japanese were driven out, suffering their worst defeat of the war when several thousand troops were annihilated. The Japanese occupied Suchow May 20, and pursued the enemy, capturing Kweiteh, Lanfeng, and Kaifeng.

The Yangtze valley offensive began in mid-May when the Japanese advanced from Wuhu 70 m. up the river to Hofei. They captured Anking, June 12, but encountered a barrier of sunken barges 40 m. beyond, at Matang, which withstood attack for 11 days until July 5. Hukow was taken July 10 and Kiukiang fell July 26, but another barrier at Wusueh-Matowchen defied attack for two months. The Peiping-Hankow railway was cut 88 miles N. of Hankow, Oct. 8. Outflanking Yangsin, which was abandoned Oct. 17, the Chinese lost control of the Canton-Hankow railway, a main source of supplies. On Oct. 25, the Japanese entered the three Wuhan cities, Hankow, Hanyang, and Wuchang, which the retreating Chinese had virtually destroyed. Of 1,500,000 inhabitants only 400,000 remained. Shortly before the fall of Hankow, the National Government was moved to Chungking, almost 1,000 m. inland. The Japanese advance along the Kiukiang-Nanchwang railway gained only 50 m.

The offensive in South China was designed to check the flow of munitions to China by way of the Canton-Hankow railway. On May 10 to 13, 1938, the Japanese took Amoy. In June, Canton was subjected to a ruthless air bombardment, killing or wounding 8000 civilians. The Japanese landed 30,000 men on Bias Bay (on the mainland opposite Hong Kong) on Oct. 12, cut the Canton-Kowloon railway, and occupied Waichow on Oct. 15. Circling to the northwest, they entered Canton, Oct. 21.

Throughout the year, the Chinese employed very effective guerrilla tactics which were mainly responsible for large Japanese casualties, and in counterattacks much territory previously lost was regained by the Chinese, especially in Shansi Province.

The Tokyo government more and more refused to consider foreign rights in China, advising other powers to adapt their attitude to new conditions. France temporarily barred all shipments to China from Indo-China in return for a Japanese promise not to invade Hainan Island, about 700 m. from the Philippine Islands; Japan occupied the island, however, in 1939. Indo-China, after the fall of France in 1940, during World War II, barred shipments to China permanently. Germany stopped munitions shipments to China and ordered military advisers home. Soviet deliveries were limited, while Great Britain and the United States increased theirs, most shipments coming by way of the Burma Road (q.v.).

Japanese efforts to subjugate China were pushed relentlessly throughout 1939, but with few of the gains registered in preceding years. The fall of Nanning and Nanchang was offset by unprecedented Japanese defeats. Stubborn Chinese resistance and guerrilla warfare made slow but encouraging progress. A firm Chinese stand blocked Japanese advances in northwest Hupeh and southwest Honan.

Differences between Japan and other countries increased gradually; while the British government seemed to be pursuing a policy of appeasement, Washington refused to yield to Japanese threats and violence. On July 26, 1939, the United States renounced the Japanese-American treaty of commerce of 1911.

The year 1940 witnessed Japan's first major military reverses. After advancing about 100 m. from Canton into northeastern Kwangtung Province in Dec., 1939, the Japanese were halted early in Jan. and in the middle of the month were driven back to the environs of Canton in a disastrous retreat.

More successful were the Japanese contingents which launched an offensive from Hankow northwest through Hupeh. They captured Siangyang, June 3. Ichang, the most important river port between Hankow and Chungking was taken, June 11. Air attacks on Chungking began in May, and throughout the summer the city was subjected to almost daily raids. On Sept. 30, the Japanese began to raid Kunming, capital of Yunnan Province and a key point on the Burma Road.

Three major campaigns and numerous minor ones were fought in 1941. Advances from Sinyang were forced back by the Chinese. An offensive launched on the Chungtiao range drove the Chinese back from their positions on the north bank of the Yellow River, but the Chinese managed to escape and inflicted casualties on the enemy estimated at 30,000. For the third time since 1938 the Japanese tried unsuccessfully to gain Changsha, capital of Hunan Province.

After passage of the "Lend-Lease Bill" in March, 1941, American supplies to China increased. On Dec. 8, 1941, a day after the Japanese attack on Pearl Harbor, China formally declared war on Japan, Germany, and Italy, and the Sino-Japanese War thus merged into World War II (q.v.). The American volunteer airmen in China, known as the "Flying Tigers", and commanded by Gen. Claire L. Chennault (q.v.), formed the nucleus of the newly established U.S. 14th Air Force, fighting with the Chinese army, and Chiang Kai-shek, with American officers on his staff, was appointed commander in chief of all allied forces in what was now the Chinese theater of World War II. On Jan. 1, 1942, China signed the Declaration of the United Nations.

The loss of Burma to Japan in the spring of 1942 and other United Nations losses in the Pacific region were severe blows to China, increased China's difficulties in getting American "Lend-Lease" supplies, and opened a new line of conquest to the invader all along the Burmese border. The acquisition by Japan of military bases in Indo-China, 1940–41, and Thailand, 1941, further endangered the Chinese stand. Nevertheless, the Chinese mustered a fighting force of about 5,000,000, including guerrilla bands and ill-trained men. During 1942, China passed from the defensive to the offensive; noteworthy are the campaigns at Changsha, Hunan Province, in which the Japanese suffered severely, and the recapture of airfields in Chekiang Province.

The period 1942–43 again saw the Chinese making some headway in the defense of their country. They resisted a Japanese offensive along the Hupeh-Hunan border, southwest from Ichang and northwest from Tungting Lake (end of May, 1943). The victory was described by the Chinese authorities as one of the greatest in the war.

The end of 1944 saw China facing its darkest hour. The Japanese had split China from north to south, penetrating into the provinces of Anhwei, Kiangsi, Hunan, Kwangsi, and Kwangtung, and also greatly strengthening their hold on the coast between Shanghai and Canton. Dismay was felt by American military leaders at the loss to the Japanese of about a dozen airfields, which had been constructed at great cost as bases for raids against the Japanese mainland and Japanese positions in China.

The Chinese armies, with American aid, assumed the offensive during 1945. In the last weeks of the war they drove the Japanese back in many areas, inflicting heavy losses.

In August, 1945, China and the Soviet Union concluded a thirty-year treaty which provided that Manchurian railways be jointly owned and operated, that Port Arthur be made a joint naval base, that Dairen become a free port, and that China recognize the independence of Outer Mongolia. The Soviet Union promised, in return, not to interfere in Chinese internal affairs and to support only the Nationalist government.

China after World War II. With the collapse of Japan later in August, the Communist and the Nationalist armies raced to the areas of N. China and Manchuria which had been under occupation by the Japanese. Utilizing American transport facilities, the Nationalist forces took over Shanghai and many other leading cities. They failed, however, to extend their control to large sections of the hinterland. Despite its assurances of noninterference in the recently signed treaty, the Soviet Union delayed the entry of Nationalist troops into Manchuria, while permitting the Chinese Communists to infiltrate the region and to equip themselves with Japanese arms. Toward the end of 1945, when the Soviet troops began to withdraw from Manchuria and the Nationalists made their entry, the Chinese Reds were strongly entrenched in many strategic areas. The ensuing encounters of the rival forces marked the resumption of civil war after a nine-year truce.

In 1946 the Nationalists were confronted not only with the problem of defeating the Communists but also with urgent tasks of economic reconstruction and government reform. Although the United Nation's Relief and Rehabilitation Administration (U.N.R.R.A.) and the United States provided vast quantities of badly needed supplies, the Kuomintang made little headway on reconstructon.

Efforts at government reform also proved fruitless. A Kuomintang-dominated National Assembly approved a new constitution on Dec. 25, 1946. Few provisions of the document, which was designed to assure China a democratic, efficient, and honest government, were effectuated.

The tempo of the Kuomintang-Communist struggle meanwhile had mounted. Because the civil war was the chief obstacle to reconstruction and reform, bringing hostilities to a speedy conclusion was essential. In view of the weakness of the Nationalist government and the growing strength of the Communists, it had become increasingly evident that a Kuomintang military victory would be enormously costly, perhaps impossible, and that an attempt should be made to mediate the struggle.

Deeply concerned with the course of events in China, the U.S. government appointed General of the Army George C. Marshall, former U.S. Army chief of staff, special envoy to the Chinese government with the task of arranging a settlement between the warring sides. General Marshall held the first of a series of conferences in Chungking with Nationalist and Communist spokesmen in January, 1946. Though the negotiations soon resulted in a truce and tentative plans for the merger of the Communist and Nationalist

armies and the formation of a coalition government, hostilities were resumed in mid-February. Marshall obtained another cease-fire agreement in June, but fighting began again the following month and spread swiftly to many parts of N. China. In November negotiations were suspended, and General Marshall returned to the United States, his mission a failure.

During 1947 Nationalist forces won major victories in Shantung and Shensi provinces, but suffered severe losses in Manchuria. At the end of the year the Communists controlled almost the whole of that region.

The civil war reached a new level of intensity during 1948, with the Nationalists experiencing many serious defeats. The gravity of the Nationalist position was emphasized when, in November, Chiang Kai-shek appealed directly to U.S. President Harry S. Truman to rush more military equipment to China. Truman replied that the question of additional help would not be considered until April, 1949, when the $463,000,000 China-aid program was due to expire.

Tientsin, a major defense bastion, fell to the Reds on Jan. 15, 1949. On Jan. 30 they captured Peiping, which subsequently became the Communist capital under its original name, Peking. With the abandonment of Nanking, the Nationalist capital, in April, effective resistance to the Communists collapsed. Shanghai fell in May, Canton in October, and Chungking in November. The Reds captured the island of Hainan in May, 1950, and they gained control of Tibet a year later, completing their conquest of all of China, except for certain small offshore islands and the large island of Formosa (Taiwan). The Nationalist government and remnants of its armies had withdrawn to the latter at the end of 1949. (For subsequent developments in the Republic of China, see FORMOSA).

There were many reasons for the Nationalist defeat. In a White Paper, issued in August, 1949, the U.S. State Department accused the Nationalist government of ineptitude, corruption, and failure to make effective use of American aid, which had totaled more than $2 billion since the end of World War II. Among other reasons for the debacle were the disruption of production and normal life by the long years of foreign and civil war, a runaway price inflation and an increasingly onerous tax burden, the poor leadership and low morale in the Nationalist armies, and the defection of leading generals to the Communists. Perhaps the most important reason for the defeat of the Nationalists was their lack of vigor in combating landlordism, usury, official corruption, and foreign domination. The Kuomintang government recognized these evils and developed remedial programs, but, having failed to produce positive results, it lost the confidence of the Chinese people. In contrast, the Communists did act resolutely to satisfy popular demands for eradication of these evils.

The "People's Republic of China" had been proclaimed in Peking on Sept. 21, 1949, at the opening session of the Chinese People's Political Consultative Conference, a provisional legislature. The Conference adopted a new "organic law" for governing the country, and the veteran Communist leader Mao Tse-tung (q.v.) was elected head of state. Mao's chief lieutenant, Chou En-lai (q.v.), was appointed premier and foreign minister.

The new regime proceeded immediately to transform the economic, social, and political life of China. Using methods of extreme brutality, it expropriated the landlords and well-to-do peasants, divided their land among the poorer peasants, and harassed the urban middle class until their resistance to control was broken. Hundreds of thousands of landowners, businessmen, and intellectuals were executed as reactionaries. Many more were sentenced to slave labor camps. People were encouraged to spy upon and denounce their friends and relatives. Ingenious methods of "brainwashing" were employed to secure confessions of guilt.

The poorer peasants were not permitted to enjoy ownership of their newly acquired land for long. They were induced, in many cases compelled, to form co-operative associations, which then by stages were converted into collective farms with the state as sole proprietor.

An ambitious Five-Year Plan was inaugurated at the beginning of 1953. Besides collectivization of agriculture, its principal goals were rapid industrialization, expansion of production in all fields, and strengthening of the national defense.

The first nationwide elections under the Peking regime were held in 1953–54. The Communist Party won overwhelmingly, though certain minor parties obtained representation. In September, 1954, the first All China People's Congress convened and adopted a new constitution to replace the "organic law" of 1949. The Congress elected Mao Tse-tung chairman of the government. General Chu Teh, head of the armed forces, was elected vice-chairman and Chou En-lai was reappointed premier and foreign minister.

Toward the end of 1955 the Communists,

reflecting increasing confidence in the stability of their regime, began to moderate their harsh methods of rule. Under the new policy emphasis was placed on persuasion rather than on terror.

The 8th Congress of the Chinese Communist Party met in Peking during September, 1956. Party leaders announced at this Congress, the first since 1945, that all the major goals of the first Five-Year Plan had been achieved a year ahead of schedule. More than 95 percent of the peasants were members of collective farms. Industrial production had risen 204 percent between 1952 and 1956 and agricultural output had expanded by 19 percent in the same period. The armed forces, though reduced substantially in size, were much better equipped, and therefore stronger, than ever before. Communist Party membership had increased 900 percent since 1945 to a total of about 10,735,000.

Together with boasts of successes, there were confessions of serious errors and excesses, especially in the administration of justice. It was admitted that many thousands of people had been unjustly convicted and brutally treated. Spokesmen for the regime promised a complete codification of laws and a greater concern for individual rights under the law.

Objectives of the second Five-Year Plan, for the years 1958–62, were revealed at the Congress. Industrial production in 1962 was scheduled to be double that of 1957, and a 35 percent rise was planned in agricultural production. Earnings of peasants and workers would be increased more than 25 percent. The whole nation was promised a better and easier life. However, the Party leaders admitted that two or three more Five-Year Plans would be required to place China in the first rank of industrial powers.

The Peking regime had scored important successes meanwhile in the field of foreign policy. During its first year as a sovereign state the People's Republic had been recognized by the Soviet Union and the other communist states, and by India, Great Britain, and many other nations. The United States, which continued to support the Nationalist regime in Formosa, withheld recognition.

Less than six months after its inception the People's Republic concluded an alliance with the Soviet Union. Formalized in a thirty-year treaty signed in February, 1950, the alliance became the keystone of Chinese Red policy. In supplementary agreements concluded in 1952 and in 1954, the Soviet Union made major concessions to Communist China, including the abrogation of Soviet privileges in

Manchuria that had been granted by Chiang Kai-shek in the treaty of 1945.

The Korean War (q.v.) marked the emergence of Communist China as a world power. Despite disavowals by the U.S. government and the United Nations of hostile intentions toward Communist China, the Red regime adopted an increasingly threatening posture as the U.N. forces in Korea moved toward the Chinese border in the fall of 1950. The Chinese Communist government ordered its soldiers into the conflict on a mass scale late in October. This provocative action, accomplished without direct reprisal by the U.N. allies, was followed by others, including "germ warfare" charges against the United States, "brainwashing" of American prisoners of war, and bold intransigence during negotiations.

After the conclusion (July, 1953) of the Korean truce the Peking regime, a mainstay, since its formation, of the communist-led insurgents in Indochina, greatly accelerated the flow of military equipment to the rebel forces, insuring the ultimate French defeat there. At the Conference on Far Eastern Affairs held (April-July, 1954), in Geneva, Switzerland, Chou En-lai, the Chinese Communist delegate, was the chief architect of a cease-fire agreement relinquishing over 70,000 sq.m. of Indochinese territory to communist North Viet-Nam. As a result of Chou's diplomacy the Peking government became a dominant force in Southeast Asia and its international prestige generally was much enhanced.

In August, 1954, Chou En-lai officially declared that the "liberation" of Formosa was one of the principal tasks of his government. Early the following month the Communists began an artillery bombardment of Quemoy, a Nationalist-held island off the coast of Fukien Province. The Communists later attacked Matsu, the Tachens, and other Nationalist-held islands. The Nationalists retaliated with air and naval raids against the mainland. Intensification of the Red offensive against the offshore islands early in 1955 gave weight to reports that the Communists were massing an invasion force for an all-out attack on Formosa itself. The United States responded by heavily reinforcing its naval and air forces in the Formosa area. Late in January the U.S. Congress approved a resolution giving the President discretionary power to use American armed forces in defense of Formosa. In February the Nationalists, with the help of the U.S. Seventh Fleet, evacuated the Tachens. There followed a *de facto* cease-fire in the Formosa area.

At the Asian-African Conference of twenty-two Asian and seven African states, held in April, 1955, at Bandung, Indonesia, Chou En-lai, as the Chinese delegate, stated a willingness to confer directly with the United States on the Formosa issue. This conciliatory move was followed by the release of four of fifteen American fliers captured by the Chinese during the Korean War. In July the United States and Communist China agreed to hold high level discussions in Geneva on mutual differences, including the repatriation of detained nationals on both sides. These talks, which proceeded intermittently beginning at the end of July, 1955, led to the release of the other fliers and of additional Americans imprisoned in China and to the granting by the United States of exit visas to a number of procommunist Chinese students. Nevertheless, full agreement was not reached on any major issue.

Following the Bandung Conference, meanwhile, Communist China improved its relations with nations of the neutralist bloc. It won (May, 1956) recognition from Egypt, concluded (September) a treaty of nonaggression and assistance with Nepal, and entertained (October) the president of Indonesia, obtaining his approval of its foreign policy.

The Chinese Communist internal situation was marked by widespread unrest among various elements during 1957. On Feb. 27, 1957, Mao Tse-tung advised the Chinese to "let a hundred flowers blossom and a hundred schools of thought contend". The people, at first hesitant, began to voice criticism with unprecedented frankness. In June, many critics were charged with treason, and a number were executed. In January, 1958, the Communists reported that 100,000 counter-revolutionaries and rightists had been "dealt with" during the preceding two years.

Chou En-lai resigned as foreign minister on Feb. 11, 1958, but retained the premiership. In December it was announced that Mao Tse-tung would not seek re-election as chairman of the republic. The National People's Congress, in April, 1959, chose Lin Shao-chi, former chairman of the standing committee, to replace him. Mao remained chairman of the Politburo.

The conflict between Communist China and the Nationalist regime of Formosa was intensified in August, 1958, when the Communists reopened fire on the islands of Quemoy and Matsu (see FORMOSA: *History*).

A revolt against the Chinese occupation broke out in Lhasa, Tibet, on March 17, 1959, but was soon suppressed. In August a serious border dispute arose between Communist

China and India, as Chinese troops penetrated Indian territory. A meeting between Indian Prime Minister Jawaharlal Nehru and Chou En-lai in April, 1960, was inconclusive. The Chinese complained in a diplomatic note delivered to India on March 22 that the Indian attitude on the disputed border region amounted to a summary rejection of a peaceful solution. India had insisted that as a prerequisite to discussion of the issue Chinese troops withdraw from the territory, amounting to about 12,000 sq.m., which India claimed.

In 1960 and 1961 Communist China suffered from famine conditions. The official government explanation was that an unprecedented combination of natural disasters, including floods and droughts, had been responsible: Foreign intelligence sources, however, maintained that at least a portion of the deficiency in food production was due to demoralization of the peasantry because of the virtual abolition of private agricultural enterprise. Evidence for this view was seen in the decentralization of authority over agriculture, announced on April 10, 1960, as well as in the payment of larger percentages of peasant earnings in cash and the granting to peasants of permission to farm small plots for their own benefit. The famine conditions were alleviated by massive Chinese purchases of grain from abroad, notably from Canada; it was believed that the purchases drastically reduced the extremely limited foreign exchange possessed by the regime.

Ideological differences appeared to arise between the Chinese Communists and the Soviet Union in the late 1950's. In general the Chinese maintained that the Soviet theoreticians were wrong in asserting that Communist and capitalist countries could co-exist in peace and in expecting that Communism would prevail in additional countries without the waging of war. Except for some of the Communist parties in the Far East, the Chinese achieved few adherents to their views in the world Communist movement, save for the regime in Albania. The Soviet rupture of diplomatic relations with Albania in December, 1961, was widely interpreted as a covert attack on the Chinese Communists.

T.S.

CHINA CLAY. See KAOLIN.

CHINA SEA, a part of the Pacific Ocean, off the E. and S.E. coasts of Asia, extending from Japan to the eastern end of Borneo and the southern end of the Malay peninsula. The island of Formosa divides the China Sea into two parts; the northern is called the East China Sea, and the southern, the South China

Sea, or, frequently, simply the China Sea.

In the northwest the East China Sea merges with the Yellow Sea. The Ryukyu Islands mark the southeastern limits of the East China Sea. The most important port on this sea is Shanghai, and the principal river draining into it is the Yangtze.

The South China Sea is partly enclosed on the east by the Philippine Islands and Borneo. In the southwest it merges with the Gulf of Siam, and on the west it is separated from the Gulf of Tonkin by the island of Hainan. The South China Sea increases in depth from the south, where much of it has a depth of less than 1000 ft., to the north, where soundings of more than 13,000 ft. have been made off the Philippine island of Luzon. Typhoons sometimes endanger navigation on the South China Sea. The chief ports on this sea, or close to it, include Manila, Singapore, Bangkok, Saigon, and Canton; and the largest rivers draining into it are the Meekong and the Si, or "West River".

CHINA WOOD. See TUNG.

CHINCH BUG, common name of *Blissus leucopterus,* a small black bug with white wing covers, belonging to the family Lygaeidae. It is common in the U.S., Central America, and the West Indies, and is most destructive to grains and grasses of all kinds. In the eastern U.S. it is the principal insect enemy of lawns and hay fields, and in the Mississippi Valley it attacks corn and small grains. Its depredations cost many million dollars annually. Two generations mature each year, the first in early summer, and the second in August or September.

CHINCHILLA, common name for a South American rodent of the genus *Chinchilla,* particularly *C. lanigera.* The chinchillas are found in the Andes Mountains in Chile, Peru, and Bolivia, at altitudes of 8000 to 12,000 feet. With the viscacha they form the Chinchillidae family, related to the cavies.

The common chinchilla is a squirrel-like animal about 10 inches long exclusive of the bushy, 6-inch tail. Its ears are large and almost hairless. With its short front legs it holds the roots and grasses on which it feeds; its long hind legs enable it to hop about among the rocks with great agility.

Chinchillas are covered with dense fur of the utmost softness, mottled gray on the back and whitish on the underside. They were formerly slaughtered by the thousands for their fur, and by the 1920's, when protective laws were adopted, the animal was almost extinct. Chinchilla farms were subsequently started in South America and the United

States. The present-day chinchilla industry is highly successful due to the hardiness of the animal and to its fecundity, the female producing an average of four offspring per year.

CHINESE ART. Chinese art is a homogeneous and continuous development, the beginnings of which rival the Egyptian and Babylonian in antiquity, and its development has continued into the present day. China occupies the same important and influential position in the art of the Far East, as Greece in the Occident.

Painting. The origin of painting, which is the most important development of Chinese art, is found in calligraphy, Chinese script being written with the brush and requiring highly artistic execution. Only fluid colors are used on highly absorbent materials, such as silk or paper, upon which no change or retouching is possible. Unlike Occidental painting, Chinese is essentially romantic rather than naturalistic in character. Its purpose is not to represent facts, but to suggest a poetic idea. Although exquisite in color, its chief beauty is one of line. It is decorative in character, avoiding modeling and shadows.

The T'ang period (618–907 A.D.), under the influence of Buddhism, was the age of classic figure painting, with Buddha and the sages as principal subjects. The human figure was decoratively conceived, not naturalistically, but with wonderful power of expression. The chief characteristic of Buddhist painting was a grand rhythm of line and arrangement; the colors were bright and harmonious. Wu Tao-tsü, one of the greatest of Chinese painters, flourished during the period. This age saw the further development of landscape painting in two great schools: the southern, which was romantic and literary in character, and the more naturalistic northern. At the head of the former was Wu Wang Wei; of the latter, Li Ssŭ-hsün.

Chinese painting, however, reached its highest point of excellence in the Sung period (960–1280). The era was notable for historical, genre, and religious painting, but was most famous for its development of the art of landscape painting. In general, the landscapes of the Sung period do not strive for naturalistic accuracy, but excel in suggesting moods or feelings; for purely esthetic qualities they have never been surpassed anywhere. Among the most important landscape painters of the era were Hsü Shih-Ch'ang, Ma Yüan, and Hsia Kuei. The emperor Hui Tsung (reigned 1101–25), a painter himself, stimulated the art by official recognition and patronage. He established an academy and a gallery which housed a collection of 5000 paintings. Among examples of Sung painting in museums of the United States are "Sage in Meditation" (Museum of Fine Arts, Boston) and "The Emperor Wên Meets the Sage Tzü-Ya" (Freer Gallery, Washington, D. C.).

The Mongol dynasty emphasized realism. Genre, flowers, birds, and insects were favorite subjects. In the early Ming period (until about 1500), elegance replaced simplicity; yet such painters as Lin Lang of the Ming period are worthy of comparison with those of the great age of Chinese painting. One of the finest collections of Chinese paintings in the western world is that of Charles Lang Freer, which he presented to the Smithsonian Institution, Washington, D.C., in 1906. Other important collections are those in the British Museum, London; the Musée Guimée, Paris; the Metropolitan Museum of Art, New York City; and the Boston Museum of Fine Arts.

Architecture. Architecture in the usual sense is not known to have been carried to important results in China before the appear-

The Forbidden City, Peking, presents a view of traditional Chinese architecture. The pink walls of the city enclose several palaces, which are reached by flights of white marble steps.

Eastfoto

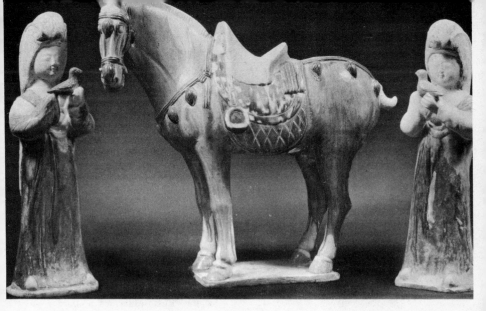

Chinese ceramics, tomb figures of the T'ang dynasty (618 to 905 A.D.). A lady falconer stands on either side of a horse. The three statuettes are coated in glazes of several colors.

ance there of the Buddhist influence in the course of the first century A.D. Then Indian types were introduced, and the Taa, or pagoda, appeared. No pagodas of this early date have been identified. The present-day Chinese pagodas are usually constructed of brick, concealed in many cases by an elaborate facing of massive tiles which are embossed with richly painted sculptured designs. Some pagodas are constructed chiefly of stone. A number of pagodas are 13 stories high, but this height is exceptional.

The typical home of the wealthy Chinese consists of a group of small one-story buildings interspersed with gardens, all within a bounding wall. Precisely the same tendency is visible in the temples of China, the "pagodas" or tower-like structures of whatever form being decorative and symbolical accessories.

Sculpture. Carving in stone was practiced in China from an early date, but a monumental sculptural style was first developed with the coming of Buddhism. Temples, similar to those in India, were adorned with rock-cut images of Buddha and his disciples, carved in the Greco-Indian manner. A typical example of such a temple with a multitude of carvings is at Tatong (Shansi) dating from the 5th century. Buddhas of stone were characteristic of the T'ang period. Jade carvings are of great elaboration, as where a single piece containing 250 cubic inches is wrought into two complete vases, side by side and

separated from one another except for connecting leaves and twigs cut out of the solid mass.

Bronzes. In the modeling and casting of bronzes, especially those of a decorative character, the Chinese are unexcelled. The development of the art has lasted uninterruptedly for a period of 3000 years. These bronzes have been preserved in such numbers that it is possible to form an adequate idea of the development of the art.

Ceramics. The Chinese are generally recognized as among the best makers of pottery in the world; from prehistoric times to the middle of the 14th century they were unsurpassed in this art. The pottery of the Han period (206 B.C.-221 A.D.) was simple, sturdy, and covered with a greenish glaze. That of the T'ang period was characterized by a greater variety of color as well as of objects. The period was especially notable for its figurines of birds, animals, and people, designed for tombs; these figures, made of clay, were glazed or painted in green, yellow, or brown. The pottery of the Sung period was usually of porcelain, generally glazed in monochrome, and was characterized by simplicity of decoration. Especially notable were the bowls and vases of this period, almost translucent in texture and with simple decorations in low relief under the glaze. The Sung pottery best-known among Western nations is the *celadons*; these porcelain objects, with their soft green color and smooth glaze, often resemble ob-

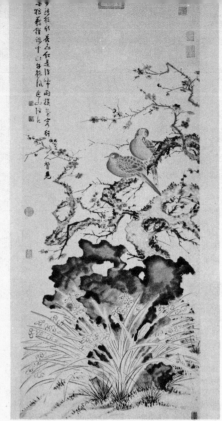

Philadelphia Museum of Art
Birds and flowers on a hanging scroll (from the period of the Ming dynasty)

CHINESE LANGUAGE

guages. It is not, however, the only language spoken within the geographical limits of China. For example, various aboriginal languages, the history of which is not well known, are spoken in the southwestern provinces. In addition, along most of China's western, southern, and northern boundaries there are languages related to the tongues of neighboring countries; among these are Thai, Tibetan, Turki, and Mongol. However, these non-Chinese languages of China are spoken by only about 20 million persons as compared with about 430 million who speak languages of the Sinic, or Chinese, family.

The Chinese language comprises scores of languages, or dialects, of varying degrees of mutual unintelligibility. Scholars usually group these dialects into five main divisions, namely, Mandarin, Wu, Min, Hakka, and Cantonese. Mandarin is spoken in about three quarters of the land area of China, extending to the Russo-Manchurian border in the northeast and to the large cities and trading posts in the southwest. The other four dialects may be pictured as occupying a broad coastal belt stretching between the figures 3 and 7 on a clock. Because of the extreme density of population in this part of China, the number of persons speaking these dialects is larger than the size of the area suggests. Wu is spoken in southern Kiangsu and most of Chekiang; Min, or Fukienese, in Fukien and eastern Kwangtung; Hakka in northern Kwangtung and southern Kiangsi; and Cantonese in southern Kwangtung and Kwangsi. The last three are also the languages of Chinese populations settled in such foreign countries as the United States (including Hawaii), the Philippines, and Malaya.

The historic center of the Mandarin dialect is in the north-central part of China, along the Yellow River, whence it has spread by migrations, some relatively recent. It was spread culturally also during the past five or six centuries by the imperial administration, which appointed all important officials from Peking, the capital. Mandarin, specifically the dialect of the Peking area, thus served as a common language for the Mandarin, or ruling class, and increasingly for all educated Chinese. During the 20th century strong efforts have been made to teach Mandarin as a compulsory second language in all schools. With increased use of radio and motion pictures as nationwide media of communication, its spread has been much accelerated.

All of the Sinic languages are characterized by extreme simplicity in apparatus. In fact, those languages are simpler even than English,

jects of jade. Chinese ceramics reached their highest development during the Ming dynasty (1368–1644). The aim of Ming pottery was in general a complex richness of effect, in contrast to the simplicity of Sung pottery; the Ming potters achieved this aim by the use of different colored glazes and enamels and of elaborate pictorial design. The art of ceramics was greatly encouraged by the emperors of the Ming period, who established imperial kilns for its production.

A very extensive literature on Chinese art, much of it written contemporaneously with the great art epochs, exists in Chinese. Works on this subject accessible to Occidental readers are, for the most part, of recent date.

CHINESE GORDON. See GORDON, CHARLES GEORGE.

CHINESE LANGUAGE, collective term for a number of closely related languages, often called dialects, which are spoken in China. Chinese is a member of the Sino-Tibetan or Indo-Chinese (q.v.) family of lan-the least inflected of the Indo-European languages. Chinese does not use inflections to indicate number, case, gender, tense, or mode. In the absence of inflection, the relations between words may be indicated by various particles of speech placed between them; actually the chief determinant of such relations is a fixed pattern of word order. As in English, the order of the principal parts of a sentence is subject-verb-object. However, Chinese differs strikingly from English in that Chinese places all modifiers, of whatever length, before the modified word. Consequently, Chinese has no equivalent for the relative clause or for the adverbial phrase following a verb. For example, "The man whom I saw yesterday playing with the children" must be expressed as "The I yesterday saw with-the-children-playing man."

Simple as the structure is, the language presents much difficulty to the foreigner because of characteristics that arise from its sound system. Almost all words are monosyllables, and because few consonantal combinations are permitted at the beginning and only *n* and *ng* at the end, there are fewer than five hundred different syllables available with which to communicate meanings. This limitation is partly met by an elaborate use of "tones". Basically, there are three tonal inflections with which a word may be uttered; namely, level, rising, and falling. These inflections may be combined with two or more differences of pitch level to produce further distinctions. For example, the tones for Mandarin are level, high rising, low rising, and falling.

Even with tonal distinctions, only some 1200 different-sounding root words are available. Hence, whenever the context itself does not prevent ambiguity, further means must be used, the most important of which is the joining up of synonyms. Thus, an English-speaking person might say "John buys flower-blossom" to show that he does not mean "John buys flour-bread"; in Chinese the ways in which this is done do not depend on the individual's ingenuity but are prescribed largely by tradition and must be learned, too.

These difficulties are little reflected in the written language, for Chinese characters are not alphabetic, but the writing system itself confronts the student, Chinese as well as foreigner, with enormous difficulties of its own. Its use is restricted to a small percentage of the population. There are many hundreds of written characters, or ideograms (see WRITING), each of which symbolizes a separate object or concept, rather than a word. The characters function somewhat as the Arabic numerals do in most modern languages; for example, the symbol "4" conveys the same meaning to all literate Europeans, but is read "four" in English, "quatre" in French, and "vier" in German. Hence, a Chinese newspaper article is equally intelligible in Canton and Peking, although the respective spoken versions of the identical material can be understood only by those who know the particular dialect in which it is rendered.

At various times attempts have been made to introduce alphabetical systems which would make the written language correspond to the spoken and facilitate mastery of the written language. Such attempts have had little success, not only because of conservative opposition but because the present universal written language, representing a communications system of great cultural and national importance, would be lost if a phonetic system were adopted.

In an attempt to reform and modernize the language, the Communist government of China launched in the 1950's a campaign designed to win popular acceptance of a common spoken and simplified phonetic written language.

Chinese shows little tendency to borrow words from foreign languages, largely because it lacks an alphabet, and thus cannot spell out new words just as they sound to the ear. Instead, the language exhibits great originality in coining new expressions out of its own stock of word roots. Thus it expresses "electricity" by extending the connotation of its word for "lightning"; by the same device "telephone" becomes "lightning-talk", and "telegraph" becomes "lightning-report". Picturesque though this device may appear, it constitutes a serious defect in the language because it leads to awkward and complicated phrases instead of the relatively simple technical terms used in other languages throughout the world.

CHINESE LITERATURE, writings produced in the Chinese language (q.v.).

In general, there are two distinct traditions in Chinese literature: the literary and the vernacular, or colloquial. Literature in the colloquial language can be traced back more than a thousand years before the Christian Era and has flourished almost continuously until modern times. It found its major expression first in poetry and later in drama and fiction, but it includes histories and popular stories and tales, as well. Nevertheless, this folk and vernacular literature long was considered beneath the notice of men of letters, who came from the scholar-official class and were the arbiters of literary taste. Their own polished and highly stylized writings set the standards for the orthodox literary tradition, which began about two thousand years ago, during the time of the Han rulers. In the 16th century A.D. certain critics became aware of the significance and value of vernacular literature, but it was not until the 20th century that it succeeded in gaining the support and esteem of the intellectual class as a whole. During the last half century this revaluation has continued, and many folk poems, plays, and stories have been rescued from oblivion; some are regarded presently as great works of literature. These writings, together with the Confucian classics, have aroused considerable interest among Western writers and translators. See CONFUCIANISM.

Chinese literature may be divided into three major historical periods, which roughly correspond to those of Western literary history: the classical period, from the 6th century B.C. through the 2nd century A.D.; the medieval period, from the 3rd to the end of the 12th century; and the modern period, from the 13th century to the present. Although this division is more or less arbitrary, it follows the main current of literary development in China.

Classical Period. As has been indicated, literature in the vernacular tradition originated before the classical period, but it was left unrecorded until classical times. A few scattered poems preserved then bear the imprint of the legendary emperors of prehistoric ages. Aside from such works of dubious authenticity, the earliest recorded examples were produced probably during the 14th century B.C.

The classical period in Chinese literature corresponds to the same period in Greek and Roman literature. Its formative stages comprise the two hundred years from the 6th to the 4th century B.C. This phase encompassed the work of Confucius (K'ung-tzu), Mencius (Meng-tzu), Lao-tzu, Chuang-tzu (fl. 4th cent. B.C.), and many other great Chinese philosophers. It culminated in the compilation of the Confucian classics, some of which have been attributed to remote antiquity, and other philosophical treatises. In the following centuries of the classical period the Confucian canon was fixed and Confucianism became the orthodox teaching of the people. A classical tradition that was to last until the present time was thus established.

The most important literary work in the Confucian canon is the *Classic of Poetry*, which partially includes an anthology of ancient poems written in four-word verses and composed mostly between the 10th and the 7th centuries B.C. Instead of glorifying gods and heroes as does most ancient literature, many of these poems sing of the daily life of the peasants, their sorrows and joys, their occupations and festivities. The poems represent the earliest vernacular tradition in Chinese poetry with characteristic simplicity of language and emotion and make up about one half of the book, the other half being dynastic songs and court poems. The latter give a colorful picture of the life and manners of the Chinese feudal nobility, just as the folk poems depict the simple, humble, and yet bountiful life of the peasantry.

The aristocratic, or court, style finds its best expression, however, in a group of poems known as the verses of Ch'u. A feudal state in south-central China, Ch'u was the home of Ch'ü Yüan (343–277 B.C.), the first great Chinese poet. A noble by birth, Ch'ü Yüan wrote *Li Sao* ("Encountering Sorrow"), a long, autobiographical poem full of historical allusions, allegories, and similes, essentially lyrical in expression. What makes the poem great is the intimate revelation of a poetic soul in agony because it has failed in its search for a beautiful ideal. Other poems by Ch'ü Yüan are equally rich in images and sentiment. He thus created a type of romantic poetry entirely different from the simple, realistic poetry of the Confucian classics.

During the four hundred years of the Han dynasty (206 B.C.-220 A.D.) both the romantic and realistic modes developed into schools of poetry which had many followers. The verses of Ch'u, which were irregular in form, led to a new literary type, the *fu*, or prose poem. On the other hand, from the four-word verse of the *Classic of Poetry* evolved five-word and seven-word verse forms, all of which are called *shih*. Chinese poetry was further enriched by the folk songs collected by an institution called the Music Bureau (Yüeh-fu), founded about the 2nd century B.C.

Chinese prose, which had produced earlier the aphoristic sayings of Confucius, the eloquent disputations of Mencius, and the romantic essays of Chuang-tzu, made great progress during Han times. The *Historical Memoirs* of Ssu-ma Ch'ien provided the pattern for a long series of dynastic histories compiled over a period of about two thousand years. In political and moral philosophy, the Confucian scholars also set the precedent for the literary tradition in Chinese prose. In this period of the Han rulers, the scholars were incorporated into the state bureaucracy. Appointments to all important official positions were based upon mastery of the Confucian classics, as revealed in state examinations. This practice continued with few interruptions until the 13th century A.D. and hardened the literary tradition into a national cult.

Medieval Period. From the beginning of the medieval period in the 3rd century until the 7th century China was divided into warring states. It suffered invasions by Tartar tribes as well as civil war. Nevertheless, these early centuries of the Middle Ages in China were by no means as unenlightened and sterile in literary production as was the corresponding period in the history of western Europe known as the Dark Ages. The spread of Buddhism (q.v.) from India, the invention of printing, and the flowering of poetry and prose illuminated the cultural horizon of the entire period and made it one of the most brilliant in Chinese history.

In times of social and political upheaval the poets found refuge and consolation in nature. Some of them were hermits who created a field-and-garden school of poetry. Others produced some of the best Chinese folk lyrics, such as the love poems attributed to Tzu-yeh, a woman poet; the *Ballad of Mulan*, celebrating the military adventures of a woman soldier disguised as a man; and *The Peacock Flew to the Southeast*, a long narrative of tragic family love, written in plain but vivid language.

The greatest Chinese poetry was created during the T'ang dynasty (618–907 A.D.), which ushered in a time of peace and prosperity that declined, however, toward the end of the period. Despite the passage of more than ten centuries, as many as 49,000 T'ang poems by 2200 poets have survived. The three most famous poets were Wang Wei (699–759), Li Po, and Tu Fu. They started their lives in the early splendor of the T'ang era, but lived through the subsequent troubled years of war and rebellion. Hardship and adversity only served, however, to give mellowness to their talents. Wang Wei, a meditative philosopher and painter with Buddhist inclinations, depicted the serene aspects of nature's beauty. It has been said that there is poetry in his pictures and there are pictures in his poems. Li Po, a leader of the romantic school, rebelled against the conventions of poetry and society. Frenzied and unfettered, his fancy

roamed to the realm of the immortals, whence, he claimed, he had been exiled to this world. He was at his best when, in an ethereal and spontaneous melody, he sang of love and friendship; of the weird, majestic, and awe-inspiring aspects of nature; and of wine, which exhilarated his spirits. His friend and rival Tu Fu was a poet of different mold, conscientious and painstaking in his efforts to achieve startling realism in particular lines of his verse. A humanitarian and historian, Tu Fu recorded faithfully and intimately his wordly attachments, his family affections, and an infinite love for his fellow men. The realism of Tu Fu's work influenced another T'ang poet, Po Chü-i (772–846), who conceived of poetry as a vehicle for criticism of life and for satire on the evils of society. In later centuries this moralistic tendency, developed by other poets, was broadened to include didactic and philosophical disquisitions, but in general Chinese poetry remained essentially lyrical.

Rhyme had always been a typical feature of Chinese poetry but the verse forms did not become well established until this period of the T'ang poets. The typical poem of the T'ang period has a regular five-word or seven-word line, with the rhyme falling on the even lines and occasionally on the first line. There are, however, two major styles in this poetry: the ancient style, characterized by simpler language and less rigid versification; and the "modern" style, requiring balanced structure, specific arrangement of poetic tones, or voice modulations (see CHINESE LANGUAGE), and a definite number of lines, either four or eight. Since the number of lines was so limited, the modern style emphasized compactness and suggestiveness in poetic expression. It is this allusive and often cryptic style with which readers of English translations are most familiar.

In the T'ang period there emerged also a new poetic form, the *tz'u*. Though each *tz'u* may have lines of varying length, the number of lines as well as their lengths are fixed according to a definite rhyming and tonal pattern. The writing of *tz'u*, which is like putting new words to old popular melodies, requires a great deal of skill.

Chinese prose also prospered in the T'ang dynasty. Chief among the T'ang prose masters was Han Yü (768–824), who advocated a return to simple and straightforward writing in the classical style. This was a reaction to the artificial, euphemistic prose of his time. As a result of Han Yü's efforts, political and philosophical treatises, informal essays, and tales of the marvelous (*ch'uan-ch'i*) were all written in the neoclassical style. The tales of the marvelous represent some of the early specimens of Chinese literary fiction. Although written in sophisticated prose, they provided materials used by the popular entertainers of later periods.

The first group of tales written designedly in the vernacular tradition appeared in the T'ang period. In an attempt to spread their religion, Buddhist preachers wrote stories for the common people in colloquial language. Thus was evolved a form of narrative known as *pien-wen*, sometimes translated as "popularization", which marked the beginning of popular fiction, as opposed to folk tales, in China.

Although few examples of the ancient tradition of storytelling had been preserved, a revival of interest in the art took place in the 11th century and it was practiced with greatly improved skill. During the medieval period storytelling became a popular form of entertainment, and the stories told by the professional entertainers, each of whom specialized in a certain type, not only were written down but also were printed in story books (*hua-pen*).

Miming, singing, and dancing had existed from ancient times, but the drama proper developed only during the later Middle Ages. As early as the T'ang period, however, actors had been prominent among the popular entertainers and were organized into professional companies. Theaters were built that could accommodate as many as several thousand people, to whom professional actors offered their wares. Some of the best entertainers might be summoned to perform also in the houses of the wealthy and noble. In later times a number of wealthy families had their own theatrical companies. The court generally supported private troupes of actors, musicians, and dancers to give special performances for the emperor and his guests on festival occasions.

Music, dancing, puppet shows, and shadow plays shared in popularity with the regular drama among the Chinese theatergoers. In the 12th century the "variety play" (*tsa-chü*) was created; it was so named because of its combination of various dramatic elements such as the comic, the lyrical, the musical, and the choreographic. This type of early play was soon forgotten and supplanted by the more mature and sophisticated drama of later times.

Modern Period. The modern period began with the growth of a vigorous vernacular literature which preceded by several centuries the appearance of modern vernacular literatures in the West. The growth of Chinese fiction and drama during the Yüan (Mongol) dynasty (1234–1368) may have been due to the weakening of the Confucian grip on Chinese letters after the abolition of the literary examination, which had become so stereotyped that it stifled creativeness. Although the examination was afterward resumed and the literary tradition was further strengthened in later centuries, vernacular literature continued to develop through the modern period until it finally coalesced with the main currents of a new and more inclusive literary movement in the early days of the 20th century.

Since the 13th century Chinese drama has followed a pattern of local development, with the most popular of local dramas assuming national importance. The Yüan drama, essentially a creation of northern China, relies upon northern dialect in dialogue and song. The lute is the chief instrument used, and the songs, which constitute the poetic portion of the play and are generally considered more important than the dialogues, are written in the *ch'ü*, a new poetic form more flexible and expressive than the previously mentioned *shih* of the Han period and the *tz'u* of the T'ang period. A Yüan play has four parts, corresponding to the four acts of a Western play; there is often an additional short act which serves as a prelude and sometimes as a sort of interlude. The Yüan drama is therefore about the length of an Elizabethan play, and, like it, essentially popular in nature and poetic in style.

With the shift of the economic center to the Yangtze River valley, during the Ming dynasty (1368–1644), the southern drama began to overshadow the northern in popularity. It differs from the northern drama not only in form but also in the kinds of song melodies and musical instruments used, chiefly the flute. The southern play has thirty to fifty sections and takes much longer to perform. In particular, the southern drama known as K'un ch'ü, which developed in the Soochow district, became very popular between the 15th and the 19th centuries, when it was challenged by a new northern drama (Ching hsi) which flourished in Peking. This new drama, however, is entirely different from the Yüan. It lacks specific literary quality and is notable mostly for its acting, singing, and dancing.

In the 14th century the art of fiction reached a new height in China. Two of the earliest Chinese novels of this period, *San-kuo chih* ("Romance of the Three Kingdoms"), a historical novel of wars and warriors, and *Shui-hu chuan* ("Water Margin", known to the West as *All Men Are Brothers*), a novel of the adventures of bandit-heroes, may be called the prose epics of the Chinese people. As composite works of folk art created from oral tradition and bearing the stamp of genius of a number of writers, they differ from the works of individual novelists. Generally, Chinese novels of both types are immensely long, vast in scope, and vivid in characterization and description. All these characteristics are found also in *Hung-lou meng* ("Dream of the Red Chamber"), a realistic domestic novel by Ts'ao Hsueh-ch'in (1715?–63). It depicts in exuberant detail the prosperity, decline, and fall of a rich official family of the 18th century.

Many important collections of short stories appeared in the 17th century. The collections consisted either of compilations handed down from an earlier period or of works by contemporary writers. Like the novels, the stories are colloquial in style and realistic in presentation, giving a faithful and intimate picture of Chinese society. The most popular anthology is *Chin-ku ch'i-kuan* ("Marvelous Tales of the Past and Present"), consisting of forty stories.

As the modern age progressed the vernacular tradition developed remarkably. Conventional literature, on the other hand, was less fruitful, although it continued to be cultivated by members of the scholarly gentry, some of whom were fine writers. Literary orthodoxy, was, however, no longer capable of producing more than stereotypes lacking in freshness and originality. This decline in the literary tradition continued until the beginning of the 20th century, when it became obvious to Chinese writers that they had to seek new inspiration for their creative efforts. Stimulated by the literature of the West and broadened in their literary horizons, Chinese writers, led by Hu Shih (1891–   ), started a literary movement known as the Chinese Renaissance in an attempt to combine the vernacular heritage of their own literature with traditions of the West.

After fifty years of experiment in this direction, contemporary Chinese literature has come of age and shown considerable creative vitality. During the first half of the 20th century Chinese writers used literature as a mirror to reflect the seamy side of life, as a weapon to combat the evils of society, and as a form of propaganda to spread the message of class struggle. By wielding their trenchant essays and stories like big sticks to attack traditional society, writers like Lu Hsün (real name Chow Shu-jen, 1881–1939) helped to advance the socialist revolution. But, although the spirit of Chinese literature changed, the background, characters, and events depicted remained typically Chinese.

CHINESE MUSIC, the body of vocal and instrumental music composed and played by the Chinese people. The nature and aims of Chinese music may best be understood in terms of the culture which produced it. For several thousand years that culture has been dominated by the teachings of the Chinese philosopher Confucius (q.v.), who conceived of music in the highest sense as a means of calming the passions and of dispelling unrest and lust, rather than as a form of amusement. It was also the traditional Chinese belief that sound influences the harmony of the universe. Consequently, for the Chinese absolute pitch (q.v.) held more meaning than it did for any other culture in the world; significantly, one of the most important duties of the first emperor of each new dynasty was to search out and establish the true standard of pitch. A result of this philosophical orientation was that until quite recently the Chinese despised music when performed for the purpose of entertainment; musical entertainers were relegated to an extremely low social status.

Melody is the predominant feature of Chinese music, and it is dictated by the sound inflections of the Chinese language. The tonal curve of Chinese melody corresponds, therefore, approximately to the tonal curve, or rising and falling pitch, characteristic of the spoken language. The inflections frequently give rise to extremely complicated melodic figurations. The same melodic patterns obtain in both vocal and instrumental music.

The composers of Chinese music usually employ scales quite different from the diatonic scale familiar to Western ears; as a result Chinese music tends to sound eerie and bizarre to Westerners. Most Chinese music is based on either of two scales, namely, the five-tone (pentatonic) scale, in which the notes *mi* and *fa* are separated by a minor third rather than by a semitone, or the seven-tone (heptatonic) scale, in which the note *fa* is raised. The pentatonic scale was employed in composing the refined, traditional music of past centuries. The heptatonic scale is used a great deal in folk music, notably that of northern China.

The Western concepts of harmony and polyphony are entirely alien to Chinese music. The scant harmony employed consists only of octaves, fourths, and fifths, but more frequently Chinese orchestras play in unison. Chinese rhythm is also dissimilar to that of Western music. Not only is it much freer, but often it is left to the discretion of the individual performer or ensemble.

Chinese musical instruments traditionally have been classified according to certain key materials used in their construction, namely metal, stone, silk, bamboo, gourd, clay, skin, and wood; of these, the stone and wood instruments are obsolete. The silk instrument, or *ch'in*, a kind of zither equipped at one time with silk strings, is still popular among a small circle of scholar-musicians. The ancient Chinese belief that music is meant not to amuse but to purify one's thoughts finds particular expression in the cult of the *ch'in*. A famous *ch'in* scholar once said, "Though the *ch'in* player's body be in a gallery or in a hall, his mind should dwell with the forests and streams."

History. Chinese music is as old as Chinese civilization and, like that civilization, it reached its zenith many centuries ago. Unfortunately most Chinese music has been lost; it is known to posterity mainly from literary records rather than from musical scores.

In the Chou dynasty (1122–222 B.C.), music was one of the four subjects which the sons of noblemen and princes were required to study, and the Office of Music at one time comprised more than 1400 people. During the Ch'in dynasty (221–207 B.C.) music was denounced as a wasteful pastime; almost all musical books, instruments, and manuscripts were ordered destroyed. Despite this severe setback, Chinese music experiencd a renaissance during the Han dynasty (206 B.C.-219 A.D.), when a special Bureau of Music was established to take charge of ceremonial music. During the reign of Ming-Ti (58–75 A.D.) the Han palace had three orchestras comprising in all 829 performers. One orchestra was used for religious ceremonies, another for royal archery contests, and a third for entertaining the royal banquets and harem.

During the T'ang dynasty (619–906) Chinese music reached its peak. Emperor T'ai-Tsung (597–649) had ten different orchestras, eight of which were made up of natives of various foreign tribes; all the royal performers and dancers appeared in their native costumes. The imperial court had also a huge outdoor band of nearly 1400 performers. A gradual decline in the quality of Chinese music took place subsequently. The often-quoted Chinese expression *"li yüeh lun wang"*, meaning "rituals and music have been lost", describes the feeling of those people who, during later centuries, longed for the lost musical art of the T'ang and other dynasties.

During the first half of the 20th century Chinese music was considerably influenced by the music of the West. Three major schools of thought arose in response to this influence. The first school aimed at reviving the old thousand-piece orchestras which once enchanted ancient princes and sages and opposed the invasion of Western music. The second school concerned itself almost exclusively with Western music. The last school of Chinese music took great pride in traditional Chinese musical culture, but did not hesitate to apply to it Western techniques of composition and performance.

During the 1950's Western influences penetrated Chinese music to an unprecedented extent. The Chinese Communist regime, established in 1949, gave special prominence to Russian music. Whether China can assimilate Western influence and still maintain a fundamentally Chinese musical culture remains an unanswered question.

CHINESE PHILOSOPHY, collective designation for the various schools of thought originated by Chinese scholars and sages. The history of Chinese philosophy extends from at least the 6th century B.C. to the present period. Many of the important works of Chinese philosophy became the sacred scriptures of the various religions practiced in China, particularly Confucianism, Taoism, and Buddhism. This article deals only with the nonreligious aspects of Chinese philosophy; for the relationship of the various systems to religious faith and practice, see the articles on the several religions.

Chinese philosophy is less systematic than that of the West, being predominantly a body of aphorisms and maxims about human relations and of cryptic utterances about the nature of reality. Although Chinese philosophy includes metaphysical and epistemological speculations, its primary concern is with man, his relations with others, his place in society. Its special genius lies in the profundity of its insights into social relations, which frequently exhibit subtleties and nuances unknown to Western thought.

The concern with man derives in large measure from the social conditions prevailing in China during the Chou dynasty (1122 B.C.-255 B.C.). By the 8th century B.C. the power of the house of Chou had waned; China was in a state of turmoil engendered by foreign invasions, agrarian revolts, and feudal strife. Under these circumstances thoughtful Chinese, including some of the rulers of the various feudal states into which China was divided, sought guidance in the conduct of their affairs. Their needs were met in part by wandering scholars who offered their services as officials and advisors to the various courts. Many of the scholars were shallow and opportunistic careerists seeking to advance themselves by their skill with words and in sophistical reasoning. However, many others were serious thinkers who were genuinely interested in developing and applying principles by which human affairs best might be regulated. Some of the serious thinkers founded academies and schools in which the particular principles they posited were taught and elaborated. Because of the large number and varying doctrine of the schools, the period is known in the history of Chinese philosophy as that of the Hundred Schools.

The most important of the schools was that founded by Confucius (q.v.), who served for a time as adviser to the court of Lu, a feudal state in what is now Shantung Province. Confucius and his followers attempted to formulate standards of righteous and cultivated behavior and of proper relations among the elements of society, e.g., between ruler and ruled, children and parents, husband and wife, living and dead. They insisted on ceremony as the basis of good relations, but emphasized that all relations must be imbued with *jen* (goodness) to have validity. They took the family, the basic unit of society, as their model for all social relationships. Thus, the ruler is conceived as the father of his subjects, the landlord as the father of his tenants, the employer as the father of his workers. The influence of Confucianism has been primarily responsible for the importance of the family and for the prevalence of paternalism and nepotism in Chinese life.

The two most prominent of the early Confucianists were Mencius (q.v.) and Hsün Tzŭ (about 300–235 B.C.). Mencius is best known for his penetrating insights into the minds of men; in fact, he anticipated some of the findings of present-day psychology. Hsün Tsŭ is important mainly for having established the Confucian canon and for having codified the teachings of Confucianism. Both scholars elaborated, and laid great stress upon, the classic doctrine, attributed to Duke Wen of Jou (fl. 11th cent. B.C.), of the mandate of Heaven. According to this doctrine, Heaven supports righteous sovereigns, and it is therefore wrong to rebel against them; but Heaven withdraws its support from evil and unworthy rulers. The success of a revolt thus proves that the mandate of Heaven has been withdrawn and transferred to a successor.

A rival school, called Taoism, was founded by the legendary sage Lao-tzu (q.v.). The aphorisms attributed to him are cryptic, paradoxical, and mystical in character and are subject therefore to varying interpretations. It is clear, however, that the Taoists taught men to "follow Nature" and warned against replacing the "Way of Nature with the Way of Man". They preferred a simple, primitive society in which government would do the least possible amount of governing and people would be left alone. Rejecting ceremonies, conventions, and all artificiality, the Taoists advocated a life of simplicity and spontaneity.

In the fugal development of Chinese philosophy, Taoism first sounded the countersubject to the Confucian subject. Confucianism is basically social; Taoism is naturalistic and individualistic. Confucianism is realistic and practical; Taoism is mystical and quietistic. Confucianism subordinates nature to man; Taoism subordinates man to nature.

Nonetheless, the two philosophies have much in common. Both reject metaphysical speculation and center their attention on humanity. The ideal of both is the sage who achieves a morally perfect life and, in doing so, helps bring about a more perfect society. Confucianism and Taoism are complementary rather than conflicting; each simply addresses itself to different aspects of the same fundamental humanism.

Among the other major schools of thought of the ancient period are Mohism, the yin-yang doctrine, logicism, and legalism. Mohism, founded by Mo Ti (fl. 5th and 4th centuries B.C.), taught obedience to the will of Heaven and to earthly rulers, universal love for all, and self-sacrifice for the commonweal. Mo Ti opposed elaborate ceremonies and all luxury and ostentation and urged that people be kept to the path of "universal love" by fear of punishment for deviating from it.

According to the yin-yang doctrine, elaborated by Dzou-Yen (fl. 4th century B.C.), all phenomena are the result of the interaction of two cosmic forces, the yin, or the passive force, and the yang, or the active force. The relations of night and day, shade and light, winter and summer, female and male, sorrow and joy, are all manifestations of the interplay of yin and yang. This concept became one of the most popular in Chinese thought.

The logicians specialized in analyzing philosophical concepts and in investigating the connection between symbol and reality. Their work exhibited great analytical subtlety, but the opposition of the other schools, which charged the logicians with deliberate sophistry, brought them into disrepute. Chinese philosophy thus was denied the benefits of what might have been a most valuable contribution.

The legalists, led by Shen Dao, Shen Buhai, and Shang Yang, all of whom flourished in the 4th century B.C., opposed abstract speculation and advocated a well-ordered society strictly controlled by law, force, rewards and punishments, and statecraft rather than by moral principles or moral suasion. Essentially opportunistic in their approach, they sought mainly to strengthen the state. Eventually legalism became the most powerful of the schools. With its help and guidance, the state of Ch'in gained control of China and started a new dynasty in 255 B.C. As a reward, the first Ch'in emperor gave the legalists a virtual monopoly in philosophy. In 213 B.C. almost all nonlegalist books were burned and the "Hundred Schools" were suppressed. However, in 206 B.C. the Ch'in dynasty was supplanted by the Han (206 B.C.-220 A.D.), and some of the old schools were revived.

After several decades of intense rivalry among the leading schools Confucianism finally emerged as the state doctrine in 136 B.C. From that time until 1906 the Confucian classics were the standard texts in schools, and government officials usually were selected by competitive examination based on those works. Thus, Confucianism dominated Chinese education, government, and society for some two thousand years.

Despite its triumph in 136 B.C., or perhaps because of it, Confucianism remained sterile for centuries. To gain prestige and influence, it absorbed and took credit for the notable doctrines of all other schools, including the Mohist, legalist, and yin yang. Frequently these doctrines were incompatible with those authentically Confucian; the result was a corruption of texts and a confusion of teaching. The most important preoccupation of the Confucianists during the period of sterility was an effort to reconcile the conflicting views of human nature of the early sages, Mencius and Hsün Tsŭ, who held respectively that human nature is basically good and that it is basically evil. The generally accepted conclusion among scholars was that human nature is fundamentally good, but that weaknesses

of the flesh, giving rise to bad desires, are the source of evil. Another solution, proposed by Han Yu (768–824), was the doctrine of the "three grades", i.e., that some men are born good, others are born neither good nor bad, and still others are born bad.

Meanwhile Buddhism had been introduced into China from India at about the beginning of the Christian Era and had been widely adopted as a religion by the common folk. In the 4th century Buddhist teachers began to propagate their philosophical doctrine in China. They were able to make that doctrine intelligible and attractive to Chinese students by presenting it in Taoist terms. In the following century an effort was made to teach the Buddhist doctrine in a fuller and more authentic way. However, the Indian concepts were not suited to the Chinese temperament. As the various schools of Indian Buddhism gradually fell into disfavor, Chinese scholars developed four indigenous schools of Buddhist thought. The Hua-yen and the T'ien T'ai schools, which entertained similar views, regarded the world of ideas and the material world as one and taught that all things are involved in each other. The Pure Land school propagated the doctrine that all persons possess Buddhalike attributes and that, by virtue of these attributes, all persons could be saved. The most important school of Chinese Buddhism is the Ch'an, or meditation, school (better known in the West by its Japanese designation, Zen Buddhism (q.v.). In this school sudden ineffable flashes of intuition are depended upon to resolve the paradoxes of existence. In place of rational thought, it urged upon its devotees the method of "directly pointing to the human mind, seeing one's own nature, and becoming Buddha in this very body". Zen Buddhism has won many adherents in the West, particularly since the end of World War II.

Buddhism is the final strand out of which the fabric of classic Chinese philosophy is woven. The three main schools of thought, Confucianism, Taoism, and Buddhism, profoundly influenced and modified each other. Confucianism influenced Buddhism toward concern for the whole of society and acceptance of the doctrine of the inherent goodness of human nature. Taoist mysticism and quietism, especially the doctrine of tranquility of mind, contributed much of Zen Buddhism. Indeed, Zen and other schools of Chinese Buddhism absorbed Taoist philosophy to such an extent that Taoism eventually ceased to exist as a separate philosophical discipline and became only a popular religion.

Finally, under Buddhist influence Confucianism was transformed into Neo-Confucianism, which dominated Chinese thought from the 11th to the 20th century.

Neo-Confucianism arose in response to the challenge of Buddhist metaphysics, which exposed the lack of a metaphysical foundation for Confucian ethics. Neo-Confucianism took two main forms, rationalism and idealism. The basic concept in both is *li* (principle), understood as inherent in all phenomena. Li is the Confucian counterpart of the Buddhist void, which the Confucianists attacked as vague and abstract.

Rationalist Neo-Confucianism reached its peak in the work of Chu Hsi (1130–1200), regarded by scholars as the greatest of Neo-Confucianists. He taught that there are two fundamental realities, li and *ch'i* (matter-energy). Li is the unifying force, connecting all things, giving them meaning. Ch'i is the substance of things; it serves to differentiate and individualize things, and therefore to make them inaccessible to reason, which can understand only uniformities. The world then is a well-ordered system governed by the harmonious interaction of li and ch'i. The path of wisdom and of morality lies in pursuing li to the utmost, searching for it behind the manifold manifestations of ch'i. Chu Hsi had a large following, and his interpretation of Confucianism was adopted officially as standard in the 15th century.

Opposition to rationalist Neo-Confucianism arose in Chu's own time, notably in the works of Lu Hsiang Shan (1130–93), founder of the idealist school of Neo-Confucianism. Insisting that li was not in things but in the mind, Lu propounded the dictum: "The universe is my mind, my mind is the universe." Instead of Chu's "path of study and inquiry" into the principle underlying things, he urged reliance upon understanding and exercising of one's own moral nature.

Idealistic Neo-Confucianism reached its zenith in the teachings of Wang Yang-ming (1472–1529), who held that man's mind is inherently good, that it is identical with li, and that one can therefore intuitively know the good. Positing unity of thought and action, he taught that to know the good is to practice it. In his emphasis on intuition, Wang reflected the influence of Zen Buddhism. Yet Wang was not a meditative monk, but an active statesman who urged courageous and forthright action to meet the crisis of his time. His teachings served as the inspiration to a dynamic approach to life for about 150 years, but then lost its vitality.

In revolt against the speculative tendencies of both rationalist and idealist Neo-Confucianism, Yen Yuan (1635–1704) and Li Kung (1659–1733) stressed learning through practice rather than thought. They thus helped to liberate the Chinese mind from its preoccupation with speculative philosophy. Another revolt against Neo-Confucianism was initiated by Tai Tung-yuan (1723–77). Whereas both rationalist and idealist Neo-Confucianism had regarded principle as good and desire as evil, Tai argued that both were good when in harmony with each other. Conceiving the universe as an unending process of creation, he held that there could be no creation, whether in human society or in the world of nature, without desire.

During the ensuing centuries Chinese philosophy, becoming increasingly humanistic, emphasized the importance of experience and action and treated the Confucian classics less as Holy Writ than as records of human experience. The greatest Confucian of recent times, K'ang Yu-wei (1858–1927), hailed Confucius as a reformer and, in his name, obtained (1898) imperial sanction, which was soon voided, of a series of far-reaching political reforms.

In recent decades the main problem for Chinese philosophy has been that of coming to terms with Western thought without losing its own identity. The first important contacts with Western thought had occurred during the T'ang dynasty (618–907), when visitors from all parts of the civilized world mingled freely at the imperial court. Subsequently the Jesuits exerted some influence on Chinese thought, particularly in the 16th and 17th centuries, but their influence was transitory. Not until late in the 19th century did Western thinking begin seriously to affect the course of Chinese philosophy. The impact of Western philosophy became especially marked after the fall of the Ching dynasty in 1911. Numerous works by Western philosophers, such as the Germans Immanuel Kant, Friedrich Nietzsche, and Karl Marx, the Frenchman Henri Bergson, and the Americans William James and John Dewey, were translated into Chinese and studied assiduously by Chinese students. During the 1920's and the 1930's Chinese scholars began to revise and reconstruct the classic philosophies, particularly rationalistic and idealistic Neo-Confucianism, in the light of Western logic and metaphysics. Many experts, both Western and Chinese, saw much originality and great promise in this development. Meanwhile Marxism had grown in strength and influence in China.

After the Communist seizure of power in 1949 it became the official philosophy of the Chinese state, thus overshadowing all non-Marxist philosophies, whether Chinese or Western. Marxism soon won a measure of popularity in China because, like all of Chinese classic philosophy, it is centered in man and society.

CHINKIANG, port and city of Kiangsu Province, China, on the Yangtze R. and the Grand Canal, about 40 miles E. of Nanking. Because the Yangtze is filling with silt at Chinkiang, and commercial use of the Grand Canal has diminished, the importance of the port is declining; but it still serves as a distributing center for imported goods. Chinkiang was the capital of Kiangsu Province from 1928 to 1949. Pop. (1953 est.) 201,400.

CHINNAMPO or **NAMPO,** seaport of Korea, on the w. coast, about 25 miles s.w. of Heijo, of which it is the port. After the defeat of Japan in World War II, Chinnampo was included in the Soviet zone of occupation of Korea. Pop. (1948) 82,162.

CHINOOK, the name given in the northwestern part of the United States and western Canada to a strong, warm, and dry south or west wind which comes from the Rocky Mountains. Similar in character to the Swiss *Föhn* winds, it is caused by compression of the air due to descent after crossing the mountains. In early spring it melts the snows very quickly, but its effects are observable only in the valleys. The name is derived from the Chinook Indians, in whose territory the phenomenon was first observed.

CHINOOKS, a tribe of Indians, now nearly extinct, on the Columbia R., on the w. coast of North America, but gathered into small reservations in Washington and Oregon. They number about 600. European traders found their language difficult to learn and to pronounce, and developed the so-called *Chinook jargon,* consisting of words from French, English, and Nootka, Chinook, and other Indian tongues.

CHINOOK SALMON. See SALMON.

CHINQUAPIN. See CHESTNUT.

CHINWANGTAO, town and seaport of Hopeh Province, China, on Liaotung Gulf, about 130 miles N.E. of Tientsin, which it serves as a winter port when the Tientsin harbor is ice-bound. Chinwangtao was built by the Kailan Mining Administration as a shipping point for the coal mined in the Kaiping coalfields about 100 miles in the interior. In 1901 the town was opened to foreign trade. It is one of the chief coal-shipping centers of the Far East. Pop. (1953 est.) 186,800.

CHIOGGIA, seaport and episcopal see in Venezia Province, Italy, about 18 m. by sea s. of Venice, and 35 m. by rail N.E. of Rovigo. It is built on piles and is surrounded by the Lombardo Ship Canal. The Vena Canal, which is crossed by nine bridges, cuts it in two, and it is connected with the mainland by a stone bridge, 800 feet long, with 43 arches. The cathedral dates from 1633, the Board of Trade building from 1322. The inhabitants are known for their quaint customs, costumes, and dialect, and the fisheries have long been important. The other principal industries are flax spinning, shipbuilding, and the manufacture of sails, bricks, candles, and lace. Although the name Chioggia comes from the Roman *Fossa Claudia,* it is built on what was probably the site of the ancient Roman town of Portus Aedro. In 1110 Chioggia became subject to Venice. In the naval war of 1377–80 between Genoa and her allies and Venice, Chioggia was taken by the Genoese and Hungarians in 1379, but was recaptured by the Venetians in 1380. Pop. (1951) 47,876 .

CHIOS (Gr. *Khios*), an island and department of Greece, in the Ægean Sea, about 8 m. off the w. coast of Asiatic Turkey. It is about 30 miles from north to south, and 8 to 15 miles wide. The capital and chief town is Chios (pop. in 1951, 24,361), a seaport on the E. coast. In the north the island is mountainous, but in the south the land is open and fertile. Gum mastic, from which a liqueur is made, and wine are the principal products of the island. Other products include olives, figs, and oranges. Coastal trade is an important economic activity. Industry includes the mining of antimony and calamite, marble quarrying, and tanning.

The island contains relics of ancient times when it was an important Greek state, the home of noted poets and sculptors, and a participant in the wars which marked the history of ancient Greece and Rome. Chios was occupied by the Seljuk Turks in the 11th century A.D., and later became a possession, successively, of the Venetians, Genoese, and Turks. During the Balkan War of 1912 it again became a Greek possession. Area of department, 348 sq.m.; pop. (1961) 62,223.

CHIPMUNK (originally *chitmunk,* from Algonquian Indian, *atchitamon,* "headfirst", from its scurrying habits), or HACKEE, common name for American rodents of the genera *Tamias* and *Eutamias* which are intermediate between the common or tree squirrels and the ground squirrels or spermophiles. The eastern chipmunk is *T. striatus;* the western chipmunks are divided into several species, of which *E. quadrivittatus* is the commonest.

The chipmunk is one of the most familiar animals in North America, living in stone walls and stumps and feeding on a wide variety of foodstuffs, including grain, nuts, birds' eggs, and insects. It is frequently seen along old fences and hedgerows, especially near woods, and lives in a burrow, where it stores for winter use large quantities of such food as small nuts and acorns, and where it remains in a nest until spring, frequently appearing, however, on warm days during winter.

CHIPPAWA, village in Welland Co., Ont., Canada, on the Niagara R., about 5 miles s. of Niagara Falls. At Chippawa during the War of 1812, on July 5, 1814, an American force of 1900, under General Jacob Brown, defeated 2100 British troops, commanded by Gen. Phineas Riall. Pop. (1961) 3256.

CHIPPENDALE, THOMAS (about 1718–79), English cabinetmaker, born in Yorkshire, the son of John Chippendale, a carver and picture-frame maker. He established a factory in London in 1749 and became noted for the furniture he designed and manufactured. The Chippendale style combines solidity with grace, and elaborate decoration with delicacy. Among the articles of furniture he made were beds, settees, mirrors, bookcases, escritoires, and tables; he was most famous for his chairs (see CHAIR). In 1754 he published *The Gentleman and Cabinet Maker's Director*, a book containing 160 engravings of furniture designs, which subsequently were widely copied and imitated. Chippendale is generally regarded as the most important of English furniture makers. After his death his furniture business was carried on by his son, Thomas Chippendale II.

CHIPPEWA. See OJIBWAY.

CHIQUITO (Sp. diminutive of *chico*, "small"), a group of South American Indian tribes constituting a distinct linguistic stock, living between the headwaters of the Mamoré and the Paraguay rivers, in eastern Bolivia. They are of small stature, a possible explanation of their name.

CHIRICAHUA NATIONAL MONUMENT, a national monument in Cochise Co., S.E. Arizona. It was established in 1924, and embraces an area of over 10,500 acres in three canyons. The region is noted for its fantastic rock formations, among which are gigantic monoliths of rhyolite. Prehistoric pictographs have been found in the natural caves of one of the canyons.

CHIRICO, GIORGIO DI (1888–   ), Italian painter, born in Greece. He studied art in Athens, in Munich, and in Italy. Early in his career he was strongly influenced by the allegorical works of the Swiss painter Arnold Böcklin (1827–1901). In Di Chirico's most important and effective period, dating from about 1908 to 1917, he painted landscapes of empty city squares and still lifes of illogically juxtaposed objects, creating a sinister, disturbing mood. He achieved this effect in part by means of unusual lights and distorted shadows and by the barrenness of his canvasses, which causes the few visible objects to assume heightened, even menacing significance. Among the representative works of this period are "Nostalgia of the Infinite" (Museum of Modern Art, New York City) and "Melancholy and Mystery of a Street" (private collection, New York City). In 1919 Di Chirico's work became more naturalistic and conventional, but he resumed the haunting style of his first period in 1925. He then produced a series of scenes dominated by faceless, mannequinlike creatures, many holding ancient temples in their laps.

Di Chirico is considered one of the outstanding Italian painters of the 20th century. He gave incalculable impetus to the surrealist movement, and deeply influenced many con-

Balanced rock formation popularly known as Punch and Judy, in Chiricahua National Monument in southeastern Arizona
National Park Service

temporary artists, including the French painter Yves Tanguy and the Spanish painter Salvador Dali. Di Chirico's other well-known works include "Conversation" (Museum of Modern Art, New York City) and "Anguish of Departure" (Albright Art Gallery, Buffalo, N.Y.).

CHIROMANCY. See PALMISTRY.

CHIROPODY. See PODIATRY.

CHIROPRACTIC, system for curing human ailments by manipulation of the spine, for the purpose of adjusting subluxations (dislocations) of the vertebrae. This system is based on the theory that all disease is traceable to organic malfunctions of the nerves, which in turn are due to various nerves being squeezed by subluxations. Chiropractic practice includes the use of all recognized diagnostic methods and is conducted with regard for environmental, nutritional, and psychotherapeutic factors. It includes various procedures designed to restore or maintain normal nerve function.

Chiropractic was founded about 1895 by Daniel David Palmer (1845–1913), a Canadian who had been practicing magnetic healing in the United States. In 1898 he opened the Palmer School of Chiropractic in Davenport, Iowa. Eight chiropractic colleges in the United States, each offering at least four years of post-high-school training, were accredited by the National Council on Education in 1962. The practice of chiropractic is today accorded official recognition in most of the States, although not generally given the same status as the practice of medicine. Headquarters of the National Chiropractic Association are located in Webster City, Iowa. In 1962 the World Chiropractic Congress was formed.

CHIROPTERA. See BAT.

CHIRU, or PANTHALOPS, a species of antelope (q.v.), *Pantholops hodgsoni,* inhabiting the pine forests and elevated open plains of Tibet, in regions bordering on the snow line. It is about 5 feet in length, and 3 feet high at the shoulder. The color of the animal is a pronounced reddish fawn with some black, and the coat is thick and woolly. Like its relative the saiga, the chiru has a peculiarly swollen nose.

CHISHOLM, JESSE (1806?–68), American pioneer trader and interpreter, born in Tennessee. His mother was a Cherokee Indian. In his youth, he accompanied one of the Cherokee migrations westward, eventually settling at Camp Holmes, on the Canadian River. Fluent in 14 Indian languages, he acted as interpreter and mediator at numerous conferences between the Federal Government and the Indian tribes of the Great Plains, among whom he was active as a trader. After a brief period as a representative of the Confederacy during the American Civil War, he settled among Indian refugees in Kansas. He subsequently moved westward, settling near the mouth of the Arkansas River. In 1865 he made a trading trip southward from this region to the upper Washita R., in what is now Oklahoma. The route which he traveled soon became famous as the Chisholm trail, which figured prominently in the development of the cattle-raising industry on the western plains.

CHISHOLM CASE, in American history, a legal proceeding which led, through the enactment of the 11th Amendment to the U.S. Constitution, to a limitation on the jurisdiction of the Federal courts. Initiated in 1792 in the United States Supreme Court, the case was brought against the State of Georgia by Alexander Chisholm, a citizen of South Carolina, in connection with an inheritance of which he was the legatee. The Supreme Court took jurisdiction under Article III, Section 2, of the Constitution, which conferred jurisdiction on the Federal courts in cases between a State and citizens of another State. The State of Georgia challenged both the right of citizens to sue State governments and the jurisdiction of the Supreme court in such cases. A Supreme Court ruling affirmed the Court's jurisdiction in cases of that type. On March 5, 1794, Congress passed the 11th Amendment, which was ratified by the States, and was declared in force January 8, 1798. It removed from the jurisdiction of the Federal courts those cases in which citizens of one State are the plaintiffs and the government of another State is the defendant. The Amendment left intact the jurisdiction of the Federal courts in cases in which the government of a State is the plaintiff and the citizen of another State is the defendant. See COURTS IN THE UNITED STATES.

CHISWICK. See BRENTFORD AND CHISWICK.

CHITA, a Region of the Russian Soviet Federated Socialist Republic, in S.E. Siberia. The principal towns include the Regional administrative center Chita (pop. in 1959, 171,000), through which the railway from the U.S.S.R. to Manchuria passes; Arbagar; Chernov; Nerchinsk; and Petrovsk. Much of the territory of the region, which consists principally of high tableland, is enclosed by the Argun and Shilka rivers, which flow in a generally northward direction and converge to form the Amur River. In the fertile valleys, three quarters of the cultivated area is devoted to the raising of wheat and oats. Other crops include rye, hay, and flax. Cattle, sheep, and pigs are raised, and butter and other dairy products are produced. The forests are worked for lumber and are a source of furs.

The mineral resources of the Region include brown coal (lignite) and lead; iron, tin, and tungsten ores; molybdenum; arsenic compounds; precious stones; and gold. Industry in Chita Region, highly developed under the first three Five Year Plans of the Soviet government, includes the smelting of 65% of all the tin produced annually in the Soviet Union; coal mining at Arbagar, Chernov, and Nerchinsk; metalworking at Nerchinsk; the production of iron, steel, and machine tools at Chita and Petrovsk; flour milling; woodworking; and the manufacture of leather goods. As a result the population increased by 73% from 1926 to 1939. Area, 168,200 sq.m.; pop. (1959) 1,039,000.

CHITON, a common name for marine mollusks, of the order Polyplacophora, particularly those of the genus *Chiton*. The shells are boat shaped and consist of a median series of symmetrical plates folding over each other and implanted in the mantle, the marginal zone of which is studded with spicules. The chitons are limpetlike in habits. Only very small species are found on the Atlantic coast, but larger species, 3 to 4 inches in length, are found in Florida and the Gulf of Mexico. The genus *Cryptochiton*, 8 or 10 inches in length, is found on the California coast.

CHITRAL, name of a feudatory mountain State and of its capital, in the province of West Pakistan, Pakistan. Chitral State borders on Afghanistan. In the 18th century, it was dominated by the Chinese, and for a time was an important Buddhist center. The capital, situated on the Kunar or Chitral River, about 20 miles N.E. of the Afghan border, is noted chiefly as the scene of a struggle, in 1895, between a besieged British force and Chitrali hillmen, in which the native hillmen were defeated. Area of State, 4000 sq.m.; pop. (1961) 113,057.

CHITTAGONG, headquarters and port of Chittagong District, East Pakistan, Pakistan. The city is situated on several small hills, on the Karnaphuli R., 12 m. from its mouth on the Bay of Bengal, and is the terminus of the Assam-Bengal railroad. The district is a long, narrow strip lying between the Bay of Bengal and the hill tracts of Chittagong and Arakan. The city was an important commercial center under the Portuguese, and

came into possession of the British East India Company, with Bengal proper, in 1760–65. Originally a part of Arakan, it was claimed 60 years later by the Burmese Emperor, as a dependency of that territory—a claim which constituted one of the grounds of the War of 1824. Following the lapse of British paramountcy in India, in 1947, and as a result of a provincial plebiscite in Bengal, in that year, the district and city of Chittagong were included in East Bengal, Pakistan. Agriculture is the chief industry of the district; its products include rice, jute, gunny, tea, and hides, which are exported through the city of Chittagong. Area of district, 2750 sq.m.; pop. (1961) 2,982,931. Pop. of city (1961) 364,205.

CHIVALRY, in the Middle Ages the body of customs and ideals relating to the duties and privileges of knighthood. It owed its development partly to feudal usages, and partly to the Church, which adopted and altered the customs of chivalry to further its own control of society. See FEUDALISM.

According to the medieval conception of chivalry, no one was born a knight (q.v.). The candidate was sent, at the age of about seven, to act as page or valet in the household of a knight. There he obtained his education, and when old enough became a squire. The duty of the squire was to attend the knight in battle or in tournament, to care for his horse and weapons, and to act as his aid. In time the squire might be made a knight. At first the distinction could be conferred by any knight; later the monarchs claimed the sole right to confer knighthood. The age when the squire became a knight varied; there are cases where the honor was conferred on boys of 10 or 11, but later it was usually deferred until at least the age of 21. At the end of the 12th century, chivalry was influenced by the romances of Arthur, Charlemagne, and other famous heroes. Manners became less brutal, and a spirit of knight-errantry prevailed. It became the fashion to be rash, imprudent, and extravagant in conduct. The *Orlando* of Ariosto and Cervantes' *Don Quixote* have made familiar the follies of declining chivalry. Chivalry was at its height in the 12th century, in the 14th was declining rapidly, and in the 15th was thoroughly decadent. Knight and squire gradually became mere titles of honor which might be hereditary.

CHIVE, or CIVE, a plant, *Allium schoenoprasum,* of the Lily family. It is a member of the same genus as the leek and onion, a perennial, ½ to 1 foot in height, with very small, flat, clustered bulbs forming a tuft. The radical leaves are tubular, tapering, and nearly as long as the leafless flowering stem, which is terminated by a hemispherical, many-flowered umbel of bluish-red or flesh-colored flowers. A wild variety of this plant grows on the banks of rivers, and in marshy or occasionally flooded places in the middle latitudes of Europe and Asia, and on the northern borders of the United States. Chives are commonly cultivated in kitchen gardens, and are used for flavoring soups and stews and for embellishing salads. Their properties are very similar to those of the onion. The part used is the young leaves, which bear repeated cutting during the season.

CHIVERS, THOMAS HOLLEY (1809–58), American poet, born near Washington, Ga. Between 1840 and 1849 he was associated with Edgar Allan Poe. After Poe's death (1849) the fact that Chiver's *Eonchs of Ruby* (1851) resembled the poetry of Poe caused critics to accuse Chivers of plagiarism. In turn, Chivers charged that Poe had plagiarized from him. Some modern critics believe that Poe's *Ulalume* and *The Raven* were influenced by Chiver's work, especially by his poem *Isadore.* Among Chiver's writings are the books of verse *The Path of Sorrow* (1832) and *The Lost Pleiad* (1845), the poetic drama *Conrad and Eudora* (1834), and the prose work *Search After Truth* (1848).

CHKALOV, now **ORENBURG,** name of a Region and of its administrative center, in the Russian Soviet Federated Socialist Republic. The eastern part of the Region constitutes the eastern extremity of Europe. The Region is hilly and consists of semi-desert steppes, made arable only by intensive fertilizing. The valleys of the principal rivers, the Ural and the Sakmara, are fertile. Wheat and sunflower seeds are the principal crops. In the Region cattle, horses, sheep, and goats are raised; meat, milk, honey, and wool are produced; and copper is mined.

The city, situated on the Ural River at its confluence with the Or, about 200 miles s.w. of Magnitogorsk, is an important industrial center. It contains railway repair shops, sawmills, breweries, and factories for the production of metal goods, bricks, frozen meat, cattle products, sheepskin, and bristles. The city developed around a fort, erected in 1735, during the struggle of the Czarist government against the Bashkir and Kirghiz peoples of the surrounding regions. During the revolution of 1917 the city was the scene of considerable fighting. Area of Region, 47,400 sq.m.; pop. (1959 est.) 929,000. Pop. of city (1959 est.) 267,000.

CHLOË, a pretty, sportive shepherdess in the Greek romance *Daphnis and Chloë,* by Longus. She has become the stock idyllic heroine. The name and character appear in Sidney's *Arcadia,* in Fletcher's *Faithful Shepherdess,* in Prior's poems, and elsewhere.

CHLORIDES, the salts of hydrochloric acid (q.v.).

CHLORINE (Gr. *chloros,* "green"), an element, symbol Cl, at. no. 17, at. wt. 35.457, m. p. — 102° C. (— 152° F.), b. p. — 35° C. (— 31° F.). At ordinary temperatures it is a greenish-yellow gas which may be readily liquefied, an absolute pressure of 100 lbs. per sq. in. sufficing at 20°C. (68°F.). The gas has a strong, irritating odor and is a violent poison; it was the first substance used as a poison gas in World War I, but was soon replaced by more lethal substances (see GAS WARFARE).

Although free chlorine does not occur in nature, its compounds are among the commonest minerals, and it is the 12th most abundant element in the earth's crust.

Chlorine compounds have been known since earliest historic times inasmuch as sodium chloride, common salt, is necessary to the maintenance of life in both man and animals. Elementary chlorine was first isolated by the Swedish chemist K. W. Scheele in 1774; Scheele, however, thought that this greenish gas was a compound, and it was not until 1810 that the English chemist Sir Humphry Davy proved that it was an element, and gave it its present name.

Chlorine is an active element, reacting with water, organic compounds, and many metals. Three oxides have been prepared: Cl_2O, ClO_2, and Cl_2O_7. Chlorine will not burn in air, but it will support the combustion of many substances; an ordinary paraffin candle, for example, will burn in chlorine with a smoky flame. Chlorine and hydrogen may be kept together in the dark, but react with explosive violence in the presence of light. Chlorine solutions in water are familiar in the home as bleaching agents.

In addition to chlorine compounds, which are produced in large quantities, almost 1,000,-000 tons of free chlorine are produced annually in the U.S.; during World War II about 1,-200,000 tons were produced each year. Most of this chlorine is produced as a by-product of the manufacture of sodium hydroxide (caustic soda) by the electrolysis of salt, the remainder as a by-product of other electrolytic processes. Most chlorine is sold as a liquid, which is regularly shipped in special tank cars. The pulp and paper industry consumes two thirds of all the chlorine produced, while one quarter of the production goes to the textile industry and for sanitation.

CHLOROFORM, the name given to trichloromethane, $CHCl_3$, because of its supposed relation to formic acid; analogous names have been given to iodoform, bromoform, and fluoroform. It is a colorless liquid, half again as dense as water and of about the same viscosity; it has a heavy, ethereal odor and a burning sweetness of taste, being about 40 times as sweet as cane sugar. It is almost insoluble in water, but is freely miscible with organic solvents, being itself an important solvent for gums, resins, fats, elements such as sulfur and iodine, and a wide variety of organic compounds. Its m.p. is $-82°F.$ $(-63°C.)$; its b.p. is $142°F.$ $(61°C.)$.

Chloroform may be prepared in several ways: by the action of chlorine on methane, which yields an impure product; by the action of bleaching powder on acetone, a convenient laboratory method too expensive for commercial use; by the action of chlorine on alcohol, the former industrial method; or by the action of iron and acid on carbon tetrachloride, the principal current industrial method.

Chloroform was discovered in 1831, and in 1847 was used as an anesthetic in one of the first experiments on surgical anesthesia. It is an efficient general anesthetic, and has the advantage (as compared to ether) of being noninflammable. However, in the presence of light it tends to decompose, yielding the highly poisonous compound phosgene; and even when pure it causes fatal cardiac paralysis in about one out of 3000 cases, so that it is seldom used today for anesthesia. It is occasionally used in medicine for internal administration as an antispasmodic and carminative, and for external application as a constituent of liniments.

CHLOROMYCETIN. See ANTIBIOTIC.

CHLOROPHYCEAE, or ISOKONTAE, one of the four classes of algae (q.v.). They usually contain chlorophyll and no other pigment, so that their appearance justifies their common name, "green algae". The group includes the simplest algae, probably the forms from which the higher plants have been derived. The class is divided by scientists into six to eight orders, of which Volvocales, Protococcales, and Confervales are the most important.

The most primitive of the green algae are the aquatic Volvocales, which are distinguished from all other green algae by the fact that the vegetative cells have cilia and are therefore motile. The forms of Volvocales range from isolated cells to complex spherical colonies. The Protococcales include a very heterogeneous assemblage of forms and are evidently closely related to the Volvocales. They occur mainly in fresh water and range from an extreme aquatic habitat to occurrence in moist places, such as tree trunks or shaded earth. They differ from the Volvocales in the fact that the vegetative cells have no cilia and are therefore quiescent. Their range of form is also from a solitary cell to a complex colony, the water net being an extreme expression of colony formation. The Confervales are also a very artificial assemblage, including aquatic and usually filamentou forms. All of them produce swimming spores and have some form of sexual reproduction.

CHLOROPHYLL, a green pigment present in most plants. It is usually associated with other plant pigments, particularly xanthophyll and carotene. In some small plants, chlorophyll is distributed throughout the protoplasm of the plant cell, but in most plants it is restricted to certain definite portions of the protoplasm called chloroplasts.

In the presence of sunlight, a plant is able to use chlorophyll to combine carbon dioxide with water, producing starch and oxygen. This process is known as photosynthesis (q.v.), and is the ultimate source from which is produced all the food consumed by every plant and animal. Chlorophyll is absent from some plants, notably the fungi and a few flowering plants such as the Indian pipe. Such plants, since they cannot manufacture their own food, must be parasitic (drawing their food from another living organism) or saprophytic (drawing their food from the bodies of dead organisms). Chlorophyll is never found in animals (except in minute plants living within the animals) and animals must therefore subsist on plants or on other animals.

The amount of chlorophyll in the leaves of flowering plants is generally from 0.2 to 1.0 gram per square meter of surface (one ounce for every 34 to 170 square yards). It is constantly being formed and destroyed within the plant, and is formed only in the presence of sunlight, so that a plant such as celery may be "blanched" (bleached) by keeping it in the dark for a few weeks. Chlorophyll is destroyed by excessive light, and plants may also be blanched in this way.

Chemically chlorophyll consists of two compounds: chlorophyll a, $C_{55}H_{72}O_5N_4Mg$, m.p. about 150°C. (302°F.); and chlorophyll b, $C_{55}H_{70}O_6N_4Mg$, m.p. about 183°C. (361°F.). They are greenish black solids, insoluble in water. Although similar to one another in properties, they may be separated by taking advantage of their slightly different solubilities in certain organic solvents. They are both similar in structural formula to hemin, the active constituent of the hemoglobin of blood.

The production of chlorophyll became an important industry when, in 1952, various tooth-paste manufacturers, claiming that the substance had remarkable breath-cleansing properties, began to make it a dentifrice ingredient. By the middle of 1953 chlorophyll-impregnated chewing gums, lozenges, dog rations, and other "deodorizing" products were available to the public. As a result of statements by several leading scientists denying the claim that chlorophyll eliminates odors, the advertising campaign soon lost its appeal.

CHLOROPLAST, in botany, the protoplasmic body found in green plants and distinguished by the green pigment chlorophyll. Chloroplasts are developed only in the cells to which a sufficient amount of light penetrates; therefore in the larger plants they are found only in the cells near the surface. The absorption of light by 6 to 10 cell layers is so complete that neither chlorophyll nor chloroplast is developed below that level. Chloroplasts originate from pre-existent structures of the same kind. Unspecialized protoplasmic organs known as plastids multiply by direct division as the cells divide. Later those plastids in the superficial cells may become chloroplasts.

The structure of the chloroplast, like that of other protoplasmic organs, is not definitely known; but it appears to be vacuolate, i.e., to consist of a firmer colorless portion enclosing many minute spaces filled with chlorophyll; but just how the latter is related to the colorless portion, and whether dissolved or not, is not satisfactorily determined. See PHOTOSYNTHESIS; PROTOPLASM.

CHLORPROMAZINE, phenothiazine compound used as a drug for its sedative effect upon the central nervous system. Developed by French scientists in 1950, the compound was found in laboratory experiments on animals to prevent shock and to produce the effects of hibernation. The drug was later applied by French surgeons in a new technique of anesthesia for operative cases likely to react badly to ordinary anesthetics. It was introduced into the United States in 1954 under the trade name Thorazine and subsequently applied as a tranquilizing drug for several diverse conditions.

Chlorpromazine is successful in the symptomatic treatment of mental patients, particularly in the manic phases of schizophrenia; see MENTAL DISORDERS. It is used also

as an aid in psychotherapy and in the treatment of alcoholism (q.v.). Because the drug prolongs and intensifies the effect of narcotics, when given to cancer patients it enables them to obtain relief from pain with smaller doses of morphine. Chlorpromazine is effective also in the control of nausea, vomiting, and persistent hiccuping. Favorable results have been obtained from the administration of the drug in cases of migraine (q.v.). A combination of chlorpromazine and reserpine (q.v.), another tranquilizing drug, has been used successfully in the treatment of hypertension (q.v.).

Chlorpromazine must be administered with caution because of the possible side effects. Among the atypical reactions to the drug are a serious form of anemia, hepatitis, and a tremor resembling that of Parkinson's disease (see PALSY). Another tranquilizing drug, called promazine, which is derived from chlorpromazine, provides encouraging results with fewer side effects.

CHLORTETRACYCLINE. See AUREOMYCIN.

CHOATE, JOSEPH HODGES (1832–1917), American lawyer and diplomat, born in Salem, Mass. As a trial lawyer he became widely known and after 1865 conducted many famous cases, including the successful defense of Gen. Fitz-John Porter, the Tweed Ring prosecution, the Tilden will contest, the Chinese exclusion cases, and the Bering Sea dispute, in which he represented the Canadian government. From 1899 to 1905 he was U.S. ambassador to Great Britain. In 1907 he was first U.S. delegate to the International Peace Conference at The Hague.

CHOATE, RUFUS (1799–1859), American lawyer, born in Ipswich, Mass., and educated at Dartmouth College. He took up the study of law, entering the Cambridge Law School in 1821 and subsequently moving to the office (in Washington) of William Wirt, then attorney general of the United States. From 1825 to 1827 he served in the Massachusetts State legislature, first as a representative, then as a senator. He was elected to the U.S. House of Representatives in 1830 and served until his resignation in 1834 to resume legal practice in Boston. In 1841, Daniel Webster having become secretary of state, Choate was elected to serve out his term in the United States Senate and represented Massachusetts until 1845.

CHOCOLATE, a preparation made from the beans of the cacao, and used as a flavoring and as an ingredient of beverages and various kinds of confectionery (q.v.). Chocolate was brought to Europe by the Spaniards, who learned its use from the Mexicans at the time of the invasion by Cortes in 1519. It was introduced into England about 1657. In the U.S., chocolate was first manufactured at Milton Lower Mills, near Dorchester, Mass., in 1765. In recent years the U.S. has consumed about half of the world production of chocolate; the amount imported annually totals about 650 million pounds. See CACAO; COCOA.

CHOCTAW, North American Indian tribe of the Muskhogean (q.v.) linguistic stock, originally located in territory now included in Georgia, Alabama, and southern Mississippi. Culturally, the Choctaws ranked high among the Indian tribes of the Southeast, and were generally friendly in their relations with the American colonists. In colonial times the Choctaws were called "flatheads" by the French, with whom they were frequently allied against the British. This designation referred to the structure of their skulls, flattened, according to tribal custom, by keeping heavy sandbags on the heads of their infants. The Choctaws also had unusual burial rites, disinterring the deceased after a few days and preparing the skeletons for preservation. Between the close of the American Revolution and 1830, the Choctaws ceded their tribal territories to the United States, accepting lands in Indian Territory and other benefits in exchange. Most of the tribe migrated to the new lands along with the Chickasaws, before 1837. In Indian Territory they organized a government, becoming, with the Creeks, Seminoles, Cherokees, and Chickasaws, part of the Five Civilized Tribes or Nations. They liquidated their tribal organization in 1906, when they accepted American citizenship. The Choctaws now number about 16,500, of whom approximately 15,000 live in the State of Oklahoma. The other 1500 are inhabitants of the State of Mississippi. See AMERICAN INDIANS: *Southeastern Area.*

CHOGSET. See CUNNER.

CHOISEUL, DUC ÉTIENNE FRANÇOIS DE (1719–85), French statesman, known in early life as Comte de Stainville. He fought in the War of the Austrian Succession, but did not attain prominence until he won the favor of Madame de Pompadour. While she lived his advancement was continuous. He was made lieutenant general in 1748. In 1756 he was sent as ambassador to Rome, where he adjusted with Pope Benedict XIV the dispute over the sacraments. In the same year he went to Vienna, entrusted with the mission of uniting Austria with France against Prussia.

He was the author of the Family Compact

(*pacte*), an agreement negotiated in 1761, which brought about the alliance of all the Bourbon crowns against foreign aggression. His reputation was enhanced by his success in suppressing the Jesuits, whom Madame de Pompadour had come to hate no less than did the nation. His patroness died in 1764, but Choiseul continued to direct both the internal and external affairs of France. He was a skillful courtier and shrewd diplomat, and so controlled the intrigues of European courts that Catherine II of Russia gave him the name *le cocher de l'Europe* ("the coachman of Europe"), but in 1770 Madame du Barry caused his dismissal. After 4 years of retirement, on the accession of Louis XVI, he returned to Paris, where he lived until his death.

CHOKECHERRY, common name of those cherries which have an astringent taste, particularly those species in the section. *Padus* of the genus *Prunus,* considered by some botanists to be a separate genus. The common chokecherry, *P. virginiana,* and the wild black cherry, *P. serotina,* are found throughout the U.S. east of the Rocky Mountains. They may become pests through harboring tent caterpillars which breed on chokecherry and then attack more valuable trees. See CHERRY.

CHOLERA, name of several common human diseases, particularly a malignant tropical disease (see CHOLERA, ASIATIC), all of which are characterized by copious "rice-water" diarrhea, vomiting, and prostration. The name is also applied to certain diseases of domestic animals, of which the most important are fowl cholera (q.v.) and hog cholera.

CHOLERA, ASIATIC, also called malignant, epidemic, or algid cholera, a severe infectious disease endemic in India and some other tropical countries, and occasionally spreading to temperate climates. The first stage, which is known as cholerine, is characterized by diarrhea, restlessness, nausea, and chills. The patient may gradually recover from these mild symptoms, but more often, after a few hours or days, the patient develops violent diarrhea with the characteristic "rice-water stools", painful vomiting and muscular cramps, thirst, and circulatory failure resulting in collapse. This stage may result in death in as short a period as one hour. Even if the patient recovers, after a day or two, from this stage of the disease, the possibility of fatal relapse, or of pneumonia or other secondary infections, remains for weeks, and the patient is faced at best with a long, slow convalescence. The average mortality, if the disease is not treated by modern methods, is about 50 percent.

The causative agent of Asiatic cholera is a vibrio (comma-shaped organism), *Vibrio comma*, discovered in 1883 by Robert Koch (q.v.). Virtually the only means by which a person can be infected by this germ is through ingestion of food or water contaminated by the stools of cholera patients. Prevention of the disease is therefore a matter of sanitation. Cholera epidemics swept through Europe and the United States in the 19th century, but did not recur in those areas after improvement of the water supply. Control of the disease is still a major medical problem in several Asian countries. A serious epidemic occurred in India in 1953; it was spread by floods which contaminated the water supply over wide areas. The disease caused 59 deaths in Calcutta, and medical authorities instituted (1954) mass inoculations of the city's population with an immunizing vaccine. The vaccine, composed of killed cholera bacteria, affords temporary immunity for a period of about five months.

Modern methods of treating cholera have reduced the average mortality to 25 percent. Early hospitalization is vital, as transfusion of blood plasma is required to counteract the loss of blood fluids. Present-day therapy includes also the administration of sulfadiazine.

CHOLESTEROL, or CHOLESTERIN, a complex alcohol, $C_{27}H_{45}OH$. It is a white solid, soluble in organic solvents but almost insoluble in water; it melts at 300°F. (149°C.) and decomposes at about 680°F. (360°C.). Chole*sterol* belongs to the group of compounds known as sterols, and is related to such other sterols as vitamin D, the male and female sex hormones, and the hormone of the adrenal cortex. Although cholesterol is known to be of considerable physiological importance, its biochemistry is still obscure. In recent years research has established a close relationship between cholesterol and arteriosclerosis (see ARTERY: *Disease of the Arteries*). In advanced stages of the disease, cholesterol is deposited in artery walls, leading to a theory that arteriosclerosis is caused by faulty metabolism of the substance. Cholesterol is present in many foods common to the daily diet, such as milk, cream, butter, and egg yolk, but it is also synthesized by the body from foods which do not contain the substance. Nevertheless, as a precautionary measure, limitation of the amount of cholesterol in the daily diet is recommended by medical authorities for individuals in middle life, when the disease is most likely to occur.

Cholesterol or its derivatives are secreted through the oil glands of the skin and act as a lubricant and protective covering for the hair and skin. The grease extracted from raw wool consists largely of esters of cholesterol. This grease, known as lanolin, is widely used in commercial products, particularly in cosmetics.

CHOLON, city of the Republic of Viet-Nam, situated about 4 miles s.w. of Saigon. Cholon is a shipping point for rice from Cambodia. Rice milling is the chief industry of Cholon; other industries include tanning, dyeing, sawmilling, copper founding, and the manufacture of rubber, glass, bricks, and soap. Pop. of Saigon and Cholon (1959 est.) 1,383,000.

CHOLULA or **SAN PEDRO CHOLULA,** town in the state of Puebla, Mexico. It is situated about 7000 ft. above sea level, on the plateau of Anáhuac, about 55 miles E.S.E. of Mexico City. It contains the remains of the ancient pyramidal Aztec temple of Quetzalcoatl (q.v.). In ancient times it was an Aztec religious center. The Spanish conquistador Hernando Cortes, who visited Cholula (then known as Chololan) in 1519, noted that the city contained 20,000 houses and many temples. Pop. (1950) 11,616.

CHOPIN, FRÉDÉRIC FRANÇOIS (1810–49), Polish composer and pianist, born in Zelazowa Wola, near Warsaw, of a French father and a Polish mother. He began to study the piano at the age of 4, and at the age of 8 played at a private concert in Warsaw. Later he studied harmony and counterpoint at the Warsaw Conservatoire. He was precocious also as a composer; his first published composition is dated 1825. In 1829 in Vienna he gave his first concerts as a piano virtuoso and from 1830 to 1831 lived in that city. From 1831, except for brief absences, he lived in Paris, where he became noted as a pianist, teacher, and composer. He formed an intimate friendship with the writer Baronne Dudevant, better known as George Sand (q.v.). In 1838 he began to suffer from a lung ailment and George Sand nursed him in Majorca in the Balearic Islands, Spain (1838–39), Paris, and Nohant until continued differences between the two resulted in an estrangement in 1846. Thereafter his musical activity was limited to the giving of several concerts in 1848 in Paris, Scotland, and England.

Chopin is generally considered the greatest of all composers of music for the piano. He is at his best in pieces for solo piano, which include études, impromptus, scherzos, nocturnes, ballades, preludes, and forms derived

Culver Service

Frédéric Chopin (from a portrait by the 19th-century Dutch artist Ary Scheffer)

from the dance, such as the waltz, polonaise, and mazurka. His music, romantic in nature, is characterized by exquisite melody of great originality, refined harmony, subtle rhythm, and poetic beauty. It exerted great influence on other composers, notably Franz Liszt, Richard Wagner, and Claude Debussy. Chopin's 206 published compositions include 55 mazurkas, 27 études, 24 preludes, 19 nocturnes, and 13 polonaises. Among his compositions in larger form are the *Concerto in E Minor* and the *Concerto in F Minor,* both for piano and orchestra, and the *Sonata in B-Flat Minor.*

CHORALE, a melody to which hymns or psalms are sung in church by the congregation in unison. The Roman Catholic church service has from early times contained chorales, but the name is generally applied to those in the style introduced by Luther into the German Protestant church in the 16th century. Realizing the great power of music to awaken religious emotion, he determined to carry his reforms into the music of the church service. He selected simple tunes from many sources, sacred and secular, and arranged them to fit the hymns and psalms used in the service. Some were ancient Latin hymns; for example, the chorale *Herr Gott, Dich Loben Wir* is adapted from a song of praise by St. Ambrose. German songs furnished material for many others. The most important of the early collections of chorales

was that published by Luther and his friend Johann Walther, in 1524, called the *Enchiridion.* Chorales were intended always to have an organ accompaniment, which was usually contrapuntal, and as time went on these accompaniments were made more and more elaborate by the organists. Originally chorales were strongly rhythmical in character. By a gradual process of change, however, this rhythmic element has disappeared, and chorales are now sung in notes of almost uniform length. Probably the most famous of all chorales is the one popularly accredited to Luther himself, *Ein' feste Burg ist unser Gott.* It appears in one of Bach's cantatas and in Mendelssohn's *Reformation Symphony,* is heard in Wagner's *Kaiser Marsch,* and forms an important theme in Meyerbeer's opera *Les Huguenots.* Bach's works abound in chorales.

CHORDATA, one of the great phyla of the animal kingdom, the members of which include the most highly developed animals, and are characterized by the possession, at some time during their embryonic or postnatal development, of a notochord, a dorsal nervous system, and gill clefts. The notochord is a longitudinal, elastic rod which acts as an axial skeleton; in vertebrates, including man, it is replaced by the vertebral column during embryonic development, and only small remnants of it are found in the form of intervertebral disks. The dorsal nervous system in vertebrates is represented by the brain and spinal chord. The gill clefts, persistent in fish, are found in all vertebrates at an early embryonic stage.

The Chordata are virtually coextensive with the Vertebrates (q.v.), but include also a few interesting forms which are neither vertebrate nor invertebrate, notably *Balanoglossus,* the Ascidians (qq.v.), and *Amphioxus.*

CHOREA. See SAINT VITUS'S DANCE.

CHORION. See EMBRYOLOGY: *Nutrition and Respiration.*

CHORUS, among the early Greeks, a festal dance, accompanied by music. Through its development in the Attic theater the word came to mean particularly the group of dancing singers who took part in the rendering of a play, and was also applied to the parts of the composition itself which they performed. In the time of the Attic tragedy the chorus consisted of 12 or 15 persons, in character befitting the scene and nature of the plot. At pauses in the acting the chorus, with an accompaniment of dancing movements, sang lyrical passages having reference suggestively to the subject and progress of the drama and serving to heighten and solemnize the impression produced by the actors. In Elizabethan drama the name of chorus was given to a character whose role was to comment on the action of the play, usually in a prologue or epilogue. In modern drama the chorus is a group of dancers who provide an appropriate accompaniment for the action of a musical play.

In music, the chorus is a vocal composition in which each part is sung by a number of singers, as distinguished from a duet, trio, or quartet, in which each part is sung by a solo singer. The term also denotes the entire body of vocalists performing a choral composition. Choruses may be written for one part (unison), two, three, four, five, or six parts. Eight-part choruses are almost invariably double choruses, consisting of four parts each. Works written for 12, 16, 20, and more parts are really four-part works written for a number of choruses. The greater the number of parts, the more the individuality of each part is destroyed. Hence modern composers rarely write for more than double chorus. The foundation of all choral writing is the four-part chorus.

CHORZÓW, or KRÓLEWSKA HUTA, city of Katowice Province, Upper Silesia, Poland, about 45 miles N.W. of Kraków. It is situated in a district noted for the production of coal, iron, and lumber. Industrial establishments in Chorzów include iron and zinc works, rolling mills, and factories for the production of glass and bricks. The city was originally a German village, founded in 1797; in 1869 it became a town and was known as Königshütte. Following the defeat of the Central Powers in World War I and the consequent division of Upper Silesia between Germany and Poland, Königshütte became a Polish city. Pop. (1960 est.) 146,700.

CHOSEN. See KOREA.

CHOSHI, town and port of Chiba Prefecture, E. Honshu Island, Japan, on the Tonegawa R., 72 m. by rail E. of Tokyo. The chief occupation is the manufacture of fish oil. Pop. (1960) 91,470.

CHOU EN-LAI (1898–   ), Chinese revolutionist, born in Huaian, Kiangsu Province, and educated at Waseda University, Japan, and at Nankai University, Tientsin. At the age of twenty-one he received a one-year jail term for participating in a student uprising in Tientsin. He spent the four years after his release (1920) studying and traveling in Europe. During his absence he became a member of the newly created Chinese Communist Party. Returning to China in 1924, he joined the Kuomintang, the national revolutionary

party headed by Sun Yat-sen (q.v.). The latter appointed him director of political training at the Whampoa Military Academy. In March, 1927, during the victorious Kuomintang campaign in north China, Chou En-lai organized and led a successful proletarian insurrection in Shanghai. The dominant anticommunist Kuomintang faction, under the leadership of General Chiang Kai-shek (q.v.), seized control of the city soon thereafter, and Chou En-lai was sentenced to death. He managed to escape, however, and participated in Red underground activities until 1931, when he became political commissar of the Chinese Red Army. In this capacity he played a key role in the historic "Long March" of the Communist forces from south to northwest China and in the negotiations (1936) which laid the basis for united Kuomintang-Communist action against the invading Japanese. He subsequently served as military adviser to Chiang Kai-shek. Following the resumption of the Chinese Civil War he was the chief Communist delegate to the futile mediation conferences attended by U.S. General of the Army George C. Marshall.

Chou En-lai was elected vice-president of the Chinese Communist Party in 1948 and to the Party secretariat early in 1949. On the formation (September, 1949) of the "People's Republic of China" he was appointed premier and foreign minister. He figured prominently in the diplomatic developments attending the Korean War (1950–53) and represented Communist China at the Geneva Conference on Far Eastern Affairs, which effected (1954) an armistice in the war in Indochina (q.v.). Chou En-lai resigned as foreign minister in 1958 but retained the office of premier. See also CHINA: *History.*

CHOUGH, any bird of the genus *Pyrrhocorax* in the Crow family. The beak is longer than the head, strong, arched, and pointed. The tail is slightly rounded. The common European species is sometimes called the Cornish chough, or red-legged crow. The chough occurs on some parts of the British seacoasts, but almost exclusively confined to situations where there are high cliffs. It lives in societies, like the rook, and feeds on insects, berries, grubs, and grain. It is easily tamed.

CHOUTEAU, RENÉ AUGUSTE (1749–1829), and JEAN PIERRE (1758–1849), American pioneers and fur traders, born in New Orleans. They were brothers. In 1763 René Auguste accompanied the fur trader Pierre Laclède on an expedition authorized by the French government of Louisiana to trade west of the Mississippi River, since the east shore had been ceded to England. The expedition resulted in the establishment of a post, in 1764, from which the city of St. Louis developed. Laclède, René Auguste, and Jean Pierre, who had been brought to St. Louis, remained in that city, establishing a trade in fur with the Indians which became the leading enterprise of its kind in the Southwest. In 1796 Jean Pierre, who had been granted exclusive trading rights with the Osage Indians, founded the first permanent settlement in what is now the State of Oklahoma, at Salina. After St. Louis became part of the U.S. as a result of the Louisiana Purchase (1803), Jean Pierre was appointed U.S. agent for the Osages, and René Auguste was made chairman of the city's board of trustees.

CHOW or **CHOW CHOW**, a dog of ancient Chinese origin, akin to the Eskimo dog. The chow is a compact, powerful dog whose characteristic appearance is one of scowling independence. It has a thick, coarse coat, which may be of any of several clear colors, such as white, yellow, red, or black; a large head, carried erect; a short muzzle; a broad, black nose; and a blue-black tongue. Its eyes are deep-set and dark; its chest broad and deep; its tail well set up and held close to the back; its forelegs straight and its hindlegs heavy and muscular. The chow was introduced into England in 1780, and the first club to specialize in its breeding was established in England in 1895. The dog made its first exhibition appearance in the United States at a show of the Westminster Kennel Club in New York City in 1890. It is a popular pet and watch dog.

CHRÉTIEN DE TROYES or **CHRESTIEN DE TROYES** (fl. late 12th cent.), French poet, born probably in Troyes. He belonged to the troubadour school that originated in southern France, and is remembered chiefly for his contributions to the Arthurian Cycle (q.v.). These include *Perceval le Gallois,* which introduced the legend of the Holy Grail; *Erec et Enide; Le Chevalier au Lyon; Le Chevalier à la Charette,* in which Lancelot du Lac was introduced; and *Le Roman de Cligès.* Wolfram von Eschenbach, the German epic poet, used *Perceval le Gallois* as the basis of his *Parzival,* the work from which Richard Wagner drew the material for the libretto of the opera *Parsifal.*

CHRIST, a Greek term found in the Septuagint, where it translates varied forms of the Hebrew verb *māshakh,* "to anoint" (most frequently the nominal form *māshīakh,* "an anointed one", whence the English term *Mes-*

The face of Christ, from the painting "Saint Veronica's Veil" by the modern French artist Georges Rouault

siah is derived). The Hebrew conception of anointing was derived from the ancient magical idea that the application of oil endowed the person or object with certain superior and even supernatural qualities. In early Israel the custom of anointing was thus in recognition of the endowment of the person with the qualification for exalted office. It was applied, not only to the priests (Lev. 4:3) as intermediaries between God and man, but also to the kings (1 Sam. 2:10) as representatives of God in the theocracy and as thus assuming in their person priestly functions. Later, it was applied to the prophets (1 Kings 19:16) and was referred to even in connection with the patriarchs (Ps. 105:15). In the development of the Messianic thought it came to be narrowed down to the redeemer and restorer of the Jewish nation (Ps. 2:2).

In the New Testament, the word *Christ* is used both as an appellative and as a proper name. In both cases it occurs either with or without the article, either alone or in combination with other terms and names. Always when used as a proper name, and frequently when otherwise used, it is a designation of Jesus of Nazareth, as the expected Messiah of the Jews. It is from this application of the term that its English meaning is derived. See CHRISTOLOGY; CHRISTIANITY; JESUS CHRIST; MESSIAH.

CHRISTADELPHIANS, also known as BROTHERS OF CHRIST and as THOMASITES, a religious sect of the United States, Canada, and Great Britain, founded in the United States in 1848 by John Thomas, M.D. (1805–71). He was at first a member of the Campbellites or Disciples of Christ (q.v.). But being "convinced by a study of the Bible that the cardinal doctrines of the existing churches correspond with those of the apostate Church predicted in Scripture", he established what he considered the only true Church. He formed his followers into societies which until the outbreak of the Civil War had no distinctive name. The one now held was selected when their members claimed exemption from military duty on the ground of conscientious opposition to war. The principles of the sect are thus stated: The Old and New Testaments are equally important; God will restore to immortal life all who love Him in this life, but those who have not accepted this immortal principle cease to exist at death; there is no personal devil; Christ is the son of God, deriving from the Deity moral perfection, but from His mother a human nature; He has the threefold character of prophet, priest, and king; the first office He fulfilled by His life and death on earth, and now as priest He mediates before the Deity; as king He will return to earth and reign over all the world from the throne of David in the Holy Land. In the United States the Christadelphians, in a recent year, had about 115 churches and a membership of about 2800.

CHRISTCHURCH, city and capital of the provincial district of Canterbury, South Island, New Zealand, situated on the Avon River about 5 miles from the Pacific coast. It is the commercial center of a fertile agricultural region in which grain and sheep are produced, and has railway connections with Lyttelton, a port 8 miles to the S.E., Dunedin, Blenheim, and other points on South Island. Exports consist mainly of wool and frozen mutton. Its chief industries are meat packing, and the manufacture of woolen goods, boots, clothing, furniture, and agricultural implements. Notable structures in the city include a Gothic cathedral with a tower 240 feet in height, and a procathedral of the Roman Catholic Church. Christchurch is the see of the New Zealand bishopric of Canterbury and the seat of Canterbury University College, a division of the University of New Zealand. The city was founded in 1851 by members of the Canterbury Association, a British colonizing society closely affiliated with the Church of England. Pop. (1961 est.) 220,500.

CHRIST CHURCH COLLEGE, a college of Oxford University, in England, founded as Cardinal College in 1525, by the English churchman Cardinal Thomas Wolsey. Following Wolsey's removal (1529) from high office, Cardinal College was suppressed by Henry VIII. Three years later, the king endowed, in its place, a new foundation called King Henry VIII's College. Substantial improvements to the foundation were authorized by King Henry in 1546, when it was merged with the cathedral of the newly-created diocese of Oxford, an arrangement that still obtains. By the terms of Henry's charter, the composite institution was provided with a dean, 8 canons, 100 students (later increased to 101), and the cathedral staff. Various modifications were subsequently adopted, the most recent in 1882, when new statutes reduced the number of students. In addition to a dean, the foundation now has 6 canons, 5 of whom are university professors, 29 exhibitioners, about 325 undergraduates, and 60 scholars, including 3 who are elected annually, according to a custom established by Queen Elizabeth I, from Westminster School, one of the oldest public schools in England. The total membership of Christ Church exceeds that of any other college of the university.

Notable among the many points of interest at Christ Church is the cathedral, used also as the college chapel, parts of which date from the 8th century. Large sections of the structure were completed late in the 12th century by the Normans. The college quadrangle, designed by Wolsey, is popularly known as Tom Quadrangle, a designation derived from the fact that the clock bell in the gate tower was dedicated to St. Thomas of Canterbury. At 9:05 p.m. daily, when the college gates are closed, the bell tolls 101 times, once for each member of the early student body. Among the many famous graduates of Christ Church are the philosopher John Locke; William Penn, founder of Pennsylvania; the playwright and poet Ben Jonson; the theologian John Wesley; and Sir Robert Peel and William Ewart Gladstone, prime ministers of England. See OXFORD UNIVERSITY.

CHRISTIAN. See CHRISTIANITY.

CHRISTIAN I (1426–81), King of Denmark (1448–81), King of Norway (1450–81), and King of Sweden (1457–64, 1465–67, 1470–71). He was the son of Theodoric, Count of Oldenburg, and Hedwig of Schleswig and Holstein. Christian founded the Oldenburg dynasty in Denmark, succeeding Christopher III of Bavaria as king. The Union of Kalmar (1397), under which Denmark, Norway, and Sweden had been united, was practically dissolved when Christian became king of Denmark. However, Denmark and Norway were reunited when he ascended the Norwegian throne. Christian seized the Swedish throne, but was able to enforce his authority in Sweden only at intervals from 1457 until his final expulsion in 1471. In 1479 he founded the University of Copenhagen in the Danish capital.

CHRISTIAN II (1481–1559), King of Denmark (1513–23), King of Norway (1513–23, 1531), and King of Sweden (1520–23), born in Nyborg. He was the son of John I (Hans) of Denmark, whom he succeeded as King of Norway and Denmark. In 1515 he married Isabella, a sister of Charles V, Holy Roman Emperor. In 1520 he overthrew the regent of Sweden, Sten Sture the younger, and thereafter was crowned King of Sweden. His violent rule, however, and especially his massacre in Stockholm of the foremost men in Sweden (November 8–10, 1520), roused such a spirit of opposition in that country that he was speedily driven out by the young national leader Gustavus Vasa (later King Gustavus I of Sweden). In Denmark also, a popular revolt drove Christian for refuge to the Netherlands. Later he returned to Norway and was proclaimed king in 1531. Captured the following year during negotiations with King Frederick I of Denmark, he spent the rest of his life in prison.

CHRISTIAN III (1503–59), King of Denmark and Norway (1534–59). He was the son of Frederick I of Denmark (q.v.), who had been elected to the throne to replace Christian II. Christian III established Lutheranism as the state religion in Denmark, defeating the strong Catholic party and confiscating its lands and properties. He expanded the Danish fleet, centralized internal government, established the hereditary right of his line to the Danish crown, and raised Denmark to a position of power and security.

CHRISTIAN IV (1577–1648), King of Denmark and Norway (1588–1648). He was the son of Frederick II. Christian ruled through regents from 1588 to 1596. He fought two wars with Sweden (1611–13, 1643–45); the first was successful, but by the second he lost much Norwegian territory. Christian entered the Thirty Years' War in 1625 as a northern champion of Protestantism, but his army suffered (1626) a severe defeat. He encouraged the arts and sciences, commerce, and exploration. A Danish colony was established in the East Indies during his reign. In 1624, after fire had destroyed Oslo in Norway, Christian refounded the city as Christiania,

by which name it was known until 1924, when the Norwegians restored its medieval name.

CHRISTIAN V (1646–99), King of Denmark and Norway (1670–99). He was the son of Frederick III. Christian created two orders of nobility consisting of officials and members of upper-middle-class families and outranking older noble families, by contempt for whom he won popular acclaim. The government was under the guidance of his chancellor Count Peter Schumacher Griffenfeld until 1676, when the king sacrificed the chancellor to the latter's opponents and imprisoned him for life. Thereafter, despite thorough centralization of the military and civil administrations, the financial condition of the government deteriorated because of royal extravagance and an unsuccessful war with Sweden (1675–79). A Norse code of laws, begun by Frederick III in 1661, was completed by Christian in 1683 and hence was called the Christian Code.

CHRISTIAN VI (1699–1746), King of Denmark and Norway (1730–46). He was the son of Frederick IV. Christian won notoriety by constructing costly edifices to gratify his consort's extravagant whims.

CHRISTIAN VII (1749–1808), King of Denmark and Norway (1766–1808), the son of Frederick V (q.v.). In 1766 he married Caroline Matilda (q.v.), the sister of King George III of England. Christian's behavior, from the time of his childhood when he had been brutalized by his tutors, was always conspicuously eccentric, and he had a reputation, during his reign, for imbecility and complete moral incompetence. This was due, in part, to his dependence on the will of others, particularly of his physician and minister, Count Johann Friedrich von Struensee (q.v.), whom he allowed to assume absolute control of the government and, later, had beheaded. In 1784 he became completely insane and Crown Prince Frederick later (as King Frederick VI) took over as regent. During Christian's reign serfdom was abolished, trade was fostered, the Schleswig-Holstein Canal was constructed, and improved roads were built.

CHRISTIAN VIII (1786–1848), King of Denmark and Norway (1839–48). He was the nephew of Christian VII. Christian served as viceroy of Norway in 1813 and was chosen king of Norway in May, 1814, after the Norwegians had rejected the Peace of Kiel, which ceded Norway to Sweden. However, an invading army forced him to abdicate within five months. Christian lived in retirement from 1815 to 1831 and then served as a Danish councilor of state until his accession to the throne of Denmark. The most important event of his reign was his proclamation in 1846 that Schleswig and Holstein, of which the Danish kings long had been dukes, were indissolubly united to Denmark.

CHRISTIAN IX (1818–1906), King of Denmark (1863–1906). He was the fourth son of William, Duke of Schleswig-Holstein-Sönderborg-Glücksborg, and the Princess Louise of Hesse-Cassel, a direct descendant of Christian III of Denmark. In 1852, with the consent of Frederick VII (q.v.), then King of Denmark, a council of the great Powers recognized Christian as his heir apparent; Frederick thus arranged his succession because, having no male heirs, he brought to an end the male line of the house of Oldenburg, rulers of Denmark since 1448 (see CHRISTIAN I). On the death of Frederick, Christian became king. The following year (1864), the Schleswig-Holstein (q.v.) problem, which had concerned Denmark for many years, came to a head; Denmark was forced to war against Prussia and Austria for the two duchies and, after being defeated, to renounce its claims by the Treaty of Vienna. In domestic affairs Christian IX's reign was marked by a struggle between liberal and conservative political elements for control of the Folketing, the lower house of the Danish Rigsdag or parliament. Christian sided with the conservatives but when the liberals gained control of the Folketing he consented to the formation of a liberal ministry. By his wife, Louise, Princess of Hesse-Cassel (1817–98), he had six children. Of these, the eldest, Frederick, succeeded him on the throne of Denmark as Frederick VIII; Alexandra married the Prince of Wales, later King Edward VII of England; Dagmar married the Grand Duke Alexander of Russia, later Emperor Alexander III; and George became George I, King of Greece, Christian IX's grandson, Charles, became (1905) King of Norway, as Haakon VII.

CHRISTIAN X (1870–1947), King of Denmark (1912–47) and of Iceland (1918–44), born at Charlottenlund, Denmark. He married Alexandrine, Duchess of Mecklenburg, in 1898, and had two sons: Frederick, the crown prince, born in 1899, and Knud, born in 1900. Christian succeeded his father, Frederick VIII. Notable events of his reign were his approval in 1915 of a new constitution which gave women the right to vote and in other ways broadened suffrage rights; the sale of the Danish West Indies to the United States in 1917; the granting of sovereign rights to Iceland in 1918; and the entrance of Denmark

into the League of Nations, 1920. However, the most important event of his reign is considered to be the return of North Schleswig from Germany to Denmark, 1920, by means of a plebiscite. Under his rule more than 2500 sq.m. of waste land were reclaimed to agriculture; a Danish merchant marine was developed; and world-wide Danish commercial enterprises were launched. In World War II, during the German occupation of Denmark (1940–45), King Christian led the Danish people in passive resistance to efforts of Germany to make Denmark part of the German "new order" in Europe. Christian X ceased being King of Iceland on the establishment of the Republic of Iceland, 1944.

CHRISTIAN ART, EARLY, those phases of the art of the Christian Church and religion which precede the triumph of iconoclasm (8th century) in the East and the coronation (800 A.D.) of Charlemagne as Emperor of the West.

Architecture. There was very little opportunity for a characteristic style in the architecture of the earliest Christians. Constantine in 313 gave Christians freedom to erect places of worship. Of the architecture before that date the catacombs (q.v.) in Rome form the chief basis for study. In the 4th century the basilical (see BASILICA), or oblong form of church construction, came into most common use. The large churches built on this plan were among the foremost monuments erected. Christian architects faced the problem of creating a large interior for worshiping multitudes, in contrast with ancient worship, which was practiced in the open air, or carried on individually or by sacrifices in the temples. In pagan temples nearly all the artistic efforts had been concentrated on the exteriors. Christian art neglected the exterior, leaving it of bare brick, conditioned in its form entirely by the interior arrangements and proportions. The general composition of the early buildings consisted of a columnar vestibule to a high, encircling wall; a square open court, or atrium; and an open porch with three doors leading into an oblong interior divided into three or five aisles by rows of columns supporting either a straight architrave or a line of arches. The dominant note of the interiors was not form, light, and shade, but color, given by mosaic (q.v.) pictures or frescoes (see FRESCO) on the upper part of the walls, marble veneer or wainscot on the lower part, elaborately patterned marble floors, and rich hangings between the columns.

Fine examples of architecture were created from the earliest period until the 6th century. While the Roman Empire still retained vitality, imperial funds were used lavishly in building and decorating churches. The later barbarian invasions, however, and the consequent decline of civilization in the West prevented new artistic developments and perpetuated the early style in Italy, Gaul, Spain, and Germany far into the Middle Ages. The basilical type of church prevailed in many regions until the 12th century. In the East, where civilization had continued uninterruptedly on a high level, the Early Christian style characteristic of the period between the 4th century and the first part of the 7th century, and known as Early Byzantine, continued to flourish. The Early Byzantine style reached its highest point in the 6th century church of St. Sophia in Constantinople (now Istanbul). The style had never been so uniform as in the West, however, and during the period of iconoclasm it gradually was transformed into the style known simply as Byzantine.

The following are some of the basilicas which remain wholly or in part (century indicated in each case): In *Rome,* Santa Maria Maggiore (5th), San Paolo fuore le Mura (5th), Santa Sabina (5th), San Pietro in Vincoli (5th), San Lorenzo (6th, old part), Sant' Agnese (7th), Santa Maria in Cosmedin (8th), Santa Prassede (9th), San Martino ai Monti (9th); in *Ravenna,* San Teodoro (5th), San Francesco (5th), San Apollinare Nuovo, San Apollinare in Classe (6th); in *Spoleto,* San Agostino (6th); in *Perugia,* San Pietro (6th); in *Istanbul,* St. John (5th); in *Bethlehem,* Church of the Nativity (4th); in *Thessalonika,* St. Demetrius (probably 5th); in *Kalat Seman* (Syria), St. Simeon Stylites (6th).

An equally important type of early Christian church was built on a concentric plan, i.e., circular, polygonal, or even equilaterally cruciform. Among the finest examples of this type are St. Sophia, mentioned above, and St. Irene, both in Istanbul; San Lorenzo in Milan; and San Vitale in Ravenna. The concentric plan was used also for baptisteries, chapels, sacristies, mausoleums, and other religious edifices. All of these buildings are comparable to such Roman structures as the Pantheon, or the temple of Vesta or Minerva Medica, but they were not so imposing or built on so large a scale.

For materials of construction, bricks were commonly used in the West, including the Greek provinces, precluding sculptured decoration, because no marble facing was used. But in parts of the Orient, especially in Syria, local stone replaced brick, and there was a great deal of carved detail. There also the normal types of the classic orders, lavishly followed farther west, were varied by many new forms, not only connected with Persian and Byzantine ornament, but seeming to foreshadow Romanesque and Gothic foliage and ornament. In Syria also variety and inventiveness of architectural plan, composition, and form were shown. The masterpiece of the school is the monastery of St. Simeon in Kalat Seman.

Sculpture. As Rome declined, sculpture in the round was abandoned because of the association of statues with idols. An abstract style of relief scuplture was developed as a means of achieving an expression of greater spirituality. The carvings on the Arch of Constantine, the base (all that remains) of the Column of Theodosius at Istanbul, and the imperial portraits of the 4th century are all examples of this abstract style. Some of the works of sculpture which do not reveal abstract influence are of pre-Constantinian date. Such are the statue of St. Hippolytus and that of the Good Shepherd in the Lateran Museum and a few of the sarcophagi. The last-named form the bulk of early Christian marble sculpture during the 3rd, 4th, and 5th centuries, after which there was very little sculpture on a large scale of any sort. These sarcophagi, after the fashion of those of the earlier Etruscans and pagan Romans, had a line of reliefs covering face and sides, or sometimes two superposed rows of figures. Many subjects were usually crowded together, although sometimes such scenes as the crossing of the Red Sea, or Jonah swallowed by the whale, occupy the entire front. The scenes are selected with evident relation to funerary ideas and belief in future life. The sarcophagi in Ravenna show most effectively the ceremonial and hieratic style, based on symmetry, rhythmic composition, and presentation of figures frontally, which is common to the sarcophagi of the 5th and 6th centuries. To this time probably belongs the last colossal statue of antiquity, the bronze emperor found at Barletta. Numerous chalices, patens, reliquaries, and other small objects, made of ivory and precious metals and used in religious services, are of particularly high quality.

Painting and Mosaics. The painted ornamentation of the earliest crypts in the Roman catacombs, such as those of Domitilla and Priscilla, show that not until the middle of the 2nd century was there a definite style of Christian painting. The technique was exactly the same as in contemporary pagan monuments; but a system of symbolism to express Christian faith was in process of formation. Everything that could be regarded as a symbol of the resurrection and of salvation was represented, whether in the form of animate and inanimate symbols, such as the phoenix, the fish, or the bread; or of symbolic scenes, such as Noah, Daniel, or the three children in the furnace. The catacombs continue throughout the 4th century to furnish practically the entire material for study, because the churches of this period still in existence have partly or entirely lost their paintings. The earliest known Christian church with frescoes is the chapel of Dura (3rd century). These frescoes are in the museum of Yale University.

The art of mosaic painting began to flourish at this time, and rapidly displaced fresco painting in the larger and richer churches. The desire to tell the people all the main facts of religious history led to the invention of a series of chronological illustrations of the events of the Old and New Testaments, which, originating as early as the 5th century, were handed down, almost unchanged, for about 1000 years. The mosaics of Santa Maria Maggiore in Rome, with their scenes from Genesis (about 430), show the early phase of the style. The historic series, however, became subordinate to the dogmatic, as in the later mosaics (about 500) in San Apollinare Nuovo, in Ravenna, portraying the life of Christ.

The two typical Italian schools of mosaics are those of Rome and Ravenna, the former representing the Latin, the latter partly the Byzantine style. In Rome the mosaics of Santa Sabina (5th century) and Santi Cosmo e Damiano (about 530) are the finest of the Roman style; but the influence of the Byzantine style is shown a little later in the churches of San Teodoro and San Venanzio. The Ravenna series is richer in the 5th and 6th centuries, with its two churches of San Apollinare, San Vitale, the two baptisteries, the archiepiscopal palace, and the tomb of Galla Placidia, filled with mosaics by the best artists of the Greek school.

Among other notable objects of early Christian art are the luxurious purple manuscripts, such as the Genesis of Vienna and the Gospelbook of Rossano (both 6th century). The use of the gold ground, which they made popular, revolutionized mosaic painting and made its figures as clean-cut as those of a Greek frieze.

See CATACOMBS; CATHEDRAL; SYMBOLISM.

CHRISTIAN CHURCH, name of a former religious denomination in the United States. The Christian Church originated in three religious dissenting movements. The first was led by James O'Kelly who, in 1792, withdrew from a conference of the Methodist Episcopal Church held in Baltimore, Md., and, in the following year, founded his first Christian Church near Chapel Hill, N.C. The second movement was that initiated by Abner Jones and Elias Smith, who broke from the Baptist church and organized new churches in Lyndon, Vt., and Portsmouth, N.H., in 1801. The third was that of a group of Kentucky ministers, led by Barton W. Stone, who withdrew about 1801 from the Presbyterian church and formed a new denomination with beliefs similar to those of the groups in Vermont, North Carolina, and Virginia. The three groups eventually united on the basis of the following common "Principles": "(1) Christ is the only head of the Church; (2) the Bible alone is a sufficient rule of faith and practice; (3) Christian character is the only basis of membership; (4) every member has the right to interpret Scripture for his own life; (5) 'Christian', to the exclusion of all sectarian designations, is a sufficient name for the followers of Christ; and (6) the goal of the Church is the union of all followers of Christ."

In 1929 the Christian Church had 1283 church organizations, 110,326 members, 1047 ministers, 1324 Sunday schools, 801 Christian Endeavor societies, and 307 women's societies. It sponsored home and foreign missions, educational work, publications, evangelism, Christian unity, social service, and other general activities. It also maintained eight educational institutions, including Franklinton Christian College in Franklinton, N.C., for Negro boys and girls.

In 1931 the National Council of the Congregational Churches and the General Convention of the Christian Churches united, first by separate votes and then by joint vote, to form the General Council of the Congregational Christian Churches. In 1957 the Congregational Christian Churches acted with the Evangelical and Reformed Church to form the United Church of Christ (q.v.). The merger was completed in 1961, when a constitution was adopted.

The membership of the Congregational Christian Churches in 1960 was over 1,400,-000, and the churches numbered about 5500. The periodicals of the two denominations also were combined, being issued under the title of the *Congregationalist and Herald of Gospel Liberty,* a publication later known as *Advance.* The denomination also publishes *Minister's Quarterly* and *Social Action.* The Congregational Christian General Council has headquarters in New York City. F.S.B.

CHRISTIAN ENDEAVOR SOCIETIES, organizations established originally for the promotion of Christian life and service among young people and later adapted to people of all ages. The first society of this nature was the Young People's Society of Christian Endeavor, organized by Dr. Francis E. Clark in 1881 in the Williston Congregational Church in Portland, Me. In 1961 the combined membership of the thousands of Christian Endeavor Societies in the world was estimated at more than 1,000,000. The societies exist in more than 60 nations and have members from more than 80 religious denominations. The World's Christian Endeavor Union, established in 1895, holds conventions from time to time in various parts of the world. The distribution of information and the publication of literature of international interest are the functions of the International Society of Christian Endeavor, with headquarters in Columbus, Ohio. Among its publications is the monthly magazine *Christian Endeavor World*.

CHRISTIANIA. See OSLO.

CHRISTIANITY, the religion centered in Jesus Christ (q.v.) as the supreme revelation of God and as Lord of his followers, and based upon his teachings. Christianity comprises three principal divisions: the Roman Catholic Church (q.v.; see also EASTERN RITE, CHURCHES OF THE); the various Protestant churches organized as a result of the Reformation (q.v.); and the Holy Orthodox Catholic Apostolic Eastern Church, which includes the various organizations adhering to the Byzantine rite (see ORTHODOX CHURCH). Although these different Christian churches together embrace a wide diversity of beliefs and practices, they embody in some way three elements pertaining to Jesus, a story, a doctrine, and a life. The story, known as the Gospel (q.v.), comprises the events associated with Jesus' life and ministry. The doctrine is that Jesus is in some sense a unique person, the Son of God, through whom man can live in the right relation to God. The life is that which the Christian pursues in imitation of Jesus' life; that is, in accordance with Christ's teachings and dominated by love for God and for one's fellow men.

Relations of Christianity to Judaism.
The life of Jesus and the origins of Christianity stand against the background of Judaism (q.v.; see also JEWS) in the time of the early Roman empire, before the destruction of Jerusalem (q.v.) and the temple in 70 A.D.; see TEMPLE: *Temple at Jerusalem*. Jesus was himself a Jew, and Christianity regards him as the culmination and fulfillment of all that is foreshadowed and foretold in the law of Moses (see TORAH) and in the Hebrew prophets. Indeed, the very name "Christ" (q.v.) is a Greek translation (*Christos*) of the Hebrew term *Messiah* (q.v.), which means "the anointed one". Thus Christianity claims to be the full and final development of Judaism and accepts the teachings of the Hebrew Old Testament as completed and fulfilled by the New Testament. In orthodox Christian belief both the Old and New Testaments are inspired writings representing, without mutual contradiction, successive stages in God's revelation. Thus Christianity, like Judaism, is a revealed religion and, in particular, the reflection of additional and completed revelation. The law of Moses was God's law, and Christ, by obeying it perfectly as the representative of his people, ended the need to continue repeating its ceremonies. Christ's death, viewed as a sacrifice (q.v.) and as the fulfillment of all Old Testament sacrifices, supersedes those ceremonial offerings. Although the destruction of the temple was a national tragedy for the Jews, it was not so considered by the Christians, for they believed that Jesus Christ had ended the temple's usefulness. See BIBLE; BIBLE, INTERPRETATIONS OF THE.

The Essential Characteristics of Christianity. All religions share some sense of man's dependence upon a supernatural being or force and of the need to improve man's relations with the supernatural. Christianity, as well as other religions, extols and requires also such virtues as patience, self-denial, forgiveness, and love. However, Christianity claims to be unique among religions in teaching that man's hope is found not in man's merit but in God's love, perfectly expressed in Jesus Christ and offered freely to all men. Christianity is particularly characterized both by its universalism in attempting to extend this doctrine to all mankind and by missionary activity as its principal method of spreading the Gospel.

Universalism. Perhaps the most striking development in the evolution of Christianity from its Jewish origins was the transition from a national religion to a universal religion. The Old Testament teaches the universal supremacy of God, but his revelation essentially is restricted to the Jewish nation. In Christianity, God's revelation and blessing are conceived of as extending to all nations and races. Jesus himself taught and ministered primarily within the limits of his Jewish environment. However, the love of God for man which he proclaimed and demonstrated, and the love for God and one's fellow man which he enjoined, were extensions of Old Testament teachings that transcended national boundaries, and the universal character of his teachings and work soon was recognized by many of his followers. The earliest followers of Jesus found it distasteful to associate with gentiles but nevertheless felt that it was appropriate and even necessary to preach the Gospel to them. For a time there was dispute about receiving gentile converts without also requiring them to become Jews, but the principle prevailed that Christianity is free from Old Testament ceremonial laws. This principle, enunciated explicitly and unambiguously by the Apostle Paul, became the basis of the universality of Christianity.

Missionary Activity. As a universal religion, Christianity is also supremely a missionary religion. The missionary genius of Christianity stems from the belief that a harmonious relationship between man and God depends upon Jesus Christ and from the motive of love for all men that he exemplified and expected of his followers. In consequence, the preaching of Christ to all men is justified and even required. The same belief and motive underlie the vast and incomparable Christian enterprises of charity, medical services, education, and social work.

Other religions, notably Islam and Buddhism (qq.v.), have spread far beyond their original locales, but their extension has come about largely through unplanned diffusion, incidental contacts, or outright conquest rather than through missionary activity. Christianity is unique in its conscious and organized effort, inherent in it from the beginning, to make disciples of all men everywhere. Although conquest and conversion often have been associated with each other in the propagation of the faith, they have never been inseparable and should not be confused; the missionary effort of Christianity has been equally vigorous apart from military or political considerations.

Basic Doctrines. Despite diversity in belief and practice, the major branches of Christianity subscribe as a whole to certain basic doctrines, particularly those summarized in the so-called Apostles' Creed (see CREED). There is far from universal agreement on a precise statement of such doctrines, and there are widespread reservations about the validity of their traditional expressions or about their importance for defining Christianity. Yet the very presence of Christianity implies some belief about God and his revelation, man and sin, the person and work of Christ, the church, and the purposes of God for the future.

Revelation. God has revealed himself and his will as recorded in the Bible. According to orthodox Christians, the writers of the Bible were divinely inspired and preserved from error; according to some other Christians the Bible represents the imperfect spiritual gropings of men seeking for truth. The Bible is, in any case, Christianity's first source of information about God's dealings with men.

The Trinity. God is recognized as an eternal and infinite spiritual being; furthermore, the main stream of Christian teaching subscribes to the doctrine of the Trinity (q.v.), i.e., that there is one God existing in three equal eternal persons, the Father, the Son, and the Holy Spirit (see HOLY GHOST).

The Natures of Man. Man is believed to have both a physical and a spiritual nature, and to be spiritually immortal. Man has sinned against God and therefore fails to achieve an adequate fellowship with God (see SIN); statements of Christian faith differ widely, however, in their emphasis on or depreciation of man's guilt in relation to God's righteousness and man's inability to rectify his position before God.

The Natures of Christ. Historical statements of the doctrine of Christ maintain that the Son of God, the eternal second person of the Trinity, appeared in history in a human nature; two distinct natures, divine and human, are thus forever inseparably associated in his divine person; see CHRISTOLOGY. The miraculous virgin birth of Jesus, the miraculous character of many of his works, and his physical resurrection (q.v.) and ascension into heaven are doctrines particularly emphasized by orthodox segments of Christianity.

Reconciliation. The purpose of Christ's incarnation and life was the reconciliation of God and man. Views of the nature of this reconciliation differ as widely as views of man's sin, guilt, and inability to rectify his position before God. In one view, man's need is compatible with the concept that Jesus proclaimed an already existing reconciliation which man simply had failed to recognize before. Another position is that the life and death of Jesus are an example of love and self-denial which man should and can emulate, and that reconciliation is present when man tries to follow that example. The most orthodox doctrine maintains that Jesus in his life obeyed God's law perfectly on behalf of his people, and that his death is a substitutionary atonement (q.v.) for man's awful sin and guilt before a holy God. Christ's redemptive work is applied to man by the work of the Holy Spirit in regeneration and sanctification. Man's response to God's love includes repentance and faith in Christ as his saviour. Reconciliation is completed by God's declaration that the believer is just in God's sight.

Fellowship. Christian doctrine includes the necessity of fellowship among Christians, which is expressed in the organization of the church. Admission to the church involves the sacrament of infant or adult baptism (q.v.), with confession of faith as a prerequisite for adults. The fellowship of confessing Christians with each other and with Christ reaches its highest expression in the sacrament of the Lord's Supper (q.v.). Baptism and the Lord's Supper are the only two sacraments recognized by Protestant churches, but the Roman Catholic Church considers matrimony, confirmation, penance, holy orders, i.e., ordination, and extreme unction (qq.v.), i.e., the last rites of the church, to be sacraments as well; see SACRAMENT. The worship of the Roman Catholic Church is centered in its observance of the Lord's Supper or the mass (q.v.), although preaching and public prayer also are practiced. In most Protestant churches, on the other hand, worship is centered in the preaching of God's word and in prayer. Participation by all members in prayer or testimony is strongly encouraged in some churches, and is associated often with a direct working of the Holy Spirit in individual believers.

The Kingdom of God. Finally, Christianity looks toward the extension and final triumph of the Kingdom of God. This is viewed by some Christian groups as the gradual and perhaps never perfected development of Christian influence in the world. However, orthodox Christians expect the physical return of Christ from heaven, a final judgment, and eternal glory for believers but eternal punishment for those who continue in sin; see HELL; PARADISE; PURGATORY.

Differences in Doctrine and Worship. Among the major organizational divisions of Christianity, the Eastern Orthodox Church and the Roman Catholic Church agree in most points of doctrine and worship. but the various communions of the former do not accept the supremacy of the Church of Rome and its bishop the pope (see PAPACY). Accordingly, although those communions accept many of the doctrines enunciated by the Roman Catholic Church since their separation from it in 1054 A.D., they do not consider such doctrines essential to Christianity.

Roman Catholicism and Protestantism differ most basically on the issue of the authority that must determine doctrine and life.

Catholicism considers the church as the final authority under Christ and teaches that the authority of Scripture is derived from that of the church. In precise opposition to this, Protestatism has maintained historically that Scripture is the final authority under Christ and that the authority of the church is secondary. The Roman Catholic view of ecclesiastical authority is the basis not only for the doctrine of the primacy of the Church of Rome and the infallibility (q.v.) of the pope in his official pronouncements, but also for such other distinctively Catholic teachings as the perpetual virginity and sinlessness of Mary (see IMMACULATE CONCEPTION), the mediation of Mary and the saints in prayer, and the transformation of the sacramental bread and wine into the literal body and blood of Christ (see TRANSUBSTANTIATION). The Protestant doctrine of the supreme authority of Scripture, on the other hand, has permitted the development of divergent and even contradictory interpretations of Scripture, each claiming to be the true interpretation. There has been a further tendency in Protestantism to neglect the authority of Scripture entirely and to replace it with the authority of individual or collective Christian experience.

Protestant Denominations. The major Protestant denominational divisions, such as Lutheranism, Presbyterianism and the Reformed churches, Congregationalism, Methodism (qq.v.), and the Baptist churches (see BAPTIST), have their roots in real disagreements in doctrine and organization. Distinctively Lutheran doctrines include the real presence of Christ in the sacramental elements and the teaching that baptized infants are necessarily saved unless they consciously and explicitly renounce their faith as adults. In accordance with Calvinist theology (see CALVINISM), Presbyterian and Reformed groups, organized into presbyteries and synods with local congregational representation by elders, stress the absolute sovereignty of God in electing those whom he will save and in applying his salvation to them; see PREDESTINATION. Congregationalism historically shares this theology, but differs in maintaining the autonomy of each local congregation. Baptist churches also are congregational in government, but distinctively teach that only confessing adults, and not their infant children, may be baptized, and only by immersion. Methodism maintains the independent ability of man to choose or reject salvation.

Attempts Toward Resolving Differences. At present, elements of unity that cross denominational lines are at least equal in significance to disagreement. Many American Protestant bodies have entered into joint action in the National Council of the Churches of Christ in the United States of America (q.v.), and interdenominational co-operation on the international level, including the participation of the Eastern Orthodox Churches, is found in the World Council of Churches (q.v.). Some other denominations believe that these councils and their participants have rejected or neglected doctrines essential to Christianity, and therefore have formed their own councils. Still other denominations have avoided all such interdenominational affiliations. Some bodies as a whole, as well as individual congregations and persons in every major denomination, profess a strictly orthodox belief based on the infallibility of Scripture and strongly emphasizing the atoning death of Christ and a personal experience of salvation. Some of these churches and persons are widely known as "fundamentalist" (see FUNDAMENTALISM), particularly when their beliefs are associated with evangelistic fervor (see EVANGELICAL) and certain rigid social prohibitions. Less orthodox groups look upon fundamentalism as virtually a worship of the Bible rather than of God; their own emphasis tends rather to a united Christian approach to current community and world problems without insisting on rigid confessional agreement. See also CHURCH, HISTORY OF THE CHRISTIAN; RELIGION: *The Religions.*

W.E.W.

CHRISTIAN METHODIST EPISCOPAL CHURCH, formerly COLORED METHODIST EPISCOPAL CHURCH, Protestant denomination organized in Tennessee in 1870. On matters of doctrine and polity the denomination is in full agreement with the Methodist Church (q.v.). A quadrennial General Conference is the chief policy-making body, and spiritual jurisdiction is exercised by nine bishops. The many interests of the church are promoted by a Commission on Race Relations, a Women's Connectional Council, and boards of evangelism, kingdom extension, Christian education, and lay activities.

The denomination maintains missions in Africa, South America, and the West Indies. Its official organ, the weekly *Christian Index,* is published in Jackson, Tenn.

The Christian Methodist Episcopal Church was formed by Negro members of the Methodist Episcopal Church, South, who withdrew from the parent body by mutual agreement after the Civil War. The right of the Southern Negroes to worship in churches of their own, if they so desired, was first recognized by the Methodist Episcopal Church, South, in 1866, and the proposal to organize an independent Negro denomination was given final approval four years later. The new denomination, known as the Colored Methodist Episcopal Church, held its first General Conference in December, 1870, in Jackson, Tenn. On Jan. 3, 1956, the name was changed officially to Christian Methodist Episcopal Church.

In 1961 the Christian Methodist Episcopal Church, reporting 444,493 members and 2523 separate churches, was the fourth-largest Methodist denomination in the United States.

CHRISTIAN REFORMED CHURCH, religious denomination in the United States and Canada representing largely secession movements from the Reformed (Dutch) Church in 1822, 1857, and 1882. The doctrinal standards are the same as those of other Reformed churches of Dutch origin, viz., the Heidelberg Catechism, Belgic Confession, and Canons of Dordrecht. In 1961 it had 572 churches and a membership of 250,934. Few of the churches use the Dutch language in divine services; half a dozen use some German; a constantly increasing majority employs English in its worship. Mission work is carried on in South America, Africa, China, and among the Indians in New Mexico.

CHRISTIANS. See CHRISTIAN CHURCH; DISCIPLES OF CHRIST.

CHRISTIAN SCIENCE, a religion founded by Mary Baker Eddy (q.v.) at Boston, Mass., in 1879, the doctrines of which were expounded by her in *Science and Health with Key to the Scriptures* (1875). The church based on her teachings is the Church of Christ, Scientist. Christian Science purports to be the science of God and His universe, including man; and the science of salvation from all evil. According to Christian Science, sin, disease, death, want, suffering, and all the phenomena of evil have only a relative existence in human experience, not an absolute reality. Christian Science affirms that every aspect of evil is a phase of error and can be overcome by comprehending that only that which is of God has any reality. The church maintains that its faith and practice are based directly upon the words and work of Christ Jesus, as distinguished from the creeds and customs that originated after the time of Christ, and that it has restored the healing power of primitive Christianity. The church has no clergy, its services being conducted by *readers*. The most important feature of the work of the denomination, the service of healing, is done by members, termed *prac-*

titioners, who are specially trained for the work.

The organization of the Church of Christ, Scientist, consists of "The Mother Church", at Boston, Mass., and "branch churches", and "societies" where the number of Scientists is not large enough to form a church. In 1961 there were more than 3200 Christian Science churches and societies in the world; of these, 2470 were in the United States. The church by-laws prohibit the reporting of membership figures for publication.

The Christian Science Publishing Society issues *The Christian Science Journal* (a monthly magazine in English which includes directories of churches and practitioners), the *Christian Science Sentinel* (a weekly magazine in English), *The Christian Science Monitor* (an international daily newspaper), and *The Herald of Christian Science* (a magazine issued monthly in German and French, and quarterly in Danish, Dutch, Italian, Norwegian, Portuguese, Spanish, Swedish, and English-Braille). The church uses also the media of radio and television; weekly programs are broadcast in the United States and abroad.

CHRISTIANSTED, seaport on the N. coast of the island of St. Croix, in the Virgin Islands.

Ward Allan Howe
The First Church of Christ, Scientist, "The Mother Church" of the faith, in Boston, Mass.

©The Christian Science Publishing Co.
Mary Baker Eddy, American religious leader and founder of Church of Christ, Scientist

Cattle and sugar cane are raised in the surrounding region. Christiansted is the seat of the Municipal Council of St. Croix. Before the U.S. bought the Virgin Islands from Denmark in 1917, the town was the capital of the Danish West Indies. Pop. (1960) 5137.

CHRISTIE, AGATHA MARY CLARISSA (about 1895–), English author, born in Torquay, of an American father and an English mother. She was a prolific writer of detective fiction and the creator of the fictional detective, Hercule Poirot. Among her detective stories are *Murder of Roger Ackroyd* (1926), *Thirteen at Dinner* (1933), *Murder in the Calais Coach* (1934), *Mystery of the Blue Train* (1935), *Hercule Poirot* (1936), *Murder in Mesopotamia* (1936), *And Then There Were None* (1939), *Triple Threat* (1943), *Death Comes at the End* (1944), *Remembered Death* (1945), *There Is a Tide* (1948), *Mrs. McGinty's Dead* (1952), *Pocket Full of Rye* (1954), *What Mrs. McGillicuddy Saw* (1957), *Cat Among the Pigeons* (1959), and *The Pale Horse* (1961). She has written several plays, including *Witness for the Prosecution*, produced in 1953. In 1956 she was made a Commander of the Order of the British Empire. See DETECTIVE STORY.

CHRISTMAS, in the Christian Church, an annual festival, held on December 25, to celebrate the Nativity, or birth of Christ. The origin of the festival is unknown. Scholars believe that it is derived in part from the pre-Christian rites of Germanic and Celtic tribesmen held in celebration of the winter solstice; see YULE. Christmas festivals, generally observed by Christians since the 4th century, include heathen customs such as the use of holly, mistletoe, Yule logs, and wassail bowls. The use of Christmas trees probably originated among the Romans of pre-Christian times from whom it spread to the Germanic peoples and thence to the peoples of the British Isles. In later times Christmas celebrations acquired a wide secular and social significance, expressed in many countries in the exchange of gifts and greeting cards and the suspension of school and work. Dutch settlers brought to the New World the custom of celebrating St. Nicholas' (Santa Claus') day on Christmas Eve.

CHRISTMAS ISLAND, name of two widely separated islands: **1.** An irregularly shaped island in the Indian Ocean, about 190 miles s. of the western part of Java. It consists principally of a plateau, about 1000 ft. above sea level, and is the top of a huge mountain extending about 14,000 ft. beneath the surface of the sea. The greatest length of Christmas Island is about 11 miles and its greatest width is about 9 miles. It was colonized by the British, mainly with Chinese and Malays, to work the island's large deposits of calcium phosphate rock. In 1900 it was incorporated in the Settlement of Singapore Island, which in 1946 became the Crown Colony of Singapore. In World War II it was occupied by the Japanese. It became an Australian dependency in 1958. Area, about 60 sq.m.; pop. (1961 est.) 3099. **2.** The largest atoll of the Pacific Ocean, about 1150 miles s. of Honolulu. Its circumference is over 100 miles. It was annexed by Great Britain in 1888, and after 1919 was included in the Gilbert and Ellice Islands Colony of the British Empire. Area, about 222 sq.m.; pop. (1960 est.) 453.

CHRISTMAS ROSE. See HELLEBORE.

CHRISTOLOGY, technical term in theology, signifying the doctrine of the person of Christ, or the answer to the question of the relation of divine and human nature in Christ. The elements of the problem may be said to have been given by the original and unvarying conviction of the Church. That Christ was man, was too plain to be denied by any. But no less plain did it seem from the beginning, to the Apostles (John 1:14), that He was truly divine. On the subtleties of this problem they did not dwell; but it never occurred to them to divide His personality. When more careful reflection was forced upon the Church, the question was

therefore merely one of adjustment of accepted truths. In the Greek theology there was a subordination of Christ to the Father, but in the Latin Church, Christ is put on an exact equality with the Father. In the Reformation the Protestant Church maintained two natures in one person and jealously affirmed allegiance to the Christology of the historic creeds. See ATHANASIAN CREED.

CHRISTOPHE, HENRI (1767–1820), King of Haiti, born a slave on the island of Grenada. Going to Haiti, he joined the Negro insurgents against the French in 1790, and soon, because of his gigantic stature, energy, and courage, became a leader among them. By Toussaint L'Ouverture (q.v.) he was appointed brigadier general. In 1802 he defended Cape Haiti against the French. He and Gen. Alexandre Sabès Pétion secured the overthrow of the short-lived government of Jean Jacques Dessalines (q.v.) in 1806; and in 1807 Christophe was appointed president of Haiti. Civil War commenced between him and Pétion; but in 1811 Christophe was proclaimed King of Haiti, as Henri I, and ruled with vigor and not without success. But his avarice and cruelty led to an insurrection; deserted by his bodyguard and all his nobles, he shot himself. He left a code of laws which he called the "Code Henri".

CHRISTOPHER, SAINT (probably 3rd cent.), saint of the Roman Catholic and Greek churches, said to have lived in Syria and suffered martyrdom under the Emperor Decius (249–251). According to tradition he was 12 ft. tall and of prodigious strength. In the pride of his strength he would serve only the mightiest upon earth. While in the service of a king, seeing his master's dread of the devil, he became the devil's servant. One day, however, he saw the devil trembling before the image of Christ, and he resolved to serve Christ only, undertaking to carry Christian pilgrims across a river. One day Christ Himself came to him in the form of a child to be carried over, but the burden grew heavier and heavier, until it was almost too much for Christopher to reach the farther shore. "Marvel not, Christopher," said the child, "for with me thou hast borne the sins of all the world". Saint Christopher (Gr. *Christophoros,* "Christbearer") is usually represented carrying the infant Christ and leaning on a great staff. The Greek Church celebrates his festival on May 9, the Roman Catholic on July 25.

CHRISTOPHER NORTH, pen name of John Wilson (q.v.).

CHRIST'S COLLEGE, a college of Cambridge University (q.v.), in England, endowed in 1505 by Lady Margaret Beaufort, Countess of Richmond and Derby, and mother of King Henry VII. At the time of Lady Margaret's grant, which was sufficient to subsidize a master, 12 fellows, and 47 scholars, God's House, founded in 1439, was annexed to the new school. Original structures of the college include one believed to have been designed by the famous English architect Inigo Jones. Among celebrated graduates of Christ's College are the poet John Milton, the philosopher Henry More, the theologian William Paley, and the naturalist Charles Robert Darwin. The college now has a master, 22 fellows, about 30 scholars, and approximately 300 junior members in residence.

CHRIST, SECOND ADVENT OF. See SECOND ADVENT OF CHRIST.

CHRIST'S-THORN. See JUJUBE.

CHRISTUS or **CRISTUS,** PETRUS (about 1400–73), Flemish painter, born at Baerle, North Brabant. He was reputedly a pupil of Jan and Hubert van Eyck (qq.v.) and his style and technique are modeled on theirs. He is believed to have visited Italy and to have instructed Antonella da Messina in the technique of oil painting, which he learned from the van Eycks. Among the works of Christus are "Portrait of Edward Grimston" (Earl of Verulam Collection, Gorhambury, England), "Madonna with Saints" (Städelsches Kunstinstitut, Frankfort), "Pietà" (Brussels Gallery), and "Deposition from the Cross" and "Portrait of a Carthusian Monk" (both in the Metropolitan Museum of Art, New York City).

CHRISTY, HOWARD CHANDLER (1873–1952), American illustrator and painter, born in Morgan Co., Ohio. He studied art in New York City at the National Academy of Design under William Merritt Chase and at the Art Students' League. During the Spanish-American War (1898) he established his reputation by war illustrations published in Scribner's Magazine, Harper's Magazine and Collier's Weekly. He illustrated many magazine serials and the works of James Whitcomb Riley, Richard Harding Davis (qq.v.), and other American writers. Christy was a noted portrait painter. Among the prominent people whose portraits he painted were Theodore Roosevelt, Warren G. Harding, Calvin Coolidge, Mary Roberts Rinehart, Benito Mussolini, Will Rogers, and Fritz Kreisler. His large historical painting "Signing the Constitution" is in the Capitol, Washington, D.C., and another, "Gen. Anthony Wayne's Treaty with the Indians at Greenville, Ohio", is in the State Capitol, Columbus, Ohio.

CHROMATOGRAPHY, analytical technique used for the chemical separation of mixtures of substances. The technique, which depends on the principle of selective adsorption (see COLLOIDAL DISPERSION), was discovered in 1906 by the Russian botanist Michael Tswett (1872–1919). In the course of research on plant pigments he poured a petroleum-ether extract of green leaves over a column of powdered calcium carbonate in a vertical glass tube. As the solution percolated through the column the individual components of the mixture migrated downward at different rates of speed, so that the column became marked with horizontal bands of colors, called a chromatogram; each band corresponded to a different pigment. An important modification of this basic technique was introduced in 1941 by the British biochemists Richard L. M. Synge and Archer J. P. Martin.

CHROMITE, or CHROME IRON ORE, a mineral belonging to the spinel (q.v.) group, consisting of ferrous chromite, $FeCr_2O_4$. It crystallizes in the isometric system and has hardness 5.5 and sp. gr. 4.5. It is found in irregular brownish-black or black grains or octahedral crystals. Chromite is the world's principal ore of the important metal chromium (q.v.), and is mined extensively in Turkey, New Caledonia, Yugoslavia, the U.S.S.R., Greece, Southern Rhodesia, and the Philippine Islands. Production in the United States in 1961 was about 82,000 tons, mined principally in Montana. During World War II domestic production exceeded 100,000 tons per year. In 1961 the U.S. imported 1,323,000 tons. In addition to its use as an ore, chromite is an important constituent of refractory bricks for metallurgical furnaces.

CHROMIUM, a metallic element, symbol Cr, at. no. 24, at. wt. 52.01, sp. gr. 7.1, m.p. 1615°C. (2939°F.), b.p. 2200°C. (3992° F.). It was discovered in 1797 by the French chemist Louis Nicolas Vauquelin (1763–1829), who named it chromium (from Gr. chroma, "color") because of the many different colors of its compounds.

Chromium is a common element, making up about 1/3000th of the earth's crust, and being surpassed in abundance by only seven metals. Chromium may replace part of the aluminum or iron in many common minerals. Workable ores, however, are rare, chromite (q.v.) and crocoite being the only ones of importance.

In chromites and chromic salts, chromium has a valence of 3. Most of these compounds are green; some are red or blue. Chromic oxide, Cr_2O_3, is a green solid. In chromates and dichromates, chromium has a valence of 6. Potassium bichromate, $K_2Cr_2O_7$, is a red, water-soluble solid which, mixed with gelatin, gives a light-sensitive surface useful in photographic printing processes. The chromates are generally yellow, the best-known being lead chromate, $PbCrO_4$, an insoluble solid widely used as a pigment under the name Chrome Yellow. Chrome Green is a mixture of Chrome Yellow with Prussian Blue. The colors of numerous precious stones, including emeralds and rubies, are due to chromium compounds; see ARTIFICIAL GEMS. Compounds of chromium are also used as mordants in dyeing, and as tanning agents in leather manufacture.

CHROMOSOME, in cytology, the unit structure formed by the chromatin of the cell nucleus formed during cell division. It carries the genes, which determine the hereditary characteristics of the cell or organism. Normally, the body cells of each species contain a specific number of chromosomes. This number is halved in the reduction cell division producing the sperm and egg, and is restored by fertilization, half the number coming from each parent. Variation in the number may be induced artificially, especially in plants, where multiples of the normal chromosome number may be produced by treatment with colchicine. See CELL; HEREDITY.

CHROMOSPHERE, the upper layer of the sun's atmosphere, a body of gases at high temperature and very low pressure, with a normal depth of about 6000 miles. The prominences, jets of incandescent gas which occasionally shoot up from the sun's surface to heights of hundreds of thousands of miles, arise in the chromosphere.

The chromosphere normally consists primarily of hydrogen, helium, and calcium. However, when there is a violent disturbance in the lower layers, other materials are brought up into the chromosphere, and its spectrum then shows the presence of iron, sodium, titanium, and numerous other elements. See SUN.

CHRONICLES, BOOKS OF, a portion of the Old Testament, in the third part of the Hebrew canon, recapitulating the history of 2nd Samuel and the Books of Kings, with omissions and additions. The Hebrew name means "events of the days"; the Septuagint entitles it *Paralipomenon* ("things passed over"); Eusebius of Cæsaria called it a *"Chronicon* of the whole divine history", whence its present name. In contrast to the older histories, which were written from the prophetic standpoint, Chronicles shows a strongly Levitical tendency. Most modern scholars hold its date to be about 330 B.C. or later, at the beginning of the Greek supremacy in Asia.

CHRONOLOGY, science dealing with division of time into regular periods, the arrangement of events in order of their occurrence, the assignment of events to their correct dates, and the reconciling of discrepancies in dates due to variations in the systems employed in modern and ancient times.

Astronomical chronology is based on celestial phenomena and the laws governing their order, occurrence, and duration. The dates of celestial phenomena can be determined quite accurately. By reckoning backward, the date of a historical event can often be verified or determined with precision if it was associated with an astronomical event. See ASTRONOMY.

Geological chronology, covering the entire history of the earth, is a science dealing with periods of time ranging into the millions of years. Time scales of these magnitudes are determined, in part, by studying rates of sedimentary deposition. Thus, the thickness of sediments in lakes and oceans or of the sedimentation from wind-blown (aeolian), glacial, or other special processes holds a clue to the passage of time. Akin to the deposition rates of sediments is the erosion rate of rocks and whole mountain ranges, from which sedimentary deposits ultimately derive. Erosion rates, too, yield clues useful in geological chronology. In geology, stratigraphic relations are vast; immense layers of sedimentary stone covering whole regions and often thousands of feet thick may be studied for chronological clues. The interpretation of fossils in such stones is one method used in deriving dates (see PALEONTOLOGY). Properly, the study of sedimentary rock deposits and related fossils in order to establish geochronological dates is called stratigraphic geology. One of the first age determinations for the earth was based on presumed annual additions to the salt content of the oceans. Recently, measurement of the disintegration of radioactive elements in rocks has led to previously unhoped-for accuracy in long-period geological dating. See EARTH: *Age of the Earth*; GEOLOGY, SYSTEMATIC.

Though advanced civilizations are often dated through political chronology (see below), early man and some primitive cultures are dated in ways more akin to the chronological methods used in geology. Thus archeologists note very carefully the order of successive deposits (stratigraphy) containing human artifacts. The principle of stratigraphy assumes that in undisturbed strata the younger (more recent) layers overlie the older (earliest) layers. This relation is often referred to as the law of superposition. The stratigraphic method valuable in archeological dating parallels the stratigraphic method in geology. Thickness of deposits, in archeology as in geology, is one of the factors in time determination. Occasionally, in the case of very ancient men, their burials or their artifacts occur in such a manner that actual geochronological methods help determine the age of the deposit. A very promising method for dating human cultures is the carbon-14 (C^{14}) method. Based on the fact that living organisms take up a naturally occurring radioactive form of carbon during their lifetimes, the C^{14} method permits investigators to determine how much of this radioactive carbon still remains in an organic specimen found with any cultural remains. This determination relates directly to the time lapsed since the specimen was buried, and relatively accurate dates may be worked out from this information.

Chronologists invoke, as well as assist, other sciences. Dendochronology is a method for dating based on counting the number of annual growth rings formed in trees. In this manner, the original log beams in many ancient southwestern U.S. pueblos and cliff dwellings were dated. Dendrochronology thus relates to botany. Less obvious is the relation of chronology to meteorology. Paleoclimatology is a branch of the weather sciences which studies ancient climates.

Political chronology deals with the history of mankind. In the most primitive stage of chronology, a nation referred its history to the lifetime of some central figure, such as the king. This system gave a complete chronology of each individual reign, but the history of the nation was often left incomplete by the lapse of time between the death of a king and the accession of his successor, and by the omission of obscure or unpopular kings from the written records. As political chronology developed, historians instituted *eras,* from national, ecclesiastical, or scientific motives, each era being dated from an outstanding event or a convenient date called the *epoch* of that era.

In ancient Babylon, continuous chronology begins with the birth of King Sargon I, about 2637 B.C. (earlier archeologists placing the date as much as a millennium earlier), and a fairly complete list of kings has been compiled to the first dynasty of Ur, extending back to 3000 B.C. and possibly beyond. The Chaldean astronomers discovered the cycle known as the Saros, a period of 223 lunations

(slightly over 18 years) which is still important in the calculation of eclipses. The chronology of ancient Egypt begins with the reign of Menes, first king of the first dynasty, about 3400 B.C. The Egyptian year began with the rising of the star Sirius but, since their civil year contained 365 days exactly, the Egyptians were compelled to use the Sothic cycle, a period of about 1460 years from one coincidence of the civil with the astronomical year to the next. Such a coincidence occurred about 140 A.D., but it is uncertain whether the first cycle started about 2780 or 4240 B.C.

The Era of the Olympiads of the Greeks was reckoned from July 1, 776 B.C., and Greek astronomers introduced the Metonic cycle of 235 lunations (almost exactly 19 years), and also the Callippic cycle of 940 lunations (even closer to 76 years). In Roman chronology the Era of the Founding of the City (*ab urbe condita,* or A.U.C.) dates from April 22, 753 B.C., and the Julian Era dates from the reform of the calendar by Julius Cæsar in 45 B.C. Under the Empire, in 312 A.D., Constantine introduced a cycle of 15 years called *Indiction.*

The Christian Era, now used almost exclusively throughout the Western World for civil chronology, was introduced in 533 A.D. by Dionysius Exiguus, who fixed the birth of Christ in the year of Rome 754. It is now generally agreed that the beginning of the era should have been fixed a few years earlier.

Scriptural chronology is extremely uncertain because various local chronologies were used at different times by scriptural writers, and different systems were used by contemporaneous writers. The Jewish Mundane Era, with the epoch 3761 B.C., was not used until the 15th century A.D., and the dating of the creation was given by Archbishop James Ussher as 4004 B.C., in the 17th century. The Mohammedan Era dates from the Hegira, July 16, 622 A.D., but since the year is based on lunar months, and is of variable length, the reconciliation of its dates with those of the Gregorian calendar is extremely complicated. See also NEW TESTAMENT CHRONOLOGY.

The epoch of the Christian Era is too recent an event to be a convenient reference point for technical calculations. Joseph Scaliger in 1582 proposed that the epoch of the Julian Era be fixed at January 1, 4713 B.C. at noon. The beginnings of the cycles used in ancient times coincided at this time, and the date was sufficiently remote to furnish a reference point to which all other chronological systems might be compared. The Julian cycle contains 7980 years of 365¼ days, but computation by years is seldom used, and the days are numbered consecutively; thus, Julian Day 2,436,205 began at noon on January 1, 1958.

In many cases, astronomical chronology is used to verify or correct dates given in history for political events. For example, by reckoning backward, the time and place may be fixed for the occurrence of a remarkable eclipse, such as the eclipse reported by the Greek scientist Thales as causing the suspension of a battle between the Medes and Persians, which was found to have occurred on May 28, 585 B.C. Scottish history furnishes another instance: when King Haakon IV sailed from Bergen with his Norse fleet to punish the king of Scotland, he put in at Ronaldsvoe in Orkney, and there the sun appeared as a thin, bright, ring. Sir David Brewster found that an annular eclipse of the sun was visible in Orkney on August 5, 1263, about one o'clock. Such verifications in chronology are dependent upon the testimony of contemporary writers, or on information which is derived from inscriptions found on coins, medals, or monuments.

In the history of Western civilizations, the principal problems of chronology lie in the reconciliation of dates in the various ecclesiastical calendars, such as the Julian, Gregorian, and Mohammedan. For example, an article appeared in the *Edinburgh Courant* of February 19, 1706. The article was an abridgement of one published in the *London Gazette* of February 13, 1705, which, in turn, was a translation from the *Amsterdam Gazette* of February 22, 1706. All three were published in the same week. The discrepancy in year was caused by the fact that Scotland and the Low Countries began the year on January 1, while England, until 1752, began the year on March 25. The discrepancy in days was caused by the use of the Gregorian calendar in the Low Countries, while, at that time, England and Scotland still adhered to the Julian calendar. See CALENDAR; DAY; MONTH; YEAR.

CHRYSANTHEMUM, the common and scientific name for flowers of a genus in the family Carduaceae. None of them are native to the New World, but some 200 species are known from Europe, Asia, and northern Africa, and some naturalized species are among the commonest American wild flowers. Notable among the latter is *C. leucanthemum,* the white, ox-eye, or common daisy, which is not a daisy at all (see DAISY). Many of the species of chrysanthemum have been under cultivation for as long as 2000 years, and

W. Atlee Burpee Co.

Tricolor chrysanthemum, Chrysanthemum carinatum

numerous hybrids have been developed, so that the nomenclature of these flowers is exceedingly complex.

Chrysanthemums, like all the other plants in the same family, have composite flowers; that is, the blossom is actually made up of many flowers. In the common daisy, for example, the yellow center or *disk* is composed of numerous tube-shaped flowers, and each of the white *rays,* incorrectly called petals, is a strap-shaped flower. The individual ray flowers and disk flowers are called florets.

Those plants which are most commonly thought of as chrysanthemums, the commercial or florists' varieties and the garden "mums", have large, globular heads in which the ray flowers are greatly multiplied, while the disk flowers are unnoticeable or even absent. Several of the Oriental species have this habit of growth, and numerous hybrids have been developed. These hybrids have blossoms up to 8 in. in diameter, double, semidouble, or single, and the individual florets, which grow erect, incurved, or reflexed, may be quilled, twisted, or flat. The terms *pompon* and *button* are applied to small, globular flowers, the term *anemone* to flowers with twisted rays, and the term *decorative* to loose, open flowers with flat, grooved, or tubular rays. Where tubular rays are open and flattened at the tips, the plants are called *spoon mums.* Other varieties are sometimes described as "feathery", "plumed", or "spidery". These flowers are produced in all shades of bronze, brown, purple, red, pink, yellow, and white.

In addition to their ornamental uses, commercial use has been made of several species, particularly the pyrethrums, from the flowers of which an important insecticide is prepared. The leaves of the costmary have been used as food, and as a flavoring for beer. The feverfew owes its name to its former medicinal use as a febrifuge. B.S.P.

CHRYSOBERYL, a mineral used as a gem stone, consisting of beryllium aluminate; it crystallizes in the orthorhombic system, and has hardness 8.5, and sp. gr. 3.7. It was considered a precious stone by the ancients, and was called "Oriental topaz", a name now used for the yellow sapphire. Although its hardness is greater than that of the emerald, a precious stone, it has little luster, fire, or brilliancy, and is now considered a semiprecious stone. In color chrysoberyl varies from yellow through green to brown; some varieties show a secondary red color when viewed in certain lights.

Three varieties of chrysoberyl are used as gems: an emerald-green variety called alexandrite; a plain yellowish-green variety which is sometimes incorrectly called chrysolite; and a green variety called cymophane, with marked chatoyancy, which is the best-known and most valuable variety of cat's-eye (q.v.).

CHRYSOLORAS, MANUEL (1355?–1415), Greek scholar, born probably in Constantinople. In 1393 the Byzantine Emperor Manuel II Paleologus sent Chrysoloras to Italy to enlist aid against the Turks. Chrysoloras settled in Italy and became a pioneer in the dissemination of Greek culture in what was then the western world. From about 1395 to 1398 he was professor of Greek in Florence and made notable translations of the works of the Greek poet Homer and the philosopher Plato. Chrysoloras died while en route to attend the Council of Constance (see CONSTANCE, COUNCIL OF) as a representative of the Greek Church. His *Erotemata sive Quæstiones* (published posthumously in 1484) was the first Greek grammar used in western Europe.

CHRYSOSTOM, SAINT JOHN (about 345–407), a Father of the early Christian Church, born at Antioch. He studied oratory under the rhetorician Libanius, and began the career of an advocate. Dissatisfied with this, he studied for three years with Bishop Meletius, by whom in his twenty-third year he was baptized. After six years spent as a monk in the mountains near Antioch, he was ordained deacon by Meletius in 381, and presbyter by Bishop Flavianus in 386. The eloquence, earnestness, and practical nature of his preaching secured for him the reputation of the greatest orator of the ancient Church. In 398 the Emperor Arcadius made him Patriarch of Constantinople. His preaching against vices excited the enmity of Theophilus, Patriarch of Alexandria, and the Empress Eudoxia, who banished him from the capital in 403. He was soon recalled, to be banished again, in 404, to Cucusus, in the desert parts of the Taurus Mountains, where he labored to convert the Persians and Goths in the neighborhood. A sect sprang up after his death called *Johannists,* who refused to acknowledge his successors; nor did they return to the general communion until 438. The surname Chrysostom (Gr. *chrysostomos,* "golden mouthed") was first used in the 7th century. St. Chrysostom's works are numerous, and include homilies, commentaries, epistles, treatises, and liturgies. His feast day is Jan. 27th.

CHUB, popular name for several fishes, particularly *Leuciscus cephalus,* a member of the Carp family. It is bluish black on the upper parts, white on the belly, and golden yellow on the cheeks and gills. It rarely exceeds 5 lbs. in weight. It occurs in the rivers of England, southwest Scotland, Europe, and Asia Minor. It spawns in April and May. The name is also applied to several American species of this family, particularly the horned dace (see DACE). The chub is of little value as food.

CHUBUT, Territory of s. Argentina, extending from the Andes Mts. in the west, where it abuts on Chile, to the Atlantic Ocean on the east. Most of the surface east of the fertile valleys of the Andean foothills is a grassy plain, suitable for grazing and farming, in which the government encourages colonization by Argentinians and immigrants. The Territory is traversed from west to east by the Chubut River, at the mouth of which, on the Atlantic Ocean, is the Territorial capital, Rawson. Petroleum is produced in Chubut. Area, 65,337 sq.m.; pop. (1960 prelim.) 142,195. See PATAGONIA.

CHUKCHI, a people living in the extreme northeast of Asia. The reindeer Chukchi dwell in the interior about the Kolyma River; the sea (or fishing) Chukchi, the great majority, inhabit the coast of the Arctic from Bear

Island to East Cape, while on the Pacific side they have mingled with the Eskimos. They are tall and rather light-skinned, and differ somewhat in form and features from the typical Mongolians, with whom they are allied by speech. The Chukchi have a wealth of folklore and mythology with traces of Eskimo influence. Their belief in a violent death as a prerequisite to immortality was, until recently, the cause of a practice known as *kamitok,* the pious slaughter of the aged by their children. Some of the Chukchi accepted Christianity. Since 1930 the land of the Chukchi has formed the Chukot National District of Soviet Russia, with its capital at the small port of Anadyr. Area of district, 254,991 sq. m.; pop., about 15,000.

CHULA VISTA, city in San Diego Co., Calif., on San Diego Bay, 5 miles s. of the city of San Diego. It has over 2 miles of bay waterfront. Lemons, celery, and flowers are raised in the vicinity, and in the city are aircraft factories (parts and assembly). Pop. (1960) 42,034.

CHUNGKING, city and river port of Szechwan Province, China, on a rocky peninsula in the Yangtze R., at its confluence with the Kialing, about 750 miles w.s.w. of Nanking. It is the leading port, commercial center, and distributing point of western China. Since 1890, when it was opened to foreign trade, its imports have included metals, kerosene, soap, textiles, and dyes. Its exports include tea, rice, tobacco, salt, sugar, wax, wood oil, musk, medicinal plants, silk and silk products, cotton yarn and cotton products, all produced in the surrounding region; and timber, wool, skins, and hides from the mountain regions beyond the Min River to the west.

The history of Chungking goes back more than 4000 years and is an integral part of the history of the Hsia, Chou, Ch'in, Yuan, and Ming dynasties (see CHINA: *History*). In February, 1923, it became a municipality of the Chinese republic; and following the outbreak of hostilities with Japan, Chungking, on Nov. 20, 1937, became the temporary capital of China. In 1940 it was made an official auxiliary capital and its limits were enlarged by the inclusion of adjoining communities. On May 1, 1946, the Chinese government transferred the capital from Chungking to Nanking. The population of Chungking in 1931 was 635,000; in 1961 it was estimated to be 2,165,000.

CHUR (Fr. *Coire*), capital of Grisons Canton, E. Switzerland, situated on the Plessur R., 74 m. by rail s.E. of Zürich. It lies in the valley of the upper Rhine, 1950 ft. above sea level, and is surrounded by mountains. Chur was settled by the Romans as *Curia Rætorum.* As an episcopal see it dates from the 4th or 5th centuries. In the western portion, or old town, is the cathedral church of St. Lucius, completed in 1282, on the site of an older church. It contains paintings by Dürer and Holbein. In the same quarter stands the palace of the Roman Catholic bishop, and nearby is the episcopal seminary, erected on the remains of a 6th-century monastery. Chur was noted early as an important trade center on the route from Italy to Germany. The present-day town has an active trade in wine and agricultural products. Pop. (1960) 24,825.

CHURCH (Gr. *kyriakon,* "the Lord's house"), a term meaning both a building devoted to public worship, especially Christian, and a body of worshipers who adhere to the same beliefs, rites, and ecclesiastical authority.

Architecture and Buildings. In its strict meaning, a church building is an ecclesiastical building in which full service can be performed and the sacraments administered. A church differs from an oratory and chapel (q.v.), where only prayers can be offered and the sacraments cannot usually be administered.

The early Christians had no separate buildings for worship, but met for this purpose in private houses. The gatherings at cemeteries on the anniversaries of the deaths of martyrs probably gave rise to the earliest special buildings for religious services, chapels connected with cemeteries outside city walls, and often built also at the entrance to catacombs. In the 3d century, in addition to the cemeterial places of worship built outside city walls, parish churches for more extensive worship were built inside the walls; and both were of considerable size. Later, two additional and distinct types of churches came into existence, the episcopal church or cathedral, in which the bishop had his seat; and the conventual church, also called abbey church, which was attached to a monastery. All these types of churches still exist today. Ranking above the episcopal church is the metropolitan church, that of an archbishop or patriarch. In the Roman Catholic Church, ranking above the metropolitan church is the pontifical church, the Lateran Basilica in Rome, the seat of the Pope.

A church building consists of two essential parts: the *nave,* for the congregation, and the *sanctuary,* for the clergy. The *nave* is the central part of the church, usually extending from portal to choir or chancel, and flanked by side aisles. The *sanctuary* is the part of the church in which the principal altar is placed. The original form of the Christian religious gathering, the *agape* or love feast, was a meal eaten in common and accompanied by song and prayer; so little fixed liturgy was prescribed that until the 3rd and 4th centuries the clergy and laity were not separated. The semicircle of the *apse,* adapted from the hemicycle of the Roman basilica, held the presbyters and bishop; and in front of it was placed the *altar*; beyond the altar the *choir* held the readers and singers, separated from the nave of the church by a parapet, which inclosed the pulpits or ambones. The nave itself was at first generally single, but the form of the basilica, with its side aisles separated by columns was soon adopted, and the men were placed in one aisle, the women in the other. In the Orient, however, the women were placed in galleries. The use of martyrs' relics, soon required by Church regulations in every church, led to the construction of a shrine to contain them in or beneath the altar. This shrine developed, between the 6th and 8th centuries, into a monumental *crypt,* sometimes filling the entire space beneath the church, but more often only that under the choir, the pavement of which was thus raised above the level of the nave. Churches are generally placed so that the apse faces east and the façade west. But the earliest practice was the reverse.

The similarity between the form of the early church and that of the already existing public and private basilica (q.v.) is self-evident. The church building was oblong, with a semicircular east end. In some large early churches the form of a T was given to the plan by the addition of a cross arm between apse and nave. The nave itself was flanked by one or two aisles on each side. Sometimes the aisle was carried around the apse, converting it into a circular or octagonal east end. Small chapels radiated from this aisle, and the apse was made as high as the choir. The façade, usually at the west end, took the outline of the nave and aisles. Near it or connected with it was a bell tower, which became an integral part of the architectural composition. In the Carolingian period, under monastic influence, the plan of churches was changed into the form of the cross, bringing in the *transept.* Later the choir was so enlarged as to rival the nave in size in many Gothic cathedrals. Other forms of churches were also built in the medieval pe-

riod. These included concentric churches, either round or polygonal, such as San Stefano Rotondo, in Rome; churches in the form of a Greek cross, such as San Marco, in Venice; and single-nave churches, sometimes domed as in Byzantine architecture, or sometimes vaulted or flat-roofed, as in Dominican and Franciscan churches.

Church furniture and decoration were important features. A church in the Middle Ages was covered with instructive sculptures or paintings, and planned by the ecclesiastics. Mosaics, frescoes, tapestries, and painted-glass windows within, sculptured reliefs and statuary without, were used in profusion. St. Bernard carried on a crusade for simplicity, which was successful only within his own order of Cistercian monks. A second reaction against church magnificence came with Protestantism. But with the growth of Protestantism also came new developments in church building. The cathedral of St. Paul in London, erected (1695–1710) by the architect Sir Christopher Wren (q.v.), served as a model for many churches built in America during Colonial and early post-Revolutionary days. After the Gothic revival of the 19th century, many beautiful parish churches in that style were built both in Europe and America. Among the many notable churches built in modern times, in the Gothic or other styles, are the Westminster Cathedral (Roman Catholic) London; Sacré-Cœur de Montmartre (Roman Catholic), Paris; Trinity Church (Protestant Episcopal), New York City; St. Patrick's Cathedral (Roman Catholic), New York city; Cathedral of St. John the Divine (Protestant Episcopal), New York City; St. Thomas Church (Protestant Episcopal), New York City; the Mormon Tabernacle, Salt Lake City, Utah; the First Church of Christ, Scientist (Christian Science), Boston, Mass.; and the Riverside Church (Baptist), New York City. See ARCHITECTURE; CATHEDRAL.

Hierarchy and Organization. A church is generally defined by Western theologians, in accord with the Articles of the Church of England, as "a congregation of faithful men, in which the pure word of God is preached, and the sacraments be duly administered in all those things that are of necessity requisite to the same." The Roman Catholic Church emphasizes in addition the "rule of legitimate pastors", and subjection to the Pope, the Bishop of Rome, as Vicar of Christ. Under these general definitions great variety in organization is recognized. The *papal* government makes all authority finally dependent upon the Pope. The *episcopal* government is administered by bishops, who are essentially equal in honor and authority, although there may be archbishops who have a certain priority and jurisdiction over other bishops. The *presbyterian* government puts authority in the hands of elders, ministerial and lay, elected ultimately by the congregation. The *congregational* government puts the entire authority over each local congregation of believers in that congregation alone.

Various dogmas are held as to the manner in which the life of the Church is perpetuated: that maintained by the great majority of Christians, the members of the Roman Catholic, Eastern, and Anglican churches, is known as the theory of apostolic succession; while the Protestant churches in general postulate no formal system of handing down the Church from age to age. See APOSTOLIC SUCCESSION; BISHOP; CONGREGATIONALISM; CREEDS.

CHURCH, FREDERICK EDWIN (1826–1900), American landscape painter, born at Hartford, Conn. Among his chief works are "The Ægean Sea" and "Heart of the Andes" (Metropolitan Museum, New York City), "Cotopaxi" (New York Public Library), and "The Great Falls at Niagara" (Corcoran Gallery, Washington, D.C.).

CHURCH CALENDAR, a table containing the holy days, saints' days, and festivals of a church, with the dates of the civil calendar on which they occur. In the Christian churches the calendar contains the fixed feasts, which, like Christmas, recur on the same date each year, and the movable feasts, which depend on the date of Easter (q.v.). The most important of the early church calendars was compiled by Furius Dionisius Philocalus about 354. After the Reformation, the German Lutheran Church retained the Roman calendar. The calendar of the Church of England contains the daily Scripture lessons, the holy days of the Church, and some Roman festivals which have been retained because of popular custom. The calendar of the Protestant Episcopal Church in the U.S. retains only those festivals which have a scriptural origin. See METONIC CYCLE; SAINT.

CHURCH DISCIPLINE, the means employed by the Christian Church, besides the ministration of word and sacraments, to secure on the part of its members a faithful adherence to their profession. Under the Decian persecution strict rules were made for the restoration of apostates. These rules remained in force till the 5th century, but a reaction followed that led to extreme laxity, and the gradual secularization of discipline

continued. Public canonical penances were gradually abolished except in cases of flagrant public offenses, and their place was taken by private penance and the application of indulgence (q.v.). The extreme punishments in the Middle Ages were the Greater Excommunication (see EXCOMMUNICATION) for the individual, and Interdict (q.v.) for the community.

In the Protestant churches public confession of sins which caused public scandal, and submission to public rebuke, were sometimes required. Practices like those of the primitive Church were established in many churches after the Reformation, but they have fallen into disuse. The power of exclusion from the Lord's Supper, and from church membership, is, however, generally retained. Ministers or other officials are, upon giving offense in their doctrine or conduct, suspended from their functions or altogether deposed from their office. The exercise of church discipline belongs to a hierarchy, or to the officials assembled in church courts, or to the members of each congregation, according as the church is Episcopalian, Presbyterian, or independent in its church government.

In the United States, church discipline is administered exclusively by church officials and judicatories. If the rights of property and of personal liberty are illegally invaded, under pretext of administering church discipline, the civil courts have authority to afford redress. See CIVIL CHURCH LAW.

CHURCHES OF ASIA, seven. See SEVEN CHURCHES OF ASIA.

CHURCHES OF CHRIST, group of churches having no over-all organization and first recognized as a separate religious body by the U.S. Bureau of the Census in 1906. Members consider themselves true Christians in direct descent from the primitive Christian church and not members of a modern denomination. The churches follow an extreme form of congregational polity, holding that the local body of worshipers is the only organization sanctioned by the New Testament. No general conference or assembly is held, consequently, and there are no central headquarters. The affairs of each church are managed by an elder assisted by a deacon. Both are chosen from the membership by the full congregation.

The Churches of Christ do not ordinarily collaborate with each other in educational, missionary, and charitable work. With the assistance of voluntary associations of private individuals, the churches separately maintain missions in about fifty countries and operate orphanages and homes for the aged, twenty colleges and numerous schools in the United States, including the Abilene Christian College in Abilene, Texas, and ten schools and colleges outside the U.S. One of their best-known periodicals is *The Gospel Advocate,* founded in 1855.

Members approve only those religious tenets and forms for which specific authority can be found in the New Testament. Accordingly, their worship consists of a standard, fivefold pattern of reading and preaching from the Scriptures, the commemorative celebration of the Lord's Supper, prayer, the singing of hymns unaccompanied by the organ or other instrumental music, and contributions for church support. Belief in Christ as the Son of God, repentance of sin, and baptism by immersion are requirements for membership.

The pioneer Churches of Christ congregations originally were counted among the Disciples of Christ (q.v.). During the latter part of the 19th century some congregations of Disciples began to install organs for musical accompaniment at divine services and to relax membership requirements. Conservative congregations, objecting strongly to these innovations and to alignment with missionary societies, gradually withdrew from the Disciples. By 1906 the conservative churches had become completely independent. There are presently Churches of Christ congregations in all 50 States. The congregations are most numerous in Alabama, Arkansas, Kentucky, Oklahoma, Tennessee, and Texas.

In 1960 membership totaled about 2,250,-000 in 18,500 separate congregations.

CHURCHES OF GOD IN NORTH AMERICA, a religious denomination in the United States. Its doctrines agree generally with those of the Baptists. It originated in revivals which took place under the preaching of the Rev. John Winebrenner, a German Reformed Church pastor, at Harrisburg, Pa. In 1830, the members adopted a basis of organization, the leading points of which were that the believers in any given place are, under the divine order, to constitute one body; that division into sects and parties under human names and creeds is contrary to the spirit of the New Testament; that the believers of any community, organized into one body, constitute God's household or family, and should be known as the Church of God; that the Scriptures, without note or comment, constitute a sufficient rule of faith and practice, while creeds and confessions tend to divisions and sects; and that the ordinances of immersion in water in the name

of the Trinity, the washing of the saints' feet, and the partaking of bread and wine in commemoration of the suffering and death of Christ, are binding upon all believers. The words "Church of God" in the titles of the church's elderships (annual conferences) or general elderships (general conferences) were changed in 1896 to "Churches of God". The denomination has a college at Findlay, Ohio, a collegiate institute at Fort Scott, Kans., an academy at Barkeyville, Pa., and a bookstore and publishing house at Harrisburg, Pa. It sustains missionaries and has an active Woman's Missionary Society. In 1960 it had about 380 churches and 37,500 members.

CHURCH, FATHERS OF THE. See FATHERS OF THE CHURCH.

CHURCH GOVERNMENT. See CHURCH; CHURCH DISCIPLINE; BISHOP; PRESBYTERIANISM.

CHURCH, HISTORY OF THE CHRISTIAN. With respect to time, the history of the Christian Church is divided into three periods: *Ancient, Medieval,* and *Modern.* The first period dates from the birth of Christ to the time of Constantine; the second, from that epoch to the Reformation; and the third, from the Reformation to the present day.

The beginning of the Christian Church dates from the Pentacostal effusion of the Holy Spirit (about 33 A.D.), when the first confessors of Christ formed a public community. Its nucleus was the first Jewish Christian community at Jerusalem under the "pillar-apostles" James, Peter, and John. As members were quickly enlisted, especially from the Jews of the Dispersion, the organization of the Church began with the appointment of seven deacons, including Stephen, the first Christian martyr. The elements of the primitive faith were to a certain extent unified and systematized by the Apostle Paul, whose missionary journeys (about 40–58 A.D.) began the evangelization of Europe.

The Roman empire maintained the view that there could be no worship of God apart from the state, and, when the early Christian Church refused to take part in the state worship as requiring idolatry, it became a *religio illicita,* and was proscribed and persecuted. The persecution continued with varying degrees of intensity until 260 A.D., when Gallienus declared Christianity a *religio licita.* For forty years the Church had peace, and flourished on every side. Diocletian, however, by four edicts of progressive severity, from 303 to 304, made a final desperate effort to annihilate Christianity throughout the empire, even decreeing torture for all Christians. The succession of Constantine in 313 delivered Christendom from its last Roman persecutor.

From that time on, the principal enemy of the Church was internal dissension. The Montanists, claiming new inspirations by the Holy Spirit, caused the convocation of the first synods, held in Asia Minor about 170. Such assemblies became common in the various provinces of the empire by the 3rd century. The controversy over the date of Easter (q.v.) disturbed the Church for a century and a half, and was finally settled at the Ecumenical Council of Nicæa in 325. At the same council, the dogma of the Trinity gained its first victory over the teachings of Arius, by the combined influence of Athanasius and Constantine, and completed its triumph at the second Ecumenical Council at Constantinople in 381. After this the Church was distracted by controversies over the teachings of Origen, the doctrines of Apollinaris the Younger, the disputes between the schools of Antioch and Alexandria over the literal interpretation of the Scriptures, the Nestorian (q.v.) controversy, the Monophysite heresy, holding that Christ had a single nature, the Monothelete heresy, holding that the two natures of Christ had a common will, and the controversy over Iconoclasm (q.v.). These discussions continued from the 4th to the 9th centuries in the Eastern Church, while in the West, theological interest centered in the conflict between the teachings of St. Augustine and Pelagianism (q.v.).

Meanwhile paganism was steadily suppressed. In the West, Christianity rose with renewed vigor from the ruins of the old empire, by the conversion of the Teutonic and Slavonic nations. During the period of waning political influence in the decaying Roman empire, the social power once held by the Roman officials gradually passed to the Christian bishops.

At the beginning of the 8th century, Christendom was threatened by Mohammedanism from the Near East and Spain, and by the ancient idolatry of the Saxons spreading once more across the Rhine. The victory of Charles Martel at Tours (732) gave a final check to the Saracens in the West, but the subjugation of the Saxons by Charlemagne took thirty-two years (772–804), and their conversion to Christianity gradually followed.

The temporal dominion of the Papacy (see PAPAL STATES) grew under the rule of the Carolingian kings from the middle of the 8th century. About the same time dissension between the churches of the East and the West

increased. Interference by the Eastern emperors in the controversies of the Church led to confusion in the relations of church and state, and widened the breach between East and West. Photius, Patriarch of Constantinople, laid down the dogmatic basis of the Schism in 867, and the severance was completed in 1054, when the papal legates laid the Roman anathema on the altar of St. Sophia in Constantinople.

In the 13th century the Church was at the zenith of its power. Heresy was treated as rebellion against the state as well as against religious authority, and the Inquisition was established for the permanent repression of dangerous heretics. Such unrestricted power soon brought about reverses. The worldliness of certain popes, the removal of the papacy to Avignon with its subjection to French policy, and the opposition to papal authority by secular rulers, both princes and bishops, laid the foundations of the 16th-century Protestant Reformation (q.v.), which divided Christendom into two hostile camps.

The Counter Reformation began in Bavaria in 1563, and quickly spread. Led by the order of the Jesuits, it continued with great success until the middle of the 17th century. It was favored in Germany by the Peace of Augsburg, which had been signed in 1555, but in France the issue was for some time in doubt. Four religious wars had ravaged the country, and during the reign of Henry III religious dissension gave rise to five civil wars. However, liberty of conscience was extended to French Protestants by the Edict of Nantes in 1598.

From 1555 the ecclesiastical position of each German territory was dependent on the religious convictions of its ruler, and the members of the Lutheran Church had political equality with "the old religion"; but the exclusion of the "Reformed" from that provision led to the isolation of Lutheranism from the struggles of Protestantism in France, the Netherlands, and England. Stability was attained only after the struggle of the Thirty Years' War, when, at the Peace of Westphalia, Catholics and Protestants agreed to recognize each other's rights to existence. In the Lutheran Church many of the Roman ceremonies were retained, and congregational organization was neglected; whereas the Reformed churches were organized on a congregational basis.

In England, the Reformation was conducted on more "Catholic" lines than on the Continent. The Book of Common Prayer was introduced, and a confession of faith in forty-two articles was drawn up. After a period of persecution under Mary Tudor (see MARY I), the Anglican Church was established under Queen Elizabeth in the closest union with the state. English Puritanism was a commingled form of liberalism with pietism, partly political and partly religious. It opposed the ceremonial elements which the Church of England retained after its separation from Rome. The working principle of Puritanism was reformation through the members of the church itself, as opposed to reformation originating with the crown.

The reformation in Scotland had received from John Knox a strictly Calvinistic stamp. The Protestant nobles (called the "Lords of the Congregation") entered in 1557 for the first time into a "Covenant" (see COVENANTERS) and the Scotch Confession of Faith was ratified by the Scottish parliament in 1560. The efforts of Mary, Queen of Scots, to win Scotland back to Roman Catholicism were fruitless. The first National Covenant "against all kind of Papistry" was signed by king and people in 1581, and frequently renewed. In 1592 the Presbyterian constitution was established. After the accession of Charles II, Episcopacy was re-established both in England and Scotland. In 1662, two thousand ministers were deprived of their posts for refusing to subscribe to the second Act of Uniformity. In the same reign other oppressive legislation increased the civil disabilities of both Nonconformists and Roman Catholics. The persecution continued until 1689, when the Act of Toleration extended religious liberty to dissenters.

In Germany the reaction from the violence of the Thirty Years' War and the lifeless orthodoxy of the succeeding century took the form of Pietism, which stressed personal sanctification rather than the Reformation doctrine of justification by faith.

The founders of English Pietism, or Methodism, did not aim at any new doctrine or order, but only sought, like the German Pietists, to deepen spiritual life. Methodist societies began to be organized in 1739. About the end of the 18th century the influence of the Methodist movement extended into the Established Church, and issued in the formation of the Evangelical party, a spiritual development of the Low Church party, which, centering in Cambridge, became for a while the most energetic group in the Church of England. At Oxford, which had been the center of the High Church party since the time of Archbishop Laud, the Tractarian movement began about 1833. Although the movement was opposed by church authorities

and several of its leaders were converted to Roman Catholicism, it continued under the leadership of Edward B. Pusey (q.v.). See OXFORD MOVEMENT.

In Ireland, the Anglican Church, which had received the entire ecclesiastical endowment taken from the Irish clergy by James I, was disestablished and disendowed in 1871 by the Irish Church Act of 1869.

In the American Colonies, many of the early settlers, who had left the Old World to escape religious persecution, granted the freedom of conscience they sought to other denominations within their settlements, while many others did not. It was not until the adoption of the constitution, with its guarantee of religious freedom, that liberty of conscience was assured. For subsequent development of the Church in the U.S., see separate articles under the titles of each church and denomination.

CHURCHILL, JOHN, 1st DUKE OF MARLBOROUGH (1650–1722), English soldier, born in Musbury, Devonshire. In 1672–73 he served with distinction under his patron, the Duke of York, who commanded the English troops sent to assist King Louis XIV of France in his war against the Dutch. In 1682, Churchill, then a colonel, was created Lord Churchill of Eyemouth in the Scottish peerage, and three years later was made Baron Churchill of Sandridge, Hertfordshire in the English peerage. During the rebellion led by the Duke of Monmouth and the Earl of Argyll, in 1685, Churchill was second in command of the forces of King James II, and was made a major general. Later, on learning that James intended to make Roman Catholicism the state religion of England, Churchill conspired with Prince William of Orange against James. When William landed in England in 1688, Churchill was made a lieutenant general by James and sent to fight William, but instead he deserted to the latter. In 1689 William III made Churchill a privy councillor and created him Earl of Marlborough.

Twice during the following years, in 1692 and again in 1696, the Earl of Marlborough was charged with treason because of his close relations with James, who was then living in exile in France, but nothing came of the accusations. During the War of the Spanish Succession (see SPANISH SUCCESSION, WAR OF THE), Marlborough, who was commander in chief of the armies of England and Holland, was created 1st Duke of Marlborough, in 1702, as a reward for his brilliant victories over the French. His greatest triumph in that war was the victory won in the battle of Blenheim (q.v.).

In 1711 Marlborough, whose wife and political associates had incurred the animosity of Queen Anne, was accused of embezzling public funds, was removed as commander in chief, and was stripped of the public offices which he had been given in gratitude for his military exploits. He lived abroad from 1712 to 1714. In the latter year, following the accession of George I to the throne of England, Marlborough returned to England, where his military rank was restored to him.

CHURCHILL, RANDOLPH HENRY SPENCER, usually called LORD RANDOLPH CHURCHILL (1849–95), English statesman, third son of the 7th Duke of Marlborough, born at Blenheim Palace. He was educated at Eton and Oxford, and entered Parliament in 1874 as as member for Woodstock. He was a passive member until 1880, when the Conservative defeat roused him to action as the leader of the "fourth party", a small band of militant Conservatives. He distinguished himself as a ready, unconventional debater, attracting particular attention by his criticism of Gladstone's foreign and domestic policy. He became prominent as chairman of the Conservative Union (1884), and in 1885 unsuccessfully attempted to defeat John Bright in Birmingham, but returned to Parliament for South Paddington. From June, 1885, to January, 1886, he was secretary of state for India, his period of office being marked by the annexation of Burma. For six months in 1886 he was chancellor of the exchequer, but resigned. He was the exponent of a progressive program for the Conservative Party which became known as "Tory democracy", and had a considerable following of young Conservatives. In 1892 he traveled in South Africa, and wrote *Men, Mines, and Animals in South Africa.*

CHURCHILL, WINSTON (1871–1947), American author, born in St. Louis, Mo., and educated at the United States Naval Academy. Annapolis, Md. He is noted for his American historical novels. Among his writings are the novels *Richard Carvel* (1899), *The Crisis* (1901), *The Crossing* (1904), *Coniston* (1906), *Mr. Crewe's Career* (1908), *A Modern Chronicle* (1910), *The Inside of the Cup* (1913), *A Far Country* (1915), and *The Dwelling Place of Light* (1917) ; and a book on ethics based on study of the Old Testament, *The Uncharted Way* (1941).

CHURCHILL, SIR WINSTON LEONARD SPENCER (1874–   ), British statesman and author, born at Blenheim Palace, Oxfordshire,

British Information Services

Sir Winston Churchill

and educated at Harrow and Sandhurst. He was the elder son of Randolph Henry Spencer Churchill. In 1895 he was attached to the Spanish army in Cuba as a war correspondent. He fought with the British army in India (1897) and the Sudan (1898).

On the outbreak of the Boer War (1899) he went to the Transvaal, and was taken prisoner by the Boers while acting as correspondent for the London *Morning Post*. He was imprisoned at Pretoria, but later escaped. In 1900, he was elected a member (Conservative) of Parliament for Oldham. He opposed Joseph Chamberlain's tariff reform proposals, and in the sessions of 1904–05 acted with the Liberals. He became parliamentary secretary for the colonies under the Campbell-Bannerman ministry in December, 1905, and in the general election of the following month he became a member (Liberal) of Parliament for Manchester, Northwest. He then became undersecretary of state for the colonies, was promoted to the cabinet in 1908 as president of the Board of Trade, made home secretary in 1910, and first lord of the admiralty in 1911. An excellent orator, known for his brilliant repartee, Churchill became one of the most prominent Parliamentary speakers.

At the outbreak of World War I, Churchill became first lord of the admiralty. He was blamed for the Dardanelles disaster of 1915 (see WORLD WAR I: *The Turkish Front*), and forced to resign. He was then appointed chancellor of the Duchy of Lancaster. After brief service in the army, he was made minister of munitions (1917–18). Subsequently Churchill served as secretary of state for war and for air (1918–21). He was secretary of state for the colonies (1921–22). From 1924 to the advent of the Labour government in June, 1929, he was chancellor of the exchequer in the Conservative ministry, having turned from the Liberal Party in order to oppose socialism. In 1925, under his administration, Great Britain returned to the gold standard.

In the period preceding World War II he was an active opponent of the policy of appeasement of the Axis dictators, which had been followed by the British government under Prime Minister Neville Chamberlain (q.v.). At the outbreak of the war, Churchill became first lord of the admiralty in September, 1939; and in May, 1940, after the British defeat in Norway, he became prime minister.

By his speeches, including that in which he uttered the now-famous words "I have nothing to offer but blood, toil, tears, and sweat", by his measures to combat possible invasion, and by his ability to enlist the cooperation of foreign governments opposed to Germany, Churchill played a great part in leading his nation to victory over the Axis.

In August, 1941, Churchill and the President of the United States, Franklin D. Roosevelt, met on shipboard in mid-Atlantic and together drew up the declaration of American-British international policy known as the Atlantic Charter (q.v.). Subsequently Churchill took part in other important conferences of Allied Powers, notably at Casablanca, Morocco, at Teheran, Iran, and at Yalta, U.S.S.R. Following the defeat of his party in the general election of July, 1945, he resigned as prime minister and became leader of the opposition in Parliament. He became prime minister again in 1951 after the Conservative Party victory of that year. In 1953 he was knighted and was awarded the Nobel Prize for literature. Due to his advanced age, Churchill resigned the prime ministership in April, 1955; he was elected to the House of Commons in May and re-elected in October, 1959.

Churchill became the first honorary U.S. citizen in history by act of the U.S. Congress in April, 1963.

He is the author of *Lord Randolph Churchill* (1906); *The World Crisis* (4 vols., 1923–29); *Marlborough, His Life and Times* (6 vols., 1933–38); volumes of speeches, including *The Unrelenting Struggle* (1942), *The*

End of the Beginning (1943), *Onwards to Victory* (1944), *Dawn of Liberation* (1945), *Secret Session Speeches* (1946), *In the Balance* (1952), and *Stemming of the Tide* (1954); *The Second World War* (6 vols., 1948–53); *Painting as a Pastime* (1950); and *A History of the English-Speaking Peoples* (Vol. 1: *The Birth of Britain*, 1956; Vol. 2: *The New World*, 1956; Vol. 3: *The Age of Revolution*, 1957; Vol. 4: *The Great Democracies*, 1958).

CHURCH LAW. See CANON LAW.

CHURCH MUSIC. See RELIGIOUS MUSIC.

CHURCH OF CHRIST, SCIENTIST. See CHRISTIAN SCIENCE.

CHURCH OF ENGLAND or ANGLICAN CHURCH, the Christian church in England, dating from the introduction of Christianity into that country; and more specifically the branch of the Christian church which, since the Reformation, has been the established church of England (see ESTABLISHMENT, ECCLESIASTICAL). The earliest unquestioned historical evidence of an organized Christian church in England is found in the writings of such early Christian Fathers as Tertullian and Origen in the first years of the 3rd century, although the first Christian communities probably were established some decades before that time. Three British bishops are known to have been present at the Council of Arles in 314. Others attended the Council of Sardica in 347 and that of Ariminum in 360, and a number of references to the church in Roman Britain are found in the writings of 4th-century Christian Fathers.

The ritual and discipline of the early British church were largely those introduced by the Celtic and Gallic missionaries and monks (see CELTIC CHURCH), but after the arrival of St. Augustine, or Austin, and his missionary companions from Rome in 597, and the ensuing fusion of Celtic and Roman influences, the Celtic forms gradually gave place to the liturgy and practices of the Roman West. During the next four centuries the church in Saxon England exhibited the same lines of growth and development characteristic of the church everywhere in the early Middle Ages. After the Norman Conquest (1066), continental influence in England strengthened the connections between the English church and the papacy. The vigorous assertions of power successfully made by popes from Gregory VII to Innocent III, between the late 11th and the early 13th centuries, were felt in England, as elsewhere, and clerical influence and privilege were widely extended in secular as well as ecclesiastical affairs. Several times during the medieval period English kings sought to limit the power of the church and the claims of its independent canon law, but without success until the reign of Henry VIII. See ENGLAND: *History*.

The acts of the Reformation Parliament between 1529 and 1536 mark the beginning of the Anglican Church as a national church independent of papal jurisdiction. Vexed at the refusal of Pope Clement VII to annul his marriage to Catherine of Aragon, Henry VIII induced Parliament to enact a series of statutes denying the pope any power or jurisdiction over the Church of England. He thus reaffirmed the ancient right of the Christian prince or monarch to exercise supremacy within the affairs of the church within his domain. He cited precedents in the relations of church and state in the Eastern Roman Empire and in those that had once existed in the West up to the days of Charlemagne. Revolutionary though his action was, Henry VIII received the support of the overwhelming majority of Englishmen, clerical and lay alike. Support was given chiefly because no drastic change was made in the Catholic faith and practices to which England was accustomed. After King Henry's death the influences of religious reform were felt more strongly in England, and in 1549 the first Anglican *Book of Common Prayer* (q.v.) was published and its use required of the English clergy by an Act of Uniformity. (See UNIFORMITY, ACT OF.) The second Prayer Book, reflecting more strongly the influences of continental Protestantism, was issued in 1552, followed shortly by the Forty-two Articles, a doctrinal statement similar in tone. (See ARTICLES, THE THIRTY-NINE.) Both were swept away upon the accession (1553) to the throne of Mary Tudor, who returned England to a formal obedience to the papacy which lasted until her death five years later.

A settlement of the religious controversy came when Queen Elizabeth I succeeded Queen Mary in 1558. Most of the ecclesiastical laws of Henry VIII were revived, a new Act of Supremacy (see SUPREMACY, ROYAL) defined more cautiously the crown's authority in the church, and another Act of Uniformity established the use of a *Book of Common Prayer* that avoided the Protestant excesses of the second Prayer Book. See REFORMATION: *England*. During the reign of Elizabeth I, the Puritans (q.v.) increased their power and became more insistent in their demands for further reform in the Church of England in the direction of the Protestantism of Geneva and other continental centers. After the

accession of the first Stuart monarch, James I, in 1603, this agitation for religious change became closely associated with the struggle of Parliament against Stuart absolutism. By 1645 the Parliament party was strong enough to outlaw the use of the Prayer Book; in 1649 King Charles I was executed and the monarchy temporarily overthrown.

In 1662, after the Restoration (q.v.) of Charles II, the use of the Prayer Book, revised to essentially its present form, was required by another Act of Uniformity. One more attack was made on the establishment of the Anglican Church when King James II attempted to reintroduce the practice of Roman Catholicism in England. However, he lost his throne to William I and Mary II in the ensuing revolution of 1688. See GREAT BRITAIN: *History*.

Since the 17th century the Anglican Church has been the scene of successive movements which have considerably broadened it, both spiritually and ecclesiastically. In the 18th century the Evangelical Revival infused a new sense of piety and of personal consecration into the popular religion of the established church, arousing men to a deeper understanding of Christian responsibility toward missions, religious education, and the social and moral evils of the times. Foremost in this movement was the work of John Wesley and his followers, many of whom left the Church of England to become Methodists (q.v.). During the 19th century a movement was launched by a group of Oxford churchmen for the purpose of recalling the Church of England to the Catholic elements in its spiritual heritage which had been preserved through the years of the Reformation. Despite the fears of Low-Churchmen that this High Church revival might lead to beliefs and practices too close to those of Roman Catholicism, the Oxford Movement (q.v.) prospered, transforming the face of the English church. It gave a new emphasis to the dignity and beauty of religious observances and to the central place of worship; and it enlarged the theological concern of the church for the ancient Catholic and Apostolic character of the ministry and the sacraments, for its pastoral ideals, and for the meaning of its fundamental central credal affirmations. That the Evangelical Revival and the Oxford Movement could both occur within the Church of England illustrates the breadth and flexibility of the Anglican tradition of faith and practice. Some members of the English church find their piety and church practice akin to those generally characteristic of Protestantism; others prefer a greater adherence to sacraments in the church and to a liturgical experience closer to that of the Catholic tradition of Christendom. This inclusiveness has often caused controversy and tension within the English church, but most Anglicans believe that the genius of Anglicanism is the comprehensive spirit with which it holds together diverse emphases in the unity of one church.

The foundation of an independent Protestant Episcopal Church (q.v.) in the United States of America dates from the time of the American Revolution, when members of the Anglican Church in the former colonies could no longer give their allegiance to the mother church overseas. From that time on the Church of England gradually became the center of a group of churches known today as the Anglican Communion. In addition to the churches of England, Ireland, and Wales, and the Episcopal Church in Scotland, there are separate and independent Anglican churches in Canada; the United States; Australia; New Zealand; western, central, and South Africa; India; China; Japan; and the West Indies. These churches and their numerous missions are located in nearly every area of the world, many of them among peoples of diverse origin who have become naturalized to Anglo-Saxon culture. They constitute a communion bound together in the common faith and practice inherited from the Church of England.

The doctrine of the Church of England is found primarily in the *Book of Common Prayer,* containing the ancient creeds of undivided Christendom, and secondarily in the Thirty-nine Articles, which are interpreted in accordance with the Prayer Book. Appeal is made to the first four General Councils of the Christian Church, as well as generally to Holy Scripture as interpreted by "the Catholic Fathers and ancient bishops". The Church of England differs from the Roman Catholic Church chiefly by the denial of the claims of the papacy both to jurisdiction over the church and to infallibility as promulgator of Christian doctrinal and moral truth; by the rejection of the distinctively Roman doctrines and discipline; and by the use of vernacular languages in its liturgies. It differs from the Eastern Orthodox Church to a lesser degree. On the other hand, the Anglican Church and its sister churches in the Anglican Communion differ from most Protestant churches by requiring episcopal ordination in the Apostolic succession for all their clergy; by the structure and tone of their liturgical services, which are translations and revised versions of the pre-Reformation services of the church; and by a spiritual orientation in which a Catholic sacramental heritage is combined with the Biblical and evangelical emphases that came through the Reformation.

CHURCH OF GOD. See CHURCHES OF GOD IN NORTH AMERICA.

CHURCH OF JESUS CHRIST OF LATTER-DAY SAINTS. See MORMONS.

CHURCH OF THE BRETHREN, sect related to the Baptist movement both historically and in doctrine. As a group they are known also as Dunkers or Dunkards (from Gr. *tunken,* "to dip"), from the baptismal ceremony practiced by the group. In this ceremony the believer is dipped three times, face forward, once at the mention of each name of the Trinity, after the baptismal formula in Matt. 28:19. The Dunker movement was an offshoot of the Pietist movement in Germany in the late 17th century. (See PIETISM.) The first Dunker congregation was organized at Schwartzenau, Germany, in 1708, with Alexander Mack, a Pietist, as its minister.

The persecution of the sect by the German state church drove the Dunkers to Wittgenstein. From 1719 to 1729 the sect emigrated to America. Its first church in what is now the United States was organized in 1723. The Dunkers are most numerous in Pennsylvania, Maryland, Virginia, Ohio, Indiana, Illinois, Iowa, Missouri, Nebraska, Kansas, and North Dakota. They are mainly farmers. In recent years the denomination has expanded to include many prosperous city churches. The denomination supports a number of colleges.

In doctrine the Brethren are strictly orthodox. They hold the Bible to be the inspired and infallible word of God, and accept the New Testament as their only rule of faith and practice. They believe in the Trinity, in the divinity of Christ, in the Holy Ghost, and in future rewards and punishments. Faith, repentance, and baptism are held to be the conditions of salvation. In practice they follow closely the Scripture teaching and observe the primitive simplicity of the apostolic church. They enjoin plainness of dress, settle difficulties among themselves without going to law, affirm instead of taking oath, refrain from participation in politics, oppose secret societies, advise against the use of tobacco, and have a rule more than a century old against the manufacture, sale, and use of intoxicants. As early as 1782 they prohibited slavery, and vehemently denounced the slave trade.

Communion is observed in the evening, after a full meal called the Lord's supper.

Before the supper the ordinance of foot washing is observed, the brethren washing one another's feet, and the sisters performing the same service among themselves. After supper, before the communion is taken, the sexes extend the right hand of fellowship and exchange the kiss of peace. Bishops (or elders), ministers, and deacons are elected by the congregations. Congregations are organized into State districts, and both elect delegates to the annual conference, which is the chief ecclesiastical body and where the freest discussion of all questions coming before the assembly is permitted. The final decisions are rendered by a two-thirds vote of the churches.

In 1881–83 the church suffered the loss of about 8000 members by a division in its ranks, resulting in the secession of two parties, known as the Old-Order and Progressive Brethren. The former objected to the advance the church was making in educational, missionary, and Sunday-school work, while the latter insisted that the church was too conservative. After some years of contention these parties withdrew from the mother church and formed separate organizations. The mother church is known today as the Church of the Brethren (Conservative Dunkers) and consists (1960) of about 1075 churches and 200,000 members. The Progressive Brethren, or Progressive Dunkers, are known as the Brethren Church, and have about 25,350 members. Another Dunker sect is composed of the German Seventh-Day Baptists. See BAPTIST.

CHURCH OF THE NAZARENE, Protestant denomination created by the merger of numerous Holiness sects, and organized in its present form at Pilot Point, Tex., in 1908. The Church is governed by the representative system. Local congregations select their own pastors and send delegates to an annual district assembly. The denomination's principal governing body is the General Assembly, attended by lay and ministerial delegates from the district assemblies. The General Assembly, which meets once a year, vests administrative responsibility in five general superintendents and a 24-member general board. The international headquarters of the Church are in Kansas City, Mo.

The Church of the Nazarene maintains home and foreign missions, supports eight colleges and a theological seminary, and issues a number of publications, including the well-known weekly *Herald of Holiness* and special periodicals for young people.

Members adhere to articles of faith generally accepted by evangelical Protestant churches and especially to those articles espoused by John Wesley, founder of Methodism. Their chief doctrine is that of entire sanctification, or Christian perfection. Other tenets include the Second Coming of Christ, the resurrection of the dead, and the Last Judgment. The sacraments of baptism and the Lord's Supper are recognized. The Bible is revered as the all-sufficient religious guide.

The present Church of the Nazarene represents the union of many churches, most of which had participated in the post-Civil War Holiness movement to restore the emphasis on Wesley's doctrine of Christian perfection. The original Church of the Nazarene was founded in Los Angeles, Calif., in 1895. Following mergers with other Holiness bodies the enlarged denomination adopted the name Pentecostal Church of the Nazarene. In 1908 at Pilot Point, Tex., the Holiness Church of Christ, founded in that city four years earlier, merged with the Pentecostal Church of the Nazarene to give the denomination subtantially its present form. The word "Pentecostal" was dropped from the denomination's name in 1919. In 1961 the Church of the Nazarene reported 315,647 members and 4486 separate churches in the United States.

CHURRIGUERESQUE ARCHITECTURE, term for an architectural style, derived from the name of Don Jose Churriguera (1650–1723), royal architect in the reign of Charles II of Spain. The Churrigueresque style was an extreme development of the Renaissance and baroque (q.v.) styles which preceded it, and was marked by fantastically lavish ornamentation of the exteriors and interiors of churches and of other large buildings. It was the prevailing style in Spain in the first part of the 18th century. During the same period in Mexico it was combined with Aztec and other native architectural styles.

CHU TEH (1886–   ), Chinese communist leader, born in Szechwan, and educated at Göttingen and Moscow. He joined the Chinese Communist Party in 1927, and in 1931 became commander in chief of the Chinese Red Army. Following the victory (1949–50) of the communists in the civil war in China, Chu Teh was appointed a member of the People's Revolutionary Military Council, the "supreme military command of the state". He was deputy chairman of the People's Republic from 1954 to 1959, when he became chairman of the Standing Committee of the National People's Congress.

CHUVASH AUTONOMOUS SOVIET SOCIALIST REPUBLIC, a constituent republic of the Russian Soviet Federated Socialist Republic. It borders on the Mordovian A.S.S.R.

on the w., the Mari (Marii) A.S.S.R. on the N.E. and E., and the Tatar A.S.S.R. on the S.E. The Volga River crosses the extreme northern part of Chuvashia in a general west-to-east direction. Cheboksary (pop. in 1939, 31,040), on the Volga, is the capital of the republic. The construction of ships' engines, lumbering, shipbuilding on the banks of the Volga, the generating of electricity by water power, and the manufacture of textiles are important industries in Chuvashia. The principal industry, however, is agriculture; wheat, flax, hemp, potatoes, pigs, goats, sheep, and cattle are raised. The Chuvash people comprise principally Turco-Tatars and Finno-Ugrians. Chuvashia was created an autonomous area in June, 1920, and an autonomous republic in April, 1925. Area, 7066 sq.m.; pop. (1959 est.) 1,098,000.

CIANO DI CORTELLAZZO, COUNT GALE-AZZO (1903–44), Italian Fascist statesman, educated at the University of Rome. In 1925 he entered the diplomatic service, and in 1930 he married Edda, daughter of Premier Benito Mussolini. As Mussolini's son-in-law and the son of Admiral Costanzo Ciano (1876–1939), the first president of the Chamber of Fasces and Guilds, Ciano became influential in Fascist circles in Italy and a member of the Fascist Supreme Council. From 1934 to 1935 he was secretary of state for press and propaganda. He served as a flier in the Italian war against Ethiopia (1935–36) and also during World War II. In 1936 he became minister of foreign affairs, serving until February, 1943, when Mussolini named him ambassador to the Vatican. The same year Ciano was one of the group of Fascist leaders who helped bring about the overthrow of Mussolini. In January of the following year Ciano was tried in Verona, then still held by the Fascists, for plotting Mussolini's overthrow and was executed by a firing squad.

CIBBER, COLLEY (1671–1757), English actor and dramatist, born in London, and educated at the free school at Grantham, in Lincolnshire. In 1688 he was a volunteer in the forces under the Earl of Devonshire in support of the Prince of Orange. On the stage, Cibber took the leading parts in many comedies, and soon establishd his reputation as an actor. Meanwhile he was writing comedies. *Love's Last Shift* was produced in 1696, followed by 29 more plays. As playwright and comedian he was closely connected with Drury Lane Theatre, of which he became manager in 1710. His adaptation (*Nonjuror,* 1717) of Moliere's *Tartuffe* as the story of a rebellious English priest, won the approval of

King George I, and may have caused his selection as poet laureate in 1730. He retired from the stage in 1733, though he occasionally reappeared. His later poems exposed him to ridicule. Alexander Pope made him the hero of the new *Dunciad* (1742). After retiring from the stage, Cibber began his famous *Apology* (1740), an autobiography.

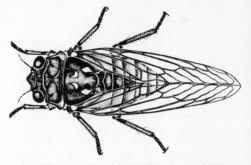

Seventeen-year cicada, Cicada septendecim

CICADA, common name for any of the homopterous bugs of the family Cicadidae, typified by the genus *Cicada.* The family is composed, for the most part, of large insects, very few measuring less than 1 inch across the open wings, while many are as large as 7 inches. The fore wings are usually transparent, but in some forms are highly pigmented, especially with black and yellow. About 800 species are known, mostly tropical.

In the United States the two commonest forms are the dogday harvest fly, *C. tibicen,* and the periodical cicada or 13 to 17 year locust, *C. septendecim.* The harvest fly is the black-and-green cicada that appears annually in midsummer, making characteristically shrill noises during the heat of the day. This form matures in two years, but since there are usually two different broods, one appears every year. The periodical cicada requires from 13 to 17 years for development, dependent chiefly upon the temperature of the locality in which it breeds. See LOCUST.

CICERO, town in Cook Co., Ill., adjoining Chicago and forming its largest suburb. It is an industrial center, noted for the production of telephone equipment, pumps, printing machinery, engravers' supplies, castings, and forgings. Cicero is the site of Morton Junior College. Pop. (1960) 69,130.

CICERO, MARCUS TULLIUS (106–43 B.C.), sometimes referred to as TULLY, Roman orator, statesman, and man of letters, born at Arpinum. He was the son of a Roman knight. As a youth he studied oratory, literature, and philosophy in Rome; among his mentors were the poet Archias, Diodotus the Stoic, Philo, Molo of Rhodes, and Quintus Mucius Scævola. He fought for a short period under Lucius Cornelius Sulla in the Social War (89 B.C.), and supported Sulla in his war against Gaius Marius. After several years of activity in the forum defending private citizens, he traveled to Greece and Asia, where he continued his studies. He returned to Rome in 77 B.C. and began his political career two years later by becoming quæstor, with the assignment of supervising the Sicilian corn supply. In 70, after election as curule ædile, he prosecuted Gaius Verres, the former governor of Sicily, for corruption and obtained an impeachment. He was prætor in 66.

Although Cicero's family did not belong to the Roman aristocracy, he was supported in the competition for the consulship in 64 by most rich and powerful Romans out of distrust of his aristocratic but less respectable rival, Lucius Sergius Catilina (q.v.), called Catiline. Cicero was elected, and during his administration a plot organized by the disgruntled Catiline to overthrow the government was uncovered and suppressed. In the next years the career of Gaius Julius Cæsar, who became consul in 59, conflicted with that of Cicero, who was forced to leave Rome in 58 as a result of Cæsar's intrigues. After a year in Macedonia Cicero was triumphantly recalled and was persuaded to support the party of Pompey (see POMPEIUS) and Cæsar. He occupied himself with literature until 51, when he accepted an assignment to govern the province of Cilicia as proconsul. He returned to Rome in 50, in time to attempt to reconcile Cæsar and Pompey, who had become bitter enemies. During the Civil War he supported Pompey; but after the latter's defeat he accepted Cæsar's overtures of amity. While Cæsar ruled Rome, Cicero lived as a private citizen and wrote extensively. After Cæsar's assassination (44), however, Cicero returned to politics, attacking Mark Antony (see ANTONIUS, MARCUS) Cæsar's successor as leader of the *populares*, and supporting the cause of Octavian (later the Emperor Augustus, q.v.); but when Octavian, Marcus Aemilius Lepidus (d. 13 B.C.), and Antony formed the Second Triumvirate in 43, Cicero's name was included among those chosen for liquidation. He was killed after an unsuccessful attempt to escape by sea.

As a statesman Cicero was more honest than effective. Although he undoubtedly had the welfare of Rome at heart, and on occasion was capable of firmness, his career was one of alternate vacillation and obstinacy. He was at first admired, then respected, but more often ignored during the bitter struggles that eventually took his life.

As an orator Cicero represents a mean between the Attic simplicity of Demosthenes and the so-called "Asiatic" floridity of his former rival, Hortensius. Ancient rhetoricians classified him with the Rhodian school of eloquence. He had both the natural gifts and the training to become an outstanding orator. The one defect in Cicero's oratory was perhaps a lack of sincerity and of genuine conviction.

As a man of letters Cicero created a rich prose style which became the standard by which all other Latin prose is now tested and compared. He added greatly to the vocabulary of his own language, giving currency to striking and picturesque words and phrases which were new to formal literature.

Cicero was a facile writer. He dealt with many subjects in many departments of intellectual interest. Nearly all of his philosophical works were borrowed from Greek sources, but his style has a lucidity and grace rare in the Greek philosophical writers. His works have been of great service to the modern world, because they have preserved much of Greek philosophy which might otherwise have remained unknown or known only imperfectly. His rhetorical works, written in the dialogue form, are of value, first, as the production of an accomplished rhetorician, and second, for the richness of the historical material contained in them.

Among the minor works of Cicero two, a treatise on old age (*De Senectute*) and one on friendship (*De Amicitia*), have always been admired, both for their style and urbane, cultivated tone. Highly important are four collections of letters written by Cicero to various acquaintances and friends, and numbering in all 774 pieces; there are, besides, 90 letters addressed to Cicero. These letters were not collected by Cicero nor did he intend that they should be published. They represent, therefore, a spontaneous self-revelation of their author.

The orations of Cicero now extant are 57 in number, of which the most famous are the four against Catiline, the 14 so-called Philippics against Antony, the oration on behalf of Archias, and two legal orations.

CIDER, the sweet or fermented juice of apples, used as a beverage and also for making vinegar. Fermented, or hard, cider contains only 2 or 3 percent of solids (instead of 12 to 15 percent as in the apple juice), and from 2 to 8 percent of alcohol. Cider brandy, or applejack, is derived by distillation from fermented cider. It contains 40 to 50 percent alcohol. For cider vinegar, see VINEGAR. See also APPLE.

CID, THE, also called EL CID CAMPEADOR (Span., "The Lord Champion"), whose real name was RODRIGO (or RUY) DÍAZ DE BIVAR (about 1040–99), Spanish soldier of fortune and legendary hero, born at Bivar, near Burgos. He is first mentioned in 1064, during the reign of Ferdinand the Great of León. Under Sancho II, son of Ferdinand, he became standard bearer and commander of the royal troops. In a war between the two brothers Sancho II and Alfonso VI of León, a stratagem suggested by the Cid secured the victory of Sancho at Llantada over his brother, who was forced to seek refuge with the Moorish king of Toledo (1071).

Upon the assassination of his friend and patron, King Sancho, he required the next heir, Alfonso, to clear himself by oath of any participation in his brother's murder before the nobles of León and Castile should do homage to him. By this act he incurred the new monarch's enmity; the politic king, however, concealed his hatred in the hour of danger, even consenting to the Cid's marriage with his cousin Ximena, daughter of Diego, Count of Oviedo. But when Alfonso thought the services of the Cid no longer necessary to his own safety, he lent a willing ear to the latter's personal enemies, and banished him in 1081. The Cid then joined the Moorish king of Saragossa, in whose service he fought against both Moslems and Christians. He frequently defeated the King of Aragon and the Count of Barcelona, the latter of whom, Berenguer Ramón II, he took prisoner.

The Cid was again reconciled to Alfonso, but in a short time was condemned to a second exile. In order to support his family and numerous followers, he was forced to fight against the Moors, over whom he gained a victory, and took Valencia in 1094, ruling for five years until his defeat by the Moors, at Cuenca, shortly before his death.

His widow held Valencia till 1102, when she called upon her cousin the Emperor for aid. He went with a strong army, but being unable to hold the city, set fire to it, took Ximena with him and carried away the remains of the Cid, which were later buried in the monastery of San Pedro de Cardeña, near Burgos.

Not long after his death the Cid became a figure in legend, and an epic poem, the *Poema del Cid,* was written in his honor, about 1140. In this and other literary works, the hero was depicted as a chivalrous hero, the champion of Spanish national aspirations.

The *Poema del Cid* was the first and best of many Spanish literary efforts, mostly in ballad form, based on the Cid legend. The story first appeared in French as early as 1600, and was the subject of an important tragedy, *Le Cid* (1636 or 1637), by the playwright Pierre Corneille. In modern times the legend was made the subject of an opera, *Le Cid* (1885), by the French composer Jules Massenet.

E.F.

CIENFUEGOS, originally FERNANDINA DE JAGUA, a city and seaport of Santa Clara Province, Cuba, on the s. coast, at the head of the bay of Jagua 230 m. by rail E.S.E. of Havana. The region surrounding the city is one of the most picturesque and fertile in Cuba. Sugar cane is the chief crop; coffee and tobacco are also grown, and cattle are raised. In the vicinity is a botanical experiment station of Harvard University. Cienfuegos is one of the chief commercial cities and seaports of Cuba, and is a center of the sugar trade. Near the entrance to the bay of Jagua, first visited by Columbus, is the Castillo de Jagua, a fortress erected in 1740–45 as a protection against Caribbean Sea pirates. The city was founded in 1819. During the Spanish-American War it was blockaded by two warships of the United States fleet under Admiral Schley. Pop. (1961 est.) 107,526.

CIERVA, JUAN DE LA (1896–1936), Spanish aeronautical engineer, born at Murcia. He was trained as an engineer, graduating from the Civil Engineering School in Madrid in 1918, but before this time he had become interested in aviation, entering a rebuilt bomber in a government competition in 1913. In 1919 he began experiments on a plane supported by a large rotor instead of by wings, in an attempt to increase the safety of aviation by constructing a plane which could remain airborne at low speeds. These experiments culminated in success after five years, and in 1925 he demonstrated his plane, which he called the autogiro, in England. Companies were quickly formed in England and America to commence manufacture of autogiros, which were constantly improved until World War II, when they were generally superseded by helicopters. De la Cierva received many honors, including the Guggenheim Medal in 1932 and 1933, and the Great Cross of Naval Merit from Spain in 1935. He was also a Chevalier of the French Legion of Honor. He wrote *Wings of Tomorrow* (1931). See AUTOGIRO.

CIGARS and **CIGARETTES.** See TOBACCO.

CIGNANI, CONTE CARLO (1628–1719), Italian painter, born in Bologna. He was the pupil of Francesco Albani, whose influence is visible in his earlier works, such as the frescoes in the Palazzo Publico, Bologna. Later Cignani was influenced by the Carracci, Correggio, and Guido Reni, as seen in his frescoes in Rome. His best-known works are "Assumption of the Virgin", a fresco in the dome of the cathedral of Forli, on which he worked for twenty years; and the oil paintings "Joseph and Potiphar's Wife" (Dresden) and "Pera and Cimon" (Vienna).

CILIATA. See INFUSORIA.

CILICIA, name of an ancient country of Asia Minor, and of a modern region of s. central Asiatic Turkey, extending along the N. and N.E. shores of the Gulf of Alexandretta, from the Taurus Mts. to the Amanus Mts., which separate it from Syria. The western part of Cilicia is mountainous and forested; much of the eastern part consists of hilly, rock-strewn, and fertile plains. The principal river is the Cyndus.

In ancient times, during the period (6th–4th cent. B.C.) when most of Asia Minor was under the control of the Persian Achæmenids, Cilicia was either an independent kingdom paying tribute to Persia or part of a Persian satrapy. After Alexander's conquests, during the Hellenistic period (4th–2nd cent. B.C.), most of Cilicia was part of the Seleucid Empire. Eastern Cilicia was conquered by the Romans in 103 B.C., and all of Cilicia became a Roman province in 64 B.C. Under the Romans the region was noted for the export of *cilicium,* cloth made of goats' hair, much prized in the manufacture of tents. In the 1st century A.D. the Apostle Paul lived in the city of Tarsus in Cilicia. Other important ancient cities in Cilicia were Seleucia, Soli, and Adana. The province remained in Roman hands until its capture in the 7th century by Arabs. In the 11th century it became the center of the important kingdom of Lesser Armenia. In the 15th and 16th centuries Cilicia became part of the Turkish Empire. The region is included in the modern provinces of Içel, Seyhan, and Maras.

CILICIAN GATES (Turk. *Gülek Bogaz*), name of a narrow pass in the Taurus Mountains of s. central Asiatic Turkey, through which passed, in ancient times, a highway from the west to the city of Tarsus (q.v.) in Cilicia. It was traversed by Cyrus the Younger and Alexander the Great.

CIMABUE, GIOVANNI (about 1240–about 1302), Florentine painter and mosaicist, born in Florence. He was one of the most impor-

tant artists of his time, breaking with the formalism of Byzantine art (q.v.) then predominant in Italy, and introducing a more lifelike treatment of traditional subjects into both painting and mosaic work. He was the forerunner of the realistic Florentine school of the early Renaissance. His most important pupil was Giotto. Among Cimabue's works are the fresco "Madonna with Angels and St. Francis" (in lower church of St. Francis, Assisi), and a number of frescoes in the upper church; the painting "Madonna Santa Trinità" (Florence Academy), and a mosaic of St. John (Pisa Cathedral).

CIMAROSA, DOMENICO (1749–1801), Italian dramatic composer, born in Aversa, near Naples. He studied music at the Conservatorio Santa Maria di Loreto, Naples. In 1772 his first opera, *Le Stravaganze del Conte,* was produced at Naples and made his reputation. In 1787, by invitation of Catherine II of Russia, he took up residence in St. Petersburg as court composer; he later was court *kapellmeister* at Vienna and then *maestro di capella* at Naples. He wrote in all over 60 operas, and also a number of masses, cantatas, and oratorios. He is best known for his comic operas, characterized by a wit and merriment that earn comparison with the music of Mozart. Cimarosa's masterpiece is considered to be the comic opera *Il Matrimonio Segreto* (1792); it is the only one of his works played today. His other operas include *L'Italiana in Londra* (1774), *Le Astuzie Feminili* (1794), *Penelope* (1795), and *Achille all' Assedio di Troja* (1799).

CIMARRON RIVER, river of the s.w. United States, about 650 m. long. It flows from the Raton Mountains in the N.E. section of New Mexico across the s.E. corner of Colorado, and thence generally eastward through Kansas and Oklahoma, where it empties into the Arkansas River about 20 miles W. of Tulsa. The Cimarron waters an agricultural region in which large numbers of livestock are raised, and important crops of corn and wheat are produced.

CIMBRI, a Teutonic people who first came into contact with the Romans in the province of Noricum (Carinthia and Carniola) in 113 B.C. They were victorious in several engagements, and were only prevented from devastating Italy by their defeat by Gaius Marius on the Raudii Campi (101 B.C.). When the battle was lost, their women killed themselves and their children. Cæsar represents the Aduatici of Belgium as the descendants of the Cimbri and Teutons. Tacitus speaks of a people bearing the name of Cimbri, few in number, but of great reputation, that sent ambassadors to Augustus. They lived, according to Pliny and Ptolemy, on the peninsula called from them the Cimbric Chersonese, now Jutland.

CIMICIFUGA, genus of perennial herbs of the family Ranunculaceae, commonly called bugbane because their malodorous white flowers are supposed to be repellent to insects. They grow in rich, moist, shady soil. The commonest, *C. racemosa,* also called black snakeroot or black cohosh, reaches a height of eight feet; it is sometimes cultivated in wild gardens. *C. simplex,* reaching a height of three feet, is used in shady borders. An extract of the roots of *C. racemosa* is used in medicine as an antispasmodic, diuretic, and expectorant, and in cardiac diseases, where its action is similar to that of digitalis.

CIMMERIANS. 1. In Homeric poetry, a mythical people living in the Far West, on the shores of the ocean, where the sun never shines and perpetual darkness reigns. **2.** A historical people, whose country lay along the northern shore of the Black Sea, including the Tauric Chersonese, and who at an early period made inroads into Asia Minor. There were presumably several such invasions, but the accounts are confused. They were driven from their homes, probably in the 7th century, by the Scythians, and overran Asia Minor. On this occasion they plundered Sardis and destroyed Magnesia, but failed in an attempt on Ephesus.

CIMON (about 507–449 B.C.), Athenian general and statesman, the son of Miltiades, the conqueror at Marathon. In conjunction with Aristides, his patron, he was placed over the Athenian contingent to the allied fleet, which, under the supreme command of the Spartan Pausanias, continued the war against the Persians (477 B.C.). His greatest exploit was his encounter with a Persian fleet of 350 ships at the river Eurymedon (466), when he destroyed or captured 300, and defeated the land forces on the same day. He succeeded in driving the Persians from Thrace, Caria, and Lycia. Following a revolt of the Helots of Sparta, against whom he took sides with the Spartan troops, he lost the confidence of his allies and was dismissed. Later the democracy headed by Pericles ostracized him. Upon his recall he was instrumental in obtaining a five years' armistice between the Spartans and the Athenians. He died during a renewed struggle against the Persians.

CINCHONA, or CHINCHONA, genus of trees of the order Rubiaceae (suborder Cin-

chonaceae), yielding the medicinal bark variously known as Peruvian bark, Jesuits' bark, China bark, or cinchona bark, from which the important alkaloids quinine (q.v.) and its congeners are obtained. All the cinchonas are evergreen trees, with laurel-like, entire, opposite leaves; stipules which soon fall off; and panicles of flowers, which, in general appearance, resemble those of lilac or privet. The flowers are white, rose-colored, or purplish, and very fragrant.

The species first discovered was *C. officinalis* of Ecuador and Peru. Important are *C. calisaya* of Bolivia and S.E. Peru, and *C. succirubra* of the west slope of Chimborazo, a mountain peak in west-central Ecuador. The trees are felled as near the root as possible, so that none of the bark may be lost. The bark, after being stripped off, is carefully dried and packed. The quilled form of the thinner bark is acquired in drying. The practice of destroying the tree for the bark made the tree rare in its native habitat. However, in 1859 cinchona was introduced into the East Indies, where it has been so widely cultivated that these islands, particularly Java, have become the center of world production of cinchona bark.

CINCINNATI, county seat of Hamilton Co., Ohio, situated in the s.w. corner of the State on the N. bank of the Ohio River, opposite Covington and Newport, cities in Kentucky, and opposite the mouth of the Licking River. It is about 270 miles S.E. of Chicago, Ill., 125 miles s.w. of Columbus, Ohio, and about equidistant, by water, from Pittsburgh, Pa., where the Ohio River begins, and Cairo, Ill., at the confluence of the Ohio and the Mississippi.

Cincinnati is the second-largest city in Ohio, ranks twenty-first in population among the cities of the United States, and is a leading commercial and industrial center. It is serviced by 8 trunk-line railway systems, including the Pennsylvania, Baltimore and Ohio, and Erie railroads; by barge and steamboat lines connecting with Ohio and Mississippi river ports; by motorbus and truck lines; and by the major airlines, which operate from a modern, municipally-owned airport. Five bridges, three of which are railway bridges, span the Ohio at Cincinnati. The Ohio River Bridge, which leads to Covington, Ky., ranks among the largest suspension bridges in the United States, with a channel span of 1057 feet.

The site of the city, 71.9 sq.m. in area, consists of two terraced plateaus, extending inland from the river lowlands to a semicircular range of hills surrounding the city. Extreme elevations of the hills, where the suburbs and better residential sections are located, average about 475 feet above river level. The middle levels, where the business district is situated, range between 50 and 100 feet above the river. The area contiguous to the riverfront, which is about 25 miles long, is the shipping center of the city, and contains numerous docks and wharves, warehouses, and industrial establishments, as well as several slum areas. Many industries and most of the railroad yards are concentrated in Mill Creek, a valley on the western edge of the city.

Iron and steel manufacturing is the chief industry of Cincinnati. Other important industries include soap making, meat packing, printing, and the manufacture of playing cards, machine tools, rolling-mill products, motor vehicles and parts, radios, tobacco products, men's and boys' clothing, boots and shoes, bakery products, paper products, and pottery.

Cincinnati has a large number of notable structures, the most prominent of which are the Carew Tower and Union Central buildings, both 495 feet in height. The Union Terminal, utilized for passenger traffic by the trunk-line railway systems entering the city, is one of the most modern structures of its kind in the world. Among other important landmarks are the City Hall, the County Courthouse, the Chamber of Commerce building, and the Federal building. Cincinnati Churches, which total about 400, include several imposing structures, notably the Church of St. Francis de Sales, the First and Second Presbyterian churches, St. Paul's Methodist Episcopal Church, St. Paul's Protestant Episcopal Pro-Cathedral, St. Monica's Cathedral (Roman Catholic), and Avondale Synagogue.

The municipal park system, comprising about 3700 acres, contains approximately 125 recreation areas and parks. Mount Airy Forest, the largest of these, with an area of 1300 acres, contains an arboretum. Eden Park, 185 acres, commanding an excellent view of the Ohio River, has several interesting features, including a conservatory, the city water reservoir, and Navigation Monument, which was erected in 1929 to commemorate completion of a navigable Ohio River channel between Pittsburgh, Pa., and Cairo, Ill. Eden Park contains also the Cincinnati Art Museum, and the Art Academy. Other well-known parks include Ault Park, 230 acres; Burnet Woods Park, 116 acres; Alms Memorial Park, which has a statue of Stephen Collins Foster, cele-

brated American song writer; and Mt. Echo Park. The Zoological Garden, about 60 acres in extent, has an interesting collection of animals.

Cincinnati has many educational and cultural facilities, including a modern public-school system, a large number of parochial schools, an art academy, the Ohio Mechanics Institute, which is a technical and vocational-training school, and several schools of higher learning. Outstanding among these are the University of Cincinnati (see CINCINNATI, UNIVERSITY OF); Xavier University, founded in 1831, and Our Lady of Cincinnati College (for women), both Roman Catholic schools; and Hebrew Union College, founded in 1875, and one of the leading theological seminaries in the United States. In addition, the city, long noted for its musical activities and institutions, is the seat of Cincinnati Symphony Orchestra, founded in 1872; and contains the Cincinnati College of Music and the Cincinnati Conservatory of Music, both units of the University of Cincinnati, which provide courses of study for the general public. The Cincinnati Art Museum has several important collections, notably the Mary M. Emery Collection of Old Master Paintings, the Herbert Greer French Collection of Print Masterpieces, collections of Oriental, Medieval, and Greco-Roman sculpture, and examples of American Indian art and craftsmanship. The public library of Cincinnati operates many branches throughout the city, and in a recent year contained 1,424,969 volumes. Various libraries with large collections of books on specialized topics are also maintained in the city.

Cincinnati has a city-manager form of government, adopted in 1924 by an amendment to the city charter of 1917. It provides for a city council consisting of 9 members, who are elected at large biennially by proportional representation, and who in turn select a city manager. The latter, who is administrative head of the city, serves for an indefinite term. The presiding officer of the council, who is elected from its membership, has the title of mayor.

Temporary fortifications were erected on the site of Cincinnati in 1780 by an expedition commanded by George Rogers Clark (q.v.), then campaigning against hostile Indians. The first permanent settlement in the area was established in 1788, when a group of settlers acquired 740 acres of land from John Cleves Symmes. In the following year the settlers laid out a village, naming it "Losantiville". This word was coined from French and Latin terms meaning "city opposite the mouth of the Licking". Federal troops constructed a blockhouse, named Fort Washington, in the village in 1789. The next year Losantiville was renamed Cincinnati, in honor of the Society of the Cincinnati (q.v.), and made the seat of newly-established Hamilton County. By 1792, when the first church and school were built, the village was a flourishing community, with a population of several hundred, and more than 30 commercial establishments. Cincinnati was incorporated as a town in 1802. Shipping, already an important industry, increased steadily in the following years, particularly after the introduction, in 1811, of steam navigation on the Ohio River. In 1819 the town, with a population of about 9800, was incorporated as a city. Large numbers of immigrants, including many Germans, settled in Cincinnati during the next few decades, contributing immensely to the economic and cultural development of the community. A symphony orchestra was organized in 1825. The Miami Canal, which linked the city with Middletown, Ohio, was completed in 1827, further stimulating commercial and industrial activity. The first railroad from the city began operations in 1843. By 1850 the population totaled 115,000, and Cincinnati was known as the "Queen City of the West".

Cincinnati was long prominent as a station on the Underground Railroad (q.v.), and during the American Civil War its citizens remained loyal to the Union. Disastrous floods damaged the city in 1883 and 1884. In 1884, too, a serious outbreak of mob violence broke out because of discontent with corrupt city officials; 45 persons were killed and considerable property was destroyed. The Centennial Exposition of the Ohio Valley, celebrating the 100th anniversary of the settlement of the city and State, was held in Cincinnati in 1888. The city was again partially inundated in the Ohio River flood of 1937, but the damaged areas were quickly repaired. Pop. (1960) 502,550.

CINCINNATI, SOCIETY OF THE, hereditary organization with headquarters at Washington, D. C., founded by American and foreign officers of the Continental Army in May, 1783. Its stated purposes were to perpetuate mutual friendships and to provide relief to members in need and to widows and orphans of fallen officers. Membership in the organization is limited to direct or to collateral descendants of Continental officers who completed three years of honorable service in the American Revolutionary War, or who were honorably discharged for disability. The activities of the society, which has affiliated organizations in each of the 13 original States and in France, include the endowment of scholarships, maintenance of a historical museum at general headquarters, and the promotion of patriotic projects.

The name of the organization is derived from that of Lucius Quinctius Cincinnatus (q.v.), a Roman patriot. Although George Washington served as its first president, the society quickly became unpopular throughout the country. Many Americans, including Benjamin Franklin and Thomas Jefferson, regarded it as the beginning of a hereditary aristocracy in the United States, dedicated to subverting the Republic. Fears of this kind led to a declaration by the State Legislature of Massachusetts that the organization was "dangerous to the peace, liberty, and safety of the Union". Opposition to the society also led to the formation of Tammany (q.v.) societies in New York and other cities. A number of the State Cincinnati societies went out of existence before the end of the 18th century, but by 1902 all of these had been reconstituted.

CINCINNATI, UNIVERSITY OF, coeducational, municipally controlled institution, located in Cincinnati, Ohio. It was chartered by the State in 1870, becoming the first municipal university in the United States. The practical study of industrial techniques to supplement academic engineering training, a new educational development, originated at the university in 1906. Similar programs are now offered also in the Colleges of Business Administration and of Design, Architecture, and Art. Both the College of Law and College of Medicine date from 1819, when those institutions were founded as Cincinnati College and the Medical College of Ohio, respectively. Among other components of the university are McMicken College of Liberal Arts, College of Education and Home Economics, College of Nursing and Health, College of Pharmacy, College-Conservatory of Music, University College, Graduate School, Evening College, and Summer School. The university conducts branch and extension work and maintains several laboratories for scientific research. In 1962 enrollment totaled 20,500, including 10,306 full-time students; the faculty numbered 1553. The library contained about 810,000 bound volumes.

CINCINNATUS, Lucius Quinctius (fl. 5th cent. B.C.), Roman general and statesman. Most of the data concerning him is legendary. He was reputedly a consul, about 460 B.C., and participated in the patricians' war (462–54) against the plebeians. About 458, he became, by decision of the Roman Senate, dictator of the Republic, charged with rescuing a Roman army which faced annihilation by the Æqui. He defeated the enemy within 16 days and resigned the dictatorship. Vested again with dictatorial power in 439, he suppressed an incipient plebeian insurrection, and killed the traitor Spurius Melius.

CINDERELLA, heroine of a universally told fairy tale. The story centers about a young girl mistreated by her stepmother and stepsisters. Through her fairy godmother's miraculous intervention, Cinderella attends a ball given by the prince of the realm, and, for the occasion, her fairy godmother magically transforms a pumpkin into a coach, mice into horses, lizards into footmen, a rat into a coachman, and rags into a glittering gown. Cinderella is warned, however, to leave the ball by midnight lest all her fine things revert to their original form. Leaving in haste at the stroke of midnight, she loses one of her small glass slippers. The prince, who has fallen in love with Cinderella, instigates a search throughout his realm for the maiden whose foot fits the glass slipper. Eventually he finds and marries Cinderella.

The English version is an adaptation of a story by the French writer Charles Perrault. In the original tale the heroine wears a fur slipper (Fr. *pantoufle en vair*), but the English translator apparently mistook *vair* for *verre* ("glass"). The story appears in German lore in the 16th century, and is among the fairy tales of the German mythologists Jacob and Wilhelm Grimm. It is the subject of the opera *La Cenerentola* by the Italian composer Gioacchino Rossini. The Russian composer Serge Prokofiev wrote the score for a ballet based on the fairy tale.

CINERARIA (Lat., "ashy"), scientific name for a genus of plants of the Thistle family, and common name for several plants formerly included in this genus but now classified in the closely related genus *Senecio*. The genus *Cineraria* now contains only about 25 species, all indigenous to South Africa. The plants most commonly called cinerarias in the U.S. are the numerous varieties and hybrids of *Senecio cruentus,* a native of the Canary Islands. These plants are shortstemmed, wooly, perennial herbs, with large, heart-shaped leaves covered with down. Their daisylike flowers show various shades and combinations of blue, white, and red, and often bloom so profusely as to cover the foliage completely. They may be cultivated in gardens in warm climates but are more commonly raised as greenhouse or pot plants. The dusty millers, *S. cineraria* and *S. leucostachys,* are also called cinerarias.

CINGALESE. See SINGHALESE.

CINNA, GAIUS HELVIUS (d. 44 B.C.), Roman poet. He was a friend of Gaius Valerius Catullus, and according to some accounts was at one time a tribune. He is best known for having been killed by a mob on the occasion of Cæsar's funeral when he was confused with Lucius Cornelius Cinna, one of Cæsar's assassins. This episode is dramatized in Shakespeare's play, *Julius Cæsar.*

CINNA, LUCIUS CORNELIUS (d. 84 B.C.), Roman patrician, one of the principal supporters of Gaius Marius. After Sulla had driven Marius from the city, he allowed Cinna to become consul, providing that he swore not to disturb the constitution. Cinna, however, impeached Sulla (87 B.C.). He and Marius next declared themselves consuls after proscribing many Roman citizens. Cinna was slain by his troops at Brundisium, while preparing to attack Sulla. His daughter Cornelia was the wife of Julius Cæsar. His son, Lucius Cornelius Cinna, who was prætor in 44 B.C., was one of those who participated in the assassination of Caesar.

CINNABAR, a mineral mercuric sulfide which is the only commercial source of mercury. It is bright red in color, crystallizes in the hexagonal system, and has perfect prismatic cleavage. The hardness of cinnabar is 2½ and its specific gravity more than 8. The mineral is comparatively rare, and usually occurs in the form of veins in sedimentary rocks. Important deposits of cinnabar are found in Spain, Italy, Mexico, China, and California.

CINNAMON, a spice, the dried bark of several species of tree belonging to the genus *Cinnamomum* in the family Lauraceae. The best-known species, *C. zeylanicum,* is indigenous to Ceylon; it is now cultivated in many other tropical countries, but the variety grown in Ceylon is superior in taste. Saigon cinnamon, *C. loureirii,* which is grown in Indochina, is almost as good as Ceylon cinnamon, but Chinese cinnamon is decidedly inferior.

In cultivation the cinnamon tree is trained to grow four to five stems. When the bark begins to turn brown, these stems, which may be 8 feet tall and 2 inches in diameter at the base, are harvested and new ones are trained to grow in their place. After being stripped of leaves and twigs, the inner and outer bark are removed. As the bark dries it forms rolls called quills, the smaller of which are inserted into the larger, and when fully dry, are tied in bundles for shipment.

Cinnamon is yellowish brown, has a peculiar, fragrant odor, and a sweetish, aromatic, pungent taste. It has been used since early times as a spice in many culinary preparations. Its aromatic qualities are due to a volatile oil, *oil of cinnamon,* which may be extracted from the bark by distillation. This oil varies in color from yellow to cherry red, the yellow being the purest and the most highly esteemed. It consists principally of cinnamic aldehyde. Both cinnamon and oil of cinnamon have been employed medicinally as carminatives and as aromatic stimulants.

CINQUECENTO, term for the art style which arose in Italy about 1500, and which belongs mainly to the 16th century. It is characterized by the revival of classical taste in all departments of culture, and is frequently used in the same sense as the word *renaissance,* especially as applied to decoration. Among the great *cinquecentisti* in art are Michelangelo, Raphael, Correggio, Titian, Leonardo da Vinci, and Benvenuto Cellini; in poetry the more notable names are those of Berni, Ariosto, and Tasso.

CINQUE PORTS, ancient collective name of the five English Channel ports: Sandwich, Dover, Hythe, Romney, and Hastings. They were enfranchised during the 11th century by Edward the Confessor. William the Conqueror subsequently granted them the privileges of an almost independent state, under command of a warden, with a court at Dover Castle. Winchelsea and Rye were added later. Until the reign of Henry VII their chief function was the supply of the country's naval contingent. In the latter half of the 13th century, during the reign of Edward I, they provided 57 fully equipped ships and frequently extended their powers to equipping piratical expeditions. Following the revolution of 1688 their privileges were gradually abolished, the jurisdiction of the Lord Warden ceasing in 1835.

C.I.O. See CONGRESS OF INDUSTRIAL ORGANIZATIONS.

CIPHERS AND CODES. See CRYPTOGRAPHY.

CIPRIANI, GIOVANNI BATTISTA (1727–85), Italian painter, draftsman, and engraver. He studied in Florence, and later went to England, where he lived most of his life. He painted pictures and mural decorations for private mansions and public buildings and was one of the original members of the British Royal Academy. He is chiefly important as a draftsman for Francesco Bartolozzi's engravings and mezzotints, and helped to form the style of the English mezzotint engravers of the 18th century.

CIRCASSIANS, a people of northwestern Caucasia, calling themselves the Adygei or Adighe, and also referred to as the Cherkesses, a term of Russian origin meaning "brigands". They are found today chiefly in the Adygei and Cherkess Autonomous Regions of Soviet Russia, and form a non-Indo-European language group. They are of the Caucasian race (with Tartar and other intrusive elements), are related in varying degrees in language and racial origin to many other mountaineer peoples of Caucasia and Transcaucasia, and are mainly Mohammedan in religion.

The Circassians are proverbially a handsome people, the men hardy and brave, and superb horsemen, and the girls so famous for their beauty that under the old Turkish regime they long adorned the harems of sultans, pashas, and rich Turks. Prior to the Russian conquest of Caucasia in the second half of the 19th century, the Circassians were divided into clans ruled in peace and led in war by princes, but they enjoyed considerable democracy and individual freedom. When the Russian conquest was completed, many Circassians left the Caucasus and migrated to various parts of Asiatic and European Turkey. Those left in the Caucasus numbered about 150,000. See CAUCASIA.

CIRCE, in Greek mythology, a sorceress who lived in a valley of the island of Æaea, surrounded by humans she had transformed into wolves and lions. According to Homer's version, she transformed the companions of Odysseus (Ulysses), who visited her island, into swine, and tried to exercise the same enchantment on him. Protected by a magic herb Hermes had given him, Odysseus withstood her sorceries, and forced her to disenchant his followers. He then remained with her a year, and learned from her how to converse with Tiresias in the "land of shades" about his future, and how to avoid dangers that beset his homeward journey. Later writers placed the island of Circe in the Tyrrhenian Sea, and still later it was identified with the Circean promontory, modern Cape Circeo, on the coast of Littoria Province, Italy.

CIRCLE, in geometry, a plane figure bounded by a curved line, the circumference, which is everywhere equally distant from a point within it called the center. The space enclosed is called the area of the circle. Any line drawn through the center and terminated by the circumference is a diameter. A radius is a straight line from the center of a circle to its periphery. The segment of any straight line intercepted by the circle is called a chord; and a chord is said to divide the area into segments, which are equal if the chord is a diameter. An arc is a section of the circle, or of its circumference.

The circle belongs to the class of conic sections, and is derived from the right cone by cutting the cone with a plane perpendicular to its axis. The circle is almost always employed in measuring or comparing angles, because angles at the center of a circle are proportional to the arcs on which they stand. The easiest subdivision of a circumference is into six equal parts, because then the chord of the arcs is equal to the radius. Divide one of these arcs into 60 equal parts, and the degree is obtained. A degree is divided into 60 equal parts called minutes, and each minute into 60 parts called seconds. The Babylonians thus produced the sexagesimal scale. According to this scale 90 degrees represents a right angle, 180 degrees a semicircle, and 360 degrees, four right angles, the entire circumference. The supposed number of days in the year led to division of the circle into 360 parts, for use in astronomical instruments.

Of all plane figures having the same perimeter the circle contains the greatest area. Of all plane curves the circle alone has the same curvature at every point. The ratio of the circumference to the diameter is a constant designated by the symbol π. This ratio is approximately 3.141592; and 3.1416, and even 3 1/7, are sufficiently accurate for ordinary purposes. Archimedes described it as lying between 3 1/7 and 3 10/71.

The center of a circle is a center of symmetry, and any diameter is an axis of symmetry. Concentric circles, that is, those having the same center, never intersect. Circles are similar figures, and their areas are proportional to the squares of their radii or diameters. Arcs of a circle are proportional to the angles subtended at the center, and conversely. This property forms the basis of angular measure.

In co-ordinate geometry the circle ranks as a curve of the second order and belongs to the conic sections. Constructions of Euclidean geometry being limited to use of two instruments, the straight edge and compasses, the circle and straight line are the two basic elements of plane geometry. The expression *to square the circle* means to construct geometrically a square equal in area to a given circle, or to state in terms of its radius the exact area of a circle; see GEOMETRY, ANALYTIC. See also CURVE.

CIRCUIT COURTS OF APPEALS. See COURTS OF APPEALS.

CIRCUIT, ELECTRIC. See ELECTRIC CIRCUIT.

CIRCULATION OF THE BLOOD, in anatomy and physiology, the course of the blood from the heart through the arteries, capillaries, and veins, and back to the heart. Of the four chambers of the heart, two pertain to the circulation of venous blood, and two to that of arterial blood. Blood from the whole body is brought to the right auricle of the heart by two large veins, the superior vena cava and the inferior vena cava. By contraction of this chamber the blood is forced through the right auriculoventricular opening into the right ventricle, and this by its contraction drives the blood to the lungs. The blood is prevented from returning into the auricle by the tricuspid valve, which completely closes the auriculoventricular opening during contraction of the ventricle. In its passage through the lungs the blood is oxygenated, and then is brought back to the heart by the four pulmonary veins, entering the left auricle. When this contracts, the blood is forced into the left ventricle, and then by ventricular contraction into the aorta. The mitral valve prevents regurgitation into the auricle, and the semilunar valve at the beginning of the aorta stops any reflux into the ventricle. Similar valves are present in the pulmonary artery.

The aorta divides into branches and these in turn divide into smaller ones, until the whole body is supplied by a minute arterial plexus, or network; the smallest arteries divide into a finer network of still more minute vessels, the capillaries, which have extremely delicate walls, so that the blood can come into closest relation with the fluids and tissues of the body. In the capillaries the oxygen is given off, the nourishment furnished to the body elements, and the waste products taken up into the blood. The capillaries then unite to form a venous plexus, and later form small veins which unite with each other to form larger ones, until all the blood is finally collected into the superior and inferior venae cavae, and thus brought to the heart again.

In addition to the pulmonary and systemic circulations, described above, there is another subsidiary to the venous system, known as the portal circulation. A certain amount of the blood of the intestines is collected into the portal vein and carried to the liver, where it traverses a capillary network in intimate relation with the liver cells. There important changes are effected in the blood, which is highly charged with foodstuffs recently absorbed in its passage through the intestinal capillaries. The blood is collected a second time into veins, and carried to the inferior vena cava, where it again joins the general circulation. In its passage through other special organs the blood undergoes further modifications. See ARTERY; BLOOD; BLOOD PRESSURE; HEART; KIDNEY; SPLEEN.

The heart's action consists in successive alternate contraction (systole) and relaxation (diastole) of the muscular walls of the auricles and ventricles. During the period of relaxation the blood flows into the two auricles from the veins, and they are gradually distended, while a certain amount of blood passes on into the ventricles through the auriculoventricular openings. At the end of this period the auricles are completely dilated, and their muscular walls contract and force nearly the entire contents into the ventricles. This action is sudden, and takes place in both auricles simultaneously. Reflux of the blood into the veins is counteracted by the mass of blood in the veins. The force of blood flowing into the ventricles is insufficient to open the semilunar valves, but distends the ventricles themselves, still in a condition of relaxation. The tricuspid and mitral valves float upward on the blood current, and close readily at the beginning of ventricular contraction. The ventricular systole follows immediately the auricular systole. The contraction is slower, but far more forcible, and entirely empties the ventricular chambers at each systole. The apex of the heart is thrown forward and upward with a slight rotary motion, and this impulse (the apex beat) is detected between the fifth and sixth ribs. For a short time after the ventricular systole the whole heart is at rest. The entire cycle, therefore, can be divided into three periods: in the first the auricles contract, in the second the ventricles contract, and in the third both auricles and ventricles remain at rest.

The heart has two sounds with every beat, and these are followed by a short pause. The first sound is dull and protracted, and coincides with the ventricular systole.

The second sound, shorter and much sharper, is probably dependent on the sudden closure of the semilunar valves. Diseases of the heart valves modify these sounds. In the healthy adult the heartbeats number about 72 a minute; but many factors, e.g., exercise, cause wide variations, even in health.

The impulse of the blood, when it enters the arteries at the moment of ventricular contraction, can be felt in all the superficial arteries of any considerable size; and this is called the pulse (q.v.). For clinical purposes it is usually felt in the radial artery on the outer side of the wrist.

With the microscope, circulation of the blood can be observed in superficial capillaries. Red blood corpuscles are seen moving along rapidly in the middle of the blood current, while the white ones advance more sluggishly along the walls of the capillaries. The capillaries present a far larger surface with which the blood comes in contact than do the other blood vessels, and therefore offer the greatest resistance to the progress of the blood, so that the capillaries greatly influence the circulation.

It is estimated that a portion of the blood can complete its circulation in half a minute. The circulation begins at a very early period in fetal life. See LYMPHATICS.

E.J.B.

CIRCULATORY SYSTEM, group of organs concerned with the transport of body fluids to all cells throughout the organism. In a unicellular organism, such as the ameba (q.v.), the cell surface is directly in contact with the environment from which food supplies are obtained and into which the waste materials are released. In multicellular animals only the outer layer of cells is in direct contact with the environment, so that specialized structures are necessary for the transport of nutrients and waste materials within the body. Hence, circulation is accomplished in the single-celled Protozoa, the lowest division of the animal kingdom, without any special circulatory apparatus; an increasingly complex circulatory system is required in higher animals in order to maintain the tissue fluids in a constant state throughout all parts of the body.

In the sponges, which attain great size, water canals penetrate all parts of the organism, delivering food and oxygen to every cell and carrying away its waste materials. In the Coelenterata, such as the hydra (q.v.), the body wall is only two cells thick. The outer layer of cells is in direct contact with the environment and the inner layer is in contact with the fluids of the gastrovascular cavity, which opens to the exterior at one end. In flatworms (q.v.) the gastrovascular cavity is branched and contains fluids which function in digestion and in circulation. The fluids of the cavity are set in motion by the cilia of the lining cells.

In the Mollusca (q.v.) the body is so large and the muscular system so well developed that more effective transportation is required. In the dorsal part of the animal there is a thick muscular tube comprising two auricles and a ventricle which constitutes a propelling organ, or heart. The heart surrounds the alimentary tract, so that nutrients may pass through the wall of the gut into the circulating fluid. From the heart the circulating fluid is carried to the mantle and to muscles and glands. The fluids in these structures and in the gills make their way to the heart usually by the aid of cilia. Oxygen is obtained both in the thin-walled mantle and in the gills. The Mollusca possess a fairly specialized circulatory system consisting of a contractile heart, arteries, tissue spaces, and veins.

Among segmented animals the annelids (see ANNELIDA) have a well-defined circulatory system with a main dorsal vessel and a median ventral vessel, and circular transverse vessels in the body wall. Vessels supply the alimentary tract, in which the blood absorbs nutritive fluids; others supply the body wall, parapodia, or gills, in which the blood is oxygenated. Propulsion of the blood is effected by peristaltic contraction of the dorsal vessel, which has valves in its walls to prevent back flow. A number of annelids have a well-developed system of contractile vessels (hearts) which provide connection between the major dorsal and ventral longitudinal vessels.

In the Crustacea (q.v.) there is a dorsal vessel, or heart, which pumps blood back and forth within the body cavity. The higher Crustacea, such as the lobster, have vessels which lead to the brain, muscles, gills, and alimentary tract, from which the blood is returned to the heart by blood spaces. In insects (see INSECTA) the heart consists of a delicate pulsating tube which helps to circulate the blood through tissue spaces. In most insects blood is not involved in the transportation of respiratory gases. Oxygen is carried from minute openings in the body wall directly to the tissues by means of many small branches called the tracheae. The circulatory system of arachnids (see ARACHNIDA) is similar to that of insects, but arteries may be present, and the blood is involved in oxygen transport.

In vertebrates (q.v.) the organs of circulation are the heart, arteries, veins, and lymphatics. The heart in the lowest of the vertebrates and in embryonic life (see EMBRYOLOGY) is at first divided into two chambers with valves between them to prevent the backward flow of blood. One chamber, the auricle, receives the blood; the other, the ventricle, expels it again to the body. By further modification a distinct chamber called the *sinus venosus* develops at the venous end, and the *bulbus arteriosus,* a dilated part of the aorta (q.v.), arises at the arterial end. This type of primitive heart is permanent in many fishes.

With the development of lungs, and consequently of the pulmonary artery and veins, the primitive heart is much changed. In amphibians (q.v.) the heart consists of two auricles and a single ventricle. Blood from the lungs enters the left auricle while the right auricle receives blood from the body tissues. Because of the single ventricle, the blood from these two sources is somewhat mixed. In many amphibians the ventricle is continued in a spirally twisted division called the *conus arteriosus.* This structure achieves the partial separation of the venous blood and the arterial blood.

Among reptiles, an incomplete ventricular septum exists in lizards, snakes, and turtles, but a complete septum in crocodiles. The blood from the right ventricle passes into the pulmonary artery, and that from the left ventricle into the aortic arch. There are fewer valves in the heart, and only one row at the beginning of the aorta and pulmonary artery.

In birds and mammals there are two auricles and ventricles, that is, auricular and ventricular septa are complete. The ventricles are the larger and have more strongly developed walls. The blood from the head, heart, and body passes into the right auricle; the blood from the lungs flows into the left auricle (see CIRCULATION OF THE BLOOD).

The lymphatic system of elasmobranchs, amphibia, and, to some extent, of birds and reptiles, is provided with lymph hearts. In fish and amphibia there are large lymph spaces, but from birds onward lymph vessels with well-defined trunks are present. The main lymph vessel is the thoracic duct, which empties in mammals into the left subclavian vein; in reptiles and birds lymph trunks divide to enter the precaval veins. The vessels, like the veins, are provided with valves which prevent a reflux of the lymph fluid. The lymph, like the blood, is composed of fluid and corpuscles. Lymphatic tissue occurs in fishes and amphibia, but lymph glands proper appear along the course of the lymph vessels probably first in birds. In lymphatic tissue or glands the leucocytes, or white corpuscles of the blood, and lymph develop. See also BLOOD; BLOOD PRESSURE; HEART; LYMPHATICS.　　　　　　　　　　　　　　E.J.B.

Culver Service

Circus Maximus, with chariot race in progress on the great U-shaped track

CIRCUMCISION (Lat. *circumcidere,* "to cut around"), the cutting off of the male prepuce, or of the corresponding tissues of a female. Since ancient time circumcision of males has been widely practiced as a religious rite. The initiatory rite of Judaism, circumcision is also practiced by Mohammedans, and signifies spiritual purification. Three thousand years before Christ it was familiar to the Egyptians, who circumcised boys between the ages of six and fourteen. The ceremony is portrayed in a drawing on a temple at Karnak; and most of the mummies are found to have been circumcised. Circumcision was known to the Babylonians, the Colchians, to some Phenicians, and apparently also to the Edomites, Ammonites, and Moabites. Further, it appears among many African tribes, among Mexicans, Indians of South America, and among the islanders of the Pacific Ocean. It may have served, like tattooing, to mark the circumcised person as qualified to take part in sacred rites. It may also have had a sacrificial character. Primitive nations, however, constantly substitute some partial mutilation for the sacrifice of the whole person.

It is uncertain whether the clans which afterward formed the people of Israel knew the custom before they entered Palestine.

After the exile, circumcision assumed a new significance in the eyes of the Jews, since the Babylonians and Persians, who ruled over them, practiced no such rite. It became the special sign of the covenant between God and His chosen people, and their devotion to it grew in proportion to the contempt it excited in their Greek and Roman oppressors. In the 2d century A.D. the Roman government sought to discourage the practice.

According to the Levitical law, every Jewish male had to be circumcised on the eighth day under penalty of being ostracized from the congregation of Israel. Strangers had to circumcise their males if they wished to partake of the Passover. In case of necessity the rite might be performed by women. Modern Jews employ a *mohel* or official who has the requisite surgical skill. The child is brought to the door of the room and handed to the mohel, who after prayer circumcises the child, and having drunk a glass of wine, gives it its name and blesses it.

Circumcision was excluded from the Christian community after a memorable struggle. Many of the Jewish converts wished to impose circumcision on Gentile Christians, and, though forbidden to do so by the first Council at Jerusalem, continued to urge the rite. At present the Abyssinian Church alone among Christian bodies recognizes circumcision as a religious rite.

Circumcision existed among the Arabs before the time of the Prophet; and though not mentioned in the Koran, is practiced with much ceremony in all Mohammedan populations. The Arabs in Egypt have their boys circumcised at the age of five or six; among the peasants the age varies from twelve to fourteen. Circumcision of females is practiced in Egypt, Abyssinia, West Africa, Arabia, and other countries.

In modern medical practice, circumcision of males is a minor operation involving removal of a portion of the prepuce. It is performed in infancy for purposes of hygiene, or for remedial purposes in adults.

CIRCUS MAXIMUS, a Roman circus located between the Palatine and Aventine hills, and the principal amusement place from the early days of the Republic to the early days of the Empire. It was reconstructed and enlarged by Julius Cæsar. In its outer dimensions the Circus Maximus was about 2000 feet long and 625 feet wide, and its arena was about 1850 feet long and 280 feet wide. It had three tiers of seats, with room for about 200,000 spectators. See CIRCUS, ROMAN.

CIRCUS, MODERN, an area for public exhibitions, usually circular and enclosed by a tent, with tiers of seats for spectators. The entertainment offered at a circus consists generally of displays of horsemanship; exhibitions by gymnasts, aerialists, wild-animal trainers, and performing animals; and comic pantomime by clowns. The term "circus" is also applied to the performance itself and to the troupe of performers.

The first modern circus was staged in London in 1770 by Philip Astley, an English cavalry officer. From the early days of the modern circus, troupes often traveled to foreign countries and to the American colonies. An English troupe known as Rickett's Circus played in New York City in 1795. The small British circus, making its way from town to town in a caravan of small wooden structures on wheels, has flourished since the days of Astley. Large circuses with elaborate spectacles are given today in England and on the European continent in large permanent buildings of the more important cities. Notable among buildings of this type are the London Hippodrome, the Cirque de Paris, and the Cirque d'Hiver of Paris.

The earliest important American circus exhibitor was Rufus Welch, who lived in the first quarter of the 19th century. In 1826 the Mount Pitt Circus gave performances in New York City in a building seating 3500. Other important American circuses of the first half of the 19th century were those of Van Ambrugh and Dick Sands. The L. B. Lent Circus, which flourished during and following the Civil War, was the first large circus to utilize rail transportation. Among showmen of the middle of the 19th century who played important parts in the development of the American circus were Adam Forepaugh, the Sells brothers, and Dan Rice. Not until the last third of the century, however, did the elaborate and costly type of circus known today come into being. In 1869 W. C. Coup organized a circus, the largest of the period, which gave performances in two rings. Coup and Dan Costello, another showman, formed a partnership with Phineas T. Barnum (q.v.), an internationally known exhibitor, and in

Early 20th-century circus advertisement

1871, in Brooklyn, N.Y., the three opened a huge circus advertised as "The Greatest Show on Earth". Ten years later this circus was combined with one owned by James A. Bailey, one of the best organizers the circus has ever known. The new (Barnum and Bailey) circus was so huge that it gave its shows in three rings. In 1884 another notable group of circus exhibitors, the Ringling brothers (Albert C., Otto, Alfred T., Charles, and John), organized their first circus. They took over the Forepaugh-Sells Circus in 1906, and in 1907, when both Barnum and Bailey were dead, bought the Barnum and Bailey Circus. In 1919 they merged this circus and their own into one enormous circus organization.

Over 30 circus troupes tour the United States each year, traveling by rail. The circus season extends from late April to November. A frequent feature of the American circus has been the preliminary parade of the performers and animals through the streets of the city or town where performances are to be given.

CIRCUS, ROMAN (Lat. *circus,* "a ring" or "a circle"), in ancient Rome, the roofless enclosure, oblong in shape, rounded at one end and open at the other, in which horse races and chariot races were held. The Roman circus was an adaptation of the Greek hippodrome. The term is also applied to the events taking place in the enclosure. Gladiatorial combats, combats between wild beasts, and combats between men and wild beasts, usually held in the arena of an amphitheater (q.v.), were also sometimes held in circuses. Tiers of seats surrounded the circus except at the end where the stalls for the horses and chariots were located. In the center of the circus, extending lengthwise almost from end to end, was a low wall, the *spina*, around which the riders or charioteers rode. The Roman populace often demanded bread and circuses (*panem et circenses*) from political candidates. Pompey the Great (see POMPEIUS) is said on one occasion (55 B.C.) to have sponsored five days of circus games during which 500 lions and 20 elephants were killed. From the fall of the Roman Empire to the end of the Renaissance, the Roman circuses were gradually dismantled for their building stones. Few traces have remained of any of them except the Circus Maxentius in Rome. See CIRCUS MAXIMUS; CIRCUS, MODERN.

CIRRIPEDIA. See CRUSTACEA.

CIRRUS. See CLOUD.

CIRTA. ancient city of northern Africa and capital of Numidia under King Syphax. Following the defeat of Syphax by the Romans, about 203 B.C., it became an important Roman colony. In 310 A.D. it was sacked by the troops of Marcus Aurelius Valerius Maxentius. The Emperor Constantine subsequently rebuilt the town (313 A.D.), renaming it after himself. Its site is occupied by Constantine, Algeria.

CISALPINE REPUBLIC, a former state of northern Italy, created by Napoleon Bonaparte on July 9, 1797, during the French Revolutionary Wars, by the union of the Cispadane and Transpadane (q.v.) republics. It had an area of more than 16,000 sq.m., on both sides of the Po River, and a population of about 3,500,000. Milan was the seat of government. The Republic maintained an army of 20,000 French troops.

In 1802 the Cisalpine Republic became the Italian Republic, with Bonaparte as its president. In 1805 the Italian Republic changed its name to the Kingdom of Italy, and Bonaparte became king of the new state. In 1815, following the final defeat of Bonaparte, the kingdom became a part of Austria; and later in the 19th century, following the unification of Italy, was included in the Italian kingdom.

CISTERCIAN, the name of a monastic order founded by Saint Robert de Molesme (d. 1111), abbot of a Benedictine monastery at Molesme in Burgundy. In 1098 Robert led a group of monks from Molesme to Cîteaux (anc. *Cistercium*) near Dijon; there Count Odo of Burgundy built a monastery for them in a swampy forest, and Robert's followers

established a community devoted to the strictest observance of the rule of St. Benedict. By command of the Pope, Robert returned in 1099 to Molesme; but his successor, Alberic (who died in 1109) succeeded in having the order confirmed. St. Bernard (see BERNARD OF CLAIRVAUX), with thirty companions, joined the Cistercians in 1113. Two years later he became the first abbot of Clairvaux, which became the center of his influence. Before the end of the 12th century the order had 800 abbeys.

When St. Bernard directed the order, he wrote and preached against the current artistic extravagances in the construction, decoration, and furnishing of churches. The austere and holy life of the early Cistercians won them respect and a vast influence throughout Christendom. They produced few great writers, but were indefatigable in collecting and copying manuscripts for their libraries. In practical matters, the order was important in the growth of the wool industry in England. After this golden age a period of decline followed. The rule was less strictly observed; many disorders crept in toward the end of the 14th century, and by the middle of the 15th century the order had split into several congregations. The habit of the order is a white robe with black scapulary.

In England their earliest establishment was Waverley Abbey (1128), near Farnham, in Surrey. Among other English abbeys were Woburn, Tintern, Furness, Fountains, Kirkstall, and Rievaux; among the Scottish, Melrose, Dundrennan, Kinloss, Glenluce, Culross, Deer, Balmerino, and Sweetheart or New Abbey. The chief French abbeys were La Ferté, Pontigny, Clairvaux, and Morimond, the last of which had 700 dependent benefices. Port Royal des Champs was the most celebrated of the Cistercian nunneries. The French Revolution reduced the Cistercians to a few convents in Spain, Poland, Austria, and Saxony. The last remnant of the order in France was expelled in 1880. See MONASTIC ART; MONASTICISM.

CISTUS, or ROCKROSE, a genus of thalamifloral dicotyledons in the family Cistaceae. Many species of *Cistus* are cultivated in Mediterranean countries for the beauty of their large flowers, which resemble the wild rose and are red, white, lilac, yellow, or frequently of two colors. The yellow rockrose, or frostweed, common on dry hillsides in eastern U.S., belongs to the related genus *Helianthemum*.

CITADEL, THE, State-controlled military college of South Carolina, situated in Charleston. An accredited school of arts and sciences, it provides courses of instruction leading to bachelor degrees in engineering, liberal arts, and business administration. Residence in campus barracks is compulsory, and students are subject to military discipline. The Citadel was founded in 1842 as the South Carolina Military Academy. In 1865, during the Civil War, Federal troops occupied the barracks, forcing the school to close. It was reopened in 1882, and given its present name in 1910. In 1962 enrolled students totaled about 2000; the faculty numbered 139.

CITHÆRON or **ELATEA,** a mountain range of Greece, extending eastward from the Gulf of Corinth, in the department of Attica and Bœotia. Mt. Cithæron, 4626 ft. above sea level, the highest peak of the range, is covered with pine forests. On its northern slope are the ruins of the ancient city of Platæa (q.v.). Mt. Cithæron is famous in Greek mythology as the scene of mystic Dionysian rites, and as the site of the mutilation and abandonment of the infant Œdipus by his father, the Theban king Laius.

CITIZEN (Lat. *civis,* "citizen"), in its most general sense, an individual member of a political society, or state; one who owes allegiance to, and may lawfully demand protection from, the government. The more general sense of the term "citizen" is more closely in accordance with the original meaning of the word. In the free republics of classical antiquity, the term "citizen" signified, not a resident of a town, but a free, governing member of the state, just as the term *civitas,* from which we derive our "city", signified, not merely a local municipality (*urbs*), but the state at large. The Greek idea of citizenship as expressed by Aristotle held a citizen to be a person with the right to participate both in the legislative and the judicial functions of the political community of which he was a member. This right was jealously guarded, and was rarely conferred on those of foreign birth. In Rome there were two classes of citizens— one class with a share in the sovereign power, i.e., capable of attaining the highest offices of state and the other possessing only the private rights of citizenship which included, however, the privilege of voting in the public assembly. As in the United States and other modern states, citizenship in Rome, though usually acquired by birth, could be attained by naturalization or special grant of the state.

In the United States the word "citizen" is used in its broadest sense. The same person may be, and usually is, a citizen of the United States and of the State in which he resides. The two are not, however, necessarily coexistent; for an inhabitant of one of the Territories or of the District of Columbia is a citizen of the United States without being a citizen of a State. The reverse, however, is not true; no person who is not a citizen of the United States can be a citizen of one of the States. The idea of citizenship does not necessarily involve the right of voting or of other participation in political activity, as in the Greek conception of the term; for minors may be citizens, although excluded from all direct political activity. A citizen of the United States may be either native-born or naturalized. By a Congressional act of 1922, the citizenship status of a married woman no longer follows that of the husband. A naturalized citizen is one who was originally a subject of a foreign state, but who has become a citizen of the United States under the acts of Congress bearing on that subject. A person who is naturalized is admitted to all the privileges and duties of citizenship; and his naturalization includes that of any minor, but not of adult, children resident at the time in the United States.

In regard to the dual relation of citizenship in the Federal government and in the State in which a person resides, a citizen of the United States owes his first and highest allegiance to the Federal government. The word "citizen" is often loosely used as synonymous with resident or inhabitant. State laws conferring the franchise upon aliens who have filed declarations of intention to become citizens are often regarded as conferring citizenship. Where a law passed for a particular purpose makes such loose use of the word, and where no question of constitutional rights is involved, the courts will interpret the word.

See NATURALIZATION; SUBJECT.

CITRIC ACID, $C_3H_4OH(COOH)_3$, a white solid, soluble in water and slightly soluble in organic solvents; m.p. 153° C. (307° F.). Solutions of citric acid in water are slightly more acidic than solutions of acetic acid. Citric acid or its salts (citrates) are found in many plants, particularly in the juice of citrus fruits, from which it can be obtained by treatment with lime. The resulting calcium citrate is soluble in cold water but insoluble in hot water. Citric acid is regenerated by treatment of calcium citrate with sulfuric acid. Much of the citric acid of commerce is made today by fermentation of sugar by a particular bacillus, *B. nigrus citrianus.*

Citric acid is used in foods and beverages to yield a pleasantly acid flavor. Several citrates are used in medicine, the best-known being the purgative citrate of magnesia. The property of citric acid of forming soluble complexes with several of the metals leads to its use as a component of Benedict's solution, where it holds copper in solution, and in certain dyeing operations, where it holds iron in solution.

CITRON, a tree, *Citrus medica,* native to N. India, cultivated in the south of Europe and other warm countries for its fruit. The fruit is large, warty, and furrowed. The pulp is acid and is used in the preparation of cooling drinks, but the part chiefly valued is the thick and tender rind, which is preserved or candied. From this also is procured the fragrant oil of citron or oil of cedrate, used by perfumers. In the United States the name citron is applied to a variety of melon resembling in appearance the watermelon, but having a firm, white, inedible core. The rind is used for preserves, like that of the true citron.

CITRONELLA, a fragrant ethereal oil used by perfumers directly and also as an adulterant. Derived from *Andropogon Nardus,* it is a grass oil. The application of citronella oil to the skin is recommended for repelling insects. The name citronella is also given to the horse balm, a plant, *Collinsonia canadensis,* of the Mint family.

CITRUS, a genus of plants of the family Rutaceae, consisting of 30 or more species of trees and shrubs, most of which bear spines or thorns and are natives of India and Asia, but many of which are now commonly cultivated in all warm climates for their fruit. This genus includes the orange, citron, lemon, lime, bergamot, shaddock, pomelo, and forbidden fruit. Citrus trees are distinguished by numerous stamens, irregularly united in bundles by their filaments, a pulpy fruit with a spongy or leathery rind, and smooth seeds. The leaves and the rind of the fruit abound in volatile oil. The flowers also contain volatile oil and emit a peculiar fragrance.

Most species of *Citrus* cannot withstand frost, and their cultivation is restricted to warm climates. However, their resistance is somewhat increased by grafting to hardier stock, and semihardy hybrids and varieties have been developed. The annual U.S. production of citrus fruits averages about 190 million boxes valued at about $350 million. The orange crop accounts for some two thirds of the total production; tangerines, lemons, and grapefruit make up most of the remainder.

CITY, generally a large center of population organized as a community. The ancient Greek city-states were independent communities, or states, consisting of a chief town and its immediate neighborhood. The cantons of which the Swiss federation is composed are not unlike cities in this sense. The Latin word *civitas,* from which the word "city" is derived, also denotes a community having administrative independence. Later the idea prevailed that a city was identical with a cathedral town, probably because bishoprics were usually situated in the chief centers of population. Accordingly, when Henry VIII of England established new sees in boroughs, he made these into cities. In Great Britain, "city" presently is merely a complimentary title conferred by the king upon important towns.

In the United States, a city is a chartered municipal corporation whose chief executive officer is usually known as mayor. There has been, however, an increasing tendency to engage professionally trained city managers to supervise city functions. The legislatures of the various States have prescribed different requisites for the granting of city charters, a principal condition being that in respect to size of population. City charters vary in the degree of power they confer on the municipal authorities, the measure of local autonomy being usually, though not always, regulated by the number of inhabitants. See MUNICIPAL GOVERNMENT.

With the exception of cities such as Washington, D.C., and Canberra, Australia, which were built as administrative seats, the city has always been the center of commercial and industrial development; but its origin is to be found among agricultural people who possessed fertile lands and built themselves walled towns, or took possession of some naturally fortified places, such as the Acropolis of Athens, in order to protect themselves from the attacks of predatory tribes. Within the city, exchange and handicrafts and various industries arose. Babylon and Egypt possessed many of these small communities. They were situated on rivers and the seacoast, and soon became centers of commerce. Large cities were a prominent feature of the ancient world. The most notable were Thebes, Memphis, Babylon, Nineveh, Susa, Tyre, Carthage, and Jerusalem. Alexandria is said to have contained over 500,000 inhabitants, and Rome was still larger. As capital of the Eastern Roman Empire, Constantinople succeeded Rome as the principal city in Europe. In the Mohammedan East, during part of the Middle Ages, Bagdad, Damascus, and Cairo led in population, while Cordova was the greatest city of the Mohammedan West and, for a time, of all Europe. At the beginning of the

16th century, Europe had six or seven cities of 100,000 or more inhabitants; at the end of that century, it had thirteen or fourteen such cities. The development of cities in Europe was one of the features of the break-up of the feudal social order. During the 17th century, although the population of Europe remained stationary, that of the cities increased.

A remarkable fact of the 19th and 20th centuries has been the constant increase in urban life at the expense of the rural districts. Cities have grown proportionally in respect to the total national populations. This is true not only of countries in which industry is highly developed, but also of countries whose economy is primarily agrarian. The principal causes of modern urban growth have been the development of mechanical industry, the improvements in transportation, and mechanization of agricultural labor.

Throughout the world the remarkable growth of great cities, as well as their manner of growth, is of special significance. It is important to note that territory adjacent to and economically dependent upon a large center continues to grow rapidly, and the increased size of modern cities is due to suburban extensions. In the older portions of the city, the population is displaced by business and industrial expansion; rapid-transit facilities remove the residential portions to outlying districts, where better living conditions are possible; and the congested wards remaining within the city do not grow, except where there is an influx of immigrants from countries with low standards of living, or of persons from economically depressed regions of the same country. See CITY PLANNING.

Since 1928 there has been a new historic phenomenon with respect to cities: their planned construction as industrial centers near sources of raw materials. In the Soviet Union, over 350 such cities have been built. After World War II cities everywhere in the world continued to expand far beyond their political boundaries. This has given rise to vast new governmental and quasi-governmental agencies to deal with the problems of metropolitan areas. Representatives of city governments, as well as of private interests, frequently participate in such bodies. Typical of interurban agencies are those concerned with the problems of such areas as the London region and the Chicago Sanitary District.

In the United States, in 1910, there were 178 cities with populations of 25,000 to 100,-000; 31 with populations of 100,000 to 250,000; and 19 with 250,000 or more inhabitants. In 1960, U.S. cities with populations of 25,000 to 100,000 numbered 378; cities with populations of 100,000 to 250,000 numbered 79; and cities with 250,000 or more inhabitants numbered 51. In 1890, 15.4 percent of the population of the United States lived in cities of 100,000 and over. In 1960 about 70 percent of the total population was urban.

WORLD'S LARGEST CITIES

	Rank	City Proper Population	Metropolitan Area Population
Tokyo	1	8,305,000	9,675,000
New York	2	7,780,000	10,695,000
Shanghai	3	6,900,000	....
Moscow	4	6,260,000	6,295,000
Bombay	5	4,145,000	4,150,000
Peking	6	4,010,000	....
São Paulo	7	3,825,000	....
Chicago	8	3,550,000	6,220,000
Rio de Janeiro	9	3,405,000	....
Berlin	10	3,240,000	....
Mexico City	11	3,225,000	4,325,000
Tientsin	12	3,220,000	....
London	13	3,195,000	8,170,000

CITY COLLEGE, THE, municipally controlled, coeducational institution of higher learning of New York City, located in the borough of Manhattan. It was founded as the Free Academy in 1847. By an act of the New York State legislature in 1866, the college became known as the College of the City of New York. In 1929, when this name was adopted to designate New York City's four City College. In 1961 the complex of municipal colleges was renamed the City University of New York. Baccalaureate degrees are offered in the liberal arts and sciences; business and public administration; civil, mechanical, and electrical engineering; architecture; and education. Masters' degrees are offered in the liberal arts, the various branches of engineering, education, and business and public administration. Evening sessions were instituted in 1909 and summer sessions in 1917. Adult courses are given by the college in many of the city's museums and libraries. The college is administered by the Board of Higher Education of the City of New York and receives its principal financial support from the city and State of New York.

The college was located originally at 23rd Street and Lexington Avenue, in the borough of Manhattan. In 1907 it was moved to 139th Street and Convent Avenue; this is now the site of the College of Liberal Arts and Sciences and the School of Engineering and Architecture. In 1930 the small original building was replaced by a sixteen-story structure which now houses the School of Business and Public Administration. Admission to the college is restricted to residents of New York State. No tuition fees are required of New

York City residents; residents of New York State pay tuition fees unless their field of study is teacher education. To gain admission, applicants must have obtained excellent grades in high school. Undergraduates of the college are required to maintain high scholastic averages. In the 1962 fall term 32,992 students were enrolled, including 10,969 full-time students; the faculty numbered 1683 and the library of the college contained 488,838 bound volumes. See COLLEGE OF THE CITY OF NEW YORK.

CITY OF REFUGE, in the law of the Old Testament, a town reserved as a temporary asylum for homicides fleeing from the vengeance of the avenger of blood. The phrase refers particularly to the Jewish form of the right of asylum. Asylum once having been gained, the responsibility for the crime was transferred to the community protecting the wrongdoer, the compensation due being a money payment, with the amount regulated by law. According to Biblical law, there were six cities in which any one who committed murder unintentionally could find an asylum. (Num. 35). If the murderer reached any of these cities, he was safe from the blood avenger. In the days of Greek and Roman supremacy many cities of Syria enjoyed special privileges as asylums. According to Josephus, Jerusalem was included in the number. When a fugitive from the avenger of blood reached one of these cities, he was tried. If the fugitive was found guilty of wilful murder, he was put to death, but if he was found innocent, he was returned to the city of refuge, where he had to remain till the death of the high priest, otherwise the avenger might still slay him.

CITY OF THE SUN. See BAALBEK.

CITY PLANNING, the scientific designing and laying out of cities and towns, or parts thereof, to meet manifold public needs. It involves not only architectural and engineering considerations, but is also concerned with the social, economic, and physical condition of the inhabitants.

Proper city planning provides efficient and safe means of transportation. It provides also for the economic distribution of public utilities, public buildings, and parks and recreation centers, and for adequate, more healthful, and less expensive housing. City planning divides the city into districts or *zones* for purposes of residence, business, and industry, and guards against haphazard and piecemeal growth of the municipality by controlling the development of new land subdivisions.

Until recently, however, city planning was confined to the laying out or remodeling of street systems and open spaces. The three main types of street plans are (1) the rectangular, gridiron, or checkerboard; (2) the radial or diagonal, which is more properly called the radial and circular, or polygonal; and (3) a combination of the first two. To these may be added the designedly irregular plan.

The simplest street plan is the rectangular, since it is easily laid out and mapped or otherwise recorded, and lends itself readily to the transfer of property, besides making for directness of travel, as compared with winding streets. Radial street plans facilitate the movement of street traffic to and from central points, but give many awkwardly-shaped lots and make it necessary to turn many corners to get to points not on the radial streets. The radial or diagonal plan, superimposed on the rectangular plan, has some advantages, but is still likely to leave many awkwardly-shaped parcels of land. The designedly irregular type of street plan, largely a modern innovation and not yet widely used, is admirably adapted to local conditions in some cities, having the streets laid out quite irregularly, on curves following contour lines. Berkeley, California, is a good example of such configuration.

The Romans, like the Greeks, laid out cities on the rectangular plan, also taking advantage of natural features; but whereas the Greeks did not hesitate to modify or abandon the regularity of their plans, in order to use hillsides or rocky eminences to give grandeur and emphasis to their public buildings, the Romans often went to great labor and expense to level the sites of their cities. The characteristic feature of Roman colonial cities was the *castrum,* or military camp, which was quadrangular with four entrance gates. Greek and Roman writers and philosophers, as well as architects, wrote of the ideal city. Cities of the Middle Ages grew either around an ecclesiastical center, or under the protection of fortifications. However, one can hardly speak of conscious city planning as existing in those times. It was during the Renaissance that architects developed many constructive ideas for city planning, especially in Italy and France, and later also in Germany.

The Renaissance led Italian towns in the 16th century to straighten and widen their streets and lay out public places. Rome was rebuilt in this period. The movement extended to France. In Germany, also under the influence of the Renaissance, the irregular city development of the Gothic period began to give way to more regular street plans. Notable examples are Mannheim and Karlsruhe. In Scotland the new portion of Edinburgh, dating about 1768, presents a fine example of systematic city planning.

After the fire of 1666 the great architect Sir Christopher Wren laid out a new city plan for London. A combined radial and rectangular street plan, with St. Paul's Cathedral as the main focal point, was proposed. The plan was sanctioned by Parliament, but its execution was prevented by the opposition of merchants and others who were anxious to rebuild immediately and who opposed the delays and difficulties of reparceling the land.

A notable example of American city planning is the city of Washington, D.C. The national capital was planned in 1791 by Pierre Charles L'Enfant (q.v.), under the direction of George Washington and after a study of many European cities. The base plan of Washington is rectangular, superimposed by a network of diagonal streets, with numerous parks, open spaces, and commanding sites for Federal buildings. The main focal point is the Capitol.

A bold reconstruction of the plan of Paris, under the direction of Georges Eugène Haussmann, Prefect of the Seine, and based on the design of the architect Dechamps, was carried out from 1852 to 1870. The plan made use of diagonal streets and great central avenues which provided means of communication through a network of streets. Esthetically the plan was effective in supplying grand vistas, closed with notable public buildings and historic monuments. The success of this scheme was largely due to the creation and perpetuation of a city-planning or art commission. Berlin, beginning in 1862, also followed a systematic street-plan system.

The outbreak of World War I brought a sudden check to city-planning activities in England and the Continent. But even before the war was over, city and town planning for the devastated regions of France and Belgium was actively taken up. The British Parliament in 1919 made important amendments or supplements to its Housing and Town Planning Act of 1909. Some amendments were designed to meet the great housing shortage, while others were intended to give municipalities broader planning authority than they had possessed under the 1909 Act, besides requiring them to enter upon certain projects which before had been left to their option. In 1919, France, too, enacted its first city-planning law. By 1921 nearly all the Canadian province had passed city-planning acts applying to their municipalities. By early 1922 more

than thirty American State Legislatures had enacted laws concerning some phase of city planning. By 1932 there were 828 municipalities in the United States with planning departments. In 1940, 284 cities, over 30,000 in population, maintained planning or zoning departments.

St. Louis, Cleveland, and various other cities have made, through planning commissions, extensive studies of their need for wider and more continuous streets, along both radial or diagonal and also circumferential lines, and as a result major street plans have been adopted or proposed. Major city-planning improvements in Chicago since 1909, some of which were for the main thoroughfares, have had an estimated cost of over $230,000,000.

Between 1930 and 1940 city planning in Europe relapsed. Nothing of importance happened in France. In England some smaller workers' settlements were built, but showed no new principles beyond those embodied in the suburban residential "garden cities", or "industrial home towns", of the architect Raymond Unwin. In Italy, Benito Mussolini built some small villages for political reasons and publicized them widely, but actually these added nothing to further development. In Germany, there was a halt to the fine planning activities of the Weimar Republic which had created exemplary settlements following the ideas of Bruno Taut, Ernst May, and many other architects of the same generation.

Only the Netherlands and the Scandinavian countries furthered modern development by building co-operative settlements which embodied modern hygienic, social, and technical ideas.

The greatest changes took place in the United States. Public opinion had remained passive for a long time, but in 1934 the practical possibilities provided by the Federal Housing Administration considerably encouraged group and multifamily housing projects. Young architects began working in this field; and slum clearance, public playgrounds, and recreation areas progressed in connection with the development of parkways and highways. Washington, D.C., New York, Los Angeles, Detroit, Philadelphia, and many smaller cities in the South developed excellent projects. Opposition arose between those recommending general decentralization and dissolution into individual family units, and those favoring, for economic reasons, multiple dwellings nearer the places of work within the city limits.

The change-over of American industry to

the war program of World War II necessitated a great effort to house the flow of workers in the rapidly growing war industry. Unfortunately, the necessities of war did not permit long-range planning; hence a provisional makeshift character prevailed. The only resulting progress was the furthering of technique and methods of housing prefabrication.

Regional planning received increasing attention since papers on the subject were presented to the National Conference on City Planning at its meeting in 1919. Until 1924, the subject had not gone beyond the study and report stage. By far the most notable undertaking of this kind, under the name, "Plan of New York and Its Environs", (changed later to "Regional Survey of New York and Environs") was begun early in 1921 and first publicly announced in May, 1922. The regional survey embraced some 5500 square miles, centering around New York City and having a resident population of some 10,000,000 living in over 400 communities. The committee, in 1930, published a summary of its work. During 1923 the Regional Planning Association of America was formed.

After some years of study, and particularly just before World War I, it became evident that proper city planning depended on zoning; that is, upon determining, subject to reasonably frequent modification, what parts of a city shall be devoted to residences of various types, such as single, semidetached or apartments; what part to business; what to manufacturing; and where a few classes of industry actually or likely to be nuisances, but essential to a large city, shall be allowed. Permissible heights of buildings, and percentage of lots built upon are taken into consideration. Upon the use and height of buildings, and the percentage of ground covered by them depend density of population; street widths; kinds of pavement; size of water mains and sewers; transportation facilities; size, location, and character of schools; and playgrounds and parks, telephone and light service.

The fact that zoning requires no construction outlay and comparatively little operating expense, and that it prepares the way for the more orderly, economical, and efficient construction of several kinds of municipal works, facilitated zoning at a time when many other municipal activities were almost at a standstill. Although not known by that name at the time, zoning in America was begun as early as 1904 by Boston, as a result of the State legislation of 1898 and 1904 which empowered Boston to limit the height of buildings near the Public Library on Copley Square. In 1930 practically every town and city of any consequence in the United States had zoning ordinances.

The grouping of public buildings into civic centers has been one of the chief concerns of American city planners, and provides a large number of examples of the execution or partial execution of city plans. Cities that have led in this respect have been Washington, Cleveland, San Francisco, and Denver. At Springfield, Mass., the "municipal group" includes a campanile flanked on either side by a city hall and auditorium.

Planning in most municipalities in the United States today is done by a city-planning commission composed of municipal officials and interested citizens who are appointed to the commission by the mayor or city manager, and are given funds to engage city-planning experts.

The use of official planning commissions by local governments is largely an American contribution to the field. Planning in the United States is less exclusively concerned with architecture than it was at the turn of the century and as it continues to be in many European countries. The problems of land economics, real-estate values, and the market mechanism are given much more weight in the mid-20th century than ever before. Although esthetic considerations have not lost their importance, a planner or a group of planners rarely concentrates on producing a "plan" as an architect produces a blueprint for a house. The emphasis is placed upon planning as a process for reckoning with the increasing complexities of city life. In subdividing a community or adding a shopping center, or in developing part of an existing area, such as a slum section, planners take into account the pertinent social, economic, cultural, and physical features of the locality to be improved. National organizations concerned with planning include the American Society of Planning Officials, at Chicago, Ill., the American Institute of Planners, at Cambridge, Mass., and the American Planning and Civic Association, with headquarters at Washington, D.C.

See CITY; HOUSING.

CIUDAD BOLÍVAR, river port and capital of Bolívar State, Venezuela, on the Orinoco R., about 240 m. from its mouth. It is the commercial and trading center of the Orinoco basin, and exports the principal products of the region: gold, diamonds, hides and skins, balata gum, tonka beans, chicle, lumber, tobacco, and bitters. The city was founded in 1764 as San Tomás de la Nueva Guayana, but was popularly known as Angostura ("narrows"). It was there, in 1824, that a physician first made the famous Angostura bitters. In the 19th century the city was, for a time, the headquarters of the nationalist revolutionary movement for freedom from Spain, and, in 1849, received its present name in honor of Simon Bolivar. Pop. (1961) 64,133.

CIUDAD JUÁREZ, a city in the state of Chihuahua, Mexico, on the Rio Grande R., opposite El Paso, Texas, with which it is connected by bridges. It was founded about 1681 and was formerly called El Paso del Norte. Ciudad Juárez has a large tourist trade with visitors from the United States, and is the northern terminus of the Mexican Central Railway. Pop. (1960) 294,373.

CIUDAD TRUJILLO, now **SANTO DOMINGO,** capital of the Dominican Republic, in the National District of Santo Domingo, situated at the mouth of the Ozama R. It is an important center of Caribbean and oceanic steamship lines, and of air lines flying the routes between North and South America. The city was founded in 1496 by the Spanish, who named their settlement Santo Domingo, and is the oldest extant settlement of the New World. In 1930 it was almost entirely destroyed by a hurricane, but was subsequently rebuilt. In 1936 it was renamed Ciudad Trujillo, after President Rafael Leonidas Trujillo

Dominican Republic Consulate
The tomb of Christopher Columbus, in the cathedral of Santa María, Ciudad Trujillo

Molina; it was again named Santo Domingo in November, 1961. Pop. (1960 prelim.) 367,053.

CIVET CAT or **CIVET,** common name for carnivores of the family Viverridae, connecting the cats with the hyenas, and having the body elongated in some of the species as much as in the weasel tribe. The head is also long and the muzzle sharp. The ears are short, broad, and rounded. The feet have five toes, and the claws are only semi-retractile. The civet preys on birds, small quadrupeds, and reptiles, and is regarded as a benefactor along the Nile River because of its appetite for crocodiles' eggs. It is commonly kept in confinement for the sake of its civet, a secretion used as a fixative in perfumery. The secretion is removed from a sac near the genital organs about twice a week by means of a small spatula, and is obtained most abundantly from the male, especially after he has been irritated. A dram is a large quantity to obtain at a time. After being cleaned of hairs, washed, and dried, civet is ready for the market. The animals kept for the purpose of providing civet are fed on raw flesh; the young partly on farinaceous food. The chief source of supply of dried civet is northern Africa.

CIVIC CROWN, one of the most valued honors among the Romans. It was given for saving the life of a citizen in battle, provided that in so doing the rescuer slew the opponent, and maintained the ground on which the fight had taken place. The crown consisted of a wreath of oak leaves, with pendant acorns. The recipient had the right to wear it always. When he appeared at the games, the spectators rose in his honor, and he was excused from all troublesome duties and services.

CIVIL AERONAUTICS ADMINISTRATON. See FEDERAL AVIATION AGENCY.

CIVIL AERONAUTICS BOARD, independent, quasi-judicial federal agency headed by five members appointed by the President with the consent of the Senate. A full term for a member is six years, with the President annually designating one member as chairman and another as vice chairman. The Board initially was responsible for carrying out the mandates of the Civil Aeronautics Act of 1938. This act was superseded by the Federal Aviation Act of 1958, which provided for the continuation of the Board as an independent agency. Board decisions affecting domestic air transportation are final, subject only to judicial review, and not subject to review by any executive department or agency; decisions affecting international air transportation must have Presidential approval.

The Board performs three chief functions: (1) regulation of the economic aspects of domestic and international United States air-carrier operations, including the issuance of certificates for scheduled and supplemental air-carrier service, approval of passenger and freight tariffs, and setting the service rate and subsidy amounts for scheduled air carriers; (2) participation in the establishment and development of international air transportation by consulting with and assisting the Department of State in the negotiation of agreements with foreign governments; and (3) promotion of safety in civil aviation, including investigation and analysis of accidents involving civil aircraft.

CIVIL DEFENSE, organized preparation for the protection of civilian lives and property and of the means of economic productivity during and immediately after an enemy aerial attack. Primary responsibility for civil defense in the United States rests with the States and Territories and their political subdivisions. The Federal Civil Defense Administration, established in 1951, serves the State and local agencies as an adviser and co-ordinator and as a clearing house for research and information.

The F.C.D.A. is headed by an administrator appointed by the President and by and with the consent of the Senate. He presides over a twelve-man Civil Defense Advisory Council appointed by the President.

National headquarters of the administration are in Battle Creek, Mich. The agency maintains a liaison office in Washington, D.C., and seven regional offices.

The Federal agency drafts the over-all plans for use by the local civil-defense units, provides the communications system for warning of an impending attack, stores needed emergency supplies in strategic places, and keeps a 200-bed mobile hospital unit in readiness for service in any part of the country. Under its direction special research programs are carried on to estimate survival possibilities under all conditions. Within prescribed limits, the agency helps the States finance certain civil-defense projects. The F.C.D.A. has the power to delegate various responsibilities to other Federal agencies and, in the event of the declaration of a state of civil-defense emergency by the President or the Congress, to exercise unusually broad powers.

Unpaid, part-time volunteers man the various services of civil defense. In 1955 they totaled about 4,500,000. Their duties include watching for hostile aircraft; organizing the evacuation of threatened communities; fighting fires; rescuing trapped persons; giving medical care to the injured; helping the police to maintain order; overseeing the purity and availability of water and food; sheltering the homeless; and repairing damaged utilities and industrial plants.

Tests have shown that a nuclear or even a thermonuclear attack does not cause the total destruction of a target area. To insure maximum safety in the event of an attack, each family should take the precautionary measures recommended by civil defense authorities. Some of the important measures may be summarized as follows:

(1) Build a family shelter or provide one in the basement; or, if an apartment dweller, learn the exact location of the shelter nearest home. Any shelter during an attack is better than none.

(2) Store flashlight, can opener, battery-operated AM radio, emergency cooking and sanitation equipment, and a week's supply of food and water in the shelter.

(3) Have at least one member of the family take Red Cross instruction in First Aid and Home Nursing. Keep a first-aid kit handy.

(4) Learn the air-raid warning signals; stay under cover until civil-defense authorities announce that it is safe to come out.

(5) Learn the facts about radioactive fallout so that its hazards can be reduced.

(6) During an emergency, tune the radio to CONELRAD, 640 or 1240 kilocycles, the channels reserved for all official announcements. Do not attempt to use the telephone.

The need for civil defense was dictated by the threat of modern aerial warfare to civil populations. Germany, Japan, and Great Britain began to organize civilians against possible air raids before the outbreak of World War II, and British experience in the early years of the war formed the basis for the earliest civil-defense plans of the United States.

The first U.S. agency charged with responsibility for civil defense was established in June, 1941. That agency, the Office of Civilian Defense, developed a dual program designed to promote the formation of protective units on the local level and the participation of civilians in other phases of the war effort. During World War II millions of Americans functioned as air-raid wardens, auxiliary fire fighters, victory gardeners, bond salesmen, and the like. An Office of Civil Defense Planning was established in 1948. The national emergency engendered by the Korean War led to the establishment of the present Federal agency. In 1953 U.S. civil-defense organizations were assigned the further responsibility of co-ordinating rescue operations in areas endangered by large-scale natural disasters, such as those caused by forest fires, floods, tornadoes, hurricanes, and earthquakes.

CIVILIAN CONSERVATION CORPS or **CCC**, a Federal agency set up in April, 1933, for the purpose of establishing a program for the conservation of the natural resources of the country: timber, soil, and water; and to provide work and training for unemployed young men.

At first the agency was officially known as Emergency Conservation Work, but when Congress extended its period of operation in June, 1937, the popular name, Civilian Conservation Corps, was made official. In 1939, the agency became part of the Federal Security Agency. In June, 1942, Congress voted to abolish the Corps within twelve months; a Presidential order for liquidation followed about six months later.

While the CCC was in operation, it provided for the enrollment of unmarried men, between the ages of 17 and 23, who were U.S. citizens in need of employment. During the 9¼ years of its existence, about 3 million men received employment on its projects, which are estimated to have added between 1½ and 2 billion dollars of value to the national domain, at a cost of under 3 billion dollars. Among its achievements were the planting of about 3 billion trees, the building of about 4000 fire observation towers, the laying of telephone lines, and the building of forest trails. The primary purpose, however, was the provision of employment and training for the enrollees.

CIVILIZATION, advanced state of a society possessing historical unity and a basic cultural homogeneity. This article is concerned with the problem of identifying specific societies which, because of distinctive achievements, are regarded by historians as separate civilizations. Distinctive features of the various civilizations are discussed elsewhere in the encyclopedia (see below).

The historical perspective in which civilizations, rather than nations or states, are seen as the significant units is of relatively recent origin. Since the Middle Ages the perspectives of most European historians have been determined notably by religious or national points of view. The religious viewpoint was predominant among European historians until the 18th century and continued to be prominent subsequently. Regarding the Christian reve-

lation as the most momentous event in the annals of mankind, they viewed all history as either the prelude to or aftermath of that event. The early historians of Europe had little occasion to study other cultures except as curiosities or as potential areas for missionary activity. The national-bias viewpoint developed in the early-16th century, largely on the basis of the political philosophy of the Italian statesman and historian Niccolò Machiavelli, for whom the state was the proper object of historical study. However, after that period the many historians who chronicled and celebrated the histories of the national states of Europe and America rarely dealt with societies beyond the realm of European culture except to describe the subjection of those societies by the more progressive and dynamic European powers.

Historians became increasingly interested in other cultures during the Age of Enlightenment; see ENLIGHTENMENT, AGE OF. The development in the 18th century of a secular point of view and principles of rational criticism enabled the French author and philosopher Voltaire and the French jurist and man of letters Charles Louis de Secondat, Baron de la Brède et de Montesquieu to transcend the provincialism of earlier historical thinking. Their attempts at universal history, however, suffered from prevalent biases. They tended to deprecate and ignore irrational customs and to imagine that all men were inherently rational beings and therefore very much alike.

Early in the 19th century philosophers and historians identified with the romantic movement criticized the typically 18th-century idea that men everywhere and at all times were the same; see ROMANTICISM. The German philosophers Johann Gottfried von Herder and Georg Wilhelm Friedrich Hegel emphasized the profound differences in the minds and works of human beings in different cultures, thereby laying the foundation for the comparative study of civilizations.

According to modern historians of civilizations, it is impossible to write a fully intelligible history of any nation without taking into consideration the type of culture to which it belongs. They maintain that much of a nation's life is affected by its participation in a larger social entity composed often of a number of nations or states sharing many distinctive characteristics traceable to a common origin. It is this larger social entity, an ethnic and cultural rather than a political entity, which such historians con-

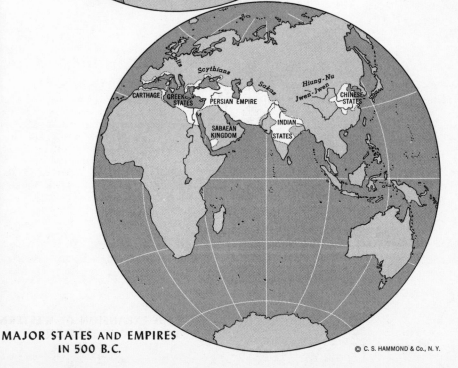

THE CRADLES OF CIVILIZATION
3000-1000 B.C.

MAJOR STATES AND EMPIRES
IN 500 B.C.

© C. S. HAMMOND & Co., N. Y.

MAJOR STATES AND EMPIRES IN 400 A.D.

MAYAN STATES

Germans
Slavs
Huns
Teutons
White Huns
KOKURYO
JAPANESE EMPIRE
WESTERN ROMAN EMPIRE
EASTERN ROMAN EMPIRE
Kanggü
KUSHAN STATES
WEI EMPIRE
SUNG EMPIRE
YAMATAI
Berbers
KINGDOM OF GHANA
Nubians
SASSANID EMPIRE
GUPTA EMPIRE
PYU
FUNAN
LANGKASUKA
Hindus
YAVADVIPA
TARUMA
AXUMITE KINGDOM
HIMYARITIC KINGDOM
Hindus
SINHALA
PALLAVA CONFEDERACY

THE EXPANSION OF WESTERN CIVILIZATION 1600 A.D.

Spaniards
JAPAN
KOREA
TIDORE
TERNATE
MING DYNASTY OF CHINA
BRUNEI
MACASSAR
AZTEC EMPIRE (1519)
Russians
ANNAM
MAYAN STATES (1527)
French
RUSSIAN EMPIRE
BUKHARA
BURMA
SIAM
MATARAM
English
MUGHAL EMPIRE
Spaniards
PERSIA
ATJEH
Moluccas
Spaniards
OTTOMAN EMPIRE
MOROCCO
Portuguese
Dutch
INCA EMPIRE (1533)
BORNU
ETHIOPIA
SONGHOY EMPIRE
HAUSA
BAGUIRMI
DARFUR
Portuguese
Dutch

sider the truly meaningful object of historical study. In modern times the living civilizations increasingly have impinged upon one another to the point that none pursue separate destinies and all may be considered participants in a common world civilization.

Some historians have professed to see certain striking uniformities in the histories of civilizations. The German philosopher Oswald Spengler, in *Decline of the West* (1918–22), described civilizations as living organisms, each of which passes through identical stages at fixed periods. The British historian Arnold Joseph Toynbee, in *A Study of History* (10 vols., 1934–54), also discerned a uniform pattern in the histories of civilizations, although he is not so rigid a determinist as Spengler. According to Toynbee, a civilization may prolong its life indefinitely by successful responses to the various internal and external challenges which constantly arise to confront it. However, many historians are exceedingly skeptical of philosophies of history derived from an alleged pattern of the past. They are particularly reluctant to base predictions about the future on such theories.

Although historians acknowledge the difficulty of delimiting precisely a particular society and correctly labeling it a civilization, they employ the term "civilization" with reference to a number of past and present societies which manifest distinctive cultural and historical patterns. Some of these civilizations are the Peruvian, which originated about 1500 B.C. (see PERUVIAN ARCHEOLOGY); the Mexican, about 600 B.C. (see MAYAS; AZTECS; MEXICO); the Far Eastern, which originated in China about 1500 B.C. and spread to Japan about 600 A.D. (see CHINA: *History;* JAPAN: *History*); the Indian, about 1500 B.C. (see INDIA: *History*); the Egyptian, about 4000 B.C. (see EGYPT: *History*); the Sumerian, about 3000 B.C., followed by the Babylonian, about 1700 B.C. (see SUMER; BABYLONIA); the Minoan, about 3000 B.C. (see MINOAN CULTURE; CRETE); the Semitic, about 1500 B.C. (see SEMITES; SYRIA: *History;* JEWS); the Greco-Roman, about 1100 B.C. (see GREECE: *History of Ancient Greece;* ROME); the Byzantine, which originated in the 4th century A.D. and spread to Russia (see BYZANTINE EMPIRE; RUSSIA; ORTHODOX CHURCH); the Islamic, 8th century (see ISLAM); and the Western, arising in Western Europe in the early Middle Ages (see EUROPE: *History;* CHRISTIANITY). See also articles dealing with various aspects of the cultures cited, e.g., BABYLONIAN ART; EGYPTIAN ARCHEOLOGY; INDIAN RELIGIONS; SUMERIAN LANGUAGE AND LITERATURE.

CIVIL LAW, term used in several senses, as follows. **1.** The *jus civile* of ancient Roman law (q.v.), that is, the law of Rome as distinguished from, for example, the *jus gentium,* the law applying to the peoples of the Roman world. **2.** The Roman law of medieval times, as embodied and systematized principally in the Justinian Code (see CODE), and as differentiated from canon law (q.v.). **3.** Modern private law, as distinguished from administrative law and from international law (qq.v.). When used in the sense of modern private law, the term civil law (written Civil law) is applied to the body of private law of those countries in which the legal system is based on the ancient Roman law, as modified by medieval and modern influences. But the term is also employed to distinguish those codes of the law which deal with civil relationships (such as citizenship, marriage, divorce, and certain contractual relationships) from other codes such as those dealing with criminal law and maritime law (q.v.).

Civil law is typified by the Code Napoléon (q.v.), the first great code of modern times, and is the law of a great part of the world. The law of Great Britain, the United States, and a number of other countries is based on English common law (q.v.) which differs from Civil law in origin and in important respects. English common law, however, has been markedly influenced by Civil law in a number of important respects, such as the theory and practice of habeas corpus (q.v.). In the United States the influence of Civil law is manifest in the law of Louisiana, which is based directly on that of the Code Napoléon. The Commonwealth of Puerto Rico and the Territory of Hawaii are administered under Civil law.

CIVIL RIGHTS and **CIVIL LIBERTIES,** in constitutional democracies, the guarantees enjoyed by every individual of the equal privileges of citizenship, including the exercise of his proper political functions, his free access to public facilities, and the security of his person and property against arbitrary action by the government. The terms "civil rights" and "civil liberties" are general expressions with no precise or technical meaning in law. The term "civil rights" refers usually to political rights. The unequal limitation of the political functions of certain minorities has not been uncommon in the evolution of modern democracy. For example, in Great Britain Catholics and Jews could not sit in Parliament until 1829 and 1858, respectively. In the United States the political rights of Negroes have been infringed frequently by State and local governments and private groups. The term "civil liberties" refers to all those privileges of the citizen which do not pertain directly to the exercise of political functions, for example, freedom of speech and association. In the United States the civil liberties of citizens are embodied in the Bill of Rights (q.v.), which comprises the first ten amendments to the Constitution; see CONSTITUTION OF THE UNITED STATES. The guarantees of freedom of speech and of the press and the safeguards of fairness, such as due process, in judicial proceedings have been the most significant and controversial of these liberties in the political history of the United States; see SPEECH, FREEDOM OF; PRESS, FREEDOM OF; DUE PROCESS OF LAW.

History. The history of the concept that human beings have inalienable rights and liberties that cannot with justice be violated by others or by the state itself is identical with the history of democracy (q.v.). The concept may be traced back to the philosophers of ancient Greece and the early formulators of Christian doctrine. In his funeral oration for the Athenian soldiers who died during the first year of the Peloponnesian War, the Athenian commander, statesman, and orator Pericles stressed the value of free discussion as a desirable preliminary to any wise action. The Greek philosopher Socrates, when he was sentenced to death by an Athenian court, chose to die rather than renounce his right to speak his mind in the search for wisdom. Somewhat later the Stoic philosophers formulated explicitly the doctrine of the rights of the individual; see STOICISM. There are traces of libertarian doctrine in the Bible and in the writings of the Roman orator and statesman Marcus Tullius Cicero and the Greek essayist and biographer Plutarch, but such ideals did not gain a permanent place in the political structure of the Roman Empire and all but disappeared during medieval times.

Individual freedom can survive only under a system of law by which both the sovereign and the governed are bound alike. The idea of government limited by law received (1215) effective expression for the first time in the Magna Charta (q.v.), which checked the growth of the power of the English king. The principles of the Magna Charta did not stem from any democratic or equalitarian philosophy, nor from any belief in the value of free discussion. The charter was a treaty

between the king and the nobility which defined their relationship to each other and laid the basis for the concept that the king himself was subject to the law rather than outside it. However, the ideas of absolutism and divine right persisted, and throughout the reigns of the Tudor and Stuart (qq.v.) monarchs there was fierce and often bloody conflict between the crown and Parliament.

On the European continent the struggle between authoritarian and libertarian principles developed in religious rather than in secular terms. During the Reformation (q.v.) freedom of religious belief and practice became a burning issue in every part of Western Christendom. However, the proliferation of divergent religious doctrines did not usher in an era of toleration; Unitarians were burned as heretics in England as late as 1612 (see UNITARIANS AND UNITARIANISM). Intolerant sectarianism was as widespread among the dissenters as among the orthodox. Not until the end of the 18th century did the ideals of religious toleration take firm root in Western civilization.

Libertarian ideals first found systematic philosophical expression during the 17th and 18th centuries. As a result of the English, American, and French revolutions those ideals were embodied in the structure of national governments. In England the struggle between Parliament and the absolutist Stuarts culminated in the so-called Glorious Revolution (q.v.) of 1688. King James II was expelled and the new king, William III, gave royal assent to the Bill of Rights of 1689, which guaranteed constitutional government. Subsequently the king's prerogatives were limited by statute and legal custom. The constitutional system was given philosophical expression in the English philosopher John Locke's writings, which influenced profoundly the founders of the United States.

The 17th century was marked also by a great flowering of individual freedom in Great Britain. The courts of Star Chamber and High Commission, which had become repressive agencies of the king and the established church, were abolished (see STAR CHAMBER, COURT OF; HIGH COMMISSION, COURT OF). In the common-law courts (see COMMON LAW) the judges became more concerned for the rights of those accused of crime than judges of former times had been. Inquisitorial examination of the accused was abolished and certain procedural safeguards were established. The abuses of press censorship moved the English poet and prose writer John Mil-

The Magna Charta, which King John of England was forced to sign in 1215, contains the historic basis for English civil liberties: "No freeman shall be taken and imprisoned or disseized or exiled or in any way destroyed, nor shall we go upon him nor send upon him, except by the lawful judgment of his peers and by the law of the land."

ton in 1644 to write *Areopagitica: A Speech for the Liberty of Unlicensed Printing*, a classic argument for a free press.

The English colonists brought the concepts of limited government and individual freedom to the New World. The early laws of Virginia, Massachusetts, Connecticut, Pennsylvania, and other colonies reflected the same interest in the reform of criminal procedure that was then manifest in England. A notable event in the history of civil liberties in America was the successful defense in New York in 1735 by the Philadelphia lawyer Andrew Hamilton of the printer and publisher John Peter Zenger (q.v.), who had been charged with seditious libel for criticizing the colonial government in his publication the *New York Weekly Journal*.

During the 18th century libertarian trends in France matched and eventually outpaced those in Great Britain and America. The events leading up to the American and French revolutions inspired a number of writings which laid the foundations of modern ideas of civil liberties. Among their authors were the French philosophers Voltaire and Jean Jacques Rousseau, the British politician and reformer John Wilkes, the British jurist and philosopher Jeremy Bentham, the Anglo-American political philosopher and writer Thomas Paine, and the American statesmen Thomas Jefferson, John Dickinson, and James Otis. The French Declaration of the Rights of Man and of the Citizen (q.v.) and the American Bill of Rights (q.v.) formally established libertarian principles as the foundation of modern democracy.

Because of the close connection between the concepts of individual freedom and the birth of republican government in France and the United States, civil liberties often are regarded as an integral part of democratic government. In fact, however, the basic principles of limited government and personal freedom were developed in England at a time when political power was closely held by an aristocratic upper class. Similarly, in America, many of the founding fathers were aristocratic-minded men who did not favor democracy in the modern sense. Conversely, recent history offers numerous examples of countries which are democratic in the sense that political power is vested formally in representative assemblies chosen by means of widely distributed elective franchises, but in which the enforcement of law is arbitrary or despotic and minorities have few, if any, safeguards against the tyranny of majorities. Nevertheless, individual freedom often has been secured and safeguarded by the establishment of republican institutions.

The civil liberties guaranteed by the First Amendment to the U.S. Constitution include freedom of speech, press, assembly, and religious exercise. The Fourth Amendment protects the privacy and security of homes and personal effects and prohibits unreasonable searches and seizures. Amendments Five to Eight protect persons accused of crime; these amendments guarantee, for example, right of trial by jury, the right to confront hostile witnesses and to have the assistance of legal counsel, and the privilege of not testifying against oneself. The Fifth Amendment contains also the general guarantee that no one shall be deprived of life, liberty, or property without due process of law. These amendments were binding originally only on the Federal government, but to a considerable degree their provisions became obligatory on the States by virtue of the Fourteenth Amendment, adopted in 1868, which extended the so-called due-process clause to the State governments.

Generally speaking, religious freedom has not been a grave problem in the United States, although there were serious outbreaks of anti-Masonic feeling in the early 1830's (see FREEMASONS) and of anti-Catholic feeling in the 1850's, when the Know-Nothings (q.v.) exploited the wave of anti-Irish sentiment that followed the extensive Irish immigration of those times.

The most serious problems concerning civil liberties have arisen during periods of national emergency. It was chiefly fear of and hostility toward revolutionary France that led to the enactment by Congress in 1798 of the Alien and Sedition Acts (q.v.), which not only stripped aliens of nearly all their civil rights but also gravely threatened freedom of speech and the press by prohibiting what was termed "false, scandalous and malicious writing" against the government, the Congress, or the President of the United States. The constitutionality of these laws was never passed upon by the Supreme Court; the laws were not re-enacted after the expiration of the two-year period for which they were adopted.

During the Civil War President Abraham Lincoln gave his principal military officers wide authority to arrest civilians for disloyal speech or acts. The courts were powerless to intervene, although these arrests were frequently arbitrary and plainly contrary to the Bill of Rights. Again, after World War I fear and hatred of the newly established Communist government in Russia led to the harassment by the U.S. Department of Justice of suspected subversives in the so-called Palmer raids, named after Attorney General Alexander Mitchell Palmer (1872–1936).

The rise of National Socialism (q.v.) in Germany, the world-wide spread of commu-

nism (q.v.), the economic depression that followed the 1929 collapse of the stock market, and other causes combined to produce new manifestations of concern for the internal security of the United States. The Federal legislative and executive machinery for dealing with disloyal acts and utterances was enlarged greatly. In 1940 Congress passed the Smith Act, which proscribed the advocacy of force and violence as a means of bringing about basic governmental changes. After World War II Congress adopted the Internal Security Act of 1950, which established a new Federal agency for the identification and repression of so-called subversive persons and organizations. In 1954, pursuant to the Communist Control Act of that year, Congress outlawed the Communist Party as an organization, although membership in the party was not expressly made criminal.

Congressional and State investigating committees conducted numerous and widely publicized hearings at which thousands of individuals were questioned concerning their political activities and associations and about their connections, if any, with the Communist Party. Among the legislators most prominently identified with this type of investigation were Senators Patrick McCarran (1876–1954) of Nevada and Joseph R. McCarthy (1909–57) of Wisconsin.

The so-called due-process clauses of the Fifth and Fourteenth amendments have been invoked often in behalf of property rights. The great public utilities and industrial combines have made them the basis for legal attacks on rate regulation and other forms of governmental control which their officers regarded as confiscatory or unreasonable. In addition, the Fifth Amendment privilege against self-incrimination has often been invoked since World War I, especially by persons accused of subversive activities, of criminal activities such as gambling and extortion, and of improper administration of labor unions.

The most critical civil-rights issue in the United States has always concerned the status of the Negro minority. As slaves, Negroes were entirely without civil rights. After the Civil War, adoption of the Fourteenth and Fifteenth amendments to the U.S. Constitution and passage by Congress in 1868, 1872, and 1875 of Civil Rights bills (q.v.) made legal provision for the civil rights of the newly emancipated Negroes. During the period of reconstruction (q.v.) the Federal government and the dominant Republican Party made vigorous and sustained efforts to establish the political equality of the Negro. Military forces were sent into the Southern States to enforce the new laws. These efforts aroused the bitter opposition of the Southern Whites, who feared the profound changes that would result if the former slaves, constituting a majority of the population in many areas, achieved political and social equality. In 1877, as the result of a political compromise between the Republican Party and the Southern leaders of the Democratic Party, Federal troops were withdrawn from the South and the era of reconstruction came to an end.

In the following two decades laws and practices to bring about segregation and the disenfranchisement of the Negro came into force throughout the South. It was a time of discriminatory legislation and unlawful violence; see NEGROES IN THE UNITED STATES; KU-KLUX KLAN; POLL TAX. Separate facilities for Whites and Negroes became part of the basic structure of Southern society, especially in the fields of transportation and education. In 1896, in a decision involving the segregation of Negro and white passengers on railroad trains, the Supreme Court approved the doctrine that the provision of "separate but equal" public facilities for Negroes did not infringe their civil liberties.

During the first half of the 20th century the Negroes in the United States considerably improved their economic condition and participated to an increasing extent in the political and cultural life of the country. These advances were accompanied by mounting public demands for the enforcement of their civil rights. On May 17, 1954, the U.S. Supreme Court, reversing its decision of fifty-eight years earlier, held that compulsory segregation of Negroes in public schools is unconstitutional under the Fourteenth Amendment because it denies Negroes equal protection under the laws. It directed, in the circumstances it reviewed, that desegregated educational facilities be furnished "with all deliberate speed".

This decision aroused considerable racial tension in the South, and many Southern politicians denounced the Supreme Court's decision as arbitrary and legally groundless. So-called White Citizens' Councils were formed in many communities to prevent the enforcement of integration. The most celebrated instance of overt defiance of the decision took place in 1957, in Little Rock, Ark. There President Dwight D. Eisenhower ultimately dispatched Federal troops to enforce a Federal court order directing admission of a few Negro students into a theretofore "white" high school. Elsewhere, desegregation decrees have generally been complied with. However, the Southern States have attempted, through legal delays, to postpone desegregation of their public schools as long as possible; by 1962 there had been only token desegregation in North Carolina and Louisiana, and none in Alabama, Mississippi, and South Carolina.

Meanwhile, civil rights for Negroes has become a major national political issue. In 1957 Congress enacted the first Federal civil-rights legislation since the reconstruction period. The Civil Rights Act of 1957 called for the establishment of a U.S. Commission on Civil Rights and authorized the U.S. attorney general to bring Federal court actions to enforce the voting rights of Negroes. This legislation was strengthened in 1960, and a number of law suits have been instituted.

Until recently the legal battles on behalf of civil rights and civil liberties were for the most part waged or supported by private organizations such as the National Association for the Advancement of Colored People and the American Civil Liberties Union (q.v.). In the last few years there have emerged new groups particularly active in the field of civil rights. Prominent among these have been the Congress of Racial Equality, the Southern Christian Leadership Conference, and the Student Non-violent Coordinating Committee. The latter groups have been instrumental in sponsoring so-called "sit-ins" and "freedom rides" designed to challenge the segregation or exclusion of Negroes in restaurants and in bus and railroad terminals throughout the Southern and border States. See also LIBERALISM.

T.T.

CIVIL RIGHTS BILL, in American history, a bill passed by Congress in 1866, as one of the Reconstruction measures for the purpose of securing equal civil rights for all citizens of the United States, and particularly for the purpose of placing the freed slaves in the South on an equal political footing with the whites. It provided that Negroes might have recourse to the courts, hold personal property, and in other ways exercise the full rights of citizenship. Although it was passed, over President Johnson's veto, there was some doubt as to its constitutionality; therefore, after the ratification of the 14th Amendment to the Constitution, a Civil Rights Bill similar to that of 1866 was passed by Congress in 1870. A third Civil Rights Bill, prohibiting discrimination against Negroes by innkeepers, common carriers, and places of amusement, and asserting Federal jurisdiction in the enforcement of the law, was passed in 1875 but was declared unconstitutional in 1883.

CIVIL SERVICE, name generally given to paid nonmilitary service in nonelective office in the executive branch of government. The term does not apply properly to service in the legislative and judicial branches, although in the United States some employees of the latter two branches are subject to provisions of the Civil Service Act. In certain countries, notably Great Britain, the term "Civil Service" is used to denote only positions in the national government; in others, including France and the United States, it is applied to governmental positions on all levels, from federal to municipal. Civil-service employees in most modern countries are selected by competitive examination. As a rule they also enjoy certain rights and privileges not always available in private industry, such as job tenure, and pensions on retirement. However, these distinguishing features of civil-service positions are relatively recent in origin.

Until the second half of the 19th century, elected government officials in most countries regarded appointive posts under their jurisdiction as political prizes, to be distributed among influential or faithful supporters. The first significant departure from this practice occurred in Great Britain in 1855, when examinations were conducted, by government order, among selected candidates for certain minor positions. The categories of jobs filled in this fashion were gradually extended, and in 1870 a policy of open competitive examinations for most posts in the British Civil Service was adopted.

In the United States, the Constitution of which vests the President with extraordinary powers in the selection of executive department personnel, President George Washington set a precedent of appointing Federal employees almost solely on the grounds of ability. His successor President John Adams was similarly beyond reproach in exercising his powers, until his last night in office. Fearing that newly elected President Thomas Jefferson would appoint extremists among his Democratic followers to a number of offices recently established by Congress, he filled the offices with Federalists. These and other appointees of Adams were promptly dismissed from office by Jefferson. By the time that President Andrew Jackson took office, merit figured only secondarily in executive department appointments. During Jackson's administration the policy of political patronage in Federal employment was intensified, partly as a result of Jackson's belief that rotation of government jobs was an essentially democratic practice. For many years thereafter virtually all appointive positions in the executive department were political plunder, belonging to the party in power. The abuses inherent in this system, which became popularly known as the "spoils system" (q.v.), were especially pronounced during the three decades following 1845. Washington, D.C., became the mecca of a multitude of Federal office-seekers.

Although an attempt to deal with the problem was made in 1853 by Congress, which adopted legislation requiring candidates for certain Federal jobs to submit to examination, various shortcomings in the provisions and administration of the law foredoomed it to failure. Another bill, directing the President to take remedial action, was passed in 1871. In that year, President Ulysses S. Grant appointed a Civil Service Commission, assigning it the task of drafting a code of hiring procedures. Congress withdrew its financial support, however, in 1873, before the Civil Service Commission could effectuate a program.

Public indignation over the spoils system gradually developed, meanwhile, throughout the country, leading to the establishment, in 1877, of the New York Civil Service Reform Association, and to the founding of similar organizations in other cities. President James A. Garfield's assassination in July, 1881, an act of revenge by an unsuccessful candidate for a Federal post, transformed the question of civil service reform into a national political issue. The National Civil Service Reform League, established in 1881, shortly before Garfield's death, led the subsequent fight for Congressional action. In 1883 Congress passed the Civil Service Act, sometimes referred to as the Pendleton Act, legislation which created the foundations of the American Civil Service system. Among the major features of the act are provisions for the selection of civil service personnel by open competitive examinations; guarantees to civil service employees against coercion in any form for political reasons, or solicitation in government buildings or by other Federal employees for political purposes; and allocation of civil-service appointments to the States and Territories in proportion to population. Administration of the act was assigned to an appointive board of three members (no more than two of whom could belong to the same political party) called the Civil Service Commission (q.v.), which was empowered to frame the necessary rules and regulations. In addition, the President of the United States was authorized to determine, by executive order, the classes of positions subject to the commission's jurisdiction. In 1883 the total number of positions was 13,900, slightly more than 10 percent of all positions in the executive branch of the government. Succeeding chief executives placed additional positions in the competitive service, which in 1962 covered more than 86 percent of all executive department posts and 91 percent of those in the United States.

Available civil-service positions are filled from lists of qualified candidates who are chosen according to the merit system developed by the U.S. Civil Service Commission. Candidates are graded by points up to 100 according to fitness, as determined in open competitive examinations. These are held, as the needs of the service require, under the supervision of the Civil Service Commission, which has a central office in Washington, D.C., and regional offices in ten principal cities throughout the United States.

From time to time the Congress of the United States has enacted legislation designed to improve the original Civil Service Act. Notable among these laws are: (1) the Lloyd-La Follette Act, passed in 1912, which guarantees civil-service employees the right of membership in labor unions, provides that agencies must acquaint discharged employees with the reasons for their removal from the service, and grants discharged employees the right to answer charges against them; (2) the Civil Service Retirement Act, passed in 1920 and amended several times since then, which provides annuities for employees who retire and benefits to survivors of deceased employees; (3) the Classification Act, passed in 1923 and subsequently amended, which provides a plan for classification of positions and for rates of basic compensation; and (4) the Hatch Act, passed in 1939, which prohibits active participation by civil-service personnel in political campaigns. The Veterans' Preference Act, passed by Congress in 1944, authorizes the commission to grant disabled veterans or their wives, and widows of veterans, an increase of ten points in the eligible ratings they earn by competitive examination. It also authorizes the addition of five points to the eligible ratings of nondisabled veterans who compete for positions. The Federal Salary Form Act of 1962 established the policy that Federal salaries shall be comparable with private-industry salaries.

The career civil service operates under a "career-conditional" appointment system. After being selected for appointment as a result of competitive examination, employees must complete three years of service before they are advanced to full career tenure. This minimum period enables the government to determine whether their further services are needed and allows employees time to demonstrate their competence and interest in their work. Once employees have acquired full career tenure they receive preference in retention when layoffs occur.

Civil-service employees enjoy a variety of employment benefits, including a contributory retirement system, an incentive awards program that includes cash bonuses for useful suggestions, low-cost group life and health insurance plans, and paid vacations and sick leave. Most agencies have systematic-promotion plans and career development and training programs.

On June 30, 1962, there were 2,484,654 civilian employees in the executive branch of the Federal government, 2,356,079 of whom were full-time employees and 128,575 part-time. Of these, 2,324,209 were stationed in the United States, including 234,598 in the Washington, D.C., metropolitan area. The Department of Defense employed 43 percent of all executive-branch employees, the Post Office Department 24 percent, and the Veterans Administration 7 percent.

Civil service reforms in the United States were not confined to the Federal government. In 1883, the year Congress passed the Civil Service Act, the New York State legislature adopted a similar bill, placing administrative employees of the State under the merit system. This was extended by statute to the incorporated cities of the State in the following year. In 1884 the Massachusetts State legislature enacted civil-service legislation which applied to State and municipal employees.

Merit systems are presently in effect in 30 States, and several, including California, Colorado, Louisiana, and Michigan, have State civil-service provisions in their constitutions. Beginning in 1940 the United States government required the establishment of State merit systems for employees in all State departments which receive Federal grants for salaries. It has been estimated that as many as 65 percent of the 1,600,000 full-time State employees reported by the Federal Census Bureau are civil-service employees.

CIVIL SERVICE COMMISSION, UNITED STATES, independent agency of the Federal government, established by act of Congress on Jan. 16, 1883. See CIVIL SERVICE. The commission consists of three members who are appointed by the President of the United States and who serve overlapping six-year terms. Not more than two of the members may belong to the same political party. Activities of the commission include the following. (1) Administering examinations to test the merit and ability of applicants for positions in the competitive service, and establishing standards for evaluating the qualifications of Federal employees who are being considered for reinstatement, promotion, and transfer. (2) Classifying Federal positions into grades according to duties and responsibilities. (3) Exercising leadership in Federal personnel management by raising standards and by recommending improvement in personnel laws, regulations, policies, and methods. (4) Administering the Veterans' Preference Act of 1944, under which past military service is a basis for preference in Federal employment. (5) Conducting investigations of the loyalty, character, and background of Federal employees and of applicants for Federal positions. (6) Administering a program of employee benefits that include life and health insurance, paid vacations, sick leave, and a retirement plan, and that also seeks to recognize and reward superior performances and achievements. (7) Administering laws and regulations which restrict political activity by Federal civil-service personnel and by certain State and local governmental personnel in positions financed by Federal funds.

CIVIL WAR, THE AMERICAN, sometimes known as the War of Secession, and also as the War Between the States, the war fought between eleven seceding States and the United States government from 1861 to 1865. The basic cause of the struggle was the fact that the United States had since its foundation developed into two distinct sections with opposing interests. The North was chiefly a manufacturing and commercial region, with small farms, whereas the South was mainly an agricultural region, with large plantations. From 1820 the two sections, which differed more and more in their needs and their outlook on political questions, clashed violently on two issues. One was the question of the extension of slavery into the territory of the United States not yet organized into States. (See ABOLITIONISTS; DRED SCOTT CASE; MISSOURI COMPROMISE; REPUBLICAN PARTY; SLAVERY.) The other was the question of states' rights

(q.v.). The quarrel over these two issues grew more and more bitter and finally resulted in the war. The immediate cause of the war was the decision of eleven States of the Union to repudiate their allegiance to the Union and to establish a Southern Confederacy. See CONFEDERATE STATES OF AMERICA.

The seceding states, in the order of their secession, were South Carolina (December 20, 1860); Mississippi (January 9, 1861); Florida (January 10, 1861); Alabama (January 11, 1861); Georgia (January 19, 1861); Louisiana (January 26, 1861); Texas (February 1, 1861); Virginia (April 17, 1861); Arkansas (May 6, 1861); North Carolina (May 20, 1861); and Tennessee (June 8, 1861). The slave States of Delaware, Maryland, Kentucky, and Missouri, and the western counties of Virginia repudiated the action of the Confederate Convention. This section of Virginia was later (June 20, 1863) admitted to the Union as the State of West Virginia.

South Carolina's declaration (December 20, 1860) that "the union now existing between South Carolina and other States under the name of the United States of America is hereby dissolved" was tantamount to a declaration of war. On December 26, Major Robert Anderson, commanding the United States forces in Charleston harbor, fearing an attack on Fort Moultrie, transferred to Fort Sumter, a stronger fortification in the center of the harbor. With the arrival of the steamer *Star of the West* with supplies for the fort, the first hostile shot of the war was fired on January 9, 1861, by the Confederates, who drove the vessel off.

On February 4, 1861, a congress of representatives of all the Southern States that had passed ordinances of secession before that date, met at Montgomery, Ala. It adopted a provisional constitution and elected Jefferson Davis of Mississippi President of the "Confederate States of America" and Alexander Hamilton Stephens of Georgia, Vice-President. Abraham Lincoln was inaugurated President of the United States on March 4, 1861. On April 8 Davis called for 20,000 volunteers. Meanwhile Confederate forces had seized Forts Moultrie and Pinckney in Charleston harbor. On April 12, under Brigadier General Pierre Beauregard, they began a bombardment of Fort Sumter, and two days later Major Anderson surrendered.

On April 15 Lincoln called for 75,000 volunteers and on the 19th he proclaimed a blockade of the Southern ports. The Confederacy passed a general conscription law. The Federal arse-

Bombardment of Fort Sumter by Confederate forces (April 12, 1861)

nal at Harpers Ferry, Virginia, was seized by the Confederates under General Letcher on the 19th, and on the 20th the U.S. Navy Yard at Norfolk, Virginia, was taken, with a vast quantity of war material and supplies.

The North had far superior material resources than the South, but at the beginning of the war suffered several disadvantages. John B. Floyd, Secretary of War in President James Buchanan's administration (1857–61), had dispersed the United States regular army of over 16,000 officers and men to distant parts of the country. He had also been instrumental in transferring quantities of arms and ammunition from Northern to Southern arsenals. When the war broke out, most of the ships of the U.S. Navy were at foreign stations by direction of Buchanan's Secretary of the Navy, Isaac Toucey. In addition, a considerable number of U.S. Army officers who came from Southern States resigned and entered the Confederate Army. The most notable of these officers was Colonel Robert E. Lee. He declined Lincoln's offer of the field command of the armies of the North, and became commander in chief of the Confederate forces of his native State, Virginia.

Lee concentrated the main body of his troops at Manassas Junction, 33 miles s.w. of Washington. On May 24 Northern troops crossed the Potomac into Virginia, occupying Alexandria. On July 11 and 13 General George Brinton McClellan gained control of N.W. Virginia for the North by defeating the Confederates at Rich Mountain and at Carrick's Ford. On July 4 a special session of Congress had voted 500,000 more men and $500,000,000 for the prosecution of the war.

The Union hoped that the quick mobilization of its men and money would result in a speedy termination of the war. But the South demonstrated that the North had underestimated the Confederacy's fighting spirit when Confederate forces under Generals Beauregard and Joseph E. Johnston defeated Union forces under General Irvin McDowell in the first Battle of Bull Run (q.v.), July 21, 1861. Immediately after this Union defeat, General McClellan was appointed commander in chief of the Army of the Potomac and quickly organized and trained the new recruits. In the closing days of the year, war almost broke out between the North and Great Britain because a United States frigate took from a British steamer the Confederate commissioners to England and France respectively, James Murray Mason and John Slidell. British protests finally resulted in the release of the two men.

Toward the end of 1861 a fourfold Union plan of campaign for the war developed: the winning of the doubtful border States to the Northern cause; a blockade of Southern ports on the Atlantic and the Gulf of Mexico; the opening of the Mississippi River to Union forces; and the capture of the Confederate capital, Richmond, Virginia.

In the West, Union forces under Brigadier General Nathaniel Lyon had secured Missouri for the Union by a series of engagements, which ended, however, in the defeat of Lyon's army and his own death at Wilson's Creek, near Springfield, Mo., on August 10. General

Ulysses S. Grant's forces captured the Confederate camp at Belmont, Mo., but they were soon driven back by the Confederates under General Gideon J. Pillow. In January, 1862, the Union army under General George H. Thomas defeated Confederate troops at Prestonburg and at Mill Springs, Ky. The North won an important victory in February when General Grant, with the aid of a naval force under Commodore Andrew H. Foote, captured Fort Henry, on the Tennessee River, and Fort Donelson, on the Cumberland. The latter was taken with nearly 15,000 prisoners and 40 cannon. This Union victory broke the Confederate line of defense across Kentucky. The Confederates then established a new line along the route of the Memphis and Charleston Railroad. Corinth, Mississippi, was the center of the line; Memphis, Tennessee, the left flank; and Chattanooga, Tennessee, the right. In April, General Grant began a movement upon Corinth in order to cut the Memphis-Charleston railroad line. On the march his troops were surprised at Shiloh on the Tennessee River by Confederates under Generals Beauregard and Albert S. Johnston. A bloody two-day battle ensued (April 6–7). (See SHILOH, BATTLE OF.) Only the arrival of re-enforcements under General Don C. Buell enabled Grant to turn what appeared to be a certain defeat into a partial victory. General Johnston was killed in this battle and the Confederate command fell to Beauregard, who retired to Corinth.

Corinth surrendered on May 30 to General Henry W. Halleck, in command of the Union armies in Missouri, and Memphis was taken by Halleck on June 6. Even before these successes, Union forces, in April, by capturing New Madrid, Mo., and forcing the evacuation of Fort Pillow, Tenn., on the Mississippi River, opened up the Mississippi as far south as Vicksburg. Working from the south in the campaign to open up the entire Mississippi, Union naval forces under Admiral David D. Farragut captured New Orleans at the end of April. During the last months of 1862 the main efforts of the Union armies of the Mississippi and the Tennessee, now under the command of General Grant, were directed to capturing the Confederate stronghold, Vicksburg, Miss., the so-called "Gibraltar of the West". But, for the time being, the operations of General Grant and General William T. Sherman against Vicksburg were unsuccessful. See VICKSBURG, CAMPAIGN OF.

In the meantime heavy fighting had been taking place in the East. The objective of the Army of the Potomac was Richmond. De-ciding to approach the Confederate capital from the S.E., early in the spring of 1862 McClellan moved his troops into the peninsula formed by the James and York rivers. Advancing towards Richmond, he defeated the Confederates at Williamsburg (May 5) and at Fair Oaks (May 31–June 1). A large Union army under General McDowell attempted to join McClellan's forces for an assault on Richmond, but was held back by Confederate forces under General Thomas J. "Stonewall" Jackson, operating in the Shenandoah Valley. By June 25th McClellan's outposts were no more than 4 miles from Richmond, but General Lee attacked before McClellan could advance further. In the Seven Days' Battle (q.v.) June 26–July 2, Lee succeeded in stopping McClellan's advance, but, although he inflicted heavy losses, could not prevent the Union forces from establishing new bases on the James River. General Halleck was summoned from the West and made commander in chief of the Union armies in place of McClellan, who had been relieved of that position in March while remaining in command of the Army of the Potomac.

The action then shifted to northern Virginia, where the Confederates under Lee, Jackson, and General James Longstreet defeated the Union army under General Nathaniel Pope in the second Battle of Bull Run (q.v.) on August 29–30, and drove Pope back upon Washington. Lee advanced across the Potomac into Maryland. General McClellan, who had superseded Pope, checked Lee in the Battle of Antietam (q.v.), Md., on September 16–17, and forced him back across the Potomac. McClellan's success encouraged President Lincoln to issue the Emancipation Proclamation (January 1, 1863) decreeing the freeing of all slaves in the rebellious States.

General Ambrose E. Burnside, who had on November 7 replaced McClellan as chief of the Army of the Potomac, unsuccessfully attacked Lee at Fredericksburg, Va., December 13. Burnside was replaced by General Joseph Hooker, who was defeated by Lee at Chancellorsville, Va. (May 2–4, 1863), and voluntarily gave up the command. The death in this battle of "Stonewall" Jackson, one of the most brilliant strategists the war produced, made the victory a costly one for the South. Lee followed up his success by invading Maryland again. Early in June he entered Pennsylvania. General George G. Meade, now in command of the Union army, pursued Lee, and the two armies met in the Battle of Gettysburg (q.v.) July 1–3, 1863. The result of the battle was a decisive Union victory. Lee

Culver Service

President Lincoln and his cabinet at the first reading of the Emancipation Proclamation

Bettmann Archieve

Final moments of the Civil War. Above: Union forces under General Sherman reach the climax of the "March to the Sea." Right: General Robert E. Lee leaves Appomattox Court House (April 9, 1865) after surrendering his sword to General Ulysses S. Grant

A review of Union troops in Washington at the close of the Civil War

retreated across the Potomac again and took up a position on the Rapidan River. Except for some heavy skirmishing, no more fighting took place in the East in 1863.

In the southwest, Grant laid siege to Vicksburg in May, 1863, and on July 4 the Confederate General John C. Pemberton surrendered with his army of 30,000. The Mississippi was now entirely in possession of the Union armies and the Confederacy was split in two. The struggle for the border States, Kentucky and Tennessee, had been marked by Union victories at Perryville, Ky., on Oct. 8, 1862, and at Murfreesboro, Tenn., Dec. 31, 1862, to Jan. 2, 1863. On Sept. 9, 1863, Union forces under General William S. Rosecrans occupied Chattanooga, Tenn., but on Sept. 19–20 were defeated in the Battle of Chickamauga (q.v.) by the Confederates under General Braxton Bragg. General Grant was now placed in command of all Union armies in the West. On Nov. 23–25 the Confederates were defeated in the Battle of Chattanooga (q.v.). At the close of 1863, Union forces held Arkansas, Kentucky, Tennessee, a large part of Louisiana, Mississippi, and Florida, as well as the Rio Grande frontier of Texas, and had control of the Mississippi River.

On March 9, 1864, General Grant was made commander in chief of all Union armies in the field. He placed General Sherman in command in the West and South. The Union strategy now was for Grant to operate against Lee in the East and for Sherman at the same time to drive General Joseph E. Johnston's forces eastward and, after cutting through the Confederacy to the Atlantic, to turn and move north. In pursuance of this plan Sherman left Chattanooga on May 7th and forced Johnston back through Georgia to Atlanta. He took Atlanta on September 2, then marched 300 m. to the Atlantic, laying waste the country on a 60-mile front. This was Sherman's "March to the Sea". He took Savannah on Dec. 20–21. His victories, together with the taking of Mobile, Ala., by Admiral Farragut in August, 1864, put an end to Confederate power in the South. On April 13, 1865, Union troops entered Raleigh, N.C., and on the 26th Johnston surrendered to Sherman.

Meanwhile Grant had been facing Lee in Virginia. Early in May, 1864, Grant's forces entered the "Wilderness", the densely wooded country west of Chancellorsville. The fighting in this region was practically continuous from the 5th to the 21st and included the Battles of Cold Harbor and Spotsylvania Court House (q.v.). The Northern casualties were particularly heavy. At Cold Harbor alone Grant lost 10,000 men in killed and wounded.

Grant transferred his base to the James River, his objective being to take Petersburg and then to move upon Richmond from the s.e. He dispatched General Philip H. Sheridan to expel from the Shenandoah Valley the Confederates under General Jubal A. Early. During this operation (Sept. 19–Oct. 19) occurred Sheridan's famous ride from Winchester to Cedar Creek (q.v.). Grant pressed the siege of Petersburg from June to October, when the army went into winter quarters. In February, 1865, the struggle was resumed. Grant won a victory at Five Forks on April 1, took Petersburg the next day, and on April 3 captured Richmond. Lee, his army weakened by casualties, desertions, and the lack of new conscripts, surrendered at Appomatox Court House on April 9. With his surrender, the Confederacy collapsed. On May 4, General Richard Taylor, commanding the Confederate forces in Mississippi and Alabama, surrendered to General Edward R. S. Canby. Confederate General Edmund Kirby-Smith surrendered the forces in Texas on May 26. Jefferson Davis escaped from Richmond, but was captured by Union cavalry at Irvinsville, Ga. on May 10.

The naval history of the war was of comparative unimportance. The navy of the South consisted mainly of raiders, although it also had a force of gunboats and a number of rams. The navy of the North was considerably larger in all categories, and was constantly engaged in enforcing the blockade; it also acted as auxiliary to the land forces. One of the most important naval actions of the war was the taking of New Orleans in April, 1862, by a Union fleet under Admiral Farragut after the cutting of a chain across the river below the city and a fierce battle with the defending forts. Also important was the Battle of Mobile Bay, August, 1864, in which a Union fleet under Farragut defeated a much smaller Confederate fleet, destroyed two forts, and took the city of Mobile.

Several notable naval engagements need mention. Foremost was the drawn battle between the ironclad ships, the Union ship *Monitor* (q.v.) and the Confederate ship *Merrimac*, at Hampton Roads, Virginia, on March 9, 1862. Neither vessel could sink the other. The battle was significant in naval history for demonstrating the comparative invulnerability of ironclads. Two other spectacular events were the destruction off Cherbourg, France, of the Confederate raider *Alabama* by the *Kearsarge* (June 19, 1864); and the torpedoing of the Confederate ram *Albemarle* in the Roanoke River by Lieut. William B. Cushing (October 27, 1864).

Union forces during the war numbered over 2,500,000. Total Union casualties were 359,528, of which number 110,070 were killed in battle or died of wounds, 224,586 died of disease, and 24,872 of other causes. The total number of Confederate troops in the war is estimated by various historians at from 600,-000 to 900,000. Confederate killed and wounded are estimated at about 134,000: The defeat of the Confederacy was nearly inevitable. The resistance of the agricultural South, skillful and fierce though it was, had to break before the superior resources in men, materials, and money of the industrial North.

CIVITAVECCHIA, a fortified seaport in the Province of Rome, central Italy, situated on the Tyrrhenian Sea, 37 miles n.w. of the city of Rome. The fortifications date from the 16th and 17th centuries.

Civitavecchia is the ancient *Centum Cellæ,* founded by the Roman Emperor Trajan, in whose honor the city was sometimes called *Trajani Portus.* It was destroyed by the Saracens in 812 A.D., but was rebuilt in 889 and received the name Civitavecchia ("old city"). In the vicinity of the town are sulfur springs and the remains of ancient baths. Present-day Civitavecchia is of considerable commercial importance. It contains cement and calcium plants, imports cereals and coal, and exports salt. Pop. (1954) 35,100.

CLACKMANNANSHIRE, smallest county of Scotland, situated at the head of the Firth of Forth. Its terrain is mountainous, with extreme elevations of about 2300 feet. The principal river is the Devon. The chief industries are coal mining, brewing, and the manufacture of whisky, woolen goods, and furniture. Sheep, oats, wheat, barley, and potatoes are the leading agricultural products. The county seat is Clackmannan (pop., about 3000), and Alloa (pop., 1961 prelim., 13,895) is the largest town. Area of county, 55 sq.m.; pop. (1961 prelim.) 41,391.

CLAIBORNE or **CLAYBORNE,** WILLIAM (1589?–1676?), American colonist, prominent in the early history of Virginia and Maryland. He was born in Westmorland, England, went to Virginia as surveyor in 1621, and in 1625 was appointed secretary of state for that colony. He founded a trading post on Kent Island in 1631, and was represented in the General Assembly of Virginia. Later the island was included in the grant to George Calvert, first Lord Baltimore, whom Claiborne had bitterly opposed in London.

Its possession remained a subject of animated controversy between Maryland and Virginia until 1776. After the execution of Charles I, when Virginia and Maryland had decided in favor of Charles II, Claiborne obtained an appointment on the commission chosen by Oliver Cromwell to reduce them to submission (1651). Governor William Berkeley, of Virginia, was removed from office, and Claiborne became secretary of state of Virginia, under the new governor, Richard Bennett. In Maryland all Catholics were promptly removed from office, an act which caused considerable friction until 1658, when the province was restored to Lord Baltimore. After the Restoration, in 1660, Claiborne ceased to have influence at court, and he died in obscurity.

CLAIMS, COURT OF, in the Federal judicial system of the United States, a court established by Congress in 1855. Its jurisdiction includes all claims against the United States arising out of a contract with the Federal government or from a Congressional enactment or Federal executive order. It also handles claims referred to it by Congress and counterclaims made by the Federal government against persons making claims in the Court of Claims against the government. The Court of Claims has no equity jurisdiction. It consists of a chief justice and four associate justices, appointed for life by the President with the approval of the Senate; and holds one session annually, in Washington, D.C.

In a number of States, the Court of Claims is either a special court, or a county court sitting as a court of claims, to audit and ascertain claims made against the county, and to provide for their payment out of taxes.

CLAIR, RENÉ (1898–   ), French motion-picture director, producer, and writer, born in Paris. His real name was René Chomette. He directed a number of silent motion pictures, including *The Crazy Ray* (1923), *Entr'acte* (1924), and *The Italian Straw Hat* (1927). He is noted particularly for the series of sound motion pictures he directed in France from 1929 to 1934, *Sous les Toits de Paris* (1929), *Le Million* (1931), *À Nous la Liberté* (1932), *14 Juillet* (1932), and *Le Dernier Milliardaire* (1934). In these pictures music, speech, atmosphere, and action are combined with finesse and charm. In England he directed *The Ghost Goes West* (1935), and in the United States, *The Flame of New Orleans* (1941), *I Married a Witch* (1942), *It Happened Tomorrow* (1944), and other pictures. After World War II he resumed his career in France, where in 1947 he wrote, produced, and directed *Le Silence Est d'Or* (Eng., *Man About Town*). He was coauthor and director of *La Beauté du Diable* (1952; Eng., *Beauty and the Devil*) and *Les Belles*

de Nuit (1954; Eng., *Beauties of the Night*), and was author and director of *Les Grandes Manoeuvres* (1955; Eng., *The Grand Maneuver*) and *Porte des Lilas* (1957; Eng., *The Gates of Paris*). Clair has been a member of the French Academy since 1960.

CLAIRVAUX, village in the department of Aube, France, situated on the Aube River, about 40 miles. E.S.E. of Troyes. It is the site of the famous Cistercian abbey founded in 1115 by Saint Bernard of Clairvaux (q.v.), who presided over it until his death, in 1153. Only one of the original abbey structures remains, the other existing buildings having been constructed in the 18th century. The abbey now serves as a penitentiary, as it did during the French Revolution.

CLAIRVOYANCE, in spiritualism and psychical research (qq.v), the alleged ability to see by extrasensory perception objects and events distant in time or space. The related alleged ability to hear by extrasensory perception sounds distant in time or space is usually distinguished from clairvoyance and termed clairaudience. Clairvoyance is said to occur most often in a state of trance, mesmeric or somnambulistic.

The phenomena that seem to transpire at times during the state of trance, in which the subject or medium describes what he apparently sees or foresees, are neither well established nor understood. Among those who believe that an act of clairvoyance actually takes place on such occasions, three explanatory theories exist. Some believe that the clairvoyant is a peculiarly sensitive person, whose mind and organs of speech are, for the time being, directed by some departed spirit. Others believe that the clairvoyant is able, without any such direction, to see objects and occurrences beyond normal vision. A third group consider that the results are to be explained by telepathic communication, not between departed spirits and the subject or medium, but between his mind and the minds of one or more living persons. However, the term clairvoyance as used today excludes extrasensory perceptions through telepathy.

Apparent clairvoyance is used by certain professional theatrical entertainers. While the entertainer is blindfolded on the stage, an assistant passes among the audience, holds up objects offered to him, and requests the blindfolded entertainer to name them. The entertainer does so, apparently by the exercise of clairvoyant powers. In reality, while he is making his requests, the assistant uses code words that reveal to the person on the stage the identity of the object.

CLAM, name commonly applied to many species of bivalve (q.v.) mollusks, particularly those which are edible, belonging to the class Pelecypoda. These mollusks burrow wholly or partially into sand or mud by means of a hatchet-shaped muscular foot. Many species of clams are eaten in Asia and Europe. In the United States the clams commonly preferred for consumption are the round or hard clam, *Venus mercenaria,* and the long or soft clam, *Mya arenaria.*

The hard clam is known in New England as the quahog, so named by the American Indians who used the inner shell as wampum. The quahog is native to the coastal waters from the Gulf of St. Lawrence as far south as the Gulf of Mexico. As this species does not burrow deeply, it may be obtained by raking the ocean bottom beyond the low-tide mark. The shell is thick, heavy and heart-shaped. Small and medium-sized quahogs are marketed as littlenecks and cherrystones respectively and are usually eaten raw. Fully grown quahogs are used mainly for chowder.

The soft clam has a comparatively thin, elongated shell. It is found buried in the sand between tidemarks along the northern Atlantic coast, as far south as North Carolina. When disturbed this clam ejects a spurt of water and withdraws to safer depths in the sand. It is obtained by digging in the sand at low tide and is eaten steamed, fried, and in chowders.

Other edible clams in the United States include the surf or hen clam, *Spisula solidissima,* which ranges from Nova Scotia to South Carolina, and the ocean quahog, *Arctica islandia,* found in deep waters from Newfoundland south to Cape Hatteras. The razor clam, *Siliqua patula,* abounds on the Pacific coast. The giant clam, *Tridacna gigas,* found on the coral reefs of the Indian and Pacific oceans, is the largest extant Mollusca (q.v.); it may weigh as much as 500 lbs. and yields about 20 lbs. of edible flesh.　　P.S.G.

CLAN (Gael. *clann,* "children", i.e., descendants of a common ancestor). This word became incorporated with the English language as early as the 17th century, to mean a body of men bound together by common ancestry or other ties. While also used for some of the Irish septs, it came to be applied almost exclusively to the several communities of the Scottish Highlanders, as divided from each other topographically and by distinctive surnames. It was used in the 16th century to designate the freebooters of the Border as well as the Celtic tribes of the Highlands; both were known for predatory habits, and separa-

tion into communities. The assumption of a common surname was general, but by no means universal. Men of different origin enlisted under chiefs as men now enlist in a regiment.

It was the policy of the old law of Scotland to require all the Highland clans to have some accredited representative to act as security at court for their good conduct. Clans that could find no security were called "broken clans" and their members were outlaws. The Macgregors were a celebrated broken clan, whom the law pursued for centuries.

Rebellions caused the British Government to break up the clans. Their members were disarmed and were forced to cease wearing distinctive costumes. At present practically no traces of the clans remain, except those of sentiment, as represented by the various clan societies.

CLARE, county in Munster Province, Republic of Ireland, on the w. coast to the N. and w. of the Shannon R. The terrain is hilly, especially in the N. and E. sections of the county, with extreme elevations of about 1750 feet. Ben Dash, a peak in the w. central region, is 8727 feet above sea level. Numerous lakes and marshes are situated in the interior. Along the River Shannon in the s. are large areas suitable for cultivation and pasturage. The coast is generally rugged, Liscannor Bay being the only safe anchorage on the Atlantic. The estuary of the Shannon contains a number of good harbors, notably the mouth of the Fergus River. Fishing is the chief activity in many of the coastal communities. Agricultural activity, mostly small-scale, consists mainly of stock farming. The principal crops are oats and potatoes. Hosiery, flannel, and frieze fabrics are the only manufactured products of importance, and flagstone, slate, and marble are quarried. Various mineral deposits, including iron, coal, manganese, and lead, occur in the county, but none of these is productive.

The county has a large number of old castles and abbeys, several ancient towers, and numerous raths and cromlechs. Ennis is the county administrative center. Other important towns include Kilrush (pop. in 1961, 2861), Ennistimon (10,932), and Kilkee (1392). Area of county, 1231 sq.m.; pop. (1961) 73,702.

CLARE, name of an English earldom and of a distinguished English family, founded by the Norman RICHARD DE CLARE (d. 1090), also called Richard Fitz-Gilbert, who became 1st Earl of Clare. One of Richard's five sons, ROBERT, founded the house of Fitz-Walter, from which was descended Robert Fitzwalter (q.v.), leader of the barons against King John. Another son, GILBERT, was the ancestor of the earls of Pembroke, including Richard Strongbow. Other members of the family became earls of Hertford. GILBERT (d. 1230), 7th Earl of Clare, 5th Earl of Hertford, also inherited from his mother the title of Earl of Gloucester and married the daughter of the 2nd Earl of Pembroke; one of England's most powerful nobles, he was among the 25 barons administering the provisions of the Magna Charta. His grandson, GILBERT (1243–95), 9th Earl of Clare, fought in the feudal wars of the reign of Henry III and married the daughter of King Edward I. This earl's daughter, ELIZABETH, endowed University Hall, Cambridge University; the institution was thereafter known as Clare Hall, and is now Clare College. Elizabeth's granddaughter, ELIZABETH DE BURGH (d. 1363), inherited the vast Clare estates, including the so-called "Honour of Clare", in Ireland, after which County Clare was named; she married the son of King Edward III, Lionel of Antwerp, whose title of Duke of Clarence (q.v.), created in 1362, was derived from Clare.

CLARE, JOHN (1793–1864), British poet, born near Peterborough, Northamptonshire. The son of a poor farmer, he was forced to go to work at an early age, and during his young manhood he tried to earn a living as farmer, servant, apprentice gardener, militiaman, and lime burner. The publication in 1820 of his first volume of poetry, *Poems Descriptive of Rural Life and Scenery,* brought him fame and a measure of financial security. His later works were less successful, however, and he soon was impoverished again. After 1837, when he suffered a serious head injury, he was confined in an insane asylum. His poems, which deal with rustic scenes and the incidents of village life, earned him the title "Northamptonshire Peasant Poet". He was strongly influenced by *The Seasons,* the masterpiece of the Scottish poet James Thomson. Clare's other works include *The Village Minstrel and Other Poems* (1821), *The Shepherd's Calendar* (1827), and *The Rural Muse* (1835).

CLARE COLLEGE, a college of Cambridge University (q.v.), Cambridge, England, founded as University Hall in 1326. In 1338 Elizabeth de Burgh, Countess of Clare, granted an endowment to the Hall, which was then renamed Clare Hall in her honor. Several scholarships at Clare College are still supported by interest from Lady Clare's orig-

inal grant. Most of the college structures were erected between 1638 and 1715, a fire in 1521 having destroyed the original buildings. In 1856 "College" was substituted for "Hall" in the official designation of the school. Celebrated graduates include Hugh Latimer, martyr of the English Reformation, Ralph Cudworth, English philosopher, and John Tillotson, English theologian. According to a college tradition, Geoffrey Chaucer also graduated from Clare Hall. Besides a master, 11 fellows, and a number of scholars, the college has about 300 junior members in residence.

CLAREMONT, city in Los Angeles Co., Calif., 35 miles E. of metropolitan Los Angeles. The chief industry is citrus-fruit packing and shipping. Claremont is the site of Pomona College, a coeducational institution founded in 1887; Scripps College, for women, founded in 1926; Claremont Men's College, founded in 1946; and Claremont College, founded in 1925 and serving as the graduate school of the group. Pop. (1960) 12,633.

CLARENCE, title of an English dukedom usually held by a younger son of the royal house. It was first created in 1362 for LIONEL OF ANTWERP (1338–63), third son of King Edward III, in honor of Lionel's wife, the heiress of the so-called "Honour of Clare", a vast domain in Ireland (see CLARE). Lionel became governor of Ireland; his administration was undistinguished. Through his daughter, Philippa, who married Edmund de Mortimer (1351–81), the 3rd Earl of March, Lionel of Antwerp was an ancestor of King Edward IV. The poet Geoffrey Chaucer served Lionel as a page. The title was created anew in 1412 for THOMAS (about 1388–1421), second son of King Henry IV. Thomas fought alongside his brother, Henry V, in France during the Hundred Years' War, and died without heirs. The title was created a third time in 1461 for GEORGE (1449–78), brother of King Edward IV. George became lord lieutenant of Ireland at the age of 13. During the War of the Roses he first supported his father-in-law, the Earl of Warwick, and Henry VI of Lancaster against Edward IV, then deserted to the side of Edward IV. After Warwick's death he seized the latter's estates and became Earl of Warwick. Suspected of seeking the crown, he was imprisoned, condemned by Parliament, and executed. His son, Edward (1475–99), Earl of Warwick, was imprisoned at the age of 10 and beheaded by order of King Henry VII. Many of these personalities are familiar through the historical plays of Shakespeare. The title was revived in 1789 for WILLIAM, third son of

King George III, who became William IV (q.v.); and in 1890 as the dukedom of Clarence and Avondale, with ALBERT VICTOR (1864–92), eldest son of Edward VII, as first and only duke.

CLARENDON, EARL OF. See HYDE, EDWARD.

CLARENDON, CONSTITUTIONS OF, the name given to 16 laws adopted at Clarendon in Wiltshire, England, in 1164, by a council of bishops and barons summoned by King Henry II. By these laws, King Henry II attempted to restrict the temporal power of the Church, and to establish the superior authority of the royal courts over ecclesiastical courts. The laws were resisted by the Church, and a number of them were not enforced. But others had an important bearing on the development of English law, constituting permanent gains to the civil power. The enactment of the "constitutions" brought to a crisis the dispute between Henry II and Thomas à Becket (q.v.). The lodge at which the laws were proclaimed is known as Clarendon Lodge.

CLARE, or **CLARA, OF ASSISI,** SAINT (1194–1253), Italian nun, born in Assisi of a rich and noble family. At the age of eighteen she heard St. Francis of Assisi preach and, inspired by his eloquence, determined to devote her life to the service of Jesus Christ. With the help and advice of St. Francis and despite the opposition of her family, she founded that year the religious order of Franciscan nuns known as the Order of the Poor Ladies (called later "Poor Clares"). See CLARES, POOR. She was canonized in 1255 by Pope Alexander IV. Her feast is celebrated on Aug. 12.

CLARINET, wood-wind instrument consisting essentially of a cylindrical tube equipped with a mouthpiece containing a single beating reed (q.v.), and having a bell-shaped open end. Clarinets are of various sizes and pitches. In the ordinary clarinet the tube is made of wood or ebonite and has 13 keys and 20 side holes, which provide the instrument with a natural chromatic scale of 2 full octaves plus a sixth. By cross-fingering, however, a skillful clarinetist can obtain another higher octave, making the total range of the instrument 3½ octaves. Clarinets in present-day use are mainly the small soprano clarinet, generally pitched in B♭, the larger bass clarinet, pitched an octave lower than the soprano, the intermediate alto clarinet in E♭, and the large pedal or contrabass clarinet, pitched an octave lower than the bass instrument.

The development of the clarinet is generally attributed to the German wood-wind manufacturer Johann Christoph Denner (1655–1707). According to some authorities, he adapted a medieval wind instrument known as the chalumeau, the range of which encompassed only one octave in the low register. Although the French composer Jean Phillippe Rameau had written for the clarinet in 1751, its introduction as a significant instrument in symphonic and chamber music is generally credited to the German composer Wolfgang Amadeus Mozart. In the 20th century the clarinet became a favored instrument in jazz, concert, and military bands.

CLARK, CHAMP (1850–1921), American politician, born in Anderson Co., Ky., and educated at Kentucky University, at Bethany College, and at the Cincinnati Law School. In 1873–74 he was president of Marshall College, W. Va. After holding various political offices in Missouri, he was elected a member (Dem.) of the U.S. House of Representatives, serving continuously (with an interim of two years, 1895–97) from 1893 to 1921. He was speaker of the House (1911–19) and was one of the leading candidates for the Democratic presidential nomination in 1912, being defeated only after William Jennings Bryan gave his support to Woodrow Wilson.

CLARK, FRANCIS EDWARD (1851–1927), American Congregational clergyman, born at Aylmer, Quebec Province, Canada, and educated at Dartmouth College and Andover Theological Seminary. He held a Congregational pastorate at Portland, Me., from 1876 to 1883, and subsequently was a pastor of Phillips Church, South Boston (1883–87). In 1881 he organized the Williston Young People's Society of Christian Endeavor in his church at Portland. From this developed the United Society of Christian Endeavor, founded in 1887, and the World Union of Christian Endeavor, founded in 1895. Clark became president of each of these organizations at their foundation, and also editor of their official organ, *Golden Rule* (after 1897 called *Christian Endeavor World*).

CLARK, GEORGE ROGERS (1752–1818), American Revolutionary soldier and frontiersman, born in Albemarle Co., Va. He represented Kentucky in the Virginia Legislature, and subsequently led the expedition which conquered Illinois Co. Starting from the fort at Louisville in June 1778, he forced General Hamilton, the English commander at Detroit, to surrender (February, 1779). After founding Fort Jefferson (1780), he spent the remaining years of the war in fighting the British and the Indians, especially the Shawnees, whom he completely defeated. For these services he was made brigadier general of Virginia militia. His conquest of the Northwest enabled the United States government to claim, in the peace negotiations of 1782–83, all the territory between the Mississippi and the Alleghanies. His memoirs were published in 1843.

CLARK, MARK WAYNE (1896–   ), American army officer, born in Madison Barracks, N.Y., and educated at the U.S. Military Academy and other American military institutions. He served in World War I and World War II, beginning as a second lieutenant in 1917 and advancing through the ranks to a permanent rank of major general in 1946. During World War II, he was in 1942 appointed commander in chief of the U.S. Army Ground Forces in Europe. That same year he was the leader of a secret mission to the French colonies in North Africa to obtain information to facilitate the Allied invasion of North Africa. In November, 1942, Clark was deputy commander in chief of the Allied forces during that invasion. In 1943 and 1944 he was in command of the U.S. 5th Army during the invasion of Italy and the capture of Rome. He was U.S. high commissioner for Austria from 1945 to 1947, and subsequently held commands in the U.S. From April, 1952, to October, 1953, Clark served as commander of U.S. forces in the Far East and U.N. supreme commander in Korea. He retired on Oct. 31, and was appointed president (from 1954) of the Citadel, a military college of South Carolina. He wrote *Calculated Risk* (1950) and *From the Danube to the Yalu* (1954).

CLARK, TOM CAMPBELL (1899–   ), American jurist, born in Dallas, Tex., and educated at Virginia Military Institute and at the University of Texas. After practicing law in Dallas, he served from 1927 to 1932 as civil district attorney of Dallas County. He began his career in federal government service in 1937 as a special attorney in the U.S. Department of Justice, in which he subsequently gained prominence for his work in the anti-trust division; from 1943 to 1945 he was in charge of the criminal division. In the latter year he became attorney general of the United States. President Harry S. Truman appointed him an associate justice of the U.S. Supreme Court in 1949.

CLARK, WILLIAM (1770–1838), American soldier and explorer, born near Charlottesville, Va., the brother of George Rogers Clark (q.v.). He entered the army in 1791, and from 1804 to 1806 shared with his friend Meriwether Lewis (q.v.) the command of an exploring party which, leaving St. Louis in May, 1804, crossed the continent, reaching the mouth of the Columbia River in November, 1805, and arrived at St. Louis on its return in September, 1806. (See LEWIS AND CLARK EXPEDITION.) Clark was commissioned brigadier general of militia in 1807, served as Indian agent for the Territory of Upper Louisiana, was governor of Missouri Territory from 1813 to 1821, and acted as superintendent of Indian affairs at St. Louis from 1822 until his death. In 1828 he laid out Paducah, Ky.

CLARKE, CHARLES COWDEN (1787–1877), English author and scholar, born in Enfield, Middlesex, the son of a schoolteacher who numbered the poet John Keats among his pupils. Charles Clarke was a friend of Keats and of other contemporary writers, including Percy Bysshe Shelley, Charles Lamb, and Leigh Hunt. His wife, MARY VICTORIA COWDEN-CLARKE (1808–98), a daughter of Vincent Novello became his literary collaborator in *The Shakespeare Key* (completed in 1868). He was chiefly known for his lectures on literary matters, which formed the basis for his writings, including *Shakespeare's Characters* (1863) and *Molière's Characters* (1865). Mary Cowden-Clarke was the author of *The Girlhood of Shakespeare's Heroines* and of a definitive work, *The Complete Concordance to Shakespeare* (1844–45); she also wrote an autobiography, *My Long Life* (1896).

CLARKE, JOHN (1609–76), English preacher, one of the founders of Rhode Island, born at Westhorpe. He emigrated to Boston in 1637, but the following year, as a sympathizer with the exiled Anne Hutchinson, he was driven out of Massachusetts Bay Colony; Roger Williams welcomed him to the settlement of Providence Plantations. Clarke settled on the island of Aquidneck, and there founded a Baptist church at Newport in 1640, one of the earliest in America. In 1651 he accompanied Roger Williams to England, as an agent for the Colony, and after remaining there for twelve years obtained from King Charles II a second charter for Rhode Island, which secured the right of personal liberty in matters of religion. On his return he resumed the care of the Newport church, and remained its minister until his death. He was a member of the General Assembly from 1664 to 1669; was deputy governor in 1669 and 1671, and afterward codified the Rhode Island laws. He has been called "the Father of American Baptists".

CLARKE, SAMUEL (1675–1729), English metaphysician and clergyman, born at Norwich, and educated at Caius College, Cambridge. In 1706 he became chaplain to Queen

Anne, and in 1709 rector of St. James's, Westminster. By his work on the Trinity (1712), in which he denied that that doctrine was held by the early Church, he raised a protracted controversy. Clarke was a vigorous antagonist of the Deists of his time; he wrote against materialism, empiricism, and necessitarianism; and maintained the essential immortality of the soul. He taught that the fundamental truths of morals were as absolutely certain as the truths of mathematics. His most famous work is *Discourse Concerning the Being and Attributes of God,* originally the Boyle Lectures of 1704–05, containing his *a priori* proof of the existence of God.

CLARK FORK, river about 700 miles long, rising in w. Montana. It flows N.W. into Lake Pend Oreille, in northern Idaho, and thence across the N.E. corner of Washington into the Columbia River.

CLARKSBURG, county seat of Harrison Co., W.Va., on the w. fork of the Monongahela R., about 60 miles S.E. of Wheeling. The surrounding region is noted for its resources of natural gas, oil, coal, limestone, and clay, and also produces livestock and corn. Fuel and glass products are manufactured in the city. Clarksburg was settled in 1772. It was named after the explorer George Rogers Clark, and was the birthplace of General Stonewall Jackson. Pop. (1960) 28,112.

CLARKSDALE, county seat of Coahoma Co., Miss., situated 77 miles S.W. of Memphis, Tenn., and 14 miles E. of the Mississippi R., in an alluvial delta known for the richness of its soil. Clarksdale is noted particularly as a market for cotton, and also for cottonseed oil, hardwood lumber, mules, and dairy products. Pop. (1960) 21,105.

CLARKSVILLE, county seat of Montgomery Co., Tenn., on the Cumberland and Red rivers, about 200 miles N.E. of Memphis. It is noted as a market for dark tobacco, and ships also large quantities of wheat, corn, and livestock. In the city are foundries, and factories manufacturing cigars, snuff, canned goods, flour, and clothing. Clarksville was founded in 1784. It is the site of the Austin Peay Normal School and a State agricultural experiment station. Pop. (1960) 22,021.

CLARK UNIVERSITY, a coeducational, privately-endowed institution in Worcester, Mass., founded in 1887 by Jonas Gilman Clark, a businessman of that city. The university, which at first was for postgraduate work only, was organized by Granville Stanley Hall (q.v.) who was its first president (1888–1919). In 1902 Clark College was founded, offering courses leading to the A.B. degree. In 1921 the Graduate School of Geography was established. In 1961 the enrollment was 2018, including 1014 full-time students, and the faculty numbered about 150; the library contained 233,000 volumes.

CLARY. See SAGE.

CLASSICAL ART. See GREEK ART AND ARCHITECTURE; ROMAN ARCHITECTURE; ROMAN ART.

CLASSIFICATION, in biology, the grouping of animals and plants in hierarchic groups in accordance with their similarities in structure and their evolutionary relationships. The science of classification is called taxonomy (q.v.). In the most widely accepted present system, all living things are classified in two "kingdoms" (see ANIMAL). Each kingdom is divided into phyla, each phylum into classes, each class into orders, each order into families, each family into genera, and each genus into species. These groups may be further subdivided; for example, families may be grouped in superfamilies and suborders, all within one order. Where relationships and differences justify further subdivision, the terms series and tribe may be used.

A species is usually defined as consisting of those individuals which are generally similar and can mate, producing fertile offspring (see BREEDING). Local variants of a species are called subspecies or varieties. The scientific name of an organism consists of the generic and specific names, together with the varietal name (if any), and sometimes the name of the discoverer. For example, the reindeer, *Rangifer tarandus* (Linn.), belongs to the animal kingdom, phylum Chordata, subphylum Vertebrata, class Mammalia, superorder Ungulata (hoofed animals), order Artiodactyla (cloven-hoofed animals), series Ruminantia, suborder Pecora (true ruminants), family Cervidae (deer), genus *Rangifer* (reindeer and caribou), species *tarandus;* and was first given its present scientific name by Linnaeus. Articles on all of the above groups will be found under their scientific or common names. For classification of animals and plants respectively, see ZOOLOGY and BOTANY.

CLAUDE, GEORGES (1870–1960), French chemist and physicist, born in Paris, and educated at the École de Physique et de Chimie. In 1897 he demonstrated that acetylene gas, which normally explodes under even moderate pressures, could be safely stored under pressure if dissolved in acetone. Today a large proportion of the acetylene used for welding is stored in this manner. Claude was also one of the first to work with neon, and in 1910 suggested the use of neon lamps. His most important work was the development of a process (announced in 1917) for synthesizing ammonia under high pressure; see NITROGEN FIXATION.

CLAUDE, JEAN (1619–87), French Protestant preacher, born at La Sauvetat-du-Drot. He taught theology at a Huguenot institution at Nîmes; after losing his position there because of his extreme religious views, he obtained a pastorate near Paris. There he engaged in controversy with Catholic theologians, including Pierre Nicole and Jacques Bénigne Bossuet. When the revocation of the Edict of Nantes was proclaimed in 1685, ending the period of toleration for Huguenots, Claude was given one day to leave France. He went to Holland, where he wrote an account of the plight of the Huguenots.

CLAUDEL, PAUL LOUIS CHARLES (1868–1955), French diplomat, poet, dramatist, and essayist, born in Villeneuve-sur-Fère, and educated at the École de Droit and the École des Sciences Politiques, in Paris. During the greater part of his life he served in the diplomatic corps, notably as consul (1894–1909) in China and as ambassador to Japan (1921–25), the United States (1926–33), and Belgium (1933–35).

Claudel's writings express his faith in Roman Catholicism, the religion in which he was born and to which he became ardently attached after 1886. His first published work, the drama *Tête d'Or* (1889), concerns the incapacity of man without God. His first collection of verse, the volume of prose poems *Connaissance de l'Est* (1900), praises the glory of God in all creation and expresses an exoticism reflecting Claudel's experiences in China. The plays *Partage de Midi* (1906), in which human passion is seen as a vehicle for heavenly love, and *L'Annonce Faite à Marie* (1910), an allegory based on the mystical spirit of the late Middle Ages, are considered Claudel's theatrical masterpieces. Some of his most powerful and magnificent poetry, conceived technically in psalmic rhythms, his characteristic mode of verse, is found in *Cinq Grandes Odes* (1910) and *La Cantate à Trois Voix* (1914). Among his other writings are the plays *La Ville* (1890) and *Le Soulier de Satin* (1921); and the prose works *Positions et Propositions* (1928–34) and *Conversations dans le Loir-et-Cher* (1937). He was elected to the French Academy in 1946. His correspondence (1899–1926) with the French writer Andre Gide (q.v.) was published in 1952.

Claudel's finest work combines the inspiration of religious mysticism with a varied experience of the world and human nature and a profound scholarly knowledge of literature. As a dramatist he is concerned primarily with spiritual conflict and the salvation of the soul. His poetry, written in a rhapsodic style ranging from rhetorical brilliance to simple tenderness, attempts to celebrate the divine spirit of the universe and man's participation in it.

CLAUDIAN, or CLAUDIUS CLAUDIANUS (fl. 400 A.D.), Roman epic poet, born in Egypt. He went to Rome about 395, and became a protégé of the Roman general and statesman Flavius Stilicho, whom he honored in his poetry. Much of Claudian's work is of high quality; scholars consider him the last important poet of the Latin classical school, and regard his accomplishments as remarkable in view of his non-Roman origin and the state of Roman culture in his time. Claudian's best-known work is the *Rape of Proserpine;* he also wrote epics and panegyrics celebrating the deeds of the Emperor Honorius and the wars against the Germans and Goths.

CLAUDIUS, the name of an eminent Roman clan (*gens*), the most important members of which were: **1.** APPIUS SABINUS INREGILLENSIS CLAUDIUS (fl. 500 B.C.), founder of the family, originally named Attus Clausus. He was consul in 495; the secession of the plebeians the following year (see ROME: *The Republic: Conquest of Italy*) was caused by his rigid enforcement of the laws on debt. **2.** APPIUS CLAUDIUS CRASSUS (fl. 450 B.C.), public official. He was consul in 471 and in 451; in the latter year he was appointed to an extraordinary board of ten officials (*decemviri*) to codify the laws. Taking advantage of his office, he caused a girl, Virginia, whom he was unable to seduce, to be declared the offspring of a slave, hoping thus to possess her. Her father, a centurion, unwilling to accept the disgrace, then killed her, and an uprising occurred resulting in the fall of the *decemviri* and the death in prison of Claudius. **3.** APPIUS CLAUDIUS CÆCUS (fl. 300 B.C.), official, orator, and author. Occupying the office of censor, which permitted him to change civic statutes, he consistently favored the plebeians, making it possible even for former slaves to participate in elections and become senators. During his administration the rules governing legal actions and holidays, which had been accessible only to officials and priests, were made public; this action also increased popular control of the government. He is perhaps best known for the highway named after him, the Appian Way (q.v.), built during his tenure of office. In 307 and in 296 he served as consul; in 295 he became prætor, thus reversing the usual order of officeholding. Perhaps his major contribution to Rome was to lay the foundation of Latin prose composition; his answer to Cineas, an emissary of King Pyrrhus of Epirus, who sought to impose harsh conditions after a military victory, was the first-known nonpoetic writing in Latin. **4.** Publius Claudius Pulcher (fl. 250 B.C.), naval commander, son of Appius Claudius Cæcus. As consul in 249 B.C. he commanded a fleet against Carthage during the First Punic War. The defeat of this fleet near Drepanum was attributed to Claudius's contempt for an omen. He was tried for high treason and severely fined. **5.** Appius Claudius Pulcher (d. about 48 B.C.), administrator and orator. He was prætor in 57 and as proprætor governed Sardinia the following year. In 54 he became consul, and in 53, as proconsul, governed Cilicia. During the Civil War he supported Pompey the Great (q.v.) against Cæsar. **6.** Publius Claudius Pulcher, brother of Appius Claudius Pulcher usually known as Clodius.

CLAUDIUS, or Tiberius Claudius Drusus Nero Germanicus (10 B.C.–54 A.D.), Roman Emperor, born at Lugdunum (Lyons). His father, Drusus, was a younger brother of Tiberius Claudius Nero Cæsar (later the Emperor Tiberius). Until Claudius reached the age of 47 he held no important public office; ancient historians depict him as neglected and ridiculed during the reigns of Tiberius and Caligula. When the latter was assassinated in 41 A.D., Claudius was proclaimed emperor by the prætorian guard. The first acts of his reign gave promise of mild and just government; but in 42, when a conspiracy against his life was detected, he allowed himself to fall under the influence of his wife Messalina, who practiced cruelties and extortions without restraint. Claudius expended enormous sums in building, especially in the construction of the famous Claudian Aqueduct. This great work occupied 30,000 laborers during eleven years. Aside from the excesses perpetrated under the influence of Messalina, Claudius's reign was that of an able administrator, both in civil and military affairs. Mauretania was made a Roman province, the conquest of Britain was commenced, and progress was made in Germany. Judea and Thrace also became Roman provinces during his rule. His administration was characterized by a decline in the power of the nobility and the practice (later commonplace) of granting responsibility and wealth to the personal followers of the emperor, including former slaves.

In 48 A.D. Claudius ordered the execution of Messalina, who had indicated her contempt for him by publicly going through a mock marriage with a lover. He then defied widespread disapproval by marrying his niece, Agrippina, under whose influence he deprived his son Britannicus of his heritage, adopting instead Agrippina's son, Nero (q.v.). Shortly thereafter Claudius was poisoned, presumably by Agrippina. After his death he was declared a god, according to the practice adopted a short time earlier. Claudius was described by ancient historians as stupid and malicious, but modern scholars tend to discount their hostile testimony and to estimate him as a shrewd and able ruler.

CLAUDIUS, or Marcus Aurelius Claudius, called Gothicus (214–70 A.D.), Roman Emperor, born in Illyria. He served as an officer in the Roman army, commanding the troops on the Illyrian border, and as a provincial governor, during the reigns of Decius, Valerian, and Gallienus. On the death of Gallienus (268) the soldiers of Claudius' command chose him emperor. His reign was marked by wars against the Alamanni and Goths; his victory over the latter at Naissus won him his agnomen of Gothicus.

CLAUSEL or **CLAUZEL,** Comte Bertrand (1772–1842), French army officer, born at Mirepoix. During the French Revolutionary Wars he entered the army as a volunteer in 1791 and rose to the rank of general within three years. He served on many fronts, and commanded the French army in Portugal in 1809. His accomplishments during the Peninsular Campaign were especially brilliant. With the final defeat of Napoleon (1815) he fled to America, and lived at Mobile, Ala., as a refugee under sentence of death. He was permitted to return to France in 1820, served in the legislature from 1827 until 1830, and with the accession of Louis Philippe was placed in command of an army engaged in the conquest of Algiers. In 1831 he was made a marshal of France, although the campaign in Algiers was temporarily abandoned; upon its revival he was again placed in command, and was unjustly blamed for a defeat at Constantine in 1836. The following year he retired to private life.

CLAUSEWITZ, Karl von (1780–1831), Prussian soldier and military theorist, born at Burg. During the French Revolutionary Wars, he served in the campaigns in the Rhineland in 1793–94, and was commissioned an officer during the siege of Mainz. He afterward attended a military academy for young officers in Berlin, and later, in 1806, during the Napoleonic Wars, was captured by the French in the Jena campaign. Clausewitz returned to Prussia in 1809, became the military instructor of the crown prince and departmental chief in the Ministry of War; and assisted General Gerhard Scharnhorst in reorganizing the Prussian army. In 1812–14 he served in the Russian army against Napoleon and, after re-entering the Prussian service, fought in the Battle of Waterloo. In 1818 Clausewitz was made a major general, and from 1818 to 1830 was director of the Allgemeine Kriegschule.

Clausewitz's collected works were edited by his wife and published in ten volumes under the title of *Hinterlassene Werke über Krieg und Kriegführung* (1832–37). Seven of the volumes are devoted to military history, but Clausewitz's fame as military theorist rests on the first three, published under the title *Vom Kriege* ("On War"). In these volumes he related war to politics ("War is a continuation of politics by other means"), and reduced military operations to a strategic science. *Vom Kriege* strongly influenced the thinking of military men in many countries. Clausewitz's ideas were influential in shaping the plans of the German military before and during World War I, but were subsequently largely discarded by Adolf Hitler in preparing for and fighting World War II.

CLAUSIUS, RUDOLF JULIUS EMANUEL (1822–88), German mathematical physicist, born at Köslin. He was educated at the universities of Berlin and Halle, and taught at Berlin, Zurich, Würzburg, and Bonn. He was one of the founders of the science of thermodynamics (q.v.), being the first to enunciate (in 1850) the fundamental law that heat cannot flow from a colder to a hotter body. He was also one of the first to apply the laws of thermodynamics, particularly the concept of entropy, to the theory of the steam engine. He also took an important part in the development of the kinetic theory of gases (q.v.), and his theory of electrolysis anticipated in part the ionic theory of Arrhenius. His writings include *Die Potentialfunktion und das Potential* (1859) and *Die Mechanische Wärmetheorie* (1876).

CLAVERHOUSE. See GRAHAM, JOHN.

CLAVICHORD, a musical instrument of the harpischord (q.v.) family and one of the predecessors of the pianoforte. The clavichord was square shaped and had a keyboard of four octaves and strings of brass wire. The strings were set in vibration by small, upright, flat-ended metal pins, known as tangents, located at the inner end of the keys. The clavichord was in vogue from the 15th to the beginning of the 19th century. In modern times clavichords are sometimes used in concerts of music of that period.

CLAY, an earth or soil which, plastic and tenacious when moist, becomes permanently hard when baked or fired. The clays owe their origin to the decomposition of various rocks, and consist chiefly of aluminum silicate and other ingredients, which vary in character with the nature of the parent rock. Common clay is a mixture of kaolin (q.v.) or China clay (hydrated clay), and the fine powder of some felspathic mineral, which is anhydrous and not decomposed. Clays vary much in plasticity, all being more or less plastic when moistened with water, and capable of being molded into any form. The plastic clays are used for making pottery of all kinds, bricks and tiles, tobacco pipes, firebricks, and other products. (See CERAMICS; POTTERY.) The following are the commoner varieties of clay and clay rocks: *China clay*, or *kaolin*; *pipeclay*, very like kaolin, but containing a larger percentage of silica; *potter's clay*, not so pure as the preceding; *sculptor's clay*, or *modeling clay*, a fine potter's clay, sometimes mixed with fine sand; *brick clay*, an admixture of clay and sand with some ferruginous matter; *fire clay*, containing little or no lime, alkaline earth, or iron (which act as fluxes), and hence infusible or highly refractory; *shale* (q.v.), a laminated clay rock; *clay slate*, an indurated cleaved clayrock; *loam*, a nonplastic mixture of clay and sand; and *marl*, a clay containing much calcareous matter. Clay at the deepest sea bottom is largely of animal origin.

CLAY, CASSIUS MARCELLUS (1810–1903), American politician, born in Madison Co., Ky., and educated at Yale University. He was elected three times to the State legislature as a Whig, but was defeated in the 1841 election, largely because of his antislavery position. In 1845 he founded an antislavery newspaper, *The True American,* at Lexington, Ky., and after the plant was destroyed by a proslavery mob, continued to publish it from Cincinnati. He severed his connections with the Whigs in 1850, and supported the newly founded Republican Party in 1856, continuing his support during the candidacy of Lincoln in 1860. From 1861 until 1869, except for one year, he was U.S. minister to Russia. In disagreement with Republican reconstruction policies he supported the Democratic Party during the candidacies of Greeley (1872) and Tilden (1876), returned to the Republican fold in

1884 on Blaine's behalf, and aligned himself with the minority ("gold") faction of the Democrats in 1896.

CLAY, HENRY (1777–1852), American statesman, born in Hanover Co., Va., in a district known as the "Slashes"; whence he derived his first popular nickname of "The Mill Boy of the Slashes." His father was a Baptist clergyman, who died when young Clay was only 4 years old. From his 14th until his 18th year he worked in a retail store in Richmond. In 1795 he was employed as a secretary by Chancellor George Wythe of the High Court, and studied law in the office of the attorney general in Richmond; at the age of 20 he was admitted to the bar and, leaving Richmond, began practice in Lexington, Ky. His boldness, ardor, and frankness soon won him a host of friends, and he quickly attained more than a local reputation as a jury lawyer. In 1799 he was a member of the convention which revised the constitution of the State. Here he first took a definite stand, with some loss of personal prestige, in opposing the perpetuation of slavery. He soon regained his popularity, however, by his effective attacks upon the much hated Alien and Sedition Acts (q.v.). He steadily gained in reputation as an orator and a lawyer. Finally, he gave up the practice of criminal law, which was always distasteful to him, the more so because of his success in defending persons accused of murder, not one of whom was ever convicted. Clay once said, "I fear that I have saved too many who ought to be hanged."

In 1803, Clay was returned to the Kentucky legislature. In 1806 he was appointed to fill an unexpired term in the United States Senate, where at once he became a national figure, showing great ability in debates and as a member of important committees, but his term lasted for only a few months, and he declined to be a candidate for the next Congress, preferring to continue his law practice in Kentucky. He had already appeared before the Supreme Court of the United States and was now widely known. In 1808 he was re-elected to the State legislature, where he became speaker. At this time American feeling had been deeply stirred by the impressment and blockade policy of Great Britain. The Kentucky legislature sought to pass a law providing that no decision of any British court nor any British work on law should thereafter be cited as an authority. This resolution certainly would have been passed by an immense majority had not Clay left the speaker's chair and delivered an impassioned appeal against it. Nevertheless, Clay took the lead among those who favored a war with Great Britain, and he and John C. Calhoun (q.v.) soon became known as "the War Hawks". In 1809 Clay was again appointed to fill a vacancy in the U.S. Senate, where he championed the protection of American industry, but opposed the plan for chartering a United States Bank on the ground that such a measure was corrupt and unconstitutional—an opinion which he afterward reversed, thereby subjecting himself to much criticism.

In 1811 Clay was sent to the U.S. House of Representatives, where he was immediately chosen speaker. His bold and vigorous course did much to precipitate the War of 1812, for the prosecution of which he advocated an increase in the army and other measures which greatly enhanced his popularity. In 1814 he was one of the commissioners sent to negotiate a treaty of peace (Treaty of Ghent) with Great Britain, being associated with John Quincy Adams, James Asheton Bayard, Jonathan Russell, and Albert Gallatin. Upon his return in 1815 he received a magnificent reception, and was soon offered a mission to Russia, but declined it so that he might enter once more the House of Representatives, to which he had been re-elected in his absence and of which he once more became speaker.

In 1816 Clay urged the passage of a moderately protective tariff bill and the resumption of specie payments; while with Calhoun he helped pass an act providing for internal improvements and succeeded in having it made a law over the veto of President Madison. In 1817 Clay was again chosen speaker of the House. He now ardently advocated the recognition by the United States of the South American republics which had declared their independence of Spain and of whose interest Clay remained consistently a vigorous champion. As speaker he was one of the few prominent statesmen who sharply criticized the administration of President Monroe during what was popularly known as "the Era of Good Feeling". In 1820 there was brought about the Missouri Compromise (q.v.), which for the time, insured fairly harmonious relations between the North and the South. In 1821 Clay effected an arrangement by which Missouri might be admitted as a slave State, but on the understanding that citizens of other States should be permitted to settle in Missouri. These arrangements gave Clay a third popular nickname, "The Great Pacificator". Two years later, Clay refused a further re-election to Congress and for a time engaged in highly profitable legal practice, being retained as permanent counsel for the Bank of the United States in Ohio and Kentucky. He did not, however, long remain outside the sphere of national politics. In 1823 he was once more elected to the House and was again chosen speaker. He had for many years been regarded as eligible for the Presidency, and in 1824 he became a candidate, his competitors being Andrew Jackson, William H. Crawford, and John Quincy Adams. In the election no candidate received a majority of the electoral votes, Clay standing fourth upon the list. Therefore, when the election was thrown into the House, Clay's name could not be presented according to the Constitution, and he gave his personal support to Adams, who was chosen. Clay thereby gained the title of "President Maker". When Adams subsequently appointed Clay as secretary of state, a great outcry arose to the effect that the appointment was the result of a corrupt bargain between himself and Adams, a charge which the character of the two men ought to have been sufficient to refute, but which, nevertheless, long cast a blight upon Clay's reputation for political integrity.

Clay retired with Adams after the latter's defeat in 1829, but two years later was elected to the Senate. In 1832, he was unanimously nominated by the Whigs, as a candidate for the Presidency, but was overwhelmingly defeated by Jackson. In the antislavery agitation he lost few opportunities of opposing the administration of Jackson.

During the Democratic administration of Martin Van Buren, Clay led the opposition to an independent treasury system, but the movement was unsuccessful. In 1840, much to his chagrin, he failed to receive the Whig nomination for the Presidency, but loyally supported General Harrison, after whose election Clay endeavored successfully to repeal the subtreasury act, but was unsuccessful in his endeavor to have a new United States Bank incorporated. A law incorporating such a bank was passed by Congress, but was vetoed by President Tyler, who had succeeded Harrison.

Clay resigned his seat in the Senate (1842), and two years later was again nominated for the Presidency against James K. Polk of Tennessee. The Presidency was lost to Clay because he had hesitated to take firm ground against the annexation of Texas. He was therefore opposed by the abolition party ("Liberty Party"), which supported James G. Birney. Clay's defeat was extremely bitter to him and was absolutely crushing to those who had followed him so loyally for many years. Never again was there any real chance of his securing the one great prize for which

he had contended; like Daniel Webster, he was doomed to disappointment in the Convention of 1848 which nominated General Taylor. In that year, however, he was re-elected to the Senate and did everything in his power to allay the increasing friction between the Northern and the Southern States, which grew fiercer and more intense after the close of the war with Mexico. Clay now showed his spirit of patriotism; his series of resolutions, known as the Compromise of 1850 (see COMPROMISE MEASURES OF 1850), undoubtedly postponed for at least a decade the outbreak of a civil war. Clay, like Webster, was censured as showing weakness in his willingness to compromise; but time made clear the wisdom of his action. The 10 years which followed the Compromise strengthened the feeling of nationality which both Clay and Webster had done their best to foster and to stimulate, and made possible, for the time being, the preservation of the Union and the transformation of the United States into a compact and permanent political entity.

By his eloquence and his grasp upon the imagination of his countrymen, Clay stood forth as the embodiment of national unity, and has become known as one of the greatest of American party leaders. The principle for which he contended was a positive one, and he fought for it with all the ardor and brilliancy of his nature. The last incident of importance in his career was his interview, shortly before his death, with Lajos Kossuth (q.v.), when he warned the Hungarian patriot of the futility of soliciting the interference of the United States in the internal affairs of Europe and declared the policy of the U.S. in dealing with foreign nations to be that of non-intervention in the affairs of Europe, as set forth by George Washington in his Farewell Address.

CLAY, LUCIUS DUBIGNON (1897–   ), American soldier, born in Marietta, Ga., and educated at the U.S. Military Academy. On his graduation (1918) from the military academy he was commissioned in the Corps of Engineers. His early career included service as an instructor at West Point, duty with an engineer unit in the Canal Zone, and various engineering assignments in the United States. He was on the staff of the chief of engineers from 1933 to 1937. Following the entry of the U.S. into World War II Clay advanced rapidly in grade, rising from the rank of colonel in 1941 to that of lieutenant general in 1945. During this period he was successively chief deputy of staff for requirements and resources, assistant chief of staff for materiel, Army Service Forces, and assistant to War Mobilizer James Francis Byrnes. Clay became General Dwight David Eisenhower's deputy in charge of civil affairs in the U.S. occupation zone of Germany in April, 1945. From March, 1947, when he attained the temporary rank of full general, to May, 1949, he was U.S. military commander in the European Theater and military governor of the U.S. occupation zone in Germany. He retired in 1949. In 1961–62 Clay served as President John F. Kennedy's personal representative in West Berlin; he held the rank of ambassador. Among his writings is *Decision in Germany* (1950).

CLAYBORNE, WILLIAM. See CLAIBORNE, WILLIAM.

CLAY PLANTS. See ROCK PLANTS.

CLAYTON, county seat of St. Louis Co., Mo., 4 miles w. of St. Louis. Manufactured products include chemicals, pencils, matches, concrete blocks, clay products, stoves, and electrical supplies. Concordia Seminary, a men's institution controlled by the Lutheran Church, is located there. Pop. (1960) 15,245.

CLAYTON, HENRY DE LAMAR (1857–1929), American legislator, born in Barbour Co., Ala., and educated at the University of Alabama. After serving as U.S. district attorney from 1893 until 1896, he was elected to the U.S. House of Representatives, where he remained until 1915; during the last four years of his incumbency he was chairman of the House Judiciary Committee. He is best known for his sponsorship of the financial measure known as the Clayton Act (q.v.), passed in 1914. From 1915 until his death he was U.S. district judge in Alabama.

CLAYTON, JOHN MIDDLETON (1796–1856), American legislator and jurist, born at Dagsboro, Del., and educated at Yale University. He was first elected to the U.S. Senate for the 1829–35 term, during which, although he was a Whig, he supported Jackson on the question of nullification (q.v.). He was re-elected, but served only one year; from 1837 until 1839 he was chief justice of Delaware. His second term in the U.S. Senate, beginning in 1845, was cut short when he accepted the office of secretary of state under President Taylor in 1850. His administration is chiefly notable for the negotiations with Great Britain on the subject of canal construction in Central America, culminating in the Clayton-Bulwer Treaty (q.v.). He served his third term in the U.S. Senate from 1853 until his death.

CLAYTON ACT, statute adopted by the U.S. Congress in 1914 to make illegal certain monopolistic practices which were then common in finance, industry, and trade. It was enacted, as an amendment to the Sherman Antitrust Act (q.v.), in response to widespread public demand that free competition be restored; this demand resulted in part, from sensational disclosures of monopolistic control of finance and industry, made, in 1913, by a Congressional investigating committee headed by Arsène Pujo. The committee disclosed that interlocking directorates were common among the largest banks, insurance companies, and corporations of the United States. The committee revealed that 180 directors of the largest banks and investment-banking houses in the country held 746 directorships in 134 corporations with a total capital of 25 billion dollars.

The Clayton Act limited interlocking directorates: directors of banks and other financial institutions such as trust companies, operating under Federal law and having resources in excess of 5 million dollars, were forbidden to serve as directors in other banks or trust companies; directors of corporations engaged in interstate commerce and having resources of more than a million dollars were prohibited, in certain cases, from serving in other companies engaged in interstate commerce; and corporations were forbidden to acquire stock in other companies in the same line of business.

Among other provisions of the Clayton Act were two of especial interest to management and labor in the United States. These were the provisions of the law relating to the use of injunctions in labor disputes. Theretofore, Federal court decisions, sustained by the Supreme Court, had held that boycotts, organized by workingmen, of the products of firms whose employees were on strike, were illegal restraints of trade under the Sherman Antitrust Law (q.v.). The Clayton Act limited the use of injunctions in labor disputes and also provided, for the first time, for jury trials in certain cases arising from the violation of such injunctions.

The benefits anticipated by labor under the Clayton Act were not realized, however. Subsequent court decisions extended the use of injunctions in labor disputes: before passage of the Act, injunctions had been available only to the government as a remedy against illegal restraint of trade; the Clayton Act, the courts held, made injunctions available to employers as a remedy for injuries suffered during labor disputes as a result of illegal restraints of trade by their employees. And, in 1921, the Supreme Court ruled that, under the Clayton Act, primary boycotts (boycotts of firms whose employees were on strike) were legal; but it ruled simultaneously that secondary boycotts (boycotts of firms not on strike but using the struck firm's products) were illegal. Dissatisfaction with the situation resulting from these decisions led to the enactment, in 1932, of the Norris-La Guardia Act, seriously restricting the use of injunctions in labor disputes. See BOYCOTT; INJUNCTION; TRUST.

CLAYTON-BULWER TREATY, a treaty between the United States and Great Britain, signed April 19, 1850, by John M. Clayton, U.S. secretary of state, and by Sir Henry Bulwer, ambassador of Great Britain to the U.S. It dealt with the construction of a canal across the Isthmus of Panama, and declared that neither power was to "obtain or maintain for itself any exclusive control over the said ship-canal", and that no part of Central America not already occupied by European powers was to be colonized. The treaty led to frequent disputes until 1881, when Secretary of State James G. Blaine first took up the present attitude of the United States, and contended that any canal built in Central America must be under the political control of the United States. After this, the treaty became obsolete and was finally annulled by the Hay-Pauncefote Treaty (q.v.) of 1901.

CLEANTHES (3rd cent. B.C.), Stoic philosopher and poet of ancient Greece, born at Assos, in the Troad. While supporting himself by manual labor, he attended the lectures of the Stoic philosopher, Zeno, and became Zeno's successor as leader of the Stoic school after 263 B.C. Of more than 50 works he is said to have written, only fragments are extant, preserved in the writings of Stobæus, Diogenes Laertius, Seneca, and Cicero; the most important of these is called the *Hymn to Zeus*.

CLEARINGHOUSE, an institution, found principally in banking and in railroading, to facilitate settlement of accounts among its affiliates. Banking clearinghouses enable their member banks to offset credits and debits among themselves, and to pay off balances with a minimum of time, effort, and use of cash. Each bank which is a member of a clearinghouse sends there daily all checks which represent claims upon other members. A settlement sheet is prepared by the representatives of each bank which shows the net result of the exchange of claims between the banks. If the claims presented by one bank exceed the total claims presented against it, the clearinghouse pays over the balance; in the reverse case, if the claims presented by a

bank are exceeded by the claims presented against it, the bank has to pay the balance into the clearinghouse.

Payment of balances to a clearinghouse is sometimes made in cash. Another form of payment is the deposit of drafts, drawn by debtor banks, with the clearinghouse, which deposits them with a member bank and issues to creditor banks its own drafts against these deposits. A number of clearinghouses use currency to pay balances; others issue certificates, negotiable only by member banks, against gold and other forms of money which had previously been deposited in the clearinghouse vaults.

The Federal Reserve Banks of the United States act as clearinghouses for their member banks. And they apply the same principle among themselves in balancing their accounts through the Gold Settlement Fund, supervised by the Federal Reserve Board.

In the United States the first clearinghouse was that of New York established in 1853. The business transacted by that house since then has assumed enormous proportions. In 1854, the year following its establishment, the clearings of the New York Clearinghouse aggregated $5,750,455,987; in 1962 the clearings totaled $851,407,372,060. The New York Clearinghouse is the most important of the approximately 325 clearinghouses in the United States.

Clearinghouses act for their members in dealing with out-of-town banks. A number of clearinghouses make examinations of the books of their member banks, independently of the usual Federal and State audits, and investigate the soundness of the loans and discounts of member banks. Reports are confidential and are given only to the investigated banks. The attention of the investigated bank is directed to assets considered too great a risk by the examiner. These practices have the effect of establishing confidence among the member banks as a result of the protection afforded them by uniform expert supervision. See BANK AND BANKING.

Railroad clearinghouses have been established on the same principle as those of banks, to settle the balance due to or by each company in respect of such matters as through traffic, running powers, and tickets available by different routes. There is in London one general clearinghouse for all the railroad systems of Great Britain, with a staff of about 2000 clerks. It was opened in 1842. There is another in Dublin for the Irish railroads. Several clearinghouses exist in the United States, each operating within a definite area, over and above the various pools and commissions which preform similar functions. The working of a clearinghouse is more complicated in the case of railroads than of banks, and necessitates the placing of inspectors at junctions (where different lines converge) to make a record of the traffic. The adjustment of the rates to be paid by each company in respect of traffic sent over other lines and of running powers is determined by mileage. The clearinghouses may also be charged with apportioning among the various companies the payments made by the government for such matters as the transport of mails, and may also act as bureaus for facilitating the discovery of lost goods.

CLEARWATER, city and county seat of Pinellas Co., Fla., situated on Clearwater Bay, about 22 miles w. of Tampa. It is a shipping point for citrus fruits, flowers, and fish, and is noted as a winter resort. Clearwater has a commission form of government. It was incorporated as a city in 1891. Pop. (1960) 34,653.

CLEARWING, any of the small, transparent-winged moths in the family Aegeriidae (formerly called Sesiidae), common in temperate climates throughout the world. The larvae of all species are borers; some hibernate in their burrows in the stems of trees and garden plants; others emerge at the end of the summer to spin a cocoon. The most destructive species of clearwing are *Conopia tipuliformis,* the currant borer, and *C. exitosa,* the peach borer.

CLEBURNE, Patrick Ronayne (1828–64), Confederate Army officer, born in County Cork, Ireland. After three years' service in the British army he emigrated, in 1849, to the United States, settling in Helena, Ark. There he was admitted to the bar and became a successful lawyer. When the Civil War broke out he enlisted as a private in the Confederate Army, and rapidly rose to the rank of major general. He commanded a brigade at the Battle of Shiloh, and showed great gallantry at Chickamauga. He received the thanks of the Confederate Congress for his distinguished services, and was styled "The Stonewall of the West". He was shot while leading a charge at Franklin, Tenn.

CLEFT PALATE, congenital abnormality of the roof of the mouth, often associated with harelip (q.v.). The abnormality results when the two palatine parts, which normally fuse to form the palate during the third month of gestation, remain wholly or partially separated. Cleft palate represents a serious handicap, as it interferes with swallowing and, in extreme cases, may prevent the infant from obtaining adequate nourishment. In addition, the abnormality causes severe speech difficulties, especially in the articulation of the consonant sounds.

Cleft palate is one of the most common of congenital deformations, occurring in about 0.14 percent of births. The factor of heredity long has been recognized as a cause of cleft palate; the defect appears more frequently in some families than in others. According to a study conducted in 1956, cleft palate also may be caused if the mother is subjected to physiological or severe emotional stress during the third month of pregnancy. It was found that mothers of children with the defect had suffered during that period from physiological stress caused by German measles, chicken pox, or diabetes, or from traumatic experiences, such as a death in the family. In laboratory experiments, cleft palate was produced in the offspring of 87 percent of mice subjected to stress during the period of fusion of the palatine bones in their embryos. However, when the pregnant mice were fortified against stress with massive doses of vitamins B_6, B_{12}, and C, the incidence of cleft palate was markedly reduced. Medical researchers believe that these vitamins also may prevent the condition in humans.

Surgery to correct cleft palate usually is undertaken in infancy or early childhood. If treatment is delayed beyond the second year, the problem of correction also involves speech re-education.

CLEISTHENES (late 6th cent. B.C.), Athenian statesman, belonging to the family of Alcmæonidæ. The family, exiled from Athens by the Pisistratidæ (see Pisistratus), was restored at the instance of the Delphic oracle. Cleisthenes found the Athenian oligarchy hostile to him, and sought the support of the democratic faction. To further his aims he brought about a fundamental reconstruction of the Athenian political system, which established him among the principal lawgivers of antiquity. The ancient tribes, based on family relationships, and which formed the stronghold of the aristocracy, were replaced with new tribes artificially formed from all the inhabitants of districts situated in various regions of Attica; thus, according to Cleisthenes' organization, each tribe had members from the city, from the inland countryside, and from the seacoast. The ancient *boule* (q.v.) became a council of 500 members, 50 from each of the 10 tribes. Admission of resident aliens (metics) to citizenship was facilitated, and the institution of ostracism (q.v.), by which unpopular political figures might be exiled, was inaugurated.

Cleisthenes' regime was interrupted by an attack launched by the ally of the oligarchs, King Cleomenes I of Sparta, who drove Cleisthenes and 700 families out of Athens, in 510 B.C.; but after Cleomenes' capture by the democratic faction, Cleisthenes and his followers returned. The cause of his ultimate decline from power is not known; it may have been through ostracism, as the ancient historian Ælian recounts.

CLEISTHENES OF SICYON (early 6th cent. B.C.), ruler of the ancient Greek city of Sicyon. The Dorian inhabitants of that city had suppressed the Ionian portion of the population with the aid of Dorians from Argos; but Cleisthenes, an Ionian, became ruler, or tyrant, of the city and used his authority to foment a war on behalf of the oracle of Delphi against the city of Crisa, which had levied tolls against pilgrims to Delphi. As a result of the victory of Delphi in this, the First Sacred War, new games were established by the Amphictyonic League (q.v.), including a chariot race, which Cleisthenes won (582 B.C.). He established similar games at Sicyon. Cleisthenes' daughter married one of the most powerful of his contemporaries, Megacles of Athens, head of the family Alcmæonidæ; their son was the lawgiver Cleisthenes (q.v.).

CLEMATIS, a genus of plants of the Ranunculaceae, having four colored sepals, no corolla, and for fruit numerous one-seeded achaenia with long, generally feathery, awns. The species are numerous, consisting of herbs or shrubs with climbing stems; they are scattered over the temperate countries of the world, and possess more or less active caustic properties. Many of the varieties are popular in perennial vines, grown in gardens in the U.S. to cover fences and arbors. *C. virginiana* and *C. paniculata* are popular, small, white-flowered forms. Other species bear flowers attaining a diameter of 4 to 8 inches and a range of color from white to blue or red; among these are *C. languinosa, C. montana,* and *C. viticella.* From the last two species have been derived the beautiful Jackmani types of hybrids. Several shrubby, herbaceous, nonclimbing forms of *Clematis* are also cultivated.

CLEMENCEAU, GEORGES (1841–1929), French statesman, born at Mouilleron-en-Pareds, Department of La Vendée. Although he was educated as a physician, he became interested in politics and journalism. His sympathies were republican, and France under Napoleon III was uncongenial; he sailed in 1866 for the United States, where he taught school (at Stamford, Conn.) and wrote articles for Paris newspapers. In 1869 he returned to France, in time to participate in the overthrow of the Second Empire and the establishment of the Third Republic.

At first he was involved in the municipal politics of Paris, serving as mayor of the district including Montmartre (18th arrondissement), then as a member of the municipal council from the same district. He was president of the council when he was elected to the Chamber of Deputies in 1876. For his first thirty years in national politics he adhered to the extreme left, constantly criticizing the government in power and on several occasions precipitating the overthrow of cabinets; but he refused to accept any ministerial position himself. He favored the separation of Church and State; opposed the policy of securing colonies in Asia and Africa; resisted the monarchists of all groups; and supported Dreyfus in his struggles for justice against the anti-Semites and army bureaucrats. He was first defeated as a candidate for the Chamber in 1893, probably because of his opposition to a proposed alliance with Russia; he returned to politics as a senator in 1902, on a Radical Socialist platform.

Clemenceau did not confine his activity to politics; in 1880 he founded a newspaper, *La Justice,* of which he remained editor for 20 years. He also established a weekly magazine, *Le Bloc* (1900–02), and in 1903 founded a daily newspaper, *L'Aurore,* which became a vehicle for his anticlerical campaigns.

A decisive change occurred in 1906, when Clemenceau accepted the cabinet post of minister of the interior; the same year he used military force to break a strike of miners resulting from a mining disaster in the Department of Pas-de-Calais. This incident and his defense of his action decreased his following among the workers, and his loyalties thenceforth were increasingly rightist. From late 1906 until 1909 Clemenceau was premier of France; under his government close relations with England, forecasting the World War I alliance, were established. In 1911 Clemenceau was again elected senator, and from this time well into the war years he devoted himself to warning the French that they were menaced by Germany, and that their military establishment was in no condition to meet that menace. Aside from a constant reiteration of this message in the legislature, he used the pages of his latest journal, *L'Homme*

Libre, established in 1913, to denounce Germany and the inefficiency of the French army; when the newspaper was suppressed after the outbreak of war in 1914, it reappeared two days later as *L'Homme Enchaîné.* His agitation continued throughout the first years of the war, and late in 1917 Clemenceau again became premier of France, at a time when the country was reeling under the attack of German armies. His administration was bold and ruthless, earning him the nickname of "The Tiger". Despite opposition he made Ferdinand Foch marshal of France and organized the nation for an all-out effort for victory. After the armistice he persisted in his uncompromising position, holding that the Germans should be rendered incapable of further warfare. Together with Prime Minister Lloyd George of England and President Woodrow Wilson of the United States he participated in the postwar diplomacy which resulted in the Treaty of Versailles; his influence was directed toward ensuring the security of France by the imposition of severe terms on the conquered countries, and his policy is believed to have generally prevailed over the more idealistic attitude of Wilson. In 1920, failing to receive a nomination for the presidency, he retired from public life, but he continued his activity as editor, writer, and public speaker, touring the United States in 1922. Among Clemenceau's writings are *Au Soir de la Pensée* (1927) and *American Reconstruction, 1865–70* (1928).

CLEMENS, SAMUEL LANGHORNE (1835–1910), American writer, better known under his pseudonym, MARK TWAIN. He was born in Florida, Mo., and when he was 4 years old his family took up residence in Hannibal, Mo. There he received a common-school education. After his father's death in 1847, young Clemens became a printer's apprentice and later wrote for the Hannibal *Journal,* a newspaper owned by his brother Orion. Subsequently Samuel Clemens was a journeyman printer and then a steamboat pilot on the Mississippi River, until the Civil War put an end to travel on the river. In 1861, after serving for a short time as a Confederate volunteer, he went to the Territory of Nevada, where he worked in the silver mines. In 1862 he became a reporter on the Virginia City (Nevada) *Enterprise* and in 1863 began signing his articles with the pen name "Mark Twain", a phrase meaning "two fathoms deep" which was used by leadsmen of Mississippi river boats in taking soundings. The following year he went to California, where he soon took up residence in San Francisco

Culver Service
Samuel Clemens, better known as Mark Twain

and became part of the group of noted writers, including Bret Harte and Artemus Ward, who contributed to the *Golden Era,* a celebrated newspaper and literary journal of the time. In 1865 the publication in the New York *Saturday Press* of Mark Twain's humorous sketch of frontier life, *The Celebrated Jumping Frog of Calaveras County,* brought him national recognition as a writer. The sketch was republished in his first book, *The Celebrated Jumping Frog of Calaveras County and other Sketches* (1867).

He lectured in New York City and elsewhere, and in 1867 visited France, Italy, and the Holy Land. He wrote of his travels in *Innocents Abroad,* published in 1869, a book in which he showed lack of reverence for certain aspects of European culture which usually impress an American tourist. In 1870 he married Olivia L. Langdon and established himself in Hartford, Conn. Much of his best work was written from 1869 to 1889, including *Roughing It* (1872), an account of his early adventures as a miner and journalist; *The Gilded Age* (with Charles Dudley Warner, 1873), a satire on post-Civil War days; *The Adventures of Tom Sawyer,* published in 1876, a story of boyhood adventure in a town on the Mississippi River; *A Tramp Abroad* (1880), an account of a walking trip through the Black Forest of Germany and the Swiss Alps; *The Prince and the Pauper* (1882), a

Culver Service

Huckleberry Finn, one of the most beloved of Samuel Clemens' characters (illustration by the American artist Edward Windsor Kemble)

satire on the social evils of England in Tudor times; *Life on the Mississippi,* published in 1883, an autobiographical account chiefly of Mark Twain's experiences as a river pilot; *The Adventures of Huckleberry Finn,* published in 1884, a sequel to *Tom Sawyer; A Connecticut Yankee at King Arthur's Court,* published in 1889, a satire on feudal England; and other works.

In 1884 he became a partner in the publishing firm of Charles L. Webster and Co., which profitably published the *Memoirs of General Grant* and the *Life of Pope Leo XIII.* Subsequently, however, the firm went into bankruptcy (1894) and in 1896 Clemens made a lecture tour of the world to pay off his debts. *Following the Equator* (1897) describes the tour. His work during the 1890's and 1900's is characterized by a feeling of pessimism and bitterness and on the whole shows a loss of freshness and invention. The best of his works of this period are *The Tragedy of Pudd'nhead Wilson* (1894) and *Personal Recollections of Joan of Arc* (1896). Others of his later writings are *The Man That Corrupted Hadleyburg* (1899), *What Is Man?* (1906), and *The Mysterious Stranger* (posthumously published, 1916). His *Autobiography* was published in 1924.

Mark Twain's best work is characterized by broad, irreverent humor, realism, love of democracy, and hatred of sham and oppression. His was a voice of social protest at a time when American life was in the grip of the conventionalism and Philistinism of the epoch of industrial expansion following the Civil War. His work, representing the equalitarian spirit of the unconventional West,

marked the end of the domination of American literature by New England writers. Mark Twain became renowned as a humorist, but his chief claim to fame as an artist rests on the books which delineate the life of the Mississippi valley in the middle of the 19th century, particularly *Life on the Mississippi, Tom Sawyer,* and *Huckleberry Finn,* generally considered as his masterpiece. Mark Twain was a world celebrity during the later part of his life; he is still widely read in the U.S. and abroad, and is regarded as one of the most characteristic and important of American writers.

CLEMENS, TITUS FLAVIUS. See CLEMENT OF ALEXANDRIA.

CLEMENT, name of 14 popes and two antipopes, of whom the most important were the following: **1.** CLEMENT I (fl. about 96 A.D.), Pope or Bishop of Rome, known as Clement of Rome or Clemens Romanus, one of the Apostolic Fathers of the Christian Church. Authorship of the celebrated Epistle to the Church in Corinth, Greece, written about 96 A.D., is attributed to Clement (see CLEMENTINES). His day is commemorated on November 23. **2.** CLEMENT V (1264?–1314), Pope from 1305 until his death, born in Villandraut, France, and educated in the arts at Toulouse, and in the law at Orléans and Bologna. His real name was Bertrand de Got. He became a chaplain to Pope Boniface VIII, who appointed him Bishop of Cominges in 1295, and Archbishop of Bordeaux in 1299. In 1309, four years after he became Pope, Clement established the papal court in Avignon, France, and two years later summoned a Council to meet at Vienne, in France, to try the Knights Templars (q.v.) for heresy. The Council did not find them guilty, but Clement abolished the order in 1312. Clement's pontificate was marked by subservience to King Philip IV of France, favoritism to his own family, the sale of offices, and oppressive taxation. **3.** CLEMENT VII (1342–94), Antipope from 1378, born in Geneva, Switzerland. Known originally as Robert of Geneva, he was a blood or marital relation of most of the great monarchs of Europe. He became a cardinal at an early age, and as the legate of Pope Gregory XI, participated, in 1377, in the suppression of a rebellion against papal sovereignty in the Romagna, Italy. In 1378, in Rome, he participated in the election of Pope Urban VI, but, later, at Fondi, took part in the second conclave of the College of Cardinals, which reconsidered the election of Urban, declared the Holy See vacant, and elected Robert to the papacy as Clement VII. Urban occupied the Vatican, Clement the papal palace at Avignon. The claimants to the papal throne excommunicated each other, removed from power rulers opposed to their claims, and engaged in military adventures to overthrow each other. This struggle, known as the Western Schism, was unresolved at the time of Clement's death. **4.** CLEMENT VII (1478–1534), Pope- from 1523, born in Florence, Italy. His real name was Giulio de' Medici, and he was the illegitimate son of Giuliano de' Medici. Orphaned at an early age, he was taken into the home of his grandfather, Lorenzo the Magnificent. He was later made Archbishop of Florence by his cousin Pope Leo X, and, in 1513, was appointed a cardinal; ten years later he was elected Pope. His pontificate was marked by a series of unsuccessful political conspiracies and military adventures with King Francis I of France against the Holy Roman Emperor Charles V. This policy resulted, in 1527, in the sack òf Rome, the besieging and ransom of Clement, and finally in the subservience of the papacy to the Holy Roman Empire. Clement's pontificate was also marked by the development of an irreconcilable rift between the papacy and England. Clement was a patron of the Renaissance artists Benvenuto Cellini, Michelangelo, and Raphael (qq.v.). **5.** CLEMENT VIII (1535–1605), Pope from 1592, born in Fano, Italy. His real name was Ippolito Aldobrandini. He was appointed a cardinal in 1585, and seven years later was elected to the papacy. He allied himself with King Henry IV of France in order to free the papacy from the domination of Spain, and, in 1598, enlarged the Papal States. In Clement's reign, a revised edition of the Vulgate (q.v.) was published; the Breviary, Missal, and Pontifical (qq.v.) were revised; the Collegium Clementinum was founded; the Vatican library was expanded; the Index was enlarged; and Giordano Bruno (q.v.) was burned at the stake for heresy. **6.** CLEMENT XIV (1705–74), Pope from 1769, born at Sant' Arcangelo, Italy, and educated by Jesuits. His real name was Giovanni Vincenzo Antonio Ganganeli. At the age of 17 he entered the Franciscan Order, and later became an instructor in philosophy and theology. Pope Clement XIII made him a cardinal in 1759, and ten years later he was elected Pope. Beset on all sides by the hostile monarchs of Europe who demanded the expulsion of the Jesuits from their countries, Clement at first resisted, but finally agreed, in 1773, to the suppression of the Jesuit Order. His action has been the subject of unending controversy, his critics accusing him

of treachery to the interests of the Church and of Catholicism, and his defenders maintaining he was motivated by the need to establish peace between the papacy and the Christian princes.

CLEMENT, JACQUES (1567–89), French Dominican friar, and religious fanatic, born in Sorbon in the Department of Ardennes. He is famous as the assassin of King Henry III of France, whom he stabbed after gaining admission to the king's private chambers as a bearer of important letters during the siege of Paris. He was immediately seized and killed by the royal guards; the king died the next day.

CLEMENTI, MUZIO (1752–1832), Italian pianist and composer, born at Rome. From 1766 onward he resided mainly in England, where he was a fashionable teacher of the piano and a concert performer, and established a successful piano-manufacturing business. Among his pupils was the British composer John Field (q.v.). Clementi made a number of tours of Europe as a piano virtuoso. As a composer he is best known for his études *Gradus ad Parnassum* (1817), a series of 100 studies which are still used for teaching the piano. He also composed a number of symphonies and 60 sonatas for the piano.

CLEMENTINES or **PSEUDO-CLEMENTINE WRITINGS,** a group of religious writings falsely ascribed to Pope Clement I (q.v. under CLEMENT), but otherwise unrelated. One of them, the earliest surviving Christian homily, was known throughout the Middle Ages as the *Second Epistle of Clement,* on the assumption that it followed the authentic first epistle addressed to the Church at Corinth. This homily was probably written in Egypt before the middle of the 2nd century. The document known as *Two Epistles to Virgins,* discussing questions arising from the practice of celibacy in the Church, is of Syrian origin, and probably dates from the 3rd century. These writings were attributed to Clement in error; but the group known as the *Homilies and Recognitions* were deliberately credited to him to enhance their prestige; their author, according to internal evidence, was a Judaic Christian, and they are first mentioned in the 4th-century *Historia Ecclesiastica* of Eusebius of Cæsarea. In them the travels of Clement and the apostle Peter form the framework for doctrinal and ethical discussions, with Simon Magus as the antagonist. Several letters forming part of the *False* or *Pseudo-Isidorean Decretals* and the so-called *Apostolic Constitutions* (q.v.) may also be classed with the Pseudo-Clementine Writings.

CLEMENT OF ALEXANDRIA, in full TITUS FLAVIUS CLEMENS (150?–220?), Greek theologian and a Father of the early Christian Church. He was probably a native of Athens, and received his education at Alexandria, where he was a pupil at the catechetical school under Pantænus. Some time after his conversion from paganism, he was ordained a presbyter. About 190, he succeeded Pantænus as head of the school, which became, under his leadership, a famous educational institution. His notable pupils included Origen (q.v.), who later achieved distinction in the early Church. Clement moved from Alexandria to Cæsarea in Cappadocia during the persecution of the Christians in the reign (193–211) of Lucius Septimus Severus. Little is known of his subsequent activities. He ranked as a saint in Roman Catholic martyrology until the 17th century, when this honor was withdrawn because of uncertainty among the Catholic hierarchy regarding his life and teachings. In the view of many scholars, Clement was the founder of the Alexandrian school of theology. According to his system, the divine Logos exhorts, educates, and perfects the true Christian. This process takes place in three stages, described respectively in *A Hortatory Address to the Greeks, The Tutor,* and *Miscellanies,* his chief works. The first is a defense of the faith; the second contains instructions in manners and morals for everyday life; the third is a discussion of various points of doctrinal theology, designed to guide the mature Christian to perfect knowledge. Clement was also the author of a number of tracts and treatises, including *Slander, Fasting, Patience,* and *Who Is the Rich Man That Is Saved?*

CLEMENT OF ROME. See Clement I under CLEMENT (popes).

CLEMSON COLLEGE, coeducational, State-controlled institution, chartered in 1889, and located in Clemson, S.C. The institution includes colleges of liberal arts, agriculture, architecture, engineering, and industrial management and textile science. The degrees of B.A., B.S., M.S., and PH.D. are granted. In 1962 enrollment totaled 4253, most of whom were full-time students; the faculty numbered about 300.

CLEON (d. 422 B.C.), Athenian politician and military leader during the Peloponnesian War (see GREECE: *Hellenic Period*). He was a son of Cleænetus. He first came into prominence by opposing Pericles, whom he caused to be convicted of maladministration of public funds. In 427 B.C., when the matter of the treatment of the inhabitants of Mytilene, who had revolted against Athens, came up for consideration in the Athenian assembly, he urged that all the inhabitants be put to death. In 425, when envoys arrived at Athens to treat of the release of the Spartan citizens shut up on the island of Sphacteria and to suggest peace, the Athenians, instigated by Cleon, imposed such terms upon Sparta that peace was found to be impossible. Later in the same year, Cleon himself was placed in charge of the operations against the island and, with Demosthenes, fulfilled his promise to end the siege within 20 days. In 422 B.C. Cleon was sent to oppose Brasidas in Macedonia and Thrace and to recover the city of Amphipolis, during the siege of which he was killed. His death paved the way for the Peace of Nicias in 421.

CLEOPATRA, the name of several queens and princesses of Egypt of the dynasty of the Ptolemies. The most famous of them was Cleopatra VII (69–30 B.C.), sometimes called Cleopatra VI. She was the daughter of Ptolemy XI Auletes, who died in 51, leaving a will wherein he named as his successors Cleopatra and her brother Ptolemy, and requested the Roman people to see his instructions carried into effect. Cleopatra, then about 17 years old, and her brother, Ptolemy XII, a child of about 12 years, succeeded jointly to the throne of Egypt, with the understanding that they should shortly marry. In the third year of their reign Ptolemy, urged by his advisers, assumed sole control of the government and drove his sister into exile. She promptly gathered an army in Syria and prepared to assert her claims. It was at this time that Pompey (see POMPEY THE GREAT), seeking refuge with the King of Egypt, after his defeat at Pharsalus, was murdered. Cleopatra seems to have been unable to make good her claim by force of arms; but, shortly after Pompey's death Julius Cæsar arrived at Alexandria and, yielding to the fascinations of the Egyptian queen, became her lover and espoused her cause. He was for a time hard pressed by the Egyptians, but ultimately triumphed, and Ptolemy lost his life. Arsinoë, the sister of Cleopatra, was carried off to grace Cæsar's triumph at Rome.

Cleopatra nominally married her younger brother Ptolemy XIII, and after settling their joint government upon a secure basis, went to Rome, where she lived as Cæsar's mistress until his assassination in 44 B.C. After Cæsar's death, having, it is said, poisoned her brother, Ptolemy XIII, she returned to Egypt. Since Cleopatra hesitated to take sides in the civil war following Cæsar's death, Mark Antony (see ANTONIUS, MARCUS) after the battle of

Philippi (42), summoned her to meet him at Tarsus in Cilicia to explain her conduct. The Roman triumvir fell victim to her charms and returned with her to Egypt. After living with her for some time, in the course of which she bore him twin children, Alexander Helios and Cleopatra Selene, Antony was compelled to return to Rome, where he married Octavia, a sister of Octavian (see AUGUSTUS). When, in 36, Antony went to the East in command of an expedition against the Parthians, he sent for Cleopatra, and she joined him at Antioch; after his defeat she met him in Syria with troops and supplies. In 34, after a more successful campaign against the Parthians, he celebrated his triumph at Alexandria and continued to reside in Egypt. In 32, Octavian declared war against Cleopatra, and Antony, in revenge, divorced his wife Octavia.

Against the counsel of Antony's advisers Cleopatra insisted on taking part in the ensuing campaign. At the naval battle of Actium (31), believing Antony's defeat to be inevitable, she withdrew her fleet from action and fled to Alexandria. On the approach of Octavian, Antony, deceived by a false report of the queen's death, fell by his own hand. Cleopatra made some attempts to bring Octavian under the influence of her charms, but, failing in this and hearing that he intended to exhibit her in his triumph at Rome, she killed herself, probably by poison, or, according to an old tradition, by the bite of a venomous serpent. Cesarion (Ptolemy XIV), her son by Cæsar, was put to death by Octavian. Her daughter by Antony, Cleopatra Selene, married Juba, King of Mauretania, who was allowed by Octavian to take under his protection his wife's two brothers, Alexander and Ptolemy. In 40 A.D. Ptolemy, son of Juba and the younger Cleopatra, was slain by Caligula, and with him ended the line of the Ptolemies. (See PTOLEMY.)

The history of Cleopatra has formed the basis for many literary works, the most notable of which are the plays *Antony and Cleopatra*, by Shakespeare, *All for Love*, by John Dryden, and *Cæsar and Cleopatra*, by George Bernard Shaw.

CLEOPATRA'S NEEDLES, the name given to two Egyptian obelisks of red syenite, which were transported from Heliopolis to Alexandria about 14 B.C., and remained there until 1877, when they were presented to the governments of Great Britain and the United States by the khedive, Ismail Pasha. One has been standing on the Thames Embankment, London, since 1878, the other in Central Park,

New York, since 1880. The latter is 69 feet high, with a base 7 feet 9 inches square, and weighs 200 tons. It is supported on four bronze crabs, reproductions from the originals preserved in the neighboring Metropolitan Museum. The obelisk bears inscriptions of Thutmose III (about 1500 B.C.) and Ramses II. The London obelisk is slightly smaller than the one in New York. See OBELISK.

CLEPSYDRA, an ancient instrument for measuring time by the flow of water through a small orifice. A simple form was used in the Athenian courts, where a speaker was allowed a certain quantity of water to drink during his speech, the quantity depending on the importance of the suit. In a more complicated form the water was allowed to flow at a uniform rate into a receptacle, on which was marked a scale of hours. Both forms were widely used in Rome, where they are said to have been introduced in 159 B.C.

CLERGY, a term generally applied to the ministers of the Christian religion in contradistinction to the laity. This use of the term is very ancient. The distinction between the clergy and the laity became more marked through the multiplication of offices and titles among the clergy; the ascription to them of a place in the Christian Church similar to that of the priests and Levites in the Jewish Church, with peculiar rights and privileges; their assumption of a peculiar dress and of official insignia; the growth of monastic institutions; and the introduction of celibacy. These notions belong to the Church of Rome.

In the Protestant churches the distinction between clergy and laity is considerably less marked. Among the privileges accorded to the clergy during the late Roman Empire and the Middle Ages was exemption from civil offices; among the rights asserted by them, and occasioning much dispute, was exemption from lay jurisdiction, even in cases of felony. (See BENEFIT OF CLERGY.) The clergy were distinguished into the *higher clergy* and the *lower clergy*. The term *secular clergy* is the designation of priests of the Church of Rome who are not of any religious order but have the care of parishes. Monks who are in holy orders are designated *regular clergy* (Lat. *regula*, "rule"). See ORDERS, HOLY; BISHOP; PRIEST.

CLERK MAXWELL. See MAXWELL, JAMES CLERK.

CLERMONT, the first successful vessel propelled by steam. It was designed by the American engineer and inventor Robert Fulton and launched on the Hudson River in September, 1807. The *Clermont* made the trip from New

York to Albany, about 150 miles, in 32 hours; in 1817 it made the same voyage in 18 hours.

CLERMONT-FERRAND, capital of the department of Puy-de-Dôme, France, 113 m. by rail w. of Lyons. It is situated on an elevation between the rivers Bedat and Allier, at the foot of a range of extinct volcanoes, crowned by the peak of Puy-de-Dôme. It consists of the two towns of Clermont and Montferrand, and is an episcopal see. It contains a 13th-century Gothic cathedral, the 16th-century house in which the philosopher Blaise Pascal was born, and the University of Clermont-Ferrand, founded in 1808. The city is a center of trade in grain and other agricultural products produced in the surrounding region. Among the principal industries of Clermont-Ferrand are the manufacture of automobile tires and other rubber products, chemicals, cereal foods, preserved fruits, jams, and candy.

Clermont-Ferrand is situated on the site of the ancient Roman city of *Augustonementum.* The town was known as *Clarus Mons* from the 9th century A.D. In the Middle Ages, Clermont was the residence of the counts of the same name, and the capital of the province of Auvergne, and became the seat of one of the oldest bishoprics of France. Several ecclesiastical councils were held there, the most remarkable being that of 1095, at which the First Crusade was decreed by Pope Urban II. Pop. (1962) 125,971.

CLEVE (Ger. *Kleve,* Fr. *Clèves*), town of North Rhine-Westphalia, West Germany, about 2 m. from the Rhine R., with which it is connected by canal, and 12 m. by rail E.S.E. of the Dutch town of Nijmegen. It is built on three hills, in Dutch architectural style. In the center of the town is the famous Schwanenburg, or Swan's Castle, said to have been founded by Julius Cæsar, and associated with the "Knights of the Swan" legend, immortalized in Richard Wagner's opera *Lohengrin.* Among other notable buildings is a 14th-century Catholic church, built in Gothic style, containing the tombs of the counts and dukes of Cleve. The town became the seat of the counts of Cleve in the 11th century, and later was the capital of the duchy of Cleves, which was created in 1417. In 1614 the duchy, which embraced land on both sides of the Rhine, came into the possession of Brandenburg (q.v.) and was afterward incorporated with the electorate. The part of the duchy east of the Rhine was ceded to France in 1795; the remaining portion was wrested by France from Prussia during the Napoleonic Wars. Both portions were restored in 1815, except for some small sections which were made part of Holland. Following the conclusion of World War II the town of Cleve was included in the British zone of occupation in Germany.

Industries in the town are the manufacture of leather, shoes, machinery, tobacco, and cotton. Mineral springs are in the vicinity and the town is frequented as a summer resort. Pop. (1960 est.) 21,500.

CLEVELAND, county seat of Cuyahoga Co., Ohio, and largest city in the State, situated at the mouth of the Cuyahoga River on the s. shore of Lake Erie, about 575 miles by rail w. of New York City and about 340 miles E. of Chicago. It is the eighth most populous city in the United States, a leading port of entry of the Great Lakes, and an important commercial and industrial center.

The site of the city, approximately $73\frac{1}{2}$ sq.m. in area, is an elevated plateau, which ranges from 75 to 300 feet above lake level and slopes gently toward the lake front. The shore line comprises about 14 m. along Lake Erie and about 6 m. on each side of the Cuyahoga, which follows an irregular course through the city. The Cuyahoga ravine is spanned by a number of bridges and viaducts, notably the Main Avenue Viaduct, completed in 1939; High Level Bridge, which has a central span of 591 feet; and the Lorain Central Viaduct. Most of the industrial establishments and railroad terminals of the city are concentrated in the low, flat areas contiguous to the river.

Cleveland is noted for the breadth of its streets and avenues, many of which exceed 130 feet in width, and for its abundance of shade trees. It has numerous individually-owned homes, and several modern public-housing developments have partially ameliorated slum conditions. In recent years large numbers of well-to-do families have established residence in Cleveland Heights, Shaker Heights, Lakewood, and other suburban communities. The business section of Cleveland is situated on the E. side of the Cuyahoga. Contiguous to the business section is the civic center. This development, the first of its kind in the United States, occupies a site overlooking Lake Erie and includes Cuyahoga County Courthouse, a Mall of 104 acres, the City Hall, the Public Library, the Federal Building, and the Public Auditorium, with a seating capacity of 16,500 persons. Close by, near the lake front, is the Municipal Stadium, with a capacity of 100,000 persons. The largest structure in Cleveland, and one of the tallest in the United States, is the Terminal Tower

Building, 708 feet above street level. Among other imposing buildings are the Ohio-Bell Telephone Building, 360 feet high; the Fenn College Building; the Cleveland *Plain Dealer* building; the Federal Reserve Bank Building; and Union Station, a railroad passenger terminal, completed in 1930 and one of the largest in the country.

The municipal park system, comprising more than 2000 acres and a series of parkways and boulevards, contains more than 30 parks. Noteworthy among these are the 113-acre Gordon Park, consisting largely of woodlands and meadows; Edgewater Park, a 125-acre recreation area including a bathing beach, bordering Lake Erie; Brookside Park, which has a zoological garden; and Rockefeller Park, containing 19 gardens landscaped in the style of the 19 foreign nations whose emigrants contributed most to the development of Cleveland. The Metropolitan Park System, maintained by Cuyahoga County and consisting of 10,000 acres, extends along the outskirts of the city.

Cleveland has many outstanding educational and cultural facilities, including a modern public-school system, several preparatory schools, and a number of schools of higher learning. Among these are Western Reserve University (q.v.); John Carroll University, founded in 1886 under the auspices of the Roman Catholic Church; Case School of Applied Science, a leading technological school, founded in 1880; and Fenn College, founded in 1881. The Cleveland Public Library, one of the most modern in the United States, contains more than 2,237,000 volumes, and the library of the Western Reserve Historical Society Museum has a notable collection of works dealing with Ohio history. Cleveland is noted also for its museums, particularly the Cleveland Museum of Art. In addition to important collections of primitive, ancient, medieval, and modern works of art, the museum has courses in art for adults and school children. The other leading museums in the city are the Cleveland Museum of Natural History, which contains 19,000 specimens of mammals, 54,000 specimens of birds, and extensive collections of insects, fossils, minerals, and precious stones; and the Cleveland Health Museum (dedicated to the promotion of good health), founded in 1936 and the first institution of its kind in the United States. The Cleveland Orchestra, a symphony organization, is another well-known Cleveland institution. Cleveland daily newspapers include the *Plain Dealer,* the *Press,* the *News,* and several foreign-language newspapers. The

city has more than 400 places of worship, predominantly Protestant, Roman Catholic, and Jewish.

In transportation facilities Cleveland is one of the leading cities of the Midwest. Seven trunk-line railroad systems, including the New York Central, the Pennsylvania, and the Baltimore and Ohio railroads, link it with all major points in the country. Transit services of the city consist of a street-railway system, motorbus lines, and interurban railroad service. The city has a modern, municipally-owned airport, and is serviced by the leading air lines. Its geographic position, convenient to the Great Lakes freight routes, gives Cleveland access to the iron-ore-producing regions along Lake Superior and to the oil wells and coal mines of Ohio and Pennsylvania. Cleveland harbor is protected by a breakwater nearly 6 m. long, and is equipped with exceptional docking and freight-handling facilities. Besides iron ore, which constitutes the largest incoming cargo, important shipments handled at the port include coal, coke, grain, livestock, and fresh-water fish. In a recent year incoming and outgoing cargoes totaled approximately 17,750,000 tons, making Cleveland the seventh in rank among the ports of the Great Lakes.

Cleveland has a leading position among the manufacturing cities of the nation, particularly in the production of pig iron and steel. Its production of steel wire, bolts, nuts, and wire nails exceeds that of any other American city. Other important industries include shipbuilding, oil refining, printing, slaughtering, and meat packing, and the manufacture of heavy machinery, cargo-handling equipment, motor vehicles and parts, hardware, electrical machinery and equipment, clothing, and knit goods. During World War II an airplane-assembly plant and an aircraft-engine laboratory were in operation in the city.

The municipal government of Cleveland is based on a charter approved by the voters in July, 1913. This provides for the nomination (and recall) of elected officials by petition, for the initiation of legislation in the same way, for a mayor elected for a two-year term, and for a city council, consisting of 33 members. Each of these is elected for a two-year term, and represents a ward. The municipality operates a water-supply system, which has a capacity of 315,000,000 gallons daily, and a sewage-purification system with a daily capacity of more than 80,000,000 gallons.

In 1796 the Connecticut Land Company, which had acquired ownership of part of the Western Reserve (q.v.) from the State of

Culver Service

Grover Cleveland

Connecticut in the preceding year, employed a party of surveyors to survey and settle the territory. This party, headed by Moses Cleaveland, a native of Connecticut, arrived at the site of the present city in July, 1796. The settlement which they established there was named in honor of Cleaveland, but the spelling was subsequently simplified. Cleveland registered little growth during its early years, and in 1810, when it became the seat of newly-formed Cuyahoga County, its population totaled only about 100 persons. The hamlet was incorporated as a village in December, 1814. Following completion, in 1827, of the first section of the Ohio Canal, the N. terminus of which began at the Cuyahoga River, the village became an important shipping center. The canal, which then linked Cleveland with Akron, Ohio, was extended to the Ohio River five years later, further stimulating commercial activity. The population increased from about 1000 in 1830 to about 4000 in 1836, the year of the incorporation of Cleveland as a city. By 1850 the city had more than 17,000 inhabitants. Shortly thereafter the first steam railroad was completed, connecting the city with points east. Ohio City, a community across the Cuyahoga from Cleveland, was annexed in 1853. During the American Civil War a number of manufacturing industries, notably iron and clothing, were established in the city, contributing considerably to its growth. In 1870 its population was nearly 93,000. Cleveland expanded steadily thereafter, annexing 8 neighboring communities between 1872 and 1923. The centennial of the incorporation of Cleveland as

a city was celebrated at the Great Lakes Exposition, held at Cleveland from June to October, 1936, and attended by about 4,000,-000 persons. The population (1960) of the city is 876,050.

CLEVELAND, (STEPHEN) GROVER (1837–1908), American statesman, and the twenty-second and twenty-fourth President of the United States. He was born at Caldwell, N.J., the son of a Presbyterian minister. In 1859 he was admitted to the bar and began to practice law at Buffalo, N.Y. After serving as mayor of Buffalo, he was elected governor of New York in 1882 by a majority of more than 190,000 votes. In 1884 he was nominated by the Democrats for the presidency of the United States. In the exciting campaign which followed, Cleveland received 219 electoral votes as well as a plurality in the popular vote, and took office as President in 1885. In his annual message to Congress in December, 1887, regarding the reduction of the surplus revenue in the national treasury, he advocated a careful readjustment of the tariff on certain manufactured articles of import, and the admission duty-free of some raw materials. The tariff issue dominated the 1888 election, in which the Democrats unanimously nominated Cleveland for re-election to the Presidency. Though he had a plurality of the popular vote, Cleveland was defeated by the Republican candidate, Benjamin Harrison. After spending 4 years in private law practice, Cleveland was renominated for President by his party, and re-elected to office in 1892. His second term was signalized by his zeal for currency reform, for the repeal of the Silver Act, and against the Republican high-tariff policies, and by a sudden intervention in the dispute between Britain and Venezuela which for a time threatened to cause war between Britain and the United States. In 1896 the Democrats repudiated Cleveland's administration, and nominated William Jennings Bryan, who was defeated by the Republican William McKinley.

CLEVELAND HEIGHTS, city of Cuyahoga Co., Ohio, situated 7 miles E. of Cleveland. It is chiefly a residential suburb of Cleveland. The community was known formerly as Turkey Ridge and Heather Ridge. Cleveland Heights was incorporated as a village in 1905 and chartered as a city in 1921. Pop. (1960) 61,813.

CLEVENGER, SHOBAL VAIL (1812–43), American sculptor, born near Middletown, Ohio. He first received attention as a stone carver in the workshop of David Guion in Cincinnati. Later, under the patronage of

Remains of a city of cliff dwellers at Mesa Verde National Park, Colorado. This spectacular setting offered the several-storied buildings some protection from the elements.

Nicholas Longworth, he visited the East, where he executed busts of Henry Clay (Metropolitan Museum, New York), Daniel Webster, Martin Van Buren, and Washington Allston (Pennsylvania Academy). His portrait bust of Webster has been used on a United States postage stamp and is considered the best likeness of that statesman.

CLÈVES. See CLEVE.

CLICHY or **CLICHY-LA-GARENNE** (anc. *Clippiacum*), a manufacturing town in Seine Department, France, forming a northwestern suburb of Paris. Its industries are the manufacture of oil and grease, chemicals, starch, soap, rubber, and glass. Pop. (1962) 56,311.

CLIFF DWELLER, a name frequently used to designate the builders of the numerous ancient cliff ruins scattered throughout the canyons and mesas of the arid Southwest, along the upper waters of the Colorado and Rio Grande rivers, in Utah, Colorado, Arizona, and New Mexico. The ruins are either upon the summits of the mesas or on shelves in the rock walls of the canyons. For a long time their origin was a subject of speculation; but recent ethnological investigation has proved that these ruins were built by the immediate ancestors of the modern Pueblo Indians, some of whom, notably the Hopi, still live upon the summits of almost inaccessible mesas, where the villages were built in former times to afford protection against the wilder Navaho and Apache tribes, by which they were surrounded.

CLIFFORD. NATHAN (1803–81), American jurist, born in Rumney, N.H. He was admit-

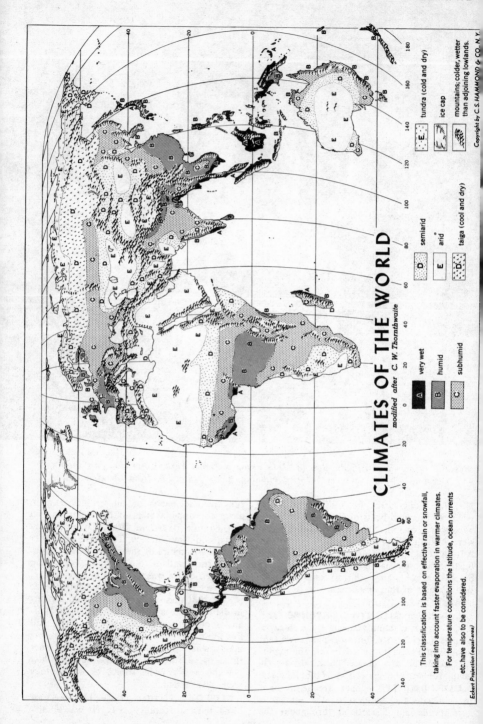

CLIMATES OF THE WORLD
modified after C. W. Thornthwaite

This classification is based on effective rain or snowfall,
taking into account faster evaporation in warmer climates.
For temperature conditions the latitude, ocean currents
etc. have also to be considered.

Eckert Projection (equal-area)

A very wet
B humid
C subhumid
D semiarid
E arid

E. tundra (cold and dry)
ice cap
mountains; colder, wetter than adjoining lowlands.
D. taiga (cool and dry)

ted to the bar, and began practice in York Co., Me., in 1827. From 1830 to 1834 he was a member of the State Legislature, and attorney general from 1834 until 1838. He served in the U.S. House of Representatives from 1839 to 1843, and in 1846 became U.S. attorney general in President Polk's cabinet. At the close of the Mexican War, as a special United States envoy to Mexico, he negotiated a treaty by which California and other territories became a part of the United States. He was associate justice of the U.S. Supreme Court from 1858 until his death.

CLIFF SWALLOW, or EAVES SWALLOW, a bird, *Petrochelidon albifrons*, of the family Hirundinidae. It is familiar throughout North America as one of the swallows which make their nests about barns and outhouses. (See BARN SWALLOW.) It is distinguished from other semidomestic swallows by its short, square tail, reddish rump, grayish breast and collar, and white forehead; and by the fact that it always builds its flask-shaped nests of mud on the outside of buildings. These swallows originally nested in colonies on rocky cliffs, but as human settlements were made near their resorts they abandoned the cliffs. In the eastern part of the U.S. the birds, through long association with man, have modified the style of their nests. They now leave off the domed roof and flasklike entrance, building only a cup.

CLIFTON, city in Passaic Co., N.J., 1 mile E. of the city of Passaic. It is a manufacturing city, with large steel, woolen, and chemical industries. Pop. (1960) 82,084.

CLIMACTERIC. See MENOPAUSE.

CLIMATE, a term employed as including not merely the conditions of a place or country with regard to temperature, but. also its meteorological conditions generally. The climate of every place on the earth's surface is determined primarily by the latitude or geographical position north and south of the equator, and by the altitude or height above sea level. Although every point on the earth's surface receives the same number of hours of sunlight in a year (barring interference by clouds), those points which are farther from the equator receive this light more obliquely, and therefore derive less warmth from it. The progressive diminution of the temperature in proportion to greater elevation is modified by many factors, so that the line of perpetual snow in mountains is far from being at the same elevation in all places of the same latitude.

Two places in the same latitude and at the same altitude may have climates totally dif-ferent, because of the local distribution of land and water and the nature of the prevailing wind. The influence of land surface is especially potent, inasmuch as the energy of the solar radiation is absorbed and transformed into heat. The air in immediate contact with the strongly heated surface is raised in temperature, expands and ascends, and has its place taken by inflowing air from the cooler regions over the oceans and seas.

The effect of solar radiation upon the water surface is quite different. The temperature is kept low because of the evaporation which takes place at the surface, while the amount of radiation which penetrates to a certain depth in the water does not raise the temperature of the surface waters more than a few degrees. Thus over continental areas the seasonal, and sometimes even the daily, temperatures vary greatly, while over oceanic and insular regions the change is comparatively small. Again, the character of the land surface has an important influence on the transformation of the solar energy, sandy deserts, for example, becoming much more strongly heated than tracts covered with vegetation.

Climate may also be influenced by prevailing winds or currents. The Gulf Stream, for example, carrying warm water from the Gulf of Mexico, renders England's climate moderate, while Labrador, at the same latitude, is made a frozen waste by the Labrador Current, carrying cold water south from the Arctic Ocean. Where the prevailing motion of air masses is from west to east, as over the U.S., much of their water content will be precipitated on the west side of any major divide. Thus, the western foothills of the Rocky Mountains have far greater rainfall than the eastern foothills at the same latitude and altitude.

The specific features that favor the growth of either plants or animals are often so obscure as to elude observation. With reference to the growth or importation of tender plants, the agriculturist needs to know the mean dates of the last frost of spring and the first frost of the autumn, the difference between which is ordinarily called the growing season. Since the establishment of the fact that the germination of seed, the growth of the plant, and the ripening of the harvest require a certain amount of heat or molecular energy, efforts have been made to determine the thermal constants for many plants and for each phase in growth. There is also a "rainfall constant" peculiar to each species of plant.

For the science of weather and its effect on climate, see METEOROLOGY.

CLIMBING FISH, any fresh-water fish of the family Anabantidae (see FIGHTING FISH), native of Africa and s. Asia. The best-known species is *Anabas scandens,* an Indian fish commonly called the climbing perch because of its resemblance to the perch in general form. It can leave pools which are in danger of drying, and travel on land, owing to the water retained in interstices connected with the gills. It is even said to climb trees by means of its spinous gill covers and by fixing its anal fin in cavities of the bark. It usually leaves the water at night when there is dew on the ground.

CLINCH RIVER, tributary of the Tennessee River, rising in Tazewell Co., Va., and flowing in a southwesterly direction through Virginia and Tennessee, joining the Tennessee R. at Kingston. Its length is estimated at over 200 miles.

CLINKER BOAT or **CLINKER-BUILT BOAT.** See BOAT.

CLINTON, county seat of Clinton Co., Iowa, on the w. shore of the Mississippi R., 138 miles w. of Chicago. Clinton was first settled in 1838 and called New York. The town was replotted by the Iowa Land Company in 1855 and renamed in honor of Governor De Witt Clinton of New York. It was incorporated as a city in 1859. Until about 1906 Clinton was important as a lumbering town. Present-day Clinton is the trade center of a fertile agricultural region, and is an important railroad and industrial city, manufacturing mill products, wire specialties, gasoline engines, locks, and cellophane. The city is the site of Mount St. Clare and Our Lady of Angels academies, both of which are Catholic schools for girls. The stage star Lillian Russell (q.v.) was born in Clinton. Pop. (1960) 33,589.

CLINTON, town in Worcester Co., Mass., on the Nashua R., about 12 miles N.E. of the city of Worcester. Its industries include book printing, and the manufacture of flashlights, perforated metals, wire cloth, insulated electric wiring, and breakfast foods. The Wachusett Dam and Reservoir, which supplies water to Boston and the Boston Metropolitan district, are located just outside the town. Clinton was originally a part of Lancaster, but was incorporated as a separate town in 1850. Government is by a board of selectmen. Pop. (1960) 12,848.

CLINTON, DEWITT (1769-1828), American lawyer and statesman, son of James Clinton, born in Little Britain, N.Y., and educated at Columbia College. After being admitted to the bar in 1788, he became secretary to his uncle, George Clinton (q.v.), governor of New York, and joined the Anti-Federalist party. He was a member of the New York State legislature, 1797-1802, and in the latter year became a member of the United States Senate, but resigned in 1803, in order to become mayor of New York City, serving with two brief interruptions, until 1815.

As a leader in civic and state affairs, Clinton contributed many services, the most lasting of which was the establishment of the New York City public-school system. He was actively interested in all scientific and social questions, encouraged steam navigation, modified the laws governing debtors and criminals, and advocated the building of the Erie Canal, a project which had been advanced by Gouverneur Morris in 1777.

The canal question became a political issue, and Clinton was elected governor of New York State on the strength of it, serving from 1817 to 1823. In this official capacity he broke ground for the work at Rome, N.Y. in 1817; and in the first year of his third term, 1825-1828, he opened the canal for navigation. Clinton was also responsible for the introduction into New York politics of the so-called "spoils system", by which members of the Council of Appointment shared equal rights with the governor in the matter of nomination.

CLINTON, GEORGE (1739-1812), American statesman, born in Little Britain, N.Y. In the French and Indian War he served as a lieutenant in the expedition against Fort Frontenac and later entered law and politics. He was made brigadier general in the Revolutionary Army, and in 1777 was elected first governor of New York, serving until 1795 and again from 1801 to 1805, when he became Vice-President of the United States (1805-12). He opposed the ratification of the Federal Constitution in the belief that it granted excessive powers to the national officers, and while presiding officer of the Senate, during his term as Vice-President, defeated by his deciding vote the rechartering of the United States Bank (1811).

CLINTON, SIR HENRY (1738?-95), British soldier, born in Newfoundland, son of George Clinton (1686?-1761), who was British colonial governor of Newfoundland from 1732 to 1741 and of New York from 1741 to 1751. He served (1760-62) with the British army in Germany during the Seven Years' War, and in America during the Revolutionary War. As major general he fought in the Battle of Bunker Hill, and took possession of New York after the defeat of Washington's forces in the

Battle of Long Island (Aug. 27, 1776). For his part in that battle he was promoted to the rank of lieutenant general and was knighted. In 1778 he succeeded Sir William Howe as commander in chief of British forces in North America, and, on his march from Philadelphia to New York, fought the unsuccessful Battle of Monmouth. In December, 1779, he led an expedition to South Carolina, and on May 12, 1780, captured Charleston. He was in constant disagreement with Gen. Charles Cornwallis (q.v.), his second in command; in 1782, after Cornwallis' surrender at Yorktown, Clinton was replaced by Sir Guy Carleton. He returned to England, soon afterward wrote the *Narrative of the Campaign of 1781 in North America* (1783). From 1794 until his death he was governor of Gibraltar.

CLIPPER, name applied to any sailing vessel to indicate that it is a very fast sailer. The name, derived probably from the colloquial verb "clip" (to move quickly), first appeared in the United States soon after the War of 1812; it was applied originally to the type of vessel formerly described as "Virginia Built" and of "pilot boat construction", but later known as the Baltimore clipper (q.v.).

By 1830 general usage had made the term synonymous with "fast-sailing". In that usage, no specific hull type or rig was indicated and the name might be applied even to a fast steamship.

In fact, the term "clipper-steamer" was applied between 1840 and 1865 to fast auxiliary steamships, but when rigged steamships went out of fashion the name disappeared also. A number of clipper-steamers were built in the United States and in Great Britain between 1845 and 1865; these vessels are also referred to in contemporary accounts as "auxiliary clippers".

After about 1845 it became the fashion to use the term in conjunction with a name indicating the cargo carried or area served by a fast-sailing vessel, and a specific rig and hull type usually were indicated. The more common types were the California clipper, China clipper, coffee clipper, opium clipper, and tea clipper. The California clipper, China clipper, and tea clipper were ship-rigged vessels with sharp ends and were designed to sail very fast. The coffee and opium clippers varied in size, might be schooner, brigantine, brig, bark, and ship rigged, and also were sharp ended for fast sailing.

The California, china, and tea clipper ships varied in degree of sharpness at the ends. The ships having the sharpest ends, i.e., those in which cargo capacity was sacrificed for speed, sometimes were called "extreme clippers". Moderately sharp-ended vessels capable of carrying more cargo than the extreme ships were called "clippers". Ships with small cargo capacity but having ends sufficiently sharp to give fairly high speed were called "medium clippers" or "half clippers". Only a small proportion of the American California and China clippers were of the extreme type; medium clippers predominated.

The American clipper ship era was of short duration, having extended from about 1845 to 1859. Very few American clippers were built after 1857 and not many were launched before 1850. All the extreme clippers were built between 1850 and 1856. In Great Britain clipper ship building continued until well into the 1870's, for the British tea trade gave employment to fast-sailing ships long after that and similar trades became unprofitable for fast American vessels. Most of the British clipper ships were of extreme models, but on the average they were smaller than the earlier American clipper ships. Some iron clipper ships were built in Great Britain, none in the United States. About 15 or 16 clippers were built in Canada, i.e., in Quebec, New Brunswick, and Nova Scotia, from 1850 to 1860. Most of the Canadian clipper ships were employed in the packet service between Great Britain and Australia. A small number of clipper ships was built in France, Germany, the Netherlands, Denmark, and Sweden.

The building of medium or half clippers extended generally from 1845 to 1860. Some vessels of this description which were built after 1860 for the coffee trade were bark rigged, but were of small size compared with the earlier California and China clipper ships. From 1850 to 1860 many sharp-ended brigantines and schooners were built on the model of the large clippers; these vessels replaced the earlier Baltimore clippers in the coastal and ocean trades.

Because of the diversity of clipper ship models, whether ships, barks, or small vessels, it is almost impossible to generalize about their appearance. As conceived popularly in the 1850's, a clipper ship was a large, ship-rigged vessel having a graceful sheer, a simple, high-arched stem fitted with a figurehead, a square or a round stern, rather low freeboard when loaded, generally very sharp ends, and an extremely large sail area. The American clipper ships depended upon proportion and line for beauty rather than upon carving and external decoration.

For a seagoing, cargo-carrying sailing vessel, the clipper ship was remarkably fast;

claims for speeds from 16 to 18 nautical miles per hour are common, and there are claims also for much higher speeds, e.g., up to 22 nautical miles per hour. The higher claims are not well enough supported by the available evidence to be wholly acceptable. There are sufficient supporting data to permit acceptance of speeds of 18 to 20 knots; however, it is very doubtful that many ships exceeded 17 knots, even though some held records for quick passages over the long courses used by the clipper ships. Although ships were known to be able to reach speeds in excess of 15 knots, it is notable that few fast vessels held records for the long passages. The records were held by potentially slower ships which were able to maintain a relatively high average speed for long periods.

The size of the American clipper ships of the 1850's ranged from about 150 feet to 250 feet in length. Only 6 noted American clipper ships were more than 250 feet long, and the longest, the *Great Republic,* was 302 feet long. Only 30 clipper ships out of about 370 or more vessels classified as American clippers were between 210 feet and 250 feet long. The most common length appears to have been about 185 feet.

The American clipper ships usually carried from 25 to 50 men in the crew. The captains and mates were picked men, as a rule, and were required to drive the ships as fast as possible. The shipping industry highly valued speed and fast passages, which accounts for the many sailing records made during the clipper ship era.

The American clipper ships generally were strongly built; iron was strapped over the frames and on the sides of the inner keel, or keels, in many instances. Although suffering much damage in spars, rigging, sails, and topside fittings due to hard driving, which made them expensive to maintain, clippers commonly lasted well. An active life of twenty-three to forty-eight years is recorded for some record-holding clipper ships.

The clipper era ended when the transoceanic carrying trade was affected by the reduced freight rates made possible by the introduction of the steamship. Thereafter only sailing vessels capable of carrying very large cargoes could be operated profitably.

H.I.C.

CLISTHENES. See CLEISTHENES.

CLIVE, ROBERT, BARON CLIVE OF PLASSEY (1725–74), English general and statesman, born in the parish of Moreton Say, Market Drayton, Shropshire. In 1743 he accepted the position of "writer", the lowest rank of employee, in the East India Company (q.v.) and assumed his duties in Madras. During the first two years (1746–48) of the series of 18th-century wars in India between England and France, Clive joined the British army as an ensign and displayed conspicuous military ability in several engagements. In 1751, with a force of 200 Europeans and 300 Sepoys, Clive, then a captain, captured Arcot, a French stronghold 65 miles w. of Madras, compelling the French to give up their siege of the British-held town of Trichinopoly. However, the French and their Indian allies, numbering 10,000, then laid siege to Clive in Arcot. After an 11-week defense in the citadel of the town, Clive and his small band, with the help of reinforcements, drove off the French, pursued them, and defeated them. These and later victories of Clive broke the French power in southern India and gave the British a stronghold in that region. In 1753 Clive returned to England, where he was treated as a hero. In 1756 he was in India again, as governor of Fort St. David. In June of that year, Siraj-ud-daula, the Nawab of Bengal, captured Calcutta from the British and reputedly committed the atrocity of the Black Hole (q.v.) of Calcutta. In February of the following year, Clive, with a force of 1900, defeated the nawab and his army of 34,000 and recaptured Calcutta. By this time, war had again broken out between the French and the British, and Clive captured Chandernagor, the principal French settlement in India. On June 23, 1757, Clive led British forces to a notable victory over the allied forces of the French and Siraj-ud-daula at Plassey (see PLASSEY, BATTLE OF); this victory permanently broke the French power in India. Clive had conspired against the nawab with Mir Jafar, the nawab's general, and following Siraj-ud-daula's death after the battle, the British made Mir Jafar the ruler of Bengal.

After further military successes against the French and the natives, and after suppressing a Dutch attempt (1759) to colonize part of India, Clive returned to England (1760). He had by then acquired through spoils and through presents from native rulers a fortune of at least £300,000, and also had received an annuity of £27,000 from Mir Jafar. He was a member of Parliament from 1760 to 1764 and was elevated to the Irish peerage in 1762. In 1765 he returned to India as governor and commander in chief of Bengal. He put an end to the disorder and corruption which had developed while he was away, restored discipline to the armed forces, and reformed the civil service. The great achievement of his third period in India was, however, his obtaining (1765) from the Mogul emperor of India, Shah Alam, who in 1759 had fled from attacks by other Indian rulers to the protection of the British in Bengal, a firman (decree) giving the British East India Company sovreignty over all of Bengal. Clive also obtained firmans establishing the Company's control over the Carnatic and Deccan regions of India. By these decrees the empire of British India was established.

Ill-health forced Clive to resign his office. On his return to England (1767), the enemies he had made in India and England accused him of having used his offices in India for personal enrichment, and caused Parliament, of which he was again a member, to impeach him. He defended himself brilliantly, but though Parliament acquitted him (1773) of the charges, the acquittal was so qualified as to make him feel disgraced. This feeling, continued illness, and addiction to opium at length resulted in his suicide.

CLOCKS AND WATCHES, mechanical devices used to measure or indicate the passage of time. A clock, which is larger in size than a watch, is usually intended to be kept in one place; a watch is designed to be carried or worn. Both types of timepiece require a source of power and the mechanical means of transmitting and controlling it, as well as indicators to register the lapse of time units.

Throughout history time has been measured by the movement of the earth relative to the sun and stars; see ASTRONOMY. The earliest type of timekeeper was the sundial (q.v.), described by the Chaldean astronomer Berossus about 500 B.C. Measuring shorter periods than the day and night later was accomplished in many other ways and with increasing precision. The methods of measuring short intervals, such as hours, were exceedingly crude in antiquity. In ancient China it was done by burning a knotted rope and noting the length of time required for the fire to travel from one knot to the next. Elsewhere the notched candle was used. Other early devices include the hourglass (q.v.), in which the flow of sand is utilized to measure time intervals, and the water clock, or clepsydra (q.v.), in which the flow of water indicates the passage of time.

The exact historical origin of the mechanical clock is obscure. Water clocks became more complicated, even to the inclusion of gearing about 135 B.C. by the Greek inventor Ctesibius of Alexandria. Eventually a weight falling under the force of gravity was substituted in time devices for the flow of water.

Until the 14th century a time-measuring instrument was known as a horologium, or hour teller. The name "clock", which originally meant "bell", was first applied in its present sense to the huge, mechanical time indicators installed in the bell towers of the Middle Ages.

Mechanisms. In a clock the source of power may be weight, a mainspring, or an electric current. Except in electric clocks, periodic adjustments, such as lifting the weight, or tightening the spring, are required. The motive force generated by the power source is transmitted by a gear train and regulated by a pendulum or a balance wheel. The time may be reported audibly by the striking of a gong or chime and is registered visually by the rotation of wheels bearing numerals or by the position of hands on a dial.

A watch generally utilizes a coiled spring as its power source. The power source of the electric watch, which was introduced in 1955, is a tiny battery; see *Electric Timepieces,* below. As in spring-powered clocks, the mechanical watch conserves energy by means of a gear train and a balance wheel regulates the motive force. In self-winding watches the mainspring is tightened automatically by means of a weight on a rotor which responds to the normal arm movements of the wearer.

Electric Timepieces. In the electric clocks used in present-day homes, a small motor runs in unison with the power-station generator, regulated to deliver an alternating current of precisely 60 cycles per second. Electric currents may be used also to keep the movements of several clocks synchronized with the pendulum in a master clock. Special clocks, designed to run on direct current delivered by storage batteries, are used in automobiles.

The newly developed electric wrist watch is powered by a tiny battery capable of functioning for two years, after which it can be replaced.

Precision Timepieces. Carefully constructed mechanical timepieces known as chronometers are precision devices used by navigators to determine their longitude at sea and by astronomers and jewelers for checking time. The first successful chronometer was constructed in 1761 by the English horologist John Harrison. These portable instruments are mounted in a box on gimbals so as to maintain the delicate movements in a level position.

Another precision timekeeper is the chronograph which not only provides accurate time but also registers elapsed time in fractions of a second. There are various forms of chronograph, including the telemeter, which measures the distance of an object from the observer; the tachometer, which measures speed; the pulsometer, which determines the pulse rate; and the production counter, which indicates the number of products made in a given time. The timer, or stopwatch, a form of chronograph used in athletic contests, shows elapsed time without providing the time of day.

Atomic Clocks. The most precise time-measuring devices are atomic clocks, which are based on detection of the internal vibrations of atoms within molecules. Because these vibrations are independent of such external conditions as the rotation of the earth, atomic clocks are used currently in many fields of scientific research, especially in astronautics (q.v.), and in the development of intercontinental ballistic missiles; see GUIDED MISSILES. Atomic time may be recognized eventually as the international standard for scientific investigations.

Historical Development. Clockworks were initially heavy, cumbersome devices. A clock built in the 14th century by Henry De Vick of Württemberg for the royal palace (now the Palais de Justice) in Paris was powered by a 500-lb. weight that descended a distance of 32 ft. The apparatus for controlling its rate of fall was so crude that the clock was inaccurate. Clocks of that period had dials with only one hand, which indicated the nearest quarter hour.

A series of inventions in the 17th and 18th centuries both increased the accuracy of clockworks and reduced the weight and bulk of the mechanisms. The Italian physicist Galileo Galilei had described late in the 16th century the property of a pendulum (q.v.), known as isochronism, stating that the frequency of the swing is determined solely by its length. In 1657 the Dutch physicist Christian Huygens showed how a pendulum could be used to regulate a clock. Ten years later the English scientist Robert Hooke invented an escapement which permitted the use in clocks of a pendulum with a small arc of oscillation. The English clockmaker George Graham improved the escapement and the English inventor John Harrison developed a means of compensating for variations in a pendulum's length resulting from changes in temperature. These and other improvements made possible the development of the highly accurate chronometer.

Watchworks were not made until coiled springs were introduced as a source of power. There is evidence that this type of spring was used in Italy by 1450. About 1500 Peter Henlein (or Hele), a locksmith in Nuremberg, Germany, began producing portable timepieces known popularly as Nuremberg eggs. In 1525 another craftsman, Jacob Zech of Prague, invented a fusee, or spiral pulley, to equalize the uneven pull of the spring. Other improvements which increased the accuracy of watches included a spiral hairspring, invented about 1658 by Hooke, for the balance wheel, and a lever escapement devised by the Englishman Thomas Mudge about 1756.

Minute and second hands in addition to hour hands, and crystals to protect both the dial and hands, first appeared on 17th-century watches. Jeweled bearings to reduce friction and prolong the life of watchworks were innovations of the next century.

Craftsmanship of a high order was required to manufacture accurate, durable clocks and watches before the introduction of machine-made parts. To acquire the necessary skill, apprentices worked under the guidance of master clockmakers. The Paris Guild of Clockmakers was organized in 1544 to control the art of clockmaking and apprenticeship. A guild known as the Clockmakers Company, founded in London in 1630, is still in existence. The Netherlands, Germany, and Switzerland produced many fine craftsmen whose work was noted for beauty as well as for a high degree of mechanical perfection.

The clock often was considered a decorative as well as useful instrument. Early clocks were highly ornamented. Many bore sculptured figures, and clockworks were used in the towers of medieval Europe to set into motion huge statues, e.g., representations of the saints. Cuckoo clocks, containing carved-wood birds, which emerge and "sing" to tell the time, were made in the Black Forest of Germany as early as 1730 and are still popular. Some early English clocks were made in the form of lanterns or bird cages. The grandfather clock, which has the pendulum and weight exposed beneath a gear housing at the top of a tall cabinet, was designed before machine-cut gears were introduced; it continues to be a popular ornamental clock. French mantel clocks, often encased in marble, and Netherlands wall clocks long were prized possessions in many American and European homes.

Watches originally were shaped like drums or balls and were worn suspended from a belt or kept in a pocket. Wrist watches became popular as watchworks became smaller.

Switzerland, world renowned for several centuries for the production of fine watches,

CLOCKS

presently exports more timepieces than any other nation. Many Swiss watches are made in the homes of craftsmen all over the country, and hundreds of small factories help keep Swiss watch production at high levels. It is a boast of highly trained modern Swiss watchmakers that they can turn $5 worth of steel into $5000 worth of hairsprings. Some Swiss watchworks are tiny enough to fit into pencil ends or in earrings.

U.S. Production. European clockmakers and watchmakers brought their skills to colonial America, and much of the mechanical ingenuity which has distinguished all American industry was originated by them. In 1650, before the introduction of the pendulum clock, there was a clock in a Boston church tower. The first public clock in New York City was built in 1716 by Joseph Phillips for the City Hall at Nassau and Wall streets, and a clock was installed in Independence Hall in Philadelphia by 1753.

Mass production of clocks with interchangeable parts began in America after the Revolutionary War. Because of the scarcity of metals, well-seasoned wood was utilized for the movements. These clockworks sometimes were used in bartering transactions. In the early 1800's, Simon Willard of Roxbury, Mass., patented the popular banjo clock and Eli Terry of Connecticut evolved a shelf clock called the pillar-and-scroll clock, which required winding only once a day.

Watches were not produced in significant volume in the United States until about 1800, when Thomas Harland of Norwich, Conn., established a factory with a capacity of 200 units a year. In 1836 the Pitkin brothers of East Hartford, Conn., produced the first American-designed watch and the first containing a machine-made part. Despite its reputation for accuracy and durability, the manufacture of this watch was discontinued as a result of the depression of 1837, which temporarily crippled American industry.

During this period, however, Chauncey Jerome of Bristol, Conn., devised a rolled-brass clock movement which could be sold at a low price. Such innovations, together with the economies of mass production, soon made the United States the leading clockmaking country of the world. As production increased, competition reduced the price of a clock to $1 or less, and for the first time nearly every family could afford a clock.

Watches also became cheaper as production rose. The American horologists Aaron Dennison and Edward Howard, working in Massachusetts, invented and perfected automatic

Wide World
Old tower clock in Bremgarten, Switzerland

production machinery in the 1850's. New designs reduced the number of parts required. Watches wound with keys were replaced after 1875 by stem-wound types. The first Waterbury, a famous American pocket watch, sold for less than $4; it was followed by the $1 Ingersol and the Ingraham.

The electric clock was an American innovation of the early 1900's. Henry Warren, a resident of Ashland, Mass., is credited with inducing producers of electric power to time the alternating-current cycles carefully so that synchronous motors could be used in living-room and kitchen clocks. The electric wrist watch has been in volume production in the United States since 1956.

Scientific advances in metallurgy and other fields have led to many improvements in timekeeping devices of all types. The mainsprings of present-day watches are made from metals that resist breakage and rust, synthetics have replaced precious stones in jeweled bearings, and cases have been perfected which seal out both dust and moisture. Other special-purpose watches include the Braille watch for the blind, which has sturdy hands not covered with a crystal and raised dots on the dial to mark the hours; the alarm watch for the pocket or wrist which functions as a portable, tiny alarm clock; and the calendar watch, which shows the day of the month and, sometimes, the day of the week. New sources of power, such as sunlight or other forms of radiant energy, are being investigated in current horological research. Experiments with vibrating quartz crystals and atoms are in progress for the development of precision timekeeping devices for the future.

CLOISONNE. See ENAMEL.

CLOISTER, a covered passage or ambulatory extending along the walls of certain portions of monastic and collegiate buildings. The cloister usually ran along three or four sides of a quadrangular area, which was called the *cloister garth.* That of Salisbury, one of the finest in Great Britain, is 195 ft. square. The upper portions of the arches above the mullions were often glazed; and sometimes, in later times, even the whole arches, so that they became a row of windows, as at Gloucester. Cloisters were used for exercise and recreation. Occasionally when wholly glazed they had cells or stalls for study on the inner side; and very frequently a stone bench may still be seen, which extends along the same side. So characteristic were they of the religious houses, that the term cloister came to be used in a general sense for the whole establishment.

CLOSED-SHOP AGREEMENT, collective-bargaining agreement between a trade union and an employer, containing the stipulation that employees of the shop or enterprise shall be union members. By the terms of a closed-shop agreement, all union members must remain in good standing in the union as a condition of continued employment, union members may be discharged only with the union's consent, and all new personnel added to the employer's working staff must be hired through the union. About 30% of all workers in American industries which had collective-bargaining agreements with trade unions formerly were covered by closed-shop contracts. The Labor Management Relations Act, better known as the Taft-Hartley Labor Law, which was enacted by the U.S. Congress on June 23, 1947, banned the negotiation of closed-shop contracts after August 23, 1947. Under the law, such agreements concluded prior to its passage were valid for the term of the contract, and agreements concluded between June 23 and August 23, 1947, were limited to a term of one year. See UNION-SHOP AGREEMENT.

CLOSURE, in parliamentary practice, a rule of procedure for bringing a protracted debate to a close. The French word *clôture* was used originally to designate this procedure and is still sometimes used. In Great Britain the rule had its origin in 1882, when the policy of obstruction followed by members of the Irish Home Rule Party in Parliament made legislation impossible. It was then decided that, at the request of 40 members, the Speaker might declare debate closed, and call for a vote on the question under discussion. As modified in 1887, the rule permitted the Speaker to cut off discussion at the request of 200 members, or at the request of 100 if fewer than 40 members voted in the negative. In the United States House of Representatives, and in the State legislatures, a protracted debate may be brought to an end by moving the "previous question". This was the method used in the United States Senate until 1917, when a small group of senators by prolonged speechmaking or filibustering prevented the passage of the armed ship bill. On March 8, 1917, a special session of the Senate adopted a closure rule. The rule was amended on March 17, 1949, and again on Jan. 12, 1959. The rule, as amended in 1959, provides that if a motion signed by 16 senators to end debate on any pending measure, motion, or other matter is presented to the Senate, the presiding officer must submit it to the Senate for a vote two days later. If two thirds of the senators present and voting vote for the motion, the matter pending must be disposed of (before other business is considered), with no senator speaking on it for more than one hour. The original Senate closure rule had referred only to pending "measures" (i.e., legislative bills); the 1949 amended rule, in addition, specifically included motions and other matters, which, it was thought, had not been governed by the original rule. The 1949 rule differed both from the original rule and the 1959 rule in providing for closure by vote of two thirds of the entire Senate rather than by two thirds of the senators present and voting.

CLOTHES MOTH, any moth the larva of which eats wool and similar materials, and may thus damage clothing, carpets, furs, and even cotton fabrics. Clothes moths are sometimes called simply "moths"; however, most moths are harmless to fabrics, and damage can almost invariably be attributed to one of three species of the family Tineidae. The adults of these species have a wingspread of from one half to three quarters of an inch; these adults do not eat, and are harmful only insofar as they produce eggs which hatch into clothes-eating larvae.

The common clothes moth *Timea pellionella,* is a small, brown moth, with darker brown spots on the forewings, whose larvae live within a case composed of bits of the food material bound together with silk. The larva of another, the carpet moth, lives within a winding gallery made up of bits of carpet or other cloth held together with silk. The species *Tincola biselliella* has a naked larva that spins a little silk over its food material, but makes neither a case nor a gallery. When the moth is ready to pupate, it spins a cocoon which is composed of fragments of cloth bound together by silk.

In recent years methods of moth control have been improved, notably through the development of the insecticide D.D.T. (q.v.). Among the new preparations is a D.D.T. solution, known as EQ-53, which was made available in 1953; added to the wash water, the solution mothproofs such washable woolens as blankets, socks, and sweaters.

CLOTHING. See COSTUME.

CLOTILDA, SAINT (475–545), the daughter of Chilperic, King of Burgundy. In 493 she became the wife of Clovis I (q.v.), King of the Franks. She was responsible for the conversion of her husband to Christianity. After he died (511), she entered a monastery at Tours, and was canonized a few years after her death. Her remains were buried in the Church of St. Geneviève in Paris. Her feast is celebrated June 3.

CLOUD, condensed form of atmospheric moisture consisting of small water droplets or tiny ice crystals. Clouds are the principle visible phenomena of the atmosphere. As such, clouds represent a transitory, but vitally necessary, step in a cycle which includes evaporation of moisture from the earth's surface, transport of this moisture into higher levels of the atmosphere, condensation of water vapor into cloud masses, and final return of water to the surface in the form of precipitation.

The formation of clouds is caused by cooling of the air, which results in the condensation of invisible water vapor to produce visible cloud droplets or ice particles. (See METEOROLOGY: *Cloud Physics.*) Cloud particles range in size between approximately 5 and 75 microns (.0002 and .003 inches). The particles are so small that they are easily sustained in the air by very light vertical currents. The different cloud forms result partly from the temperature at which condensation takes place. When condensation occurs at temperatures below freezing, clouds are usually composed of ice crystals; those which form in warmer air usually consist of water droplets. Occasionally, however, "supercooled" clouds contain water droplets at subfreezing temperatures. The air motion associated with cloud development also affects formation. Clouds which develop in calm air tend to appear as sheets or stratified formations, whereas those which form under windy conditions, or in air with strong vertical currents, have a chaotic or towering appearance.

The first scientific study of clouds began in 1803, when a method of cloud classification was devised by the British meteorologist Luke Howard. The next development was the publication (1887) of a classification system which later formed the basis for an *International Cloud Atlas* (1896). This atlas, considerably revised and modified through the years (most recently in 1932), is now used throughout the world.

Clouds perform a very important function in modifying the distribution of solar heat over the earth's surface and within the atmosphere. In general, because reflection from the tops of clouds is greater than reflection from the earth's surface, the amount of solar energy reflected back to space is greater on cloudy days. However, even though most solar radiation is turned back by the upper layers of the clouds, some radiation penetrates to the earth's surface, which absorbs this energy and in turn re-radiates it. The lower parts of clouds are opaque to this long-wave earth radiation and reflect it back earthward. The result is that the lower atmosphere generally absorbs more radiative heat energy on a cloudy day due to the presence of this "trapped" radiation. By contrast, on a clear day more solar radiation is initially absorbed by the earth's surface, but when re-radiated this energy is quickly dissipated because there are no clouds. Disregarding related meteorological factors, the atmosphere actually absorbs less radiation on clear days than on days when it is cloudy.

Cloudiness has considerable influence on man's activities. Rainfall, which is so important for agricultural activities, has its genesis in the formation of clouds. The marked effect of clouds on visibility at flight levels proved to be a major difficulty during the early days of the airplane, a hazard which was alleviated with the development of "instrument flying", which permits the pilot to navigate even when in the midst of a thick cloud. The sharp increase in consumption of electricity for lighting during cloudy days represents one of the major scheduling problems faced by the electric-power industry. Indirectly, certain clouds present hazards in the form of lightning and hail, which can cause death and property damage.

Classification. Clouds are divided into four main families on the basis of their height above the ground: high clouds; middle clouds; low clouds; and clouds with vertical development which may extend through all levels. The four main divisions are further subdivided into genera, species, and varieties, which describe in detail the appearance of clouds and the manner in which they are formed. There are more than one hundred different kinds of clouds. Only the primary families and most important genera are described below.

High Clouds. These are ice-partical clouds, found at average levels of 5 miles or more above the earth. There are three principal genera in the family. *Cirrus* clouds are isolated, feathery and threadlike, often with hooks or tufts, and arranged in bands. *Cirro-stratus* clouds appear as a fine, whitish veil, occasionally exhibiting a fibrous structure, and producing halo phenomena when between the observer and the sun or moon. *Cirro-cumulus* are fleecy clouds, small white balls and whisps, arranged in groups or rows. Cirro-cumulus and cirrus clouds are known popularly by the descriptive phrase "mackerel scales and mares' tails".

Middle Clouds. These are water-droplet clouds ranging in altitude from about 2 to 4 miles above the earth. Two principal genera are included in the group. *Alto-stratus* clouds appear as a thick gray or bluish veil, through which the sun or moon may be seen only diffusely, as through a frosted glass. *Alto-cumulus* are dense, fleecy clouds, in the form of balls or puffs somewhat larger than cirro-cumulus. The sun or moon shining through alto-cumulus clouds may produce a corona, or colored ring, markedly smaller in diameter than the halo.

Low Clouds. These clouds, also composed of water droplets, are generally less than a mile high. There are three principal forms. *Strato-cumulus* consists of large rolls of clouds, soft and gray looking, which frequently cover the whole sky. The cloud mass is usually not very thick so that blue sky often appears between breaks in the cloud deck. *Nimbo-stratus* clouds are thick, dark, and shapeless. They are precipitation clouds from which, as a rule, rain or snow falls continuously. *Stratus* clouds are sheets of "high fog". They appear as flat white blankets, usually less than 2000 feet above the ground. When they are broken up by warm, rising air, the sky beyond is usually seen to be clear and blue.

Clouds with Vertical Development. This cloud type ranges in height from less than a mile to more than 8 miles above the surface of the earth. There are two main forms. *Cumulus* are dome-shaped, "wool-pack" clouds most often seen during the middle and latter part of the day when solar heating produces the vertical currents necessary for their formation. These clouds usually have flat bases and rounded, cauliflowerlike tops. *Cumulo-nimbus* are thunderstorm clouds, popularly called "thunderheads"; they are dark, heavy-looking clouds rising like mountains high into the atmosphere, often showing an anvil-shaped veil of ice clouds (false cirrus) at the top. Heavy, abrupt showers are usually associated with thunderheads.

An anomalous, but exceptionally beautiful, group of clouds contains the *nacreous* or mother-of-pearl clouds, which are 12 to 18 miles high, and the *noctilucent* clouds, 32 to 35 miles high. These very thin clouds may be seen only between sunset and sunrise and are visible only in high latitudes.

The development of the high-altitude airplane has introduced a species of artificial clouds known as *con-trails* (condensation trails). They are formed from the condensed water vapor ejected as a part of the engine exhaust gases.　　　　　J.C.T.

CLOUDBERRY, a plant, *Rubus chamaemorus,* in the Rose family. It is a member of the same genus as the blackberry (q.v.), but has a herbaceous single-flowered stem without prickles. The plant is of low growth, 8 to 10 inches in height; the leaves few, large, lobed, and kidney-shaped; the flower large and white; the fruit orange red, equal in size to a brambleberry, and of an agreeable flavor. It is a native of the northern parts of Europe, Asia, and America.

CLOUD CHAMBER, a laboratory device for observing the movements of individual atoms, ions, or electrons. It was invented in 1912 by C. T. R. Wilson (q.v.), and has since been one of the most important tools of atomic physicists.

The cloud chamber consists of a steel box several inches in diameter, with a glass top (through which photographs can be taken) and a movable bottom which can be dropped rapidly to cause expansion of the air within. The chamber is filled with moist, dust-free air, and when the bottom is dropped the air expands, so that the temperature drops below the dew point. At the lower temperature it cannot hold as much water vapor, and this vapor condenses in the form of mist. However, the condensation process in the supercooled vapor cannot normally start unless a center is created by a speck of dust or an electrically charged particle.

If a photograph is taken a fraction of a second after the expansion, it will normally show nothing; but if an electron or ion has just passed through the air, leaving a trail of charged particles behind, each of these particles will form a droplet, and the photograph will show a trail of mist. The trail will be straight, thick, and dense if formed by a heavy nucleus, such as an alpha particle; thin and irregular if formed by an electron; and of medium thickness if formed by a proton. By placing the cloud chamber in a strong magnetic field, the electron or ion can be made to follow a curved path, the radius of the curve being a measure of its velocity.

The first artificially induced transmutation was discovered with a cloud chamber. An alpha particle, striking a previously motionless nitrogen nucleus in the center of the chamber, produced a moving oxygen nucleus and a proton, the photograph showing a forked trail with a short, thick branch created by the newly formed oxygen nucleus and a long, thin branch by the proton. Two fundamental particles, the positron and the meson, were first detected in cloud-chamber photographs taken in the course of cosmic-ray research. See COSMIC RAYS.

A similar nuclear-particle detector known as the bubble chamber was invented in 1952 by the American physicist Donald A. Glaser (1926–). This device utilizes superheated liquids for bubble formation, just as the cloud chamber uses supercooled gases for droplet formation. An ionizing particle passing through the superheated liquid initiates the development of a string of bubbles along its path. Both types of chamber are used in similar applications. Compare SCINTILLATION COUNTER. G.T.S.

CLOUET, name of a family of French portrait and miniature painters of Flemish origin. The elder JEAN CLOUET (d. 1490) was employed by the duke of Burgundy. JEAN CLOUET, the younger (about 1485–1545), was court painter, and valet to Francis I of France. His son, FRANÇOIS (1510–72), succeeded him at the court of Francis I, and held the post under Henry II and Charles IX. The portraits painted by François are distinguished by delicacy of form, pale simple tones, French elegance, and Flemish love of detail. His drawings may be found in the National Library, Paris, in the British Museum, and in various private collections in England.

CLOUGH, ARTHUR HUGH (1819–61), English poet, born at Liverpool. His early childhood was spent at Charleston, South Carolina, but in 1828 he returned to England, entering school at Chester, and later studying at Rugby under Dr. Thomas Arnold. He graduated from Oxford University, and was a fellow at Oriel College there until 1848. After this protracted period of academic life he spent 5 years traveling, administering a hostel in London and lecturing; in 1852 he visited Ralph Waldo Emerson at Cambridge, Mass. The following year he settled down to a position in London as examiner in the Education Office, remaining there until poor health forced him to travel again in 1860. He died while in Italy. Although none of his poetry was of great importance, he was a prominent literary figure in his time, the friend of such men of letters as Benjamin Jowett and Matthew Arnold. Much of his verse is experimental, as was *Tober-na-Vuolich* (1848), written in hexameters, and the *Amours de Voyage* (1849), a romance in verse. His death inspired Arnold's lament, *Thyrsis*.

CLOVER, or TREFOIL, any plant of the leguminous subfamily Papilionoideae of the genus *Trifolium,* which comprises about 250 species. Clovers are native to every continent except Australia and vary considerably in habit of growth, some trailing along the ground, while others reach a height of three feet. The flowers, ranging in color from white to red and purple, are borne in dense heads. The leaves of the clover are normally 3-lobed, but occasional 4-lobed specimens are found. Included in the genus are both annual and perennial species.

In agriculture, the clovers are of great importance as hay and pasture plants. They are also extensively used as green manure because, like other leguminous plants, their roots contain bacteria which are able to fix atmospheric nitrogen. When the clover is plowed under, the nitrogen in the plants is made available to the soil. A number of clovers, none of them native to this country, are grown on farms in the U.S. The commonest is red clover, *T. pratense,* introduced from Europe. When mixed with timothy or other grasses it forms a good hay for rotation farming on fertile, well-drained soils. Alsike clover, *T. hybridum,* a perennial with an erect stem and a rosy flower, is favored for hayfield and pasture use on soils of indifferent fertility. The familiar white clover, *T. repens,* is excellent for pasturage but is seldom used as hay, since its yield is small. It is often found in lawn-grass mixtures. Except in natural pastures, the native clovers find little agricultural use. Only four native species appear in the eastern half of the U.S., among them *T. stoloniferum,* a perennial with a purple flower and long runners growing from the base of its stem, and the low-growing *T. carolinianum,* also with a purplish flower. There are at least 50 clover species native to western U.S.

One of the peculiarities of many of the common species of clover, including red clover, white clover, and alsike clover, is that the plants are incapable of fertilizing themselves. They are cross-fertilized from flower to flower by the pollen carried by insects, particularly by bees. A further peculiarity of the red clover is that the nectar is situated too deeply in the flower for the short proboscis of the honeybee to reach it. Red clover is visited and pollinated only by bumblebees.

A number of other plants in the same subfamily are sometimes called clovers, though they are not members of the genus *Trifolium.* Among them are the sweet clover, *Melilot,* bush clover, *Lespedeza,* and tick clover, *Desmodium;* prairie clover, *Orthocarpus,* is a member of the Figwort family.

CLOVES, the dried flower buds of the clove tree, *Caryophyllus aromaticus,* or *Eugenia caryophyllata,* of the family Myrtacae. The clove tree is from 15 to 40 feet high, evergreen, with a beautiful pyramidal head. The flowers are small, but produced in great profusion in cymes. The leaves, flowers, and bark have an aromatic odor. The ripe fruit resembles an olive in shape, but is smaller in size. It is of a dark red color, and sometimes appears commercially in a dried state under the name of "mother cloves". It has an odor and flavor similar to cloves, but much weaker. The flower buds are the principal product of the tree. They are gathered, and are dried by exposure to the smoke of wood fires, and to the rays of the sun. When first gathered they are reddish, but change to a deeper brown color. The clove tree is a native of the Spice Islands, but is now cultivated in Sumatra, Réunion, Mauritius, some parts of the West Indies, and elsewhere.

The properties of cloves depend chiefly on an essential oil (oil of cloves) which forms one fifth or one sixth of the whole weight and is used for flavoring. The oil is obtained by repeated distilling; it has a hot acrid taste, is light yellow when pure, and brown red when not so carefully prepared. It is sometimes used in medicine as a stomachic, and as an admixture of purgatives to prevent griping. In dentistry it is used as an anesthetic and, because of its mild antiseptic properties and pleasant taste, to flavor dentifrices. Being one of the least expensive essential oils, it is also used in industrial perfumery, for example, in the scenting of soaps.

CLOVIS, county seat of Curry Co., N. Mex., about 95 m. by rail s.w. of Amarillo, Tex. It is a trade center for a poultry, cattle, and wheat region. In the city are large poultry hatcheries, butter-processing plants, and feed-grinding mills. Clovis has a commission form of government. Pop. (1960) 23,713.

CLOVIS I, or (Ger.) CHLODWIG (about 466–511), King of the Franks, and first important ruler of the Merovingian (q.v.) dynasty. He succeeded his father, Childeric I, as king of the Salian Franks in 481. He began his career of consolidating the Frankish dominions by a victory in 486 over Syagrius, a former Roman governor who had made himself ruler of a territory in northern Gaul. By 493, when he married the Burgundian princess Clotilda, he had conquered numerous petty princes whose territory had surrounded his capital at Soissons. He next came into conflict with the Alamanni, who inhabited territory east of his domains; according to a legend, it was only by invoking the God of his Christian wife, Clotilda, that he defeated this enemy. There is little doubt that Clotilda was instrumental in his conversion, and he was baptized by St. Remigius in 496. He was now the champion of orthodox Christians in every part of Gaul, and was supported effectively by the Church in all his campaigns. He continued to fight the Alamanni, who were completely conquered by 506; the next year the Visigoths were decisively beaten, and their king, Alaric II, was killed by Clovis in a battle near Poitiers. He made Paris the capital of the Frankish kingdom, which now included all of present France except portions in the south. Clovis' alliance with the Church was symbolized by his presiding over the Council of Orleans in 511. According to the Salian custom, he divided his kingdom among his four sons.

CLOWN. See CIRCUS, MODERN.

CLUB, an association of persons which meets periodically for social intercourse or to promote a common interest in literature, politics, science, sports, or other matters. Some clubs are proprietary, that is, they are owned and run for profit by an individual or individuals. Clubs owned by their members are usually managed by a committee or governing board and officers elected by the members. The number of members of a club is generally limited. New members are usually elected by vote of the membership after a committee of members has first passed on their applications. The revenue of a club is derived mainly from the entrance fees and annual dues of the members; additional revenue is sometimes derived from the sale of food and drink to the members.

Clubs existed in the ancient world, particularly in Greece and Rome, where they were known respectively as *hetaireia* and *sodalitas*. They were formed for religious purposes, or for promoting the mutual interests of persons following the same trade. Some Greek and Roman clubs took an active part in politics. The earliest-known club in England was *Le Court de Bone Compagnie,* organized in the reign of Henry IV (early 15th century). According to accounts given by the poet Thomas Hoccleve, this club resembled the dining club of today. The most famous of early English clubs was the *Bread Street Club* of Elizabethan times, reputedly founded by Sir Walter Raleigh. It met at the Mermaid Tavern in Bread Street, London; among its members were William Shakespeare, Francis Beaumont, John Fletcher, and other literary notables of the time. Another well-known club of that period was the *Apollo,* founded by Ben Jonson; its meeting place was the Devil Tavern in London. Among the notable clubs of the 17th century was the *Calves' Head Club,* established about 1649; its members met annually on the anniversary of the execution of King Charles I and dined, among other things, on calves' heads, which represented for them the heads of the King and his supporters. The first English political club was the *Rota,* established in 1659 at the Turk's Head in New Palace Yard, London.

The middle of the 17th century saw the establishment in London of coffeehouses. These were natural clubrooms, and at the beginning of the 18th century a great increase took place in the number of clubs in London. Two famous periodicals of the time, the *Tatler* and the *Spectator,* give accounts of some of the clubs. Among them were the *October Club*; the *Green Ribbon Club,* or *King's Head Club*; the *Scriblerus Club,* founded by the satirist Jonathan Swift; and the *Kit Kat Club,* which numbered among its members the Dukes of Marlborough and Devonshire, Sir Robert Walpole, Joseph Addison, and William Congreve. A number of associations known as *Mug House Clubs* were among important political clubs of the early part of the 18th century. Another noted club of the 18th century was the *Sublime Society of Beefsteaks,* the members of which included William Hogarth, Richard Brinsley Sheridan, and the Duke of Clarence. The most famous club established in the 18th century was the *Literary Club* or *The Club.* It was founded in 1764 by Sir Joshua Reynolds and Dr. Samuel Johnson. *The Club,* which met at the Turk's Head, London, and which is still in existence, had among its early members Edward Gibbon, James Boswell, and Oliver Goldsmith. After

the end of the Napoleonic wars in 1815, the need for recreation centers for the servicemen who thronged London led to the establishment of various service clubs, many of which still exist.

Modern London has numerous clubs. Among its important social clubs are the *Cocoa Tree* (established 1746), the *Grosvenor Club* (1883), and the *Piccadilly* (1893). Political clubs include the *Carlton* (1831), the *Reform* (1834), the *Conservative* (1840), and the *City Liberal* (1874). Among clubs devoted to the arts and sciences are *The Athenæum,* found in 1823 by a committee which included Sir Walter Scott and Thomas Moore; the *Press Club* (1882); the theatrical clubs the *Garrick* (1831), and the *Green Room* (1877); the *Arts Club* (1863); the *Royal Societies Club* (1888); and the *P.E.N. Club* (1921). The important clubs composed of university graduates are the *United University* (1822), the *Oxford and Cambridge* (1830), the *New Oxford and Cambridge* (1883), and the *University for Ladies* (1887). Among well-known clubs devoted to sports are *The Jockey* (1750); the *Prince's Racquet and Tennis* (1833); the *Alpine Club* (1858); the *Turf* (1868); the *Kennel Club* (1873); the *Renelagh* (1894); the *Royal Automobile Club* (1897); the *National Sporting Club*; the *Leander*; the *Thames*; and the *Royal Yacht Squadron.* The *St. James Club* (1857) is a club for diplomats.

In France, political clubs were centers of violent political activity during every important revolutionary period. The most notable political clubs of the French Revolution were the *Club des Jacobins,* the *Club des Cordeliers,* and the *Club des Feuillants.* They were suppressed by Napoleon in 1799. The best-known club of the 1848 revolution was the *Société Centrale Républicaine.* Political clubs flourished in Germany, Italy, and Spain in the same periods as in France. They were suppressed by statute in Germany in 1793 and 1832. Clubs for the promotion of good government later arose in many German cities, especially Berlin. The social club on the English order never found wide acceptance on the Continent. Paris, however, has two fashionable and exclusive social clubs, *Le Cercle de la Rue Royale* and the *Jockey Club.*

In the United States a number of clubs were founded in the latter part of the 18th century, including the *Sans Souci Club* of Boston (1785) and the *Hoboken Turtle Club* (1797). Among the important clubs founded in the 19th century before the Civil War were the *Union Club* (1836) and the *Century Association* (1847), both of New York City, and the *Somerset Club* of Boston. In 1863 the *Union League Club* was founded in New York City by members of the Republican Party to encourage support of the Federal government; other clubs of the same name were organized in Philadelphia and other cities. However, clubs did not become widespread in the United States until after the Civil War. Since the 1860's numerous clubs representing the most varied activities of American life have come into being, and their number is constantly increasing. Particularly notable is the development of women's clubs, of which there are now thousands in the United States, and the growth of the country club. The latter is usually both a social club and a sport club, and in the smaller cities and towns of the United States is a center of social life the year around.

CLUBFOOT or **TALIPES**, deformity caused by shortening of one or more muscles or tendons of the foot. If the deformity is not corrected, it becomes aggravated by shortening of the ligaments and alteration in the shape of the bones. In the majority of cases the condition is congenital, and at the time of birth only the muscular structures are affected. At this stage the condition may be remedied by comparatively simple means, but if it is allowed to progress, the deformity is extremely difficult to correct. Flatfoot or splayfoot is a type of clubfoot known technically as talipes planus.

CLUB MOSS, common name for ferns of the family Lycopodiaceae, of which the only important genera are *Lycopodium* and *Selaginella*. These low, mosslike, evergreen plants are widely distributed throughout the United States and other temperate and tropical climates. Some tropical species grow on the trunks of trees, as well as on the ground. Reproduction of these plants, which is similar to that of most ferns, is accomplished by spores (asexual cells) which ripen underground into a sexual reproductive organ from which the new plant grows. The spores are copious, and constitute lycopodium powder, a yellow, inflammable powder used in the manufacture of fireworks, and in pharmacy as an absorbent of blood and other fluids. *L. clavatum* is the common club moss, or running pine; *L. complanatum,* and sometimes other species, are called ground pine; and *L. selago* is the tree moss, fir club moss, or foxfeet. Fossil species, many of gigantic size, have been found in Upper Silurian, Devonian, and Carboniferous strata.

CLUBROOT, or ANBURY, a disease to which turnips, cabbages, cauliflowers, rutabagas, and allied plants are liable, and which often causes serious damage, destroying the crop of entire fields. It is called clubroot because of the knobs or tubercular excrescences which form upon the root. The root often becomes divided into a number of parts, each in some small degree swelling separately by itself, whence the popular name, "finger-and-toe disease". The disease is caused by the fungus *Plasmodiophoro brassicae,* which multiplies with great rapidity in the cells of the host. This acts as a stimulus, causing the roots to assume their strange appearance. The fungus is capable of remaining in the soil for a number of years.

CLUJ (Hung. *Kolozsvár,* Ger. *Klausenburg*), city and capital of the region of the same name, Rumania, on the Somos Mic R., 200 miles N.W. of Bucharest. It is an episcopal see of the Eastern Orthodox, Uniate, and Reformed churches. Among the principal buildings of Cluj are the church of St. Michael, a Gothic structure erected in 1396–1432; the house, now an ethnographical museum, in which Matthias Corvinus, King of Hungary, was born in 1443; a Reformed church, constructed in 1486; the Batthanyi palace, residence of the former princes of Transylvania; and the University of Cluj, founded in 1872. Industrial establishments in the city include textile and paper mills, sugar refineries, breweries and distilleries, and earthenware, soap, and candle factories.

Historians believe that Cluj is built on the site of the ancient Roman settlement of Napoca. Saxons (Germans) settled there in 1178 A.D., and became Lutherans during the Reformation. They left the city in the 16th century, during the Counter Reformation, following the establishment of the Uniate Church. Magyars then became the predominant national element in the city. During the following centuries Cluj was the seat of government of the principality of Transylvania, eastern Hungary. In 1918 Cluj became a Rumanian city as a result of the cession of Transylvania to Rumania. In 1940, during World War II, northern Transylvania, including Cluj, was ceded to Hungary at Hitler's dictation, but was recovered by Rumania in 1945 at the end of the war. Pop. (1960 est.) 161,931.

CLUMBER SPANIEL, breed of spaniel (q.v.), named after an estate of the English duke of Newcastle, at which it was bred after having been introduced into England from France about 1720. The clumber spaniel has a large, massive head; long ears; large, hazel-colored eyes; short legs; a heavy body; and a short, heavy tail. The coat of the dog is dense and silky and in color is either lemon and white or orange and white. The male is between 55 and 65 pounds in weight; the female, from 35 to 50 pounds. The clumber is slower moving than other sporting spaniels, but is an excellent finder and retriever of game.

CLUNY or **CLUGNY,** town in the department of Saône-et-Loire, east central France, on the Grosne River, about 13 miles N.W. of Macon. In Cluny are the ruins of a Benedictine abbey (founded in 910) which contained a church 650 feet long and 130 wide, at one time the largest ecclesiastical building in Europe. The former abbot's palace is today the town hall and is used also as a museum and library. Other notable structures of the town are the church of Notre Dame (Gothic, 13th century), the church of St. Marcel, with its Romanesque spire of the 12th century, a number of medieval houses, and remains of the old fortifications. The principal industries are the quarrying of limestone, and the manufacture of paper, leather, pottery, and yarn. Cluny was the birthplace of the painter Pierre Prud'hon. Pop. (1962) 3711.

CLYDE (Welsh *Clwyd* "strong", "far heard"), the third largest river of Scotland, widely celebrated for the romantic beauty of its scenery. Its headstreams are the Daer Water and the Potrail Water, which rise in Lanarkshire near the border of Dumfriesshire, and several small streams of the semicircular range of the Hart, Queensberry, and Lowther hills. The Clyde drains the counties of Lanark, Renfrew, and Dumbarton, and the area of its basin is 1481 sq.m. It flows in a general northerly direction for a little more than a third of its total length of 106 miles and then in a general northwesterly direction, past or through the towns and cities of Lanark, Hamilton, Rutherglen, Glasgow, Renfrew, Clydebank, and Dumbarton. Near the latter place it becomes an estuary, the Firth of Clyde. In this course it receives the Medwin, Cornwath, Mouse, Calder, North Calder, Kelvin, and Leven rivers. Near Lanark, extending for about 4 miles, are the celebrated falls—the Bonnington, Corra, Dundaff, and Stonebyres Linns—the largest in Scotland. Their total descent is 230 ft., Corra Linn, the grandest fall, descending 84 ft. in 3 cascades. Below Stonebyres Linn the Clyde descends at the rate of 4 ft. per mile.

From its source to the falls the Clyde is noted as a fishing stream, but from the falls to its mouth it is the most important commercial river of Scotland. Below Glasgow it expands into an estuary navigable by the largest ves-

sels, and near Renfrew is the junction of the Clyde with the Forth and the Clyde Canal which connects the Firth of Clyde with the Firth of Forth on the east coast of Scotland. The falls of the Clyde furnish power for many mills, especially textile mills, and nearer the river's mouth are the largest and most important shipbuilding yards of Scotland.

CLYDE, BARON. See CAMPBELL, SIR COLIN.

CLYDEBANK, town of Dunbartonshire, Scotland, on the Clyde R., 6 m. by rail N.W. of Glasgow. In 1941, during World War II, the town's shipbuilding yards, engineering works, and distilleries were largely destroyed by bombing. Pop. (1961 prelim.) 49,654.

CLYDESDALE HORSE. See HORSE: *Breeds.*

CLYTEMNESTRA, in Greek legend, daughter of King Tyndareus of Sparta and of Leda; half sister of Helen of Troy; and wife of Agamemnon, King of Mycenæ. Her children by Agamemnon were Iphigenia, Orestes, and Electra. Because of her grief at the sacrifice of Iphigenia at Aulis and her fury against Agamemnon for bringing his handmaid Cassandra home from the Trojan War, Clytemnestra, with the help of her lover Ægisthus, murdered the king and his captive girl. These events and their consequences, including the matricide of Orestes, were the themes of several Greek tragedies.

CNIDUS or **GNIDUS,** an ancient city of Caria in Asia Minor, located at the end of the promontory of Triopion, partly on the headland and partly on Triopion Island or Cape Krio. A bridge and a causeway connected both parts of the town, which were walled and which had a total length of about a mile. Cnidus, historians believe, was founded by the Lacedæmonians. It was one of the six cities of the Dorian Hexapolis (league) and an important commercial center. In 466 B.C. it became subject to Athens. Cnidus was reputed to have been favored by the goddess Aphrodite. A statue of her by the sculptor Praxiteles was placed in the temple dedicated to her. At Cnidus in 394 B.C., the Persians under the Athenian admiral Conon defeated a Spartan fleet commanded by Pisander and broke the power of Sparta in Asia Minor. The Persians granted autonomy to Cnidus as the Romans did at a later date. The subsequent history of Cnidus is unknown. Its site abounds in ruins of its ancient glory.

CNOSSUS. See KNOSSOS.

CNUT. See CANUTE.

COACH, a four-wheeled, horse-drawn carriage, formerly employed extensively to carry passengers. Fundamental features of coach design include a heavy body, suspended on springs and equipped with side doors and front and rear seats; a roof which forms part of the body, and an elevated driver's seat attached to the front of the body. The name is derived from that of Kocs, a town in Hungary, where vehicles of this kind were first made, probably in the 14th century. In the initial stages of its development, the coach was elaborately designed, and was used mainly by the European nobility and royalty, and for purposes of state. The bodies of these early coaches were suspended from iron standards on the axles by means of leather straps, in lieu of springs. The first coach made in England was constructed for the Earl of Rutland in 1555. A few years later Queen Elizabeth acquired a vehicle of similar design. Toward the end of the 16th century, the coach superseded the stage for the transportation of passengers and goods and became generally known as the stagecoach. The vehicle, designated by this name, was subsequently introduced in America, where it figured prominently in early intercity and interstate transportation. An extensive network of stagecoach routes had been established in England by 1750, and in 1784 the British government began the transportation of mail over these routes. As a result of improved roads, stagecoaches on many of the British lines were averaging, by the beginning of the 19th century, a speed of about 10 miles an hour. This speed was frequently exceeded on many of the American runs, notably those in the western frontier region. The railroad gradually superseded the stagecoach as a means of transportation, but the term "coach" is still applied to railway carriages in the U.S. and England and often to motorbuses in the United States.

See CARRIAGE.

COACH DOG. See DALMATIAN.

COACHWHIP SNAKE, a colubrine snake, *Masticophis flagellum,* found in the southern and western parts of the U.S. It has a slender, tapering, brownish body about 7 ft. in length and its scales give it the appearance of being made of braided leather, like a whip. The coachwhip snake is extremely agile and can glide over open ground at a speed almost as great as that of a running man.

COAL, rock composed of petrified vegetable matter, used largely as a fuel. In remote geological times, and particularly in the Carboniferous Era between 350 and 270 million years ago, many parts of the world were covered with luxuriant vegetation growing in swamps. As these plants died and subsided into the water, the water protected them from quick and complete decay. However, they gradually decomposed, giving off oxygen and hydrogen, thereby increasing the percentage of carbon in the deposit. Thus peat bogs were formed (see BOG), which in turn were buried under increasing loads of sand and mud settling from the water over them. Under the pressure of the overlying layers, through subsequent movements of the earth's crust, and sometimes through subjection to the heat of volcanic action, the vegetable matter was further compressed and hardened and its carbon content raised. The exact types of vegetation from which coal was formed are not known. Most geologists believe it was produced largely from trees or fernlike plants.

Coals are classified by rank according to their fixed carbon content, which corresponds to the amount of change they have undergone. Peat, the first stage in the formation of coal, is low in heating value, with a fixed carbon content of about 23 percent. Lignite, the lowest rank of coal, is about 30 percent carbon. Soft or bituminous coal is 43 to 85 percent carbon. Anthracite coal, which is very hard and stonelike, has a carbon content of 86 percent or more and is high in heating value. In some cases the coal-making process has continued, and has thus produced graphite that is almost pure carbon. The other components of coal are volatile hydrocarbons, and minerals which remain as ash when the coal is burned. See ANTHRACITE; BITUMINOUS COAL; PEAT; LIGNITE.

All ranks of coal are useful. Peat has been employed as a fuel for open fires for centuries, and more recently both peat and lignite have been made into briquettes for burning in furnaces. Electric-power utilities use the greatest amount of bituminous coal. In 1962, 45 percent of the total amount produced in the United States was consumed by such utilities. The steel industry is another large consumer of bituminous coal, especially of metallurgical or coking coal, and with present-day processes it takes almost a ton of coal to make a ton of steel. Several basic chemicals are recovered as by-products of coking operations. Further processing yields many derivatives from which thousands of products are manufactured. Many industries consume coal for power, processing, or heating purposes.

Coal deposits are found in nearly every region of the world, but those of present commercial importance are confined to Europe, Asia, and North America.

Great Britain, which led the world in coal production until the 20th century, has deposits in s. Scotland, England, and Wales. In w.

Europe, there are important beds in Alsace, Belgium, and the Saar and Ruhr valleys. Central European deposits include those of Silesia, Bohemia, and Hungary. The Soviet Union's most extensive and valuable coal field is that of the Donets Basin between the Dnieper and Don rivers; large deposits have also recently been exploited in the Kuznets Basin in Central Siberia. The coal fields of China, among the largest in the world, were little developed until about the middle of the 20th century.

Coal occurs in 37 States of the United States, divided into six provinces and Alaska. The eastern province, about 70,000 sq.m. in extent, includes the Appalachian fields of Pennsylvania, West Virginia, Kentucky, Tennessee, Ohio, and Alabama, and produces the greatest part of all U.S. coal. In the Gulf States of Alabama, Mississippi, Louisiana, Arkansas, and Texas, there are large lignite fields which may total as much as 78,000 sq.m., though only a small fraction of this area is worked at present. There are extensive bituminous deposits in the Mississippi valley from Arkansas to Michigan, forming another coal province with an area of about 132,900 sq.m. Lignite deposits in the Dakotas and bituminous beds in Montana and Wyoming cover about 88,590 sq.m. The Rocky Mountain coal province consists of isolated fields from the Canadian border south to New Mexico, totaling about 37,000 sq.m. On the Pacific Coast there are about 1,900 sq.m. of coal fields. The original coal reserves of Alaska are estimated at nearly 95 billion tons.

Almost all the anthracite coal in the U.S. is concentrated in a small area around Scranton and Wilkes-Barre, in Pennsylvania. The best bituminous coal for coking purposes comes from the Middle Atlantic States.

It is estimated that there are about 5115 billion tons of coal reserves throughout the world, about one third of them in North America. About half of all reserves are bituminous; only about one twentieth is anthracite, and most of this is in Asia.

Coal has been mined to some extent for more than 1000 years, and large-scale mining was practiced as early as the 18th century. The first coal mine in America was opened in Virginia during the 1740's; the mining of anthracite began in 1793. Extensive mining in this country commenced about 1820; until 1854 more than half of all U.S. coal produced was Pennsylvania anthracite.

There are two main systems of coal mining, namely surface, or strip, mining and underground, or deep, mining. Strip mining, which is a form of quarrying, is possible only when the coal seam is near the surface of the ground. In large surface mines huge power shovels and draglines are used to remove the earth and rock, called the overburden, above the seam. One new shovel has a bucket capacity of 200 tons. Smaller shovels then load the coal directly into trucks. The chief advantage of strip mining is the enormous saving of time and labor as compared with underground mining. The daily output per man in strip mines is almost double that in underground mines.

As a supplement to strip mining, or when other mining techniques are not adequate, augers are used to bore horizontally into exposed coal seams. The loosened coal then flows into a conveyor for loading into trucks. A newer development is a boring machine which can tunnel as deep as 1000 feet into the coal seam, dumping the coal into mobile conveyors which it pulls after it.

In underground, or deep, mining the coal seam is reached through vertical or inclined shafts, or through level or nearly level tunnels, depending on its location. The coal deposit is usually marked out in "rooms" which vary in size according to local conditions. The coal is cut and blasted away, leaving pillars of coal to support the roof. In the so-called longwall system of working, the entire section of the seam is removed and the roof is allowed to settle, leaving only haulage tunnels clear of the subsiding debris.

Power cutters have supplanted the traditional miner's pick. With them the miner makes an undercut about 6 inches wide and as much as 9 feet deep across the face of the coal seam, often close to the floor of the room. Then deep holes are drilled at the top of the face and charges of explosives are tamped into them. The explosive blast brings down and partially shatters a large chunk of the coal face, which is then loaded by machines into low, electrically propelled shuttle cars. These cars bring the coal to a central loading point whence it is hauled to the surface either by rail cars or by giant conveyor belts. Nearly one third of U.S. underground production of bituminous coal is mined by continuous-mining machines, which eliminate the separate steps of cutting, drilling, blasting, and loading. These huge machines, capable of mining up to 8 tons of coal per minute, tear coal from the face and load it onto built-in conveyor belts. The belts transport the coal to waiting shuttle cars or mine conveyor belts which carry it to the surface. The coal is then dumped into a preparation plant where it may be screened, washed, sorted into various sizes, and sometimes crushed before shipment.

Among the chief problems in underground mines are ventilation and roof support. Ventilation is important because of the presence in coal mines of several dangerous gases. Large fans and blowers must be used to maintain circulation of pure air. In order to prevent the spread of coal dust, which can be highly explosive, mine interiors are frequently sprayed with limestone dust, a process known as rockdusting. To provide support for the roofs of tunnels and work spaces, metal props and heavy timbers are conventional materials used. Many mines recently have introduced modern roof-bolting techniques which are aids to safer and more efficient operation. See also MINING.

Mine Labor. The trend of employment in mines has been generally downward. In 1925 a total of 748,805 men were engaged in coal mining in the United States, but in 1962 the number had fallen to about 150,000. The decrease in employment has been particularly marked in the anthracite industry. At the same time that employment has fallen, the productivity of the individual miner has increased greatly, largely through mechanization of mines. Bituminous production per man per year was 781 tons in 1925, but in 1962 it amounted to an estimated 12,832 tons.

Mine Safety. Certain hazards are inherent in coal mining because of the presence of explosive and asphyxiant gases, such as methane and carbon dioxide, and the possibility of cave-ins and falls of rock. Since 1910 the Bureau of Mines of the Department of the Interior has made a special study of mine safety. The Bureau not only tests and recommends approved types of equipment, but also studies mining techniques with a view to making them safer. An important part of its program is the instruction of miners and officials in accident prevention and first aid. The success of the safety programs of the Bureau, the mine owners, and the miners' union is reflected in accident statistics. In the year 1930, for every 100 million tons of bituminous coal produced, 346 miners lost their lives. In 1962 there were only 62 fatalities per 100 million tons mined.

Coal Production. Prior to World War II, coal production in the United States had gradually declined, though it was still far ahead of that of any other country. The cause of this decline was largely the increasing use of other fuels, particularly oil. War industry needs, however, stimulated mining, and in 1947 production reached an all-time high of 687,813,731 tons, of which 630,623,722 tons were bituminous. Production subsequently fluctuated; in 1962 it was estimated to be 439,854,000 tons. Pennsylvania and West Virginia produce about half of the country's bituminous coal, and another third comes from Kentucky, Illinois, Ohio, and Virginia.

The U.S.S.R. is the leading coal-producing nation; in 1961 its total output was 558,210,-000 tons. The United States holds second place. Other major producers are Communist China, with a 1961 output of 420,000,000 tons; West Germany, 267,396,000 tons; East Germany, 263,536,000 tons; Great Britain, 213,321,000 tons; Poland, 128,909,000 tons; and Czechoslovakia, 100,851,000 tons.

NATIONAL COAL ASSOCIATION

COALFISH, a name given to two unrelated dark-colored fishes. The coalfish of the N. Atlantic Ocean is the pollack or green cod, *Pollachius virens,* which is used as a food fish. It reaches a length of 3 ft. and weighs 25 lbs. or more. The Pacific coalfish is the beshow, *Anoplopoma fimbria,* found south of the Aleutian Islands, and also caught for food.

COAL GAS. See GAS.

COAL OIL. See PETROLEUM.

COAL TAR, a viscous black liquid produced in the destructive distillation of coal during the process of making coke (q.v.) and illuminating gas (see GAS: *Coal and Coke-Oven Gas*). It has a specific gravity between 1.0 and 1.2, and is a complex mixture of aromatic organic compounds including benzene, toluene, xylenes, naphthalene, cresols, and anthracene. The fractional distillation of coal tar to separate these compounds is an important branch of the chemical industry.

The fractions obtained from the distillation of coal tar vary somewhat with the source of the tar and with market demands. The modern tendency is to use vacua or inert gas circulation to reduce the temperature of distillation and thus increase the yield of valuable products. The products of distillation are approximately as follows: (1) *Light oil,* including benzene, toluene, and xylene, together with a certain amount of pyridine and naphthalene. The light oil boils up to approximately 170° C. (338° F.) and comprises about 25% of the tar. (2) *Carbolic oil,* made up of phenol, naphthalene and pyridine bases, forming about 10% of the tar and boiling up to 225° C. (437° F.). (3) *Creosote oil,* chiefly composed of cresols, comprising another 10% of the tar and boiling at temperatures up to 270° C. (518° F.). (4) *Heavy oil,* phenanthrene, anthracene, and carbazol, comprising about 40% of the tar and boiling up to 320° C. (608° F.). The residue left after distillation is pitch, used for road making and in the manufacture of roofing and coal-dust fuel briquettes.

When coal gas was first produced for illuminating purposes in the early 19th century, there was little use for coal tar, and it was commonly burned or used as a wood preservative. Then, as the compounds making up the tar were isolated and studied, coal tar became the basis for an entire new chemistry. Its derivatives are used today for the manufacture of dyes, medicinal products, explosives, paints, and fuels.

For the useful chemicals sometimes called "coal-tar products" see AROMATIC COMPOUNDS.

COAL-TAR DYES. See DYESTUFFS; ANILINE.

COASTAL PLAIN, any flat, low-lying geographical region situated next to the sea, but in the U.S. especially the coastal area of the U.S. Atlantic and Gulf coasts also called the Atlantic Coastal and Gulf Coastal plains.

The Atlantic Coastal Plain stretches from Maine to Florida in a strip of varying width, bounded on the east by the Atlantic Ocean and on the west by the Piedmont Plateau. The Gulf Coastal Plain is a continuation of the Atlantic plain and rims the Gulf of Mexico from Florida to Texas and Mexico, stretching also northward to include the lowlands of the Mississippi valley as far as St. Louis.

Geologically the coastal plain is of recent formation. It rose from the ocean and subsided several times during the Cenozoic era, finally emerging during the Quaternary period. The region is formed of sedimentary rocks and its emergence was so gentle that beds of Cretaceous, Tertiary, and Quaternary origin still lie horizontally in the position in which they were deposited. See UNITED STATES: *Physical Features.*

COAST AND GEODETIC SURVEY, bureau of the U.S. Department of Commerce, established in 1807 by President Thomas Jefferson under the terms of a Congressional enactment. Originally it was known as the "Survey of the Coast" and was under the jurisdiction of the Treasury Department. The present name of the bureau was adopted in 1878.

The functions of the bureau include surveying and chartering the coasts of the United States and dependencies; compilation and printing of aeronautical charts for civil aviation; tide and current surveys for making annual tide and current predictions; determination of geographic positions and elevations along the coasts and in the interior of the country in order to co-ordinate coastal surveys and to provide a framework for mapping and other engineering work; observations of the earth's magnetism for information essential to the mariner, aviator, land surveyor, radio engineer, and others; seismological investigations to obtain data for designing structures resistant to earthquakes; and gravity and astronomic observations to provide basic data for geodetic surveys and studies of the size and shape of the earth.

The principal publications of the bureau are nautical and aeronautical charts, Coast Pilots, tide and current tables, geodetic data, charts showing magnetic declination, annual lists of U.S. earthquakes, and manuals on appropriate subjects. Technical data from which these publications are compiled are obtained by a fleet of surveying ships supported by field parties engaged in geodetic, astronomic, gravity, tidal, magnetic, and seismological observations. Processing, application and dissemination of these data are carried on by an office force in Washington, D.C., and at 13 district offices located throughout the country.

COAST ARTILLERY CORPS, formerly a branch of the U.S. Army responsible for the development, maintenance, and operation of seacoast defenses. See ARTILLERY.

COAST DEFENSE, systematic protection of a country against attack at any point along its coast, involving all branches of the armed services. The term is used in the plural (*coast defenses*) to mean permanent installations which are prepared in time of peace for the protection of the principal harbors, waterways, and naval bases. Coast defenses include fortifications, controlled mine fields, and air bases along the coast and at offshore bases. In time of war such defenses are supplemented by air and naval patrols, additional mine fields, submarine and torpedo nets at principal harbors, and mobile military forces held in reserve at strategic points.

The armament of seacoast fortifications has of necessity kept pace with that of naval vessels. For example, in 1900 the heaviest coast-defense cannon used by the U.S. were the 10-inch gun, with a range of 7500 yards, and the 12-inch mortar, firing a 1000-lb. shell over shorter ranges. By World War II, these had been replaced by the 16-inch gun with a maximum range of almost 50,000 yards and the 16-inch howitzer, firing a shell weighing more than a ton. The disappearing carriage, protected only by a parapet, gave way to a development of the earlier barbette carriage, which permits greater elevation and range, and also permits protection of the installation by overhead cover against aircraft bombs and steeply falling shells of high-angle naval gunfire. During the same period air power became an important factor in coast defense. With the increased speed and range of modern airplanes, air bases located halfway across the country or far offshore on islands are within striking distance of any point on the coast, and are therefore an integral part of the coast-defense system. See ARTILLERY; FORTIFICATION AND SIEGECRAFT; MINE, SUBMARINE.

COAST GUARD ACADEMY, UNITED STATES. See UNITED STATES COAST GUARD ACADEMY.

COAST GUARD, UNITED STATES. See UNITED STATES COAST GUARD.

COAST RANGE, the mountain system which extends, with interruptions, along the Pacific coasts of the western United States and southwestern Canada. The Coast Range in Canada, north of the Strait of Juan de Fuca, consists of the mountains of Vancouver Island and the Island Range of British Columbia. These are continuations of the coastal uplifts extending from the United States, although in British Columbia the name "Coast Range" is given to the spurs of the Cascade Range. In the United States, the Coast Range begins near Santa Barbara, southern California, where it interlocks with the Sierra Nevada Range. Thence the line of elevation is continued in a general north-northwesterly direction to Cape Mendocino by two parallel ridges, about 400 m. long and from 30 to 60 m. apart. The ridge rising abruptly from the shore line is the Coast Range proper; that to the east is the Monte Diablo Range. Between the latter and the Sierra Nevada are long valleys, notably the San Joaquin. The east and west ranges below Santa Barbara, notably the Santa Inez, Santa Monica, San Bernardino, and San Jacinto, are sometimes called parts of the Coast Range, but are properly a continuation of the Sierra Nevada. At San Francisco Bay, about midway between Santa Barbara and Cape Mendocino, a great rift occurs, the ranges sloping down to the rocky hills through which this body of water has broken. There are no high peaks as far north as San Francisco Bay; the highest, near the bay, are Monte Diablo (about 3856 ft.), Mount Helena (about 4343 ft.), and Mount Hamilton (about 4400 ft.), on the last of which is situated the Lick Observatory. The peaks gradually rise in height north of San Francisco Bay, Mount Bailey, 150 miles north, being about 6357 ft. above sea level. The Coast and Sierra Nevada ranges interlock again near Mount Shasta. Farther north the Coast Range develops into isolated mountain groups, and near Oregon groups diverge to the east and connect with the Cascade Range. Farther north, the Coast Range in Oregon and Washington has less marked uplifts, the elevations averaging only from 1000 to 3000 feet. The Olympic Mountains, however, near the Strait of Juan de Fuca in Washington, include several peaks of considerable elevation, the highest being Mount Olympus, with an altitude of about 7923 feet.

The Coast Range is not a continuous mountain ridge, but a series of disconnected uplifts. Because of the extent of the range, or ranges, a wide variety of climate and vegetation is encountered. In Oregon and Washington there is heavy rainfall and the mountains are forested with fir, pine, and spruce. In California the climate is generally dry, with rainfall increasing north of San Francisco Bay; vegetation is generally sparse. Minerals mined include petroleum, quicksilver, coal, and bituminous shale.

COATBRIDGE, manufacturing town in Lanarkshire, Scotland, on the Monkland Canal, 8 miles E. of Glasgow. It lies in an important coal and iron-mining region, and is a center of Scotland's iron and steel industry. Pop. (1961 prelim.) 53,946.

COATES, ALBERT (1882–1953), British conductor and composer, born in St. Petersburg, Russia, the son of an English manufacturer. He was educated at Liverpool University, and he received his musical training at Leipzig Conservatory, where he was a pupil of Arthur Nikisch. In 1910 he was appointed chief conductor of the Imperial Opera House at St. Petersburg. After the Russian Revolution of 1917 he was placed in charge of all the opera houses of the Soviet Union. He had first appeared as a conductor in London in 1914; in 1919 he returned to take over the conductorship at Covent Garden. He made his American debut with the New York Symphony Orchestra in 1920 as guest conductor, and returned the following year. From 1923 to 1925 he was director of the Rochester Philharmonic Orchestra. In the following years he appeared as guest conductor at many concerts, including several at the Hollywood Bowl in California and at the Lewisohn Stadium in New York City. In 1943 he joined the music faculty of the University of Southern California. He was the composer of a number of operas, including *Samuel Pepys* (1929), *Pickwick* (1936), and *Gainsborough Duchess* (1941).

COATESVILLE, borough of Chester Co., Pa., on Brandywine Creek, 38 miles w. of Philadelphia. It is noted for its iron and steel industry. The Brandywine Iron Works was founded there in 1810. In 1825 this mill rolled the side plates and boiler iron for the first ironclad steam vessel, the *Codorus.* The modern Lukens Steel Mill, one of the largest plate-rolling mills in the world, is the successor of the historic Brandywine works. In Coatesville are also brass foundries, machine shops, silk mills, garment factories, and plants producing paper napkins. The region surrounding the city is noted for dairying and poultry raising. Coatesville was first settled about 1714. Pop. (1960) 12,971.

COATI, an animal of the genus *Nasua,* in the same family as the raccoon. Coatis are similar in size and appearance to raccoons, but have more slender bodies and longer tails. They have an elongated, flexible snout with which they grub in the earth for the insects and other small animals on which they feed; they also climb trees to obtain birds and eggs. Only two species are known: *N. narica,* of Mexico and Central America, with brown fur; and *N. rufa,* of South America, smaller, with red fur.

COAT OF MAIL, body armor composed of interlinked steel rings. These links averaged about three eighths of an inch in diameter, and there were two main styles. In the first, one end of the slender steel rod was flattened and pierced, the other brought to a point and turned up; the rod was then curved, the point thrust through the hole in the flat end and riveted; in the second form both ends of the rod were flattened and pierced, it was bent in a circle and the superimposed ends joined with a rivet. At the time of the Norman Conquest (11th cent.) coats of mail were loose, shirtlike garments extending from the neck to the knees, with sleeves to the elbows; the skirts were split front and back for ease in the saddle. In the days of Richard Cœur de Lion (late 12th cent.) the vogue of mail was at its height. The legs and feet were protected by mail leggings, apparently laced behind, and a coif or hood which was attached to the coat covered the head and protected the throat and the face as high as the lips. See ARMOR.

COAXIAL CABLE. See TELEPHONE: *Coaxial Cable.*

COBALT, a chemical element, symbol Co, at. no. 27; at. wt. 58.94; sp.gr. 8.9; m.p. 1480°C. (2696°F.); b.p. 2900°C. (5252°F.). This steel-gray metal was discovered by the Swedish chemist Georg Brandt in 1735. It takes a high polish; it is hard and brittle, but ductile at high temperatures.

Cobalt occurs as the arsenide, $CoAs_2$, known as smaltite or speiss cobalt; as cobalt sulpharsenide, CoAsS, known as cobalt glance or cobaltite (q.v.); and as a hydrated arsenate of cobalt, Co $(AsO_4)_2 \cdot 8H_2O$, known as cobalt bloom or erythrite. Its chief commercial sources are the silver ores of Ontario, which contain arsenides and sulfides of cobalt, and the manganese ores of New Caledonia, containing 2% cobalt oxide. Cobalt arsenide is obtained from the former ore by means of a blast furnace, and the arsenide is then transformed into the oxide, which is reduced by carbon to obtain the metal.

An alloy with steel known as "cobalt steel" is used for making permanent magnets. With tungsten carbide, cobalt forms "carboloy", a hard material used for cutting and machining steel; and alloyed with chromium, it produces "stellite", used for the same purpose.

There are several known isotopes of cobalt; the most important is the radioactive isotope (q.v.) Co-60, which has a half life (q.v.) of 5.7 years and yields intensive gamma radiation. It is widely used in industrial applications and in radioisotope therapy. See TRACERS.

COBALT, a mining town of Timiskaming Co., Ontario, Canada, situated on Cobalt Lake, 325 miles N. of Toronto. Silver deposits were discovered in the vicinity in the early 20th century, and by 1911 Cobalt had become world-famous, with 34 mines, the output of which in that year was 31,000,000 ounces. The ore beds proved shallow, however, and today silver-mining operations are greatly reduced. Cobalt, arsenic, and nickel are also mined in the vicinity of the town. Pop. (1961) 2209.

COBALTITE, a mineral cobalt sulfarsenide with isometric crystals resembling those of pyrite. It is silver white to red in color and has a metallic luster. The specific gravity of cobaltite is 6.3, and its hardness 5.5. Cobaltite occurs in association with nickel and other cobalt minerals and is mined as a cobalt ore. Large deposits are found in Sweden and in Ontario, Canada.

COBAN, capital of the department of Alta Verapaz, Guatemala. It is about 4300 ft. above sea level, and is situated 100 miles N. of Guatemala City, in the center of an important coffee-growing region. Cacao, sugar cane, and vanilla are also grown in the surrounding area. Pop. (1961 est.) 41,104.

COBB, IRVIN S(HREWSBURY) (1876–1944), American humorist and journalist, born at Paducah, Ky. As a youth he contributed to weekly magazines, and at the age of 19 became editor of the Paducah *Daily News*. His first assignment on the metropolitan press was as editor of the humorous section of the New York *Evening Sun* (1904–05); this was followed by a post on the staff of the New York *World*. From 1911 until 1922 he was on the staff of the *Saturday Evening Post*, serving as war correspondent during World War I. Later he joined the staff of *Cosmopolitan Magazine* (1922–32). He was also active as a writer for the screen and for radio, and was a prolific writer of fiction; his most popular character was the idealized Civil War veteran, the courtly and garrulous Judge Priest. Among Cobb's works are *Cobb's Anatomy* (1912), *The Escape of Mr. Trimm* (1913), *Old Judge Priest* (1915), *Speaking of Operations* (1916); *The Life of the Party* (1919), *Some United States* (1926), *This Man's World* (1929), and his autobiography, *Exit Laughing* (1941).

COBB, TY(RUS RAYMOND) (1886–1961), American professional baseball player, born at Narrows, Ga. He became a member of the Detroit club of the American League in 1905, and beginning the following year became one of the leading players of his time, breaking more records than any other player in baseball history. He played more than 3000 games in 24 years, and for the period 1907–19, except for one year (1916), he was the leading batter of the American League. He held the record for most times at bat, for runs scored, and for hits. His 1911 batting average of .420 was only equaled once (George Sisler, 1920) and never surpassed in the American League; his overall average for 24 years was .367. From 1920 to 1926 he managed the Detroit club. In 1927 and 1928 he played with the Philadelphia club of the American League, and then retired. At the first election, in 1936, of "immortals" to the Baseball Hall of Fame, Ty Cobb was the leading candidate. His autobiography *My Life in Baseball* (with Al Stump, 1961) was published posthumously.

COBBETT, WILLIAM (1763–1835), English political writer, born in Farnham, Surrey. He wrote under the pseudonym Peter Porcupine. He enlisted in the British army and during his term of service (1783–91) taught himself grammar, geometry, French, and other subjects. In 1792, to escape prosecution for his pamphlet on abuses in the army, he fled England and took up residence in Philadelphia, Pa. Here, in his newspaper, *Porcu-*

pine's Gazette, and in many pamphlets, he violently attacked the French Revolution and American democracy. He returned to England in 1800, and in 1802 he became editor of the Tory weekly journal *Political Register*. Two years later he changed his political principles and turned the journal into an advocate of radical social and parliamentary reform. From 1804 to 1817 he fought for the cause of various oppressed classes of British society. Laws passed to suppress radicalism caused him to go to America again in 1817, where he spent two years as a farmer. After his return to England in 1819, he played a leading part in the agitation for parliamentary reform which culminated in passage of the reform bill of 1832. He was a member of the first Parliament elected under the reform law.

Cobbett was noted for the sarcasm, wit, and violence of his polemic style. He was the author of nearly 50 prose works, the most important of which are *Porcupine's Works* (12 vols, 1801), *Grammar of the English Language* (1818), *History of the Reformation* (1824–27), *Rural Rides* (1830), *The English Gardener* (1829), and *Advice to Young Men* (1830).

COBDEN, RICHARD (1805–65), English economist and statesman, known as "The Apostle of Free Trade". He was born at Heyschott, in Sussex, and at the age of 15 became a clerk in a warehouse in London owned by his uncle, a calico merchant. Soon he was permitted to sell calico on the road, and in 1828, together with some friends, established an independent calico business which brought him both fortune and leisure. By 1835 he was in a position to satisfy his curiosity about foreign lands, and he traveled for three years, returning with a stock of information and much of the philosophy of free trade which characterized his thinking; this was first apparent in two pamphlets he wrote at the time, *England, Ireland, and America* (1835) and *Russia* (1836).

The first result of his teachings was the formation in 1838 of a group of seven merchants of Manchester, including Cobden, around which the Anti-Corn-Law League developed. Cobden, his constant associate John Bright (q.v.), and others in the League incessantly agitated for repeal of the duties on corn (i.e., wheat) imports as part of a campaign to decrease the cost of living (see CORN LAWS). When the repeal was carried in 1846, the major opponent to the League, Sir Robert Peel, paid tribute to Cobden as the prime force behind the victory; but the long struggle had so impoverished the leader of the League that a popular subscription was taken to restore his credit.

By 1846 Cobden had already been a member of Parliament for five years, and had indicated his position on matters other than the Corn Laws. He favored a minimum interference of government in business, opposing factory reforms and trade unions; he also opposed intervention of government in the affairs of foreign nations. Cobden's opposition to England's foreign policy was unpopular and temporarily cost him his seat in Parliament. Yet he was so respected by his opponents that one of them, Lord Palmerston, offered Cobden the post of president of the board of trade in his cabinet in 1859. Cobden's principles did not permit his acceptance, but the following year he represented England in negotiations for a commercial treaty with France promoting the free trade which he espoused. His last important political activity was in support of the North in the American Civil War, at a time when British leaders were confused and hesitant.

Cobden has been considered a typical representative of the so-called Manchester School of economics. He practiced, regardless of his own convenience or interest, the principles of *laissez-faire* which characterized that school.

COBEGO, COLUGO, or KAGUAN, a mammal of the genus *Galeopithecus.* This genus is considered to comprise an entire order of mammals, the Dermoptera, most nearly related to the Insectivora. The cobegos are sometimes incorrectly called flying lemurs. Two species are known, one living in the East Indies, and the other in the Philippine Islands. The former is smaller, but has longer ears and a larger skull.

They are slender, long-limbed, large-clawed, long-tailed, fox-headed animals, about 18 inches in length, clothed in soft, short, and protectively mottled fur, and provided with a folded extension of the skin which extends from the neck nearly to the tip of the tail and includes the feet, which are fully webbed. This parachutelike wing equals in extent that of a bat of similar size, but it is furry both above and below. In flight the cobego does not equal bats, but it can sail longer distances, and come nearer to guiding its course, than do any other "flying" mammals. It is wholly arboreal in its life; on a flat surface it flops awkwardly toward the nearest tree, the mode of progression resembling that of a seal. It becomes active mainly at twilight and in early morning. The cobego spends most of its time hanging from branches or sailing from one

tree to another, and feeds upon vegetables, leaves, and fruit.

COBHAM, LORD. See OLDCASTLE.

COBLENZ. See KOBLENZ.

COBOURG, county seat and port of entry of Northumberland Co., Ontario, Canada, on Lake Ontario, about 70 m. by rail N.E. of the city of Toronto. It possesses a good harbor, and has steamboat connections with Lake Ontario and St. Lawrence River ports. Cobourg is noted as a summer resort. Until 1890 the town was the site of Victoria University, now in Toronto. Industrial establishments in Cobourg include woolen mills, a carpet factory, a brass foundry, and chemical plants. Pop. (1961) 10,646.

COBRA, any of a number of species of snakes of the family Elapidae belonging to the genera *Naja, Ophiophagus,* and *Hemachatus.* The cobras, which are among the deadliest of the world's snakes, are characterized by an ability to extend the ribs immediately behind their heads to form a flaring hood. The snake spreads this hood when it is angry or disturbed. The range of the genus *Naja* extends from the Philippine Islands through s. Asia to Africa. The genus *Hemachatus* is confined to a single species native to s. Africa.

The most remarkable of the cobras is the king cobra, *Ophiophagus hannah,* the longest poisonous snake in existence, and regarded as the most dangerous. It averages 12 ft. in length, but it is known to grow to 18 ft. It is a thin snake, olive or brown in color, with bronze eyes having a large, glittering, round pupil. The king cobra is easily provoked to attack, and is particularly deadly because of the large quantity of highly toxic venom secreted in its poison glands; its bite can kill an elephant. It is found in the Philippines and other islands of Malaysia, s. China, Burma, and the Malay Peninsula.

The other cobra of Asia, *N. naja,* is known variously as the common, Asiatic, Indian, or spectacled cobra, or the cobra de capello (Portuguese, *capello,* "hood"). It is smaller than the king cobra, seldom reaching a length of more than 6 ft. The hood of the Asiatic cobra is proportionately much larger than that of the king cobra, and is marked in most varieties by a spectacle-shaped black-and-white pattern on the top of the hood and two black and white spots on the lower surface. The ground color of the snake is yellow to brown. This cobra is responsible for many deaths each year in India, where it is regarded with religious awe and seldom killed. According to Buddhist mythology, the cobra spread its hood over Buddha when he was asleep, and he, in gratitude, took the serpent under his protection and gave it the spectacle-mark so that it could be recognized and avoided by birds of prey. The range of the Asiatic cobra extends from the eastern shore of the Caspian Sea to China and the Malay Archipelago.

Though cobras are often regarded as Asiatic serpents, most of the species are natives of Africa. Among them is the spitting cobra, *N. nigricollis,* found from s. Egypt to the Transvaal. Different varieties of the species range in color from dull black to pink, with the lighter-colored types marked by a black band about the neck. The spitting cobra is capable of ejecting its venom from a distance of about 8 ft. into the eyes of its victims. The venom then causes temporary blindness and great pain. The ringhals, *Hemachatus haemachatus,* is also a spitting cobra. It is a dark brown or black snake with keeled scales and light rings on the neck. The ringhals is the smallest of the cobras, reaching only about 4 ft. in length. The Egyptian cobra or asp, *N. haje,* is a 4- to 6-foot snake found along the north coast of Africa.

The venom of cobras is a neurotoxin, acting powerfully on the nervous system. The high mortality from the bites of cobras in Asia has been much decreased, in some areas, by the availability of effective serum. The Haffkine Institute in Bombay and the Pasteur Institute in Bangkok produce such antivenins in quantity.

COBURG, town of Bavaria, West Germany, on the Itz River, about 30 miles N.E. of Bamberg. Located on the trade route that ran from Nuremberg northward, Coburg was an important trading center in the 15th and 16th centuries. The medieval castle of the town, containing the room occupied by Martin Luther when he was in concealment there in 1530, was restored in 1835–38 and became the residence of the dukes of Saxe-Coburg. The castle today is a museum of natural history. The principal industries of the town are the brewing of beer and the manufacturing of furniture, glass, machinery, baskets, and woolen and linen goods. Coburg also has iron foundries and sawmills. Pop. (1960 est.) 44,000.

COCA, a shrub, *Erythroxylon coca,* in the Geranium order, the leaves of which are much used by the inhabitants of Peru and Bolivia as a narcotic and stimulant. The dried leaves, which contain cocaine (q.v.) and several of its derivatives, are mixed with unslaked lime or wood ash and chewed. The properties of coca are similar to those of opium, but it is not so strong a narcotic. The shrub is cultivated in Ceylon, India, and Java, as well as in South America. It is 3 to 6 ft. high, with rusty branches, and leaves that resemble tea leaves.

COCAINE, a bitter, colorless, crystalline alkaloid, $C_{17}H_{21}O_4N$, obtained from the leaves of the coca (q.v.) plant. It can also be prepared synthetically. It was first isolated in 1855, recognized as an anesthetic in 1860, suggested for clinical use in 1879, and used as a mydriatic and local anesthetic in operations on the eye in 1884. For the next half century it was extensively used as a local anesthetic in dentistry and surgery, but since that time it has been largely replaced by newer, synthetic anesthetics.

Cocaine is a solid, melting at 98° C. (208° F.). It is slightly soluble in cold water, more soluble in hot water, and readily soluble in organic solvents. Its salts, particularly cocaine hydrochloride, are readily soluble in water, and cocaine is generally used in medicine in the form of a solution of this salt. Such solutions, however, are unstable and subject to spoilage.

The principal physiological effects of cocaine are paralysis of the sensory nerve endings and nerve trunks (resulting in anesthesia), stimulation of the sympathetic nervous system (resulting in constriction of the blood vessels and dilatation of the pupil), and stimulation of the central nervous system (resulting in exhilaration and possibly in convulsions, followed by mental and physical depression, particularly of respiration). Sleep-producing drugs, particularly barbiturates, are good antidotes against the stimulant effects of cocaine.

Cocaine is toxic, habit forming, and a narcotic. Traffic in cocaine is strictly regulated by State laws, and by a Federal law, the Harrison Act of 1915, which requires accurate accounting of its handling and disposition. Newer anesthetics, such as novocaine, which is about one fifth as toxic, are not so regulated. See ALKALOIDS; ANESTHESIA; DRUG ADDICTION; NARCOTICS.

COCANADA, officially **KAKINADA,** city and seaport of Andhra Pradesh, Republic of India, situated on the Bay of Bengal and on the Godavari R. delta, about 315 miles N.E. of the city of Madras. Navigable channels connect Cocanada with the Godavari delta canal system. In the city are rice and cottonseed-oil mills, salt works, and tobacco factories. Cotton, rice, and oilseeds are the principal exports. Pop. (1961) 122,865.

COCCIDAE, a large family of bugs, of the order Homoptera, which includes the scale insects and mealy bugs (qq.v.). Commercially the Coccidae are important for the waxes and other products made from their secretions. See LAC; MANNA; COCHINEAL.

COCCIDIA, an order of minute, egg-shaped protozoa in the class Sporozoa, which are parasitic in the liver and intestines of various fishes, birds, and mammals, including man. Species of the type genus *Eimeria* (formerly *Coccidium*) cause white diarrhea of chickens, which is responsible for the loss of almost half of the artificially-hatched and brooded chicks in the U.S.

COCCYX. See SPINAL COLUMN.

COCHABAMBA, capital of the department of the same name, in Bolivia, on the Rocha R., about 8400 ft. above sea level, at the foot of Mt. Tunari, and 127 m. by rail E.N.E. of Oruro. It is laid out with wide and regular streets and contains several large structures, notably the theater, the government building, and the hospitals of Viedma and San Salvador. Cochabamba has a university, two colleges, and several secondary schools. The city manufactures cotton and woolen goods, leather, soap, and earthenware, and also carries on considerable trade, especially in grain and Peruvian bark. Cochabamba was founded in 1563 as Oropeza. In 1847 it was created an episcopal see. Pop. (1961 est.) 91,017.

COCHIN, a breed of large domestic fowl of the Asiatic type, particularly valued for meat. They may be white, black, buff, or variegated in color; and have feathered legs which are yellow except in the black varieties, and single combs.

COCHIN, town and seaport of Kerala State, Republic of India, on the Arabian Sea, about 95 miles S.S.E. of Calicut, Kerala. It lies at the N. end of a narrow neck of land, about 12 m. long and less than 1 m. wide in many places, and separated from the mainland by inlets from the sea and by the estuaries of rivers draining from the Western Ghats. During the rainy season these backwaters are navigable, but in the dry season some are less than 2 ft. deep. As a result the harbor is barely operative during the months from May to August. At all times large vessels must anchor at sea, 2½ m. offshore. Cochin, the most important port on the Malabar coast, is the center of coconut-oil production in the state, and products made of coconuts are the chief items in the city's export trade, which includes also groundnuts and tea. Rice is imported. The industry of Cochin includes shipbuilding, sawmilling, fishing, and the manufacture of coir mats.

In 1500 the Portuguese became the first European possessors of Cochin when they seized the town. Two years later the explorer Vasco da Gama erected a factory there, and the first European fort in India was constructed in Cochin in 1503. In 1577 Jesuits published at Cochin the first book printed in India in native characters. The British settled in the town in 1634, but were driven out by the Dutch, who captured Cochin in 1663 and subsequently developed it as an important center of trade. During their conquest of India the British seized the town in 1795 but allowed the Dutch to administer it until 1814 when it became a possession of the East India Co. In 1936 Cochin was placed under the direct administration of the British government in India and given the status of a major port. Following the lapse of British paramountcy in India in 1947, Cochin was included in the Dominion of India. Pop. (1961) 35,076.

COCHIN CHINA, properly SOUTH VIET-NAM, formerly one of the states of the Associated States of Indochina, in s. Indochina, adjoining the South China Sea and the Gulf of Siam, and bordering Central Viet-Nam and Cambodia. The largest cities in the region are Cholon and the former capital, Saigon (qq.v.). Other towns include Cantho, Baclieu, and Rachgia. Saigon, about 30 miles from the China Sea, on the Saigon R., is the only large seaport, and was the chief export center for Cochin China, Cambodia, and Laos. A number of coastal towns, including Rachgia and Hatien, on the Gulf of Siam, have roadsteads.

Except for some moderate elevations in the north, the region is a low alluvial plain, extremely fertile and well watered by a number of rivers, the principal one being the Mekong, which traverses the entire region from Cambodia in a generally southeasterly direction. A large number of natural and man-made canals, called arroyos, link the river deltas, aiding in communications and in the distribution of the rich floodwaters (June to October) of the Mekong R.

The economy of the region is based on the cultivation of rice; the region is one of the greatest rice-producing and rice-exporting areas of the world. In 1952 production amounted to over 1.87 million tons; before World War II it was over 3 million tons. Other crops include sugar cane, coffee, tobacco, coconuts, betel nuts, pineapples, bananas, oranges, pepper, sweet potatoes, beans, groundnuts, corn, cotton, and rubber. Pigs, buffaloes, cattle, horses, sheep, and goats are raised, and the inland and ocean fisheries are important. Manufacturing industries are rice milling, lumbering, sawmilling, and the manufacture of soap, preserved fruits and fruit juices, automobile tires and other rubber products, and cigarettes. The chief articles of export are rice, corn, pepper, copra, fish, and rubber. Machinery, textiles, and tea are among the principal imports. Wholesale and foreign trade are largely handled by Europeans and Chinese. Finance is dominated by French interests through control of the Franco-Chinese Bank and the Indochina Bank, both situated in Saigon. An overwhelming majority of the population (1951) is Annamese, with about 678,000 Chinese and about 19,000 European civilians, chiefly French.

Cochin China before the second half of the 19th century constituted a part of China, Cambodia, and Annam successively. In 1861 the French took Saigon, and in 1862 the country was ceded to the French by the king of Annam. It became a French colony in 1867, although resistance to French rule continued until 1869. In 1887 Cochin China was included in French Indochina. During World War II the country was occupied by the Japanese. In June, 1946, Cochin China was made an autonomous republic in the newly created Federation of Indochina. A specially elected Territorial Assembly of Cochin China voted (April 23, 1949) for union with Viet-Nam (q.v.). Area of former state, about 26,476 sq.m.; pop., about 6,000,000.

COCHINEAL, a red dyestuff made from the dried female cochineal insect, *Dactylopius coccus,* a scale bug of Mexico and Central America. The insects feed on cactus, especially on *Opuntia* (or *Nopalea*) *coccinellifera,* which was at one time extensively cultivated for their sustenance. The bodies of the females swell after mating, and it is at this time that they are collected. If they are killed by dry heat, their white powdery coating is retained, and the product is "silver-gray cochineal"; if by hot water or steam, the powder is lost, and "black cochineal" is produced.

Inasmuch as a laborer can collect in one day about 10,000 insects, enough for only two ounces of cochineal, it has always been expensive, and was one of the first natural dyes to be largely replaced by cheaper synthetic dyes. A red pigment prepared from cochineal is called carmine (q.v.).

COCHLEA. See Ear.

COCHRAN, Charles Blake (1872–1951), English theatrical producer, born in Lindfield, Sussex, and educated at Oxford University. He began his career in the theater as an actor in New York City in 1892, and produced his first play, Henrik Ibsen's *John Gabriel Borkman,* in New York City in 1897.

Later, Cochran secured control over a number of leading London theaters, introducing such important continental stars as the Guitrys and Eleonora Duse to the London stage. He produced such hits as *The Better 'Ole* (800 performances, 1917–18), *Chauve Souris* (1921), *Anna Christie* (1923), *Porgy* (1929), and *Conversation Piece* (1934), and a series of revues known as *Cochran's Revues*. He was general manager of Royal Albert Hall from 1926 to 1938, and in 1934 he became governor of the Shakespeare Memorial Theatre at Stratford. His writings include *Secrets of a Showman* (1925) and *Showman Looks On* (1945).

COCHRAN, Jacqueline (1912?–), American aviatrix and business executive, born in Pensacola, Fla. At the age of fourteen she left home and found work in a beauty shop, and by 1935 she was the owner of her own cosmetics firm. In 1936 she married the American financier Floyd Bostwick Odlum (1892–), through whom she had become interested in aviation. She received her pilot's license in 1932. Two years later she entered her first major flying competition, the London-Melbourne air race, and in 1935 she became the first woman to enter the Bendix Trophy transcontinental race; she won the Bendix Trophy in 1938. During World War II she ferried bombers to Great Britain and headed the U.S. Army Air Forces training program for civilian women pilots. In 1945 she became the first civilian woman to receive the Distinguished Service Medal. Her national and international flying awards and trophies number more than two hundred. She won the Clifford Burke Harmon Trophy of the International League of Aviators on seven occasions, most recently in 1962. She was the first woman to break the sound barrier. After setting a number of records in jet planes, in 1961 she established a new women's speed record of 842.6 m.p.h. She wrote *The Stars at Noon* (autobiography, 1954).

COCHRANE, Thomas, 10th Earl of Dundonald (1775–1860), British naval officer, born at Annsfield, in Lanarkshire, Scotland. As son of the Earl of Dundonald he was known as Lord Cochrane until he succeeded to his father's title in 1831. His uncle was Sir Alexander Cochrane (1758–1832), a captain in the British Navy who was later to become British naval commander in North American waters during the War of 1812. Lord Cochrane was assigned to his uncle's ship in 1792 and was soon promoted. He distinguished himself by the capture of Spanish frigates in the Mediterranean Sea, and after the outbreak of the Napoleonic Wars was placed in command of a ship (1804). In 1807 he was elected to Parliament, where his attacks on the conduct of his superior officers made him unpopular with naval authorities. Upon the exposure of stock-market manipulations in which Cochrane appeared to be involved, he was found guilty of fraud, expelled from Parliament, and dismissed from the navy (1814).

In 1817 he entered the service of Chile, at that time engaged in a war of independence against Spain. Cochrane organized the Chilean navy and remained in command until 1822, when he took command of the Brazilian navy, remaining in that service for three years. After a brief period in command of the Greek navy, he returned to England in 1828. In 1832, after Cochrane had become Earl of Dundonald, King William IV pardoned him and gave him the rank of rear admiral in the British navy; in 1848 he was placed in command of the fleet in North Atlantic waters. He was the author of *Narrative of Services in the Liberation of Chile, Peru and Brazil* (1858) and *Autobiography of a Seaman* (posthumously published, 1860–61).

COCKATOO, common name for several genera of birds belonging to the family Psittacidae, which includes also the parrot (q.v.). Characteristics are a tuft on the head; a strong, high beak with a notch behind the point; frequently bright colors of the plumage; long wings; and loquacious habits. The cockatoos inhabit Australia, Tasmania, New Guinea, and the Malay Archipelago.

COCKCROFT, Sir John Douglas (1897–), English physicist, born in Todmorden, and educated at the University of Manchester and at St. John's College, Cambridge University. A fellow at St. John's College from 1928 to 1946, Cockcroft was Jacksonian professor of natural philosophy at Cambridge University from 1939 to 1946. From 1941 to 1944 he was chief superintendent of the British Air Defense Research and Development Establishment, and from 1944 to 1946 he served as director of the atomic energy division of the Canadian National Research Council. He was director of the British Atomic Energy Research Establishment at Harwell (1946-58) and chairman of the Defense Research Policy Committee (1952-54). In 1960 he became master of Churchill College, Cambridge, and in 1961 chancellor of Australian National University. Cockcroft is best known for a nuclear experiment, conducted (1932) in collaboration with the British physicist E. T. S. Walton, in which

H. Armstrong Roberts
Cocker spaniel

transmutation of elements was accomplished for the first time by means of artificially accelerated particles; see Atomic Energy. He was knighted in 1948, and with Walton shared the 1951 Nobel Prize in physics. Cockcroft received also the Niels Bohr Medal (1958) and the Atoms for Peace Award (1961).

COCKER SPANIEL, smallest breed of the sporting spaniel (q.v.), weighing between 22 and 28 pounds. It has a rounded skull; eyes generally either hazel or dark-brown in color; long, wide ears covered with long silky hair; straight forelegs and strong, muscular hindlegs; and a short tail. The dog has a soft, dense coat of flat or slightly waved hair, and in color is either a solid black, red, buff, cream, or liver, or a combination of black and white, black and tan, black, tan, and white, or of other colors. The dog is an excellent retriever; in recent times in the United States it has become one of the most popular of pets.

COCKFIGHTING, the sport of placing gamecocks in a pit or on a stage to fight one another. The handlers of the cocks place them beak to beak and then release them, whereupon the animals fight until one is killed, or can fight no longer, or refuses to fight. Often the cocks are equipped with spurs of silver or steel. Three types of cockfights are popular: the *single battle,* in which two cocks fight; the *main,* in which cocks are paired in an elimination tournament; and the *battle royal,* in which a number of cocks fight one another simultaneously until only one is left. Betting on the outcome of fights is usual among spectators, owners, and handlers of the cocks.

Cockfighting was practiced extensively in ancient Persia, Greece, and Rome. It was a popular sport in England for about 600 years, until prohibited by act of Parliament in 1849. It is prohibited in practically all of the United States either by State or local law. Cockfighting is still widely prevalent today in India, the Malay peninsula and archipelago, and in many Latin-American countries.

COCKLE, any bivalve (q.v.) mollusk of the genus *Cardium,* especially the common cockle, *C. edule.* Cockles have heart-shaped shells with prominent ribs, and muscular, pointed feet. About 200 species are known, most of them native to the tropics. The common cockle grows in the waters off England and is regarded as a delicacy.

COCKLEBUR or **CLOTBUR,** common name for plants of the genus *Xanthium* in the family Carduaceae. They are coarse, rough, or spiny annual herbs with heart-shaped leaves, spotted stems, and small heads of greenish flowers. The fruit is a bur with hooked bristles by which it clings to animals, thereby disseminating the seeds contained within the burs. These plants are widely distributed, growing chiefly on waste land. The burs are injurious to the wool of sheep, and efforts are made to exterminate the plants from grazing land.

The name cocklebur is also applied to the burdock (q.v.), another plant which injures the wool of sheep.

COCK OF THE ROCK, a tropical South American bird, *Rupicola rupicola,* of the family Cotingidae. The male is about the size of a pigeon; it has showy orange plumage, a large disklike crest, and a short, straight tail. The female is a dull, olive brown and uncrested. In the mating season the males gather in open spaces and court the females by engaging in a community dance, each displaying its showy plumage. Because of their attractive feathers, which are used for millinery and for making a variety of decorations, the birds have been hunted so extensively that they are becoming rare.

COCKROACH, or ROACH, any insect of the order Blattariae. Many cockroaches are household pests, particularly those of the families Blattidae and Pseudomopidae. The roaches were among the earliest winged insects to develop, judging from their fossil remains. They are nocturnal in habit and a majority of the 1,200 species known have an unpleasant odor.

The cockroaches are stout-bodied insects with long antennae, and are usually dark brown or black, though some tropical species are gaily colored. In some species the wings of the females are only rudimentary. Cockroaches are found throughout the world, but only four species are common in houses in the U.S. The Croton bug, *Blatella germanica,* is a brown or yellowish insect with wings that when folded extend beyond the abdomen. The species was named because it was observed in large numbers in New York City following the opening of the Croton aqueduct. The black beetle, *Blatta orientalis,* has a shiny, black body and wings shorter than the abdomen. The names bug and beetle for these insects are common but incorrect. The common American cockroach, *Periplaneta americana,* is long-winged, dark in color, and larger than the black beetle. The Australian cockroach, *P. australiae,* is marked by yellow stripes on the inner portion of its front wings. This insect is found in the southern States. A number of other cockroaches which live under the bark of trees occur in the U.S.; however, they are rarely seen.

Cockroaches are commonly supposed to live only in dirty surroundings, but this is not the case. The insects consume all types of human food as well as a variety of animal and vegetable substances, even including leather, paper, and bone. Hence once they are established in a house, it is impossible to starve them out or get rid of them by cleaning. They can be exterminated only by the use of poison.

COCOA, common name for a powder manufactured from the seeds of the cacao (q.v.), and for the beverage prepared by mixing the powder with milk. Cocoa differs from chocolate (q.v.) in having a substantial part of the natural fat of cacao, cocoa butter, expressed in the process of manufacture. After the fat is expressed and the cake ground, small percentages of various substances may be added, such as starch to prevent caking, or potassium bicarbonate to neutralize the natural acids and astringents and make the cocoa easy to disperse in liquids. Cocoa has a high food value, containing as much as 20% protein, 40% carbohydrate, and 28% fat. It is also mildly stimulating, because of the presence of theobromine, an alkaloid closely related to the caffeine of tea and of coffee. The terms cocoa and cacao should not be confused with coco or with coca, which are two unrelated plants.

COCOA BUTTER, a yellowish-white fat obtained from the seeds of the cacao tree in the process of making cocoa (q.v.). This fat is hard and brittle when cold, but melts at a temperature slightly below that of the human body. Cocoa butter is used in the manufacture of chocolate candy, cosmetics, salves, soap, and suppositories.

COCOANUT. See COCONUT.

COCOA PLUM. See COCO PLUM.

COCONUT, or COCOANUT, the fruit of a palm, *Cocis nucifera,* widely distributed throughout the tropical regions of the world. The coconut palm has a cylindrical stem, about 1½ ft. in diameter, and from 60 to 90 ft. high, with many rings marking the places of former leaves. At its summit it bears a crown of about twenty pinnate leaves, which generally curve downward, each from 10 to 15 ft. in length. The short racemes bear from five to fifteen or more nuts; and ten or twelve of these racemes, in different stages, may be seen at once on a tree, about eighty or one hundred nuts being its ordinary annual yield, although the best trees are said to produce two hundred. The tree bears fruit seven to eight years after the time of planting, and continues productive for seventy or eighty years, the fruit being gathered four or five times annually. This fruit provides the inhabitants of many tropical coasts and islands with a great part of their food; it is not only eaten straight from the tree, both ripe and unripe, since it is filled when immature with a pleasant milky fluid, but is also prepared in a variety of ways.

The kernel of the coconut contains more than 60 percent of a fixed oil called coconut oil, or coconut butter. The oil is an important article of commerce, being much employed for the manufacture of soaps and candles.

The root of the coconut palm possesses narcotic properties, and is sometimes chewed instead of the betel nut. The terminal bud, palm cabbage, is considered a delicacy, and trees are often cut down for the sake of it; the central part of the young stem is also succulent and edible. Its saccharine sap, toddy, like that of some other palms, is a favorite beverage in tropical countries, either in its natural state in which it is obtained from the tree, or after fermentation, which takes place in a few hours; and from the fermented sap, palm wine, a spirituous liquor, arrack, is obtained by distillation.

The dried leaves of the coconut palm are used extensively for thatch, and for many other purposes, such as the making of mats, screens, and baskets, by plaiting the leaflets. By far the most important fibrous product of the coconut tree is coir, the fiber of the husk of the unripe nut. Uses are found for the wood and fiber of the stem, the husk and shell of the nut, and the dried kernels, known as copra (q.v.).

COCONUT CRAB, PURSE CRAB, or **ROBBER CRAB,** a large tropical land crab, *Birgus latro,* found on the islands of the South Pacific and Indian oceans. It is related to the hermit crab, but has a symmetrical abdomen covered with horny plates and so requires no borrowed shell or other artificial protection. A powerful pair of pincer claws enable the crab to break open the coconuts on which it feeds. These crabs weigh as much as 20 lbs. They climb coconut palms and are reputed to pick coconuts from the trees.

COCOON, a protective covering for the eggs of some invertebrates or for insects, usually in a pupal stage. Insect cocoons are largely formed of silk. An egg cocoon is spun by the egg-laying insect, and pupal cocoons by the larva. See INSECT: *Metamorphosis.*

COCO PLUM, COCOA PLUM, or ICACO PLUM, common name for the edible fruit of a small tree or shrub, *Chrysobalanus icaco,* in the Rose family, and for the plant itself. The plant is native to tropical America and Africa; it grows to a small tree in the warmer parts of its range, and remains a shrub in the more temperate portions as, for example, in Florida. The plumlike fruit has purplish skin and white flesh.

COCOS ISLANDS, or KEELING ISLANDS, TERRITORY OF, group of twenty-seven privately owned, small coral islands in the Indian Ocean, controlled by Australia, and situated about 580 miles s.w. of Java and 1720 miles N. of Perth. Copra is the chief product. The islands are noted as the site of studies in natural history made by Charles Darwin in 1836. They were discovered by Captain William Keeling in 1609; were annexed by Great Britain in 1857; were included in the jurisdiction of the governor of Ceylon in 1878, and in the jurisdiction of the governor of the Straits Settlements in 1886; and were incorporated into the Settlement of Singapore in 1903. The islands were placed under Australian control in 1955. Area, about 5 sq.m.; pop. (1960 est.) 607.

COCTEAU, JEAN (1891–), French poet, playwright, and novelist, born at Maisons-Lafitte. Cocteau was an important French writer of the first half of the 20th century. He sponsored new movements in painting, literature, music, the theater, and the ballet; and much of his writing was experimental. He wrote poetry, novels, plays, miscellaneous works, and stories for motion pictures and ballets. In 1955 Cocteau became a member of the French Academy. Among his works are the miscellany of cartoons, prose, and verse *Le Potomak* (1919); the ballets *Le Bœuf sur le Toit* (1920) and *Les Mariés de la Tour Eiffel* (1921); the book of poems *Poésie 1916–*

23 (1924); the novel *Les Enfants Terribles*
(1929; Eng. trans., *Enfants Terribles*, 1930);
the plays *La Machine Infernale* (1934; Eng.
trans., *The Infernal Machine*, 1936), *La Machine à Écrire* (1941; Eng. trans., *The Type-
writer*, 1948), and *L'Aigle a Deux Têtes*
(1946; Eng. trans., *The Eagle Has Two
Heads*, 1948); and the motion pictures *Le
Sang d'un Poète* (1933), *Eternel Retour*
(1944), *La Bête et la Belle* (1946), and *Le
Testament d'Orphée* (1960), of which he also
directed all but the second; and the film
version of *Les Enfants Terribles* (1952). His
theories on motion pictures were published
under the title *On the Film* (1954). *Journals,*
a compendium of excerpts from his writings,
was published in 1956.

COD, any of the bony fish included in the
family Gadidae, but particularly *Gadus mor-
rhua,* the common cod. The cod has a moderately elongated body with three dorsal and
two anal fins, and a single barbel under the
chin. Cod may reach a weight of 150 lbs. or
more, but the average large specimen weighs
between 15 and 30 lbs. The fish live in N.
Atlantic waters between the latitudes of 50°
and 75°, near the bottom at depths between
10 and 120 fathoms. The Alaska cod, *G.
macrocephalus,* is found in the Pacific.

Cod are among the most important food
fishes in the world. They are caught in large
numbers on the Newfoundland Banks and off
the coasts of New England, Iceland, Scotland,
and Scandinavia. The usual method of fishing
is with many-hooked hand lines or trawls.
The flesh is often frozen, or dried and salted,
the livers are used for the production of cod-
liver oil (q.v.), and the fishes' air bladders
are a source of isinglass. About 25,000 tons of
cod are landed annually by fishermen at U.S.
Atlantic ports, almost all in Massachusetts.

CODA (It., "tail"), the concluding passage
of a musical composition, or of a movement
in a composition. Originally a single phrase
for ending a canon, it was used by the classical masters for securing an effective close.
Beethoven was the first to recognize the unlimited possibilities of the coda for the purpose of building up tremendous climaxes,
thus raising it to the place of an essential
factor in his architectonic scheme, a place
which it has subsequently maintained in the
works of later masters.

CODE, in jurisprudence, a systematic compilation of law in written form, issued by
rulers in former times, and promulgated by
legislative authority after the rise of representative governments. Early legal codes were
little more than statements of the body of cus-

toms which had obtained the force of law in
civilized communities. The earliest legal code
known in its entirety is the Babylonian cuneiform Code of Hammurabi (see HAMMURABI),
of about 2100 B.C.; it was discovered in
1901. Four fragments of an earlier Babylonian cuneiform code, known as the Code of
Lipit-Ishtar, were discovered about 1900 and
were deciphered in 1948.

Included by some legal historians among
the early codes are the Book of the Covenant
and the Book of the Law of the Old Testament. The ancient Greek city-states began codifying laws in the 7th century B.C. Of
Greek codes, that known as the Laws of
Gortyn, after the Greek lawgiver of that name,
is regarded as the closest to a systematic statement of ancient Hellenic law. The Twelve
Tables (q.v.) of ancient Roman law are often
cited as a classic example of an early code.
Other compilations of customary law include
the Hindu Code of Manu, believed to date
from about 400 A.D., and the code of the Chinese T'ang dynasty, issued in 630 A.D.

Of all the codes of antiquity, that of the
Roman Emperor Justinian I, known as the
Codex Justinianus, Justinian Code, or merely
The Code, is the one bearing the closest
resemblance to the codes of later times. It
was in part a compilation and consolidation
of statute law, but lacked the systematic arrangement and the concentration on a single
branch of the law, such as criminal or civil
law, which are essential features of later codes.
The influence of the Justinian Code was great.
Long after Rome fell, Roman law, as codified
by Justinian, continued to serve as a source
of law in Europe, in the form of Civil Law
(q.v.). Through a 13th-century Spanish code,
called Siete Partidas ("seven parts") and based
partly on the Justinian Code, the Corpus
Juris Civilis was later extended to the New
World, and, with the Siete Partidas, became
the basis for the legal systems of the greater
part of Latin America.

Modern codes are, in general, designed to
provide a comprehensive statement of the
laws in force in a single branch of the law,
in a logical and convenient arrangement and
in precise and unambiguous phraseology. Traditional modern codes include codes of civil,
criminal (qq.v.), and public law, and codes
of civil and criminal procedures.

Statesmen of modern times regard legal
codes as necessary instruments of national
unity and central authority. Napoleon planned
the Code Napoléon (q.v.), later renamed the
Code Civil, as a means of consolidating his
realm. The Code Napoléon became one of the

most important modern codes, and the basis of the legal systems of Belgium, the Netherlands, Romania, Italy, Portugal, Santo Domingo, Haiti, the U.S. State of Louisiana, and the province of Quebec in Canada. It also influenced the legal systems of a number of Latin-American countries.

Other important modern codes include the Danske Lov, proclaimed in 1683 by King Christian V of Denmark; Code Frédéric, or Gesetzbuch ("law book"), proclaimed by Frederick the Great, King of Prussia, in 1751, and renamed Landrecht in 1794; and the Gesetzbuch of Germany, issued in 1900, which influenced the later codes of Switzerland, Turkey, and China. Although not a product of secular authority, the Codex Juris Canonici of the Roman Catholic Church, which went into effect in 1917, is regarded as an important modern code; it marked the culmination of almost 1900 years of development in the field of canon law (q.v.).

In England, in which the legal system is based on common law (q.v.), the work of codification has been largely a problem of consolidating common and statute law. A pioneer in this work was the jurist Jeremy Bentham (q.v.), who died while working on a codification of constitutional law. His work influenced the later codes adopted by the British government for India; and these in turn influenced codification in England, as was evidenced by the revision of statutes and legal procedure from 1870 to 1885. The Bills of Exchange Act (1882), the Partnership Act (1890), the Sale of Goods Act (1893), and the Marine Insurance Act (1906) are regarded as true codes, because they consolidated common and statute laws in a comprehensive fashion.

In the United States, in which law is derived in large part from English common law, the problem of codification has been complicated by the existence of a multiplicity of sovereign governmental jurisdictions. The Federal government is supreme in foreign policy and in fields in which its authority is essential for the national welfare, as in interstate commerce. But its powers are sharply circumscribed by the constitutionally-established sovereignty of the States in other matters. Hence there have come into being two general sets of codes, Federal and State codes, with divergences on many points. On the other hand, largely as a result of the pioneer work of the jurist David Dudley Field, well over half of the States have adopted uniform codes of civil and criminal procedure. And all the States have enacted uniform legislation with respect to negotiable credit instruments.

Efforts made under the auspices of the League of Nations to define a code of international law were aborted by the demise of that tribunal on the outbreak of World War II.

CODEINE, an alkaloid, $C_{18}H_{21}NO_3H_2O$, found in opium. It is a white crystalline solid, slightly soluble in water and soluble in organic solvents. When heated, it gives off water and melts at 155°C. (311°F.). Chemically it is a methyl ether of morphine, and has the same general physiological effects as morphine, but to a lesser degree; in particular, it is less habit forming than morphine. It is used in medicine to reduce pain, especially in the respiratory system.

CODE NAPOLÉON, designation officially applied in 1807 to the code of French civil law, enacted in March, 1804, as the *Code Civil des Français*, and still in force. Properly, the term applies to the entire body of French law, as contained in the Five Codes promulgated between 1804 and 1810. An initial draft, completed in 1793, was formulated as the result of popular protests, following the outbreak of the French Revolution, against the extreme diversity in the laws then in force in different parts of France. This draft was rejected by the National Convention as unworthy of the Republic. Following a number of delays, the task of preparing another draft was entrusted, in July, 1800, to a commission consisting of the most eminent jurists of France, including Jean Étienne Marie Portalis. The new draft, completed by the commission in four months, encountered considerable opposition, because of its conservative features, before it was finally enacted. It was named in honor of Napoleon, who had participated in its formulation.

The Code Napoléon was a compromise between the customary law, basically Germanic, of the northern provinces of France, and the law, essentially Roman, of the southern and eastern regions of the country. In arrangement, the code corresponds to the *Institutes,* Justinian's contribution to the Corpus Juris Civilis. Among the merits of the code are its simplicity and clearness of statement. It has required many judicial interpretations, however, and has been frequently modified by legislative amendment. As a result of the Napoleonic conquests, the code was introduced into a number of European countries, notably Belgium, where it is still in force. It also became the model for the civil codes of the Canadian province of Quebec, the Netherlands, Italy, Spain, some of the South and Central

American republics, and the State of Louisiana.

CODES AND CIPHERS. See CRYPTOGRAPHY.

CODEX JURIS CANONICI. See CANON LAW.

CODEX JUSTINIANUS. See CODE; ROMAN LAW.

CODEX THEODOSIANUS. See JUSTINIAN CODE.

CODIFICATION. See CODE.

CODLING MOTH, the adult of the apple worm, *Carpocapsa pomonella.* It was introduced from Europe about 1750, and has become one of the most serious of insect pests in the U.S., attacking pears, quinces, and walnuts, as well as apples. The brown moths, just under an inch in wingspread, emerge from their cocoons about the time that the apple tree blossoms, and lay their eggs on the leaves of the tree. When the larvae are hatched they eat a little foliage and then burrow into the fruit, leaving extensive tunnels. As many as three generations may hatch in a single season. At the start of cold weather the larvae spin inconspicuous cocoons in which they pass the winter. In early spring the larvae spin thinner cocoons and enter the pupal stage, from which the moths emerge. Codling moths are common wherever apples are grown, but can be controlled by spraying the trees before the caterpillars have entered the fruit.

COD-LIVER OIL, a light yellow oil, found in the liver of the cod, which is one of the most important natural sources of vitamins A and D. It is frequently prescribed by doctors not only as a preventative for deficiency diseases, particularly in babies, but also for the nutritive value of the fat it contains. Oils with similar properties, often loosely called cod-liver oil, are obtained from the livers of the halibut, tuna, and shark. Since World War II shark-liver oil has been the most important commercial source of natural vitamin A, although commercial synthetic vitamin-A production was begun in 1948. Fish-liver oils are prepared by heating the fresh livers in steam kettles. The first oil rendered is purified by molecular distillation and used for medicinal purposes while the oil produced by continued heating is used for poultry feed and the dressing of leather. Total annual consumption of fish-liver oils in the U.S. is about 20,000,000 lbs. See VITAMIN.

CODY, county seat of Park Co., Wyo., located on the Shoshone R., at the N.W. terminus of the Chicago, Burlington and Quincy Railroad. Farming (by irrigation from the Shoshone Dam), the raising of sheep and cattle, oil refining, and the tourist trade are the chief industries. Fifty miles w. of the town is Yellowstone National Park. Cody is headquarters of the Shoshone National Forest. In the vicinity of the town are many dude ranches, and scenic places, including Shoshone Canyon, a winter sports area. Cody was named for William F. Cody ("Buffalo Bill"), and contains a Buffalo Bill Museum and monument. Pop. (1960) 4838.

CODY, WILLIAM FREDERICK (1846–1917), American guide, scout and showman, known as "Buffalo Bill", born in Scott Co., Iowa. He became one of the riders of the Pony Express at its establishment in 1860, and at the beginning of the Civil War was a government scout and guide. In 1863 he enlisted in the Seventh Kansas Cavalry against the Indians, and at the close of the war contracted with the Kansas Pacific R. R. to furnish buffalo meat to the workers on the line, in this way earning his nickname. He was an army scout again from 1868 to 1872, when he was elected to the Nebraska legislature. He served in the Fifth U.S. Cavalry in the Sioux War of 1876, and in the battle of Indian Creek killed in personal combat Chief Yellow Hand. In 1883 he organized his "Wild West Show", a representation of life on the plains, and in 1887 took the show to Europe. In 1901 he became president of the Cody Military College and International Academy of Rough Riders which was established on his lands in Wyoming. He wrote several books describing his life on the frontier, including *The Life of Hon. William F. Cody* (1879); *Story of the Wild West and Camp-Fire Chats* (1888); *The Adventures of Buffalo Bill* (1904) ; and *True Tales of the Plains* (1908).

COE COLLEGE, privately controlled, coeducational institution of higher learning, located in Cedar Rapids, Iowa, and affiliated with the Presbyterian Church. It was established as the Cedar Rapids Collegiate Institute in 1851 and was renamed Parson Seminary in 1866 and Coe Collegiate Institute in 1875. The institution was incorporated under its present name in 1881. In 1919 it absorbed Leander Clark College, of Toledo, Iowa. Coe offers courses of study leading to the degrees of B.A. and B.MUS. Special educational programs include a three-year medical technology course, a five-year nursing program, and a liberal-arts-engineering curriculum, all conducted in co-operation with other colleges and institutions. During the 1962 fall term the enrollment included 850 full-time and 58 part-time students; the faculty numbered

65. The endowment in 1962 was $4,508,423, and the library contained about 69,000 bound volumes.

COEDUCATION, a term signifying the education of members of both sexes in the same classes in schools. Coeducation, which originated in Europe, was an outgrowth of the general movement for the education of girls which became widespread there in about the 17th century; for reasons of economy, girls were admitted to some schools for boys, or schools were organized for members of both sexes to attend together. Scotland in the late 17th century and New England in colonial times had coeducation in elementary grades. Not until the 19th century, however, when changing economic and social conditions led to demand for greater educational opportunities for women, did coeducation become widespread.

In England free coeducational schools for elementary education were first established by the government in 1870. In England today boys and girls between the ages of 4 and 8 are educated together. From the age of 8 the two sexes are generally educated separately, except in rural areas where scarcity of buildings often forces coeducation through the secondary school. In Scotland all the elementary schools are coeducational. Women were first admitted to classes with men in London University in 1880, and they were granted degrees there from that year. They first attended classes with men in Cambridge University in 1881, but were not granted degrees there until 1923. Oxford first admitted women to classes with men in 1881 and permitted women to take degrees beginning in 1920. Today most English universities are coeducational, as are all Scottish universities. Most of the important universities of Eire are coeducational. Coeducation is the chief form of education in the public schools and universities of the Dominion of Canada, and it prevails in the universities of most British colonies and commonwealths.

In France coeducation in primary schools exists only in villages where there are too few primary pupils to require two teachers; in most French communes with populations over 500 there are separate primary schools for boys and girls. Only a few French secondary schools are open to women. The Soviet Union had coeducation throughout its educational system until 1943 when separate schools for the two sexes were established in the cities. Sweden, Norway, Denmark, Finland, Germany, Austria, Switzerland, Belgium, and the Netherlands have a certain amount of coedu-cation in their elementary school system. In general the universities of all European countries, including those of France, Italy, Spain, Norway, Sweden, Denmark, Finland, Switzerland, Greece, Austria, and Germany are open to women.

Coeducation reached its highest development in the United States. It originated in New England and spread through the Middle West and Northwest, and then through other parts of the United States. Today coeducation prevails in about 97% of all public elementary and secondary schools in the United States.

Coeducation in colleges is likewise widespread in the United States. Oberlin College and Antioch College, both in Ohio, admitted women from the very date of their founding, 1833 and 1853 respectively. Antioch's first president was Horace Mann (q.v.), a strong advocate of coeducation. Of Eastern universities, St. Lawrence University (1861), Cornell University (1868), and Swarthmore College (1869) were the first to adopt coeducation. The State universities of Indiana and Michigan admitted women in 1868 and 1870 respectively. Today practically all of the State universities in the country are coeducational. After the end of World War II (1945), owing to the shortage of facilities in men's colleges to accommodate the large number of veterans seeking higher education with government support, some women's colleges admitted a limited number of male students on an emergency basis. Approximately 75 percent of the accredited U.S. universities and colleges are coeducational.

COELACANTH, lobe-finned fish of the family Coelacanthidae in the order Crossopterygii. Coelacanths first appeared on the earth during the Devonian period, about 350 million years ago, and are represented today only by one genus *Latimeria*. Lobe-finned fishes are so named because they have a fleshy, scale-covered lobe at the base of the paired fins, in contrast to the ray-finned fishes in which such lobes are absent. See FISH.

In the Devonian period the primitive lobe-finned fishes called crossopterygians gave rise to the first land vertebrates, or amphibians, as well as to the coelacanths. The coelacanths are, however, a specialized branch of the crossopterygians which has remained practically unchanged since its inception. For this reason the modern coelacanth *Latimeria* is frequently called a living fossil. In addition to their lobed fins, the coelacanths are characterized by an easily recognizable lobed tail. Fossils found in many parts of the world indicate that during their long history various types of coelacanths, ranging in size from 6 in. to nearly 5 ft., inhabited lakes, swamps, inland seas, and the ocean.

Prior to 1938, because of the lack of fossil coelacanths in rocks formed later than the Cretaceous period, paleontologists thought that the coelacanth had become extinct about 70 million years ago. In December of that year a fishing trawler off the eastern coast of South Africa captured a living coelacanth, which was subsequently named *Latimeria*. Failure to discover fossil coelacanths in rocks deposited during the last 70 million years is due probably to the restriction of this genus to the permanent ocean basins where fossil remains are very difficult to find. Between 1952 and 1956 eleven more specimens of *Latimeria* were captured, all near the Comoro Island group, northwest of Madagascar.

Latimeria closely resembles its fossil ancestors, having the characteristic paired, lobe-based fins and the three-lobed tail. It is steel blue in color and attains a length of about 5 ft. and a weight of 150 lbs. Around the Comoro Islands, which appear to be its normal habitat, *Latimeria* lives on or near the rocky ocean floor at a depth of 450 ft. to 750 ft. and feeds on other smaller fishes found at such depths. Inasmuch as the coelacanths are specialized crossopterygian fishes, the anatomy of *Latimeria* provides little new information on the origin of the land vertebrates except, perhaps, in relation to the evolutionary development of limb from fin. The lobed fins of *Latimeria* are very similar to those of the primitive crossopterygian ancestors of the limbed amphibians.

R.S.

COELENTERATA, one of the phyla of the animal kingdom, usually ranked as next to the lowest of the types of Metazoa, and including the polyps, corals, sea anemones, and jellyfishes. It is characterized by the absence of a body cavity and a separate circulatory system, both of these being functionally replaced by the system of chambers or tubes into which the mouth opens. Because this system is not only digestive, but also takes the place of the body cavity, it is sometimes called the *coelenteron*. More commonly the coelenteron is called the gastrovascular cavity, since it not only serves as a stomach for digestion and, by means of its branches, as a vascular or circulatory system in conveying food (and perhaps oxygen) to all parts of the body. All the Coelenterata are more or less radially symmetrical and generally on the number 4 or 6; i.e., they can be divided in either four or six vertical planes, and the re-

sulting halves will be approximately similar. The Coelenterata may therefore be defined as radially symmetrical, unsegmented Metazoa, having a gastrovascular cavity. In most Coelenterata there is no anus, waste matter from the digestive system being ejected through the mouth. Between the endodermal lining of the gastrovascular canals and the ectodermal covering of the body is a structureless layer, known as the supporting layer, or *mesogloea*. This may be very thin and firm, or it may be very thick and gelatinous. It contains scattered nerve and muscle cells, skeletal cells, and pigment cells.

The Coelenterata are a large group, of about 5000 species, widely distributed in the oceans of all parts of the world. Only three or four species of the entire group are known to inhabit fresh water. There are two forms of coelenterates, the polyp and the medusa, both of which may develop alternately during the life cycle; see ALTERNATION OF GENERATIONS. The polyp form, which occurs in colonies, is cylindrical, with one end attached to rocks or debris on the bottom and the other end containing the mouth and the tentacles. In the medusa form the tentacles are extensions of an umbrellalike surface, and the mouth is at the center of the body, corresponding to the position of the umbrella handle.

There are three classes in the phylum Coelenterata, namely, the Hydrozoa (q.v.), in which the polyp form predominates, the Anthozoa (q.v.), consisting solely of polyp forms, and the Scyphozoa, with medusa forms predominant; see JELLYFISH.

COELLO, ALONSO SÁNCHEZ. See SÁNCHEZ COELLO, ALONSO.

COEUR D'ALENE, lake in N. Idaho, situated among the mountains of the same name. It is 22 m. long and averages over 2 m. in width. The Coeur d'Alene and St. Joe rivers enter the lake at its s. end, and the Spokane R. issues from its N. end.

COEUR D'ALENE, county seat of Kootenai Co., Idaho, on the N. end of the lake of the same name, and 33 miles E. of Spokane, Wash. Fruits, general farm crops, and dairy products are produced in the surrounding area. The city is headquarters for the nearby Coeur d'Alene National Forest; it is a center for white-pine logging operations, and for fishing and hunting activities. Pop. (1960) 14,291.

COFFEE, term applied to trees of the genus *Coffea* of the madder family, and also to the beans of these trees and to the beverage brewed from them. Of the thirty or more species of the genus only three are important, namely, *C. arabica, C. robusta,* and *C. liberica.* The shrub or small tree, 15 to 20 ft. in height at maturity, bears shiny green, ovate leaves which persist for three to five years, and white, fragrant flowers that bloom for only a few days. During the next six or seven months the fruit develops, changing from light green to red and, ultimately, when fully ripe and ready for picking, to deep crimson. The mature fruit, which resembles a cherry, grows in clusters, attached to the limb by very short stems, and contains one or two seeds, or beans, surrounded by a sweet pulp.

Cultivation. The soil in which coffee is grown must be rich, moist, and absorbent enough to accept water readily, but sufficiently loose to allow rapid drainage of excess water. The best soil is composed of leafmold, other organic matter, and disintegrated volcanic rock. Although coffee trees are damaged easily by frost, they are cultivated in temperate climates, within the Tropical zone. The growing temperatures range from 55° F. to 80° F. and average about 70° F. Altitudes of coffee plantations range from sea level to about 6000 ft. (the tropical frost level). *C. robusta* and *C. liberica* grow best at altitudes below 3000 ft.; *C. arabica* flourishes at the higher altitudes. The seeds are planted directly in the field or in specially prepared nurseries. In the latter case, young selected plants are transplanted later to the fields. Commercial fertilizers are used extensively to promote the growth of stronger, healthier trees with heavier yields. Both the trees and the fruit are subject to insect infestation and microbial diseases which may be controlled by spraying and proper agricultural management.

Production. The coffee tree produces its first full crop when about five years old. Thereafter it produces consistently for fifteen or twenty years. Some trees yield 2 or 3 pounds of marketable beans annually, but 1 pound is considered an average annual yield. There are two methods of harvesting. One is based on selective picking; the other involves shaking the tree and stripping the fruit. Beans picked by the first technique are generally processed, if water is available, by the so-called wet method, in which the beans are softened in water, depulped mechanically, fermented in large tanks, washed again, and finally dried in the open or in heated, rotating cylinders. The so-called dry method, used generally for beans harvested by the second technique, entails only drying the beans and removing the outer coverings. In either case the final product, called green coffee, is hand sorted to remove defective beans and extraneous material, and then is graded according to quality.

Coffee grows well in Java, Sumatra, Arabia, India, Africa, the West Indies, and South and Central America. South and Central America, where *C. arabica* is grown, produces approximately 80 percent of the world's supply.

Commercial Crops. The major types of commercial coffee are the *arabicas* and the *robustas.* In the Western Hemisphere the *arabicas* are subdivided into Brazils and milds. *Robustas* are produced in the Eastern Hemisphere exclusively, together with substantial quantities of *arabicas.* The Brazils consist principally of Santos, Parana, and Rio, named for the ports from which they are shipped; milds are identified by the names of countries or districts in which they are grown, such as Medellin, Armenia, and Manizales coffees from Colombia. *Robustas* and other *arabicas* are similarly identified.

Green coffee is the largest single commodity imported by the United States. Imports in a typical year in the early 1960's totaled more than 22 million bags; about 80 percent came from South and Central America. Brazil and Colombia supplied roughly 40 percent and 20 percent, respectively. The total value of green coffee imported into the United States in 1961 was $1 billion. Dollar earnings from coffee paid for 31 percent of the goods which the fifteen producing nations of Latin America purchased from the United States.

Roasting. Several varieties of green coffee usually are blended and roasted together to produce the tastes, aromas, and flavors popular with consumers. As a rule the beans are heated in rotating, horizontal drums which provide a tumbling action to prevent uneven heating or scorching. Temperatures for roasting range from about 380°F. for a light roast, through 400°F. for a medium roast, to about 425°F. for a dark roast. The end product is determined either by eye or, automatically, by sensitive heat-measuring devices. The roasted beans are cooled rapidly.

Roasted coffee may be packaged and shipped to retail stores, which custom-grind it for the customers on purchase, or it may be ground in plate- or roller-type grinding mills before shipment. These mills can be adjusted for all the more commonly used grinds, such as regular, drip, and fine grinds for home use, and urn, fine, and special grinds for restaurant and institutional use.

Ground coffee loses its unique flavor within about a week unless it is specially packaged. Plastic-and-paper combinations are popular packaging media which afford protection to freshly roasted and ground coffee. Hermetically sealed vacuum, or pressure, cans keep coffee fresh for more than a year. For best results, consumers should not buy more coffee than they can use in one week if the container is not hermetically sealed.

Beverage Preparation. The beverage is prepared by mixing ground, roasted coffee and hot water. Recommended proportions are 2 level tablespoonfuls of coffee for each 6 oz. of water. To obtain a flavorful and aromatic drink, high-quality coffee and fresh water should be used. Important factors involved are the degree of roast, a grind suited to the equipment used, temperature of the water (above 200° F.), time of exposure of coffee to the water, and the degree of separation of grounds and sediment from the beverage. For home use, percolators, drip pots, and vacuum devices are popular. Urns, vacuum devices, and cartridge-pressure equipment are commonly used in restaurants and institutions. An increasing amount of coffee is sold from vending machines in which ground coffee or powdered soluble coffee are utilized.

Chemical Composition. The beverage contains a complex mixture of chemical components of the bean, some of which are not affected by roasting. Other compounds, particularly those related to the aroma, are produced by partial destruction of the green bean during roasting. Chemicals extracted by hot water are classified as nonvolatile taste components and volatile aroma components. Important nonvolatiles are caffeine, trigonelline, chlorogenic acid, tannin proteins, amino acids, carbohydrates, and minerals. Important volatiles are organic acids, carbohydrates, minerals, aldehydes, ketones, esters, amines, and mercaptans. The principal physiological effects of coffee are due to caffeine (q.v.), an alkaloid that acts as a mild, non-habit-forming stimulant.

Soluble Coffee. Soluble, or instant, coffee powder is a relatively new but increasingly important product of the domestic coffee industry. In 1961 nearly 18 percent of the coffee imported by the United States was used for manufacture of soluble coffee. In its manufacture an extract is prepared by mixing coarsely ground and roasted coffee with hot water; the water is evaporated from the extract by various methods, including the use of spray driers or high-vacuum equipment. The resulting fine powder is packed in vacuumized, sealed jars or in cans. In preparing the beverage about 1 teaspoonful of powder is needed for each 6 oz. of hot water.

Decaffeinated Coffee. Caffeine can be removed from coffee by treating the green beans with chlorinated-hydrocarbon solvents. The beans are roasted by ordinary procedures after removal of the solvents. Decaffeinated coffee is used by persons who may be hypersensitive to the caffeine present in regular coffee.

Extracts. Liquid coffee extracts, concentrated by removing part of the water in vacuum concentrators, are used widely in vending machines and for flavoring ice cream and other food products.

Coffee Substitutes. The use of substitutes for coffee in the United States is very limited; the most important is chicory (q.v.), which is used, however, more as an extender. Under U.S. law, the addition of chicory or any other substance must be clearly stated on the brand label of coffee containers.

U.S. Consumption. According to a recent survey, coffee is used as a beverage in 98 percent of U.S. households. Annual consumption per capita is about 16 lbs. of coffee. In a recent year the total beverage consumption exceeded 160 billion cups, including a daily consumption of 99 million cups during the so-called coffee break, which has become a full-fledged institution in American industry. Nearly half the population drinks from 3 to 10 cups of coffee per day. About 3 percent of the consumer's food dollar is spent on coffee.

History. Exactly where and when coffee was first cultivated is not known, but some authorities believe that it was grown initially in Arabia near the Red Sea in about 675 A.D. There was, however, comparatively little coffee cultivation until the 15th and 16th centuries, when extensive planting of the tree occurred in the Yemen region of Arabia. The consumption of coffee increased in Europe during the 17th century, prompting the Dutch to cultivate it in their colonies. In 1714 the French succeeded in bringing a live cutting of a coffee tree to the island of Martinique in the West Indies. This single plant was the genesis of the great coffee plantations of Latin America.

PAN-AMERICAN COFFEE BUREAU

COFFEYVILLE, city in Montgomery Co., Kans., on the Verdigris R., less than 3 m. from the Oklahoma boundary and approximately 150 m. south of Topeka. It is served by three railroads, and is the industrial center of a rich agricultural area noted for grain and livestock; and also for natural gas, oil, coal, shale, and clay. In the city are oil refineries, large machine shops, flour mills, grain elevators, a milk condensery, a zinc smelter, and tile and brick plants. Coffeyville was laid out and incorporated in 1871. Pop. (1960) 17,382.

COFFIN, a receptacle, usually of wood or metal, in which a corpse is laid for burial or cremation. A coffin made of stone is called a sarcophagus (q.v.).

Coffins made of stone, wood, earthenware, glass, and papier-mâché were used by the Egyptians several thousand years before the Christian Era. Hieroglyphic writings on the interiors of a number of these coffins are known as Coffin Texts. The wooden and papier-mâché coffins are known as mummy cases.

Some American Indian tribes used canoes as coffins; others used wooden coffins or baskets, or merely wrapped their dead in blankets or buffalo robes before burial. The Australian aborigines generally buried their dead in coffins made of bark, but some used wickerwork baskets.

Among ancient European peoples, primitive stone coffins, or cists, were made by placing an unhewn flat stone at the bottom of a grave, and others on their edges to line the sides; a large stone was used as a cover. Other primitive coffins were made of tree trunks which had been split in the center and then hollowed out.

Burnt-clay coffins were used by the ancient Greeks. In the Christian Era wrought-stone coffins were used by wealthy Greeks and Romans; the latter introduced them into England, where they were used until the 16th century.

In the Middle Ages lead coffins, resembling ancient Egyptian mummy cases in shape, were used in Europe. In England and Scotland, the dead were sometimes buried in iron coffins; the poor were often interred in cloth shrouds, or were instead covered with hay and flowers, and buried in the grave.

Modern coffins, used for burial in the earth, are sometimes made of finely carved wood, or richly wrought metal; but most coffins, including those ordered in huge quantities by governments during wartime, are pine boxes, made by mass-production methods. Coffins used in cremation are burned with the bodies and are therefore generally made of light materials, such as thin wood or papier-mâché. See BURIAL; CREMATION.

COGNAC, town in s.w. France, Department of Charente, on the Charente River, 23 miles w.n.w. of Angoulême. Cognac has a 12th-century church and a castle of the 15th and 16th centuries. Its leading industry is the distillation of the brandy known as cognac. Other industries are the manufacture of bottles, and trading in cattle and grain. Cognac

was the birthplace of Francis I, King of France. Pop. (1962) 20,647.

COHAN, GEORGE MICHAEL (1878–1942), American comedian, producer, and playwright, born in Providence, R.I. He first appeared on the stage when nine years old in *Daniel Boone*. Later, with members of his family, he starred in "The Four Cohans" which became one of the most popular attractions on the vaudeville stage. He wrote musical comedies and plays, playing the lead in many. His plays include *Little Johnny Jones* (1904); *The Governor's Son* (1904); *Forty-five Minutes from Broadway* (1905); *The Yankee Prince* (1909); *Get-Rich-Quick Wallingford* (1910); *The Little Millionaire* (1911); *Seven Keys to Baldpate* (1913); *Hit the Trail Holiday* (1915); *The Tavern* (1920); *The Song and Dance Man* (1923); *The Baby Cyclone* (1927); and *The Merry Malones* (1927). He played in *I'd Rather Be Right* (1937). He wrote many popular songs, including the famous "Over There" of World War I.

COHEN, MORRIS RAPHAEL (1880–1947), American philosopher and teacher, born in Minsk, Russia, and educated at the College of the City of New York and Harvard University. After a brief period of teaching mathematics, he served as professor of philosophy at the College of the City of New York from 1912 to 1938. He was also at various times a visiting lecturer at many universities, including Columbia, Yale, and Harvard. He was noted for his studies in the philosophy of the natural sciences and in the philosophy of law. His best-known works are *Reason and Nature* (1931), *Law and the Social Order* (1933), *Preface to Logic* (1944), *Faith of a Liberal* (1945), and *Dreamer's Journey* (1950).

COHEN, SOLOMON SOLIS. See SOLIS-COHEN, SOLOMON.

COHN, FERDINAND JULIUS (1828–98) German botanist and bacteriologist, born at Breslau, and educated at the universities of Breslau and Berlin. In 1859 he became professor of botany at Breslau, serving in that position until his death. He made great contributions to the knowledge of algae, fungi, and insect and plant diseases. His greatest contribution, however, was in his studies of microscopic plants; he demonstrated that bacteria are plants, and is regarded as the founder of the science of bacteriology. He discovered the nature and principal properties of bacterial spores, and assisted Robert Koch in the preparation of his famous treatise on anthrax (1876). In 1870 Cohn founded the journal *Beiträge zur Biologie*. See BACTERIA.

COI or **SONGKOI** or (Eng.) **RED RIVER,** a river in China and in Tonkin, Viet-Nam. The river rises in the mountains of s.w. China and flows S.E. for more than 600 m., emptying in the Gulf of Tonkin through a large delta. Its main tributaries are the Black and the Clear rivers. The delta of the Coi is the most fertile and populous part of Tonkin.

COIL, INDUCTION. See ELECTRICITY.

COIMBATORE, district and city of Madras State, Republic of India. The district terrain comprises, for the most part, a level plain with an average height of 900 ft. above sea level. It is encircled by mountains except in the east, where the land extends to the Carnatic (q.v.) plain. The chief rivers are the Amravati, Bhavani, Cauvery, and Noyil. Lumbering and the production of raw silk are important industries in the district, which contains numerous canals and irrigation works necessary to the cultivation of rice, millet, pulse, cotton, tobacco, and oilseeds.

The city of Coimbatore is situated on the Noyil River, on the slopes of the Nilgiri Hills, 1437 ft. above sea level, and 305 miles by rail southwest of the city of Madras. About 3 miles east of Coimbatore is the noted temple of Perur. The city is a local educational center and contains a school of forestry, an agricultural college, and technical schools. Industry in Coimbatore includes the manufacture of textiles, fertilizers, soap, dyes, and sugar, and the processing of coffee. Area of district, 7225 sq.m.; pop. (1961) 2,525,302. Pop. of city (1961) 286,305.

COIMBRA, capital of a district of the same name, and of the province of Beira Litoral, Portugal, on a steep hill on the Mondego R., 115 m. by rail N.N.E. of Lisbon. The city is situated on the site of Æminium of ancient Roman times, but derives its name from the bishopric of Conimbriga which was moved to the site of Coimbra in the 9th century A.D. The Cid (q.v.) and King Ferdinand I of Castile captured Coimbra from the Moors in 1064. Thereafter, until 1260, it was the capital of Portugal. After 1306, the city of Coimbra was for a time the site of the university founded in Lisbon fifteen years before, and in 1537 became its permanent location.

The modern city is noted chiefly as an educational center. It contains, in addition to the university, a college of arts, a literary and scientific institute, a library of some 150,000 books, museums, and large research laboratories. Among other buildings of note are the 12th-century Romanesque cathedral, the 12th-century church of San Salvador, and the 16th-century church of Santa Cruz. Earthen-ware and combs are manufactured. Area of district, 1527 sq.m.; pop. (1960 prelim.) 444,657. Pop. of city (1960 est.) 112,199.

COINAGE. See MINT.

COINS. See MONEY; NUMISMATICS.

COKE, the hard, porous residue left after the destructive distillation of coal, used as a reducing agent in the smelting of pig iron, and as a fuel. Coke is blackish gray in color and has a metallic luster. It is composed largely of carbon, usually about 92 percent; most of the remainder is ash. When used as a fuel, it has the high heating value of 13,800 B.T.U. per pound.

Coke was first produced as a by-product of the manufacture of illuminating gas (see GAS). However, with the growth of the steel industry the increasing need for metallurgical coke made it inevitable that coke should be manufactured as a chief product rather than as a by-product.

The earliest method of coking coal was simply to pile it in large heaps out of doors, leaving a number of horizontal and vertical flues through the piles. These flues were filled with wood, which was lighted and which, in turn, ignited the coal. When most of the volatile elements in the coal were driven off, the flames would die down; the fire would then be partly smothered with coal dust, and the whole heap sprinkled with water.

A later development was the coking of coal in the beehive oven, so called from its shape. As in open-air coking, no attempt was made to recover the valuable gas and tar. As late as 1893, beehive ovens were the only devices used for coking in the U.S., but they have now been almost entirely supplanted by the modern by-product coke ovens. These ovens, usually arranged in batteries of about sixty, are narrow vertical chambers with silica-brick walls, heated by burning gas between adjoining ovens. Each oven is charged through an opening in the top with anywhere from 10 to 22 tons of coal, which is heated to temperatures as high as 1482° C. (2700° F.) for an average of seventeen hours. During this period the gases from the oven escape through another opening in the top. The coal tar (q.v.) is condensed by contact with water in a hydraulic main, while the gas, after being scrubbed with water to remove ammonia and with oil to remove benzene, is used to heat the ovens. At the end of the coking period the red-hot coke is forced by a ram out of the oven directly into a car which carries it to the quenching hood, where it is sprinkled with water. The emptying process takes only about three minutes, so that the oven is ready for recharging with little loss of heat.

In 1961 one ton of coal coked in a by-product oven yielded an average of 10,700 cu.ft. of gas, 1394 lbs. of coke, 8.7 gal. of coal tar, 19.4 lbs. of ammonia, and 3 gal. of crude light oil. U.S. coke production was about 51.7 million tons in 1961.

NATIONAL COAL ASSOCIATION

COKE, SIR EDWARD (1552–1634), English jurist, born at Mileham, in Norfolk, and educated at Cambridge University. In 1578 he was admitted to the bar, in 1589 became a member of Parliament, and in 1592, while Elizabeth I was queen, became solicitor general. Two years later he became attorney general, an appointment for which Francis Bacon was his competitor; this victory was the beginning of a long enmity between the two men. Coke's first years as representative of the crown were characterized by ruthless support of authority; his prosecution of Robert Devereux, Earl of Essex, of Sir Walter Raleigh, and of the Gunpowder Plot conspirators has been termed vindictive.

In 1606, in the reign of King James I, Coke was made chief justice of Common Pleas. Thereafter he vigorously championed the common law against all other authority, even against the royal prerogative and the privilege of the Church. In 1613, in order to silence him, the King promoted Coke to the office of chief justice of the King's Bench; but two years later Coke challenged the power of the Court of Chancery. In 1616, at the instigation of Bacon (then attorney general), charges on relatively minor issues were brought against him and he was removed from office. The following year, however, he was reappointed to the Privy Council, and after his re-election to Parliament in 1620 once again challenged royal authority. His part in the debate on the Bill of Liberties earned him nine months in prison in 1622, but was the most important contributing factor to the formulation of the Petition of Right (q.v.), which became an integral part of the English Constitution.

Coke was a stern but able judge; it was said that his colleagues echoed him so servilely that the king was forced to consult them in Coke's absence when he desired an independent opinion. His chief fame is that of a compiler of the law; his compilations took the form of *Reports* issued regularly after 1600; and four volumes of *Institutes* (1628–44), the first of which is known as *Coke Upon Littleton*. All these works were studied assiduously by generations of students.

COLA NUT or **KOLA NUT,** the seed of a large tree, *Cola acuminata,* a member of the Chocolate family, originally native to Africa and now cultivated in a number of tropical countries. The trees are evergreens about 35 ft. high, and bear the seeds in podlike receptacles. The seeds are about an inch in length, mottled brown or reddish gray, with an odor like that of nutmeg. The taste of the fresh seeds is bitter, but as the nuts age they become slightly aromatic. They contain caffeine, tannin, and theobromine, and are used extensively in the manufacture of soft drinks known as cola beverages.

COLBERG. See KOLBERG.

COLBERT, JEAN BAPTISTE (1619–83), French statesman, born at Reims. He obtained employment in the office of the War Ministry at the age of 19. In 1651 Cardinal Jules Mazarin, a former premier exiled by King Louis XIV, retained Colbert as his confidential agent at court. After Mazarin returned to royal favor, he recommended Colbert to the king for preferment. At first Colbert held no office, but as the king's adviser he secured the prosecution of the superintendent of finance for embezzlement. The office was abolished, but in effect reconstituted when Colbert was made controller general in 1665. For the rest of his life he was the leading statesman of France, holding various offices; but his power was gradually curtailed by rivals.

Colbert set about to reorganize the entire economic structure of France. Beginning with a drastic overhauling of finances, including prosecution of grafting officials and repudiation of certain bonds, he proceeded to reconstruct commerce and industry according to a grand plan. He organized trading and colonization companies, prescribing detailed rules. He established model factories, and attempted to standardize production in those already existing. Under his direction networks of canals and roads were built, seaports were fortified and a fleet consistent with France's commercial requirements was constructed. He extended his patronage to the arts and sciences, founding academies, providing pensions, erecting public buildings, and encouraging scientific cattle breeding. Many of Colbert's reforms, especially the creation of a navy and the construction of public works, were of lasting value; but most of his ventures were either unsuccessful or were undermined by the reckless extravagance or military expenditures of King Louis. The precarious financial condition of France at Colbert's death was blamed on him, and his unpopularity was such that his body had to be secretly removed from his home to prevent its abuse by a mob.

COLBY COLLEGE, coeducational, nonsectarian institution of higher learning, situated in Waterville, Me. It was known originally as The Maine Literary and Theological Institution, and was chartered, under the auspices of the Baptist Church, by the Massachusetts State Legislature in 1813, seven years before Maine was admitted to the Union as a separate State. Two years after its opening (1818), the name of the institution was changed to Waterville College. In 1867 this name was changed to Colby University in honor of Gardner Colby, a Boston industrialist, who was a generous benefactor. It was renamed Colby College in 1899. The college provides courses of study in the liberal arts leading to the degree of A.B. In 1962 enrollment was 1229 full-time and 7 part-time students; the faculty numbered 112.

COLCHESTER, city in Essex, England, on the Colne R., about 12 m. from its mouth on the North Sea, and 52 m. by rail N.E. of London. Before the Roman conquest of Britain, Colchester was the "Royal Town" of the British chief Cunobelin. When the Emperor Claudius had conquered the southeastern part of Britain, he founded on the site of Colchester a *colonia* (see COLONY) called Camulodunum, later renamed Colneceaster by the Saxons. The castle ruins in Colchester contain the largest Norman keep in England. The city has large cattle and corn markets and is the center of trade for the surrounding agricultural district. Pop. (1961 prelim.) 65,072.

COLCHICINE, a bitter, poisonous alkaloid obtained from the corm and seed of the meadow saffron or autumn crocus, *Colchicum autumnale,* an Old World plant of the Lily family. The plant has leaves up to 12 inches in length and, in the fall, large, stalkless flowers. The drug is a powerful cathartic, and also has emetic and diuretic properties. It is used in the treatment of gout and rheumatism. Colchicine has the property of doubling the chromosome numbers in plant cells and is frequently used in genetic studies. It has been successfully used to make fertile, pure-breeding plants from otherwise sterile hybrids, and to produce new varieties of plants.

COLD, COMMON, acute infectious disease of the upper respiratory tract, caused by a number of viruses. The infection affects the mucous membranes of the nose and throat, causing such symptoms as nasal congestion and discharge, sore throat, and coughing. These symptoms are typical also of other respiratory infections, caused by bacteria, and of allergic conditions, such as hay fever and asthma; therefore, the common cold is difficult to diagnose with certainty. Ordinarily it runs a mild course, subsiding spontaneously in a few days. Its medical significance lies in the possible complications which may ensue. Various diseases, such as bronchitis, pneumonia, and sinus or middle-ear infections, may arise from the cold. The lowered vitality of the body may also reactivate such diseases as tuberculosis or heart disease or rheumatic fever if the cold is complicated by a streptococcus infection. Individuals are subject to frequent cold infections. Recent cold-virus research indicates that there are several strains of each type of virus with varying degrees of virulency. Infection with one strain confers only a brief immunity to reinfection by the same strain, but gives no immunity against the other strains. It has been demonstrated that colds occur universally wherever the cold viruses have been introduced.

The common cold was formerly believed to result from exposure to cold weather or from chilling. This belief arose because the number of colds increases considerably when the temperature drops. Medical authorities hold that chilling contributes to the onset of colds by lowering the body's resistance to the viral infection.

There is no known cure for the common cold and no preventive drug has yet been found which has proved efficacious. In the early 1950's, various antihistamine drugs (see ALLERGY) were claimed to be effective in the prevention of colds if taken at the onset. Most physicians believe, however, that these anti-allergy drugs cannot affect the progress of the true, virus-caused cold. Present-day methods of treating a cold are directed toward the relief of symptoms and the prevention of complications. One or two days of bed rest is generally recommended to avoid complications, although the cold itself is not incapacitating. In addition, antibiotics are administered as a preventive measure when the cold may precipitate attacks of latent diseases.

According to recent statistics, the common cold is the primary cause of absenteeism in schools and industry. In the United States, where individuals are estimated to have an average of 2½ colds each year, the labor force loses over 150,000,000 workdays annually because of colds. As a consequence there has been in recent years an intensification of the effort to find a cure and possibly a preventive vaccine for the cold. Because only man and the ape were known to be susceptible to cold-virus infection, laboratory research was formerly limited to experiments on human beings. Such tests are difficult to control scientifically. The study of cold viruses has benefited greatly by the development of a new technique for growing cultures of the viruses outside the human body. In 1954 a three-year research project, in which the new technique was applied in the investigation of cold viruses, was launched by several institutions. The project was financed by the Common Cold Foundation, an organization founded in 1951 under the auspices of the American College of Chest Physicians and the Association of Industrial Physicians. On the basis of the research a vaccine was developed from certain strains of viruses which cause severe colds with fever and sore throat, but only a small proportion of all common colds are caused by these viruses. See also IMMUNITY; VIRUS.　　　　　　　　　H.R.M.

COLD HARBOR, BATTLE OF, one of the most sanguinary battles of the American Civil War, fought from May 31 to June 12, 1864, at Cold Harbor, Va., about 10 miles N.E. of Richmond. The battle was joined when the Union Army of the Potomac, which numbered about 102,000 men under General Ulysses S. Grant, engaged the Confederate Army of Northern Virginia, about 65,000 men under General Robert E. Lee, following Grant's successes in the Wilderness campaign. In pursuit of Lee's forces, Grant crossed the Pamunkey River on May 28, and, on May 31, confronted the Confederate Army, entrenched in positions along the line of Totopotomoy River. On the afternoon of May 31, General P. H. Sheridan launched a mounted assault on Cold Harbor, carrying and holding the Confederate positions despite fierce attacks by enemy cavalry under General Fitzhugh Lee. General Sheridan was relieved on the following day by General Horatio G. Wright, in command of the 6th Corps of the Army of the Potomac, and General William F. Smith, commanding the 18th Corps of the Army of the James. Late in the afternoon of June 1, Wright and Smith attacked Lee's positions in the face of extremely heavy fire and, after suffering a loss of about 2000 men, succeeded in capturing much of the Confederate front line. Lee's forces counterattacked on the morning of June 2, directing their main assault against the positions of the Union 5th Army Corps and taking many prisoners. Early on the morning of June 3, Grant's troops began a general advance against the Confederate line. More than 5000 Union soldiers were killed or wounded during the first hour of the attack.

These losses, particularly severe during the first 20 minutes, were probably greater than total casualties incurred during any similar period of the war. Sporadic fighting continued until 1:30 p.m. of June 3, resulting in about 2000 additional Union casualties. Both armies thereupon entrenched. From that time until June 12, when Grant withdrew across the James River, the action consisted chiefly of minor skirmishes. The losses sustained by the Army of the Potomac during the battle, which was fought on the ground where the Battle of Gaines's Mill had occurred 2 years before, totaled more than 12,700 men. Estimated Confederate losses included about 2600 killed and wounded. In the opinion of most military critics, Grant was guilty of a serious mistake at Cold Harbor, for his losses were unjustified in terms of results achieved. Grant subsequently agreed with this verdict.

COLD SORE. See HERPES.

COLDSTREAM GUARDS, a regiment in the Foot Guards or Household Brigade, the oldest in the British army except the 1st Foot, now called the Royal Scots. Raised in 1660 by General George Monck at Coldstream, in Berwickshire, Scotland, it was at first called "Monck's Regiment". Later, under the name of Coldstream Guards, it formed part of King Charles II's brigade.

COLE, THOMAS (1801–48), American painter, born at Bolton le Moors, Lancashire, England. He was brought to the U.S. by his parents at the age of 18, and became interested in painting several years later. After studying in Philadelphia and New York, he spent three years in Europe, returning to the U.S. in 1832. He devoted himself to painting allegorical and landscape pictures, the former of which he preferred. However, his landscapes, the first important pictures of American scenes, are considered his best work; he is known as the founder of the "Hudson River School" of American artists. Characteristic of his allegorical work is the series called "Course of Empire" (N.Y. Historical Society); several of his landscapes, including the Connecticut River scene "Oxbow", are in the Metropolitan Museum, New York City.

COLE, TIMOTHY (1852–1931), American engraver, born in London. He came to the U.S. in 1857, settling at first in Chicago; but, after losing all his possessions in the fire of 1871, he moved to New York. There he made wood engravings for several magazines. In 1883 he went to Europe to make engravings of the old masters, a project which became his lifework; his engravings appeared in book form as *Old Italian Masters* (1892), *Dutch and Flemish Masters* (1901), *English Masters* (1902), *Spanish Masters* (1907), and *French Masters* (1910). Thereafter he was commissioned to make engravings of the American masters in U.S. collections. He is generally considered the greatest wood engraver of his time.

COLEOPTERA. See BEETLE.

COLERIDGE, the name of a family of English men of letters and lawyers, all descended from JOHN COLERIDGE (1719–81), a parson, who became vicar of the parish of Ottery St. Mary, in Devonshire, in 1760. Among his children were two sons, JAMES COLERIDGE (1760–1836) and the poet, SAMUEL TAYLOR COLERIDGE (q.v.). James had four sons: Francis George, John Taylor, James Duke, and Henry Nelson. Of Francis George Coleridge's descendants, the most notable was his granddaughter, MARY ELIZABETH COLERIDGE (1861–1907), novelist and poet, author of *The Seven Sleepers of Ephesus* (1893) and *Gathered Leaves* (posthumously published, 1910). SIR JOHN TAYLOR COLERIDGE (1790–1875), born at Tiverton, and educated at Oxford University, was called to the bar in 1819, and became a judge of the King's Bench in 1835, serving for 23 years. He wrote *Memoir of the Rev. John Keble* (1869). His sons were SIR JOHN DUKE COLERIDGE, 1st BARON COLERIDGE (q.v.) and HENRY JAMES COLERIDGE (1822–93), who graduated from Oxford University and entered the Roman Catholic priesthood in 1855. A son of Baron Coleridge, BERNARD JOHN SEYMOUR COLERIDGE, 2nd BARON COLERIDGE (1851–1927), after graduating from Oxford University and being called to the bar, became a member of Parliament (1885–94) and judge of the King's Bench (1907–23). Samuel Taylor Coleridge had a daughter, SARA COLERIDGE, a son, DAVID HARTLEY COLERIDGE (q.v.), and another son, DERWENT COLERIDGE (1800–83), who became a scholar and headmaster of several schools. Derwent was the father of ERNEST HARTLEY COLERIDGE. Sara Coleridge married her cousin, HENRY NELSON COLERIDGE; their son was HERBERT COLERIDGE (1830–61), who graduated from Oxford University and was appointed by the Philological Society as secretary of a committee to prepare a dictionary, a project which subsequently resulted in the *New English Dictionary*.

COLERIDGE, DAVID HARTLEY (1796–1849), English poet, born at Clevedon, Somersetshire, the eldest son of Samuel Taylor Coleridge. He studied at Oxford and was elected to a fellowship at Oriel College, from which he was expelled by the authorities in 1826 on the charge of intemperance. After two years in London, he returned to the Lake Country; there he twice attempted school teaching, finally settling at Grasmere. Prematurely gray and old, he became familiar to the peasantry as "Little Hartley". He was a scholar of rare attainment, a poet of taste and felicity. His longest literary work was the preparation of an edition of the dramas of Philip Massinger and John Ford, with biographies of those authors (1840). He also wrote *Worthies of Yorkshire and Lancashire* (1836). He is best known, however, for his verse, which is singularly fine in mood and happy in expression.

COLERIDGE, SAMUEL TAYLOR (1772–1834), English poet and critic, born at Ottery St. Mary. He was the son of a scholarly pastor. His early schooling, at Christ's Hospital, left a lasting impression on him. From 1791 until 1794 he attended Jesus College, Cambridge University, except for a brief period during which he enlisted as a dragoon.

At the University he wrote a poem which was published in the *Morning Chronicle;* and he absorbed various political and theological ideas then considered radical, especially those of Unitarianism. He left Cambridge without his degree, and after meeting Robert Southey (q.v.) joined with him in a plan, soon abandoned, of founding a fraternalistic settlement in Pennsylvania. In 1795 the two friends married sisters; Southey departed for Portugal, but Coleridge remained in England to lecture. In 1796 his first volume of poetry was published. More important than either his marriage or his first publication was the friendship which began in 1795 between Coleridge and William and Dorothy Wordsworth, the principal result of which was the planning of a joint volume of poetry. This book, *Lyrical Ballads,* which appeared in 1798, was a landmark in English poetry; it contained the first great works of the Romantic School, including Coleridge's *Ancient Mariner.* The years 1797–98, during which the three friends lived near Nether Stowey, in Somersetshire, were probably the most fruitful of Coleridge's life; he wrote *Kubla Khan,* began work on *Christabel,* and wrote the tragedy later called *Remorse.*

In the fall of 1798 the friends left for a trip on the Continent, and Coleridge soon went his own way, spending much of his time in Germany. During this period he lost his early sympathy with political radicalism, and became interested in the philosophies of such figures as Immanuel Kant and Jakob Böhme, and in the literary criticism of Gotthold Lessing. He learned German, and translated Johann von Schiller's dramatic triology, *Wallenstein,* into English. By this time he had already become addicted to opiates. In 1800 he returned to England, and shortly thereafter settled with his family and friends at Keswick in the Lake Country of Cumberland. He made a tour of Scotland, spent almost a year in Malta, where he was secretary to the governor of the island, and visited Rome, returning to England in 1806. Until 1816 he spent some of his time lecturing and writing, but increasingly the opium habit curtailed his creative activity. In this period he attracted a small but loyal following for his platform appearances, especially his lectures on Shakespeare, which were partly responsible for renewed appreciation of that author after years of comparative indifference. Donations and grants supplemented Coleridge's literary income.

In 1816 Coleridge, estranged from his family and hopelessly addicted to opiates, took residence in the home of an admirer who was also a physician, James Gillman. There he occupied himself with a major prose work, *Biographia Literaria* (1817), a poorly organized series of autobiographical notes and of dissertations on many subjects, including philosophy and literary criticism, portions of which were brilliantly perceptive. The section in which Coleridge defines his views on the nature of poetry and compares them with those of Wordsworth are especially esteemed. In 1817, also, his *Sibylline Leaves* was published, and Coleridge appeared for the last time as a lecturer. Other of his writings were published while he was in seclusion at Gillman's home, notably *Aids to Reflection* (1825) and *Church and State* (1830).

Coleridge was esteemed by some of his contemporaries, and is generally esteemed today, as a lyrical poet of the first rank. His themes were usually supernatural, and he used the magic of his art to bridge the gap between the reader and the strange world of which he wrote. His poems were few in number, but unexcelled for imagery and melody. His critical prose has also retained its significance, and many passages are stimulating. To his contemporaries he was a literary giant, and his stature has scarcely decreased through the years.

COLET, JOHN (1467?–1519), English theologian, born in London, and educated at Oxford University. After traveling in France and Italy, where he was influenced by Budé and Erasmus, he returned to England in 1496 and became a priest. His lectures on the Epistles of St. Paul attracted great attention for their originality. In 1498 Erasmus visited Oxford, and Colet powerfully influenced that scholar's opinions on the proper methods of Scripture interpretation and on the value of the scholastic philosophy. In 1505 Colet became dean of St. Paul's, London, and continued to deliver lectures which gave rise to much controversy. With the large fortune he inherited on the death of his father, he founded St. Paul's School. Because of Colet's vigorous denunciation of the corruption of the clergy, charges of heresy were brought against him, but Archbishop Warham refused to support them. In 1510 Colet appointed the Mercers' Company of London managers of his school, the first example of lay management of an educational institution.

COLETTE, pen name of SIDONIE GABRIELLE CLAUDINE COLETTE (1873–1954), French novelist, born in Saint-Sauveur-en Puisaye, and educated in the local schools. In 1893 she married the French writer Henry Gautier-Villars (1859–1931), with whom she collaborated on her first novel, *Claudine à l'École* (1900; Eng. trans., *Claudine at School,* 1930), a semiautobiographical work published under her husband's pen name, Willy. This novel and the three others of the Claudine series, including *Claudine en Ménage* (1902; Eng. trans., *The Indulgent Husband,* 1935) and *Claudine s'en Va* (1903; Eng. trans., *The Innocent Wife,* 1934), were highly successful. Gautier-Villars' contributions to the series having been negligible, in 1904 she assumed

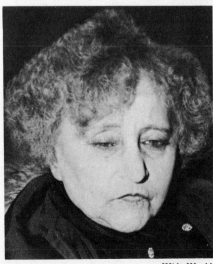

Wide World

"Colette"

the pen name Colette Willy. She was divorced in 1906, and during the next few years she performed in music halls as a dancer and continued her literary career. Her outstanding novels of this period include *L'Ingénue Libertine* (1909; Eng. trans., *The Gentle Libertine*, 1931) and *La Vagabonde* (1910; Eng. trans., *The Vagrant*, 1912). From 1910 to 1924 she was the wife of the French writer Henri de Jouvenal (1876–   ).

Chéri (1920; Eng. trans., 1929), an account of a young man's love affair with an elderly woman of doubtful reputation, and its tragic sequel *La Fin de Chéri* (1926; Eng. trans., *The Last of Chéri*, 1932), established her reputation as the leading woman novelist of France. After 1921, under the pseudonym Colette, she wrote profound studies of women in love, such as *La Seconde* (1929; Eng. trans., *The Other One,* 1931) and *Duo* (1934; Eng. trans., 1935). She married the French writer and statesman Maurice Goudeket (1889–   ) in 1935.

In addition to novels, Colette wrote numerous drama criticisms, book reviews, and fashion columns. Several of her works, notably *Gigi* (1945; Eng. trans., 1952), were adapted for the theater and for the motion pictures. In 1945 she became the first woman to be elected to the Goncourt Academy and at her death she was accorded a state funeral.

Colette is considered one of the greatest French fiction writers of the 20th century. Her work is distinguished for its penetration into the motives of characters observed against a sensuous background of nature. She is noted for a lucid and incisive literary method based largely upon remarkable powers of observation and insight. Because the emphasis of Colette's analytical realism falls equally upon objects, animals, and human beings, her detachment sometimes is criticized as cynical. However, her fame rests upon her close understanding of the moral and psychological bases of character, especially those of women, revealed in a luminous prose style wherein all details accumulate meaning.

COLEUS, genus of tropical African and Asian plants, belonging to the mint family, Lamiaceae. There are about one hundred species, several of which are extensively cultivated for their brilliantly colored, variegated foliage. The common garden coleus, *C. blumei*, is a perennial herb which grows from 2 to 3 ft. tall. It has large, regularly toothed leaves, colored variously with red, green, yellow, and purple. In a variety of this species the foliage is more brightly col-

ored and has scalloped edges, formed by deeply indented, rounded teeth. Coleuses are very popular as house plants.

COLFAX, SCHUYLER (1823–85), American statesman, born in New York City. He moved in 1836 to Indiana, where in 1845 he acquired a newspaper at South Bend, which he made the most influential Whig journal in the district. He was a delegate to the Whig conventions of 1848 and 1852, and was elected to the U.S. House of Representatives in 1854 by the newly formed Republican Party, serving until 1869, three times as speaker. In 1868 he was elected Vice-President of the United States, in President Ulysses S. Grant's first term. With his implication in the Crédit Mobilier charges of 1873, he spent the remainder of his life in political retirement.

COLGATE UNIVERSITY, an institution of higher learning for men, situated in Hamilton, New York. It was founded in 1819 by the Baptist Education Society of the State of New York as the Hamilton Literary and Theological Institution. The university was known as Madison University from 1846 to 1890, when it was given its present name in honor of James Boorman Colgate, Samuel Colgate, and their father, William Colgate (see COLGATE), its principal benefactors. Colgate Theological Seminary, one of the university schools, and Rochester Theological Seminary were merged in 1929, becoming known as Colgate-Rochester Divinity School, located in Rochester. Colgate is now principally an undergraduate institution, although graduate study is offered by certain departments. Courses of study leading to A.B. and A.M. degrees are offered. In 1962 enrollment was 1432, including 1407 full-time students; the faculty numbered about 135.

COLIC, a severe cramping pain in the abdomen. When arising in the bowel, it is spasmodic in character and is dependent upon irregular contraction of the muscular coat of the intestines. Intestinal colic is a symptom of neuralgia of the intestines, caused by cold; of mild enteritis, caused by irritating food or purgative medicine; of toxic conditions such as lead poisoning, or poisoning by the bacterial toxins of spoiled foods; or of peritonitis, appendicitis, and other diseases. Infantile colic, common in the first six months of life, is usually caused by flatulence and distention, but may be merely the result of disturbed digestion. Renal colic is pain over the kidney and through the abdominal wall, due to passage of a calculus, or stone, from the kidney through the ureter into the urinary bladder. Biliary colic is caused by the passage of a gallstone from the gall bladder into the intestines. The passage of such stones is extremely painful.

COLIGNY, GASPARD DE (1519–72), French military leader and Huguenot, born at Châtillon-sur-Loing, France. He distinguished himself in the wars which Francis I and Henry II carried on against Spain. In 1552 he was made admiral of France. During his imprisonment, after the capture of St. Quentin (1557) by the Spaniards, he embraced the views of the Huguenots (q.v.), to which the rest of his life was consecrated.

On the accession of Francis II as King of France, his mother, Catherine de Médicis, and the Guises became all-powerful, and opposed all toleration of the Huguenots. However, Coligny by his high character and his abilities succeeded, in conjunction with the heads of the Bourbon family, in effecting the treaty known as the "Pacification of Amboise" (1563), by which the Huguenots were allowed freedom of worship. This concession was gradually withdrawn by the queen mother, and the second Huguenot war broke out in 1567. After the death of the Huguenot leader Louis I, Prince of Condé, in 1569, Coligny was appointed generalissimo of the forces of King Henry of Navarre, a Protestant. Peace was concluded in 1570. Catherine, alarmed once more at the influence of Coligny over the young king, Charles IX, organized the massacre of St. Bartholomew, during which Coligny was murdered.

COLIMA, capital of the state of Colima (q.v.), Mexico, situated in the valley of the Colima R., about 50 miles E.N.E. of the port of Manzanillo, with which it is connected by rail. About 40 miles N.E. of the town is the active volcano of Colima (12,782 ft.), the eruption of which in 1941 resulted in a large loss of life. Colima has a considerable trade in farm and cattle products. Pop. (1961) 41,007.

COLISEUM. See AMPHITHEATER.

COLITIS, ULCERATIVE. See PSYCHOSOMATIC MEDICINE: *Ulcerative Colitis.*

COLLAPSE. See SHOCK.

COLLARED LIZARD, one of a genus, *Crotaphytus,* of iguanid lizards, characteristic of the dry, open regions of the s.w. United States. They are often called "collared" or "ring-necked" lizards because of the black collar around the wrinkled neck of the common Texan species, *C. collaris.* This species is found from the Ozark Mountains to Nevada and southern California and is entirely insectivorous. Although stout of body, it can run very rapidly, and very often runs upon the hind legs alone. In the deserts of the Colorado valley there lives a second species, called "leopard lizard", *C. wislizenii,* is larger, has no collar, and is noted for its fierce and greedy disposition. It eats not only blossoms, leaves, and insects, but also young horned toads, and all sorts of smaller lizards, killing and swallowing some two thirds its own size. It will even kill and devour smaller individuals of its own species. This lizard is remarkable for the fact that not only the male, but the female as well, undergoes a change of color in the breeding season (midsummer), the latter becoming salmon red on the whole abdominal region.

COLLECT, a brief, comprehensive prayer in the liturgies of the Roman and Anglican churches. It varies with the feast and the season; it is recited in the Mass or Communion Service before the epistle, and is repeated as the concluding prayer of the canonical hours (see BREVIARY). All of the earlier Christian liturgies contained such prayers, and some collects still in use appeared as early as the 4th century. In early manuscripts they were called *orationes ad plebem collectam;* in the Roman missal the term oratio is retained, while in the Anglican Prayer Book and in the vernacular the term *collect* is used. A single collect was originally prescribed, but, with the growth of the church calendar, it became customary to commemorate a festival, displaced by one of greater importance, by adding its collect to the collect of the day. The *secret* and the *postcommunion,* two other prayers similar in structure and use to the collect, are contained in the Roman missal, but are not retained in the Anglican Prayer Book, which contains almost literal translations of the Latin collects for most of its services.

COLLECTIVE BARGAINING. See LABOR RELATIONS; NATIONAL LABOR RELATIONS ACT; TRADE UNION.

COLLECTIVISM, a social economic system in which the means of production are controlled by groups of workers using them or by the state, rather than by individuals or groups of capitalists. The term is often used to designate any system favoring a more or less equal distribution of the products of industry, as opposed to capitalist control of industry or private or individual profit. In this sense collectivism differs little from theoretical *socialism;* but practical socialism is more concerned with using existing governmental structure for obtaining an equal distribution of the products of industry by such means as graduated taxation, universal insurance, and state control of industry and public utilities. Marxian socialism advocates abolition of capital and profit, to be achieved by establishing a dictatorship of the proletariat. *Communism* is a more extreme form of collectivism in which private property is abolished, as well as capital and profit. *Bolshevism*, originally the name given to the philosophy of the majority group within the Social Democratic Party in Russia, contemplates the establishment of a classless communistic society by means of a period of state socialism in which state control is at first strengthened, and later gradually eliminated. Since the Bolshevist Party changed its name to the Communist Party after the revolution in Russia in 1917, the terms bolshevism and communism are popularly regarded as synonymous. *Communalism* is a form of collectivism in which ownership and control of the means of production are vested in a smaller unit, the commune (q.v.), with corresponding reduction in the authority of the state. See separate articles on the systems mentioned. See also PLANNED ECONOMY.

COLLEGE (Lat. *collegium,* "a society"), in general usage in the United States, a designation applied to a school of higher learning, either affiliated with a university or independently constituted, which provides curriculums in the liberal arts and sciences leading to the bachelor's degree. As originally employed in Great Britain the term designated an organization, usually located near a university and endowed, which provided lodging and board for scholars. These organizations eventually became constituent, self-governing parts of the universities in which their members were enrolled. Every member of the university had to attach himself to a college; conversely, every person admitted to a college was required to matriculate in the university. Both Cambridge and Oxford universities (qq.v.) evolved in this fashion. Colleges which functioned independently of universities developed into self-contained schools. In its broadest meaning, the term denotes an association or group of persons with mutual duties, objectives, and, sometimes, certain privileges. Thus it is occasionaly applied in Great Britain and the United States to associations which have scientific purposes, for example, *college of physicians* and *college of surgeons.*

In early Roman usage, "college" signified any association of persons having a common purpose or performing a specific function. The word was synonymous in some respects with *corpus,* a corporation or body of members;

with *universitas,* a whole as contrasted with its parts; and with *societas,* a partnership. The Roman college was required to be incorporated by public authority, could possess common property, and could sue or be sued in the name of its manager. Many of these colleges were mercantile in character or were organizations of artisans similar to the medieval guilds, but there were others, with religious or political purposes, such as the *college of augurs* and the *college of pontiffs.* Similar applications of the term which have survived to modern times include *college of cardinals, college of bishops,* and *college of presidential electors.*

COLLÈGE DE FRANCE, public educational institution in Paris, founded about 1530 by King Francis I. Supported by the French government, it is under the jurisdiction of the Ministry of Public Instruction. The Collège has had an autonomous status throughout its existence, despite repeated attempts of the University of Paris to secure control. Though a royal institution, the Collège escaped suspension during the French Revolution because of its reputation for academic freedom and integrity. It offers free courses, without matriculation and examination, on a wide variety of subjects in the arts and sciences. Programs of study, none of which lead to a degree, are designed to attract scholars more mature than the average university student. Among the celebrated savants who have taught at the Collège were Petrus Ramus, Pierre Gassendi, Charles Rollin, Baron Silvestre de Sacy, Édouard Laboulaye, and Jules Michelet.

COLLEGE OF ELECTORS. See ELECTORAL COLLEGE.

COLLEGE OF EUROPE (Fr. *Collège d'Europe*), international, coeducational college, founded in 1950, and located in Bruges, Belgium. It was founded on the initiative of the International Cultural Section of the European Movement, an educational committee formed in connection with the establishment of the European Coal and Steel Community (q.v.). Supported by the governments of Belgium, the Federal Republic of Germany, Luxembourg, the Netherlands, and France, by the city of Bruges, and by the European Coal and Steel Community, the college is a graduate center with facilities for approximately forty students. Its faculty is composed of resident and visiting lecturers of many nationalities. The special objectives of the college are the study of the political, economic, social, and cultural problems encountered by the Western European Union (q.v.)

and the training of groups of young Europeans for work toward realizing the ideal of European unity. Courses are offered in the fields of diplomacy, international organizations, public service, education, and journalism. The first rector of the college was the Dutch educator Henry Brugmans; its principal publication is the quarterly *Les Cahiers de Bruges*.

COLLEGE OF THE CITY OF NEW YORK, now **THE CITY UNIVERSITY OF NEW YORK,** collective name of the seven coeducational, municipally controlled institutions of higher learning of New York City. The colleges are The City College, Brooklyn College, Hunter College, Queens College (qq.v.), Bronx Community College, Staten Island Community College, and Queensborough Community College.

COLLEGES, AMERICAN. See UNIVERSITIES AND COLLEGES, AMERICAN.

COLLEGES, LAND-GRANT. See LAND-GRANT COLLEGES.

COLLIE, a working dog originating in Great Britain, and used for herding cattle and sheep. Two varieties are known, the rough-coated and the smooth-coated. The rough-coated collie originated in Scotland in the 17th century and was used in herding sheep. It is believed that collies for sheepherding were imported into America in early Colonial times. The rough-coated collie has a flat skull tapering gradually to the eyes; eyes of medium size with an extremely alert and intelligent expression; small ears; a muscular neck with a full frill; and a moderately long tail, usually carried low. The dog has an abundant coat, usually black and tan in color, with a white collar and frill; and sometimes sable with white markings. The male of this type is about 24 inches high at the shoulder and weighs about 60 pounds; the bitch is about 22

Evelyn M. Shafer
Rough-coated collie

inches high and weighs about 50 pounds.

The smooth-coated collie originated in the north of England and was used for driving cattle and sheep to market. The coat of the smooth-coated collie is short and dense and usually black and white. The dog has almond-shaped eyes; small ears; a long, well-shaped neck; muscular, sloping shoulders; and a tail of medium length. The male smooth-coated collie stands from 22 to 24 inches high; the bitch, from 20 to 22 inches.

COLLIER, JEREMY (1650–1726), English clergyman, born at Stow with Quy, Cambridgeshire, and educated at Cambridge University. He was rector at Ampton, Suffolk, from 1679 until 1685. When King James II was deposed in favor of William of Orange in 1688, Collier joined those who refused to forswear their oath of allegiance to the former king by pledging loyalty to William, and were thus known as "nonjurors". He was several times imprisoned for his writings; in 1696 he publicly absolved two prisoners about to be executed for the attempted assassination of the king, and was declared an outlaw. Despite this status he remained an active nonjuror, and devoted his energy to criticism of the contemporary stage, attacking such playwrights as Sir John Vanbrugh and William Congreve in a dissertation, *Short View of the Immorality and Profaneness of the English Stage* (1698). This work started a public discussion which persisted for about ten years, but did little to accomplish Collier's purpose, despite considerable public sympathy. During these and later years he also compiled his *Great Historical, Geographical, Genealogical, and Poetical Dictionary* (4 vols., 1701–21), and wrote *Ecclesiastical History of Great Britain, from the First Planting of Christianity to the End of the Reign of Charles II* (2 vols., 1708–14). In 1712 George Hickes, last surviving nonjuror bishop, consecrated Collier as a bishop.

COLLINS, EDWARD TROWBRIDGE (1887–1951), American baseball player, born at Millerton, N.Y., and educated at Columbia University. He played at second base with the Chicago and Philadelphia clubs of the American League from 1906 to 1930. His lifetime batting average was .333. He was elected an immortal of baseball's Hall of Fame in 1939.

COLLINS, MICHAEL (1892?–1922), Irish patriot and soldier, born at Woodfield, Klonakilty, Ireland. From 1906 to 1916 he was a clerk in the civil service and in a London bank. He took part in the Easter Rebellion of 1916, and was captured. After his release he became one of the chief workers for Irish freedom as a leader in the Sinn Fein (q.v.) movement. In 1918 he was again arrested; later, in spite of persistent attempts to arrest him, he succeeded in eluding the police and also in helping colleagues to escape. While still a fugitive, he was elected to the Sinn Fein revolutionary parliament, and served as finance minister (1919–22). Later he was appointed commander in chief of the Irish Free State forces. On Aug. 22, 1922, he was ambushed and killed.

COLLINS, WILLIAM (1721–59), English poet, born at Chichester and educated at Winchester College and at Oxford University. In 1738, before attending Oxford, he had written the poems which earned him contemporary recognition, *Persian Eclogues,* published in 1742 and later known as *Oriental Eclogues.* After graduation from the university he continued to write verse while attempting to decide on a career. He was saved from utter poverty by a small bequest, but soon began to suffer from fits of insanity which clouded the last nine years of his life. His later work was generally neglected, but brought him the acclaim of a handful of literary connoisseurs, including the poet James Thomson, on whose death in 1748 Collins wrote a moving elegy, and Oliver Goldsmith. Of the small quantity of poetry which he wrote, such pieces as his *Ode to Evening, Ode to Simplicty,* and *The Passions* (all published between 1747 and 1750), and *Ode on the Popular Superstitions of the Highlands of Scotland* (posthumously published, 1788) suffice to place him among the fine lyric poets in English.

COLLINS, WILLIAM WILKIE, better known as WILKIE COLLINS (1824–89), British novelist, born in London, and educated privately. From 1841 to 1846 he clerked in a London firm of tea merchants. Later he was admitted to the bar. His first novel, *Antonina; or, The Fall of Rome* (1850), is a historical romance. In 1851 he met the British novelist Charles Dickens, and the two writers became close associates, each influencing the work of the other. They collaborated in writing the novel *No Thoroughfare* (1867). Collins is best known for his masterpieces *The Woman in White* (1860) and *The Moonstone* (1868), both mystery novels. Like many of his other works, these novels were first published in periodicals edited by Dickens. In later works Collins was primarily concerned with social problems.

Collins strongly influenced the technical development of the English novel, especially the detective novel, by creating a new type of fiction in which character counts for little and the greatest importance attaches to the construction of a plot designed to baffle the reader. Among his other writings are travel sketches published as *Rambles Beyond Railways* (1850–51); a series of ghost stories entitled *After Dark* (1856); and numerous novels, including *The Dead Secret* (1857), *No Name* (1862), *Armadale* (1866), *The New Magdalen* (1873), and *The Legacy of Cain* (1888).

COLLIP, JAMES BERTRAM (1892–   ), Canadian biochemist, born in Belleville, Ontario, and educated at the University of Toronto. He taught biochemistry at the University of Alberta from 1915, becoming full professor in 1922. In 1928 he became professor of biochemistry at McGill University and served until 1941, when he became professor of endocrinology and director of the Research Institute of Endocrinology. After 1946 he served as dean of the medical faculty at the University of Western Ontario and as director of the division of medical research of the National Research Council. In 1923 F. G. Banting and J. J. R. Macleod, who had received the Nobel Prize in medicine for the discovery of insulin (q.v.), insisted on sharing the prize with Collip and C. H. Best for their part in the discovery. Collip received many honors for his work in blood and tissue chemistry, especially for his contributions to the knowledge of the internal secretions of the parathyroids, placenta, pituitary, and pancreas. He was elected fellow of the Royal Society (London), and fellow of the Royal Society of Canada, of which he was president in 1942–43, and was made Commander of the Order of the British Empire in 1943.

COLLOIDAL DISPERSION or **COLLOID SYSTEM,** a mixture of two substances in which one is divided into extremely fine particles dispersed through the other. Colloidal dispersions are sometimes called colloidal solutions or colloidal suspensions, but these titles are not strictly correct, because these dispersions are actually intermediate between true solutions and true suspensions; colloidal particles are larger than the particles of dissolved substances, and smaller than the particles of suspended substances.

Colloid systems are unique in their physical properties, justifying some physicists in holding that such systems constitute a separate state of matter, comparable to solids, liquids, and gases. A colloidal system is usually considered as a two-phase system characterized by a very high ratio of interface surface to the mass or volume of the dispersed phase. Colloid systems are enormously important, both biologically and economically. Virtually all living tissue is colloidal, as are such diverse products as milk, opals, and glue. Smoke is a colloidal dispersion of a solid in a gas; fog is a colloidal dispersion of a liquid in a gas (see AEROSOL); foam is a colloidal dispersion of a gas in a liquid; emulsion is a colloidal dispersion of a liquid in a liquid. The most important case, that of a solid dispersed colloidally in a liquid is commonly called a colloidal solution or "sol". A sol which has set to form a material of jellylike consistency is called a "gel".

No sharp line can be drawn between coarse suspensions, colloidal dispersions, and true solutions. In general, if a simple suspension is allowed to stand long enough the suspended particles will settle, whereas under normal conditions a true colloid will never settle. In general, each particle in a colloidal dispersion consists of many molecules, whereas in true solutions each molecule or ion of solute is separate from every other molecule. On the other hand, some organic compounds, such as proteins, have enormous molecules, so large that each one is equivalent to a colloidal particle. Thus, a solution of a protein behaves in most respects like a typical colloidal dispersion; yet proteins have been crystallized from such solutions, which is generally a characteristic of "true" (i.e., noncolloidal) solutions.

In many respects colloid systems behave like solutions of substances with high molecular weights. Thus colloids, like all dissolved substances, have an effect on the freezing and boiling points of the solvent, but a very small one. Individual colloidal particles are often ionized or charged electrically. Thus rubber can be electroplated from latex, a colloidal dispersion, and the amount of current required is extremely small, since the current required is always in inverse proportion to particle size. A similar electrical phenomenon is the basis of the Cottrell Precipitator (q.v.) for smoke abatement.

The movement of colloidal particles through a fluid under the influence of an electric field is known as electrophoresis. An important method of electrophoresis, devised in 1937 by the Swedish biochemist Arne Vilhelm Tiselius, is used extensively in present-day studies of proteins and blood serums and in the diagnoses of diseases producing abnormalities of the blood serum.

Because of their size, colloidal particles can pass through ordinary filters, but not through the extremely fine openings in a so-called semipermeable membrane, such as a piece of parchment (see OSMOSIS). A liquid cannot flow through a semipermeable membrane, but will *diffuse* through it slowly if there is liquid on both sides. Therefore a colloidal dispersion cannot be purified by filtration, but it can be dialyzed by placing it in a semipermeable bag with pure water on the outside. Dissolved impurities then gradually diffuse through the bag while the colloidal particles remain imprisoned within it. If the process of dialysis is carried to completion, the suspension will often break down (i.e., settle), since the stability of colloidal systems depends on the electrical charges on the individual particles, and these are in turn generally dependent on the presence of dissolved impurities. See also DIFFUSION.

Although individual colloidal particles are too small to be seen with an ordinary microscope, they can be made visible by a technique called ultramicroscopy. If a colloidal dispersion is placed under a microscope and a beam of light is directed through it from one side, the path of the beam becomes visible by scattering from the colloidal particles. This same phenomenon makes the path of a beam of light visible in a darkened room, but under the microscope separate flashes of light are observed. The particles are seen to be in motion (see BROWNIAN MOVEMENT), and their speed is exactly that calculated for molecules of the size of the colloidal particles. The particles are directly visible in an electron microscope.

Because of the Brownian movement and because of repulsion between like electrical charges, colloidal suspensions will not settle out under the influence of gravity. By the use of ultracentrifuges yielding fields of force more than a million times as great as that of gravity, such suspensions can be caused to settle, and much has been learned of colloids by studying sedimentation rates and other properties of colloidal suspensions in such fields. See CENTRIFUGE; CHROMATOGRAPHY.

H.A.N.

COLMAR (Ger. *Kolmar*), capital of the department of Haut-Rhin, Alsace, France, situated on a plain in the vicinity of the Vosges Mountains, on the Logelbach and Lauch rivers, 40 miles s.s.w. of Strasbourg. Colmar is connected with the Rhine River by the Rhine-Rhône Canal. It became a free city of the Holy Roman Empire in 1226. From the 13th to the 18th century a struggle took place for control of the city's government between the democratic and the aristocratic elements of Colmar, ending finally in the victory of the democratic element. By a unilateral interpretation of the Treaty of Nijmegen (1678) which had ended the war (1672–78) of France against Holland and the Holy Roman Empire, France annexed Colmar in 1681. The city was restored to Germany at the end (1871) of the Franco-Prussian War, and returned to France after World War I by the Treaty of Versailles (1919). In World War II it was taken by the Germans in 1940 and recaptured by the French in 1945.

Among the city's notable buildings are the Roman Catholic church of St. Martin (13th and 14th centuries); the Lutheran parish church (15th century); a Dominican monastery (13th century), now a museum containing the town library; the courthouse; and the town hall. Colmar is in a rich agricultural district producing tobacco, vegetables, fruit, and vineyards. The principal industries are the manufacture of woolen, silk, and cotton textiles, starch, sewing thread, machinery, soap, candles, pipes, ribbons, and hosiery; bleaching; sugar refining; and the brewing of beer. The German painter, Martin Schongauer and the French sculptor, Frédéric Auguste Bartholdi (qq.v.), were born in Colmar. Pop. (1962) 51,779.

CÖLN. See Cologne.

COLOCYNTH, an herbaceous vine, *Citrullus colocynthis,* of the same genus as the watermelon, native to the countries surrounding the Mediterranean Sea. Its round, yellow, thin-skinned, 3-inch fruit is sometimes called the bitter apple, gourd, or cucumber. The dried pulp of the fruit contains a bitter glucoside, colocynthin, $C_{56}H_{84}O_{23}$, and is sometimes used in medicine for its purgative properties. It is poisonous in large doses.

COLOGNE (Ger. *Köln* or *Cöln*), city of North Rhine-Westphalia, West Germany, situated on the Rhine River, 325 miles S.W. of Berlin and 44 miles N.E. of Aachen. Its location at the point where the route from Paris to the N.E. of Germany is crossed by the Rhine, and also at the junction of many roads along the Rhine, has given Cologne great commercial importance. It is a railroad center and one of the chief ports of Europe.

Cologne was originally a town of the Ubii, a Germanic tribe, and was then called *Oppidum Ubiorum*. In 50 A.D. the Roman emperor, Claudius I, established a colony there and named it *Colonia Agrippina,* after his wife, a native of the town. It grew and prospered under Roman rule and subsequently under that of the Franks, who took the town about 330 A.D. The bishopric of Cologne was founded in 313 and was elevated to the rank of an archiepiscopal see by Charlemagne in 785. The archbishop of Cologne was recognized as elector of the Holy Roman Empire by the Golden Bull of 1356. During the wars of the French Revolution, the French took Cologne in 1794 and by the Treaty of Lunéville in 1801 they secularized the archbishopric and annexed the city to France. The Congress of Vienna, which met in 1814 after the final defeat of Napoleon, assigned Cologne to Prussia in 1815. In World War I the British bombed Cologne twice in 1918. Following the war, the city was general headquarters for the British army of occupation from December, 1918 to January, 1926. In World War II Cologne was the object of frequent heavy raids by Allied air forces. The old town, including the Roman and medieval parts of the city, was 90 percent destroyed, but the cathedral was only slightly damaged. After the defeat of Germany in 1945, Cologne was incorporated in the British zone of occupation.

In Roman days the town was a rectangular tract surrounded by walls. Medieval Cologne was crescent shaped and was enclosed by a rampart, walls, and gates. Inside these fortifications was a maze of narrow, crooked streets, which still exist today. Between 1881 and 1885 the fortifications were razed and a boulevard, the Ringstrasse, four miles long, was constructed on their site. Beyond the Ringstrasse is the modern part of Cologne, with wide streets, modern houses, and parks. Across the Rhine is the suburb of Deutz with which Cologne is connected by several bridges.

Cologne is noted for its university, founded in 1388, and for its churches. The Cologne Cathedral, a magnificent example of the Gothic cathedral in Northern Europe, is 443 feet long and 282 feet wide, with spires 512 feet high. It was begun in 1248 but not completed until 1880. The great bell of the south tower, the *Kaiserglocke,* cast in 1874 from French cannon captured in the Franco-Prussian War, is one of the largest in the world. The cathedral contains the shrine of the Magi, which covers the reputed bones of the three Magi, and has been the objective of many pilgrimages. Cologne's oldest church, St. Maria im Kapitol, consecrated in 1049, was destroyed by bombs. Among other important churches are those of St. Gereon (11th century), St. Kunibert (13th century), and the Jesuits' Church (17th century). The churches of St. Martin (12th and 13th centuries) and the Apostles (12th century) were destroyed by bombs. Modern ecclesiastical buildings include a Roman Catholic church in Deutz (erected 1896) and a large synagogue in the modern section of Cologne (1899).

Among the noteworthy old secular buildings was the Rathaus, the central and oldest portion of which dated from the 14th century. It contained the restored Hansa Saal, in which the first general meeting of the Hanseatic League (q.v.) was held (1366). The Gürzenich, erected in 1441–52 as a festive hall, was used from 1875 as a stock exchange. Both buildings were gutted by bombs. The Templars' Lodge, a Romanesque building of the 12th or 13th century, is now used by the Cologne chamber of commerce. Among notable buildings erected in modern times are the palatial government buildings (1830); the Municipal Museum (1855–61); the Stadtheater (1872); the Court of Justice (1886–93); the post office (1893), and the Imperial Bank (1897). A central railroad station was built in 1889–94. The city is noted for the many fine monuments which it contains. Its zoological garden, which was opened in 1860, is one of the finest in Europe.

Cologne is a center for trade in wine, oil, corn, timber, coal, porcelain, dyes, drugs, and other goods. Among the many commodities manufactured in the city are chocolate, sugar, cigars, tobacco, mineral waters, textiles, machinery, glue, soap, and the world-famous toilet water, eau de Cologne. Pop. (1960 est.) 789,300.

COLOMBIA, republic of South America, situated in the northwestern part of the continent. It is bounded on the N. by Panama and the Caribbean Sea, on the E. by Venezuela and Brazil, on the S. by Peru and Ecuador, and on the W. by the Pacific Ocean. It is the only country of South America with coasts on both the Caribbean Sea and the Pacific Ocean. The capital and largest city of Colombia is Bogotá (q.v.). The principal commercial cities are Medellín; Barranquilla, the chief international airport; and Cali (qq.v.). Other important cities are Manizales, Cartagena, Ibagué, Cúcuta, Bucaramanga, Pasto, Santa Marta, Neiva, Popayán, and Tunja. Colombia is composed of 25 major administrative units. These are the 17 departments of Antioquia, Atlántico, Bolívar, Boyacá, Caldas, Cauca, Chocó, Córdoba, Cundinamarca, Huila, Magdalena, Meta, Nariño, Norte de Santander, Santander, Tolima, and Valle del Cauca; the 4 intendencies of Arauca, Caquetá, La Guajira, and San Andrés y Providencia; and the 4 com-

Standard Oil Co. (N.J.)
Statue of Simón Bolívar, Medellín, Colombia

missaries of Amazonas, Putumayo, Vaupés, and Vichada. The area of Colombia is estimated at 439,617 square miles. The population (1961 est.) is 14,446,580.

THE LAND

Physical Characteristics. The distinguishing topographical feature of Colombia is the Andean mountain chain, situated in the central and western parts of the country, and extending from N. to S. across almost its entire length. These mountains comprise three principal and parallel ranges, the Eastern Cordillera, the Central Cordillera, and the Western Cordillera. In the north the Eastern Cordillera divides into two ranges, one extending northeastward into Venezuela, the other merging with the Sierra de Perijá, which extends northward almost to the Caribbean. On the Caribbean coast, northeast of the Sierra de Perijá, is the isolated mountain mass known as the Sierra Nevada de Santa Marta, the highest peak of which is 19,030 ft. above sea level. The central Cordillera contains the volcanic peaks of Huila, 18,701 ft. above sea level, and Tolima, 18,438 ft. About 150 m. south of the Caribbean, the Central Cordillera descends to form low marshland, covered with dense jungles. West of the Western Cordillera, extending along the thickly forested Pacific Coast, is the Cordillera de Baudó. The peaks of the Cordilleras are perpetually covered with snow; the timber line is about 10,000 ft.

East of the Eastern Cordillera are vast reaches of torrid lowlands, thinly populated and only partly explored. The southern portion of this region, called *selvas* ("rain forests"), is thickly forested and is drained by the Caquetá R. and other tributaries of the Amazon. The northern and greater part of the region comprises vast plains, or *llanos,* and is traversed by the Meta and other tributaries of the Orinoco. Between the cordilleras are high plateaus, a number of which are more than 8000 ft. above sea level, and fertile valleys, traversed by the principal rivers of the country. The principal river of Colombia, the Magdalena, flows northward between the Eastern and Central cordilleras, across practically the entire country, emptying into the Caribbean near Barranquilla after a journey of about 1000 miles. The Cauca, also an important means of communication, flows northward between the Central and Western cordilleras, merging with the Magdalena about 200 m. from the Caribbean. Between the Western Cordillera and the Cordillera de Baudó, the Atrato flows north to empty into the Gulf of Darien, an inlet of the Caribbean. In the west the Patía cuts its way through the Andes to empty into the Pacific. From the Western Cordillera the San Juan, the Dagua, and a number of other short streams make precipitous descents into the Pacific.

The coastline of Colombia extends for about 1100 m. along the Caribbean and for about 900 m. along the Pacific. River mouths along the coasts are numerous but there are no good natural harbors. The Caribbean coast is mostly swampy and the river estuaries are shallow or are obstructed by shifting sand bars or other natural impediments. The principal port is Barranquilla, on the Magdalena R., 11 m. from its mouth on the Caribbean Sea. Other important ports are the Caribbean port of Cartagena; Buenaventura, the chief Pacific port; and Tumaco, the most southerly Pacific port.

Climate. Colombia lies almost entirely in the north torrid zone. The climate, however, varies with the altitude. The low regions along the coast and the deep Patía and Magdalena river valleys are torrid and malarial. From 1500 ft. to about 7500 ft. the climate is subtropical, and from 7500 ft. to 10,000 ft. it is temperate. In the latter zone are situated most of the principal cities of the republic, including Bogotá, which has an annual mean temperature of 57° F. Above 10,000 ft. is the zone of cold climate.

Throughout the year three-month periods of rain alternate with equal periods of dry weather. The period of rain is called invierno ("winter") and the period of dry weather is known as verano ("summer"). The occurrence of these periods varies from year to year and from place to place. Along the Pacific coast precipitation is tropically heavy; in the Chocó district it rains afternoons and evenings all the year round. At Bogotá, about 8650 ft. above sea level, the annual rainfall averages about 40 inches. Dry weather prevails along the slopes of the Eastern Cordillera.

Flora and Fauna. The indigenous flora of Colombia is diverse, ranging from trees and plants common to tropical areas to those characteristic of the temperate zone. Along the Caribbean coast coconut palms and mangroves grow extensively. In the forest areas of the country, estimated at more than 150,-000,000 acres, are a wide variety of commercially useful trees. These include wax and ivory-nut palms, and trees yielding tolu balsam, copaiba balsam, rubber, balatá, chicle, cinchona, and divi-divi. Among cabinet and building woods are mahogany, lignum vitae, oak, walnut, cedars, and pine. In addition, there are plants yielding vanilla, sarsaparilla, ginger, gum copal, ipecac, tonka beans, and castor beans.

The fauna is also of great variety and includes the larger South American mammals, such as the jaguar, puma, tapir, peccary, anteater, sloth, armadillo, various species of monkey, and, on the plateaus, one or more species of red deer. Alligators, once numerous but now becoming scarce because they are hunted intensively for their commercially valuable hides, are found along the principal rivers. Snakes of several kinds are found in the low, hot regions. The condor, vulture, toucan, parrot, cockatoo, crane, stork, and a variety of hummingbird are a part of the rich avifauna.

ECONOMIC ACTIVITY

Agriculture. Colombia is primarily an agricultural country. The majority of the population is employed in crop farming and stock raising. But most of the arable land is uncultivated, and the agricultural methods in use are backward; in many areas they are primitive. Coffee is the principal crop and the main source of the country's wealth. Colombia is second only to Brazil in the annual volume

Continued on page 2254

of coffee produced, and is the world's leading producer of mild coffee. The crop is cultivated chiefly on mountain slopes between 3000 and 6000 ft. above sea level, principally in the departments of Caldas, Antioquia, Cundinamarca, Norte de Santander, Tolima, and Santander. There are more than 150,000 plantations, chiefly small, extending over approximately 880,000 acres and containing almost 600,000,000 trees. Coffee output totals about 7,200,000 bags weighing 132 lbs. each. About 88% of the coffee exported goes to the U.S. The principal crops, in addition to coffee, are sugar cane, rice, bananas, and cotton. Other crops include cereal grains, vegetables, a wide variety of tropical and semitropical fruits, including coconuts and pineapples, and cacao, tobacco, and peanuts. Plants producing fique, pita, sisal, and hemp fibers, used in the manufacture of cordage and coarse sacking material, are raised. Silkworms are cultivated. Rubber trees grow wild, but some cultivation has been undertaken.

Stock raising is centered in the valleys and plateaus of the cordilleras, in the *llanos*, and in the coastal districts. Colombia has about 12,100,000 head of cattle, 1,000,000 horses, 1,000,000 donkeys and mules, 1,114,000 sheep, 400,000 goats, and 1,727,000 hogs.

Pearlfisheries exist on the north coast, especially off the Goajira Peninsula.

Mining and Manufacturing. Petroleum and gold are the two principal mineral resources of Colombia. About 85% of the petroleum industry is controlled by American interests, principally subsidiaries of Standard Oil, and about 15% by British investors; Colombians own less than 1% of the industry. Production is centered in the valley of the Magdalena R., about 400 m. from the Caribbean, and in the region between the Eastern Cordillera and Venezuela; it amounts annually to more than 6,000,000 metric tons, half of which is shipped to Curaçao for refining. About 85% of the annual yield is exported.

Gold, mined in Colombia since Spanish colonial times, is found principally in the department of Antioquia, and to a lesser extent in the departments of Cauca, Caldas, Nariño, Tolima, and Chocó. Colombia is the leading gold producer of South America. About 60% of the annual production is controlled by foreign concessionaires. Platinum, first discovered in Colombia a little over 200

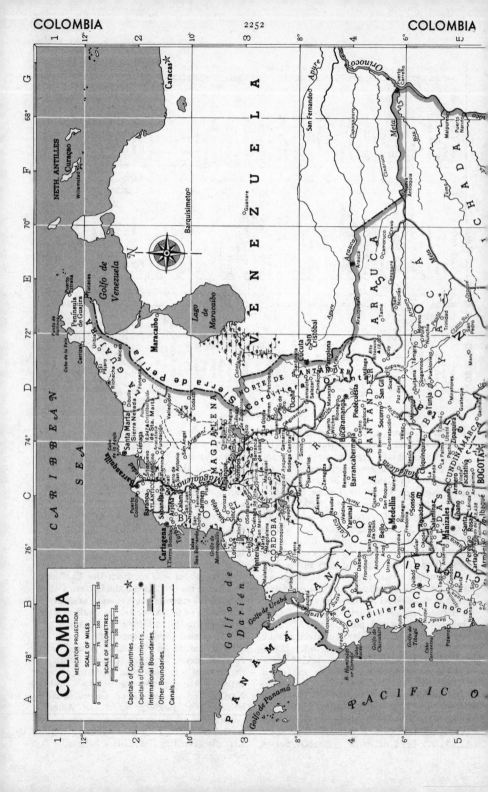

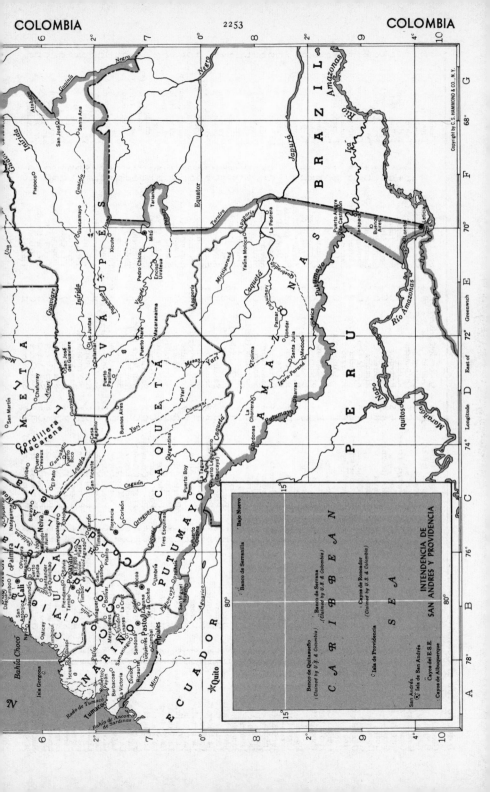

Index to Map of Colombia—cont.

years ago, is found in the auriferous sands of the San Juan and Atrato river basins. Colombia has the largest platinum deposits in the world. Total production of this metal is about 29,000 fine oz. annually. Colombia is one of the foremost countries of the world in emerald production. The chief emerald-mining centers are the government-owned Muzo mine and the American-owned, but government-controlled, Chiver mine. Other important mineral products are silver, coal, and salt. Deposits of copper, lead, iron, manganese, zinc, mercury, mica, phosphates, and sulfur are largely unworked because of inadequate transportation facilities.

Manufacturing industries in Colombia, stimulated in recent years by the establishment of high protective tariffs on imports, are generally small-scale enterprises, producing for the domestic market. About 152,000 workers are employed in about 8200 industrial establishments of 5 or more workers. Cotton-spinning mills, situated principally in the cities of Barranquilla, Manizales, Medellín, and Samacá, are the chief manufacturing establishments. Other industries include the manufacture of foodstuffs and tobacco products, brewing, and flour milling. Chemical products are becoming increasingly important, and footwear, Panama hats, and glassware are made. Electric power consumed annually amounts to about 1,276,000,000 kilowatt-hours.

Commerce. The principal exports, in the order of value, are coffee (82%), petroleum (15.5%), leather, bananas, and platinum; leading imports are machinery, vehicles, metals and manufactures, and chemical products. The United States absorbs about 81% of Colombia's exports and supplies 62% of the imports. Other export markets of Colombia are Curaçao, Germany, Canada, Sweden, the Netherlands, Trinidad and Tobago, Belgium and Luxembourg, and France. Leading sources of imports, in addition to the United States, are the United Kingdom, Germany, Belgium and Luxembourg, Canada, Curaçao, the Netherlands, and Sweden.

Communications. The difficult terrain of Colombia makes the construction of roads and railways costly. Colombia has approximately 2000 m. of railways on 17 lines, 8 of them owned by the central government or the departmental administrations of the country. Most of the national railways are feeder lines to the Magdalena R., the main transport artery of the country, navigable for about 900 m. from its mouth. The government announced in 1954 that all railways would be nationalized. The length of motor highways is about 17,000 m. Included among the auto roads is a part of the Simon Bolívar Highway, linking Caracas, Venezuela, through Bogotá and other Colombian towns, with Quito, Ecuador. Aerial transport was begun in Colombia in 1919. The national air companies annually carry over 1,388,000 passengers and about 127,000 tons of freight. Pan American World Airways, called Avianca in Colombia, connects that country with Panama, Caribbean lands, and the United States. In 1946 Colombia, Venezuela, and Ecuador jointly agreed to establish the Greater Colombia Merchant Marine; Venezuela withdrew in 1953.

THE PEOPLE

Population. About 68% of the population of Colombia is composed of descendants of intermarriages between Spanish colonial settlers, native Indians, and Negroes. About 20% of the population is white. Indians comprise about 7% of the total, and pure Negroes about 5%. The urban population is about 38%, the fertile valley and plateau of the Eastern Cordillera being the most densely populated area.

Immigration into Colombia, since the country achieved its independence in the first part of the 19th century, has been negligible, with the result that the population has been developing in the direction of racial homogeneity. The official language of the country is Spanish. In Bogotá is spoken the purest Spanish in South America. Roman Catholicism is the predominant religion.

Education. A law passed in 1934 stipulates that a minimum of 10% of the government income shall be spent on public education. However, only about 6% is allotted for this purpose. Primary education is free but not compulsory; primary and secondary school enrollment totals about 1,438,000 students annually. More than 35% of the population is illiterate. Institutions of higher learning include the National University at Bogotá, founded in 1572, nine public universities, and ten private universities.

GOVERNMENT

The constitution of 1886 and its subsequent amendments provide the basis for a highly centralized republican form of government in Colombia. Executive power is vested in a president, legislative power in a bi-cameral congress, and judicial power in a supreme court and its subordinate courts. The president is elected by direct popular vote for a four-year term, and may not succeed himself immediately. The ministers comprising the cabinet are appointed by the president, but are responsible to congress. The president also appoints the governors of the departments, the executive officers of the departmental subdivisions, called municipal districts, and the commissioners who administer the intendencies and commissaries. Congress consists of a senate and a house of representatives. The Senate consists, since 1958, of 80 members elected for four-year terms by direct popular vote. The House of Representatives has, since 1960, 152 members elected by direct popular vote for two-year terms. Supreme court judges are nominated by the president and are elected by congress. They appoint the judges of the superior courts. All citizens over twenty-one years of age, with the exception of members of the police force and of the army, are eligible to vote and to be elected to public office. Women acquired the right to vote in 1954. A one-year term of military service is compulsory for men between twenty-one and thirty years of age.

HISTORY

In 1502, on his last voyage to the New World, Columbus explored a part of the Caribbean coast of the empire of the Chibcha Indians (q.v.), now the northern coast of Colombia. He was followed by a number of Spanish conquistadores, who conquered the Chibchas and established the first permanent settlement of Europeans on the American mainland, on the site of Darien (1510), and the settlements of Santa Marta (1525) and Santa Fé de Bogotá (1538). In 1549 the former Chibcha empire was included in the Audencia of New Granada. Between 1717 and 1739 the Audencia of New Granada and the territories which later became Ecuador, Venezuela, and Panama, were included in the Viceroyalty of New Granada. Lack of economic progress, and social and political discrimination against native-born New Granadans caused intense hostility to Spanish rule. Inspired by the successful American and French revolutions of the late 18th century, the people of New Granada joined the revolutionary movement for independence which swept over Spain's New World empire in the first part of the 19th century.

In the wars which followed, Simón Bolívar (q.v.) was the outstanding revolutionary and military figure. His decisive victory over the Spanish royalists at the battle of Boyacá River (see BOYACÁ, BATTLE OF), on Aug. 7, 1819, resulted in the liberation of the former Audencia of New Granada. The Congress of Angostura, which followed, on Dec. 17, 1819, proclaimed the formation of the state of Greater Colombia, to comprise the former Audencia of New Granada, present-day Panama, and, upon their liberation, Venezuela and Ecuador. Following the liberation of Venezuela in 1821, the Congress of Cúcuta, on Aug. 30, 1821, adopted a constitution for Greater Colombia, providing for a republican form of government, and elected Bolívar the republic's first president. The new republic was short-lived. In 1831, following its dissolution, New Granada (including Panama) became a separate republic.

The history of the country as an independent state is, in large part, a record of the struggle, frequently resulting in civil war, of liberal and conservative elements to determine government policy. Political and social issues were frequently complicated by bitter controversies involving the property, legal status, and privileges of the Roman Catholic Church.

Slavery was abolished in New Granada in 1851–52. A new constitution, adopted in 1853, provided for trial by jury, freedom of the press, and other civil rights. In 1853 church and state were separated. Five years later the provinces became federal states and the name of the republic was changed to Granadine Confederation. Civil war broke out in 1861 between liberal elements, favoring greater sovereignty for the states comprising the republic, and conservative elements, fighting for a strong central government. Following the victory of the liberals a new constitution was adopted in 1863 providing for a union of sovereign states, and formally changing the name of the republic to the United States of Colombia.

In the half-century 1880–1930, conservative policies predominated. A revolt of liberal elements was suppressed in 1885. A new constitution was proclaimed in 1886 and the present name of the country, the Republic of Colombia, was chosen. The new constitution abolished the sovereign states created by the constitution of 1863, and established the present basic structure of the country. The Roman Catholic Church was made the official church.

In 1903 the Colombian senate refused to ratify the Hay-Herrán Treaty, which provided for the leasing to the United States of a strip of territory across the Isthmus of Panama for the purpose of building a transisthmic canal. A revolt broke out in Panama; United States armed forces intervened to prevent the suppression of the uprising by

Colombian troops; and the United States recognized Panama as an independent state. The strained relations which followed between Colombia and the United States were finally resolved by the Thomson-Urrutia Treaty, negotiated in 1914 and ratified in 1921. By the terms of this treaty Colombia received $25,000,000 and special transit rights for its goods across the Isthmus of Panama.

Most of Colombia's boundary disputes were settled by arbitration and without incident. But in 1932 a century-old boundary dispute with Peru almost led to war, when armed Peruvians occupied the town of Leticia, in territory ceded to Colombia by Peru in 1927. A peaceful solution of the issue was reached in 1934.

The return to power of liberal elements, which took place in the election of 1930, resulted, in 1936, in amendments to the constitution giving the government power to regulate privately owned property in the national interest; establishing the right of workers to strike, subject to legal regulation; disestablishing the Catholic Church; and secularizing public education. A new labor code adopted in 1944 provided for minimum wage scales, paid vacations and holidays, accident and sickness benefits, and the right to organize.

During World War II Colombia severed diplomatic relations with Japan, Germany, and Italy, in 1941, and with the government of Marshal Pétain of France, in 1942. In 1943 the Colombian senate declared a state of belligerency with Germany, and the republic was admitted into the United Nations. Colombia signed the formal charter of the United Nations organization in June, 1945, becoming one of the 51 original members.

On April 9, 1948, dissatisfaction on the part of the people of Bogotá with the Conservative government elected in 1946, was fanned into a revolutionary flame by the assassination, in Bogotá, of Jorge Eliécer Gaitán, leader of the Liberals and their nominee for the 1950 presidential election campaign. Angered masses of people set fire to the presidential palace and other buildings and invaded the Capitolio, where the 9th International Conference of American States was in session. The Conference was disrupted and the delegates, including United States Secretary of State George C. Marshall, fled for their lives. Revolutionary elements seized radio stations and called for a nation-wide uprising. The trade unions in Bogotá called a general strike in the city.

On April 10, the cabinet, previously composed exclusively of Conservatives, was reorganized to include an equal number of Conservatives and Liberals. Through the army, which remained loyal to the government, the reorganized cabinet gradually acquired control of the situation. On April 15 the general strike was called off. Government spokesmen and some of the delegates to the Inter-American Conference blamed Colombian communists for the uprising, but communist leaders arrested during the disturbances were soon released. According to reliable estimates over 20,000 residents of Bogotá were killed or injured and almost 800 merchants suffered serious financial loss in the fighting. Fatalities throughout the country were estimated at over 1500. Colombia was a signatory (April 30) of the charter of the Organization of American States. This document was drafted by the Bogotá Conference.

The party antagonisms responsible for the Bogotá uprising deepened during 1949, engendering a state of chronic political turbulence which occasionally resembled civil war. Tension and violence mounted steadily during the congressional election campaign, and on May 25 such campaign activities as parades and meetings were prohibited by governmental decree. The Liberals in the coalition cabinet and in other official positions resigned in protest a few days later. In the election, held on June 5, the Liberal Party retained its majority status in the House of Deputies.

Under a law effectuated in October, the date of the presidential election was advanced to November 27, 1949. Unprecedented violence, with hundreds of killings, marked the ensuing campaign. Charging the government with grave violations of election laws, the Liberal Party withdrew (October 31) its candidate and declared a boycott of the election. On November 9 President Mariano Ospina Pérez dissolved Congress and declared a state of siege. The Conservative candidate Laureano Gómez Castro was elected without opposition.

Introducing a new phase of the political struggle, a group of armed men, described by the government as "bandits", attacked (December 14) a Conservative Party rally in Cocuy, killing 82 persons. By the spring of 1950 bands of guerrillas were in action in many outlying sections of the country. On May 28 the government extended the state of siege and prorogued the 1950 session of Congress, perpetuating the Conservatives' dictatorial control of the nation.

President Gómez Castro was inaugurated on August 6. Later in August his government was proclaimed illegal by a convention of the

Liberal Party. In a manifesto drafted by the Liberal Party leader Dario Echandia the government was accused of suppressing freedom of speech, press, assembly, and movement. The manifesto charged that the government's 1949 declaration of a state of siege was designed to prevent a Liberal victory in the presidential election. The International Bank for Reconstruction and Development, an agency of the United Nations, submitted (August 12) to the government the results of an exhaustive study of the Colombian economy and proposed a five-year, $2.5-billion program for industrial and agricultural improvements, expansion of public works, and reforms of the system of taxation. In April, 1951, the Bank granted Colombia a $16.5-million loan for road construction. Additional loans were granted during the next eight months. Meanwhile the Gómez Castro government had collaborated closely with the Western democracies in the fight against communist aggression in Korea. On June 16 a battalion of Colombian volunteers, the first contingent from a South American country, joined the U.N. forces in Korea.

On September 2 the Colombian Commission of Economic Development, completing a study of the International Bank survey of national economic requirements, recommended adoption of a $1.6-billion, five-year development program. In the congressional elections, held on September 16, the Conservative Party won an overwhelming victory. The aggregate vote polled by the Communist Party and Popular Liberal Party, the only opposition groups participating, was less than 2 percent of the total. The Liberal Party boycotted the election. Due to illness President Gómez Castro received a leave of absence on November 5; Roberto Urdaneta, a cabinet minister, became provisional president.

Religious persecution, reported on occasion during 1951, became widespread in 1952. In September the Evangelical Confederation of Colombia charged that Colombians had committed over 700 anti-Protestant acts in the past three years. The government claimed several victories over the so-called bandits during the year.

In February, 1953, the Conservative Party completed the draft of a proposed new constitution for the country. Under the provisions of the document, which was to be submitted to a Constitutional Convention in June, Colombia would become a fascist state modeled after Spain. The Liberals and many moderate Conservatives bitterly opposed the changes.

Gómez Castro resumed the presidency on June 13. His government was deposed the same day by a military junta under General Gustavo Rojas Pinilla. Leaders of both political parties approved the *coup d'etat*. The Constitutional Convention met on June 15 and installed Rojas Pinilla as provisional president. He was formally elected by the Convention for a four-year presidential term on Aug. 3, 1954. The Convention also enacted legislation extending the voting privilege to women and outlawing the Communist Party.

In 1955 the government severely curtailed the freedom of the press and took steps to nationalize all newspapers. One of the worst disasters in Colombian history occurred on Aug. 7, 1956, when a convoy of munitions trucks blew up in the city of Cali. The blast killed an estimated 1000 persons and caused damage totaling $10 million.

On Oct. 11, 1956, Rojas Pinilla convened the National Constitutional Assembly. At the session, the first held in two years, a number of delegates openly denounced the restrictive policies of the government. In subsequent months Colombia was swept by a wave of violent demonstrations against the incumbent regime. However, on May 8, 1957, the assembly again elected Rojas Pinilla to a four-year term. This action by the assembly further inflamed public opinion, and on May 10, 1957, a military junta deposed Rojas Pinilla, who fled to Spain. The Liberal and Conservative parties then came to an agreement providing for twelve years' equal share of all governmental offices, including the congress and cabinet. This scheme was overwhelmingly approved in a plebiscite on Dec. 1. Early in 1958 the Liberal-Conservative agreement was extended to sixteen years and on May 4 the Liberal, Alberto Lleras Camargo, was elected president. In October Rojas Pinilla returned from exile. He was arrested and found guilty of violating the constitution and of abusing his power as president.

In 1960 Lleras Camargo announced a plan to raise national income by 5 percent a year from 1960 to 1965. He visited the United States in April, and obtained a loan of $50 million for construction of electric-power plants, railroads, and highways. The early 1960's was a period of increasing economic expansion and stability. On Aug. 7, 1962, Guillermo León Valencia, a Conservative, was inaugurated president.

COLOMBO, capital, chief port, and leading commercial city of the Dominion of Ceylon, and one of the principal ports of the world. It is situated on the w. coast of the island, near the mouth of the Kelani R. It owes its importance largely to its great breakwaters, which give shelter to a large artificial harbor. Prior to the construction of these works, begun in 1875, ocean vessels had to anchor as much as a mile from shore, exposed to inclement weather. A considerable part of the harbor has been dredged to a low-water depth of 36 ft., and Beira Lake, administratively a part of the port of Colombo, has been connected with the harbor by a canal and locks. Colombo handles most of the foreign trade of Ceylon (q.v.), and is one of the most important fueling stations for foreign steamers on the Australian and Asiatic routes.

The European business section of the city, called the Fort, occupies the site of the former fortified area. Its broad avenues and modern buildings are in sharp contrast to the narrow, crooked streets and ramshackle structures of the Pettah, or Asiatic quarter. Among the hospitals of Colombo is the Pasteur Institute. Places of worship include Christian churches, Mohammedan mosques, and Buddhist temples. The city also contains the University of Ceylon, the Ceylon Technical College, and other institutions of learning. The University of Ceylon was established in 1942 by the merger of Ceylon Medical College (1870) and Ceylon University College (1921).

The early name of the city, Kalan-totta (Kalany ferry), derived from a nearby riverferry point, was corrupted into Kalambu by the Arabs and changed to Colombo, in honor of Christopher Columbus, by the Portuguese on their arrival in 1517. The city was taken by the Dutch in 1656 and by the British in 1796. Pop. (1958 est.) 480,000.

COLON. See INTESTINE.

COLÓN, seaport and capital of the province of the same name, in Panama. It is on the Atlantic side of the Isthmus of Panama, 48 m. by rail N.W. of Panama City. Colón, geographically within the Canal Zone, is situated on Manzanillo Island, between Manzanillo Bay and Limón Bay. It is the northern terminus of the Panama Railroad and the Panama Canal.

Under the treaty of 1903, Colón (and Panama City), while remaining Panamanian territory, came under the jurisdiction of the United States in all matters relating to sanitation and public health.

The climate of the city is tropical, the mean temperature being about 80° F.; rainfall is heavy and the humidity averages about 90% during the rainy season.

The deep but exposed harbor of Colón, in Limón Bay, has been improved by a breakwater from Toro Point, erected by the Canal Commission. Docking equipment is modern. Colón was formerly either the terminus or a port of call for about a dozen steamship lines, but has lost much of its steamship business to the newer port of Cristobal (q.v.), where are located the shops of the Panama Railroad. Nevertheless, Colón is still an important port, containing large fueling stations, cold-storage plants, and warehouses. Products shipped from Colón are chiefly bananas, coconuts, pineapples, mahogany and other hardwoods, dyewoods, balata, and ivory nuts.

Colón was founded in 1850 by the builders of the Panama Railroad. For a time it was called "Aspinwall", in honor of William H. Aspinwall, one of the builders, but subsequently the name was changed by statute to Colón, in honor of Christopher Columbus, who sailed into Limón Bay in 1502. When the Canal Commission undertook its work, the population of Colón was about 3000, largely Jamaica Negroes and natives of mixed Spanish, Indian, and Negro blood. Pop. of city (1960) 59,598; of province (1960) 105,416.

COLONIA, capital of Colonia Department, s.w. Uruguay. The uplands of the department are barren, but the valleys and plains are fertile. Farming and stock-raising are the principal industries. Products include cattle, cereals, milk, butter, cheese, wine, woolen textiles, paper, sand, and gravel. The city of Colonia is noted as a pleasure resort, with a bullfighting ring and a casino. It is situated on land jutting out into the Plata R., and is about 150 miles E.S.E. of Montevideo by rail, road, or steamer, and 25 miles from Buenos Aires, Argentina, with which it is connected by ferry. The commercial importance of Colonia as a port is increasing. Other towns, with population estimates for 1958, are Carmelo (15,000), Juan La Caze (8000), and the river port of Nueva Palmira (6000). Area of department, 2193 sq.m.; pop. (1958 est.) 132,000. Pop. of city (1958 est.) 15,000.

COLONIA AGRIPPINA. See COLOGNE.

COLONIAL ARCHITECTURE, a style of architecture, with numerous local varieties, common in the latter period of the American colonies (18th century) and the early years of the Republic. It is a modification of the English Renaissance style, or Georgian. Houses, mansions, and public buildings in Colonial style are characterized by porticos with classic columns, by doorways decorated with the classic orders, and classic cornices. In general, buildings in the style have a balanced, reposeful appearance. Notable examples of Colonial architecture are St. Paul's Chapel,

New York City; Independence Hall, Philadelphia, Pa.; and the home of George Washington at Mount Vernon, Va.

COLONIAL DAMES OF AMERICA, NATIONAL SOCIETY OF, patriotic association of women organized in 1891. Its purposes include the collection of manuscripts, traditions and relics of Colonial and Revolutionary times, and the commemoration of the success of the Revolution. Membership in the society is restricted to women who are directly descended from ancestors who resided in the American colonies before 1776, and in 1958 totaled about 14,000. There is a Colonial Society in each of the 13 original States and the District of Columbia, and an associate society in each of the other States.

CÓLON ISLANDS or **ARCHIPELAGO OF COLON.** See GALÁPAGOS ISLANDS.

COLONNA, VITTORIA (1492–1547), Italian poet, daughter of Fabrizio Colonna, grand constable of Naples, born in Castello di Marino near Rome. Her youth was passed among the greatest literary persons of Italy. At 17 she married Fernando Francisco de Avolos, Marqués de Pescara, to whom she had been betrothed since childhood. Her marriage had no issue and was followed by gradual estrangement from her husband. Her separation from him at Naples and Ischia inspired many of her poems. After Fernando's death in 1525 in the battle of Pavia, her poems became deeply religious. She had a remarkable friendship with Michelangelo, who addressed sonnets to her.

COLONY, a term used in modern times to describe a territory controlled by a foreign power. This meaning of the term is an outgrowth of its earlier meaning to denote a settlement of the inhabitants of one country in another land for economic or political reasons. Among the first to establish colonies in the older meaning of the term were the Phenicians, who founded trading settlements along the North African coast and on the islands of the Mediterranean Sea. The first great colonization movement of the Greeks occurred at the end of the 2nd millennium B.C., when the migrations of peoples from the Danube River basin displaced many of the indigenous inhabitants of Greece, who found new homes in Asia Minor and in the Ægean Islands. In the first centuries of the 1st millennium portions of the invading peoples, the last of which was the Dorians (q.v.), also colonized Asia Minor, displacing indigenous peoples who in turn colonized Syria, Italy, and other Mediterranean lands. Between the 8th and 6th centuries occurred the second important Greek

colonization, caused by economic changes and political dislocations in Greece. The movement, which resulted in Greek colonies along the shores of the Mediterranean Sea from the Crimea to Sicily, was characterized by a pattern which varied only in details. When it had been determined to send out a colony, the oracle was consulted, and a leader appointed; fire was taken from the sacred flame that burned in the Prytaneum, and the new society, though virtually independent, patterned itself after the mother city. If, in turn, the new colony undertook to found a colony it went for its leader to the mother city, as custom decreed. Differing from the colony as thus described was the cleruchy (q.v.), or allotment, members of which remained in close connection with the mother city and did not form an independent community. The Athenian cleruchies had a certain measure of autonomy.

It was the policy of Imperial Rome that not only every conquered territory, but every district where Roman citizens settled, should be an integral part of the Empire. The *colonia* was one of the municipal institutions of the Empire, having its own governing corporation dependent on Rome. Roman colonies were centers for the diffusion of Roman culture and civilization.

After the fall of Rome centuries passed before colonization began again. When Venice and Genoa were at the height of their power (13th century), they sought to advance their commercial interests by settling colonies in the islands of the Mediterranean and on the shores of the Hellespont and the Black Sea. At the close of the Middle Ages the Portuguese and Spaniards became the great colonizing nations of Europe. Portugal was first in the field, establishing settlements along the west coast of Africa in the 15th century. After the discovery of the Cape of Good Hope by Bartholomeu Dias in 1488, followed 10 years later by the rounding of the Cape by Vasco da Gama, Portugal extended its settlements along the eastern coast and into India, finally penetrating to the islands of the Pacific. By the middle of the 16th century Portugal had begun the colonization of Brazil, and Spain had established its New World Empire with colonies in Cuba, and Central and South America. Neither Spain nor Portugal developed the agricultural resources of the regions they occupied, but used the colonies as a basis of profitable trade with the home country. The Spanish colonies were also vitally concerned with the mining of precious metals. They were governed by an official hierarchy, under the general direction of an executive department in Spain. The other nations of Europe—Great Britain, France, Holland, and a number of other states—subsequently colonized in America, the East Indies, and Africa.

By 1630 the British had gained a foothold in America, but the policy of Great Britain toward her American colonies was one of exploiting them as sources of raw materials and as outlets for manufactured products. Manufacturing and the development of political independence were restricted. Shipping was controlled by the mother country, which made enormous profits out of the slave trade with the colonies. As trade and manufacturing developed in the American colonies the rising class of colonial merchants vigorously resisted the restrictions imposed on them by Great Britain, and the growing conflict of interests led to the American Revolution.

During the 18th century Great Britain, despite the loss of the colonies which later became the United States of America, built up a vast colonial realm by the conquest of India and the acquisition of other territories, principally Canada, which she acquired by defeating the French in the Seven Years' War (q.v.). In the 18th century the New World empire of Spain, which had attained its peak in the 17th century, declined; and the Dutch, whose colonial realm had been founded in large part upon the conquest of the American and Asiatic colonial empire of Portugal, lost the island of Ceylon to the British during the French Revolutionary Wars.

In the 19th century Great Britain and France, chiefly because of the superiority of their sea power and manufacturing industries over those of their rivals, were the foremost empire builders in the world. Their colonial interests extended to China and other parts of the Far East, and to Africa. In Africa they were followed on a lesser scale by Germany and Belgium. By its victory over Spain in the Spanish-American War of 1898 and the resulting acquisition of the Philippines and other territories, the United States took its place among the colonial powers of the world, although American insular possessions are not usually called colonies.

In the first part of the 20th century Japan annexed Korea by treaty in 1910, and Italy acquired Libya as a result of its victory over Turkey in the war between those two countries in 1911–1912. Following its defeat in World War I Germany was stripped of its colonies in Africa and Asia (see VERSAILLES, TREATY OF). Between World Wars I and II Italy acquired Eritrea, Italian Somaliland, and Ethiopia, all in Africa; and Japan conquered Manchuria and began the conquest of China.

Following the defeat of the Axis Powers in World War II Ethiopia recovered its independence; Italy, in the peace treaty which it signed in 1947, renounced all claims to its colonial possessions; and Japan was stripped of its colonial lands. The rising tide of nationalism among the peoples of Asia and Africa who were part of the colonial empires of the big powers led to the establishment of a large number of independent and semi-independent states (see AFRICA; ASIA).

COLOR, physical phenomenon associated with the various wavelengths in the visible portion of the electromagnetic spectrum; see ELECTROMAGNETIC WAVES; SPECTRUM. As a sensation experienced by man and some animals, perception of color is a complex neurophysiological process and is not fully understood; see VISION. See also COLOR BLINDNESS.

White light is composed of electromagnetic vibrations, the wavelengths of which are evenly distributed from 16 to 32 millionths of an inch. If the intensity of these vibrations is strong, the light is white; if the intensity is less, the light is gray; and if the intensity is zero, the light is nonexistent or black. Light composed of vibrations of a single wave length in the visible spectrum differs qualitatively from light of another wave length. This qualitative difference is what is perceived subjectively as hue. Light with a wave length of .000032 in. is perceived as red, and light of .000016 in. wave length is perceived as violet. The quality of the intermediate wave lengths is perceived as blue, green, yellow, or orange, moving from the wave length of violet to that of red.

The color of light of a single wave length or of a small band of wave lengths is known as a pure spectral color or hue. Such pure colors are said to be fully *saturated,* and are seldom encountered outside of the laboratory. An exception is the light of the sodium-vapor lamps used on some modern highways, which is almost fully saturated spectral yellow. The wide variety of colors seen every day are colors of lower saturation, that is, mixtures of light of various wave lengths. Hue and saturation are the two qualitative differences of physical colors. The quantitative difference is *brilliance,* the intensity or energy of the light.

Primary Colors. The human eye is not built as a machine for spectral analysis, and the same color sensation can be produced by different physical stimuli. Thus a mixture of red and green light of the proper intensities appears exactly the same as spectral yellow, though it does not contain light of the wave lengths corresponding to yellow. Any color sensation can be duplicated by mixing varying quantities of red, blue, and green. These colors, therefore, are known as the *additive primary colors*. If light of these primary colors is added together in equal intensities the sensation of white light is produced. There are also a number of pairs of pure spectral colors called *complementary colors*, which if mixed additively will produce the same sensation as white light. Among these pairs are certain yellows and blues, greens and blues, reds and greens, and greens and violets.

Most colors seen in ordinary experience are caused by the partial absorption of white light. The pigments that give color to most objects absorb certain wave lengths of white light and reflect or transmit others, producing the color sensation of the unabsorbed light.

The colors which absorb light of the additive primary colors are called *subtractive primary colors*. They are red, yellow, and blue, which absorb green, blue, and red, respectively. Thus, if a green light is thrown on a red pigment, the eye will perceive black. These subtractive primary colors are also called the pigment primaries. They can be mixed together in varying amounts to match almost any hue. If all three are mixed in about equal amounts they will produce black. A familiar example of the mixing of subtractive primaries is in color photography (q.v.) and in the printing of colored pictures in magazines, where successive printings of red, yellow, and blue inks are used to build up an image in natural color.

The mechanism of the absorption of light by substances to produce color is obscure. It is apparently a function of the molecular structure of the substance. In the case of organic compounds, for example, only unsaturated compounds show color, and their hue can be changed by altering the compounds chemically. Inorganic compounds are generally colorless in solution or liquid form, except for compounds of the so-called transition elements, such as chromium and manganese.

Color is also produced in other ways than by absorption. The colors of mother-of-pearl and of soap bubbles are caused by interference (q.v.). Some crystals show different colors when light is passed through them at different angles, a phenomenon known as pleochroism. A number of substances show different colors by transmitted and reflected light. For example, a very thin sheet of gold appears green by transmitted light. The "fire" of certain gems, notably the diamond, is due

to the dispersion of white light into its component spectral hues, as in a prism. Some substances, when illuminated by light of one hue, absorb this light and reradiate light of a different hue, always of longer wave length. This phenomenon is called fluorescence, or, if delayed, phosphorescence (see FLUORESCENCE AND PHOSPHORESCENCE). The blue of the sky is caused by the scattering of the short wave length blue components of white sunlight by tiny particles suspended in the atmosphere. A similar scattering can be observed in a darkened movie theater. Seen from the side, the light beam from the projector appears blue, because of the smoke and dust in the air; yet the light on the screen is white. See LIGHT; OPTICS: *Physical Optics;* RADIATION.

E.C.W.

COLORADO, one of the Mountain States of the United States, bounded on the N. by Wyoming and Nebraska, on the E. by Nebraska and Kansas, on the S. by Oklahoma and New Mexico, and on the w. by Utah. Colorado is rectangular in shape, measuring about 276 m. from N. to S. and about 387 m. from E. to w.

Area (8th State in rank)	104,247 sq.m.
Land	103,922 sq.m.
Inland water	325 sq.m.
Population (33rd State in rank)	(1960) 1,753,947
	(1950) 1,325,089
	(1940) 1,123,296
Altitude	3350 to 14,431 ft.
Capital and largest city	Denver (1960) 493,887
Entered Union (38th State)	Aug. 1, 1876
Nickname	Centennial State
Motto	*Nil Sine Numine*
	(Nothing Without Providence)
Song	"Where the Columbines Grow"
Tree	Colorado blue spruce
Flower	white and lavender
	Rocky Mountain columbine
Bird	lark bunting

Physical Characteristics. The E. third of the State is a plain, underlaid by shales, sandstones, and limestones; the central part is mountainous; and the w. third consists mainly of sedimentary plateaus. The terrain is dominated by the great, complex N.-S. ranges of the s. Rocky Mountains, which are uplifted pre-Cambrian granites. Mountain building, beginning in Cretaceous times, caused the broad regional upwarping of older sedimentary formation evidenced in the Flatirons of the E. slope and the Grand Hogback on the w. Erosion of the mountains and stream deposition formed the High Plains, an extension of the Great Plains, which slope eastward gradually from about 5000 ft. at the base of the foothills to an elevation of about 3500 ft. at the Kansas-Nebraska boundary. The uniform level of the plains N. of Denver is interrupted by erosion in the s. Platte wa-

View of the civic center of Denver, the mile-high capital of Colorado, showing the City and County Building. Peaks of the Rocky Mountains fringe the western horizon.

tershed. The foothills, generally abrupt in the N. part of the State, are more broken in the S., where rock masses, eroded into fantastic forms, occur over a wide area. Glaciers have sculptured the high mountains into their present scenic splendor.

The approximate mean elevation of Colorado (6800 ft.) is higher than that of any other State except Alaska. The lowest point, with an elevation of 3350 ft., is situated in the S.E. corner of the State in the bed of the Arkansas R. Mount Elbert (14,431 ft.) is the highest peak in the State and second-highest in the United States outside of Alaska.

The E. chain of the Rocky Mountain system in Colorado consists of a series of massive abutting ranges. From N. to S., these are the Medicine Bow Range, extending into the State from Wyoming; the Front Range, in the central region; the Sangre de Cristo Mountains; and the Culebra Range, which projects into New Mexico. The most celebrated peaks of the E. chain are Longs (14,255 ft.) and Pikes (14,110 ft.), in the Front Range; both peaks served as landmarks to the gold seekers en route to California in 1848–49.

The principal chain of the Rockies in Colorado, situated W. of, and generally parallel to, the E. chain, is composed of a complex system of ranges and spurs, considerably more elevated than those of the E. chain. The crest of the W. chain, with the exception of the Front Range, constitutes all of the Colorado portion of the Continental Divide, the irregular crest separating the watersheds of Pacific and Atlantic drainage. In the N., the Continental Divide enters the State from Wyoming via the Park Range, extends eastward to the Medicine Bow Range, southward along the crest of the Front Range, then southwestward and southward through the principal ranges of the W. chain.

The main range of the W. chain of the

Rockies is the Sawatch (sometimes spelled "Saguache") Range, in which Mount Elbert is situated. The Sawatch, highest range in the State, has numerous other outstanding summits, including Mount Harvard (14,420 ft.), Mount Princeton (14,197 ft.) and Mount Yale (14,196 ft.). Also well known are the Elk, Park, and Gore ranges, and the San Juan Mountains of the W. chain. These and other ranges of the Colorado Rockies contain 54 peaks with elevation in excess of 14,000 ft. The State has 830 additional peaks over 11,000 ft. The W. third of the State is characterized by a number of high, rocky plateaus, notably the Roan, the Uncompahgre, and the White River.

There are many vital passes across the Rockies in Colorado. The State maintains 27 highway passes, all but 6 of which are open to year-round traffic. Among the important all-weather highway passes are Berthoud (11,314 ft.) and Loveland (11,992 ft.) in the Front Range, Rabbit Ears (9680 ft.) in the Park Range, Vail (10,603 ft.) in the Gore Range, and Monarch (11,312 ft.) in the Sawatch Range. The highest auto passes are the Trail Ridge High Point (12,183 ft.) in Rocky Mountain National Park and Independence Pass (12,095 ft.) in the Sawatch Range. The two highest highways in the United States are located in Colorado and are open only in summer; one leads almost to the top of Mount Evans (14,260 ft.) W. of Denver and the other leads to the summit of Pikes Peak W. of Colorado Springs. Important railroad passes are La Veta, Tennessee, and the Moffat Tunnel.

Four great elevated, structural valleys, generally referred to as "parks", extend from N. to S. through central Colorado. Each of these is enclosed by the E. and W. chains and by lateral ranges of the Rockies. The San Luis Valley, situated in the south-central part of the State, extends into New Mexico and is the largest park. Its surface, about 7500 ft. above sea level, is remarkably flat. With an area approximating that of the State of Connecticut, it is drained by the Rio Grande and is an important irrigation region. The other great mountain parks are South Park, N. of the San Luis Valley; Middle Park, s.w. of Rocky Mountain National Park; and North Park, N.W. of Rocky Mountain National Park between the Park and Medicine Bow ranges.

The sources of four major rivers, each of which figures prominently in the drainage system of the United States, are situated in the Colorado Rockies. These are the Rio Grande, Arkansas, and South Platte, which are fed from the watershed E. of the Continental Divide, and the Colorado River, which is fed from the watershed W. of the Divide. Numerous smaller streams, including many tributaries of the major rivers, flow through the Rockies. Notable among these streams are the Gunnison, the Uncompahgre, the San Juan, the Green, the Eagle, and the White rivers. The falls, gorges, and canyons which mark the precipitous descent of mountain streams in Colorado are among the scenic wonders of the State. Among the more spectacular canyons are the Royal Gorge of the Arkansas, a chasm which is spanned by the Royal Gorge Suspension Bridge (1053 ft. above the river), the highest bridge of its kind in the world; and the Black Canyon of the Gunnison, a national monument, along the sheer walls (1730 to 2425 ft.) of which are exposed rocks of all known geologic eras, including the earliest, the Archean.

Climate. Because of topographic differences, the State has many climatic variations, often occurring within short distances. Except in the mountains, a semiarid climate prevails throughout in the State. The E. plains, the most heavily populated region, receive slightly less than 20 in. of precipitation annually. The mountain areas receive annually the equivalent of 30 to 50 in., much of which is in the form of snow. The w. intermontane valleys, such as the San Luis and Uncompahgre, have desert conditions, with the annual precipitation less than 10 in. East of the Continental Divide, most of the precipitation occurs between late spring and early fall. West of the Divide the precipitation is well distributed throughout the year, with peak periods in the spring and late summer.

In the E. plains and w. valleys midsummer temperatures average 62° F. to 78° F. with warm daytime temperatures sometimes in the high 90's, but offset by cool nights. These areas average 24° F. to 34° F. in the winter. In the mountains the average temperature is in the 50's during summer and between 10° F. and 12° F. in winter. Occasional winter lows of −50° F. are recorded in high mountain valleys when the air is clear and still. Bright sunshine, clear skies, and consistently low relative humidity give the State a bracing atmosphere reputed to be beneficial to persons with pulmonary ailments. Special facilities for the treatment of such persons are provided in a number of communities, notably in Colorado Springs.

Forests, Parks, and Places of Interest. Virtually all of the wooded areas of the State are situated along the slopes of the Rockies, where the timber line averages between 11,000 and 11,500 ft. in elevation. In their most important function, these forests help to control the water supply for irrigation districts, municipalities, and industries. Grazing, timber, and recreation are other important uses of Colorado forests. The forests are well stocked with game and fish. Colorado ranks sixth nationally as a recreational-fishing area. Hunting and fishing privileges, regulated by State laws, are extended to residents and visitors. There are 11 national forests within the State borders and 1 extending into Utah. White River, San Juan, Rio Grande, Gunnison, Pike, and Arapaho are among the largest. The national forests within Colorado have a total area of 13,693,389 acres and comprise about one fifth of the total area of the State; the forests are administered by the national Forest Service.

Two national parks and 6 national monuments, located in the State, have a total area of almost 550,000 acres. Rocky Mountain National Park (q.v.), the larger, attracts over 1,000,000 visitors annually and contains year-round facilities for numerous recreational activities and for observing the spectacular scenery (including Longs Peak) and hundreds of species of flowers and animals. Mesa Verde National Park (q.v.), in the s.w. corner of the State, has many structures built by the ancient cliff dwellers, notably the Cliff Palace, the largest existing edifice of its kind. Colorado National Monument is well known for its large number of monolithic sandstone shafts, one of which, called Independence Rock, is 500 ft. high. Other national monuments noted for their scenic or historical interest in Colorado are Black Canyon of the Gunnison, Great Sand Dunes, and Yucca House; Dinosaur and Hovenweep are partly in Utah.

INDEX TO MAP OF COLORADO

◉County Seat

Continued on page 2268

COLORADO

SCALE OF MILES

State Capitals   ⊛ County Seats

Canals

Copyright by C. S. Hammond & Co., N. Y.

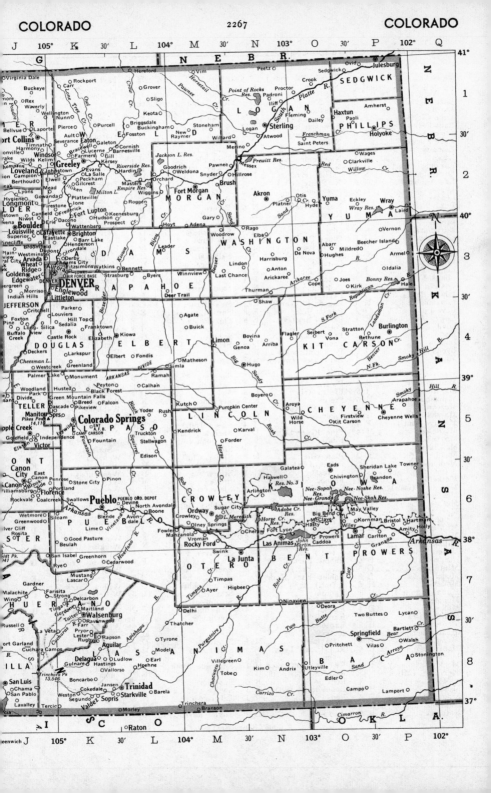

Index to Map of Colorado—cont.

◉County Seat

Among other places of interest are the Garden of the Gods (q.v.), near Colorado Springs; the Will Rogers Shrine of the Sun, on Cheyenne Mountain near Pikes Peak; the grave of Buffalo Bill, on Lookout Mountain near Golden; the highest U.S. highway, which leads almost to the summit of Mount Evans (14,260 ft.); the once-famous Cripple Creek mining area; and the opera house and museums in Central City, the once-famous gold-mining town.

Beautiful natural settings have encouraged development of a variety of annual cultural activities, among which are the Central City Summer Opera and Play Festival, the summer festivals of the Institute of Humanistic Studies at Aspen, symphony concerts at the outdoor amphitheater at Red Rocks Park near Denver, and many winter-sports programs throughout the State.

Natural Resources. *Plants.* Topography is the key to the abundance and variety of natural resources within Colorado. The natural vegetation of the E. plains is low-grass prairie, dominated by buffalo and blue grama grasses. These native grasses once sustained large bison herds but now support domestic range cattle. The most common trees found along the stream courses of the plains are cottonwood, box elder, and willow.

From the plains upward to the foothills and Continental Divide, rapid vegetation changes occur as a result of the lower temperatures. In the foothills zone (6000 to 8000 ft.) scrub oak occurs near the lower limit; other vegetation at these levels includes willow, alder, birch, blue spruce, Douglas fir, and ponderosa pine trees. The montane zone (8000 to 10,000 ft.) is distinguished by the presence of quaking aspen and lodgepole pine; ponderosa pine and Douglas fir are also present, and Englemann spruce and alpine fir grow in the upper parts of this zone. The aspen groves are particularly colorful in the fall.

The subalpine zone (10,000 to 11,500 ft.) represents the upper limits of forest growth and has some of the finest stands of timber in the State; limber pine, alpine fir, and Englemann spruce are the dominant species at these elevations. Above the timber line (11,500 ft.) is the alpine zone where only hardy, primitive vegetation such as mosses, lichens, and small tundra plants can survive.

Common wildflowers of the State include the pasqueflower, arnica, golden pea, blue larkspur, blue beardtongue, Indian paintbrush, mariposa lily, and columbine.

Animals. The fauna of the State are numerous and varied because of the diversity of habitats. On the E. plains and adjacent foothills live most of the 11,000 antelope (pronghorn) in Colorado. The once-plentiful bison is almost extinct. Prairie dog colonies are widespread. Fur bearers, game mammals, and game birds of this area include the fox, skunk, weasel, muskrat, mink, opossum, cottontail, jack rabbit, raccoon, partridge, pheasant, and prairie fowl. Their predators are the coyote, badger, ferret, falcon, owl, and duck hawk. Eastern Colorado is located on one of the major migratory bird routes. Thousands of ducks and Canada geese winter in this region. The horned lizard (horned toad), prairie rattlesnake, and many harmless reptiles inhabit this area. Rivers, lakes, and reservoirs below 7000 ft. abound in bass, sunfish, crappie, walleye, yellow perch, and catfish. In the forested montane and subalpine zones, mule deer and elk (wapiti) are numerous. Predators in this region include the bobcat, coyote, mountain lion, and many black bears. Smaller animals of the mountain forests are marten, mink, weasel, fox, beaver, porcupine, squirrel, skunk, snowshoe rabbit, and chipmunk. Bighorn sheep, saved from extinction by State conservation laws, range above and below the timber line. In the alpine zone are the cony, fox marmot, ptarmigan, marten, weasel, coyote, and bobcat. In the mountain lakes, beaver ponds, and streams, rainbow, brook, brown, and native trout are plentiful and salmon and whitefish abound.

Minerals. Colorado is one of the great mineral States of the nation. The chief metallic-mineral areas are in the Front Range mineral belt which extends s.w. from Boulder to Breckenridge, the Cripple Creek district, the central Colorado region, and the San Juan Mountain region. Gold, silver, lead, zinc, molybdenum, tungsten, and copper are the most important minerals. Uranium and vanadium occur in the carnotite sandstones near the west-central boundary. Oil and gas fields of significance are in the Denver-Julesberg Basin in the N.E., the Uinta Basin in the N.W., and the Paradox and San Juan basins in the s.w. About 1000 sq.m. of oil shale in N.W. Colorado contain an estimated 500,000,-000,000 barrels of oil. Large deposits of bituminous coal are located in the Trinidad-Walsenburg area and the San Juan River and Uinta regions. The State has the largest bituminous-coal reserve in the country. Its total coal reserves, of all types, are an estimated 250,000,000,000 tons. Other nonmetallic minerals include limestone, clay, gypsum, marble, sand, gravel, slate, peat, mica, vermiculite, fluorite, salt and sulfur-bearing pyrite. Yule marble quarried in Colorado was used to construct the Lincoln Memorial, in Washington, D.C., the Tomb of the Unknown Soldier in Arlington National Cemetery, in Arlington, Va., and many other famous structures. Gem stones found in the State include turquoise, topaz, aquamarine, garnet, agate, and amazon stone.

Soils. Colorado contains many of the major soil groups. Dark brown and brown soils occur on the E. plains and parts of the extreme w. of the State. Gray desert soils are found in the San Luis Valley and the Colorado Valley near Grand Junction. Shallow, stony soils, known as lithosols, prevail in the remaining mountain areas. In the lower elevations the soils of the State, though fertile, are low in humus and high in mineral content. Because of much soluble mineral matter, irrigated soils often become saline or alkaline. Less than 10 percent of the soil in the State is suitable for agriculture.

Water Supply. Because of semiaridity, future economic growth in Colorado will be limited by the availability of water. The Continental Divide is one of the major water catchment areas of the West. The State participates in no less than nine separate inter-State water compacts and in the planning of three major river-basin developments.

The Colorado Water Conservation Board, co-operating with the Bureau of Reclamation, U.S. Army Corps of Engineers, and U.S. Geological Survey, directs the State and inter-State water development for irrigation, power, and flood control and for industrial and domestic supply. Since the 1880's Colorado has been one of the leading irrigation states, ranking fourth in number of acres irrigated. A number of projects, notably the John Martin Reservoir and the Uncompahgre, the Grand Valley, and the Mancos developments were financed by the Federal government. The largest irrigation project in the State, financed by the Bureau of Reclamation, is the Colorado-Big Thompson Project. This development, consisting of a series of reservoirs and a 13-mile tunnel under the Continental Divide, channels impounded water from the w. side of the Rockies to farm land in the South Platte R. drainage area. It provides irrigation for about 615,000 acres. The State owns 30 trans-mountain water-diversion tunnels and ditches. The upper Colorado R. contains the largest number of undeveloped sites in the State and numerous proposals are being studied by the U.S. Congress for their development.

Hydroelectric plants, mostly privately owned, produced 1,412,000,000 kilowatt hours in the early 1960's; about 80 percent of the electrical energy in the State originates in fuel generation.

Population. Colorado had a population of 1,325,089 in 1950; in 1960 the State had a population of 1,753,947, the increase since 1950 resulting from natural population growth, civilian migration, and growth of the military population. Most of the population is situated on the plains along the E. flank of the Rockies. Four counties, Denver, El Paso, Jefferson, and Adams, have populations in excess of 120,000 and comprise almost half of the population of the State. Secondary population centers occur in the South Platte, Arkansas, and w. intermontane valleys. According to the 1960 census, the density of the population was only 16.8 people per sq.m. and 73.7 percent of the population lived in urban areas.

In 1960 the people of Colorado who were native Whites comprised about 95 percent of the population; foreign-born Whites represented 0.3 percent, Negroes 2.3 percent, Japanese 0.4 percent, American Indians 0.2 percent, and other Asians 0.1 percent of the total population. The white population is widely distributed throughout the State. The Negro population is mostly concentrated in the largest cities and the Japanese are found mainly in the irrigated, truck-gardening areas. The only Indian reservation in Colorado, the Consolidated Ute Agency, is in the s.w. part of the State; it is divided between the tribal lands of the Wiminuche Ute on the w. part of the reservation and the lands of the Southern Ute around Ignacio. The largest groups of foreign-born Whites are Mexicans, Ukrainians, Germans, and Italians.

Largest Cities. Denver (pop. in 1960, 493,-887), the capital of the State, is the largest city. The Denver metropolitan area, with a 1950 population of 563,832, expanded to a population of 929,383 according to the 1960 Federal census report. The Pueblo metropolitan area, which had a 1950 population of 90,188, reached a population of 118,707 in 1960. The principal business centers of Colorado, with 1960 populations, are Denver (493,887), Pueblo (91,181), Colorado Springs (70,194), Boulder (37,718), Greeley (26,314), and Grand Junction (18,694).

Education. *Public Schools.* Public education in Colorado is under the supervision of the Department of Education, which is headed by an elected commissioner of education. However, elected school boards in local districts exercise most of the control. Education is compulsory for all children between eight and sixteen years of age. State aid is limited to nonsectarian institutions by the constitution of 1876. In the early 1960's there were 984 elementary schools, 159 junior and 260 senior high schools, 6 schools for exceptional children, and 13 institutions of higher learning, including 6 junior colleges, supported by the public. The Emily Griffith Opportunity School, an experimental institution founded in Denver in 1916, has influenced other similar schools throughout the United States.

Public-school enrollment in the early 1960's included annually more than 250,000 elementary pupils and about 160,000 secondary pupils. During the same period there were about 9830 elementary teachers and 7960 secondary teachers.

Private and Parochial Schools. Private and parochial schools include 86 elementary schools, 35 secondary schools, 1 school for exceptional children, and 7 colleges. During the late 1950's there were about 23,900 elementary pupils and 5300 high school pupils annually enrolled in the Roman Catholic system, the largest of the parochial and private-school systems; there were about 2000 pupils in Lutheran schools.

Colleges and Universities. The outstanding State-supported institutions of higher learning include the University of Colorado in Boulder and Denver, Colorado State University in Fort Collins, Colorado School of Mines in Golden, Colorado State College in Greeley, Western State College in Gunnison, and Adams State College in Alamosa. Privately endowed universities and colleges include the University of Denver and Regis College, both in Denver, and Colorado College in Colorado Springs. The United States Air Force Academy is located near Colorado Springs also.

Libraries and Museums. There are 126 public libraries throughout the State; their combined stock totals about 1,800,000 books and their annual circulation is over 5,000,000. Largest holdings are in the newly constructed Denver Public Library. The Supreme Court Library has the best legal collection in the West.

Denver has an outstanding group of museums which include the Colorado State Museum with its collection of Pueblo Indian and early Western relics, the Denver Museum of Natural History with dioramas of ancient man and wildlife, and the Denver Art Museum. Exceptional museums throughout the State include the Henderson Museum at the University of Colorado, the Buffalo Bill Museum near Golden, the Central City Opera House Museum and Central City Historical Museum, the Koshare Kiva in La Junta, the Ute Indian Museum in Montrose, and the Mesa Verde National Park Archeological Museum.

Religion. There are more than 312,400 Protestants, about 221,550 Roman Catholics, and approximately 17,000 Jews in the State according to statistics reported by the individual faiths. Membership in the Congregational Christian Church represents about 32 percent, in the Protestant Episcopal Church about 29 percent, and in the Methodist Church about 13 percent of the total Protestant population.

Manufacturing. Since the initial settlement of Colorado the economic emphasis has shifted from mining to agriculture and then to manufacturing. Manufacturing is the leading economic activity, followed by agricultural, mining, and tourist enterprises. Between 1947 and the late 1950's the number of manufacturing establishments increased 41 percent. The greatest expansion occurred in the Denver, Boulder, and Colorado Springs areas. The greatest increases in production took place in the furniture, instrument, machinery, lumber- and wood-products, transportation-equipment, and garment groups. The chief manufacturing industries of the State process and refine agricultural and mineral products. Foremost among the industries are sugar-beet refining, canning, meat packing, smelting, petroleum refining, printing and publishing, and the manufacture of chemical products, dairy products, lumber, flour, leather goods, iron and steel, and bakery products. Others include the manufacture of clothing, furniture, pulp and paper products, stone and clay products, and machinery. The State has over 2400 manufacturing establishments with an average annual employment exceeding 70,000 production workers. However, the largest single employer is the Federal government, particularly at the Denver Federal Center.

Agriculture. Colorado, one of the leading agricultural States of the Union, is an important producer of commercial vegetables. Late in the 1950's it was one of the leading States in the production of green peas, spinach, cantaloupes, cabbage, carrots, celery, lettuce, cauliflower, and onions. In field crops the State ranks second in sugar beets, fourth in dry beans, sixth in potatoes, and seventh in winter wheat. The greatest crop acreage is devoted to winter wheat. Next in acreage are hay, barley, and corn. Hay is the most valuable crop, followed by winter wheat, corn, potatoes, and commercial vegetables. Other field and orchard crops include tomatoes, spring wheat, oats, rye, sorghum, apples, peaches, and pears. According to the 1959 Federal census the State had 33,390 farms and ranches occupying 38,813,392 acres (58.4 percent of State area), but only 5,881,446 acres actually produced crops. The majority of crop land is located on the E. plains, where winter wheat and dry field beans are the dominant crops.

Livestock. The livestock industry, one of the oldest in the State, is concentrated on the E. plains and the w. slopes of the Rockies. Cattle and sheep represent 95 percent of the total value of the livestock, cattle being most important. Colorado ranks seventh nationally in number of sheep and in wool and lamb production. Denver is the largest sheep-processing center in the nation. Other livestock include chickens, turkeys, and hogs.

Mining. Mining, although no longer the leading industry of the State, continues to be of major importance. In terms of value the State ranks seventeenth nationally in mineral production. Uranium is one of the leading metals produced, principally in the Colorado Plateau. The State produces 18 percent of the uranium mined in the United States and has 7 percent of the U.S. reserve. A mine in Colorado is the world's leading molybdenum producer and has the largest known reserves. Federal aid has encouraged exploration and production of strategic minerals such as uranium, molybdenum, and tungsten.

The most valuable mineral produced in Colorado is crude petroleum. More than 53,240,000 barrels were produced annually in the early 1960's, half of which came from the Rangely Field in Rio Bianco County. Molybdenum production, less than half the value of petroleum, ranks next in value. Other minerals produced in descending order of value are coal, cement, gravel, zinc, natural gas, sand and gravel, lead, copper, tungsten, gold, fluorspar, silver, limestone, and building stone. Important mining centers are located at Cripple Creek for gold; Redcliff for lead, zinc, and silver; Leadville for lead and silver; Uravan for uranium; Rifle for oil shale; Trinidad for coal; and Sterling for oil and gas.

Tourism. The tourist trade is the fourth-largest source of wealth in the State. Approximately 3,878,000 tourists spend more than $225,800,000 annually.

Forestry. About one third of the total area of the State, or approximately 20,000,000 acres, is in forest, of which 13,693,389 acres are in national forest. Yet the State usually ranks only thirty-second in the Union in timber production. Approximately 8,400,000 acres are in commercial stands. Of these, 79 percent are Federally controlled, 19 percent are controlled by private interests, and 2 percent are controlled by the State and various municipalities. Timber production in the mid-1950's was about 174,000,000 board feet annually; Engelmann spruce is the most important species, followed by ponderosa and lodgepole pines and Douglas fir.

Transportation. Despite mountainous terrain, Colorado has a remarkably well-developed transportation system. There are about 73,610 m. of roads and highways and city streets, of which 69,279 m. are in rural areas. There are also 8302 m. of Federally supported State highways. The remaining total mileage is under county and city supervision. Many national and local bus and motor-carrier companies provide passenger and freight service to all parts of the State.

The 15 railroad companies in the State maintain a total of over 4000 m. of track. Foremost among the operating lines are the Denver & Rio Grande Western Railroad, the Union Pacific Railroad, the Atchison, Topeka & Santa Fe Railway Co., the Chicago, Burlington and Quincy Railroad Co., and the Colorado and Southern Railway Co. The Moffat Tunnel (6.4 m.) through the Front Range shortens the rail distance between Denver and the Pacific coast by 176 miles.

Denver, Pueblo, Colorado Springs, La Junta, and Grand Junction are served by major inter-State airlines. In 1960 Colorado had 91 airfields, of which 38 were open to public use.

Communication. Colorado is well served by many communication media. Three major news-gathering agencies, the Associated Press, International News Service, and the United Press, have regional offices in Denver to serve the press and radio of Colorado and surrounding States. The Capitol Press, a news service, reports daily on activities of the State government. There are twenty-eight major daily newspapers centered in the largest cities. *The Denver Post* and *The Rocky Mountain News*, both of Denver, have the widest circulation. The weekly newspapers, most frequently located in small towns, number 141. There are 56 AM and 7 FM radio stations operating in the State. A total of 9 commercial television stations, 4 in Denver, 2 in Colorado Springs, and 1 each in Pueblo, Grand Junction, and

Montrose, are in operation. Denver also has 1 educational television station.

Government. The constitution of Colorado, adopted in 1876 and subsequently amended, provides for the initiation of legislation and constitutional amendments by popular vote. The veto power of the governor does not extend to measures initiated by the people or to measures referred to the people by the General Assembly. Amendments to the initiative and referendum law require that 15 percent of the legal voters must sign an initiated measure in order for it to be placed on the ballot a required eight months before election. All ballots cast in primary elections are party designations. At general elections, the headless ballot is provided and electors vote for each candidate individually. The State is represented in the Congress of the United States by 4 representatives and 2 senators.

Executive. The State constitution vests executive authority in a governor, lieutenant governor, secretary of state, treasurer, auditor, attorney general, and superintendent of public instruction, each of whom is elected for a two-year term. The treasurer and auditor may not succeed themselves.

The Governor's Council, an advisory body only, considers State problems, policies, and procedures and consists of the secretary of state, treasurer, director of revenue, commissioner of education, attorney general, controller, state purchasing agent, and other heads of departments as the governor may designate.

Legislative. Legislative power is vested in the General Assembly, a bicameral body consisting of a Senate and House of Representatives. The House of Representatives has 65 members who serve two-year terms; the Senate has 35 members who serve four-year terms. The General Assembly meets annually. In 1953 the General Asesmbly created by statute its own fact-finding agency, the Legislative Council. This council is made up of legislators appointed with approval of their colleagues to conduct research on problems important to the Assembly and to prepare factual reports on major issues before the Assembly.

Judiciary. Judicial authority is vested in a Supreme Court with 7 justices elected for ten-year terms; it exercises appellate jurisdiction as well as original jurisdiction in certain types of cases and exercises a superintending control over all inferior courts. The State is divided into 16 judicial districts, each of which is presided over by 1 or more district judges; there are a total of 35 such judges; who are elected for six-year terms. County jurisdiction is vested in 1 court for each county. The judge, elected for a four-year term, need not be a lawyer.

Jurisdiction involving minors is exercised by the county courts except in cities exceeding 100,000 population, in which case separate juvenile courts may be established. Only Denver has a juvenile court. Denver also has a Superior Court, established by law in 1954, for conducting trials of matters originating in or appealed from municipal, police magistrate, and justice courts within the county or city.

Local Government. Counties and towns are the chief agencies of local government. A few municipalities still operate under special-legislation charters granted by the Territories of Colorado and Kansas. Most municipalities exist under general charters from the State. Towns with less than 2000 population have a mayor and board of trustees. Most cities with populations between 2000 and 25,000 have a mayor-council type of government, but 9 have adopted city-manager government. All cities and towns with populations of 2000 or more may draft their own charters. Of these home-rule cities, 11 have council-manager governments, 2 have mayor-council types, and 1 has a city commissioner type of government.

Voting Qualifications. To be a qualified voter in Colorado a person must be registered, twenty-one years of age, a citizen of the United States, have one year of residency in the State immediately preceding the election, and have been a resident in the county for ninety days, in the city or town for thirty days, and in the precinct or ward for ten days.

History. The Pueblo Indians, descendants of the pre-historic Cliff Dwellers, and also other tribes, notably the Utes and Arapahoes, were in possession of the region in the 16th century, when it was first visited by Europeans. According to some historians, Francisco Vásquez Coronado, the Spanish explorer, led the initial expedition into the territory between 1540 and 1542. Other exploratory expeditions were undertaken by Spanish explorers during the 17th and 18th centuries. However, although Spain claimed the region, no attempt was made to colonize it.

The first citizen of the United States to enter the present State was James Purcell, a fur trader, who arrived there in 1803. In that year the U.S. Government acquired possession of nearly half of the region through the Louisiana Purchase (q.v.). Three years later Zebulon Montgomery Pike, an officer of the U.S. Army, discovered, while surveying the

Arkansas River, the peak which now bears his name. Further surveys were made in 1819–20 by Stephen Harriman Long, another American Army officer, whose memory is commemorated by Longs Peak. As a result of Long's reports, which termed the region uninhabitable, little attention was given to it until 1828, when a fur-trading post was established near the site of La Junta. Additional trading posts were subsequently established, but the territory remained generally unpopular. In the Treaty of Guadalupe-Hidalgo (1848), which terminated the war between Mexico and the United States, the U.S. Government acquired that portion of the present State situated w. of the Rio Grande.

Discovery of gold in 1858, near the site of Denver, brought large numbers of emigrants to the region. Numerous mining towns, including Denver, Boulder, and Colorado City (now part of Colorado Springs), were founded during the next 3 years. The U.S. government established the region as the Territory of Colorado on February 28, 1861. In the course of the next decade, a number of Indian tribes in the Territory, notably the Cheyennes and the Arapahoes, resisted further encroachments on their lands, precipitating a series of sanguinary conflicts with the settlers. In one of these, known as the Sand Creek Massacre, many Indians were killed. Several attempts had been made by the settlers, meanwhile, to secure admission of the Territory to the Union as a State. This was not accomplished until 1876. Exhaustion of the major known gold deposits, in 1878, caused a severe recession in the State and the desertion of many of the mining towns. This crisis was soon overcome by discovery of a process of extracting silver and lead from carbonates discarded at the gold mines. The value of the minerals produced by this process shortly exceeded that of the gold output. Renewed mining activity occurred in 1891 after Bob Womack's discovery of the great Cripple Creek gold field. Serious disputes between mine owners and the Western Federation of Miners, a labor union, occurred during the last decade of the 19th century. In 1899 the General Assembly enacted a law establishing the 8-hour day for mine and smelter workers. Although this legislation was declared unconstitutional by the State Supreme Court, in 1902 the voters adopted a constitutional amendment and obtained re-enactment of the law. Another strike of miners occurred in 1903–04, when martial law was declared and the writ of habeas corpus was suspended. One of the most serious strikes in Colorado

history occurred in 1913–14. This struggle, which involved mainly the workers of the Colorado Fuel and Iron Company, was marked by considerable violence, notably in the mining town of Ludlow.

With the introduction of sugar-beet farming and the expansion of irrigation developments early in the 20th century, agriculture became vitally important to the Colorado economy. The recent emergence of manufacturing marks the closing of the frontier and the beginning of a mature economic diversification. The State, because of its climate and scenic grandeur, became noted also as a center for tourists and convalescents.

Colorado contributed much in man power and materials during World Wars I and II. More than 125,000 men registered for armed service in World War I, and more than 130,000 young men and women entered the armed forces during World War II. The war years also brought a demand for Colorado minerals. In 1918 the great molybdenum deposit at Climax and the tungsten mines near Boulder were developed. World War II requirements stimulated the development of oil in the Rangely area. During the depression years of the 1930's unemployment was prevalent. Prolonged drought and high winds caused further hardship in the E. part of the State. Many Federal programs were initiated to bring relief to the area.

The Federal government has become vital to the State's economy. About 36 percent of the total area of Colorado is Federally owned. Currently important Federal installations include the Atomic Energy Commission plant in Rocky Flats, N.W. of Denver, the National Bureau of Standards laboratories in Boulder, and the U.S. Bureau of Mines oil shale experiment plant in Rifle. Many important military establishments are located in Colorado. The Rocky Mountain Arsenal, Fitzsimons Army Hospital, Lowry Air Force Base, the headquarters of the Continental Air Defense Command, and a U.S. Naval Air Station are all located in the Denver area. In or near Colorado Springs are the U.S. Air Force Academy, and Fort Carson.

In national politics, the Colorado electorate has demonstrated no lasting attachment to either of the majority parties. The Republicans won the Colorado electoral votes between 1876 and 1888, in 1904, between 1920 and 1928, and in 1940, 1944, 1952, 1956, and 1960. In 1960 the Republican candidate, Richard M. Nixon, received 402,242 votes; his Democratic opponent, John F. Kennedy, received 330,629 votes. D.D.MacP.